Finance Bundling and Finance Transformation

Frank Keuper • Kai-Eberhard Lueg (Eds.)

Finance Bundling and Finance Transformation

Shared Services Next Level

Springer Gabler

Editors
Prof. Dr. habil. Frank Keuper
Lehrstuhl für Betriebswirtschaftslehre,
insb. Konvergenzmanagement und
Strategisches Management
Steinbeis Center of Strategic Management
Steinbeis-Hochschule Berlin
Hamburg, Germany

Kai-Eberhard Lueg
Siemens AG, Global Shared Services
München, Germany

ISBN 978-3-658-00372-2
ISBN 978-3-658-00373-9 (eBook)
DOI 10.1007/978-3-658-00373-9

The Deutsche Nationalbibliothek lists this publication in the Deutsche Nationalbibliografie; detailed bibliographic data are available in the Internet at http://dnb.d-nb.de.

Library of Congress Control Number: 2013935228

Springer Gabler

Lektorat: Barbara Roscher, Jutta Hinrichsen

Printed on acid-free paper

Springer Gabler is a brand of Springer DE. Springer DE is part of Springer Science+Business Media.
www.Springer-gabler.de

Preface: Shared Services as a Building Block for a World Class Finance Organization

In this book, we will illustrate the journey of a Shared Services Organization from a cost-efficient transactional service provider to a trusted partner of the operational businesses within a corporation, taking *Siemens* and its transformation process as an example. Further, it provides practical insights of today, but also a visionary view of the future.

A few years ago, *Siemens* changed its regional administrative structures from individual country presences to cross-border regional 'Cluster' organizations in order to make the organizations more effective, lean and globally aligned. With regards to the global finance function, it offered the opportunity to realize additional optimization potential in the areas of governance, quality and efficiency via the creation of a Global Shared Services Organization.

The finance function is an integral part of the global *Siemens* group, being represented in the Corporate Headquarters, in the Sectors and Divisions driving the business, in its regional Cluster organization providing infrastructure and business support and – last but not least – in its captive Global Shared Services Organization rendering in-house transactional and value-add services in the area of finance and accounting.

In the past, the advantages that such a Shared Services Organization offers were not fully leveraged and the penetration rate was low. In the course of remodelling the finance organization by launching the worldwide 'Finance Bundling' program, this hidden potential was systematically addressed: using economies of scale and scope on a global level, improving cost efficiency, freeing up the businesses of administrative tasks while assuring and improving transparency, compliance, quality of books and records and reliability of internal and external reporting.

This program is well embedded in the overarching short- to mid-term strategy for our Global Shared Services Organization, which consequently pursues a three-step-approach:

- 'Lift & drop' – Transfer transactional activities from the countries and single entities to the Shared Services Organization, bundle them, establish a service mind-set and start harmonization;
- 'Change' – Focus on harmonization and standardization, start transformation and automation, leverage process improvements;
- 'Enhance, innovate & automate' – Focus on transformation and automation, portfolio expansion, and reach the status of a 'trusted adviser'.

The structure of this book also follows this approach and gives insights regarding important supporting strategies and measures.

I believe that in the future Shared Services will be *the* way modern international organizations effectively and efficiently structure and manage their administrative work across country borders.

Munich, February 2013

Joe Kaeser

Chief Financial Officer
Siemens AG

Foreword

As the market environment is constantly becoming more complex, dynamic and international, the meaning of success-oriented management of financial processes becomes much more criticial. The set-up of a competitive Finance Shared Services Organization (FSSO) focuses on the effective and efficient rendering of selected finance, accounting and controlling processes. However, in managerial literature the challenges of managing a FSSO in the different stages of its development are only discussed as subtopics. Therefore, this compilation will address systematically – based on a generic phase model of a Shared Services Organization's development – frequently arising questions related to the management of FSSO. In addition selected enablers and prerequisites for a successful development of a Shared Services Organization shall be discussed and a picture of the future of FSSO – which results in new future management implications – shall be provided.

In his introductory article *KAI-EBERHARD LUEG* explores the strategic view of the development of the *Siemens*-internal Shared Services Organization and briefly describes the relevant topics to be considered along the journey through three developmental phases: "lift-drop" (where transitions occur), the "change phase" (where service delivery is optimized) and the "enhance and innovate phase" (where innovation is embraced to expand service offerings). In his article *KAI-EBERHARD LUEG* especially emphasizes relevant key factors for successful transitions, the management of systematic process improvements, the people-focused topics of personnel and change management as well as the professional monitoring of performances. The reader's interest is drawn to the variety of topics covered in this book that can all be accessed in detail within the respective articles. Accordingly, this compilation has been subdivided into four parts.

Part 1	"Lift and Drop" – Gaining Speed and Volume for a Global Finance Shared Services Organization
Part 2	"Change" – Get to the Next Level of Shared Services Maturity and Productivity
Part 3	"Enhance and Innovate" – From a Service Provider to a Strategic Partner
Part 4	Selected Enablers and Prerequisites for a Successful Development of a Shared Services Organization

Figure 1: Structure

The first part starts with two interviews. The first one is conducted with *RALF P. THOMAS*, Chief Financial Officer of *Siemens* Sector Industry, who specifically focuses on two of the three development phases of captive Shared Services Organizations: The "bundling phase" to gain speed and volume and the following "optimizing phase" to systematically harmonize and automate processes. The interview takes the customer's perspective into consideration including perception, expectations and ultimate satisfaction towards a Shared Services Organization. The second interview explores the role of a governance function on Shared Services Organizations and was conducted with *JOCHEN SCHMITZ*, Head of Corporate Finance Reporting &

Controlling, *Siemens AG*. The focus of this interview is the area of "Accounting & Finance Services" specifically investigating the relationship of a Shared Services Organization with its governance function, Corporate Finance.

The following article by *KLAUS P. STEGEMANN*, *SIEGRID DENGLER*, *ALEXANDER RIEDEL* and *TOBIAS WEBER* revisits the global Cluster Finance Bundling project conducted by *Siemens AG* from 2009 to 2011. Its purpose is to summarize both the strategic challenges addressed by the project as well as the key cornerstones of its successful implementation. It thus provides insights and guidance on the inception and completion of a large-scale project in the field of optimizing a regional finance organization with special regard to Shared Services. *MARCELL VOLLMER* and *PETER RASPER* outline a conceptual model of transformation management including Change Management and Communication. Their model is based on a real case delivered by both authors as well as qualitative pre-studies. Thus, a holistic approach for transformation management during the entire journey in a global Shared Services Program is proposed. Based upon a wide body of scientific literature on process standardization and Shared Services *FRANK ULBRICH* explores possible trajectories of Shared Service Centers, discusses motives to move into a certain direction, and especially investigates their pros and cons. *STEPHAN BOOS* identifies key factors for the successful management of transition projects in a Shared Services environment. The first part of the compilation is completed by an interview conducted with *DAN NOVAK*, Head of the *Siemens* Accounting & Finance Services Center in the Czech Republic, which primarily focusses on the development phase of "lift-drop" and the realization of the Finance Bundling project at *Siemens* hereby especially taking the center perspective into consideration and the systematic management of the growth resulting from the bundling initiative.

The second part of the compilation starts with an article by *OTTO WENDLAND*, who describes a systematic approach to launching a process improvement program in order to meet technical as well as behavioral challenges during an evolutionary Shared Services journey as depicted in figure 1. *ANNETTE HÄUSSER* conducted an intensive literature review and 22 in-depth interviews with Shared Services Center managers to explore numerous areas in which Finance Shared Services can positively influence corporate performance. In the following interview with *OLIVER WOLF* readers gain deeper insights into performance tracking of Shared Services Centers. This matter is also discussed by *MATTHIAS LOHRMANN* and *ALEXANDER RIEDEL*. They develop frameworks to support process quality and process performance assessment. *STEFAN RÖDER* and *FRANK KEUPER* outline a conceptual model of internal customer perceptions of service quality provided by Shared Services Organizations. The model is based on a wide body of internal marketing literature as well as qualitative pre-studies. A multidimensional, hierarchical scale for measuring service quality is proposed, which is embedded in a structural model to further analyze relevant outomes of customer perceived service quality within a Shared Services environment.

At the beginning of part three *KAI ZABEL* concentrates on the extension of the Shared Services concept to smaller entities. Beginning with the benefits of Shared Services for smaller entities, he goes on to talk about generic approaches and shows how to organize the extension. In the next chapter *JOACHIM JÄCKLE* and *SEBASTIAN WOLF* deal with the concept of Shared Services as integrated business partners managing end-to-end processes. Starting with the relevant conceptual basics they especially elaborate critical transformation issues during the journey from transactional Shared Services to business partnering. *NICOLE DREHER* pays attention to a systematic concept of developing new ideas that can be added to the Shared Services portfolio and sold within a captive environment. After having selected the new service offerings, a comprehensive approach – the "6 Shared Services Ps" – is applied to systematically develop the marketing and sales strategy of new services along the Shared Services relevant areas of product, price, place, promotion, people and perception management. The measures and initiatives derived along the "6 Shared Services Ps" give a clear hands-on guidance and a practical implementation advice on how to sell services in a highly sensitive environment – thereby taking political as well as emotional obstacles into consideration. *DOMINIC STEPHENSON*, *ROMAN BECKER*, *PATRICK LANGE*, *THILO RAU* and *ALEXANDER RIEDEL* discuss the foundations, sourcing options and crucial implementation issues of Controlling Shared Services. *MARIJN JANSSEN, JÜRGEN H. M. VAN GRINSVEN* and *ANTON JOHA* focus on the challenges of combine a Center of Expertise and a Shared Services Center into a Shared Service Center of Excellence. They analyze the basic concepts and identify a case study at a financial organization, in which the operational risk management (ORM) function is organized as a Shared Service Center of Excellence. The third part of this compilation ends with two future-oriented articles. While *FRANK HELBING*, *THILO RAU* und *ALEXANDER RIEDEL* especially discuss trends and developments regarding Finance Shared Services Organizations, *KAI-EBERHARD LUEG* and *FRANK KEUPER* take a more holistic view towards Shared Services in 2020.

Part four begins with the paper by *VANESSA EGLI* exploring the way in which change management has been used, and can be used, to support the successful execution of transition projects, referring to the *Siemens* Finance Bundling global project as a specific example. The article by *SUSANNE SOMMERER* elaborates how the HR organization and the responsible management of a SSO can jointly ensure successful Personnel Management. Further, she describes important success factors and selected 'real life' HR initiatives, applied within the SSO of a multinational company. *ARWED CRÜGER* and *ANDREAS RIEDL* discuss transfer pricing requirements concerning Shared Services. Last but not least *STEFAN STEIN*, *WINFRIED RUH*, *MARCUS SELG*, *MARTIN TROST* and *ALEXANDER RIEDEL* also deal with transfer pricing aspects focussing on cross-border service provisions.

A special thanks to our authors without whose contributions this book would not have been possible. Despite the tight schedule, the authors demonstrated extraordinary commitment in putting together their practical and theoretical contributions. As always, delivery of the final proofs to *Springer Gabler Verlag* was only possible thanks to the many "helping hands" in the back-ground – on *Siemens* side especially *REGINA SCHMIDT*. We would like to take this opportunity of expressing our thanks.

The editors wish to express a further special note of thanks to *BARBARA ROSCHER* und *JUTTA HINRICHSEN* of *Springer Gabler Verlag* for their help and cooperation in publishing this book.

Hamburg/Munich, February 2013

PROF. DR. FRANK KEUPER and *KAI-EBERHARD LUEG*

Table of Contents

Introduction

Strategic Roadmap of a Global Finance Shared Services Organization

KAI-EBERHARD LUEG

Siemens AG, Global Shared Services

Executive Summary

The implementation of Shared Services structures is now in many areas and in many regions a widely accepted model to gain process efficiency and reduce costs. But the evolution is ongoing. Shared Services are increasingly being seen as a modern, effective and efficient way for multinational companies to organize and streamline their administrative structures across borders.

In theory, a Shared Services Organization (SSO) can quickly improve cost position, quality and control, and give business units flexible support by freeing them from their administrative tasks. In practice, it takes a rather long breath and systematic planning as well as stringent execution of the different development phases, each with its own challenges. This ultimately takes the Shared Services Organization to the position of being recognized as a trusted partner. This further includes that its core competencies as a provider of intelligent workflow solutions is fully recognized and utilized, in contrary to just staying a cost-effective but technically not advanced partner.

Taking *Siemens* as an example, this article reviews the specific strategic roadmap of its Finance Shared Services Organization, thereby outlining: 1) The phases of "lift-drop" with the transfer of transactional accounting tasks into Shared Services environment, 2) "Change" and the systematic process optimization and 3) The rather future-oriented phase "enhance and innovate" conducting analyses of additional service offerings and elaborating substantial innovations to reduce manual interventions in processes. The main improvement levers of the third phase will surely be in the workflow automation area.

In addition, the challenges and opportunities of an internal Shared Services provider are briefly described, thereby taking into consideration external conditions like globalization, increasing competition and emerging markets driving the need of a Shared Services Organization to actively contribute to the overall competitiveness of the company. Furthermore, the heterogeneous business requirements of a conglomerate company like *Siemens*, the various ERP systems and the continuous merger and acquisition activities challenge a Shared Services Organization on an ongoing basis. To complete this picture, internal conditions like demanding stakeholder expectations such as cost reduction and improvement of quality and transparency are analyzed.

In order to provide a practical view on the strategic development of a captive Shared Services provider, specific focus areas are identified to gain an understanding of how to successfully move from "lift-drop" to "change". Further, recommendations are given on how to initiate the "enhance and innovate phase". Therein, topics such as the key factors for successful transitions, the management of systematic process improvement, the people-focused topics of personnel and change management as well as the professional monitoring of performances are highlighted.

In summary, this article explores the strategic view of the development of the *Siemens*-internal Shared Services Organization and briefly describes the relevant topics to be considered along the journey, thereby emphasizing challenges and opportunities as well as practical focus areas. Thus, this introductory article is set up to draw the reader's interest on the variety of topics covered in this book that all can be accessed in detail within the respective articles.

1 Introduction

The business environment in contemporary times is increasingly unpredictable, for this various reasons can be quoted: higher market volatility, technological and global shifts and the facilitation of increased communication and data exchange possibilities around the world. At the time of writing, many companies are feeling the impact of a weakened global economy. To be successful in competing especially with companies evolving from emerging markets, the organization must be flexible and be able to respond to rapid market changes.

Addressing the challenge of remaining successful in a constantly changing environment, a global conglomerate has a strong need to leverage all possibilities to reduce administrative costs, increase quality, speed, flexibility and transparency, for example with the help of a Shared Services Organization.

In the reference case of *Siemens*, the global Shared Services Organization has evolved from various local and individual bundling initiatives. It started to be an in-house Shared Services provider in 2006. After several local transitions of transactional accounting activities had been successfully realized, a mandate by the managing board was given in 2009 and the world-wide transition of transactional activities into a Shared Services environment gained tremendous speed and momentum. Starting 2010, within two years more than 300 transition projects were executed. The transactional accounting tasks were transferred from more than 300 operational companies into the Shared Services Centers (SSCs) which were ramped-up around the world.

This phase was essential to establish the *Siemens* SSO within the company and to position it as an integrated part of the *Siemens* financial community. The strategic roadmap and the development phases of an internal Shared Services provider will be the key focus of this introductory article.

2 Overall Targets and Benefits of Finance Shared Services

When outlining the reasons for the implementation of Shared Services Organizations various topics are cited by experts:

- The cost reduction and realization of savings via labour arbitrage and process optimization,
- The systematic improvement of quality,
- The increase of compliance and transparency on usage, costs and performance.
- The freeing-up of business units of administrative tasks, in order to enable them to focus on core tasks.

The main expectation of stakeholders regarding the transfer of activities to a SSO is a **reduction of costs** with improved or at least unchanged quality of services. Major parts of the savings are bound to factors which cannot be easily achieved inside the normal, often decentralized company organizations as they do not have the necessary scale or capabilities to individually exploit labor arbitrage advantages, economies of scale and process efficiency improvements resulting from transactional "mass production". SSOs on the contrary are organized specifically in a way to offer the possibility to reduce costs and to improve operational efficiency.

Various estimations on the potential of cost reductions after successfully implementing a SSO are available but referring to a study of 500 major German companies of different branches, annual savings of 5 to 30 % after the implementation of SSCs were stated.[1] Transferring formerly independent local transactional processes from the business units into a centralized Shared Services Organization creates the basis for generating economies of scale. The main cost reductions are leveraged through consolidation of transactional tasks, process optimization and synergy effects, the improved quality and effectiveness, but especially through the choice of locations offering a higher cost-effectiveness. In a rather medium- to long-term view, the bundled and centralized transactional operations can become an economically attractive base for process redesigns and investments in automation.

However, it is not all about cost savings. There are further advantages resulting from the implementation of a SSO. The Shared Services model can be an attractive option as it **frees up key personnel** in the business units from basic, time consuming activities related to support processes. Thus, the business units can fully concentrate on their core activities in their value chain. The Shared Services Organization takes care of the support processes and fully concentrates on these. This means a dedicated management is established to explicitly focus on the effective and efficient execution of support processes as their core competence.

The dedicated management attention on support processes is directly linked to the next benefit of SSOs – the **improvement of quality**. This is by far the most important topic, especially in the area of financial processes, though in practice this is often not given the necessary attention it deserves. While the most important objective of Shared Services Organizations is to reduce costs in the initial period, quality improvement has become a decisive factor for the establishment of a SSO. A recent study by *PriceWaterhouseCoopers* revealed that quality improvement is considered as the most important objective for implementing a SSO from today's perspective.[2] Pooling of processes and the availability of dedicated process experts in the Shared Services environment provide the opportunity to systematically improve transactional tasks now that they are delivered by one single and focused organization. When analyzing and aggregating the demand of all the business units, it pays off to have dedicated experts working on the improvement of the process landscape.

Another benefit from Shared Services Organizations lies in the **increased transparency**. This is closely linked to the topic of compliance and adherence to company guidelines. It is easier to ensure that guidelines are being followed when focusing on one organization with standardized workflows (the SSO) rather than trying to control various business units executing the services in different manners.

---

1 Cf. *FISCHER/STERZENBACH* (2006).

2 Cf. *PWC* (2012), p. 14.

After outlining the benefits of Shared Services Organizations it needs to be highlighted that the expectations of the stakeholders need to be met in order to realize the benefits mentioned above: professional transfer of support processes to the SSCs, uninterrupted high quality in service delivery and consequent optimization of processes to realize cost reductions for the customers. Keeping in mind that the fulfillment of these tasks needs to be proven and communicated step by step, the underlying transparency of processes, cost and performance is a prerequisite to successfully compete as an internal Shared Services Organization.

3 Strategic Development Phases

The strategic development phases of captive Shared Services Organizations describe the degree of maturity and the position and role within the organization. In general, three different approaches exist to transition processes into a Shared Services environment. Each of these three approaches is divided into three steps, i.e., "lift", "drop" and "change". The phase of "change" points to the process transformation; "lift" refers to the transfer of processes from the operational business units to the SSC, and "drop" describes the integration of processes into the SSO.

- Option 1: "Lift-drop-change"
- Option 2: "Lift-change-drop"
- Option 3: "Change-lift-drop"

While the three approaches do not differ much with respect to their ultimate target, the order of the three phases makes a huge difference when it comes to an overall strategic company view. When deciding about the appropriate approach to be used the following should be considered:

- How can the knowledge transfer to the SSO be guaranteed?
- Who will be the process owner?
- How can barriers and constraints be handled in an effective and transparent way?

The decision about the best option for a company largely depends on the objectives. **Option 1** ("lift-drop-change") foresees that the SSO takes over and operates processes from the customer as they were executed before. After this, the SSO moves into the next phase and actively drives the harmonization and optimization of the processes. In case the pace of the transition is a crucial factor, a company should prefer this option. Specifically in rather big and complex organizations, the realization of the actual "change" is often much more time consuming than the actual transition. Further, in order to achieve the first results of process reallocation as fast as possible, the "lift" from customer side and "drop" to the Shared Services environment should be realized right at the beginning, securing exploitation of labor cost arbitrage, providing motivation for the "donating" entities and an economic platform for the changes to come.

Option 2 ("lift-change-drop") describes a rather uncommon method of removing processes from the business units, then optimizing them before transferring into the SSCs. This approach is rarely used since the optimization needs a relatively high effort that has to be executed in a limited period of time in order to guarantee service continuity.

Option 3 ("change-lift-drop") demands that processes are optimized first by the current process owner who is the future customer of the SSO and then transferred. This implies that the optimization is driven by the "donating" operational units. An extremely high degree of coordination among these units is required to ensure process harmonization. This option in most cases can be highly time consuming and risky because the "change" has to be completed before the actual transition is initiated. Therefore option 3 may be suitable for comparatively less complex organizations.

Looking at a complex and heterogeneous company like *Siemens*, the decision on the more suitable option can be considered as rather obvious. Project Finance Bundling reshaped the entire *Siemens* finance community in a fundamental way. It was about achieving fast results thus starting with the "lift-drop" phase driven by a central department, the governance function of the Accounting and Finance Organization. At first, the decision to follow the methodology of "lift-drop-change" offered the opportunity to realize the transition of a defined scope of services with a clear mandate of the *Siemens* managing board and after that to drive the "change" and optimize accounting processes in a systematic and transparent manner. This option offers an opportunity for the SSO to prove and demonstrate that not only a take-over of support services can be professionally managed, but also that the SSO is capable of stabilizing the business and driving the necessary changes to optimize accounting processes in a structured and professional way. The ultimate focus is then to achieve further improvements in processes which should result in savings that are handed back to customers in terms of price reductions and improvements in quality and speed.

In the following sub-chapters the phases of "lift", "drop" and "change" will be described in detail taking *Siemens* as a reference, followed by an outlook to a future additional phase called "enhance and innovate". In order to give the complete picture, enablers and prerequisites for the successful realization of these phases will be outlined.

3.1 Phase I: Lift and Drop

The "lift-drop" phase, in the case of the *Siemens* SSO, was officially initiated with the receiving of a mandate by the *Siemens* managing board. Project Finance Bundling including the transfer of specific transactional accounting processes into the Shared Services environment can be considered as the biggest change project within the finance community that has ever been realized in *Siemens*. In parallel to the transfer of transactional activities to SSCs, on a regional level, governance and controlling activities were transferred into new cross-regional Cluster organizations.

The *Siemens* internal SSO had to ensure smooth transitions from the operational business to the Shared Services Centers around the world thereby covering transactional services such as Accounts Payables, Accounts Receivables, Master Data, Inter- and Intra-Company Clearing, Cash and Bank, Asset Accounting, General Ledger and Closing and Reporting. Existing business and also the new workload had to be executed in a professional way which implied that the SSO had to ramp up a large number of employees within a short period of time.

Looking at the different players in this project it becomes clear that one of the key challenges is to satisfy all the stakeholders involved in this project. The Corporate Finance department of the company was in the driver's seat and was actively managing the variety of stakeholder interests.

At the beginning of Project Finance Bundling some of the stakeholders involved were reluctant and had doubts about the capability of the Shared Services Centers. To ensure results and mitigate their concerns, a professional project and risk management approach was taken to build up trust and confidence with all relevant partners.

The question of how this project was successfully handled from a Shared Services Organization's perspective will be dealt with in various articles of this book. A first impression of the key success factors are outlined below:

- Professional and transparent project and risk management (including systematic reporting activities, and including the "right to say no" for the SSO),
- Close collaboration amongst all parties involved (donating entities, Finance Governance, operative organizations and the SSO),
- Continuous communication on relevant next steps and issues to be solved,
- Efficient timely recruiting of personnel for the SSC,
- Training and motivation programs to keep and further develop key employees,
- Continuous controlling and monitoring.

From a strategic perspective the "lift-drop" phase was an elementary step for the *Siemens* SSO to gain pace and volume, and to prove that an internal service provider is able to successfully support such a comprehensive project and to actively drive the change of the financial operations structure within the company.

Looking back at some of the aspects learned during this project, the absolute key priority was to ensure continuous service quality supported by direct feedback and communication. This means for instance constantly accurate bookings and correct monthly and quarterly closings of the books at all times. If this cannot be guaranteed the development phase of "lift-drop" and with that the entire Shared Services concept is endangered and skeptics would rightfully put every effort in stopping such a project. Bearing in mind that the relationship between the SSO and the donating entities has to be built on trust and experience, this can be only achieved by delivering high quality services.

3.2 Phase II: Change

The next step for the internal SSO after having successfully managed the "lift" of transactional accounting activities from the donating entities and having "dropped" these tasks into the Shared Services Centers is to prove that the Shared Services Organization can be more than just a "supplier" and can actively optimize and change processes. This is an entirely new level of challenge requiring different skill-sets and appropriate trainings. Now that the transactional activities are handled in a single organization, executed in multiple global locations, the actual optimization can be realized in a faster and more structured way than in a decentralized fragmented organization.

When setting up a program to actively drive process optimization, it is crucial to understand the main interests and concerns of various stakeholders e.g.:

- The **customers** are interested in receiving agreed levels of services as defined in Service Level Agreements (SLAs) and Key Performance Indicators, thereby ensuring quality and price reductions.
- The **Corporate Finance** department with the overall governance for the accounting processes expects streamlined, harmonized and optimized transactional accounting processes ensuring highest quality levels.
- The **Shared Services Organization** intends to prove that the change can be managed in an effective and efficient way and wants to offer its employees opportunities to develop end to end process expertise.

Post bundling *Siemens* decided to start systematic improvements by way of harmonization and best practice sharing. Therefore, the *Siemens* SSO has initiated a global "Process Improvements for Accounting" program ("PIA"). It is crucial for the success of this program to closely involve all stakeholders in the program set-up and also in the execution. As a consequence, the organizational set-up of the PIA Program comprises various representatives of the customers and governance sides to safeguard all stakeholder interests.

In detail, the PIA Program includes eight projects at the time of writing in the areas of Accounts Payable, Accounts Receivable and Closing and Reporting with the focus to make current processes faster, more efficient and leaner. The projects include, for instance, in the area of Accounts Payables the scanning and automated processing of invoices, the implementation of e-invoicing, the reduction of payment runs, the reduction of efforts for payment proposal verification; and in the area of accounts receivables the harmonization of bank statements and the increase of usage of remittance advices. For Closing and Reporting the implementation of an event-driven-closing-workflow is analyzed to reduce error-prone manual processes in increasingly tight global closing time schedules. To involve process experts in this program, specific process communities are set up. They frequently meet and exchange ideas in their specific area of expertise to jointly define common practices, as for instance a standard closing process used as a basis for the implementation of an event-driven-closing-workflow.

Coming back to the various stakeholder interests, a way to ensure support from major stakeholders is the transparent four-step-approach of PIA:

1. Calculation of top-down impact estimations for chosen ideas
2. Realization of pilot projects as proof of concept
3. Calculation of bottom-up impact estimations followed by discussions and subsequently decisions by a Steering Committee whether to proceed with global roll-outs or not
4. Systematic implementation

The objective of each pilot is to ensure technical and economical feasibility before the roll-out. This is where the *Siemens* SSO is focusing on at the time of writing. Looking at the first experiences within the PIA Program it can be stated that the successful realization of "change" is highly dependent on the active support of all stakeholders involved who need to work into the same direction. The momentum necessary to drive a program of such magnitude has to be generated by the Shared Services Organization itself and as with all changes it is about transparently demonstrating the benefits resulting from the changes and convincing the parties involved of the necessity of the project to obtain their support. Especially in a captive environment, without a specific mandate by the managing board, this "selling" involves a high degree of effort on the Shared Services side. By working on this step by step, more and more promoters can be convinced and with that a broad roll-out can be financed for all initiatives where successful pilots have proven the concept.

When the first wave of the PIA Program is completed, more projects are planned in subsequent phases. After all, the systematic process optimization has to be also a continuous improvement program. Therefore, the process expert communities which were set up must not stop exchanging ideas and discussing new ways of optimizing accounting processes in the Shared Services locations, together with the customers.

3.3 Phase III: Outlook – Enhance and Innovate

The following development phase "enhance and innovate" gives an outlook on how an internal Shared Services Organization can further develop within the company. It needs to be emphasized that the first priority of the *Siemens* internal Shared Services provider remains to successfully stabilize and further improve the work that has been transferred and to ensure processes are optimized by usage of systematic programs whilst maintaining costs.

Nevertheless, it is up to the SSO to "use the momentum" and thus the position achieved within the company to think about potential new ideas – all on the transactional level – that can generate further savings for the entire company. It is crucial to mention that active portfolio enhancement is a highly sensitive topic, since again customers and stakeholders may be rather reluctant when it comes to transferring more activities from their operational business into a Shared Services environment. It is essential to note that any portfolio enhancement needs to be carefully prepared and discussed on the Shared Services side first, aligned with the respective governance functions and then implemented together with customers.

The further optimization of the current Shared Services portfolio has to be initiated in a systematic way just as it is the case for both of the phases "lift-drop" and "change". In the first place the right service portfolio enhancements need to be selected taking customer expectations and requirements into consideration. Usually, at the initial phase of developing a new portfolio element, no mandate from the central managing board is available. Both, the selection of the appropriate new services as well as the selling of these services can be considered as a challenge, and it needs to be ensured that the SSO does not go into "overselling mode".

Considering the second and even more important aspect of this development phase "enhance and innovate" it comes to the aspect of taking the change phase to the next level by implementing more and more intelligent and automated solutions that reduce manual efforts and make processes more efficient. Solutions for operating platforms (middleware) to deal with the different IT-systems within the company are to be analyzed. In the view of the author, automation will be by far the biggest lever to improve productivity and quality in the Shared Services environment in the middle and long term. Other key topics, such as user-friendly interfaces and workflows will need to be developed. More ideas are developed in close cooperation with the process communities and major stakeholders.

4 Challenges and Chances

After having investigated the Siemens SSO specific development phases, the next step is to outline challenges and chances from a practical Shared Services perspective. The *Siemens* SSO needs to continuously improve in all areas to handle the current and future challenges, both internally and externally. However, risks can also be chances. In the next pages, some examples of tools and initiatives will be highlighted which the *Siemens* SSO has employed to successfully manage these challenges.

4.1 Rapid Changes in Environmental Conditions

Most organizations face increasing competition, also from emerging countries. Competitors from low cost countries are a challenge for organizations which traditionally have their resources in high cost countries. Certainly innovation and quality are decisive factors for being competitive; nevertheless, companies need to find intelligent means to reduce costs and to offer products at competitive prices. Further, they need to be faster in adapting to environmental changes and in implementing new service and delivery structures.

While the *Siemens* SSO as an internal provider and zero profit organization is not confronted directly with competition, it nonetheless has to constantly prove its value-add by generating savings and increasing process and service quality for the company. Moreover, benchmarking with other captive SSOs is essential to ensure that even in a captive environment, the SSO can offer attractive and competitive services. Only then can the internal customers recognize the value and long-term benefit of a Shared Services Organization. Technological development is thereby absolutely crucial. In the areas of process improvement and automation, new developments enable the SSO to continuously pursue higher efficiency. Just to name a few examples: e-invoicing or self-billing based on e-enabled portals and process flows can improve operations to a great extent and can support bold moves in productivity.

Globalization and competition have a direct impact on SSOs themselves. Being dependent on the resources market in the SSC locations, Shared Services Organizations are often confronted with competitors rivaling for the same resources. Due to the fact that the flexibility of salaries is comparatively limited as the SSO concept is to some extent based on lower-cost structures, and due to the fact that tasks in the range of Shared Services are perceived as rather repetitive and not career-driven, activities around human resource management play an important role. Strategies around the attraction, development and retention of people are therefore crucial for success.

Other challenges resulting from globalization are legal regulations. SSOs which are based on the concept of transferring transactional activities from one country to a location offering higher cost-effectiveness are dependent on efficient bundling activities. When this is not possible due to legal regulations, e.g. data protection/security constraints, employment restricttions or unfavorable tax regulations, the whole concept cannot be realized. Here the degree of influence on change is rather low, however, these facts need to be equally kept in mind when planning the transfer of transactional activities. Individual projects which cannot be started due to previously unknown or underestimated legal restrictions will have a negative impact on the overall business case and savings.

4.2 Complex Organizations, Processes and IT Landscapes

Siemens is an international industrial conglomerate and by nature a rather **complex organization,** not only due to its size and heterogeneous business structure, but also to its historical growth. At the time of writing, *Siemens* is active in around 190 regions with almost 600 companies all over the world. Because of its continuously growing portfolio and mergers and acquisition activities, the organizational structure of *Siemens* contains a large variety of individual organizational structures, reaching from pure production sites to sales organizations and holdings. Several initiatives have already been implemented in order to adapt the organization to the changing needs. One of the latest global initiatives was taken in 2008 when *Siemens* reinforced the position of its Sectors (Energy, Healthcare, Industry, and later Infrastructure & Cities) and partially changed its organization from independent country presences to administrative structures bundled on the level of newly established cross-regional Cluster structures.

The complexity of the *Siemens* structure can equally be noticed in the **processes**. Financial planning (internal and external), reporting and controlling in *Siemens* are based on various processes and activities conducted by the individual companies. These differences in business processes are also due to different products and solutions offered by *Siemens* which reach from magnetic resonance healthcare systems to fossil power plants or from small motors to high speed trains. Processes and the respective IT applications used at *Siemens* are therefore equally diverse; often requirements differ depending on the company's function and business. Due to its size and complexity, *Siemens* does not only have a variety of guidelines to follow, but also a diversity of different activities due to local specifics, such as legal and offshore regulations, tax requirements, foreign currencies, data protection etc.

Referring to the **IT landscape** we can differentiate between standard ERP platforms and non-standard business-specific platforms including small company solutions. *Siemens* developed a standardized SAP platform called "Spiridon" which is an example for an internal highly integrated IT platform concept based on harmonized processes in the local sales companies. However, it is a system which is not suitable for all companies. For consolidated companies that cannot use this system or other comprehensive ERP systems, a Small Company Solution[3] has been developed. In addition to standard ERP platforms with different releases, there are

3 The Small Company Solution is a template solution that is set as a corporate standard for consolidated small and medium-sized *Siemens* companies (sales do not exceed € 50m, less than 100 SCS users) where SCS covers the logistics functionality of the various business processes and thus supports the realization of the entire accounting process.

also other non-standard ERP systems in place which vary in their system performance, data volume, functionalities, etc.

With a large variety of processes, IT systems and different needs of the customers, it is difficult to find the right balance between standardization and flexibility to adapt to customers' specific requirements. This diversity does not so much evoke difficulties in the transfer of processes but rather in the achievement of bundling effects aside from labor arbitrage. A further optimization of the finance processes of a large company, making it even better, leaner and more flexible, is therefore enormously challenging but also brings along a lot of chances for a captive Shared Services Organization.

In the *Siemens* SSO one of the first steps was the implementation of a so-called reference process house and the establishment of process handbooks which have been elaborated in close cooperation with the governance function. Additionally, in order to enable internal and external benchmarking, a global product catalog was introduced in *Siemens* comprising clearly defined portfolio elements and underlying services and products.

One initiative, to foster harmonization around the *Siemens* globe and to ensure transparent consolidated reporting on the finance level, is the Infrastructure Cost Reporting Project. A lean and globally consistent regional finance organization, offering clear roles and responsibilities based on a globally aligned activity split ensures an optimal setup of regional infrastructure in order to support the operative units in doing their business in an efficient way. Target is to provide worldwide cost transparency for infrastructure service providers.

4.3 Demanding Stakeholder Expectations

The fulfillment of stakeholder expectations is key in all development phases of a captive Shared Services Organization. When looking at these expectations in detail, the following areas can be identified:

- Realization of savings
- Quality improvement
- Development of intelligent (process) solutions
- A transparent cost/ pricing approach
- Continuous tracking and monitoring
- Adherence to compliance guidelines

When transferring activities to a Shared Services Organization the immediate customer's expectation is certainly to reduce **cost**. Taking the *Siemens* SSO into consideration it can be stated that from project Finance Bundling which lead to the transfer of transactional accounting processes into internal Shared Services Centers, *Siemens* achieved on average cost savings of 35% worldwide. The Shared Services Centers have been strategically built up in cost efficient locations in order to secure quick savings by the transfer of activities from higher cost countries. However, this requires lead time and there is of course the learning curve. Further, the deployment of new, often rather inexperienced people in the Shared Services Centers requires some temporary managed over-staffing. Further, SSOs which are represented globally make use of a systematic front-office/ back-office structure. When applying this concept one has to bear in mind that for achieving an additional savings effect by – for instance – transferring tasks from an European SSC to India, the key focus on quality needs to be maintained. Also this step needs to be closely aligned with the customer.

After completion of the transfer and stabilization, further savings which can be handed back to the internal customers are to be realized through systematic harmonization, standardization and where possible automation of the accounting processes. Due to the fact that *Siemens* SSO follows a "cost plus" charging model or in other words a "zero profit" approach, all savings are direct savings for the customers.

In order to minimize time consuming and from a company perspective unproductive internal alignment, the *Siemens* Finance Bundling Project followed a globally harmonized **costing/ pricing approach** with regard to services rendered by *Siemens* SSO, considering mandatory local tax and legal requirements. Generally transfer prices, including those which are related to internal projects, are to be calculated on an arm's length basis and need to be documented in line with the transfer pricing guidelines. They have to comply with business specific pricing rules and local requirements as well. Transfer Pricing policies need to be designed to ensure a sustainable approach by balancing global compliance with Transfer Pricing laws by mitigating relevant risk exposures whilst meeting business needs regarding efficient business processes.

In addition to being a lever for simple cost reduction, Shared Services have evolved into a comprehensive and flexible platform for improving processes, using modern enabling technologies and implementing **quality** improvement concepts. Nevertheless, especially at the beginning of a transition it is very challenging for the service provider to maintain the agreed levels of quality: new people at new locations perform the services for business units which compare the performance of the new service provider with their own past performances. So, expectations are high, not only regarding cost reductions, but also referring to quality of services. Cases have been observed where customer expectations towards outsourced services are even higher than they were when conducted in the own organization.

Referring to further demanding expectations by the stakeholders, especially concerning the stabilization of processes **continuous tracking and monitoring** of key performance indicators and operational metrics need to be ensured. Thus, underlying process quality and performance need to be transparent for the stakeholders. For the major accounting tasks handled by the *Siemens* SSO, a "quality cockpit" has been developed including 12 key performance indicators to monitor quality on *Siemens* SSO side (output KPI's) and on business partner side (directly related input KPI's). The outputs of the Quality Cockpit are displayed in a Dashboard which provides full transparency and supports fact-based discussions internally and with the customer in order to define mitigating actions where necessary, and to continuously stabilize and optimize end to end processes.

All *Siemens* entities are required to implement an effective and efficient Risk and Internal Control System within their area of responsibility. A Risk and Internal Controls organization is in place to provide all the guidance, support and expertise needed to thouroughly implement and properly run the processes. Trust and acceptance on the stakeholders' side can be achieved through the increase of transparency on usage, performance and costs of services and through the strict implementation and monitoring of all relevant internal control requirements. **Compliance** with legal requirements and ethical standards is the basis for high integrity business behavior. The overall target of the *Siemens* SSO is to be recognized as a trustworthy partner to all stakeholders.

As soon as the processes are stable, the next steps are optimization, harmonization and automation to generate further savings and improve overall quality and process efficiency.

5 Focus Areas of Implementation

A successful management of the challenges and chances described above requires a clearly defined strategy taking into account specific focus areas. They include project-related topics, such as the Professional Management of Transition Projects during the "lift-drop" phase, the Systematic Management of Process Improvements during the "change" phase and Future-Oriented Portfolio Management as a part of the "enhance and innovate" phase, as well as key enablers and prerequisites for project success, such as the Sustainable People Management and the Continuous Controlling and Monitoring.

5.1 Professional Management of Transition Projects

In the strategic development phase of "lift-drop", one of the key factors for success is the professional management of the transition projects. These projects coordinate the overall transfer of defined transactional processes from local donating entities to the receiving SSC.

For *Siemens* SSO as a captive Shared Services provider a clear mandate as well as the support and commitment from top management and governance for these projects was an important aspect. As already mentioned above, projects with such a scale are not embraced by each and every stakeholder specifically in complex and decentralized organizations like *Siemens*.

Further, it was crucial to define and align a clear service scope and project objectives. Based on the determined project goals, the management team set up rules to govern the design and implementation decisions made in the project. The key design principles contain clear-cut escalation rules and approval levels as well as formalized rules for the deviation request process, whenever a project could not be conducted according to the overall scope. Moreover, the activity split as a globally applicable standard was agreed, defining organizational process responsibilities and ensuring a consistent assignment of tasks to organizational units. The agreed principles and project scope were binding and exceptions were only possible in accordance to strict criteria and reconciliation with the governance function.

In particular, during the "lift-drop" phase which was critical in terms of the timeline, the steering committee, project team and other team members committed high efforts to the project progress and ensured consistent momentum. This commitment to agreed deliverables, timelines and active participation as well as the adherence to achieved results and decisions were key success factors. A transition guide thereby ensured the systematic processing of transition projects.

5.2 Systematic Management of Process Improvements

In the strategic development phase "change" the overall target is to leverage harmonization and if possible automation and implementation of supportive workflow tools. In order to provide adequate room for discussions and to give process improvements the necessary importance, specialized finance **process communities** were established by the *Siemens* SSO. In general, these process communities are aimed to connect people with peers and their outputs include leading practices, guidelines, knowledge repositories, technical problem- and solution discussions, working papers and strategies. The mission of the process communities is to build excellence by consolidating knowledge amongst all SSCs, facilitating communication, networking and driving consensual understanding of problems and opportunities.

The starting point for the process communities was the commitment to further improve transactional accounting processes. From there, several possible improvement projects were identified and analyzed. In order to ensure professional implementation and transparency it was decided to proceed under the roof of a systematic program. In August 2011 this led to a "Process Improvements for Accounting Founding Charter", which was discussed and agreed with all major stakeholders and customers of the *Siemens* SSO. The main improvement levers for PIA are internal quality and productivity improvement projects, harmonization of bundled processes and where feasible investment in automation. From 14 identified improvement areas 8 prioritized projects were chosen to start, based on the following evaluation criteria: easy implementation, direct quality impact, yearly cost savings and low complexity (interfaces). The overall target is to achieve quick wins through which additional savings can be achieved and where the contributors are not overstrained after an already very labor-intensive lift-drop phase.

Various tools and methodologies were introduced in the SSCs to focus on continuous improvements like six sigma, failure mode and effects analysis etc. with the main objective of providing the necessary skills to the employees to develop and maintain their focus on improvements.

A strong change culture with focus on process quality improvement and harmonization is a prerequisite to implement the necessary framework for one-time process improvements but also for continuous improvements which are crucial for sustainable success.

5.3 Future-oriented Portfolio Management

When it comes to further areas of improvement, it has to be considered that due to Project Finance Bundling and the transfer of specific transactional accounting processes, the maximum internal accessible market penetration in *Siemens* is in many cases nearly reached. This means that the SSO needs to be aware of the fact that any additional market penetration is rather limited – at least in these areas.

In the strategic development phase "enhance and innovate" the key target is to further improve accounting processes, to identify new portfolio elements – and to actively "market" them. Following the initiation of the improvement program, benchmarking projects now play an important role in the context of efficient process improvement and future-oriented portfolio management. It is important to get transparency where the organization stands, to conduct comparisons amongst the Shared Services Centers and also to benchmark with other external Shared Services providers thereby looking at cost, productivity, process designs and quality.

Getting transparency with the help of benchmarking enables the SSO to improve its performance by identifying weaknesses and strengths and deriving specific measures. As a result and to support the development from a mandated service provider to a strategic partner, opportunities to refine service offerings and to add matching new services along the core competencies can be developed. The topic of selecting the right ideas to further expand the service portfolio as well as the "marketing" of new ideas without a mandate by the managing board will be outlined and analyzed in further detail in the articles of the section "enhance and innovate".

5.4 Sustainable Change and Personnel Management

Two of the main enablers along the journey of developing a Shared Services Organization to a trusted partner are Change Management and Personnel Management. Referring to **Change Management** the SSO needs to first identify, employ and integrate new employees with a broad range of process and language skills to suit the growing customer community ("lift-drop" phase). Secondly, the Shared Services provider also needs to cope with a growing process complexity while staying on top of local compliance and legal regulations to then initiate the process optimization ("change" phase). Then during the third phase the commercial skills of the organization play a more important role in terms of identifying product refinements that will improve service offerings, increase market share and focusing on innovations that fundamentally improve the process execution. Additionally the SSO, especially the captive one, operates in an environment of high attention from various stakeholders and governance partners. The achievement of rapid organizational changes while still keeping all affected parties aligned can only be achieved by efficient Change Management practices, placing a special focus on the "people" dimension.

Taking the **Personnel Management** into consideration, generally, the SSO is widely but wrongly perceived as an industry that does not offer many individual development options but offers repetitive, low level and low paid jobs in an environment characterized by constant time and cost saving pressure. From the very beginning in a SSO it is important to consider employee activities and to think about how a successful personnel management can be ensured – considering all relevant external and internal influencing dimensions (e.g. local economic and social factors, business strategy and organizational aspects). According to the business development stages which the SSOs are living through, a strategic Personnel Management needs to set its focus on the relevant enabling Human Resources activities. In a SSO people development, retention and engagement management have to play an important role when defining the personnel management strategy: dedicated measures ensure that all required professional competencies and skills are available in time on all employee levels ("lift-drop" phase). Further, these measures need to foster talent and key player retention and keep unwanted attrition as low as possible ("change" and "enhance and innovate" phases). In particular, in the Shared Services business which is a people-driven business an efficient personnel management is one of the key enablers to constantly develop the organization.

5.5 Consequent Monitoring and Controlling

Another enabler to successfully realize the defined development phases of "lift-drop", "change" and "enhance and innovate" is the consequent monitoring and controlling. For a project like Finance Bundling this topic was an indispensible success factor. A comprehensive set of monitoring and controlling activities from high level to low level activities is required. This starts already during the project phase and has to be equally adhered to after the project closure, in the daily operations phase. Hereby, financial and non-financial indicators are to be considered.

The success of a project is dependent on the overall planning, the continuous tracking of the status and controlling of the budget. Defined quality gates are important for a transparent progress reporting. Therefore, for each phase of the project, so-called milestones are to be set up which require the fulfillment of the defined criteria and a clear documentation of the project status in order to be officially achieved. Equally for the controlling of the project costs and its payback an achievement tracking has to be established with the target to compare the actual costs with the original impact estimation. The aim is to gain an understanding about current costs compared to the target (budget) as well as an overview of the expected development of the future (forecast).

Moreover, the success of a project is also dependent on the phase after the project closure. Projects are being initialized in order to make a certain change in the operations or organization. Therefore, expectations towards the success of a project go beyond the finalization of the project. Consequent monitoring and controlling processes – to regularly check whether the project results still match to the expectations - are crucial factors for success. Performance reviews which monitor actual performance against predefined targets enable regular improvements in consistency and predictability of performance.

In daily operations, the cost factor performance and cost tracking certainly play an equally important role and require consequent monitoring. As already mentioned, projects usually raise expectations towards the future, especially in terms of an investment for future cost savings. The cost development therefore demands a continuous controlling and reporting of the financial figures in order to be able to depict medium- to long-term benefits or of course to identify unexpected costs to initiate respective mitigating actions.

In order to enhance cost and price transparency and to enable internal and external benchmarking to reach for example a first quartile cost position, in *Siemens* the project "Costing and Pricing" has been initiated. The *Siemens* captive SSO has introduced the transactional pricing model globally for all customers following the "cost plus" method in order to comply with the arm's length principle. The principle of "zero profit" for the SSO on a global basis remains unchanged. The new charging procedure will be consistent for all customers and based on consumption of products or services, giving better comparability regarding performance, productivity, and allowing more transparent comparison with other Shared Services providers (benchmarking).

6 Conclusion

To summarize, the implementation and further development of a Shared Services concept has to be planned and prepared thoroughly to ensure ultimate achievement of targeted results and thereby meeting the various stakeholders' expectations.

Considering this, the strategic roadmap of the *Siemens* Finance Shared Services Organization was developed on the basis of the three phases model: "lift-drop", "change" and "enhance and innovate". This model enabled the *Siemens* SSO to achieve in the first step service continuity and quick savings handed over to the customers, but also assures continuous service improvement and systematic exploitation of process improvements and automation in the following steps.

The realization of the strategic roadmap of a Shared Services Organization is influenced by many internal as well as external factors. Numerous challenges, such as environmental conditions, complex organizational structures, process and IT landscape complexities, change management and demanding stakeholder expectations need to be considered. Further, the SSO must also cope with many perception aspects ("service was better when my organization did the work"). So Shared Services need to be managed in a systematic and stringent manner which includes many collaboration aspects. On its journey towards a trusted partner and solution provider, defined focus areas of implementation, for instance the professional management of transition projects, the systematic process improvement or change management helped the *Siemens* SSO to succeed and to advance.

But not only the *Siemens* SSO has gained experience in comprehensive best-practice approaches in the area of systematic Shared Services development. This book intends to share the experiences, insights and thoughts of companies, of universities, and of Shared Service specialists.

Abbreviations and Terms

Center	Short for "Shared Services Center" or "Delivery Center" (*Siemens* term)
Donating entity	Legal entity or organizational/accounting unit handing over certain administrative tasks to a Shared Services Organization (or to a regional organization)
Finance Bundling	Comprehensive *Siemens* program in the areas of accounting, controlling, taxes and financial services to re-shape, harmonize and optimize the worldwide finance functions within the *Siemens* group; focus in this article is the transfer of transactional accounting tasks to the in-house Shared Services Organization
HQ	Headquarters

KPI	Key Performance Indicator
Ramp-up	Describes the development phase and corresponding activities of a Shared Services Organization when work is being transferred from one or more donating entities, requiring a corresponding increase of the service provider's internal resources in order to handle the additional volume
Receiving entity	Legal entity or organizational/accounting unit, regularly a Shared Services Organization (or a Cluster or Country organization), receiving certain administrative tasks from the donating entity
SLA	Service Level Agreement
SSC	Shared Services Center(s)
SSO	Shared Services Organization(s)

References

FISCHER, T./STERZENBACH, S. (2006): Controlling von Shared Service Centers – Ergebnisse einer empirischen Studie in deutschen Unternehmen, Nürnberg 2006.

PWC (2012): Financial Shared Service Center on the Rise Toward Valuable Business Partners – 2nd generation FSSCs, May 2012.

Part 1:

"Lift and Drop" – Gaining Speed and Volume for a Global Finance Shared Services Organization

Shared Services Generating Value for Business

Interview with *Ralf P. Thomas*

Siemens AG, Sector Industry

This interview explores the customer point of view on Shared Services Organizations (SSOs) and was conducted with Dr. Ralf P. Thomas, Chief Financial Officer of Siemens Sector Industry – which is one of the world's leading suppliers of innovative, environmentally friendly products and solutions for industry customers. More than 100,000 employees in this Sector generate a business volume of around 20 billion Euro and enable a leading market position. The Industry Sector of Siemens is one of the key customers of Siemens Global Shared Services and supports the idea of centralizing specific processes in order to generate value for the entire Siemens company.

This interview specifically focuses on two of the three development phases of captive Shared Services Organizations: The "bundling phase" to gain speed and volume and the following "optimizing phase" to systematically harmonize and automate processes. The interview takes the customer's perspective into consideration including perception, expectations and ultimate satisfaction towards a Shared Services Organization.

During the last decade, Siemens built up a Global Shared Services Organization which at the time of writing comprises approximately 6,000 people in all Business Lines, thereof roughly 2,500 employees in the area of Accounting & Finance Services.

Where do you, as the Chief Financial Officer (CFO) of the Siemens Sector Industry, and thus one of the key customers of Siemens Global Shared Services, see the main benefits delivered by a Shared Services Organization for your business?

Shared Services Organizations are commonly set up to deliver transactional services to multiple business units or functions in a consistent and standardized manner. In doing so, captive SSOs, as applicable in the *Siemens* environment, let us – the business units – benefit from four key aspects:

- Firstly, referring to the financial perspective, SSOs achieve cost reductions by bundling administrative processes. The centralization of these repetitive activities not only results in economies of scale due to the high volume of activities, but can also be leveraged by transferring certain activities to locations with higher cost-effectiveness. Further, a bundling effect is achieved by efficient allocation of tasks amongst the employees of the SSO also having a view on the critical mass aspect.
- The second benefit of SSOs is to deliver high quality in administrative support processes. By reorganizing especially transactional, repetitive tasks into a Shared Services environment, process optimization can be implemented in a more effective and efficient way. In short, the quality of support services is expected to increase considerably since a selected organization exclusively focuses on these support processes and further actively improves them.
- This automatically leads to the third benefit of Shared Services Organizations which is the fact that the SSO takes over non-core tasks from us, the business units. In doing so, our focus can be exclusively on our own core business. This certainly implies a relationship of trust; although mainly administrative tasks are transferred to the SSO, this still represents a great portion of responsibility that is being handed over as well, e.g. as seen by the transfer of crucial closing activities. As a consequence, the collaboration between the Shared Services Organization and the business units' needs to be very transparent including various routines, tools and other means of interaction amongst the involved parties and a continuous open dialogue on the actual service delivery, especially on the management level.
- The fourth benefit for the customers of a captive SSO is the transparency gained by bundling certain tasks in a selected place. Especially from a compliance perspective, it is an indispensable value for any company to ensure relevant guidelines are being adhered to in a single place rather than in various different locations.

Taking all four benefits into consideration and looking at the SSO from a company perspective, the ultimate value of Shared Services is to provide an "umbrella" under which specific processes are standardized and harmonized in a systematic and professional way, speaking a common language and adhering to the relevant legal frameworks and to company guidelines. In doing so, cost reductions can be achieved that are directly handed back to the business units.

The strategic roadmap of Siemens Global Shared Services foresees different development phases, starting with "lift-drop" and the bundling phase and after this the "change" phase mainly driven by a comprehensive process optimization program. Referring to the first phase – the bundling activities – Siemens has been undergoing a major transformation project for its finance processes.

Looking at the project Finance Bundling, how did you perceive this finance transformation from a customer perspective?

"Finance Bundling" can be considered as one of the major change projects within the entire *Siemens* history. Calling it a "finance transformation" only vaguely describes this massive project where a key factor for success was to provide the necessary manpower to make this change happen. Within project Finance Bundling, transactional accounting tasks were transferred to the Shared Services Delivery Centers around the world while at a Cluster level selected services were integrated into a new cross-border Cluster organization.

In short, it was a project involving various different stakeholders – and of course the key target was to achieve a relatively high satisfaction level amongst all concerned parties. This pluralism of interests was very complex to capture in the first place. After the different stakeholders' interests were identified, the next challenge was the "alignment" and thus developing solutions which satisfied all parties involved; hereby quality was always our top priority.

Consequently, project Finance Bundling was extremely interdisciplinary and the following parties in particular had to closely interact with each other in order to guarantee the overall success of the project:

- The "Governance" side, represented by the *Siemens* Corporate Finance department, providing the framework for the project, i.e. split of activities, guidelines, rules of collaboration and leading the project with a clear mandate by the *Siemens* Managing Board.
- The "Shared Services Organization", which had to guarantee the resources and the organizational set-up in the Centers to efficiently execute the transferred accounting processes.
- The "Customers", and thus the "activity donating" entities; people affected by the change had to be informed upfront and motivated to ensure the required degree of collaboration, particularly when it came to handing over selected processes to the SSO.

The outlined parties had to collaborate closely on the one hand, and on the other systematically handle the following critical areas:

- The "Processes Management", representing the basis for standardization, also meaning a very detailed interaction with existing business processes, preparing them in a way that standardization is actually possible.
- The "Management of Enablers", where the priority lies on IT, is a major task for *Siemens* with more than 200 ERP-systems and hundreds of other applications at the beginning of the transformation. The impact of IT must not be underestimated and is crucial for the implementation of process workflows, process standardization and automation.

- The "People Management", which is one of the key factors in service business, with the explicit focus on winning the right people and retaining them, since "things are getting done by people".

To conclude, project Finance Bundling was definitely a challenge for all parties involved and it was only possible to succeed by taking all interests and perspectives into account, and the solution was one of a closely collaborating finance community built on trust.

The "lift-drop" phase is considered as the key element for a Shared Services Organization to gain speed and volume to become a global finance Shared Services Organization.

In your opinion, how were the major challenges handled in this phase and is there anything you would recommend to an organization undergoing the same journey?

As already mentioned above, it is essential for the success of a change project such as Finance Bundling to have a clear project set-up in place involving all major stakeholders, especially the management level concerned. Without a clear statement by our Senior Finance Management Team and the company CFO the actual change would not have been executed in such an effective and fast way. This means, the top level mandate was elementary to not only initiate the project but also to "follow it through" and successfully realize the transition projects.

Further, project management combined with a strict tracking of milestones and the overall progress of the project are key factors for success. Every project of this size has at least some stakeholders doubting the success and benefit of the change. Therefore, consequent project management and controlling as well as effective risk management need to guarantee transparency of progress. As a consequence, those in doubt of the overall benefit can be constantly informed about the milestones achieved and the results of cost savings for the company. And, extremely important: priority number one was quality, always!

This again takes us to the "people" factor of this business. *Siemens* as a huge conglomerate company sells industrial automation systems, turbines, trains, infrastructure solutions etc. but at the same time *Siemens* employing around 360,000 people around the world is a social system, too. The immanent diversity can only increase efficiency and effectiveness if all people concerned "pull the same rope in the same direction". For Global Shared Services, it was a huge management task to coordinate the growth of this organization in only 1.5 years and ensure service delivery at agreed levels. In particular with regard to the capability of the Shared Services Accounting & Finance Organization, doubts were raised and quite a few stakeholders were uncertain if the *Siemens* SSO would actually be able to manage this role.

Looking back on more than 300 successfully realized transition projects and the high number of employees in new Shared Services functions, from a customer perspective it can be stated that the "lift-drop" phase has been efficiently handled and this was mainly due to systematic project management and the ability to show and prove progress at any point of time.

Now the expectations towards the Shared Services Organization are to fulfill the next step of the Shared Services journey and to ensure a systematic optimization of processes by leveraging standardization, harmonization and automation of processes.

A classic move for a Shared Services Organization is the step from bundling to actual process optimization to get to the next level of Shared services maturity and productivity. For this "change" phase Siemens initiated the so-called "Process Improvement in Accounting" (PIA) program.

How would you evaluate this step from a business perspective and what do you personally expect from this phase? How are you actively influencing this phase as one of the key stakeholders?

After having realized economies of scale out of the "lift-drop" phase and Finance Bundling, the next step is to deliver 'economies of scope' by realizing the promised process optimization; there is high expectations from the business side on this next step of maturity.

Over time, *Siemens* has developed a complex and heterogeneous process landscape in some parts of the organization. This was mainly due to the different business types performed as well as various merger and acquisition activities. Now that the *Siemens* internal Shared Services Organization is entering the "change" phase, it is a great opportunity and at the same time their responsibility to streamline, optimize and harmonize transactional accounting processes, e.g. by way of best practice sharing. I personally expect substantial improvements with regard to quality, speed, reliability, and cost of processes.

In taking over specific accounting tasks the Shared Services Organization has not only taken over a great deal of responsibility, but has also learned from the transitions and matured towards being a process expert in the field of transactional accounting processes. This expertise needs to be leveraged in the "change" phase: by collaborating on a worldwide basis to systematically standardize, harmonize and automate processes. For this phase, best practice sharing is essential since process experts are located around the world, not only on the Shared Services side, but also on the Cluster or Sector side. It is now in the hands of the Shared Services Organization to leverage this expertise by bringing the experts of a certain area together and give them the chance to create ideas to make processes leaner and both, more efficient and more effective.

The program mainly driving the "change" phase is PIA and it has to be implemented in a professional, structured and transparent way. This means that the approach needs to be very similar to that was has been achieved in the project Finance Bundling. Although the *Siemens* Shared Services Organization has actually proven the bundling concept, still the "change" phase needs to be confirmed step by step. Again, a systematic project and risk management and transparent tracking of progress is of utmost importance. Any upcoming issues need to be addressed quickly and in an open and honest atmosphere. Close teamwork between all stakeholders involved will be the essential element for PIA to be successful. The challenge is again the pluralism of interests and the satisfaction of all stakeholders involved. The only exception is that this time, the Shared Services Organization itself is in the driver's seat and since accounting processes affect a variety of other business areas, there is a high number of stakeholders to be included into the change project.

Therefore, the role of the *Siemens* Shared Services Organization within the *Siemens* financial community has changed from receiving the main workload out of project Finance Bundling ("lift-drop" phase) to a more active role of professionalizing processes under the Shared Services umbrella and thereby continuously reconciling the optimization initiatives with the relevant stakeholders.

Looking at the Siemens Shared Services Organization, the bundling project has been successfully realized ("lift-drop" phase) and the optimization of processes has been initiated with the help of program PIA ("change" phase).

Where do you picture Siemens Global Shared Services in the near future? What are your expectations towards the development of the captive Shared Services provider?

The *Siemens* Sector Industry is one of the key customers of *Siemens* Shared Services Organization, specifically in the area of Accounting & Finance and is at the same time one of the sponsors of the organization. From this point of view, my personal expectations towards the development in the near future is to "harvest what we have been sowing". This means that the split of activities as introduced with project Finance Bundling has now reached a "steady state". The highest priority should now be ensuring accuracy in the service delivery to guarantee successful closings and bookings in the delivery centers.

The stabilization of processes is certainly not an easy task, since various different factors need to be taken into consideration; employees need to be motivated and encouraged to work for the Shared Services Organization, service delivery needs to be ensured at an agreed quality level, processes need to be systematically professionalized by standardization and automation – to sum it up, the *Siemens* Global Shared Services Organization should put every effort into using and maintaining the momentum that has been created by fulfilling the promises of process professionalization in the "change" phase, ultimately resulting in further price reductions for the *Siemens* internal customers without compromising on quality.

The overall potential is at the moment not fully leveraged since the "change" phase has not been finalized yet. Therefore, management attention of all parties involved needs to be maintained and the Shared Services Organization has to continue to prove the benefits progressively.

So the big headline for the next chapter of *Siemens*' Shared Service in Finance is spelt out easily: "Walking the talk".

Dr. Thomas, thanks for this interview.

The Role of a Governance Function in a Shared Services Environment

Interview with *JOCHEN SCHMITZ*

Siemens AG, Corporate Finance

This interview will explore the role of a governance function on Shared Services Organizations (SSOs) and was conducted with Dr. Jochen Schmitz, head of Corporate Finance Reporting & Controlling. The focus of this interview is the Siemens Shared Services Organization, precisely the area of "Accounting & Finance Services" (roughly 2,500 employees). This interview will investigate the relationship of a Shared Services Organization with its governance function, in the case of Siemens Corporate Finance.

The Siemens Global Shared Services Organization which, comprises approximately 6,000 people working in the areas of "Accounting & Finance Services", "Human Resources Services" and "Supply Chain Management Services" is providing administrative services to entities within the Siemens group. The key focus of this interview will be the "Accounting & Finance" area and especially its relationship with the governance function.

By way of introduction, would you please provide some main facts on Siemens Corporate Finance and describe your own your role within the Siemens financial community?

As head of the Reporting and Controlling function within *Siemens*, I am – together with my team – in charge of ensuring efficient, best-practice financial reporting that meets both, internal and external requirements. In addition, I am in charge of the Corporate Risk and Internal Controls Department as well as the global Accounting and Controlling groups spread around the world, together with the local CFOs.

The Reporting and Controlling department is divided into five teams: the first team is responsible for the practice-oriented, easy-to-understand and fast implementation of accounting regulations as per the International Financial Reporting Standards (IFRS) and the German Commercial Code as well as the mandatory administrative and financial guidelines of *Siemens*. The second team is in charge of the financial statements and management reporting on a group level, issuing *Siemens* policies regarding the timely provision of closing-related information required for published financial statements, as well as for the internal management reporting. The third team ensures that business processes on corporate level comply with accounting and controlling regulations, that resources are deployed in a cost-effective way, and that the business figures for the corporate units are fully transparent. Further, a fourth team is in charge of the prompt editing and preparation of external financial statements that are informative, support the interests of the company and meet legal requirements as well as the demands of capital markets on the basis of the reporting provided by operating and corporate units. Last but not least we take care of performing the shareholder governance function for *Siemens* subsidiaries and issue the regulations required to perform the rights and duties that result from legal ownership.

Generally spoken, the Reporting and Controlling department of Corporate Finance can be considered as the overarching accounting and controlling governance function for the *Siemens* company, thus providing guidance and support to the *Siemens* Shared Services Organization which is considered as an 'extended operational arm'. This governance role with respect to the SSO is particularly referring – on an operational basis – to the provision of guidelines for any accounting and closing activity. On a strategic basis, the role is concerning the support in leading the SSO along the journey of becoming an important integral part of the *Siemens* financial community and thus playing a key role within the overall value chain of accounting and reporting processes. This close relationship between Corporate Finance Reporting and Controlling is underscored through a direct reporting line of the head of the "Accounting & Finance Services" arm of the SSO.

Where do you, as the head of Corporate Finance, Reporting & Controlling, and thus the Governance of the Accounting & Finance Shared Services Organization, see the main benefits delivered by an internal Shared Services Organization for Siemens? How can the SSO contribute to the overall optimization of the global Finance & Accounting Function?

The reasons for implementing a Shared Services Organization at *Siemens* were mainly twofold: We expected an increase in quality and a decrease of cost relating to administrative, repetitive tasks in the area of accounting. Referring to the **cost** aspect, it can be stated that the cost efficiency results from two reasons. Firstly, the bundling of transactional services into a central place of service delivery and with that the re-allocation of services and secondly by leveraging labor arbitrage and shifting work to locations offering a higher cost-efficiency. In realizing the major infrastructure project called 'Finance Bundling' for *Siemens*, exactly these levers were realized and a cost decrease of approximately 35 % was achieved. This move may be considered as one of the constitutional steps of the overall optimization of the **global** Finance & Accounting Function.

Considering the **quality** aspect, a Shared Services environment offers the opportunity to systematically manage and improve administrative activities as well as to further increase transparency and control - now that they are handled in one specific organization. With a clear ownership of the processes the efficient process harmonization and optimization can be realized in a faster and more efficient way. Here it is essential to note, that the quality effect can be realized if it is based on a clear assignment of competencies. Taking this as a basis, the next opportunity to increase quality is the dedicated management within the SSO, fully concentrating on the administrative processes and actively searching for measures to improve these processes. Further, committed experts help to identify and realize the improvement measures bringing in their own experiences and process know-how. Finally, the willingness of the SSO customers to actively participate in this change management process is essential for *Siemens* to achieve the full benefit. By the way, this process improvement closes the loop of 'cost' and 'quality' as they are necessary prerequisites to reduce cost going forward.

This simple statement of 'quality up and cost down' describes, in a nutshell, the value a SSO can offer within a company. In doing so, a SSO is able to actively free up operational units from non-core activities which often consume a notable degree of time. However, without a trustful relationship between the operational business units and the SSO the benefits described cannot be realized. At this point, the governance role of Corporate Finance is to support the collaboration and provide clear and comprehensible rules in a game demanding a high degree of flexibility and the willingness to realize the change.

The strategic roadmap of Siemens Global Shared Services foresees three major phases starting with "lift-drop" in the bundling phase, after this the "change" phase mainly driven by a comprehensive process optimization program and in the third phase "enhance & innovate" to actively drive automation and enhance the existing portfolio. Referring to the first phase – the bundling activities – Siemens has been undergoing a major finance transformation project.

Looking at the project 'Finance Bundling', how did you perceive this finance transformation from a corporate perspective with your function in the driver's seat of this major change project?

'Finance Bundling' can be considered as the major change project adjusting the *Siemens* finance organization according to a reshaped and streamlined overall company structure: A new cross-country Cluster organization was built up overseeing strategic accounting tasks in the respective region. At the same time, administrative and transactional accounting activities were transferred from the operational units into the Shared Services Centers.

This global project was steered from the Corporate Finance side, in particular leveraging the fact that the accounting heads in the Clusters/Regions report directly to Corporate Finance. Further, it was essential to have a stringent guidance leading the way through the realization of the change. Necessary conditions for the project success were a comprehensive project set-up to achieve the expected results as well as clear guidelines, such as the split of activities with a well defined assignment concept to the respective remaining entities such as SSO, Cluster Accounting & Controlling etc.

Moreover, the project 'Finance Bundling' was about managing expectations and systematically working on the fulfillment of the latter. This project demanded that various different stakeholders work jointly on the targeted goals and move in the same direction. In particular expectations towards the *Siemens* SSO were high since the transfer of certain accounting processes had to be successfully managed, a significant number of new employees had to be recruited, developed, retained and while doing that existing services delivery had to be ensured.

The different expectations raised by the stakeholders were only fulfilled since they were clearly outlined beforehand and permanently in focus during the project execution. In particular, consequent project management with a clear target setting, tracking of progress and monitoring of risks and issues helped to comply with stakeholders' needs. It is important to mention that doubts towards the capability of the SSO came up beforehand and not all stakeholders were confident that the major part of the project could be driven by the internal service provider. As a matter of fact, the *Siemens* SSO has managed to fulfill all expectations referring to time, quality and transparency of the transfer of services. Now it is up to the SSO and their customers, to prove that the "change" can be managed with the same professionalism.

The "lift-drop" phase is considered as the key element for a Shared Services Organization to gain speed and volume to become a global finance Shared Services Organization.

In your opinion, how was the "lift-drop" phase handled by the Siemens Shared Services Organization playing one of the major roles in this finance transformation project? What were the key success factors for this project?

In order to realize a major change project, such as 'Finance Bundling', it is essential to clarify beforehand which activities are going to be moved into which direction. Every move needs to have a reasonable explanation ultimately resulting in the long-term benefit for the company. With this allocation of tasks the working packages for all parties involved become evident and the individual work in the respective groups can be executed. This preparatory work is considered as the necessary step for a successful project completion.

The **'promoter model'** by *WITTE*[1] provides an essential approach to demonstrate the key roles that need to be installed in a project to efficiently drive change:

- The **'power promoter'** indicating and leading the way forward based on his hierarchical position thereby referring to the strategic long term benefit for the company;
- The **'content promoter'** providing the structure and concrete know-how of the underlying topic and outlining the regulations and guidance for the project due to the great expertise in the respective area of interest.

Taking *WITTE*'s promoter model into consideration the key roles can be transferred into the 'Finance Bundling' environment: The power promoter – engaging all respective parties that had to be involved – was the mandate provided by the *Siemens* Chef Financial Officer outlining a comprehensive statement that this project had to be executed in a specific period of time to ultimately achieve an increased competitiveness for the *Siemens* company.

The governance role by Corporate Finance was one of a content promoter. A detailed action plan was outlined based on the concrete split of activities including the allocation of tasks amongst all stakeholders concerned. This guiding role also led to Corporate Finance managing the project from a central side and continuously involving all stakeholders concerned.

To summarize, the two promoter roles were indispensable in realizing the change and letting the parties involved interact and collaborate within the scope of this project. The two installed promoter roles ensured the speed and drive behind the project and thus the transfer of certain transactional accounting processes into the Shared Services environment. However, looking at the receiving side and thus the SSO, consequent project and risk management and the continuous communication of progress achieved were necessary factors in completing the transfer and stabilization of a huge package of work.

A reasonable move for a Shared Services Organization is the step from bundling to actual process optimization to get to the next level of Shared services maturity and productivity. For this "change" phase Siemens initiated the so-called "Process Improvement in Accounting" (PIA) program.

What was the role of Corporate Finance when setting up the PIA-Program as a major part of the "change phase" and how is it now supporting the realization of PIA? What do you personally expect from this phase?

The PIA-program was installed as a subsequent step after having realized the bundling project. PIA reflects the next development step after the "lift-drop", on the journey to becoming a trusted strategic partner.

This project outlining the "change" phase was set up as an optimization program driven by the SSO, in close alignment with the governance function and all stakeholders involved. Right from the beginning, the governance function and thus Corporate Finance Reporting & Controlling actively influenced the set up and the choice to realize PIA as an 'inductive' program. This means that the first questions raised were those towards the existing challenges

1 Cf. *WITTE* (1973).

and to then derive the consequent improvement projects together with the respective process experts. The PIA-program is geared towards further improvement of quality, increase in flexibility and – of course – implementation of automation to further decrease cost.

The expectations from the governance side are to use the momentum that the SSO has created by successfully realizing the bundling and approaching the PIA-program with the same professionalism and sensitivity. Again, it is all about consequent stakeholder involvement and close alignment amongst all parties affected by the change. Speaking of the realization of change, here, the promoter model plays a key role in the same way it did for the project 'Finance Bundling'. The SSO has now moved into a more content-related role taking over the lead to efficiently drive process optimization as a **'content promoter'**. The governance function is – together with representatives of the customer side – obtaining the **'power promoter'** role and thus paving the way towards a consequent execution of the PIA-program.

The systematic realization of the PIA-program is considered as a crucial next step for the *Siemens* internal SSO. The SSO has proven that the transfer of certain accounting packages can be executed efficiently, now the organization is offered the opportunity to demonstrate that it can do more than the mass-business as a internal service provider, i.e. the systematic improvement of processes with a special focus on a stringent stakeholder alignment by consequent communication and involvement into the relevant changes to be realized.

One of the key elements of the vision of Siemens Shared Services is to develop from a service provider to a close partner adding value to the Siemens business. This is why the third development phase "enhance and innovate" is paving the way for portfolio enlargement and active use of automation and innovation.

Where do you envision Siemens Global Shared Services as part of the Siemens finance community in the near future? In which areas do you see the main challenges and how are you planning to influence this development from a "Governance" perspective?

Looking at the third development phase "enhance and innovate", the expectations from a governance perspective are – in the first place – to further increase the degree of automation and intensify the work on innovations in the process flow, that more and more decrease manual effort and risk of error.

With regard to the 'enhance' aspect it can be stated that similar to the procedure applied for the project 'Finance Bundling', a framework needs to be developed specifically outlining the potential scope of services offering a high strategic fit for execution in a Shared Services environment. Generally, those services should be transferred to a SSO, where a clear cost decrease may be expected, where quality and transparency can be improved, where the potential for further harmonization may be recognized and where a customer may desire to 'outsource' this process and hence focus on core activities.

After the scope of additional services, which could be delivered out of a Shared Services Center, is defined, the next step is to realize a pilot and calculate a business case to ensure the targeted cost reduction can be proven. Taking this calculation as a basis, further operational business units can be convinced of the benefit. The role of governance, specifically focusing on the third development phase 'enhance and innovate,' is to support the SSO in the realization of the planned steps, hereby taking the overall benefits to increase the company's competitiveness into consideration.

The captive set-up of the SSO has proven its efficiency during the last years, especially considering the SSO's know-how of *Siemens* specific processes and IT landscape, its close market orientation and by offering services at arm's length. Continuous benchmarking and the strategic view on the overall company benefit ensure that the SSO delivers services internally, but keeps an open eye and ear to the outside Shared Services world in order to remain competitive for the internal customers.

As a conclusion, it can be stated that the *Siemens* Finance SSO contributes to the overall competitiveness of the company by

- "lifting and dropping" transactional accounting activities in its Centers leveraging advantages of cost-competitive locations and bundling effects,
- proactive "changing" and the systematic end-to-end optimization of accounting processes, and
- "enhancing and innovating" existing processes and identifying additional services to be transferred into a Shared Services environment.

To realize each of these development steps the support and advice of the governance function Corporate Finance – in the role of a strategic business partner – can be considered as one of the crucial factors for success.

Dr. Schmitz, thanks for this interview.

References

WITTE, E. (1973): Organisation für Innovationsentscheidungen – Das Promotoren-Modell: Schwartz, Göttingen 1973.

Finance Bundling: Transforming the Finance Regional Organization of a Global Player

KLAUS P. STEGEMANN, SIGRID DENGLER, ALEXANDER RIEDEL and *TOBIAS WEBER*

Siemens AG and *KPMG AG Wirtschaftsprüfungsgesellschaft*

Executive Summary

This chapter revisits the global Cluster Finance Bundling project conducted by *Siemens AG* from 2009 to 2011. Its purpose is to summarize both the strategic challenges addressed by the project as well as the key cornerstones of its successful implementation. It thus provides insights and guidance on the inception and completion of large-scale project in the field of optimizing a regional finance organization with special regard to shared services.

The Cluster Finance Bundling project was set up in 2009 to regionally bundle finance activities and align finance function setup to corporate strategy and business challenges. Accordingly, this chapter first describes the general management objectives behind the project, the resulting challenges and how these were addressed setting clear project rules and boundary conditions. Subsequently, it details the content and application of the concepts and approaches employed to derive precise actions by defining the target state, the transition methodology and transparent financial objectives for the global finance organization. In the following, the governance and control mechanisms facilitating hassle-free concept implementation are depicted. Finally, we highlight how accountability was ensured and summarize most important lessons learned from a project management perspective.

Since the optimization of business support functions[1] is an imperative in a competitive business environment and will inevitably occur within large-scale organizational transformation projects, the article sheds light on best practices and provides useful practical insights for line and project management, consultants and professionals entrusted with related challenges. The methods and tools applied for transforming business to operational strategy and organizational concepts as well as the implementation of those concepts within a global project are lined out.

1 Initial Situation and Targets

The ever-increasing pace of change in today's world-wide markets poses tremendous requirements towards effective infrastructure services for global organizations like *Siemens AG*. Infrastructure functions like HR, IT or finance are increasingly perceived as service providers and facilitators for core business units. Their major goal is to enable the core business functions to focus on customer and market activities, and to contribute to overall competitiveness through excellence in their field of action.

To address this challenge, *Siemens* implemented a new organizational model effective from January 2008, creating three Sectors oriented at a products and solutions perspective, and 20 regional Clusters oriented at local market structures and infrastructure requirements. This new organizational setup triggered three workstreams[2] to align the group HR, IT and finance functions to the new regional infrastructure model. Besides the Cluster organizations, *Siemens*

---

1 These "back-office" or "infrastructure" functions typically comprise e.g. Finance, HR, IT, Supply Chain Management/Logistics, Procurement, Real Estate Management, etc.

2 For a "how to" guide for strategic controlling of project portfolios and the definition of multi-project-management as an element of corporate strategy implementation cf. KRAHN/SCHMIDT (2010), p. 292 et seqq.

Global Shared Services (GSS) as the groups shared services organization played a vital role. Within the global program, workstream finance initiated the Cluster Finance Bundling project[3] to optimize its organizational setup and streamline finance activities in the regions.

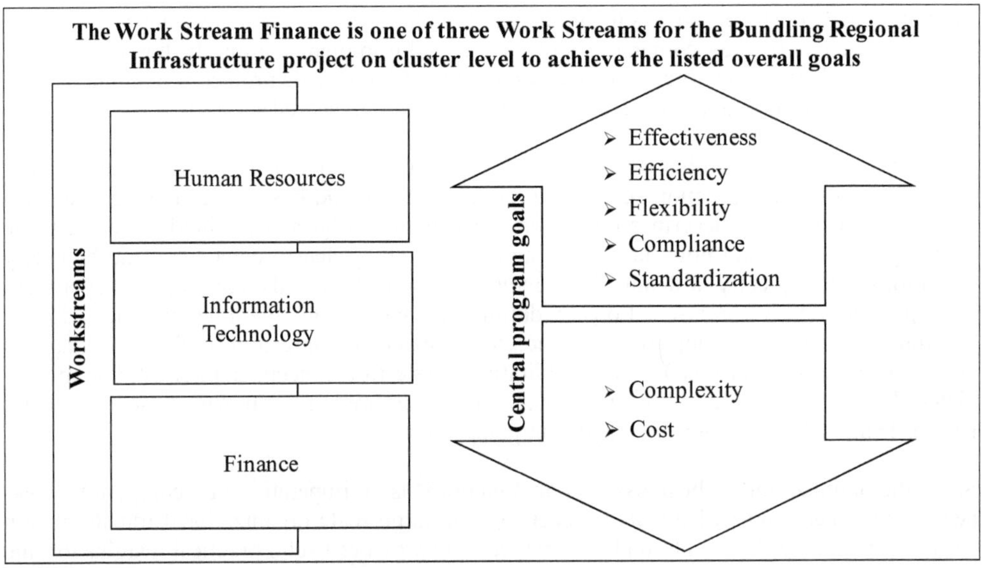

Figure 1: Overall workstream goals[4]

As summarized in figure 1, the *Siemens* CFO and finance management tasked the project team with achieving a set of goals[5] valid for all workstreams:

- *Increasing effectiveness* refers to the quality of support provided to both operational business and group management. For finance, this can be illustrated by considering the timely delivery of high quality financial statements and managing reporting on a monthly and quarterly basis.
- *Increasing efficiency* refers to controlling the operational cost of running support, general and administrative processes. *Siemens* had initiated a corresponding program to reduce SG&A cost already in 2008, and the workstreams were challenged to ensure the sustainability of the corresponding results.
- *Increasing flexibility* reflects strategic considerations on the pace of change in global markets. Infrastructure functions must be able to quickly adapt existing processes or even implement new ones. This includes the ability to flexibly scale operations to address shifts in global demand.

---

3 For the definition of a project cf. *PMI* (2008), chapter 1.2.

4 Source: *SIEMENS AG*.

5 For the derivation of project goals from strategic company objectives cf. *KAPLAN/NORTON* (1997), p. 57, and *LANGE* (2008), p. 105 et seqq., and *FIEDLER* (2010), p. 74 et seqq. For project portfolio management and selection cf. *LAPPE/EIKELMANN/CAMPANA/SCHOTT* (2010), p. 173 et seqq., and *VOIGT* (2010), p. 187 et seqq. The collection of requirements is a crucial step to determine project content and scope cf. *PMI* (2008), chapter 5.1.

- *Ensuring compliance* is of vital importance for all infrastructure functions, and for finance in particular. Local statutory, tax and capital markets regulations need to be taken into account as well as group guidelines. In this respect, transparency in the sense of defined responsibility and accountability for all processes constitutes an important prerequisite.
- *Increasing standardization* constitutes one of the most essential operational means to achieve the goals described in this section. To ensure its implementation as a long-term asset, it has been defined as a strategic objective in itself.
- *Decreasing complexity* also constitutes a vital enabler to the overall set of goals defined for the workstreams. By addressing it as a strategic objective in itself, its merits do not have to be appraised on a case-by-case basis.
- *Decreasing cost* not only refers to the efficiency of infrastructure operations as described above, but also to the overall perspective of a seamless and streamlined integration of infrastructure processes with operational business. Optimized effectiveness, for example, will also contribute to managing the overall cost base of the group, and standardization will help to control future IT architecture investment volumes.

This chapter describes how the Cluster Finance Bundling project achieved the set of goals described above. It thus provides insights on how infrastructure functions in global organizations can be re-aligned to meet today's challenges in a balanced approach between regional and business-specific requirements, at a benchmark level of excellence globally implemented and sustained. The following sections further set the scene by describing strategic cornerstones of the approach pursued defining the scope and boundaries of the project.

1.1 Cornerstones of the Approach Pursued

The new Cluster finance organization had to facilitate the enforcement of governance principles while at the same time sustainably reduce the cost baseline and support the quality of books and records. To achieve these objectives, governance responsibilities and organizational setups had to be re-defined to match the structure of Clusters and Sectors, and new globally consistent delivery models for regional Cluster and shared services organizations had to be developed and implemented.

To enable the project team to focus on straightforward implementation, a number of strategic considerations were determined as initial stipulations:

- Enable Clusters to fulfill their role as the owner of regional finance infrastructure.
  - Provide a comprehensive finance target operating model to be realized by all Clusters. Design, agree and implement a globally consistent finance organization with defined governance roles and responsibilities in line with the Cluster and Sector structure as well as business support requirements.
  - Generate a global activity split for finance processes to maximize Cluster bundling and GSS penetration.

- Fully leverage efficiency potentials from bundling and enable finance to leverage process optimization potentials arising from ERP systems adaptation and harmonization potentials.
  - By default, migrate all non-transactional processes to Cluster level and bundle remaining country-specific processes at one single country location, leveraging economies of skill in competence centres.
  - Transfer all transactional processes to GSS: maximize GSS penetration rate[6], leveraging economies of scale and exploit labour cost arbitrage potentials.
- Ensure a fast but hassle-free transformation.
  - Control implementation costs by adhering to a total payback period of less than three years. Limit implementation time to two years.
  - Define a standardized, detailed and reproducible implementation methodology to be followed by Clusters and entities ensuring high transformation speed by leveraging experience gained and lessons learned.

To achieve these cornerstones, the project needed to address several challenges:

- Organizational alignment: de-centralized legal entity and country finance organizations had to be transferred into the new Cluster setup. Collaboration between Sectors, Clusters, governance owner and GSS are a pre-requisite. The original organizational scope covered ca. 5,200 FTEs in ca. 600 legal entities across 175 countries.
- Governance harmonization: varying organizational models for regional finance functions had to be replaced by a globally standardized finance organization and activity allocation across all Clusters. Final implementation of GSS' role as sole transactional service provider had to be ensured by substantially increasing initial penetration rate.
- Sustainable cost optimization: level of savings achieved after a group-wide SG&A program was to be made sustainable. A wide spread in Clusters' cost of finance for the functional scope defined in relation to direct sales volume ranging from 0.32% to 1.1% indicated further potential.
- Quality requirements: high quality and timeliness of books and records and continuous business support had to be maintained during and after transformation. Transparency over process execution was to be ensured. Retention of key personnel needed to be managed.

1.2 Project Scope and Boundary Conditions

For addressing the organizational challenges, finance governance rules were developed to define a clear responsibility split between Sectors, Clusters, GSS and corporate as well as to assure a distinct accountability within the finance organization.[7] In order to balance business and governance requirements, clear rules were defined clarifying potential governance conflicts ("right-of-way" definitions) for a number of selected areas. Sectors were responsible for

6 The penetration rate measures realized shared services potential in respect to total potential obtainable according to service capability and global finance activity split.

7 For the inclusion of corporate environment factors into the project charter cf. *PMI* (2008), chapter 4.1.

business driven decisions, while Clusters were responsible for governance and infrastructure driven decisions. In both cases, decisions had to be in accordance with corporate guidelines and local regulations. The primary aim of the finance shared service delivery centers managed by GSS was process standardization and harmonization in order to raise service quality, increase reliability and reduce cost. Based on these targets, the penetration rate of GSS as service provider was to be increased to position GSS as a strategic business partner for all finance service functions.

Based on Cluster Finance Bundling project goals, scope and boundary conditions[8] were defined to provide a general framework for project content and decisions. It was clearly stated that all finance functions except audit, namely accounting, controlling, tax and financing as in all legal entities were in scope. By default, finance functions were to be performed at least on Cluster level with only legal and / or regulatory limitations being possible exceptions. All transactional processes were to be performed by GSS if offered. The overall implementation responsibility was allocated to the Clusters.[9]

By taking the described decisions on the project scope early on – namely the inclusion of all entities and all finance processes with the exception of internal audit – the project was free to address the resulting challenges in a solution-oriented manner. These way scope discussions could be avoided ex ante.

2 Defining Concrete Actions

This section describes the top-down design and implementation approach pursued in the Cluster Finance Bundling project, ranging from guiding and key design principles, group-wide activity splits for finance processes to a thoroughly elaborated target operating model and implementation guidelines.

2.1 Project Guiding and Key Design Principles

In order to create a globally usable methodology for the Cluster Finance Bundling project and agree key decisions amongst stakeholders at an early stage, an overall framework for scope and design was defined and documented in the central finance blueprint.[10] Core piece for this framework were the guiding and key design principles[11] which constituted a first vital step towards establishing the finance target operating model (TOM) which describes the structure and relationships that drive the future finance delivery model.

8 For general procedures to define project scope and content cf. *PMI* (2008), chapter 5.2.

9 For the de-centralization of implementation responsibility cf. *SCHUPPERT* (2010), p. 52 et seqq.

10 The central blueprint constituted the project charter cf. *PMI* (2008), chapter 4.2.

11 "The seeds of problems are laid down early [...] The review of most failed projects or project problems indicate that disasters were well planned to happen from the start" cf. *NASA* (1996), rule 15. Guiding and key design principles served as a tool for structural standardization of project content cf. *MILOSEVIC/INMAN/OZBAY* (2001), p. 10 et seq.

Project guiding principles established core project content by defining scope, exception handling and aspired bundling level. They comprised the decision to transfer processes to either Cluster level or to GSS and bundle remaining processes to the maximum extent possible at country level. Exceptions to this bundling approach should only be granted if absolutely necessary from legal or regulatory perspective and had to be approved by the steering committee.

Based on the guiding principles a set of 20 key design principles was developed. Key design principles were the ground rules reflecting overall project objectives and a binding benchmark for the validation of all subsequent project decisions. Each principle was based on a bold statement approved by the steering committee and included well-specified procedures and approval requirements for permissible exceptions. Design principles comprised e.g. strategic project objectives, process allocation guidelines including defined drop-down criteria for lower-level process allocation, personnel allocation strategy, process migration approach, service provider charging model and service provider escalation management. This set of principles constituted the basis for the development of the global finance activity split and the detailed design of the finance target operating model.

2.2 Global and Local Finance Activity Split

The development of a global activity split for finance ensured a clear and consistent assignment of tasks and operational responsibilities to Sectors, Clusters, countries, corporate functions and GSS. It provided precise directions for all 7 finance functions, 72 key processes, and 413 sub-processes in scope regarding the allocation of activities to organizational levels and service providers. Based on the key design principles, activities were generally bundled at the highest possible level to pool knowledge and realize maximum efficiency potentials with only few required exceptions remaining on local country level due to e.g. regulatory restrictions.

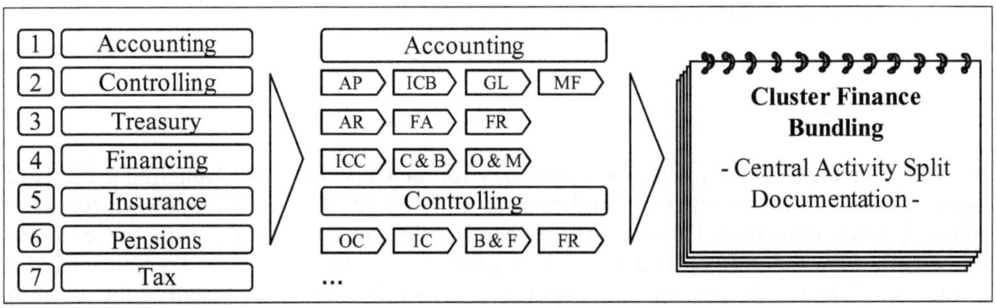

Figure 2: *Global finance activity split*[12]

12 Source: SIEMENS AG.

To ensure activity split viability a staggered piloting approach[13] was followed. At first, a core team of functional process experts developed an initial "best practice" model based on the *Siemens* process documentation which also included outside-in views. This model was then challenged and refined for optimal application by functional key experts taking a business and customer perspective. Proof of concept and refinement in detail was provided by concept application in two pilot Clusters which were chosen for representing the highest complexity in terms of business practice and scope. The final global activity split document was approved by the steering committee and communicated throughout the finance community. Before implementation each Cluster had to analyze the regional applicability of the global activity split and apply for deviations via a defined acceptance process as a mandatory step during the planning phase. After approval, deviations were documented in the local Cluster activity split document which constituted a binding and auditable standard for project implementation. The exception process[14] was handled stringently to ensure maximum global consistency.

2.3 Finance Target Operating Model (TOM)

Based on the project key design principles a common target operating model for finance was developed to facilitate a well-directed consistent optimization instead of short-term individual Cluster sub-optimization. An operating model is typically used to describe how the enterprise runs its business, across all dimensions and levels, in order to execute its strategy. It is the manifestation of the operations strategy which includes explicit choices about the best deployment of the organisation's elements to achieve the business goals. In essence, it is the delivery vehicle of business model as it is what makes the business model idea real and tangible.[15]

In a constantly changing environment there is a need for actively managing the alignment of support functions to corporate strategy and business model. To avoid repeated greenfield approaches it is recommendable to follow a methodology that combines strategic development with tactical enablement. Whilst strategic development focuses on the "What" i.e. the translation of business requirements into operating model design choices, tactical enablement focuses on the "How" i.e. developing, planning and implementing solutions that support design choices taken. Those choices typically include questions such as centralization vs. decentralization, in-sourcing vs. outsourcing, degree of standardization and integration, leveraging economies of scale or scope, etc. and are key to achieve and sustain strategy and vision.

The TOM methodology employed in the Cluster Finance Bundling project lies at the intersection between strategic development and tactical enablement as it defines and describes the delivery mechanisms required in order to globally provide finance process services to *Siemens* business and at the same time answers key questions regarding the defined organizational approach to service performance. As organizations are complex systems consisting of several different interlinked logical components, the conceptual framework for the target operating model was developed around the six dimensions services, sourcing/location, governance, people, processes and technology. This ensured that the "complex machinery" was

---

13 "Experience may be fine but testing is better. Knowing something will work never takes the place of proving that it will."; *NASA* (1996), rule 96.

14 For a general view on the management of deviations in project practice cf. *HÄLLGREN/MAANINEN-OLSSON* (2008), p. 55 et seqq., and *HÄLLGREN* (2009), p. 612 et seqq.

15 Regarding the requirement for consistent and strategy-complaint operating models cf. *KNÖPFLE* (2011), p. 4.

broken down into its logical components and the appropriate analysis and design techniques were deployed for each component to build a better model. For each dimension, high-level requirements, constraints and design decisions were documented.

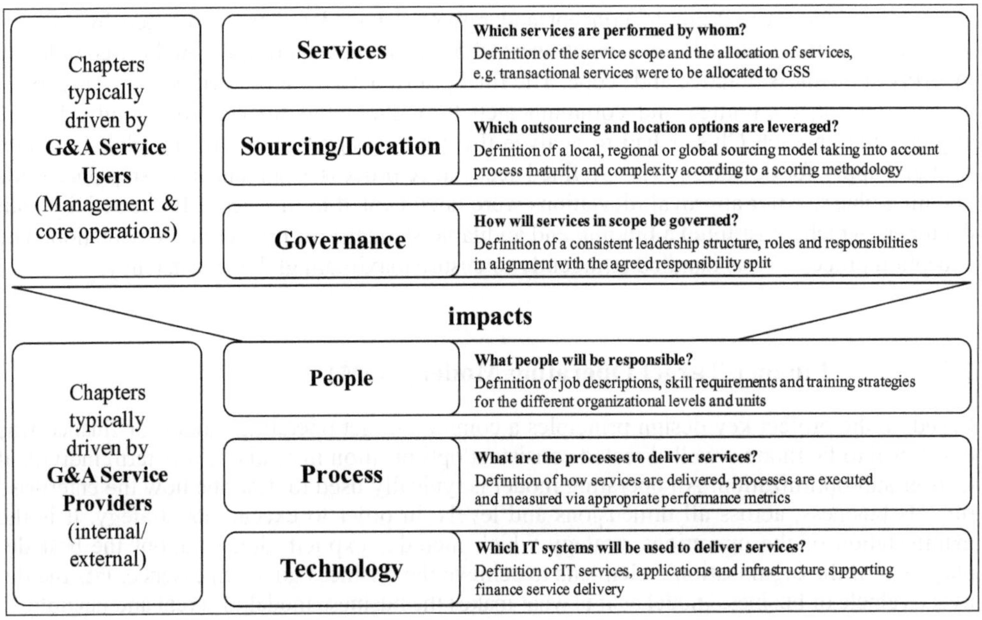

Figure 3: *Target Operating Model dimensions*[16]

The Target Operating Model for finance was developed by top management and included input from Sectors, Clusters and functional experts. It was validated by pilot Clusters representing the highest degree of complexity in the group. As a change enabler it contributed to the strategic alignment of the finance function and its customers by providing a consolidated view and common understanding of the way finance was going to perform its services. Furthermore it shed light on changes and transformations required for future success and provided the basis for business case development as well as a rationale for investment decisions.

2.4 Transition Methodology and Approach

A project of the size and complexity of Cluster Finance Bundling required a consistent global methodology and approach.[17] Therefore, the *Siemens* Implementation Guide (SImpleG) was developed. It provided comprehensive structure including milestones, deliverables, definitions and standard templates for both project phases, the planning and the implementation phase.[18] Whereas the planning period was about setting up the project and planning the transi-

---

16 Source: *KPMG MANAGEMENT CONSULTING.*

17 For the impact of project standardization on project management effectiveness; cf. *MILOSEVIC/INMAN/OZBAY* (2001), p. 9 et seqq.

18 Standardized milestones are the basis for an effective project controlling; cf. B001, *KNAPP/LEDERER* (2010), p. 279 et seqq.

tions in detail, the implementation phase dealt with the actual shift of respective finance activities to the service providers GSS and the new Cluster finance organization. For a successful and low-risk handover of tasks from the donating (process ramp-down) to the receiving entities (process ramp-up), both sides needed to be thoroughly prepared.

The SImpleG transition methodology was developed on the foundation of existing *Siemens* project and transition management knowledge comprised in three different frameworks:[19]

- The top+[20] guidelines set initial definitions and key basic principles for managing the implementation of cost-driven productivity actions at *Siemens*. It requires a strict application of defined degrees of implementation (DIs) to ensure transparency of implementation progress and the timely identification of implementation hurdles and risks.
- The PM@*Siemens* standard predetermined general project management standards, concepts and requirements.[21]
- The GSS methodology guide contributed deep know-how from former transitions of infrastructure functions including detailed procedures and tools for core deliverables such as baselining and business case.

As an integrative methodology, SImpleG combined specific technical and project management knowledge from finance functions and service provider with change management and communication-related expertise. To consider all relevant steps and activities, the methodology was centrally developed by a diverse team of transition experts and then refined during the planning phase of pilot Clusters. The deployment within a central project management platform did not only ensure global accessibility of required information but also enabled continuous improvement via an active knowledge sharing and exchange of lessons learned throughout all project phases.

19 For a comprehensive overview of general project management standards cf. *WAGNER* (2012), p. 27 et seqq.

20 The top+ office is responsible for driving and supporting business excellence and a high performance culture within *Siemens* and reports directly to the board.

21 Regarding PM@*Siemens* and the *Siemens* project community cf. interview with Dr. *JÜRGEN SCHLOSS* in *STEEGER* (2010), p. 6 et seq.

Project Phase 1: Implementation Planning on Cluster Level				
DI 1: Initiate cluster project	**DI 2: Achieve planning prerequisites**	**DI 3: Outline implementation plan**	**DI 4: Agree implementation plan**	**DI 5: Complete implementation plan**
➤ When cluster has nominated key transformation team members	➤ When baselining and function workshops are finalized	➤ When cluster has finalized project structure and scope	➤ When first draft is reconciled with receiving entities and companies	➤ When implementation plan is finalized and approved
➤ IG 1130: List of legal entity in-scope defined	➤ IG 1220: Deviations from central activity split analyzed and documented ➤ IG 1240: cluster impact estimation without one-off cost	➤ IG 1310: Draft implementation plan defined ➤ IG 1330: Cluster, Country locations defined and approved by cluster CFO	➤ IG 1420: Draft implementation plan agreed with GSS and sector headquarters ➤ IG 1430: Draft implementation plan reconciled with relevant regional companies and sector companies	➤ IG 1520: Cluster impact estimation finalized (including one off-cost) ➤ IG 1540: Implementation plan finalized and cluster CEO and CFO approval received
Project Phase 2: Ramp-up on Receiving Entity Level				
DI 1: Define project prerequisites	**DI 2: Set up ramp-up organization and roadmap**	**DI 3: Define ramp-up measures**	**DI 4: Achieve readiness for transitions**	**DI 5: Complete transitions**
➤ When receiving entity has "ramp-up" team established	➤ When receiving entity has "ramp-up" plan finalized	➤ When receiving entity has "roll-in" procedures prepared	➤ When receiving entity has core functions team ready for "roll-in"	➤ When all legal entity are transitioned into receiving entities
➤ IG 2120: Organizational set-up of receiving entity designed and approved ➤ IG 2130: Recruiting and staffing strategy defined	➤ IG 2210: Ramp-up plan for receiving entities finalized ➤ IG 2230: First communication to receiving entity done	➤ IG 2320: Master process template for detailed process analysis designed ➤ IG 2340: Standard legal entity roll-in procedures prepared	➤ IG 2410: Readiness-of-receiving-entity-Checklist finalized ➤ IG 2420: SLA KPI tracking concept defined	➤ IG 2530: Adaption of incentive systems designed ➤ IG 2540: All legal entities transitioned into receiving entities
Project Phase 2: Ramp-down on Donating Entity Level				
DI 1: Define project prerequisites	**DI 2: Set up project organization and roadmap**	**DI 3: Define transition measures**	**DI 4: Achieve readiness for hand-over**	**DI 5: Complete transition**
➤ When legal entity has nominated key transformation team members	➤ When legal entity has detailed its project plan and scope	➤ When legal entity has finalized detailed analysis and measures	➤ When legal entity is ready to transfer tasks to receiving entities	➤ When legal entity transferred all agreed tasks to receiving entities
➤ IG 3120: Project prerequisites defined with CFO ➤ IG 3150: HR informed regarding planned transition activities	➤ IG 3230: Project plan defined and aligned with receiving entities ➤ IG 3240: Define and schedule involvement of Employee Representative Bodies	➤ IG 3380: Future operating model defined ➤ IG 3396: Knowledge transfer plan and training plan defined	➤ IG 3430: Receiving Entity staff assigned, recruitment done and new employee on board ➤ IG 3490: Readiness of receiving entity signed off	➤ IG 3540: Implementation sign off achieved ➤ IG 3550: HR activities completed regarding people measures

Figure 4: Overview of DIs and selected key milestones per project phase[22]

In essence, SImpleG presented a detailed end-to-end description of required project steps from donating and receiving entity perspective that enabled local project managers and teams to understand the content and challenges of the transition program from start to end.[23] Each project phase was broken down into 5 degrees of implementation (DIs) which included a defined list of milestones to be completed. For each milestone, a deliverable sheet was developed providing the following guidance:

- ➤ A short description of the objectives of the milestone
- ➤ A list of proposed steps and activities for all stakeholders involved
- ➤ An role-bound indication of deliverable responsibility and required cooperation
- ➤ A list of prerequisites (steps and actions) required prior to milestone completion

---

22 Source: *SIEMENS AG*.

23 The SImpleG can therefore be classified as the Work Breakdown Structure (WBS), cf. *PMI* (2008), chapter 5.3. "People have reasons for doing things the way they do them. Most people want to do a good job and, if they don't, the problem is they probably don't know how or exactly what is expected"; *NASA* (1996), rule 32.

- Templates and useful documents for milestone delivery incl. quality requirements

Due to the allocation of defined activities to different DIs, global project status reporting could be standardized and compared on legal entity or Cluster level which increased overall transparency. Additionally, risks identified could be allocated to single-entity project stages and mitigation measures globally deployed via integrating new templates and information into the SImpleG online sources.

In order to manage process transition from donating to receiving entities without negatively impacting the closing process and/or the quality of books and records, two distinct approaches had been chosen. For Cluster-level bundling, a "lift-change-drop" approach was followed, so that processes were removed from providers as is but optimized before migration so that the new service provider already performed the standardized and optimized processes. This approach was best suited for processes with low to medium "quick win" standardization potential that could be achieved with low risk for process stability.

Given the high volume of transactional processes which generally had high optimization potential requiring time and effort to be leveraged, a "lift-drop-change" approach was employed for process transition to GSS. Accordingly processes were transferred as is to the delivery centers without any changes. Process standardization and optimization beyond the realization of "quick win" opportunities was out of scope for the Cluster Finance Bundling project so that maximum bundling effects could be achieved without incurring unjustifiable risk.

2.5 Baselining and Business Case

An important requirement for a sound planning and monitoring of measures and a robust target setting was transparency regarding the finance baseline.[24] Only after this planning prerequisite had been achieved by all Clusters, information about the detailed project scope was available and optimization potentials could be assessed considering the new target operating model and the local Cluster activity split. Again the piloting approach helped to validate and refine baseline and business case methodology.

From a project perspective, the following points were crucial regarding baselining and business case:

- In the first place, a business case is a pre-requisite for proper business decisions. A business case helps to view and evaluate the project in terms of what it will specifically return to the organization for the money spent and resources committed. Thus it was important to document aspired changes, cost and benefits to gain agreement of the value and the benefits associated with change and enable a monitoring of achievements.

- Once this payback is understood, identified measures can become true drivers for change. Clear goals and expectations can be shared and communicated to project stakeholders who will be responsible for implementing or supporting change and achieving the required improvements. Thus it was key to position the project as an investment, rather

[24] For a detailed overview of required current state analysis and techniques in organizational transformation projects cf. *WEUSTER* (2010), p. 28 et seqq.

than a cost, by relating the implementation requirements to quantified business potential benefits that provided clear payback and return on investment.

- Last but not least, it is the people within an organization who implement change and achieve the identified potential benefits. Therefore, identified potential benefits need to be agreed to and achieved by the organization. The purpose of the Cluster Finance Bundling business case was not to set "stretch" goals. Rather, the business case was focused on setting realistic targets which the finance community agreed to and which all participants were measured against. Viewed from this perspective, the development of the business case could be seen as a process that engages and mobilizes the organization and would later be used to monitor and measure success.

The process of establishing the baseline followed two main steps: In the first place, Clusters had to define the legal entity scope based on the corporate index of consolidated companies. This "entity in scope" register was key throughout the project as subsequent implementation planning; progress tracking and status reporting had to be performed on legal entity level. Accordingly the register was constantly updated according to changes in the corporate landscape (e.g. divestments, mergers & acquisitions). In the second place, finance function FTE and cost were assessed on legal entity level and consolidated to the global finance baseline. To ensure data consistency and keep workload for local teams manageable, all input was provided via defined interfaces into the central project management platform and detailed guidance regarding FTE and cost definition was provided. As all data was available online and stored in a database, the central team was able to ensure overall quality via automated input validations, manual analytical checks and reviews from finance management.

Results of the legal entity level baselining were integrated into the Cluster business cases which were crucial for documenting *ex ante* Cluster commitment and *ex post* project success after full target operating model implementation. Additionally, Cluster business cases created an outlook on the structure was well as the cost level of the new global finance organization and provided the basis for detailed legal entity level implementation planning. To ensure the determination of balanced efficiency targets across all Clusters, internal benchmarking was employed.

Cluster business cases followed a strict bottom-up approach and build upon two improvement levers which were closely interrelated:

- Process standardization relates to the implementation of a common global activity split based on the clear allocation of responsibility. It facilitates a standardized finance organizational model including roles and responsibilities and thus improves governance and transparency. Moreover, it constitutes the key enabler for process bundling (at service providers) and subsequent selective process optimization. Selective process optimization relates to leveraging "quick win" process efficiency potentials arising from bundling at service providers and feasible without fundamental changes to the underlying ERP systems. Examples include the use of workflow and EDI procedures.
- Bundling relates to realizing economies of scope and scale as well as labor arbitrage potentials by executing processes at the appropriate and most efficient level and location. To fully realize the potential, bundling follows a fundamental key design principle: GSS for 100 % of transactional processes, Clusters/Sectors for 100 % of non-transactional processes with high skills and communication requirements, and countries for remaining processes subject to local regulation.

Besides financial savings, Cluster business cases included a management summary outlining key financial and FTE ratios in baseline and target state, information about projected FTE movements from countries to Clusters and GSS and expected project one-off cost split between project execution cost and restructuring expenses. Cluster targets with regard to project goals were measured via a defined set of KPIs:

- Cost of finance (for functions in scope) in percent of direct business: measured the overall efficiency of the Cluster finance organization and provided a comparable basis for tracking sustainable cost reduction. Efficiency enhancement was key to sustain SG&A program savings.
- GSS Cluster penetration rate: measured realization of total potential according to global activity split (drop-down due to legal, tax and compliance reasons possible). Process transfer to GSS supported the two improvement levers.
- FTE on Cluster level in percent of country & Cluster FTE: indicated the Cluster bundling rate, i.e. Cluster process and work share. Establishing strong Clusters was key for achieving global governance.
- Cost per FTE: measured realization of labor arbitrage potentials due to process re-allocation to service providers. It reflected sourcing effects by balancing Cluster and GSS location cost.
- Country reduction in force: measured immediate project effects in terms of FTE ramp-down in local country finance organizations. FTE bundling at Cluster and GSS locations according to agreed regional activity splits was a prerequisite for achieving governance, efficiency and effectiveness goals.

Another deliverable included in Cluster business cases was a scoring of potential Cluster location options as the location decision had a long-term impact and far reaching organizational implications. The selection was made on the basis of the assessment of pre-defined criteria (e.g. labor cost, quality of life or labor environment).

Whereas Cluster project teams were responsible for the preparation of Cluster business cases, the process required a close involvement of both function responsible as well as future service provider representatives from Clusters and GSS to ensure alignment on aspirations and target state. During business case establishment, assumptions and results were repeatedly challenged by different stakeholders and the central team. Final quality assurance and reconciliation was performed by the respective Cluster CFO who then presented the results to the steering committee for approval and reconciliation. The steering committee challenged Cluster business cases based on their content, external benchmarks and internal "best practice" KPI comparison. After steering committee approval was granted, Cluster cases were consolidated to a global project business case and a scoreboard was developed to initiate a friendly competition amongst Clusters based on the central KPI "cost of finance in % of direct business". Reconciled Cluster business cases indicated a cost reduction for the finance functions in scope of 23 % with payback periods of less than three years.

3 Achieving Definite Results

In this section, we describe technical factors which contributed to the success of the Finance Bundling project. Namely, effective project governance, controlling, and risk management greatly contributed not only to an effective project execution, but also to the sustainability of project results. In this respect, appropriate change enabler tools are of particular importance.

3.1 Project Governance

Given the enormous project scale that required working with more than 150 people in many different time zones, a thorough project management concept[25] was a major factor for success or failure during both planning and implementation phase. Day-to-day business within the project could only be handled by implementing a project management framework that established clear reporting and escalation lines. Hence the flow of communication and decision making had to be reflected in an elaborated set of roles and responsibilities.[26] In addition clear interfaces between organizational units and service providers had to be established and all relevant stakeholder groups had to be included in the project organization.

To account for existing reporting lines, two project organizations were established: The central, regional and local finance community was included in the finance project organization, whereas GSS established a customer project (CP) team lead by the GSS CFO to provide optimal planning and transition support.

Representing top-management buy-in and commitment, the *Siemens* CFO and a dedicated Executive Sponsor from his leadership team acted as Project Sponsors (PS) presiding over the finance project organization.[27] They initiated the project, acted as project champion along the entire project lifecycle supporting change management efforts and ensured the availability of key resources.

The Steering Committee (SC)[28] was an active body during the project. It was accountable for key principle definition, deliverable acceptance and results validation as well as for taking strategic decisions. It consisted of Sector CFOs, Cluster CFOs and function heads.

---

25 For a comprehensive overview of project management bodies and processes cf. *DE ROOIJ* (2010), p. 17 et. seqq, and *PMI* (2008), chapter 2.

26 "Cooperative efforts require good communications and early warning systems. A project manager should try to keep his partners aware of what is going on and should be the one who tells them first of any rumor or actual changes in plan"; *NASA* (1996), rule 16.

27 "Remember who the customer is and what his objectives are (i.e. check with him when you go to change anything of significance)"; *NASA* (1996), rule 80.

28 Steering committees are important structural elements with positive influence on project success cf. *LECHLER/ COHEN* (2009), p. 42 et seqq.

The Project Team (PT) was installed as a decision body[29] and information sharing platform for business and Clusters. It defined the project strategy, discussed current issues, defined and validated potential solutions. The team was formed by Cluster CFOs, Sector head of accounting & controlling and the GSS CFO. The project team was headed by the project lead.[30]

The Project Management Office (PMO)[31] was responsible for defining and implementing the overall project methodology including guidelines and standards, budget and resource controlling, project schedule management, central risk management, blueprint maintenance, overarching topics and integration management as well as meeting and decision preparation. It was staffed with dedicated professionals and constituted the key working-level project interface to the *Siemens* organization and other projects.

The Global Cluster Coordinators (GCC) were the central link to regional Cluster teams with each Cluster having a dedicated contact person. Besides supporting Cluster project teams in all aspects of daily project work, their responsibilities included progress tracking and reporting, deliverables quality assurance, cost and benefits realization control was well as knowledge management and issue resolution.

People & Communication (PC) was set up as an independent project function to emphasize the importance of creating and sustaining a productive and goal-oriented project culture that provided project discipline.[32] It was in charge of change management and internal / external project communication except status reporting.[33]

---

29 "Never ask management to make a decision that you can make. Assume you have the authority to make decisions unless you know there is a document that states unequivocally that you can't."; *NASA* (1996), rule 69.

30 For an analysis of the impact of the role of leadership on project performance cf. *ANANTATMULA* (2010), p. 13 et. seqq.

31 For best practices in establishing, developing and implementing PMOs cf. *ANDERSEN/HENRIKSEN/AARSETH* (2007), p. 97 et. seqq. On the role of PMOs cf. *SANTOS DO VALLE/DA SILVIERA E SILVIA/PEREIRA SOARES* (2009), p. 1 et. seqq. On the value of PMOs cf. *HURT/THOMAS* (2009), p. 55 et. seqq.

32 For an analysis and recommendations for communication design for multi-disciplinary multi-national projects cf. *FOX* (2008), p. 536 et. seqq.

33 "You cannot watch everything. What you can watch is the people. They have to know you will not accept a poor job." "Always try to negotiate your internal support at the lowest level. What you want is the support of the person doing the work, and the closer you can get to him in negotiations the better."; *NASA* (1996), rule 20 and 25.

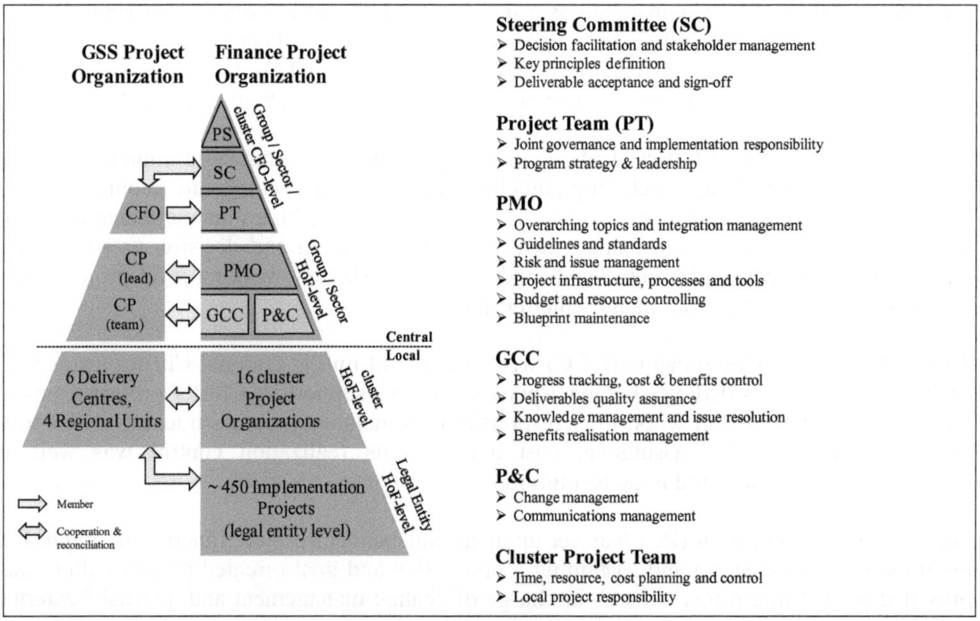

Figure 5: GSS and Finance Bundling project organization[34]

In each local Cluster project, a dedicated project lead was in charge of planning and executing the implementation of the new finance structure regionally and locally with all relevant activities. Cluster project teams consisted of a diverse team of function and project management experts and provided a single interface for central project teams to Cluster legal entities.

The project governance setup combined with robust project controlling providing up-to-date status, cost/benefit and risk information led to a close integration and reconciliation with project stakeholders and sustained organizational commitment. Having people with different backgrounds included on all levels of the project organization ensured the right mix of organizational and technical knowledge to successfully achieve the ambitious project goals. All project bodies included external consultants who supported the project from the beginning. On working level, the teams were equally staffed with *Siemens* personnel and consultants to ensure the integration of internal views and outside-in perspectives. To achieve consistent project delivery quality and optimal local support, the central consulting organization coordinated the global engagement and served as single point of contact for *Siemens* procurement and consultant related requests.

34 Source: SIEMENS AG.

3.2 Project Controlling

The general aim of project controlling[35] is to ensure the achievement of proclaimed project goals and give early indications of possible challenges and/or delays.[36] In essence, two core areas have to be covered: on the one hand, project controlling has to exercise a support function i.e. provide guidance and enable the project organization to pursue project goals.[37] On the other hand, project controlling has to exercise a control function i.e. watch over the achievement of the magic triangle magnitudes time, quality and profitability.[38] Within Cluster Finance Bundling project this came down to the simple paradigm "You get what you measure and only what gets measured gets done". Thus, project controlling primarily centered on the key aspects quality gate concept, tracking and reporting as well as cost/benefit controlling which were executed by the GCC.

These aspects were reflected on the overall objectives of the GCC project function:

- Monitoring of high-risk project steps with closing implication: following-up on the delivery of key milestones which have a strong impact on closing procedures and/or quality and timeliness of books and records.
- Implementation compliance: tracking of adherence to initial implementation planning and provision of transparency regarding progress, deliverable quality and implementation risks.
- Business case realization; tracking of targeted financial benefits achievement, i.e. adherence to Cluster impact estimation FTE and cost baseline development as well as implementation and restructuring cost projections.
- Activity split compliance: assuring compliance to global/local activity split as approved by steering committee.

According to this concept, Cluster project leads and teams were responsible for the achievement and quality of all planning and implementation deliverables required by the SImpleG milestone methodology as well as for process continuity, knowledge transfer and the achievement of their respective Cluster business cases. The central GCC were responsible for global coordination, knowledge sharing, quality assurance and progress monitoring. As total project deliverables amounted to more than 18,000 (i.e. more than 40 per legal entity in scope) a trust-based approach had to be followed balancing risk and involvement. Accordingly 8 SImpleG key milestones were selected and integrated into a quality gate concept ruling legal entity project progress (measured via standard degree of implementation 1 to 5). Defined quality, consistency and adequacy requirements were centrally reviewed for all key milestones whereas additional sample checks could be performed under risk considerations.[39] For each key milestone, defined deliverables had to be uploaded into the central project management platform as attachments to the standardized legal entity progress reporting. The uploads

---

[35] For general procedures of project schedule, cost and quality management cf. *PMI* (2008), chapter 6, 7 and 8.

[36] Cf. *FIEDLER* (2010), p. 31 et seqq.

[37] Cf. *KOREIMANN* (2003), p. 18 et seqq.

[38] Financial project controlling was performed on EVA basis. For a discussion of the Earned Value Approach cf. *BOWER/FINEGAN* (2009), p. 435 et. seqq.

[39] "Reviews are for the reviewed and not for the reviewer. The review is a failure if the reviewed learn noting from it"; *NASA* (1996), rule 39.

had to include confirmation sheets signed by key stakeholders involved in deliverable achievement. As all SImpleG deliverables were standardized, global Cluster coordinators were able to benchmark results submitted, identify and disseminate “best practice” deliverables, create a list of known pitfalls and mitigation actions and identify risks and non-compliance at an early stage.[40]

Deliverable quality control was supported via a standardized status reporting[41] process fully supported by the central project management platform. Legal entities reported milestone achievement and uploaded required key milestone documentation in real time. Bi-monthly status meetings with project management ensured alignment of progress and expectations. Comprehensive Cluster-level reporting was scheduled once a month. Besides legal-entity-level progress reporting, Cluster-level reporting addressed qualitative information regarding achievements, information and/or decision requirements, experience exchange and a description of next steps. The central part was a comprehensive risk assessment via standard categories closing quality, receiving entity readiness, donating entity readiness, employee representation and external factors which were consolidated to a central risk register. For each reporting, Cluster CFOs had to state any risks to quality of books and records or the Cluster business case separately in writing. Additionally, all legal entities not achieving milestones as scheduled or presenting significant schedule risks were logged and discussed separately to assess problem areas and jointly derive solutions. Bi-monthly meetings of project management and GCC ensured alignment of status and expectations, timely escalation of risks and reconciliation of overarching topics (e.g. vertically integrated IT systems of subsidiary groups) before escalation to steering committee. Subsequent to Cluster-level reporting the results were discussed with business, function and service provider representatives in separate meetings and calls. This ensured a company-wide alignment regarding current status and topics to be resolved. Issue could then be tackled from many perspectives as stakeholders were committed and strived for project success.

Cost/benefit controlling comprised two information sources: expected deviations to initial Cluster business cases resulting from e.g. activity split deviations or scope changes were discussed during Cluster-level reporting.[42] Impacts were documented and tracked. The cost perspective was covered via reporting of actual and forecast of Cluster-level project execution and restructuring expenses in the group’s management reporting system.[43] The tracking followed a defined process with clear approval procedures based on local posting rules and reconciled with financial reporting guidelines as well as local auditors. Deviations to expenses incurred and accruals were discussed with Cluster project leads to avoid budget overruns.

---

40 Cf. B017, p. 282 et seqq.

41 “The amount of reviews and reports are proportional to management’s understanding […] It is necessary in this type of environment t make sure that data is presented so that the average person, slightly familiar with activities, can understand it. Keeping the data simple and clear never insults anyone’s intelligence.”; *NASA* (1996), rule 41; cf. B017, p. 266.

42 “The first of trouble comes from the schedule or the cost curve. Engineers are the last to know they are in trouble. Engineers are born optimists.”; *NASA* (1996), rule 56.

43 “Most of yesterday’s projects overran because of poor estimates and not because of mistakes […].”; *NASA* (1996), rule 73.

3.3 Embedded Risk Management

The project entailed a large number of transitions resulting in a significant shift of activities and responsibilities in the accounting and financial reporting processes. Throughout the entire transformation period the highest levels of quality and timeliness of books and records needed to be assured at any time. Thus, an overarching risk management[44] process was implemented and embedded in the general project controlling and change management approach.[45]

Achieving Cluster Finance Bundling goals in a short timeframe was a challenge to all *Siemens* entities. Shifting processes, activities and responsibilities across legal entities and geographic regions whilst ensuring process continuity and high quality financial reporting involved several risks e.g. potential knowledge drain, loss of key personnel and process non-compliance. In order to manage those risks systematically, the central team decided to establish an embedded risk management approach.[46]

The project controlling approach and milestone concept reflected in SImpleG offered a structured basis for project risk management. As implementation progress could be tracked on legal entity level and milestones had to be scheduled, the central team was able to proactively identify implementation risks e.g. back-end loaded planning leading to a high number of transitions during fiscal year-end or quarterly closing procedures. In addition the milestone-based documentation of deliverables in SImpleG helped to constantly improve deliverable quality and identify key risks and mitigation measures per milestone.

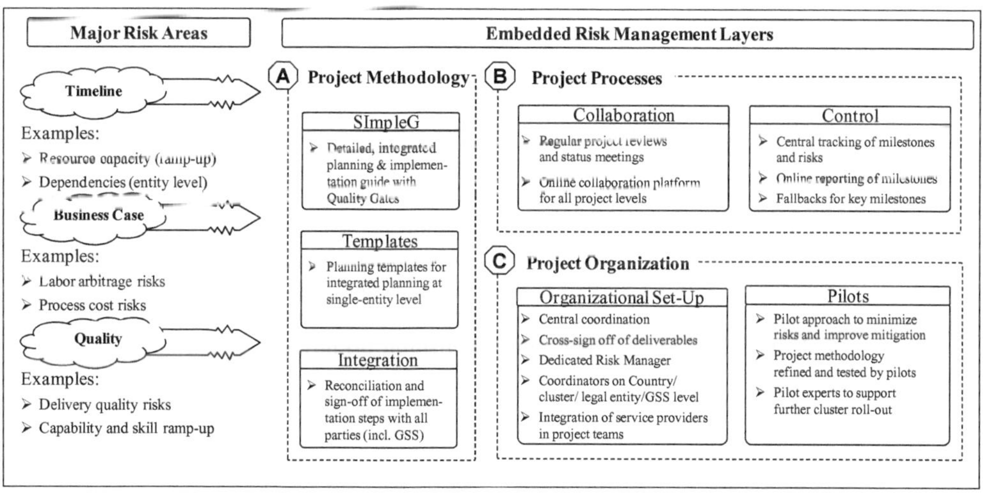

Figure 6: Embedded risk management layers[47]

44 For a review of risk management literature cf. *SANCHEZ* et. al. (2018), p. 14 et seqq.

45 For general project risk management procedures cf. and *PMI* (2008), chapter 11. On best practices for risk management in complex projects cf. *BENTA/PODEAN/MIRCEAN* (2011), p. 142 et seqq.

46 "Never male excuses; instead, present plans of actions to be taken."; *NASA* (1996), rule 100.

47 Source: *SIEMENS AG*.

Project reporting and communication enabled a constant flow of information from legal entities over Cluster project teams to the central team which consolidated, analyzed and categorized potential risks in a central register and jointly developed mitigation measures with local teams.[48] Accordingly all regular project communication was analyzed regarding its impact on key risk categories in a mapping approach to identify potential gaps. This gave the central team a general understanding of risk management coverage and enabled the definition of additional risk mitigation measures for potentially uncovered key risks.[49]

3.4 Change Enablers

Due to the scale and scope of the Finance Bundling project, appropriate and effective change management tools had to be employed to enable a successful transformation. This section describes the most important considerations in this regard.

3.4.1 Knowledge Sharing

Building a global experts network for regular exchange of project experiences was one of the major challenges with enormous influence on project success and performance. Through extensive cooperation, contribution and distribution of valuable better practices, a knowledge-sharing[50] culture and a forum for open discussion were created. To provide optimal support to the finance community throughout the project, a systematic knowledge sharing approach was established and embedded in the communication strategy.[51] The GCC and PC teams ensured effective sharing of project and operational knowledge via providing the right communication tools and platforms to enable a vivid exchange of proven project solutions.

The initial knowledge sharing during the planning phase focused on benefiting from pilot Cluster experience. As two of the most complex Clusters had been chosen as pilots, a large amount of useful experience in the form of templates, support documentation and work instructions was readily available in SimpleG and could be accessed by project managers and staff from other Clusters. Nevertheless, the key challenge consisted in sharing the tacit undocumented knowledge and experiences that pilot Cluster project teams had gained. This required broadening the idea of knowledge sharing beyond the collection, consolidation and distribution of documented knowledge and establishing a knowledge sharing culture in the project community.[52]

During implementation phase the requirement for broadening the knowledge sharing approach became obvious as implementation requirements turned out to be individual and complex, i.e. transitions differed remarkably from each other concerning their size, complexity, regulatory and legal specifics. Providing guidance and knowledge within SImpleG was useful

---

48 "Mistakes are all right but failure is not. Failure is just a mistake you can't recover from; therefore, try to create contingency plans and alternate approaches for the items or plans that have high risk."; *NASA* (1996), rule 94.

49 "Wrong decisions made early can be recovered from. Right decisions made late cannot correct them."; *NASA* (1996), rule 82.

50 On Knowledge Transfer in general cf. *ZEPPIN* (2008), p. 4 et seqq.

51 On knowledge management in a project environment cf. *POLYANINOVA* (2011), p. 34 et seqq.

52 "Things that fail are lessons learned for the future. Occasionally things go right: these are also lessons learned. Try to duplicate that which works."; *NASA* (1996), rule 93.

but did not address more specific questions or problems that transferring entities were facing.[53] Accordingly, additional methods and channels to share knowledge were required. Thus, GCC and PC established a better practice roadmap that extended the existing knowledge sharing by adding three key areas:

- Daily support: as valuable experience was collected on a daily basis by project teams all around the globe, GCC and PC established and communicated a process to collect, categorize, standardize, consolidate and share lessons learned. The process could be triggered by requests for contribution from project members, central identification of better practice by GCC during milestone reviews and/or voluntary submission of input via a proper knowledge sharing portal in the central project platform.
- Live meetings: to encourage topic-specific exchange of tacit knowledge a live meeting schedule was set up that provided Clusters project teams the opportunity to present their better practices. This channel fostered the general willingness to share as experts were highly acknowledged in the finance community.
- Transition experience campus: to broaden the stakeholder base involved in knowledge sharing, strengthen cross-Cluster and cross-function interfaces and foster mutual understanding, two-day on site campuses were conducted on several locations around the globe. Each campus included 20 to 30 stakeholders which were key for a successful transition e.g. Cluster project leads, Cluster heads of accounting & controlling, Cluster service manager, GSS and business representatives. Besides technical presentations the events included breakout sessions, panel discussions, face-to-face meetings and workshops moderated by experienced change managers and mediators.

Like project controlling, knowledge sharing was closely related to risk management. Central team members participating in the process were able to identify risks, root cause and potential mitigation measures at an early stage and gather experience that prevented the project from taking the same risk twice.

3.4.2 Central Project Management Platform

Facilitating a project platform supporting highly efficient project management, automated reporting procedures and high data quality was key to project success. Given project scope and complexity, a large number of globally distributed project members and stakeholders needed to be supported with features that enabled global collaboration and the secure exchange of enormous data volumes.[54] The "Finance Navigator" was developed as central web-based project management platform to cope with all these challenges.

---

53 "Documentation does not take the place for knowledge. There is a great difference in what is supposed to be, what is thought to have happened, and reality. Documents are normally a static picture in time that get outdated rapidly"; *NASA* (1996), rule 43.

54 On the general management of inter-team tasks and task interdependencies cf. *HOEGEL/WEINKAUF* (2005), p. 1287 et seqq.

According to PMO principles, the platform needed to fulfill the following requirements:

- All activities need to be vertically aligned
- Consistent project standards (processes, templates, reports) should to be used on all project levels
- The degree of automation had to be maximized ensuring scalability
- Information security was a prerequisite

To ensure data security and practicability, the Finance Navigator was set up as an intranet portal on the basis of Microsoft SharePoint. Server farms were hosted by *Siemens* contractors which guaranteed a rigid user authorization process and a secure log-in concept for *Siemens* collaborators. A sophisticated role-based authorization concept provided the required flexibility to tailor user rights to project role requirements and define automated workflows as well as escalation processes. Several functionalities and access to distinct areas were tied to specified user roles reducing single-user interface complexity.

Key features of Finance Navigator included:

- An eRoom (document exchange library) served as central file storage with individual access rights for folders and different file and folder search parameters.
- The milestone-based real-time reporting contained current status, issues, risks and required decisions and was linked to SImpleG methodology.
- The SImpleG methodology was reflected in a detailed step by step guide, ensuring latest content and templates with an integrated interactive navigation.
- The implementation roadmap platform provided a central overview of implementation timelines on legal entity level. Each company in scope was reflected as separate reporting item which besides milestone scheduling and status provided additional company-specific information e.g. key contacts, revenue, finance FTE, GSS potential, etc.
- A people contact database contained contact details of all internal and external project members and mail distribution lists.
- A project calendar published all project relevant meetings and events. It supported different views and Microsoft Outlook interfaces.

Additionally, Clusters could establish their own secure sub-workspaces supporting comprehensive project management and collaboration for local project management. Baselining on legal entity level was fully supported based on an integrated database accessible via different user-friendly input and output interfaces.

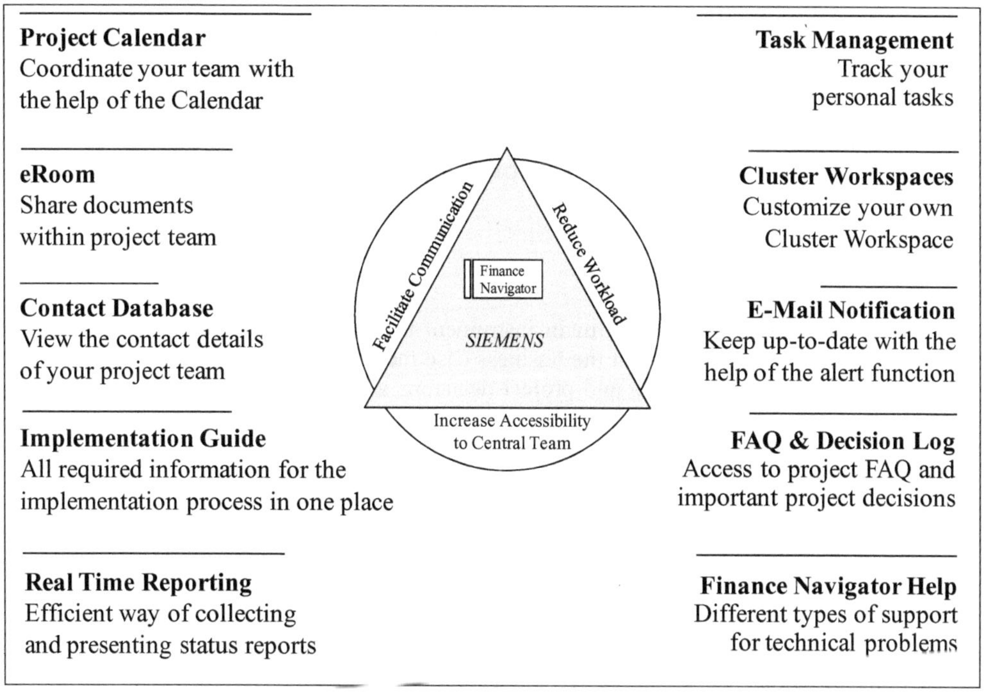

Figure 7: *Finance navigator capabilities*[55]

To support efficient and effective handling of the platform a training concept was deployed which consisted of training material and exercises for Finance Navigator administrators who were the key contacts for Cluster managers and teams. Training was cascaded from central team to local administrators to keep workload manageable.

[55] Source: *SIEMENS AG*.

4 Enabling Continuous Improvement

Besides the design and implementation of a new target operating model for the finance function, the Finance Bundling project was also tasked to ensure the sustained effectiveness of project results. This section describes the corresponding methodology.

4.1 Effectiveness Review

Cluster business cases had been a main instrument to manage decision making during the entire project. As a reference point the business case methodology provided valuable insights on the consequences of business and project decisions as well as external factors impacting the project. Those helped making the challenging project goals more modular and manageable[56], retain focus on strategic objectives and benefits rather than on activities and obtain clear lines of sponsorship.

Whilst regular reporting on performance against the target benefits produced information useful to identify shortfalls and new benefit opportunities, it was important to demonstrate transparent project results after full implementation of blueprint and activity split. According to the Cluster Finance Bundling motto "project achievements only count if they are sustainable and measurable", Cluster CFOs had to present their "Cluster achievement case" to the steering committee after successful implementation in order to proof that

- Cluster organization and target operating model had been implemented and stabilized (governance view),
- all transitions had been successfully completed (legal entity view),
- appropriate personnel had been set up in countries, the Cluster and GSS in line with initial Cluster business case (resources view),
- Efficiency, governance and effectiveness potentials with respect to business case KPIs had been realized (project goal view).

Accountability was ensured via a detailed ex-post comparison of initial Cluster business cases to final Cluster achievements which had to include explanation of key deviations in terms of process allocation and activity split compliance, FTE ramp-up/ramp-down, project budget and financial cost baseline development. [57] To proof P&L effectiveness and establish a transparent link to *Siemens* efficiency goals, all Cluster achievement cases were reconciled to financial reporting. The reconciliation included the bridging of baseline FTE to reported infrastructure FTE (resource view) and the bridging of baseline cost to reported infrastructure expenses (financial view).

---

56 On the flexibility of modular approaches cf. *KRÜGER* (2010), p. 305 et seqq.

57 "Hide nothing from the reviewers. Their reputation and yours is on the line. Expose all the warts and pimples. Don't offer excuses – just state facts."; *NASA* (1996), rule 36.

The final achievement review was a prerequisite for transparency over project achievements and continuous tracking. Sustainability was ensured by making stakeholders responsible to maintain results and share experience and lessons learned with peers.

4.2 Lessons Learned

Key lessons learned from the project relate to collaboration between local and central units, the treatment of project scope and principles as well as the management of a global business case. The securing of lessons learned from Cluster transition experience was an important step to enable the finance community to strive for further improvement and excellence. As always, success factors extended beyond a design principle-based methodology to ownership by senior finance leadership, a diverse team composition and achieving project discipline by creating a real project culture.[58]

Successful implementation requires the right mix between local commitment and central governance - implementation must be under local responsibility, but central governance is required.[59] This includes ongoing top management commitment and alignment of key stakeholders, but also a culture of mutual trust and open communication via regular and formal project reporting. Elimination of political barriers by alignment of stakeholders is as important as furture-oriented coachwork for skills and qualifications. Central toolkits – e.g. HR communication and implementation campuses – must not be a burden, but a means of support. It is essential to achieve a "getting things done" and "making it work" mentality that includes thinking about solutions instead of ways to avoid change. Accordingly the central project team never said "none of our business". If one is brave enough to say "all entities are in scope" one has to accept, that "all problems are in scope" too. The responsiveness of the project team was very high and the support effort was highly appreciated by the global organization.

A winning design principle-based methodology is characterized by an early agreement on a set of fundamental guiding and key design principles. Topics addressed included an all-in approach towards the organizational project scope, the setting of strategic project principles regarding scope, roles and aspirations, defined project rules (e.g. no delegates in meetings, shift of burden of proof) and a mandatory and standardized Cluster-level business case. This resulted in accelerated design and execution speed. The piloting approach was vital to provide proof of concept and generate stakeholder confidence.

After all – to convince people you need people. Thus ownership for the project was assumed by the senior finance leadership team which formed the steering committee and approved all decisions made during the project including any deviations from guiding or key design principles set beforehand. Accountability and commitment was passed down the whole line via Sector CFOs and Cluster CFOs to their local teams. The diverse composition of project teams integrating all required and relevant expertise ranging from functional processes, Sector and Cluster experience to GSS guaranteed that the full scope of complexity was addressed. Pro-

---

58 "Management principles still are the same. It is just that the tools have changed. You still find the right people to do the work and get out of the way so they can do it."; *NASA* (1996), rule 3.

59 "Projects require teamwork to succeed. Remember, most teams have a coach and not a boss, but the coach still has to call some of the plays."; *NASA* (1996), rule 87.

ject discipline and comprehensive project setup ensured that all functional and local stakeholders are enabled to contribute and made accountable for project progress and final success. Maintenance of project focus, commitment to agreed decisions, deliverables, timelines and business cases as well as transparency (DI quality gates) and continuous communication were crucial. Ongoing alignment and assessment of status and progress between all relevant stakeholders supported by a framework of controlling and monitoring tools contributed to project success.

Furthermore change management required the project lead and central team to go out and talk to the people personally and also take the fire personally - this can never be delegated.[60] Undoubtedly the controlled implementation of defined change required a well thought through methodology and plan behind. But personal involvement and accountability proved to be essential especially when concepts are often very black or white, but yet one has to stick to it. In the beginning this provoked, but due to strong central commitment, communication and on-site face-to-face meetings, people understood that becoming grey to early in the process would take the project nowhere as discipline is key.

What is good for the company, is good for the project – to achieve the best possible outcome for the company, the project did not limit its scope of thinking. The teams addressed topics that were not comprised in the initial project scope, but crucial nevertheless. In the course of the project an compay-wide infrastructure cost controlling was set up and implemented into the financial reporting systems. Enhanced transparency contributed to sustainably challenge and enhance infrastructure cost baselines. The contracting requirements with service providers were covered by implementing a standardized SLA tool that was later on applied to all infrastructure functions.

5 Conclusion

In this chapter, we described the Finance Bundling project at *Siemens AG* in terms of its inception and the top-down project methodology employed as well as specific tools and methods which ensured project success during design and implementation and thereafter. Lessons learned are applicable to comparable projects which address the re-alignment of infrastructure functions, in particular on a global scale and in conjunction with bundling and shared services approaches.

As of today, the target operating model for the global finance function designed and implemented by the project continues to provide value to the entire organization. Due to the committment of all parties involved as part of a complex organizational structure including Sectors, Clusters, local entities and central functions, the challenging project goals ranging from improvements to effectiveness, efficiency, flexibility, compliance and standardization to a reduced overall complexity and cost targets could be sustainably achieved.

60 "A project manager should visit everyone who is building anything for his project at least once, should know all the managers on his project (both government and contractor), and know the integration team members. People like to know that the project manager is interested in their work and the best proof is for the manager to visit them and see first hand what they are doing"; *NASA* (1996), rule 1.

References

ANANTATMULA, V. (2010): Project Manager Leadership Role in Improving Project Performance, in: Engineering Management Journal, Vol. 22 (2010), No. 1, pp. 13–22.

ANDERSEN, B./HENRIKSEN, B./AARSETH, W. (2007): Benchmarking of Project Management Office Establishment: Extracting Best Practices, in: Journal of Management in Engineering, Vol. 23 (2007), No. 2, pp. 97–104.

BENTA, D./PODEAN, I./MIRCEAN, C. (2011): On Best Practices for Risk Management in Complex Projects, in: Informatica Economica, Vol. 15 (2011), No. 2, pp. 142–152.

BOWER, D./FINEGAN, A. (2009): New Approaches in Project Performance Evaluation Techniques, in: International Journal of Managing Projects in Business, Vol. 2 (2009), No. 3, pp. 435–444.

FIEDLER, R. (2010): Controlling von Projekten, Wiesbaden 2010.

FOX, S. (2008): Information and communication design for multi-disciplinary multi-national projects, in: International Journal of Managing Projects in Business, Vol. 2 (2008), No. 4, pp. 536–560.

HÄLLGREN, M. (2009): Mechanisms of Deviation: Observations of Projects in Practice, in: International Journal of Managing Projects in Business, Vol. 2 (2009), No. 4, pp. 611–625.

HÄLLGREN, M./MAANINEN-OLSSON, E. (2008): Deviations and the Breakdown of Project Management Principles, in: International Journal of Managing Projects in Business, Vol. 2 (2008), No. 1, pp. 53–69.

HOEGEL,M./WEINKAUF, K. (2005): Managing Task Interdependencies in Multi-Team Projects: A Longitudial Study, in: Journal of Management Studies, Vol. 42 (2005), No. 6, pp. 1287–1308.

HURT, M./THOMAS. J. (2009): Building Value Through Sustainable Project Management Offices, in: Project Management Journal, Vol. 40 (2009), No. 1, pp. 55–72.

KAPLAN, R./NORTON, D. (1997): Balanced Scorecard – Strategien erfolgreich umsetzen, Stuttgart 1997.

KNAPP, A./LEDERER, A. (2010): Instrumente des Controlling bei der Steuerung von Projekten, in: *STEINLE, C./ESSELING, V./EICHENBERG, T.* (eds.), Handbuch Multiprojektmanagement und -controlling, Berlin 2010, p. 277–290.

KNÖPFLE, G. (2011): Strategie und Organisation aus einem Guss – das Schattendasein von Service- und Support-Abteilungen schadet vielen Unternehmen, in: Stuttgarter Zeitung, No. 73, 2011.

KOREIMANN, D. (2003): Project Controlling – eine vergessene Disziplin?, in: Projekt Management, No. 3, 2003, pp. 18–24.

KRAHN, T./SCHMIDT L. (2010): Strategische Steuerung von Projektportfolios am Beispiel der FinanzIT, in: *STEINLE, C./ESSELING, V./EICHENBERG, T.* (Hrsg.), Handbuch Multiprojektmanagement und -controlling, Berlin 2010, pp. 291–303.

Krüger, W. (2010): Ansatzpunkte für ein flexibles Multiprojektmanagement, in: *Steinle, C./ Esseling, V./Eichenberg, T.* (eds.), Handbuch Multiprojektmanagement und -controlling, Berlin 2010, pp. 305–318.

Lange, D. (2010): Mitwirkung und Funktionen des Controllings bei der Konzeption des Projektportfolios, in: *Steinle, C./Esseling, V./Eichenberg, T.*(eds.), Handbuch Multiprojektmanagement und -controlling, Berlin 2010, pp. 101-114.

Lappe, M./Eikelmann, T./Campana, S./Schott, E. (2010): Praxiserfahrung und Best Practices zur Projektpriorisierung und -selektion, in: *Steinle, C./Esseling, V./Eichenberg, T.* (eds.), Handbuch Multiprojektmanagement und -controlling, Berlin 2010, pp. 173–186.

Lechler, T./Cohen, M. (2009): Exploring the Role of Steering Committees in Realizing Value From Project Management, in: Project Management Journal, Vol. 40 (2009), No. 1, pp. 42–54.

Milosevic, D./Inman, L./Ozbay, A. (2001): Impact of Project Management Standardization on Project Effectiveness, in: Engineering Management Journal, Vol. 13 (2001), No. 4, pp. 9–16.

National Aeronautics and Space Administration (NASA) (1996): One Hundred Rules for NASA Project Managers, online: http://www.oliverlehmann.com/project-management-sources/Nasa-Hundred-Rules-for-Project-Managers.pdf.

PMI (2008): A Guide to the Project Management Body of Knowledge (PMBOK), 4th edition, Pennsylvania 2008.

Polyaninova, T. (2011): Knowledge Management in a Project Environment: Organisational CT and Project Influences, in: Vine, Vol. 41 (2011), No. 3, pp. 34–48.

de Rooij, C. (2010): Organisation des Multiprojektmanagement und -controlling: Praktische Erfahrungen aus einem Rückversicherungs-Unternehmen, in: *Steinle, C./Esseling, V./ Eichenberg, T.* (eds.), Handbuch Multiprojektmanagement und -controlling, Berlin 2010, pp. 17–32.

Sanchez, H./Robert, B./Bourgault, M./Pellerin, R. (2008): Risk Management applied to Projects, Programs and Portfolios, in: International Journal of Managing Projects in Business, Vol. 2 (2008), No. 1, pp. 14–35.

Santos do Valle, J./Silveira e Silvia, W./Pereira Soares, C. (2008): Project Management Office (PMO): Principles and Practice, ACEE International Transactions, Sao Paulo 2008.

Schuppert, G. (2010): Internationales Multi- Produkt- und Projektmanagement am Beispiel eines Joint Ventures in China, in: *Steinle, C./Esseling, V./Eichenberg, T.*(eds.), Handbuch Multiprojektmanagement und -controlling, Berlin 2010, pp. 51–68.

Steeger, O. (2010): „Projektmanagement und Siemens gehören zusammen" – Interview with Dr. Jürgen Schloß, in: Projekt Management aktuell, No. 2, 2010, pp. 3–10.

Voigt, V. (2010): Ausgestaltung der Projektpriorisierung – ein engpassorientierter Ansatz, in: *Steinle, C./Esseling, V./Eichenberg, T.* (eds.), Handbuch Multiprojektmanagement und -controlling, Berlin 2010, pp. 187–207.

Wagner, R. (2012): Standards für das Multiprojektmanagement, in: Projektmagazin, No. 4, 2012, pp. 27–39.

Weuster, A. (2010): Unternehmensorganisation: Organisationsprojekte – Aufbaustrukturen, München 2010.

Zeppin, M. (2008): Wissenstransfer, Saarbrücken 2008.

Managing the Transformation During a Finance Shared Services Journey

Marcell Vollmer and *Peter Rasper*

SAP AG

Executive Summary

During an implementation of Shared Services the impact on organizational change is quite often underestimated and the transformation management not properly setup.

In order to gain a better understanding of the need for a holistic transformation management approach during the planning, set-up and stabilization (further improvement) of a global Finance Shared Services Organization, this paper outlines a conceptual model of transformation management including Change Management, Organizational Development and Communication. The model is based on a real case delivered by both authors as well as qualitative pre-studies. Thus, a holistic approach for transformation management during the entire journey in a global Shared Services Program is proposed.

1 Introduction

1.1 Shared Service Center Concept

Successful companies invest in their core competencies and core processes to increase their chances of growth. Whereas in the 1990s[1], labor-intensive industrial processes in manufacturing were relocated to less expensive locations, the focus today is on standardized administrative or support processes that can be contracted out to third parties such as suppliers or individually to outsourcing providers or centralized in captive Shared Service Centers (SSC). To date, the business literature has failed to come up with a single general definition of the Shared Service Concept.[2] For our purposes the definition of *SCHULMAN* et. al. will be used, according to which the essence of the shared service concept lies in the *concentration of company resources performing like activities, typically spread across the organization, in order to service multiple internal partners at lower cost and with higher service levels, with the common goal of delighting external customers and enhancing corporate value.*[3]

So that optimization can be achieved, the critical mass must be exceeded to enable the service functions to be consolidated in terms of quality and cost. Today, more than 80% of all Fortune 500 companies have implemented SSCs. At the same time, increased efficiency and improved service quality, combined with process standardization, serve to raise customer satisfaction. Cost and complexity reduction are now considered "table-stakes" for most Shared Services Organizations. Today, it's about strategic business enablement. What does this mean? It means: global flexibility, sourcing agility, and continuous innovation.

---

1 Cf. *KAGELMANN* (2001), p. 49.

2 Cf. e.g. *FISCHER/STERZENBACH* (2006), p. 7, *PÉREZ* (2008), p. 25, *ULBRICH* (2008), p. 34, *BECKER/KUNZ/MAYER* (2009), p. 17. *ULBRICH* (2008), p. 34, notes critically by way of conclusion: "Many authors simply wrote about using shared services in organizations and, for example, how to benefit from this idea, rather than actually explaining or defining what the shared services idea is really all about." Controversy also surrounds who was the first to use the shared service concept. For instance, *ULBRICH* (2008), p. 3, claims that *JIM BRYANT* was the first to use the term in the late 1980s as part of a project at *Baxter Healthcare*, while *QUINN/COOKE/KRIS* (2000), p. 19, regard *BOB GUNN* from the consultant company *A.T. Kearney* as the originator.

3 Cf. *SCHULMAN* et al. (1999), p. 9.

Studies dating back a number of years have shown that – after IT and payroll – the greatest potential for savings is to be found in the area of finance and accounting (F&A).

Worldwide, there are approximately 4,200 multinational Shared Service Centers.[4] These include internal (captive) Shared Service Centers, which form part of a large enterprise or multinational group, as well as external (outsourced) Shared Service Centers which are often operated by Business Process Outsourcing (BPO) providers on behalf of multinational groups.

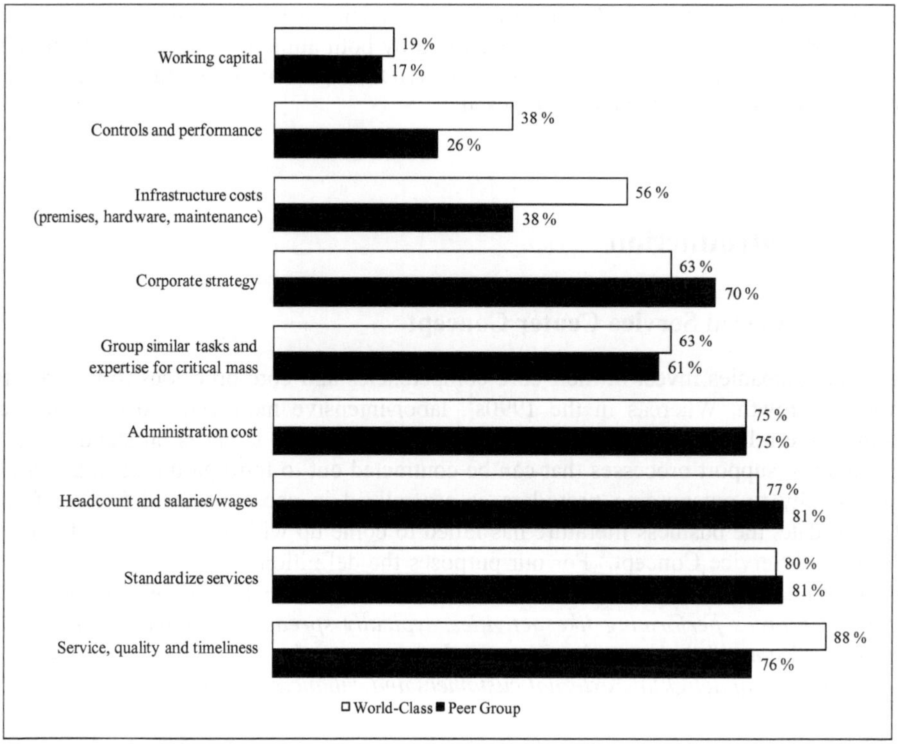

Figure 1: Reasons for setting up Shared Service Centers[5]

In terms of the functional focus, Finance Shared Service Centers are the most common, accounting for approx. 56 %, followed by IT Shared Service Centers (approx. 19 % of SSCs), HR (approx. 18 % of SSCs), with Procurement shared services organizations (approx. 6 % of SSCs) coming in last.

4 Cf. *HACKETT* SSC BPO Database.

5 Cf. *HACKETT* (2011).

The 4,200 multinational Shared Service Centers are distributed regionally as follows: 51 % Europe, 22 % Americas, 13 % Asia, 2 % Oceania and 1 % in Africa[6]. SSOs are split up into nearshore, onshore or offshore according to their geographic location, and into local, regional, supraregional, national, multinational, continental, intercontinental or global for the services to be provided according to the geographic reach.[7]

According to the integration of the SSO into enterprise workflows, a basic distinction is drawn between rigidly prescribed processes – very often workflow-based – referred to as sequence-integrated[8] services (e.g. vacation application/approval processes, travel expenses processes, payroll), and flexible processes – tailored to the situation in terms of timing, quantity and quality – referred to as sequence-independent[9] internal services (e.g. prepaid expenses and deferred income, creation of goods and services contracts, booking training courses).

To boost efficiency and reduce costs for administrative activities, *SAP AG* initiated a project to implement the organizational and process structures for a Shared Service Center for the Asia-Pacific region in 2002, which successfully went live in Singapore in 2003. Subsequently, a project for the Europe, Middle East and Africa (EMEA) region was also launched at the end of 2003; the project went into operation in Prague in January 2005. Two years later, an SSC followed in the remaining Americas region, which includes North and South America, and went into operation in Buenos Aires.

6 Cf. *HACKETT* GBS Overview & Trends, standardization in GBS & benchmarking.

7 Cf. *BECKER/KUNZ/MAYER* (2009), p. 50 et seq.

8 Cf. *STAUSS/NEUHAUS* (1999), p. 583 et seqq.

9 Cf. *STAUSS/NEUHAUS* (1999), p. 583 et seqq.

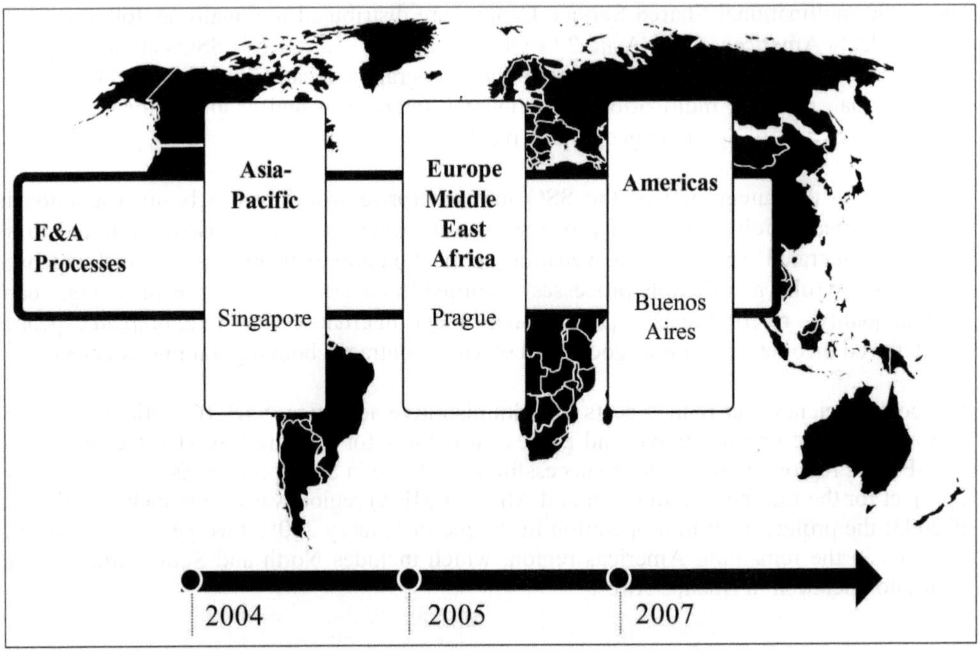

Figure 2: *Development and structure of the individual SAP Shared Services Centers from 2004 to 2007*

Shared Services aim to bolster efficiency and, in particular, deliver cost savings by providing services for customers, suppliers and all employees of the 100-plus *SAP* companies worldwide in a standardized organizational unit with defined standard processes, combined with performance management which is based on key performance indicators (KPIs) and service level agreements (SLAs). The cost savings are achieved, in particular, through bundling tasks and relocating them to low-wage locations; locally based employees are reduced while resources are built up at the low-wage location.

Overall, the aim was to reduce costs by 30 % while maintaining quality – in line with the ballpark figure of 30 % to 40 % quoted as feasible in the literature.[10]

The change management process, which accompanies or, in the authors' view must accompany, the setting up of any center, is supported by top management, executive management and employees, and forms the basis for process transfer and organizational change. The process describes the individual phases, the organization describes the setup and brings together the processing phases in groups. Both are carried out by people, by the enterprise's employees, and for that reason transformation management forms the basis for successful implementation. For *SAP AG*, the Shared Service Center also serves as a showcase for the efficient use of its own standard software.[11]

10 Cf. for instance *FROLIK* et al. (2004).

11 *SAP* software is already being used as standard in more than 75 % of Shared Service Centers (internal survey).

For everyone involved, setting up a Shared Service Center entails a host of changes and challenges. Transformation management is at the same time the key success factor as well as the aspect that tends to be neglected most frequently. This study aims to illustrate the importance of the early and targeted integration of stakeholders in terms of success when setting up a Shared Service Center. The study focuses on *SAP*'s largest Finance and HR Shared Service Center project and analyzes the time from the initial concept (2004), through the migration to the Shared Service Center for 42 international subsidiaries (2005) to completion of stabilization (2007). After a center's setup phase, the globalization of all Finance Shared Service Centers was undertaken under a standardized management structure along with the simultaneous integration of two other Shared Service Centers, as part of *SAP*'s acquisition of *BusinessObjects* in 2008 (at the time the third-largest acquisition in the IT industry).[12]

An overview of the phases and milestones is provided below.

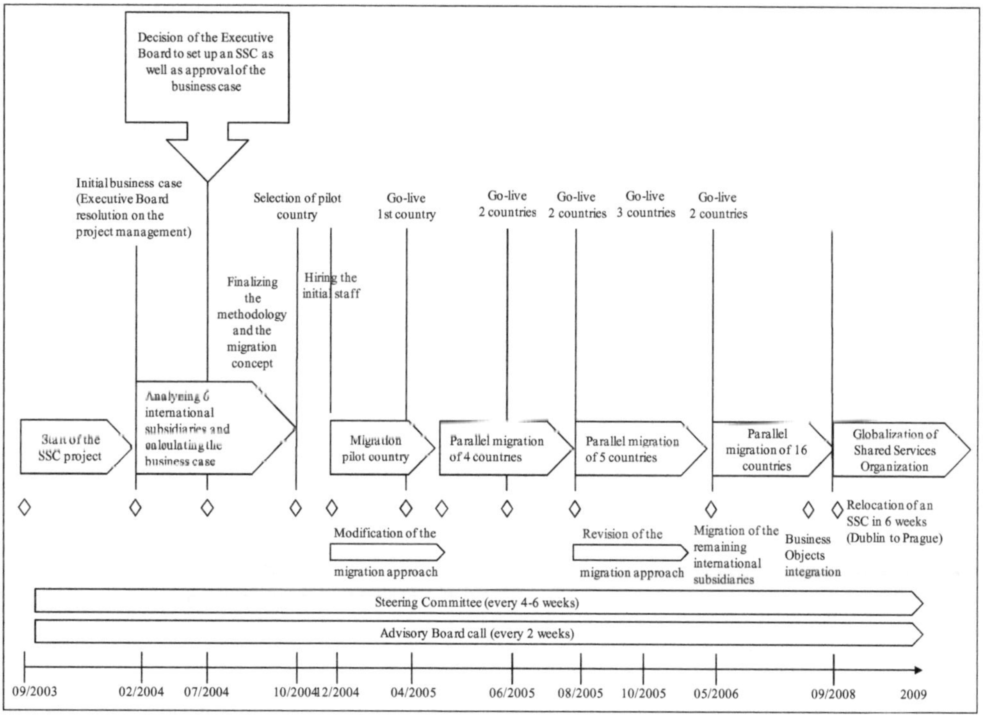

Figure 3: Implementation steps for SAP AG's Shared Services Centers from 2004 to 2009

12 Cf. online *SAP AG* (2012).

1.2 Shared Service Center Project Phases

After the initial idea and the decision to perform an analysis, the realizable potential is estimated (I), as is the feasibility of setting up a Shared Service Center with the standardization and splitting of transactional processes (II). The business case includes a detailed cost-benefit analysis and a calculation of return on investment, taking account of the time frame required. The next step involves assessing and selecting relevant locations. This is followed by the detailed planning of a serviceable and viable migration once the pilot country has been selected. The project implementation and the migration tools are tested in a pilot country, and then further planning for the remaining countries is finalized and optimized based on the experience garnered (III). Finally, all the selected Finance and Accounting processes are gradually migrated from the countries to the Shared Service Center (IV).

In the initial stage of this migration, the finance and accounting processes are standardized in the country before they are migrated to the Shared Service Center and a customer/supplier relationship is forged between the local finance department and the centralized SSO. After the critical mass of countries has been reached, processes are optimized continuously and economies of scale are leveraged using step-by-step business process reengineering (V). Thus, the Shared Service Center project can be divided into five phases, as shown in figure 4.

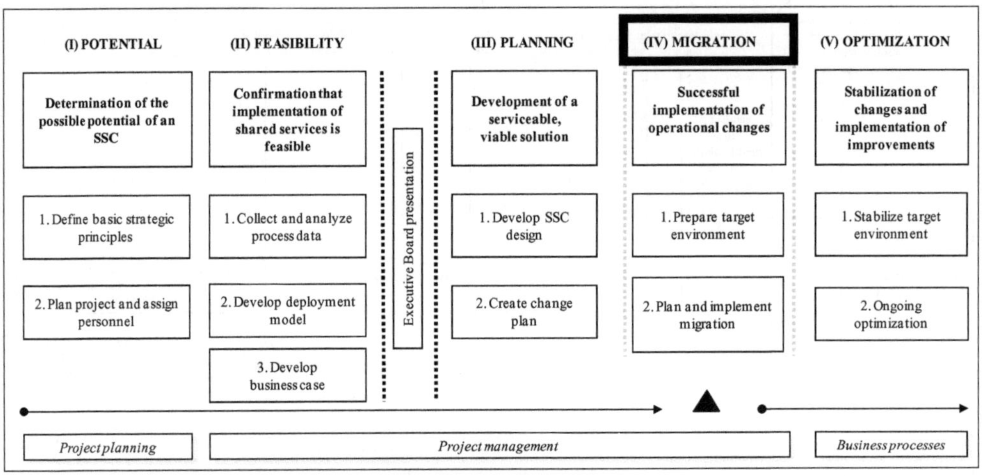

Figure 4: Project Phases and success factors

1.3 Transformation Management Aspects and Stakeholder Management

The successful implementation of the organizational and employee-related changes through a Shared Service Center project calls for *transformation management* which accompanies all the phases, in addition to the technical process and the methodology planning.

PRAMMER[13] sees transformation management as a further development of the organizational development and change management approach. He links the basic principles of both approaches and derives his transformation management approach.[14]

This paper takes a broader approach to the concept of transformation management. The authors see transformation management as the entirety of all those activities that accompany a change process. In addition to organizational development, this entails all change management activities as well as the accompanying communication. Change management, organizational development and communication must be seen as a whole throughout transformation management if these three core elements, which are associated with the successful accompaniment of change processes, are to be optimally controlled and fine-tuned.

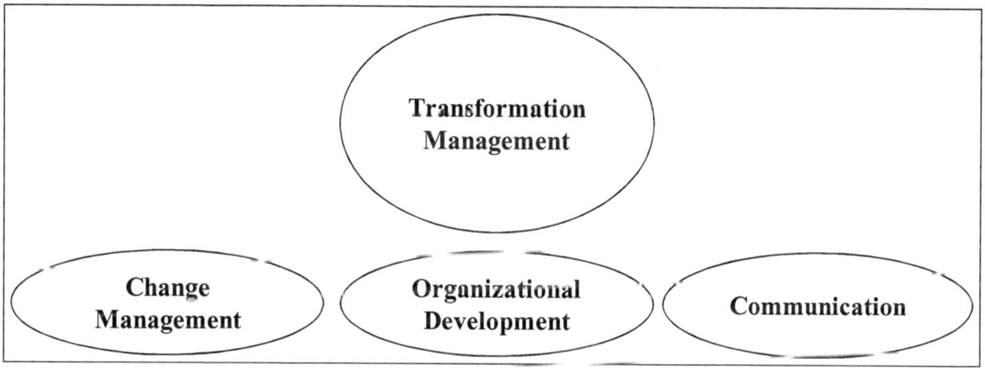

Figure 5: Components of transformation management

The following elements tend to be indicative of successful transformation management:

- Centralized management and top-management support
- A structured organizational concept
- Professional change-management accompaniment of the change process and integration of the relevant stakeholders
- A project-management approach tailored to the corporate culture
- Accompaniment through experienced communications specialists to control the distribution of information

---

13 Cf. PRAMMER (2009).

14 Cf. PRAMMER (2009), p. 29 et seqq.

Transformation management aims to prepare the organization and the stakeholders for the change. The core element is a project team that possesses a suitable mix of experience in setting up Shared Service Centers, project management skills, and expertise in planning and executing the migration. Enterprise-specific process and IT/software expertise are prerequisites for successful planning and subsequent implementation. The project leads' and project members' experience in the specialized areas is indispensable, because employees, employee representatives, and managers will critically question all decisions that stem from setting up the Shared Service Centers, and expect to be given competent answers. The integration of an experienced HR manager in project planning is recommended in order to deal with relevant transformation-management and specific employee issues professionally and promptly. An in-house communications department should be involved to professionally provide customers, executives and employees with the information they need. The ultimate goal is to ensure that the project is implemented on time. One success factor in this respect is the fully open and traceable communication of decisions and the planned implementation steps.

The coordination of collaborative project planning processes is linked closely with the usage of suitable media. The targeted usage requires knowledge of the issues that need to be communicated. The entire project team can decisively influence and thus improve transformation management by means of communication and change management if executives and knowledge experts in the enterprise are involved in putting together the business case and project planning from an early stage. A *sounding board* develops in the enterprise which enables the team to identify fears and obstacles across the company and to combat these early on by adopting suitable measures. Suitable media for informing the diverse, heterogeneous stakeholder interests and target groups include, in particular, intranet, e-mails, video and telephone conferences, employee newsletters, customer correspondence or notices, in addition to direct, personal communications.

In this context, *stakeholder management* is understood as a project management process that forms part of communication management. The identification of relevant stakeholders is known as being not an easy task when implementing projects. First, you need to define which employee groups, organizational units, or institutions are affected by the project or how they must be involved in it. The stakeholders identified can then be weighted according to importance and influence. The groups can then be summarized in a stakeholder map.

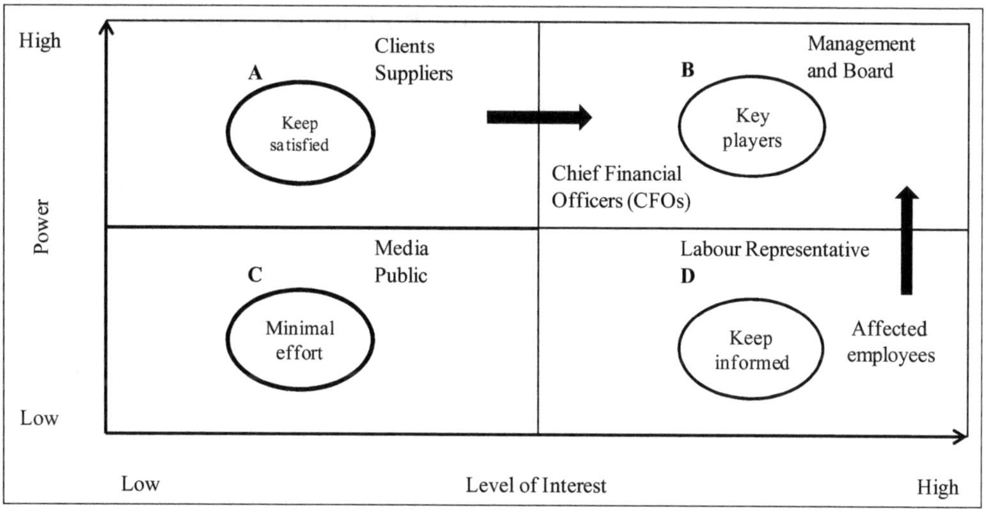

Figure 6: *Stakeholder map*

Stakeholder management provides all those involved in the project with active and proactive support and control. These include customers, employees, suppliers, the public, and the media. The following three groups are set out in detail below:

- Management and Executive Board in the function of decision-making body within the enterprise.
- Chief Financial Officers (CFOs), as local decision-makers and
- Employees as the group affected by the process change.

Stakeholder management prepares the necessary information, mainly in the form of a summary presentation with decision paper, for project management and for decisions.

The following illustrates the individual phases of project planning from the perspective of integrating the stakeholders involved in the process.

2 Process Analysis, Migration Plan and Location Decision

2.1 The Process Analysis and Assessment of the Impact on the Organization

At the start of every Shared Service Center project the question arises regarding the definition of the processes concerned and the stipulation of the countries concerned.

The *SAP AG* organization is divided up globally into three large geographic regions. There are Shared Service Centers both in Latin America and North America, in Asia-Pacific and in the EMEA (Europe, Middle East and Africa) region. 16 globally setup Shared Service Center organizations with over 30 centers exist in 2012. These include not only classic SSC areas such as IT, Finance, HR and Procurement, but also Business Research, Market Intelligence, Sales Operations Services, Knowledge Management, Marketing and Inside Sales to name only a few.

This paper was based on the Multi-Tower Shared Services project for Human Resources and Finance in the EMEA region, which was initiated in 2004 (Inside Sales was also added to the same center in 2006). In addition to the uniform management structure in the EMEA region, the limited number of time zones is one success factor for successful transformation management. Shared Service Center projects where countries from all of the world's time zones are affected pose additional challenges for daily project work. Particularly in relation to the numerous complex and sensitive issues as part of a Shared Service Center project, travel expenses are another factor that should not be underestimated in pan-continental projects. Video- or telephone conferences only tend to be a useful tool once a sound basis of trust has been built up through previous personal contact between the employees involved. Experience from current shared services projects shows that meetings via latest telepresence systems tend to come closest to a face-to-face meeting and may constitute a suitable alternative where the travel budget is limited.

When selecting the geographic area for a Shared Service Center, a purely regional approach is adopted initially in certain cases in order to analyze all German-speaking countries, for instance. *SAP AG* did not opt for this concept because economies of scale were targeted to be leveraged in the business case by taking into account a large number of countries.

In addition to the country selection, the second important decision for a Shared Service Center project is the selection of the processes to be migrated. In the case in question, all transactional HR and financial processes were selected, including Payroll, Global Mobility, HR Administration, Compensation & Benefits (HR) and Accounts Payable, Accounts Receivable, General Accounting (Finance processes) and the billing processes: Software, Education and Consulting, as well as Travel and Expense Accounting. The experiences of many other enterprises when setting up Finance Shared Service Centers demonstrated that transactional processes are particularly suitable. They include a large number of activities that can be standardized and automated, which can be differentiated clearly between international subsidiary and Shared Service Center, and which are fairly easy to learn for newly hired staff.

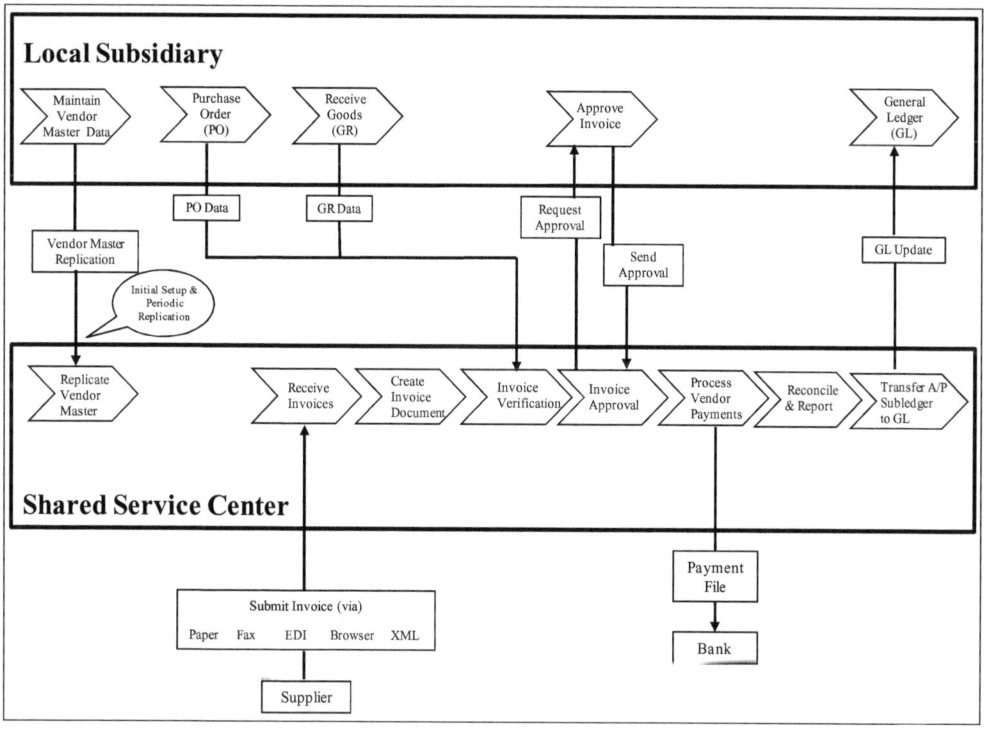

Figure 7: Procure-to-Pay process with split between enterprise and SSC

The less expertise you need to carry out the selected processes, the easier it is to build up this expertise at another location. These processes can also be easily automated and standardized to leverage efficiency benefits.

In the literature, there is no general consensus on the most effective sequence of process standardization and migration to a Shared Service Center. Should you first standardize the processes and then migrate them to the Shared Service Center or the other way round?

Both approaches have their pros and cons, but tend to be never implemented in their pure form, because a sensible middle way for the particular organization tends to be chosen. Theoretically the ideal is for the processes to be standardized as far as possible before being migrated to a Shared Service Center. This not only makes the work in the migration project easier, but also facilitates the induction of new Shared Service Center staff. This high level of standardization before migration does, however, of course come at a cost. It calls for a large number of changes to workflows and work steps before the actual migration. Implementing these changes is time-consuming and labor-intensive. Particularly if there is a need to implement new systems, which have been provided according to the standard process, the time/effort involved is considerable since it requires intensive training for users. Since the users are swapped over with the migration (employees in the subsidiaries are replaced by SSC employees), consideration should be given to whether the increased level of standardization before migration actually justifies doubling the time/effort spent on training.

The other extreme – migrating the process to the Shared Service Center without any prior standardization activities – only tends to be selected if the processes in the individual international subsidiaries are already very similar and there is a uniform system landscape. Selecting this approach if the processes in the countries differ greatly makes little sense since this would mean confronting the new Shared Service Center employees with a host of different types of process execution. In this early stage of the Shared Service Center, this would simply overstretch the staff that has not received any training whatsoever.

Since this extreme is seldom used in practice, a middle way tends to be the preferred option, as mentioned earlier. Prior to migration, standardization measures that are easy to implement are initiated, followed by the migration, and finally further standardized in the Shared Service Center as far as possible. 100 % standardization is, however, not possible mainly due to legal restrictions. The following graphic illustrates all three approaches:

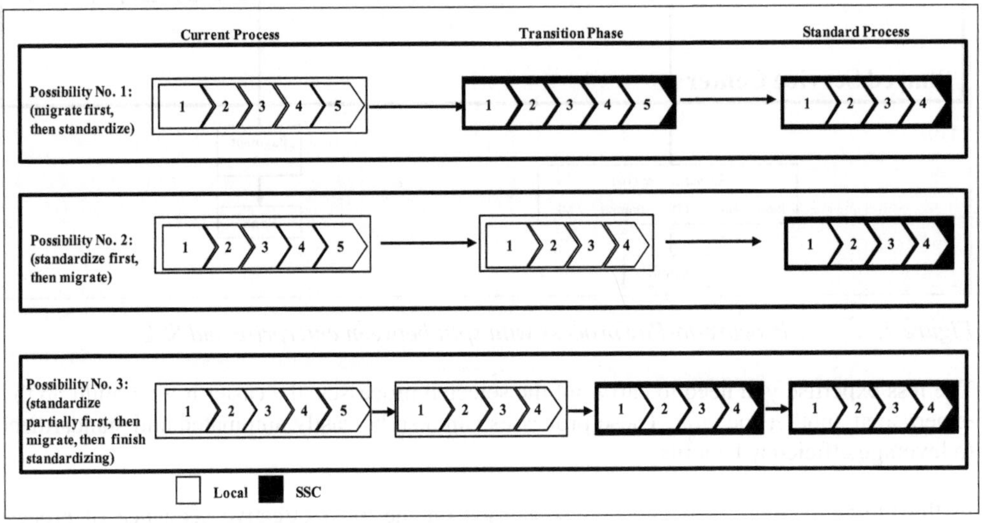

Figure 8: *Process standardization and migration to the Shared Service Center*

Another aspect associated with the process selection is the proportion of personal communication required to execute this process. A high proportion of vis-à-vis situations exists, for instance, with many controlling processes. This approach, together with a low degree of frequency of use, means that these kinds of processes are only suitable to a limited extent for the Shared Service Center.

Process manuals, which include detailed documentation of individual tasks for each process step, form the basis for the shared services process split. The process manual includes both the thematic structure of the subprocesses as well as precise detailed arrangements covering processing steps, such as assigning and posting incoming invoices in the Shared Service Center to a transaction from a process perspective. All system descriptions, such as individual functions or interfaces between people and system, are important in this respect. The process manual not only clearly defines the tasks and the distribution of tasks between the international subsidiaries and the Shared Service Center, but it also underpins the contractual basis for service provision, the service level agreement (SLA), which can be used to precisely assess and continually fine-tune the process. The detailed definition of the ideal process in the manual for a Shared Service Center has one particular feature: the *process cut*, which precisely defines the interface between international subsidiaries and the Shared Service Center (see figure 7). This relates to the division of labor in respect of individual subprocesses, but also to the necessary usage of the system and the associated data store and documentation, or the usage of raw data.

A key module for transformation management of a Shared Service Center project is the standard definition of the to-be process, the ideal process cut, and the associated organizational changes. Even if there is a uniform IT landscape (*SAP* ERP 6.0) in the case of *SAP AG*, each international subsidiary utilizes the system in a slightly modified form for various reasons. Two main reasons for differences are decisive:

1. There are specific legal features and provisions in the individual countries, which lead to different process conditions, such as data storage requirements or requirements governing the retention of original documents.
2. Another cause can be summarized under the notion of 'human creativity'. This includes the introduction and the status quo of individual workflows in the organizational units, whereby country-specific problems are mapped by means of separate solutions in the system. For instance, a corporate headquarters can only specify, control and monitor the precisely standardized procedure in all 30 international subsidiaries for each detailed process by spending an inordinate amount of time and money.

If over 40 CFOs and finance managers need to agree on a uniform subprocess, say for Accounts Payable, this decision requires a great deal of coordination. In addition to harmonizing processes and system usage across all international subsidiaries, all other process optimization possibilities are exploited before the processes are transferred to the Shared Service Center. This concerns, for instance, the usage of the latest system components or technologies, and business process reengineering (BPR).

Both internal and external benchmarks are used to identify the ideal process. To this end, the employees working in a process were assigned in all international subsidiaries. Full-time equivalents (FTEs) are analyzed for comparison purposes. This analysis establishes in the finance organization in a country which employees are engaged in which detailed processes with which proportion of full-time equivalents. This information also provides the starting point for determining the future finance organization. The full-time-equivalent analysis also provides important basic information for calculating the financial business case and is a prerequisite for defining the initial draft of the migration planning and the Shared Service Center Organization (SSO).

2.2 The Initial Draft of the Migration Planning and the Financial Business Case

A business case is a scenario calculation used to provide a business assessment of a project investment and must convincingly justify to a multinational group's executive board assumptions on costs and forecast benefits in order to be approved. The calculation of the business case requires the already complete project planning on setting up a Shared Service Center.

This step takes place, however, on a high aggregation level in some cases. The aim is to calculate as precisely as possible the costs and savings potential even at this stage.

The following assumptions are included as part of the business case:

- Definition of the to-be process and process cut
- Stipulation of the savings targets
- Migration planning: country sequence and speed in the migration
- Selection of offshore versus nearshore (or onshore) decision

The core element of the business case is planning the migration which stipulates which processes in which countries should be relocated at which point in time to the Shared Service Center. Thus all the necessary activities for setting up the Shared Service Center are determined. This concerns the hiring and training of new employees in the Shared Service Center as well as the corresponding setup of the location and the reorganization of the international subsidiaries.

Together with the full-time-equivalent analysis, which provides the precise figures for each country and each process, the costs of a Shared Service Center setup and the possible savings can be derived from the migration planning.

The costs are subdivided into the future ongoing costs of the Shared Service Center on the one hand and the project and transformation-management costs for setting up the center on the other.

Savings are calculated on the basis of the labor arbitrage between the subsidiaries and the Shared Service Center as well as through leveraging efficiency benefits associated with process standardization.

Following the migration, costs can be further reduced by means of greater process automation and further process standardization as well as economies of scale. The gradual implementation of both effects is set out below by way of example.

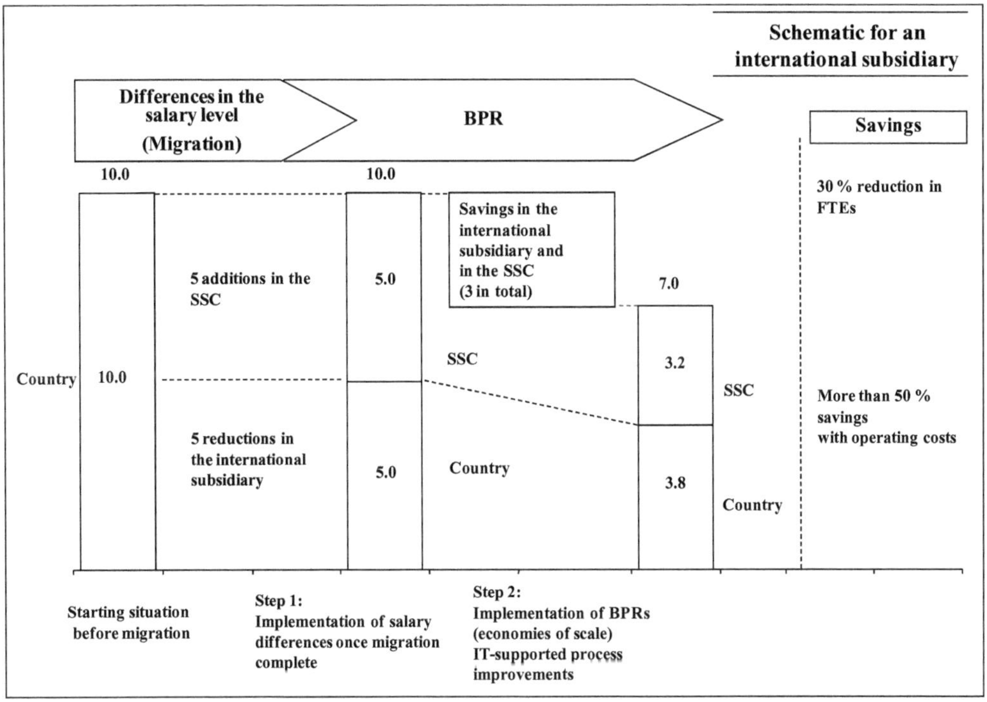

Figure 9: Implementation of the business case

From the perspective of transformation management, the creation of a financial business case and the initial migration planning must be seen as highly critical. There is a need to create a balance between the need to receive information that is as detailed as possible from employees in the international subsidiaries and, on the other hand, to minimize communications about the impending setting up of the Shared Service Center project.

The decision was taken at *SAP* to inform all employees right from the creation phase of the financial business case that such a project was in the pipeline and a feasibility study was being drawn up on the basis of which a decision would be taken regarding whether and on what scale a Shared Service Center could be set up.

Since not all eventualities can be considered in a business case, the various possibilities for setting up a Shared Service Center have been analyzed in a scenario analyses.

2.3 Scenario Analysis and Coordination Process

Various scenarios have been identified and analyzed, the pros and cons of the achieved benefits assessed and compared. Alongside the pure analysis of facts and figures, transformation management should already be considered during the business case creation process. An important aspect in this respect is the integration of the managers affected. The professional preparation for all employee-related problem areas of the Shared Service Center project is even more important.

Shared Service Center projects mean wide-ranging and, in certain areas, serious changes for employees. With a concept developed to this end (people management framework), options were defined for helping employees cope with these challenges as best as possible. An individualized skill assessment of the employees involved is always the starting point. This relates both to technical skills, such as process expertise or IT expertise and product expertise, as well as to other individual skills such as problem-solving skills or motivation. As a rule, this knowledge is already recorded in a structured format, for example in the form of annual performance appraisals.

The next step involves analyzing all the possible job offers in the respective department as well as in the enterprise as a whole, for instance using the intranet. On request, discussions with the potential new managers can be supported by the HR department. The managers involved also receive coaching in order to actively accompany and control the change process.

In a great many cases, individual employees cannot move to other departments without garnering the necessary expertise beforehand. In this case, an individual training plan was put together with input from the *SAP* University. If no suitable position can be found for individual employees within *SAP*, employees receive support during the external job search by using application training or the external networks of partner companies. This is, however, only done in very few exceptional cases since the majority of the employees affected remained with the company.

2.4 Location Decision

The question regarding the selection of the best Shared Service Center location is very critical for all stakeholders involved. Particularly for multinational groups based in Germany, any closer scrutiny of Germany as a location attracts fierce criticism from the population. Arguments for and against a German location for the Shared Service Center need to be weighed up carefully. In addition to two German *SAP* locations Walldorf and Berlin, 16 other European cities were analyzed in detail. This extensive analysis was conducted at the start with the aid of *desktop research* and support from management consultants specialized in location analysis. Cities were selected that already had experience of Shared Service Centers. A host of cost- and quality-related selection criteria were applied to these potential locations.

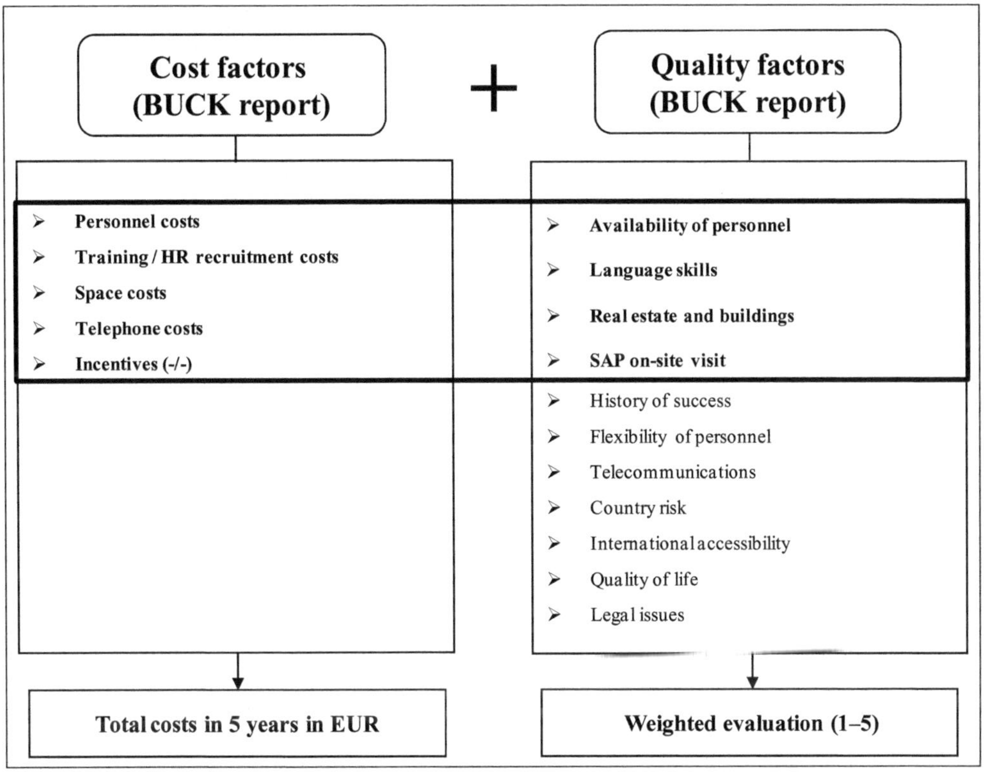

Figure 10: Selection criteria for the location decision

During the analysis one particular consideration was the availability of a sufficient number of qualified specialist staff for the respective processes in the cities. Another selection criterion was the availability of the necessary language skills in the analyzed cities. The ability of a Shared Service Center to also offer processes in the respective local languages is particularly important for processes with external customer contact. Further quality criteria include the infrastructure and the condition of the available buildings. The building's physical location and its facilities should be as attractive as possible in order to attract a sufficient number of new employees. In this respect, factors such as the proximity to the airport or to the city center, subway stations or the infrastructure near to the branch were also considered. All the quality selection criteria were compared with a host of cost selection criteria. Labor costs, training and recruitment costs at the particular location were taken into account. Other important decision-making criteria include the cost of infrastructure and telecommunications, as well as the cost of building maintenance.

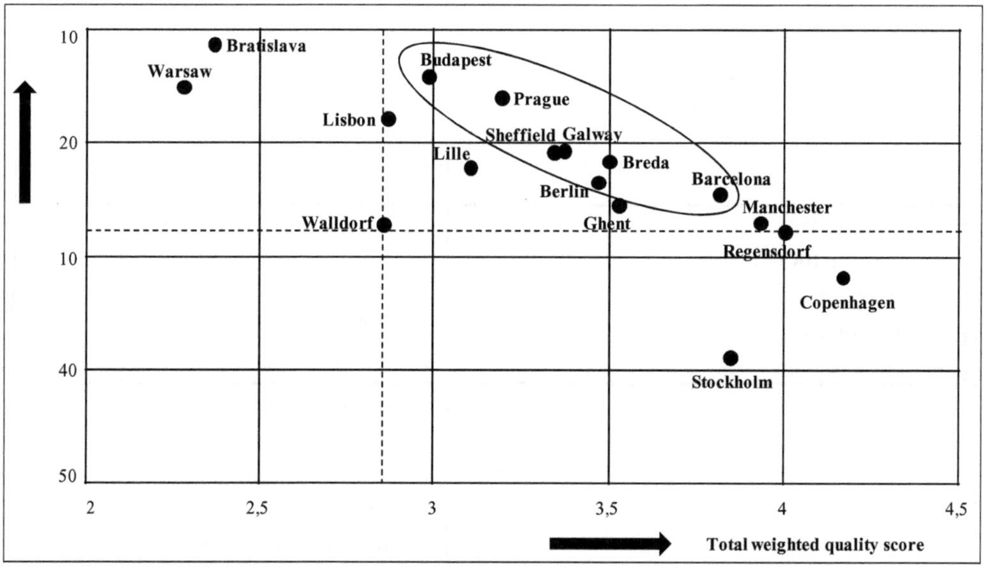

Figure 11: *Results of the location selection at a glance*

The usage of the aforementioned quality and cost criteria provided a shortlist of seven potential locations for which business case scenarios were simulated (cf. Figure 8). This shortlist was then whittled down further, leaving four cities for which all cost and quality criteria were reviewed once again locally in detail and compared with the specific quantity structures from Shared Service Center planning, for instance in relation to the number of employees in the respective processes with the necessary language skills in each case. The location decision was taken by considering economic factors such as HR and material costs in combination with qualitative factors such as the availability of staff with the necessary qualifications (financial reporting, language and system skills) as well as the necessary infrastructure. The following overview (figure 12) summarizes the analyzed quality criteria and the weighting of the location factors used for the location decision:

➢ Availability of personnel	30 %
➢ Language skills of personnel	15 %
➢ Flexibility of personnel	10 %
➢ Telecommunications	10 %
➢ Country risk	10 %
➢ International accessibility	10 %
➢ Quality of life	5 %
➢ History of success	10 %
	100 %

Figure 12: *Evaluation and weighting of the quality selection criteria for the location*

Finally only two cities fulfilled all criteria and were very close to each other: Prague and Budapest. The *SAP* managers including the Group CFO responsible for deciding on the location visited these two cities before making their final decision. Specific buildings at both locations were surveyed during this time and during the analysis. At this time, contacts were already made with the local authorities and economics ministries to sound out the possibility of support and firmly compare the qualitative and monetary aspects.

Both cities came out virtually neck and neck in the managers' assessment so that it was ultimately just nuances that swayed their decision in favor of the nearshoring location Prague.

The selection of a nearshoring location (measured in terms of the distance to the Headquarters in Walldorf) and setting up a new center without any existing infrastructure (greenfield approach) means a much larger change management overhead than selecting an existing location (brownfield approach). New staff are being hired in the low-cost location. Employees are switching to new roles in the existing locations. The change management aspect is set out below, with particular attention paid to the integration of the relevant stakeholder groups.

Related studies often note critically that the actual savings fail to live up to the expectations[15]. Through the location selection, the savings expected by *SAP* – especially through labor cost differences – were achieved, which was verified at *SAP* by the Controlling department as an independent body. Nevertheless, no or only very minor standardization and automation savings were made in the initial stage of relocation. In the following years, these savings were made through an increase in volume of up to 40 % in the four years that followed, and could be covered without adding any additional staff.

3 Transformation Management During the Planning and Piloting of a Shared Service Center Project

3.1 Planning the Migration

The initial migration approach of *SAP*'s Shared Service Center project was developed by the project team together with CFOs, finance managers, HR department managers and an external management consultancy, which was later replaced by internal consultants, in several planning workshops over a period of 3–4 months. The broad base of participants provided the necessary experience while ensuring the stakeholder groups also bought into the process. The entire project planning process – running through to the testing of the concept with the aid of an international subsidiary (pilot) – took place in three phases.

15 Cf. *LACITY/FOX* (2008), p. 17 et seq. For instance, the analysis carried out by *FISCHER/STERZENBACH* shows that the cost reduction potential hoped for by those surveyed, e.g. "Cost reduction through standardization", "Cost reduction through economies of scale", "Cost reduction through synergies" or "Cost reduction through downsizing" could not be achieved; cf. *FISCHER/STERZENBACH* (2006), p. 48.

3.1.1 Outline Migration Concept

The weaknesses of the selected processes that would be restructured were determined in a benchmark analysis. As a result, four reasons for setting up a Shared Service Center including an assessment of possible savings potential were determined: cost reduction, increase in productivity, improvement in process quality and an increase in customer satisfaction. Studies have shown that savings of an average 26 % with a simultaneous increase in productivity (up to a maximum 20 %) and a quality increase of up to 20 % could be achieved through the introduction of a Shared Service Center.[16]

The initial outline concept for the migration with four project phases was defined after opting for the business case to set up the Shared Service Center in Prague.

Phase 1 entails the preparation of an international subsidiary for the migration. A project team records the variations between defined to-be process and as-is process (gap analysis). At the same time, newly hired employees are trained on the *SAP* systems and familiarized with the corporate culture (training phase).

Phase 2 sees a start made on transferring the process-specific expertise of the local processes to employees in the Shared Service Center (transition). This know-how transfer is carried out by employees in the subsidiary, who train the newly hired employees at their work center. During the training on the job, employees sit next to each other. The employee being trained 'shadows' (hence the term work shadowing) all activities of the experienced colleague over a period of approximately 6–8 weeks. In parallel with work shadowing, the deviations determined by the project team within the processes are assessed and solutions (for instance workflows, IT system modifications, etc.) derived in order to achieve a high level of standardization.

All system and process modifications take place up to the go-live in *Phase 3* (Run) in order to ensure the subsequent migration of the processes to the Shared Service Center. Deviations from the standard process, which will have to remain due to legal or fiscal provisions, are documented and included in an annex to the process manual as a kind of operating instructions. A sign-off meeting is held before the go-live to provide formal confirmation of the documentation and handover of the processes. The international subsidiary's CFO, the head of the Shared Service Center and the project lead agree on the final documentation and sign the handover document.

The international subsidiary's processes are handled from the go-live in the Shared Service Center. Employees from the international subsidiaries provide support during the transition phase lasting several weeks in order to be able to competently answer questions or problems that may arise as well as to ensure that sufficient time is available to stabilize the modified organization and ensure high quality.

16 *SAP*-internal benchmarks based on studies conducted by *Hackett*, *Ernst & Young*, *Deloitte&Touch* and *PWC*.

Phase 4 involves process guidance for stabilization purposes based on the training (now only in the reverse role: employees in Prague execute the process and are supported by colleagues in the international subsidiary), described as reversed work shadowing.

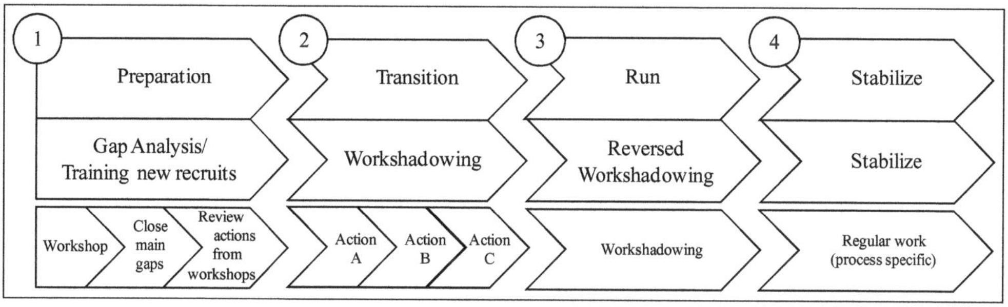

Figure 13: Project phases re. the process migration of the countries to the SSC

3.1.2 Detailed Concept and Project Organization

The development of the methodology approach and the planning of the consecutive phases were completed in the outline concept and are described in further detail in the next step. The process standard is defined for each of the 70-plus subprocesses and documented in the process description. The pilot country must be selected and the subsequent country migration planned. Before a decision must be made whether the migration is completed simultaneously country by country for all processes, the migration should be completed for each process and for all countries, or a mixture of the two options. In the case of *SAP*, the decision was made to migrate all processes for each country - with the exception of the German subsidiaries which accounted for the largest volume.

The training documentation and planning for recruitment are put together as soon as the sequence of countries has been defined and thus the number of employees to be hired with the necessary language skills has been determined. The project planning and new organization are defined and subsequently the migration sequence coordinated with all stakeholders – in particular with the CFOs directly affected by the initial migrations. The project organization consists of seven units, which are illustrated in the graphic below, in addition to the Steering Committee as the top decision-making committee and the Advisory Board:

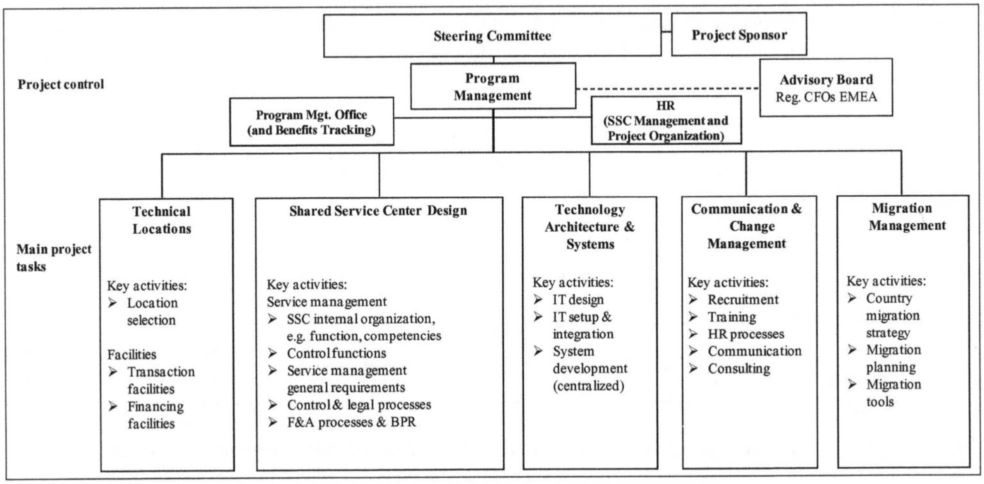

Figure 14: Project organization of SAP Finance and HR Shared Service Center project

From a transformation management perspective, two aspects need to be highlighted when it comes to putting together the detailed concept. For each process, a standard process (EMEA standard process) was described based on the process manuals, and the handing over of responsibility between the Shared Service Center and the decentralized international subsidiaries determined. The six selected processes were subdivided to this end into over 70 subprocesses, the interfaces and transitions to the Shared Service Center defined and a detailed full-time-equivalent analysis put together to accurately estimate the cost/time involved.

The defined standard process needs to be coordinated with the respective lines of business and then agreed with the CFOs and finance managers of all the countries affected by the migration. In total, over 40 stakeholders had to be involved and their consent obtained. This coordination process required early communication, mainly in the form of telephone conferences and as part of fortnightly Advisory Board calls, as well as meetings between project team, line of business and experts (for instance CFOs with a wide-ranging detailed understanding of the individual processes based on their experience).

Additional complexity was added through the stringent requirements of the *SARBANES-OXLEY* Act (SOX) introduced in summer 2002 which set out regulations governing corporate governance. In accordance with Section 404, relevant enterprise processes for financial reporting must be described in detail and control processes stipulated in order to minimize the risk of erroneous balance sheet presentation. For *SAP AG*'s Finance and Accounting Shared Service Center project, these arrangements meant the need for close coordination of the migration with the SOX project. Through the necessary minimum number of checks for each process, the migration planning had to be modified and the timing set so that the Sarbanes-Oxley Act audits could be prepared and conducted.

3.1.3 Pilot Country and Implementation

Once the planning for the time line and development of the project methodology (see detailed description of the tools in the next section) had been completed, the first migration of a country took place. Switzerland – a medium-sized country in relation to revenue and the finance organization – was selected for the piloting. The selection process took place with the involvement of all CFOs in several meetings and telephone conferences. Preparation for the selection took the shape of a recommendation from the project team and a pre-analysis of the international subsidiary. At the start, the CFO was involved and supported the approach so that the final decision could be made in the Steering Committee

3.1.4 Technical Prerequisites for Implementing a Shared Service Center

Apart from the organization design and location selection, implementing the necessary technical prerequisites constitutes a key component in successfully setting up a Shared Service Center. The usage of an enterprise resource planning system (ERP system), which sets out the transaction basis for finance and HR processes, provides the foundation in this respect. The ERP system includes both master data administration as well as system mapping of the processes with their respective subprocesses. Although there is the option of mapping the various process flows of the individual international subsidiaries in various ERP systems, optimum standardization can be achieved by means of a single ERP instance. A single ERP instance allows employees in the Shared Service Center to conduct the processes of all international subsidiaries efficiently within a single system. The introduction of a single ERP instance is, however, not always feasible depending on the complexity of the IT landscape. With multiple ERP systems, the interfaces and the access options need to be precisely defined and modified so that the processes can be conducted in the Shared Service Center.

Customer relationship management solutions are ideal for providing communications between individual international subsidiaries and the Shared Service Center. The integration of an Interaction Center module in the CRM solution sustainably increases the efficiency of communications between front- and backoffice. The Interaction Center supports an interactive call center function, which provides the employee in the Shared Service Center with tools and information in order to conduct incoming and outgoing inquiries rapidly and efficiently through the use of tickets. At the same time, the Interaction Center provides various communications channels such as e-mail, telephone, fax and mail.

The implementation of a ticketing system enables process flows to be traced and, above all, workflows to be triggered if further information is required. If the generalist on the first level is not able to resolve the problem, they forward the ticket to the relevant specialist.

The combination of the usage of ERP, CRM and Interaction Center therefore provides a possible technical base for standardizing and migrating processes from individual international subsidiaries to the Shared Service Center. IT implementation/standardization constitutes an important component in migration planning.

Further automation options, such as eInvoicing (EDI), support the entirely paperless exchange of data and information. In the case of eInvoicing, a data record is simply uploaded onto the *SAP* system rather than sending the invoice by mail. In the past or, in certain areas, even today, optical character recognition (OCR) systems are used in order to electronically read paper documents once scanned. Business analytics, automated workflows or e-billers can be used more efficiently in a centralized Shared Service Center standard than would be possible in individual international subsidiaries.

Ongoing benefits review and continual transformation management as well as communications to stakeholders are put in place in the affected countries before migration commences. To ensure that the communication is uniform and stakeholders are informed in a timely manner, the project team has developed a change management and communications approach.

3.1.5 Digression: Relocating a Shared Service Center Within Eight Weeks as Part of a Post-Merger Integration

In 2007, *SAP* acquired *BusinessObjects*. *BusinessObjects* was an independent company and market leader in the field of business analytics software with approx. USD 1.3 billion in revenue and over 6,500 employees worldwide.

The *SAP* Executive Board decided, following the conclusion of the acquisition at the end of January 2008, to transfer all processes and systems from *BusinessObjects* to *SAP*'s existing systems by July 1, 2008. The time frame was very ambitious since a total of 40 financial processes and 26 systems had to be transferred in the Financials area for 29 countries. Furthermore, 425 employees had to be trained. The very tight timetable had two reasons:

1. It was meant to create a showcase for the flexibility and speed with which *SAP* software can be introduced and a company integrated from a system perspective and
2. From mid-September no more changes to defined financial processes could be made due to the auditing preparation as part of the Sarbanes-Oxley Act; i.e. either the migration was completed before this date or the changes would have to wait until the first quarter of the following year.

The planned process and system integration was successfully implemented on time. The ambitious plan was implemented thanks to clear target orientation and good collaboration of all the employees and departments involved (cross-functional teams comprising the Financials area, IT, Shared Service, internal and external consultants), the support and prioritization of this project by the Executive Board and professional project management with a team of up to 150 employees. The project management team was also responsible for transformation management and had to ensure that all internal and external stakeholders of *BusinessObjects* were informed, the roles and tasks communicated in a timely manner to employees, and these employees were trained on the new processes and systems.

Even while process and system integration was still being implemented, the next question arose, namely organizational integration. Three months after the start of the project, the Executive Board had decided in April that the organization should also be integrated simultaneously with the system go-live. This meant that all corporate functions, including the Financials area with Financial Reporting, Controlling, Legal, Treasury, Tax, Risk & Compliance Management, Facility, Invoicing and Invoice Processing and Travel Expenses should be integrated from an organizational perspective into the existing *SAP* functions. In addition to the functional areas the continuation of the process-based *BusinessObjects* Shared Service Centers also needed to be defined. Here, the organizational integration was not so simple since there were overlaps in the task areas and processing following the process and system integration.

By 2008, *SAP*'s Finance Shared Service Centers were managed as separate organizational units under the direction of the regional CFOs. The integration of *BusinessObjects* saw the addition of another Shared Service Center in Dublin, Ireland, and a centralized financial administration function in Vancouver, Canada. A continuation of the SSCs as separate units and the extension of two additional Shared Service Centers with the same service portfolio did not seem to make sense. Instead, consideration was given to the option of merging the shared services units globally under standardized management and transferring the two financial units that needed to be integrated as a result of the acquisition into a global organization. The concept for organizational integration was finalized in May 2008 and a resolution passed by the CFO in June. Implementation was to be completed following process and system integration, with October 1, 2008 selected as the starting date to avoid having to manage too many activities at the same time.

The first stage would see the global finance shared service organization made up of three regional center organizations; in addition to the largest SSC in Prague, another center in Dublin was assigned organizationally in EMEA. This belonged to *BusinessObjects*. The centralized financial unit in Vancouver was assigned to the existing SSC in Buenos Aires for North America.

This decision effectively merged in an initial stage all existing Shared Service Centers into a single organization under a standardized management structure .Since in the SSC in Dublin and in Vancouver at *BusinessObjects* similar transactional activities were executed, which were completed at *SAP* in the existing SSCs, the decision was forced upon them to transfer the financial processes from Dublin to Prague and to complete the same transfer from Vancouver to Buenos Aires in another step.

At the end of July 2008, the team started, which set up the SSC in EMEA, to analyze in detail the possibilities of organizational integration from Dublin to Prague.

Result of the analysis: In Dublin five financial processes were conducted by 64 staff in total:

1. Procure-to-Pay
2. Travel and Expenses
3. Customer-to-Cash
4. General Accounting
5. Order-to-Cash

The first four processes with a total of 43 staff corresponded to the *SAP* standard process in accordance with the process and system integration completed on July 1. However, the process steps were completed in different ways. I.e. the tasks that were conducted in the Shared Service Center in Dublin were more extensive than in *SAP*'s SSC in Prague in the case of General Accounting, for instance. The Order-to-Cash process was not identical to the existing *SAP* process due to the differences in the business model. For this reason only the transfer of processes 1–4 was considered.

Since the provisions relating to the SOX Act also applied to the financial processes in the SSC, the relocation of the SSC in Dublin and the integrations of the financial function from Vancouver to Buenos Aires could not be conducted simultaneously. The project team devised a proposal for the staged integration and the CFO decided to go ahead with implementation at the start of August. First of all, the financial processes were to be relocated from Dublin to Prague. Since this had to be completed before the auditing preparations, only six weeks remained for the transfer.

A team was set up comprising of the shared services migration team and released employees from process and system integration to conduct the project. The team's task was to ensure that the Prague SSC's standard process is used in Dublin in order to then be able to transfer the tasks. To this end, tasks of individual countries had to be transferred to Dublin (Customer-to-Cash) and also from Dublin to a total of 8 countries (General Accounting).

43 staff in total transferred the tasks to Prague in accordance with the standard process. 250 staff were already working at this point in time in the Prague SSC, prompting the decision to assume the risk of being able to cope with the additional volume for the time being with the existing number of staff. Triggered by the global financial crisis which was beginning to be felt in mid-September in the wake of the collapse of *Lehman Brothers*, the transaction volumes fell sharply during this period, ultimately meaning that no additional staff needed to be hired. In addition, there was scaling through process standardization and automation that enabled, also in the years that followed, to manage the volume with the same number of staff.

Early, open communications with staff, professional project management and a fair arrangement with the 43 employees affected in Dublin were decisive factors in the success of the two-time transformation with process and system migration in the initial stage and subsequent relocation of four transactional processes from Dublin to Prague. Agreement was reached with all the employees involved. One group left the company in 2008, followed by another in early 2009.

The figure below provides a summary and concise illustration of the migration approach.

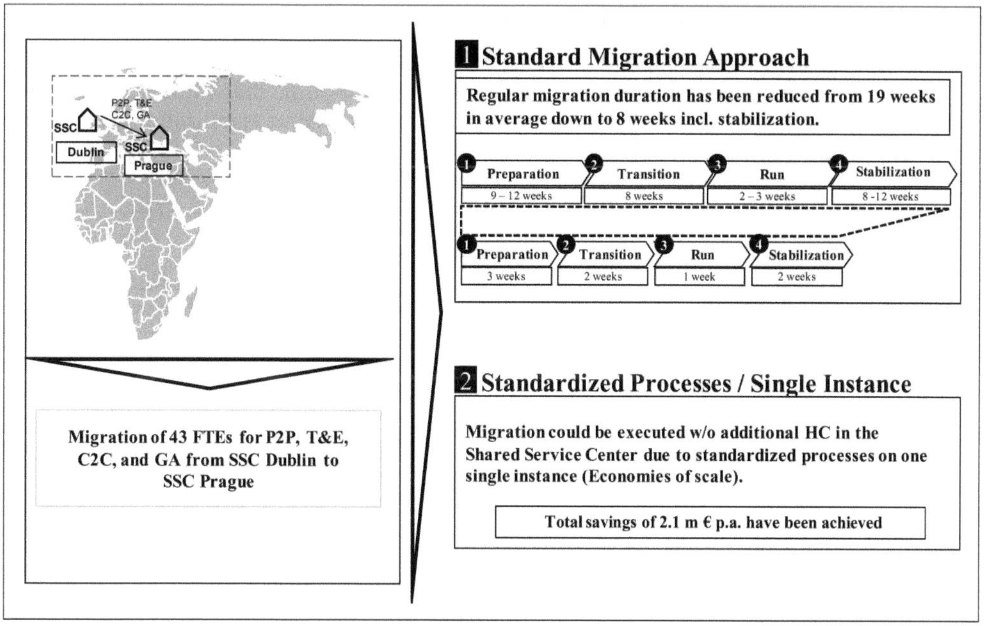

Figure 15: Relocation of a Shared Service Center from Dublin to Prague

3.2 *SAP's* Transformation Management Approach

The Transformation Management (TM) approach includes

1. Stipulating migration planning and milestones,
2. Developing tools for conducting the migration,
3. Defining the future financial and accounting organization,
4. Designing arrangements for employee change,
5. Recording job changes and, where necessary, departures of staff in a matrix and
6. Providing a local work plan for the countries.

The management level of CFOs was involved intensively for two reasons: On the one hand it was necessary to utilize their experience in order to gain input for developing the change management approach; on the other hand the buy-in of the CFOs was an important success factor not only to implement the project and, at the same time, secure proponents throughout the organization, but also since the CFOs are responsible for change management and communication in their organization.

The following describes the tools that were developed and used as components in the transformation management concept.

3.2.1 Transformation Management Planning

To perform the migration to the SSC Prague, a detailed time schedule for all the countries to be migrated was required, along with details of the duration of the individual tasks. For this, suppositions were made from recruiting through the completion of stabilization. Eight modules were defined for the planning phase:

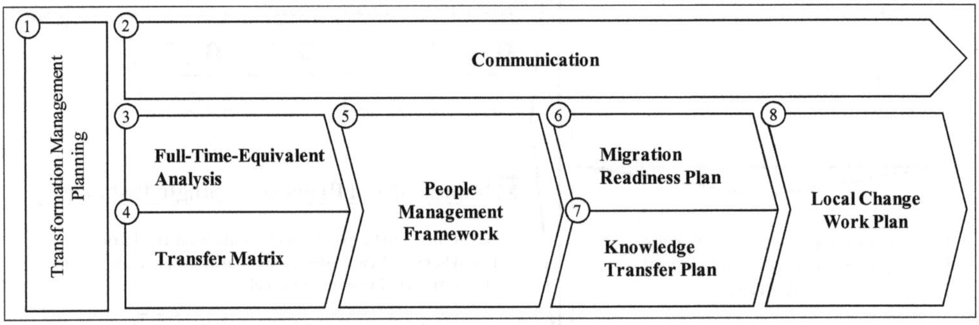

Figure 16: Change Management Controlling Toolbox

Communications measures throughout the entire project were conducted to provide support.

3.2.2 The Selected Communication Approach

Ideally, the first communication to employees about extensive transformation management projects should not take place until all decisions have already been made and the business case has been approved. In many cases, particularly with projects in which many jobs and employees are affected, this communication is almost impossible. Rumors and fears are often spread very early on within the entire organization. In this case, professional communication should set out clearly and simply how the project will develop in future. Which decisions are made at what point in time and when the communication to all employees will take place in relation to these decisions should be communicated early on in particular. The key decisions for this first employee communication relate to the impact on the organization. In any case a clear description of the project reasons and objectives should be prepared for the communication. This should set out clearly what advantages the project offers for the organization, but also what changes are required in the organization of the individual countries.

It is also important to involve the employee representatives (works council) in good time. Above all, employees are ultimately interested in how the Shared Service Center project will specifically affect their job. For this reason, the decisions should first be communicated that relate to the affected roles. By selecting the countries and processes, which are migrated to the Shared Service Center, these posts are defined precisely.

Communication about jobs should be cascaded top-down. First, all managers are informed, then the managers inform the respective employees for whom they are responsible at an employee meeting. The key communication for employees takes place in a phase as soon as the respective managers have decided how the future international subsidiary will be structured and which employees are affected in what way by the reorganization. This communication is also again conducted in the form of a communication cascade. In addition, one-to-one employee reviews are conducted individually with each employee, following on from the employee meetings in which the basic organizational changes are communicated. The employees who remain in the same role or who transfer to another existing role are informed about the course of developments. All issues are discussed jointly that have been prepared beforehand with the HR department in order to structure possible moves or changes smoothly. Particularly for employees for which a post is no longer foreseen in the future organization, it is important to manage the individual employee reviews as professionally as possible. One of the important objectives of these discussions is therefore also to talk about possible subsequent steps and point out perspectives jointly with the employee. Generally, managers are also not sufficiently prepared for these kinds of situations. It therefore makes sense for the HR department to support the managers, for instance by providing training sessions, mentoring or even coaching. Success factors in successful communication include in any case open, transparent and simple messages. Inconsistencies in internal and external communication should also be avoided.

The inclusion of the stakeholders involved in the decision-making process and subsequent migration was a critical success factor in agreeing the project contents and selecting a pilot following the Executive Board decision to conduct the project. This resulted from *SAP*'s well-established management culture in which managers are extensively involved in business decisions. An Advisory Board was set up to systematize this involvement, which provided information on project progress in fortnightly telephone conferences between project team and Managing Directors as well as CFOs in the 30 international subsidiaries and discussed decisions to be taken. This included the project methodology, migration planning including scheduling of the countries being migrated and the selection of the pilot. The agreed decision paper was then submitted to the Steering Committee and approved.

The process of drawing up the key project content and decision papers together with the Advisory Board was often felt as protracted by project employees at the start. This was in part due to the coordination process that included up to seven stages: Devising a proposal, internal coordination in the project team, coordination with the external management consultancy, presentation and discussion in the Advisory Board, revision or finalization, import into the Steering Committee through to implementation. On the other hand, there was a know-how gap between the project team, external management consultancy and Advisory Board in relation to the Shared Service Center and migration content. One success factor was the way in which this know-how gap was rapidly overcome. By creating a joint understanding of the project content, the Advisory Board's willingness to embrace changes was increased substantially. At the same time, the quality of the project results was improved substantially. By way of summary, the communication approach, which was developed jointly with the change management approach, is illustrated on a time line:

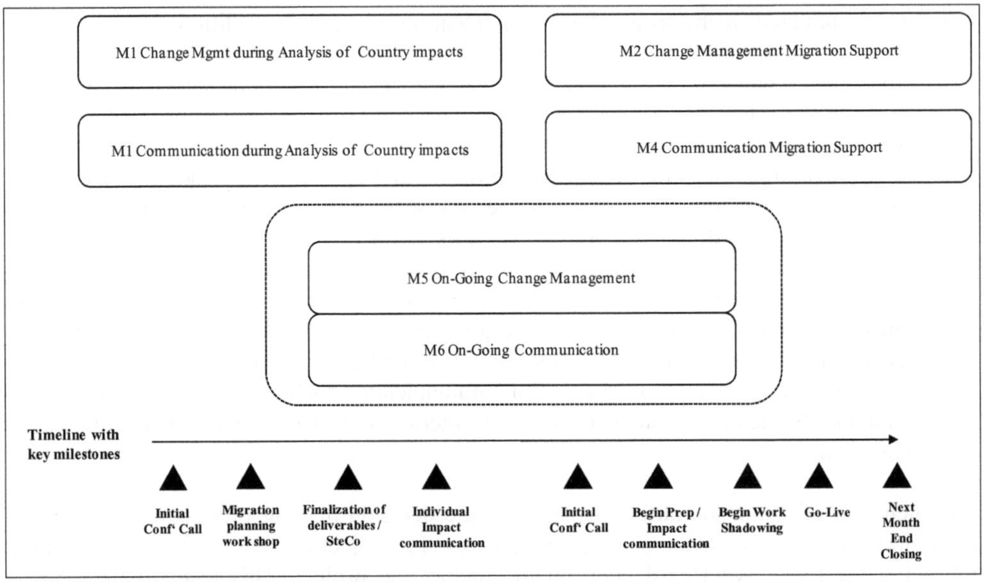

Figure 17: Timeline of the developed change management (M1, M2 and M5) and communication modules (M3, M4 and M6)

The simultaneous introduction of an incentive or bonus program for project managers, Shared Service Center managers and CFOs definitely constituted another success factor. The variable salary component was linked to the aim of a successful migration and included in the individual target agreements.

3.2.3 Full-Time Equivalent Analysis and Process Cut

The full-time-equivalent analysis provides a detailed record of the entire activities in the six processes selected for the migration (Accounts Payable, Accounts Receivable, General Accounting, Software, Education and Consulting Billing, including Travel and Expense Accounting) and also provides the basis for calculating the business case. The first step involved recording all employees and a percentage assignment of actual activities to the individual subprocesses. This was completed in the form of a time assessment of the effort of individual employees with individual processes on the basis of employees' and supervisors' empirical data. The information was validated using benchmarks from other international subsidiaries and in the form of key performance indicators (KPI), which enabled the cost and work involved to be estimated on the basis of volume data. The second step involved the process cut: the allocation of processes between Shared Service Center and international subsidiaries. One example is illustrated in the following figure:

FTE Analysis			Process Costumer to Cash (C2C)							
Job Title	Full Time / Part Time	Total FTE	Costumer Master Main-tenance	Credit Control	Manual Postings	Monitoring and Collection of Recivables	Bank Reconci-lation	Account Closing Procedure	Period Close	Manage-ment
			C2C	C2C	C2C	C2C	C2C	C2C	C2C	C2C
CFO	100%	0,00								
Finance Manager	100%	1,00				5%				5%
Finance Specialist	100%	1,00			5%					
Finance Specialist	100%	1,00				5%				
Finance Specialist	100%	1,00								
Finance Specialist	100%	1,00								
Finance Specialist	100%	1,00								
Finance Specialist	100%	1,00	5%		15%	30%	5%	10%	5%	
Temporary hourly paid	20%	0,20				20%				
			0,05	0,00	0,20	0,60	0,05	0,10	0,05	0,05
Process Cut	**SSC**				**90%**	**70%**	**95%**	**70%**	**90%**	**73%**
	LOCAL		**100%**	**100%**	**10%**	**30%**	**5%**	**30%**	**10%**	**27%**
FTE's acc. to Process Cut	**SSC**				0,18	0,42	0,05	0,07	0,05	0,04
	LOCAL		0,05	0,00	0,02	0,18	0,00	0,03	0,01	0,01

Figure 18: *Example FTE analysis for Customer-to-Cash with allocation of the process cut*

3.2.4 Transfer Matrix

All employees who are affected by the migration within the Financials department have already been entered into the transfer matrix as part of the full-time-equivalent analysis. The transfer matrix is a tool for planning and executing changes for all the employees affected. The goal is to completely map the source/target organization, and the movement data for all employees: In which area are they currently employed and where can they be deployed in future or when does the contract end. This aggregated overview provided an exact analysis of the savings in personnel costs that were achieved after the migration or at what point in time the savings (personnel costs) can be achieved.

If the employee would like to switch from their existing function in the Financials area (role) to another area, details were entered of which skills an employee has and which they need in order to be able to carry out the new role. Because only activities are entered in the transfer matrix overview and full-time-equivalent analysis that are related to the processes affected by the migration, it was now necessary to also enter activities and time factors allocated to other tasks. The complete overview was then documented in the employee role map (ERM) and the development of the employee within the organization monitored, taking training activities (upskilling) into account. The responsible manager could use this documentation to transparently map the current and future organization and, where necessary, roles to be filled.

Because the CFOs were already informed about the project some months before the actual migration, employees leaving the company were only replaced using temporary contracts or employment agencies.

3.2.5 People Management Framework (PMF)

Although in some cases many roles ceased to exist in the international subsidiaries, the number of employees who left the company is very small. This is due to the fact that, using the people management framework (PMF), all possibilities were exhausted to prevent employees from losing their jobs.

1. *Revenue growth* led to demand for employees in the Finance and Accounting area;
2. *Initial or ongoing training* enables employees to take on other tasks;
3. Natural *turnover* has led employees to leave the company;
4. Job offer in *other functional areas* in the company was accepted;
5. *Low performers* managed to be developed or have left the company;
6. Employees for which *no remit* can be found and who are helped to find a job.

These six groups form the basis that is regulated with various measures in the people management framework:

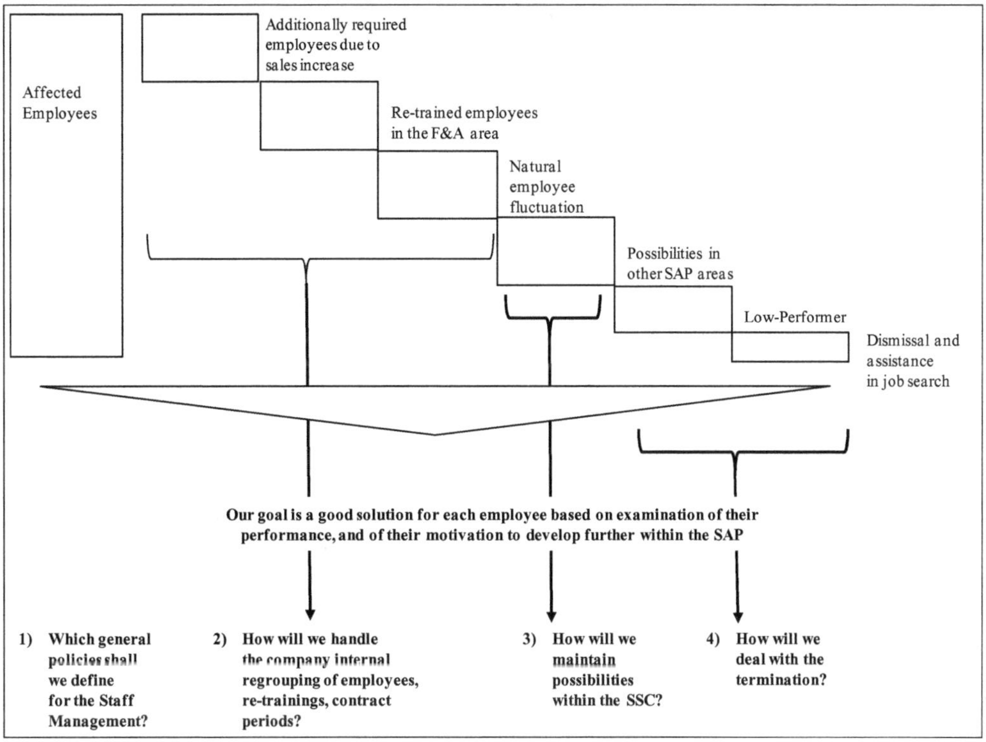

Figure 19: Stages in the People Management Framework

3.2.6 Migration Readiness Plan (MRP)

The standardization and subsequent migration of processes from an international subsidiary to a Shared Service Center requires extensive preparation. For instance, all deviations from the to-be process must be eliminated. These systems must also be accordingly modified and prepared. Not least, all those involved, customers, employees and suppliers must be informed about the new processes since all the processes to be migrated are prepared in parallel simultaneously and all tasks entered, prioritized and assigned a schedule with the aid of the migration readiness plan tool. Status and the impacts were also described through to the migration possibly being put in jeopardy. The status of the data was displayed with traffic-light symbols and discussed in the weekly telephone conference between the project team, Shared Service Center management, and the respective subsidiary with all process owners. If necessary, measures were initiated during these conferences. This setup gave all the stakeholders an overview of the status of all processes, and provided a common understanding of the migration and the associated requirements.

3.2.7 Knowledge Transfer Plan (KTP)

Employee training is a critical success factor for transferring processes to a Shared Service Center. For this training, mainly employees were selected who have already gained experience in the financials area and who have the necessary language skills. Recently hired employees received training on how to use the *SAP* systems, the fundamentals of *SAP* internal financial reporting and processes, and corporate culture. Employees in each of the international subsidiaries passed on their expertise to the employees in the Shared Service Center, ensuring knowledge transfer from the subsidiaries to the Shared Service Center. In the initial phase, the employees in the countries (senders) explained the workflows and system applications to their new colleagues (recipients) directly on the job. The sender previously entrusted with the processes continued the tasks and provided the newly hired colleague with the know-how (work shadowing). In the second phase, the previous recipient at the Shared Service Center location takes over the activities and is supported by the sender in the case of questions or problems that arise. The role allocation was reversed in the Shared Service Center with the go-live (reversed work shadowing).

To ensure that all newly hired colleagues acquired the necessary expertise to complete the tasks, the project team developed a list of topics that listed all activities within the subprocesses and that was structured according to processes. Together with the project team, the sender is responsible for communicating and testing all the individual tasks with the associated knowledge. In total, there were up to 20 employees being trained at the same time. One example can be found in the following figure:

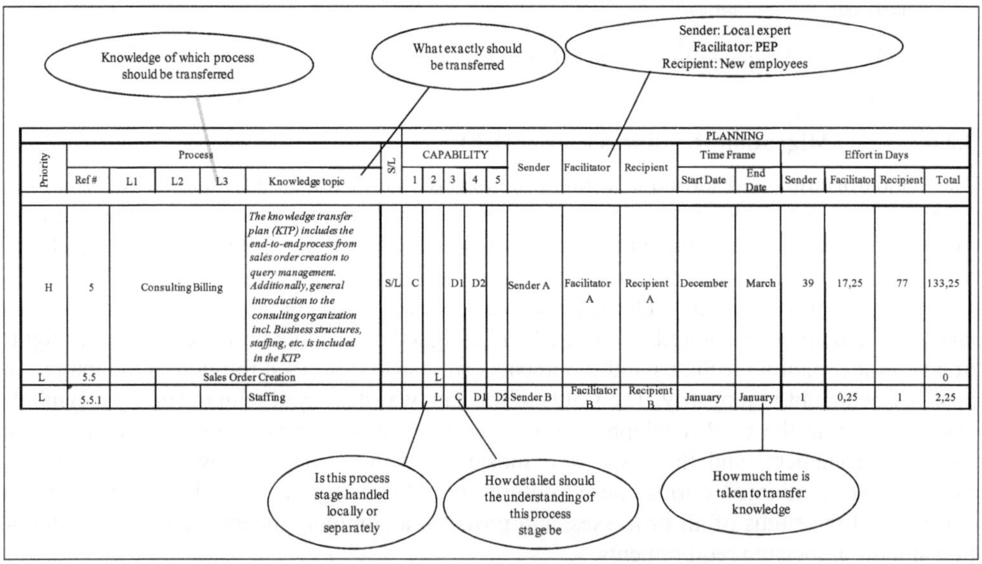

Figure 20: Knowledge Transfer Plan in the workshadowing phase

3.2.8 Local Change Work Plan

All the measures listed that led to a fundamental change in the local organization were summarized in a task list, prioritized and transferred chronologically to a project plan. This gave the local management an overview of all measures and made available a tool that provided transparency and, of course, enabled efficient implementation. The local change work plan listed the changes for the individual employees and the communication of the measures to the respective teams, as well as the requirements for the imminent migration.

3.3 Definition of the Future Finance and Accounting Organization

To align the Finance and Accounting organization to the processes changed by the Shared Service Center, the as-is state was analyzed before migration and a plan for transfer to the target organization devised. The target organization is aligned at the highest level to the processes whose transactional components is processed in the Shared Service Center:

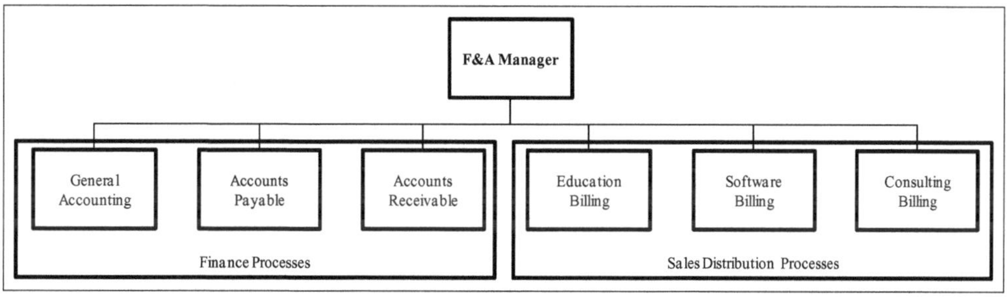

Figure 21: Future F&A organization

The country specifics were only taken into account in the second level. To optimize scarce resources, for instance employees with special language skills, the employees were gradually trained and deployed on a cross-process and cross-country basis.

3.4 Challenges for Transformation Management

Certain particularly significant challenges of transformation management should be illustrated below by way of example:

- *Training by colleagues that are affected by the downsizing*: Training the new colleagues presented one challenge. The employees in the international subsidiary were divided into two groups. One group stays in the financials organization to process the steps that remain in the subsidiary, or transfers to another functional area within *SAP*. The other group leaves the company once the migration has been completed. Employees from both groups first trained their new colleagues in the international subsidiary (work shadowing) and then in the Shared Service Center (reversed work shadowing).The supposition that problems would arise during training due to this combination of employees affected in the subsidiaries was not confirmed, because all employees were involved at an early stage and agreement reached. It was thus possible to sustain employee motivation until the migration was complete. In individual instances, requests were also received to terminate the employment contract prematurely if employees already had job offers. Other notable absences, such as illness notifications, only existed in a few exceptional cases.

- *Language requirements*: Another aspect that also presented a challenge was the recruitment of employees with the necessary language skills. For the migration from 30 international subsidiaries, 25 different languages were required. Employees with relevant language skills could not either always be obtained easily on the labor market or did not always meet the quality that the CFOs in the international subsidiaries expected. The CFOs were concerned about the acceptance of the new organizational form, in particular in those cases where processes with customers (priority 1) or suppliers (priority 2) were involved. Here, conceptual solutions were developed in several stages. On the one hand, it was agreed that the CFOs or their finance managers would hold interviews with newly hired employees in order to test the language quality. At the same time, language courses were attended in order to build on existing language skills and to receive more practice in using the foreign language. One key finding in this respect was that language skills – and not, as assumed, specialist skills – have the highest priority in recruitment. Due to the high level of standardization, it is easier to acquire process knowledge than to improve on basic language skills.

- *Team building in the initial phase of work shadowing*: To ensure that a team spirit developed between employees in the international subsidiary and employees in the Shared Service Center, great importance was placed on the integration of both employee groups, especially in the initial phase. As part of the change management concept, employee meetings were planned to prepare the international subsidiary. First, there was a joint kick-off event with personal introductions, an introduction to the upcoming tasks, and details of the time schedule. At the weekends, joint leisure activities were planned and employees got to know the city. An additional bonus was granted (key-player bonus) to cover the dual workload that certain employees took on due to their role as process specialists in several areas with multiple project running simultaneously.

- *Formal migration aspects (sign-off meetings and service level agreements)*: Formal agreements for the steps in the migration were drawn up as each step was completed. At the end of the analysis, the first sign-off meeting took place, in which the participants defined which tasks would be performed before the migration, who would perform them, and by when they would be completed (local finance organization, IT, project team, Shared Service Center). Before the go-live, the overall targets between the project team, the Shared Service Center, and the CFO were determined and, as the contractual basis for transferring the processes, the sign-off documents, in which all exceptions and deviations from the standard were defined, were signed. At the same time, a standard service level agreement (SLA) was signed in which the service level is defined. In the next step, the key performance indicators (KPIs) that enable the process quality to be measured were defined. During the meetings, there was sometimes a different understanding about how to interpret the text in the agreement. This generated some discussion, in which points that had been seen as resolved had to be discussed, rephrased, or adjusted. In the initial phase with the first countries these meetings lasted several hours. In order to improve the sign-off process in future, a dry run was held in which the document was discussed between the project team and the CFO and then worked through between the project team and the head of the Shared Service Center. While the preparation did take longer, the formal completion was shortened considerably.

- *Involvement of employee representatives:* Due to the scope of organizational change that implementing a Shared Service Center entails, we recommend involving the employee representatives extensively and at an early stage. The employee representatives were informed that a Shared Service Center was planned right at the start of the project. Later, two employee representatives joined the Steering Committee to ensure the exchange of information and make aligning the processes transparent and therefore easier. Employees who contacted the employee representatives could in this way be informed using a standardized approach and could be given competent advice. The largest international subsidiary was planned in consultation with the employee representatives from the outset in such a way that the individual processes were migrated in several waves distributed over the entire project duration. This meant that employees leaving in the meantime were replaced by temporary staff, with sufficient time available to look for suitable posts within the company.

- *Employees must be freed up:* This is basically the most critical transformation management aspect as part of a shared service project. In the company's international subsidiaries or branches, relocating tasks may mean that employees are freed up if there are no tasks elsewhere in which they can be incorporated with the necessary training. Dealing with these employees respectfully, informing them promptly and in a suitable form and motivating them also for the duration of the project and the induction of new employees, is, in addition to the company's obligation as employer, one of the challenges of transformation management in shared services projects. By informing the employees affected early on and offering support to find a new position within and outside *SAP*, *SAP* managed to successfully carry out this change. If a split did occur in individual instances, employees were offered a contract. Thanks to the host of new jobs created in the company, this was, however, rarely the case. Through open communications and fair implementation of the measures, motivation was maintained among the employees affected.

- *Employees will be hired:* New employees constitute a smaller challenge for transformation management since they neither have to give up familiar structures and workflows, nor lose their job or colleagues. Nonetheless, the new job also constitutes a change for these employees, which must be managed and accompanied from the project side. Also the fact that these new employees come into contact with old employees during the work shadowing phase and rely on their knowledge, may cause tensions, which transformation management must be clear about and which should be accompanied.

4 Shared Services and Transformation Management – quo vadis?

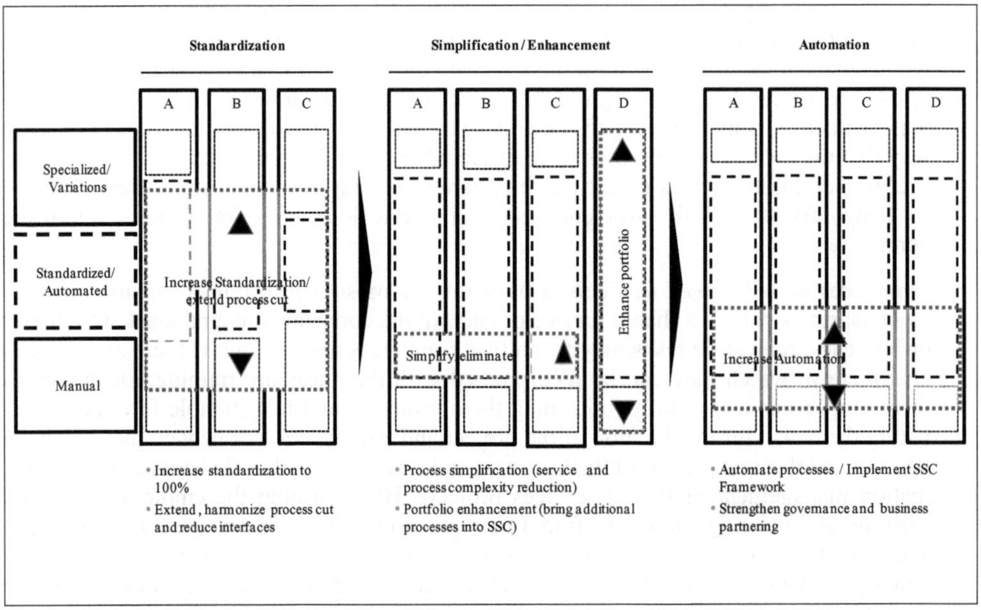

Figure 22: Our approach to move forward

Two decades have passed since the first Shared Service Center was implemented in the 1990s and, as such, it is now time to analyze how we can further develop the Shared Services approach and the associated transformation management, and take it to the next level.

While the main drivers behind the first shared services projects were essentially cost savings, which could be achieved by relocating transactional processes to a Shared Service Center, and due to the associated increase in the level of standardization, today it is also increasingly about migrating higher qualified processes to a Shared Service Center, simplifying processes already in the SSC and eliminating superfluous process steps. This step is possible since existing SSC organizations had several years to garner experience in the respective processes and are now able to also take on more complex tasks and identify superfluous or overly complex process steps. Due to labor arbitrage and standardization the cost savings potential has largely been exploited so that there is now the necessity to increase the efficiency of Shared Service Centers using other levers.

Once superfluous or overly complex process steps have been eliminated or simplified and the service portfolio extended according to the increased maturity of the SSC organization, the next step involves increasing the level of automation. This makes sense for the following reasons:

- The less manual intervention required in a process, the fewer people are needed to support the process. This capacity that is freed up in the SSC can be used to cope with an increasing transaction volume with the existing workforce (efficiency gain), to include other processes in the SSC's service portfolio or also to intensify business partnering.
- The less manual intervention required to conduct a process, the less the risk that errors are made, which are costly and may lead to compliance problems.
- Increased automation reduces the need for new SSC employees. Since it is becoming increasingly difficult for the SSCs to find suitable personnel, which boast the technical and linguistic requirements in order to be able to work successfully in an SSC, a high degree of automation of the solution is conducive to resolving this problem. At the same time however, a high degree of automation increases the complexity of the remaining jobs since these then mainly focus on exception handling, which requires a high degree of experience and knowledge.

The maximum level of automation is achieved if a transaction can be completed entirely without human intervention. This is what is known as lights-out mode. A typical process, which has the potential to be managed in lights-out mode, is the Invoice to Pay process for PO-based orders. If this process is conducted automatically, the invoice comes in electronic format from the supplier and is automatically scanned and digitized using an optical character recognition (OCR) machine. This invoice, which has been digitized by OCR, is automatically compared with the purchase order and the delivery note, posted straightaway where they match and assigned for payment, and finally archived in the ERP backend. Only invoices without a PO reference or with variations compared with the purchase order or delivery note are automatically sent to the approver via workflow and signed for payment once approved.

There are a wide range of options for partial and full automation of processes. Even apparently very complex processes with a prevalence of exceptions can be automated using the right software since this also allows exceptions to be mapped.

In the wake of increasing automation and the associated projects, the question arises for transformation management about which new challenges this entails. Here the following additional challenges for transformation management can be found, unlike SSC projects that have already been implemented:

- Previously typical Shared Service jobs were characterized by a high degree of repetitive and transactional work, with a low degree of complexity. The key criterion was often existing language skills, rather than process experience. These requirements are changed dramatically with increasing automation. Repetitive and transactional workflows will in future be completed automatically. The remaining more complex exceptions, which not only have previously called for a high degree of language skills, but also sound process expertise as well as knowledge of local specifics.
- The Shared Service Organization of the future will in all probability be a Center of Expertise, which is based wherever the greatest knowledge exists in the company (thought leadership). This tends to be found at the company's headquarters. Many existing shared services organizations have based their centers in Eastern European and Asian locations in order to maximize cost savings through labor arbitrage. Thus the centers tend to be remote from the location of the thought leaders, which you, however, need in order to set up and run the Center of Expertise. For these shared services organizations due to the

realignment of the SSC concept toward highly automated Centers of Expertise, you may need to rethink the location decision made in the past.

- By increasing the level of automation it is necessary that the enterprise's external stakeholders (e.g. customers and suppliers) also change the way in which they make contact with the enterprise. Contact via customer and supplier portals and transferring incoming and outgoing invoices via e-invoicing or also directly via the portals, are becoming increasingly important. Contact via call centers is an increasingly widespread form of internal and external customer support, which calls for an optimum software solution. That optimum solution comes in the form of call center functionality with a ticketing system built into the CRM system. In this respect, *SAP* uses a solution developed specifically for Shared Service Centers dubbed "Shared Services Framework".

5 Core Elements of Successful Transformation Management and Further Development of Content

A Shared Service Center project poses numerous challenges to an enterprise's organization. Different stakeholder groups with diverging interests must be integrated in the individual project phases and their buy-in obtained in order to ensure rapid implementation. The executions have shown that the early integration of the stakeholders constitutes a key factor in the project success. This could be illustrated by numerous examples in accordance with the individual project phases. Successful transformation management has the task of proactively accompanying the change process and ensuring target group-specific communication to all stakeholders. In the selected example it was shown that the aim was to develop a transformation management concept tailored to the business workflows and corporate culture. The early integration of stakeholders and the associated targeted information with the communication media that appeals to them directly lies at the heart of the transformation management concept in this respect.

We recommend that future Shared Service Center projects develop and consistently implement a transformation management concept in parallel to the project planning. The insights garnered from the pilot country should be integrated into the conceptual approach. The targeted communication with stakeholders is also decisive for implementing the project. The experience should be bundled and integrated into the migration approach and an update produced for the planning, tools and methodology.

Successful transformation management, with the subareas change management, organizational development and communication is the task of management, but also needs to be accepted by employees and embraced in the new task areas in the newly created organization.

In relation to the future of shared services and the trend toward Centers of Expertise, new challenges for transformation management arise, as set out in section 4. We need to prepare ourselves early on for these new challenges in order to select an optimum transformation management approach for these future projects.

Abbreviations and Terms

BPR	Business Process Reengineering
C2C	Customer to Cash
CFO	Chief Financial Officer
CRM	Customer Relationship Management
EDI	Electronic Data Interchange
EMEA	Europe/Middle East/Africa
ERP	Enterprise Resource Planning
F & A	Finance and Accounting
FTE	Full-time Equivalent, measuring unit for the workforce of one employee
HR	Human Resources
IT	Information Technology
KPI(s)	Key Performance Indicator(s)
KTP	Knowledge Transfer Plan
MRP	Migration Readiness Plan
OCR	Optical Character Recognition
PMF	People Management Framework
SLA	Service Level Agreement
SOX	*Sarbanes-Oxley*-Act
SSC	Shared Service Center
SSO	Shared Services Organization(s)
TM	Transformation Management

References

BUCK REPORT (2004): Buck *REPORT*, Internal Dokument, Walldorf 2004.

BANGEMANN, T. O. (2005): Shared Services in Finance and Accounting, Burlington 2005.

BECKER, W./KUNZ, C./MAYER, B. (2009): Shared Service Center – Konzeption und Implementierung in internationalen Konzernen, Stuttgart 2009.

FISCHER, T. M./STERZENBACH, S. (2006): Controlling von Shared Service Centers – Ergebnisse einer empirischen Studie in deutschen Unternehmen, Nürnberg/Ingolstadt 2006.

FROLIK, A./MACHACEK, K./BLOCHING, U./LEEB, G. (2004): Shared Services Center. Erfolgreicher Weg zur Senkung von Fixkosten im Unternehmen. Vortrag vor der Industriellenvereinigung Kärnten, Klagenfurt 2004.

KAGELMANN, U. (2001): Shared Services als alternative Organisationsform, Wiesbaden 2001.

LACITY,M. C./FOX, J. (2008): Creating global shared services. Lessons from Reuters, in: MIS Quarterly Executive, Vol. 7 (2008), No. 1, p. 17–32.

NEUKIRCHEN, R./VOLLMER, M. (2008): Change Management und Shared Services – Einbindung der Stakeholder, in: *KEUPER, F./OECKING, C.* (Eds.), Corporate Shared Services – Bereitstellung von Dienstleistungen im Konzern, 2nd Edition, Wiesbaden 2008, p. 399–328.

NEUKIRCHEN, R./VOLLMER, M. (2007): Controlling Toolbox für ein erfolgreiches Change Management im Finance Shared Services Projekt, in: Controlling – Zeitschrift für erfolgsorientierte Unternehmenssteuerung, Vol. 19 (2007), No. 2, p. 91–98.

PRAMMER K. (2009): TransformationsManagement – Theorie und Werkzeugset für betriebliche Veränderungsprozesse, Heidelberg 2009.

QUINN, B./COOKE, R./KRIS, A. (2000): Shared Services – Mining for Corporate Gold, Harlow/London (UK) 2000.

SAP AG (2000): Supervisory Board, online: http://www.*SAP*.com/corporate-en/our-company/*SAP*-boards/supervisory-board.epx, last update: 01.08.2012, access: 23.08.2012.

SCHULMAN, D. S./HARMER, M./DUNLEAVY, J./LUSK, J. (1999): Shared Services – Adding Value to the Business Units, New York 1999.

STAUSS, B./NEUHAUS, P. (1999): Interne Kundenzufriedenheit als Zielgröße einer Personalmanagement Abteilung, in: *BRUHN, M.* (eds.), Internes Marketing – Integration der Kunden und Mitarbeiterorientierung, Grundlagen – Implementierung – Praxisbeispiele, 2nd Edition, Wiesbaden 1999, p. 133–153.

THE HACKETT GROUP (2006): CEO Research 2006 and SSC BPO Database (status July 2012), internal document.

ULBRICH, F. (2008): The Adoption of IT-Enabled Management Ideas – Insights From Shared Services in Government Agencies, Stockholm 2008.

Shared Service Trajectories

FRANK ULBRICH

Northumbria University

Executive Summary

Numerous studies have reported on the virtues of shared services—especially cost reduction and quality improvement. Process standardization plays a prominent role in strategies to deliver those benefits. This chapter reviews previous research on process standardization and shared services to outline how unbalanced standardization causes shared service centers to transition into less effective service delivery modes. Linked to the two dimensions of service consolidation and external service receivers, such transition is likely to follow one of four distinct trajectories: (1) centralized shared services, (2) outsourced shared services, (3) collaborative shared services, and (4) decentralized shared services. Each of these trajectories negatively impacts on an organization's ability to realize its original goals, i.e., simultaneously reducing costs and improving quality. Hence, shared service centers might lose some of their positive qualities when moving toward one of the four trajectories.

1 Introduction

In response to ever enduring competition and an increased focus on cost reduction, organizations have utilized various service delivery modes to effectively and efficiently utilize resources. One such mode—shared services—promises organizations to simultaneously realize cost reductions and high levels of services quality.[1] Organizations usually accomplish these goals by uniting non-core business processes that are spread among diverse business units. To this end dedicated entities—the shared services centers—are established to consolidate and improve processes.[2] Such processes might encompass a wide range of services from one or several business functions including finance and accounting, human resources, procurement, facility management, or information systems.[3]

Traditionally, shared service centers have focused on internal service delivery. Lately, however, centralized, outsourced, collaborative, and decentralized shared service modes have become prevalent. The emergence of these four modes, it is argued, is the result of traditional shared service centers gradually shifting their properties along the dimensions of service consolidation and external service receivers—a shift that results in unbalanced process standardization, which in turn jeopardizes achieving the original goals of simultaneously reducing costs and improving quality.

This chapter outlines shared service trajectories. By doing so it contributes to gaining a deeper understanding of various delivery modes of shared services and facilitates managers in making better informed strategic decisions on shared service initiatives. The remainder of the chapter is organized as follows. The following section examines process standardization as an integral part of the shared service delivery mode. Thereafter the four trajectories caused by process standardization are expounded. The final section concludes this chapter by summariz-

1 Cf. *JANSSEN* et al. (2009).

2 Cf. *WISSKIRCHEN/MERTENS* (1999), *BERGERON* (2003), and *WANG/WANG* (2007).

3 Cf. *WEGENER* (2007) and *MCIVOR* et al. (2011).

ing the trajectories, and stating theoretical implications and recommended directions for future research.

2 Process Standardization and Shared Services

Managers are faced by a perpetual challenge to improve and standardize processes in shared service centers.[4] Standardizing processes is concerned with reviewing and identifying commonalities of a range of processes in order to design and implement best practices; i.e., processes are optimized to be performed at the lowest possible cost.[5] Creating such single, uniform processes is often seen as a main contribution of a shared service center in order to realize synergies and achieve high levels of services quality.[6]

The positive role of process standardization has been confirmed through many case studies.[7] *DAVIS* et al.,[8] for example, report that the Cabinet Office in the UK estimates a possible twenty percent cost saving on central and local government finance and accounting and human resources services by implementing shared services; and *TURLE*[9] states, "Whether it's sharing the process of council tax collection or using a single IT system for payroll, shared services provide the greater efficiency that comes through economies of scale, and the greater effectiveness that comes from adopting best practice processes," confirming the wide-spread focus on best practices and process standardization.

Further evidence for the importance of process standardization is provided by *TOMKINSON*[10] who shows that, by better understanding the purchase-to-order process, Basingstroke and Deane Borough Council in the UK were able to improve the necessary activities their staff performed, reducing the cost per transaction from £92 to £11 in their shared service center. And the global provider of telecommunications equipment and services *Ericsson* lowered the total cost for finance and accounting from "0.61% of Group net sales in 2005 to 0.34% in 2006,"[11] which was achieved through "standardizing and automatizing their financial processes"[12] and integrating them "into [their Enterprise Resource Planning] system."[13]

4 Cf. *HESKETH* (2008).

5 Cf. *WANG/WANG* (2007).

6 Cf. *SCHULMAN* et al. (1999), *CECIL* (2000), *TRIPLETT/SCHEUMANN* (2000), and *BERGERON* (2003)

7 For example, cf. *JANSSEN/WAGENAAR* (2004), *JANSSEN/JOHA* (2006a), *WAGENAAR* (2006), *JANSSEN* et al. (2007), *BECKER* et al. (2009a, 2009b), *MISKON* et al. (2009), *BORMAN* (2010a, 2010b), *ULBRICH* (2009, 2010a, 2010b), and *TOMASINO* (2011).

8 Cf. *DAVIS* et al. (2007).

9 *TURLE* (2010), p. 184.

10 Cf. *TOMKINSON* (2007).

11 *LINDVALL/IVEROTH* (2011), p. 297.

12 *LINDVALL/IVEROTH* (2011), p. 286.

13 *LINDVALL/IVEROTH* (2011), p. 289.

The examples above vividly illustrate that process standardization is often driven by optimizing processes as well as utilizing supportive information systems. Such information systems usually enable and facilitate service provision in shared service centers. They play a key role especially in shared service centers when outcomes are delivered digitally (for example, a monthly report). The kind of information system that often supports shared service centers are Enterprise Resource Planning systems. They support the centers through their ability to consolidate, standardize, and automate processes.[14] The systems are usually equipped with a wide range of standard processes, building on best practices. To utilize these best practices, many organizations simply want to adopt those suggested processes. As a consequence, Enterprise Resource Planning systems impact frequently on business process design and service delivery of shared service centers.[15]

However, processes cannot always be placed easily within the constraints of an Enterprise Resource Planning system. When this is the case process standardization might not be accomplished as simply as it appears in theory. Following a standard solution might then be inappropriate. It has therefore been noted that no one universal approach exists to gain benefits through shared services[16] and that process improvement needs to focus on organizational peculiarities and on optimizing the internal client experience too.[17]

The use of standard processes in Enterprise Resource Planning systems can also negatively contribute to the individual qualities of labor because the high degree of process standardization provided by these systems might lead to deskilling;[18] i.e., due to standardization work tasks become less challenging to deal with. Initially gathered core competence might then not be needed to perform such tasks anymore. If this is the case, it is much likely that process standardization will lead to core competence not being properly utilized and eventually being completely lost. Not utilizing or losing core competence contradicts evidently the whole idea of shared services, which advocates explicitly gathering and utilizing core competences in designated service centers.

It can therefore be proposed that excessive process standardization might have a negative impact on shared services. This view is confirmed in the general management literature that provides ample examples in which a too high level of—i.e., excessive—process standardization impedes organizations from achieving their goals. *HALL/JOHNSON*[19] provide examples where process standardization has failed and argue that a balance is needed between standardized and less rigidly controlled processes, saying, "Ironically, process standardization can undermine the very performance it's meant to optimize."

The appropriate level of process standardization might therefore vary between organizations based on their specifics needs, calling for a more balanced level of process standardization. This view, however, contradicts much previous research on shared services that almost exclusively favors the concept of relatively high levels of process standardization in order to im-

---

14 Cf. *SEDERA/DEY* (2007).

15 Cf. *LACITY/FOX* (2008).

16 Cf. *ULBRICH* (2006, 2008) and *AKSIN/MASINI* (2008).

17 Cf. *SCHULZ/BRENNER* (2010).

18 Cf. *HOWCROFT/RICHARDSON* (2012).

19 *HALL/JOHNSON* (2009), p. 60.

prove services.[20] Too much or too little process standardization, however, might be counterproductive and negatively impact on a shared service center's ability to reach its original goals. Hence, the quest is to understand when or how process standardization becomes unbalanced and what this means for the provision of shared service.

To allow academics and managers to better understand the impact of process standardization on providing shared services, this chapter outlines four trajectories that are likely to happen when process standardization becomes unbalanced.

3 Trajectories Linked to Process Standardization

Before outlining the four trajectories and how they link to process standardization, a brief account is given for how the results emerged, including a short description of the data collection method, some limitations, and important assumptions regarding the trajectories' point of origin.

Only secondary data was used in this study. To this end, case studies on shared services were retrieved and analyzed to explore the trajectories of shared services. In a first round the analysis focused on finding evidence for different levels of process standardization. In a second round the impact of process standardization on service provision was examined; in particularly looking for commonalities in how service provision was organized. By applying an inductive process, patterns emerged and four new categories of shared service modes were identified: centralized shared services, outsourced shared services, collaborative shared services, and decentralized shared services.

In a third round the analysis focused on identifying any related links to the level of standardization and type of service modes. While carefully reviewing the cases, two such links became apparent: the levels of consolidation and external service provision. The level of consolidation indicates the range of services provided by a shared services center. The higher the level of consolidation is, the lower the number of services provided. The level of external service provision indicates the relation to external service providers and receivers. A high level of external service provision means that services are retrieved from external organizational entities and/or provided to such entities.

The links between these two levels, the level of standardization, and the type of service mode are captured in Table 1. Table 1 also accounts for what is perceived the traditional—or original—shared service center, i.e., an organizational entity characterized by a medium level of consolidation, low level of external service provision, and a balanced level of process standardization.[21]

---

20 Cf. *KAGELMANN* (2001), *BERGERON* (2003), and *JANSSEN/JOHA* (2006b).

21 It shall be noted that Table 1 provides no indication of how likely it is for one trajectory to occur. The purpose of this study has been exploratory, focusing on identifying new types of shared service modes only. There is no intention to make any statements regarding which trajectory is most common or most likely to appear under certain circumstances. This kind of question is intentionally left for future research in this area.

Two assumptions were made when analyzing the cases. First, for a transition toward a different shared service mode to be happening an organization had previously an established shared service center in the traditional sense, i.e., being an organizational entity, servicing internal clients, providing a range of service based on standardized and optimized processes that have been consolidated in the shared service center.[22] Second, it was assumed that an organization's shared service center had originally emerged to address the drawbacks of a previously existing decentralized service delivery. This decentralization had led to low process standardization and dispersed service provision in the organization, i.e., the level of consolidation was low.[23]

	Level of		
	Consolidation	**External Service Provision**	**Process Standardization**
Shared service center	medium	low	balanced
(1) Centralized shared service	high	low	excessive
(2) Outsourced shared service	high	high	excessive
(3) Collaborative shared service	medium–high	medium–high	balanced–excessive
(4) Decentralized shared service	low	low–medium	deficient–balanced

Table 1: Characteristics of a traditional shared service center vs. four trajectories[24]

3.1 Centralized Shared Services

The first trajectory indicates a development toward a level of excessive process standardization. In this trajectory the level of consolidation increases toward high while a low level of external service receivers is maintained. The increased level of consolidation usually coincides with further streamlining of processes and prescribing their compulsory use. This trajectory leads to centralized shared services.

Centralized shared services allow the achievement of higher economies of scale. Consequently, a reason for moving toward this mode may be seeking to better achieve the shared service center's original goal of realizing synergies, i.e., cost reduction. Previous studies have shown that the realized cost reduction in traditional shared service centers is commonly less high

22 This assumption is considered reasonable because many organizations have progressed along this line when forming their shared service centers.

23 This assumption is based on a wide-spread consensus in the 1990s that service provision could best be performed locally to fully meet local demands.

24 To facilitate comparison, the first row shows the characteristics for traditional shared service centers.

than expected.[25] Though it appears to be possible to achieve higher economies of scale through further streamlining processes, i.e., aiming for a higher level of standardization, and prescribing the mandatory use of these services across the organization. Such service provision is similar to traditional centralization,[26] although organizations keep referring to it as shared services because centralization is usually considered an inadequate concept in terms of current management ideas. Besides, the move toward decentralization took place rather recently in many public-sector organizations, making it difficult to argue for returning to an old mode, which had been deemed ineffective only a couple of years before.[27]

Centralized shared services are less focused on clients than traditional shared service centers. Instead they focus on economies of scale, striving for offering the most efficient and effective ways to deliver services. This rational thought goes far back to ideas of scientific management,[28] driving process standardization even further. This form of excessive process standardization no longer puts the client in focus. It is purely about making the service center perform more efficiently, better contributing toward achieving synergies. As a consequence, the client–service-provider dialogue usually diminishes and clients feel less well served than before, reducing the clients' perceived service quality, contrary to the original goal of achieving a high level of service quality.

Centralized shared services, hence, seem to be too much focused on their own performance. Driven by rationality they primarily focus on tangible costs and benefits. Cost reduction, for example, is easily measured in monetary terms. A high level of service quality, however, is rather intangible and shared service centers appear to have difficulties in evaluating intangible costs and benefits. When not considering the intangible costs and benefits, they do not apply a holistic view to realize how their service provision feeds into their clients' service delivery and, ultimately, the public. Hence, moving toward centralized shared services might be driven by short-term goals of cost reduction rather than a sustainable focus.

A shared service center should therefore carefully evaluate intangible costs and benefits in its equation of determining the most beneficial service delivery mode. Special consideration needs to be given to one of the main reasons for having shared services in the first place, i.e., the level of service quality. Too much process standardization might negatively impact on the perceived service quality.[29]

3.2 Outsourced Shared Services

The second trajectory indicates a development toward a level of excessive process standardization. In this trajectory the level of consolidation increases toward high at the same time as the level of external service receivers increases toward high too, i.e., organizations turn over their service delivery to an external vendor. When moving service delivery to an external vendor, the level of external service receivers is at its highest. This trajectory leads to outsourced shared services.

---

25 Cf. *A.T. KEARNEY* (2004).

26 Cf. *KAGELMANN* (2001).

27 Cf. *ULBRICH* (2006).

28 Cf. *TAYLOR* (1911).

29 Cf. *HALL/JOHNSON* (2009).

Outsourced shared services allow organizations to take advantage of specialist capabilities that are not available in-house for providing high-quality services. This position needs to be contrasted with the original idea of shared service centers on gathering an organization's expertise in one single entity. Following the reasoning of the latter, it is suggested that shared service centers already possess capabilities similar to external vendors and that the often-mentioned advantage of getting access to specialist capabilities is overrated. However, organizations might not succeed in actually consolidating their capabilities because of transitional problems. Then an external vendor could provide such access. However, this would probably mean that the organization will lose even more capabilities,[30] exposing it even more to external service providers. It would mean that an internal problem is solved by moving it to a vendor instead of focusing on how to facilitate change and develop essential capabilities internally.[31] Hence, the contribution of outsourced shared services toward achieving higher levels of service quality is questionable.

Outsourced shared services are also seen as a means of delivering higher levels of cost reduction. *McIvor* et al.[32] note that, "Organizations have been increasingly turning to vendors to implement and manage outsourced shared services . . . to drive standardization and performance improvement." The underlying belief that outsourced shared services contribute positively to a higher level of cost reduction stems from the ability to compare, or benchmark, the original shared service center's performance with the one of an external vendor. Such benchmarking has often become possible through process standardization, which has greatly increased transparency. Such transparency facilitates assessing the efficiency of any service delivery mode, which is why internal streamlining often precedes outsourcing.[33] This streamlining might go so far that process standardization becomes excessive, completely focused on achieve higher levels of cost reduction, however,—similar to centralized shared services—negatively impacting on service quality because of the lost ability to respond to local business needs.[34]

Outsourced shared services can also facilitate organizational redesign. Modern organizations constantly restructure to align structure to strategy.[35] In public-sector organizations this is often evident when major paradigm shifts or political changes occur. An example is that public-sector organizations are asked to focus on their core business. All services consolidated in a shared service center are per definition support services, and it could be argued that the organization should not deal with them. If such restructuring of the internal corporate hierarchy is a goal per se, outsourced shared services might be a mean to accomplishing it. However, new skills are then required to manage the dependencies rather than the service center.[36]

A shared service center should carefully assess all risks associated with outsourced shared services to determine the most beneficial service delivery mode. Special consideration should be given to contractual hazards that might impede the achievement of the original goals. In particular the level of service quality might suffer when processes are excessively standard-

---

30 Cf. *Utterback/Abernathy* (1975) and *Gospel/Sako* (2010).

31 Cf. *Day/Norris* (2006).

32 *McIvor* et al. (2011), p. 448.

33 Cf. *Sako* (2010).

34 Cf. *Janssen/Joha* (2006b).

35 Cf. *Chandler* (1969) and *Kim/Mauborgne* (2009).

36 Cf. *Borman/Ulbrich* (2011) and *McIvor* et al. (2011).

ized and changes are, because of existing contracts, too costly to implement. This leads to too many standardized processes and this imbalance in process standardization might negatively impact the clients' perceived level of service quality. Through this a shared service center loses momentum, not being able to achieve a high level of service quality.

3.3 Collaborative Shared Services

The third trajectory indicates a development toward a balanced to excessive level of process standardization. In this trajectory the level of consolidation might slightly increase toward medium–high and the level of external service receivers increases toward medium–high; i.e., service delivery is aimed at providing services to clients inside and outside the organization. Depending on the homogeneity or heterogeneity of the service receivers, service standardization might be perceived as balanced rather than excessive. Because of its nature, i.e., organizations collaborating in service delivery and/or service utilization, this trajectory leads to collaborative shared services.

Collaborative shared services allow organizations to share their expertise beyond organizational boundaries with other organizations. In the public-sector setting, sharing expertise with one another is not unusual. This has led to various collaborative arrangements over the years, including shared services.[37] The advantage of such arrangements is that organizations can share "best practice and problems so as to avoid 're-inventing the wheel.'"[38] As a consequence, collaborative shared services have emerged in many countries. *MURRAY* et al.,[39] for example, report on collaborative shared services in district councils in close vicinity in the UK. Similar arrangements have also been reported from German municipalities by *BECKER* et al.[40] and *NIEHAVES/KRAUSE*,[41] referring to them as shared service networks and shared service partnerships. Other forms of collaboration include shared service organizations, which are popular forms in, for example, Canada[42] and the US.[43]

Collaborative shared services allow several public-sector organizations to collaboratively achieve higher levels of service quality and cost reductions than they could achieve on their own. Therefore these organizations agree on a collaborative mode for delivering services to all partners in the collaboration. This usually implies that processes are further standardized, which often is seen as positive as indicated by the best practice example above.

Collaborative shared services, however, can also be perceived as having a negative impact on service quality. Especially when services have been delivered quite differently prior to the collaboration, process standardization can be perceived as rather excessive, forcing service receiving entities to significantly change their work process, negatively impacting on the perception of service quality. In this case a participating organization might want the service center to adopt its specific process to be used as standard process. It is likely, though, that the

37 Cf. *JANSSEN* et al. (2009).

38 *MURRAY* et al. (2008), p. 550.

39 Cf. *MURRAY* et al. (2008).

40 Cf. *BECKER* et al. (2009b).

41 Cf. *NIEHAVES/KRAUSE* (2010).

42 Cf. *GRANT* et al. (2007).

43 Cf. *TOMASINO* (2011).

organization that "wins" over others is the one that is most powerful in the collaboration. It is therefore important to understand the dependencies in collaborative shared services[44] and assess all associate risks with this type of service delivery. One such risk is that the collaboration is not stable, usually because of the selected cost allocation model, which might lead to its disintegration.[45]

A shared service center therefore should carefully assess all risks associated with collaborative shared services. If process standardization leads to perceived lower service quality, the organization loses momentum if opting for this trajectory.

3.4 Decentralized Shared Services

The fourth trajectory indicates a development toward a deficient–balanced level of process standardization. In this trajectory the level of consolidation decreases toward a low level, although the level of external service receivers is predominantly low it might occasionally increase up to medium. Lower process standardization results in a more diversified range of services offered to clients and expert competence that might occasionally be made available to clients outside the organization. This leads to decentralized shared services.

Decentralized shared services allow organizations to better focus on clients' individual needs. An example of this trajectory is given by *Farndale* et al.[46] who describe the move from highly standardized to highly customized processes. Using Human Resources as an example, they find that service development might need to develop to highly customized processes to truly focus on clients. They explain that only through individually servicing each client, can client focus be achieved, creating the necessary foundation for clients to perceive delivered services as being of high quality. Not completely unsurprisingly, *Farndale* et al.[47] find that only about one fourth of organizations find process standardization and control of Human Resources processes important goals when implementing shared service centers.

Decentralized shared services are not to be mistaken for the pure decentralization originally associated with New Public Management. They still distinguish themselves from the traditional service delivery mode in gathering and utilizing an organization's expert competence. This competence is accumulated in the center, allowing all clients to access it. Occasionally, clients may come from outside the organization. As a result, expert competence is available to at least the whole organization rather than to a few specific entities only.

Decentralized shared services, on the other hand, cannot match the synergies of the original shared service ideal. Lower process standardization inevitably results in lower economies of scale. This seems to be accepted by organizations moving toward decentralized shared service. Such move, however, might be premature because the literature suggests that, even within Human Resources, processes can be standardized to a wide extent and can be provided through a traditional shared service center, potentially achieving cost and quality benefits.[48]

---

44 Cf. *Borman/Ulbrich* (2011) and *Ulbrich/Borman* (2012).

45 Cf. *Beimborn* (2012).

46 Cf. *Farndale* et al. (2009).

47 Cf. *Farndale* et al. (2009).

48 Cf. *Ulrich* (1995) and *Wang/Wang* (2007).

A shared service center therefore should utilize its expert competence to design more versatile services that can be delivered to various entities in the organization and positively contribute to achieving cost benefits. Such cost benefits are unlikely to be achieved in decentralized shared services. Hence, moving toward decentralized shared services hazards losing momentum.

4 Conclusion

This chapter has reviewed previous studies on shared services to outline trajectories for shared service centers. Four such trajectories have been identified (cf. Figure 1), namely (1) centralized shared services, (2) outsourced shared services, (3) collaborative shared services, and (4) decentralized shared services. Advantages and disadvantages of these four trajectories have been discussed, including possible reasons for moving in each direction, and the links to the levels of consolidation and external service receivers have been explained.

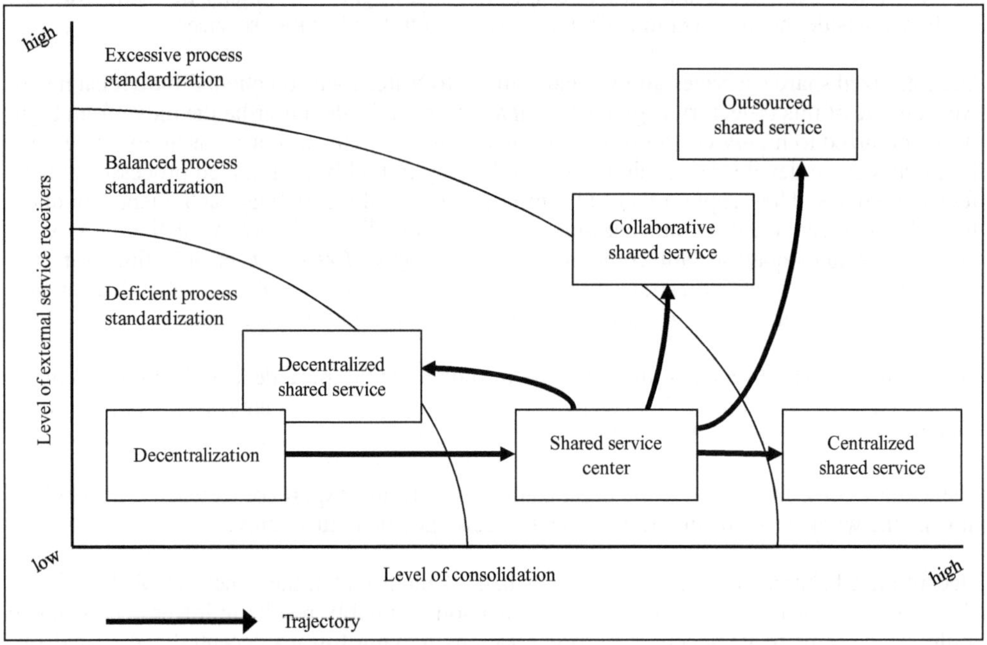

Figure 1: Trajectories of Shared Services Modes

The chapter expands the body of knowledge by synthesizing previous research and, through this, contributing to gaining a deeper understanding of different trajectories of organizational development over time. Decision-maker and heads of shared service centers can use the insights of this chapter to identify the trajectory that appears most beneficial to them based on their peculiarities and strategies. Future empirical validation of the outlined trajectories is suggested to make the findings more robust.

5 Acknowledgement

A previous version of this chapter was presented at the Eighteenth Americas Conference on Information Systems, Seattle, Washington, August 9–11, 2012.

References

A.T. KEARNEY (2004): Success Through Shared Services: From Back-Office Functions to Strategic Drivers, Chicago (IL) 2004.

AKSIN, O. Z./MASINI, A. (2008): Effective strategies for internal outsourcing and offshoring of business services: An empirical investigation, in: Journal of Operations Management, 2008, Vol. 26, No. 2, p. 239–256.

ARELLANO-GAULT, D. (2000): Challenges for the new public management: organizational culture and the administrative modernization program in Mexico City (1995–1997), in: American Review of Public Administration, 2000, Vol. 30, No. 4, p. 400–413.

BECKER, J./NIEHAVES, B/KRAUSE, A. (2009a): Shared service center vs. shared service network: a multiple case study analysis of factors impacting on shared service configuration, in: Proceedings of the 8th International EGOV Conference 2009, August 30–September 3, Linz 2009.

BECKER, J./NIEHAVES, B./KRAUSE, A. (2009b): Shared services strategies and their determinants: a multiple case study analysis in the public sector, in: Proceedings of the 15th Americas Conference on Information Systems, August 6–9, San Francisco (CA) 2009, available at: http://aisel.aisnet.org/amcis2009/14, accessed: February 29, 2012.

BEIMBORN, D. (2012): How stable are cooperative sourcing coalitions? Game theoretical analysis and experiment, in: Electronic Markets, forthcoming

BERGERON, B. (2003): Essentials of Shared Services, Wiley, Hoboken (NJ) 2003.

BORMAN, M. (2010a): Characteristics of a successful shared services centre in the Australian public sector, in: Transforming Government: People, Process and Policy, 2010, Vol. 4, No. 3, p. 220–231.

BORMAN, M. (2010b): The formation of shared services partnerships in local government to manage resource dependencies, in: Proceedings of the 16th Americas Conference on Information Systems, August 12–15, Lima 2010, available at: http://aisel.aisnet.org/amcis 2010/34/, accessed: October 10, 2012.

BORMAN, M./ULBRICH, F. (2011): Managing dependencies in inter-organizational collaboration: the case of shared services for application hosting collaboration in Australia, in: Proceedings of the 44th Hawaii International Conference on System Sciences, January 4–7, Kauai (HI) 2011.

CECIL, B. (2000): Shared services moving beyond success, in: Strategic Finance, 2000, Vol. 81, No. 10, p. 64–68.

CHANDLER, A. D. (1969): Strategy and Structure: Chapters in the History of the American Industrial Enterprise, MIT Press, Boston (MA) 1969.

DAVIS, K./FAWCETT, R./DODIMEAD, P. (2007): Improving Corporate Functions Using Shared Services, National Audit Office, London 2007.

DAY, K. J./NORRIS, A. C. (2006): Supporting information technology across health boards in New Zealand: themes emerging from the development of a shared services organization, in: Health Informatics Journal, 2006, Vol. 12, No. 1, p. 13–25.

FARNDALE, E./PAAUWE, J./HOEKSEMA, L. (2009): In-sourcing HR: shared service centres in the Netherlands, in: The International Journal of Human Resource Management, 2009, Vol. 20, No. 3, p. 544–561.

GOSPEL, H./SAKO, M. (2010): The unbundling of corporate functions: the evolution of shared services and outsourcing in human resource management, in: Industrial and Corporate Change, 2010, Vol. 19, No. 5, p. 1367–1396.

GRANT, G. G./MCKNIGHT, S./URUTHIRAPATHY, A./BROWN, A. E. (2007): Designing governance for shared services organizations in the public service, in: Government Information Quarterly, 2007, Vol. 24, No. 3, p. 522–538.

HALL, J. M./JOHNSON, M. E. (2009): When should a process be art not science?, in: Harvard Business Review, 2009, Vol. 87, No. 3, p. 58–65.

HESKETH, A. (2008): Should it stay or should it go? Examining the shared services or outsourcing decision, in: Strategic Outsourcing: An International Journal, 2008, Vol. 1, No. 2, p. 154–172.

HOWCROFT, D./RICHARDSON, H. (2012): The back office goes global: exploring connections and contradictions in shared service centres, Work Employment and Society, 2012, Vol. 26, No. 1, p. 111–127.

JANSSEN, M./JOHA, A. (2006a): Governance of Shared Services in Public Administration, in: Proceedings of the 12th Americas Conference on Information Systems, August 4–6, Acapulco 2006, available at: http://aisel.aisnet.org/amcis2006/284, accessed: February 29, 2012.

JANSSEN, M./JOHA, A. (2006b): Motives for establishing shared service centers in public administrations, in: International Journal of Information Management, 2006, Vol. 26, No. 2, p. 102–115.

JANSSEN, M./JOHA, A./WEERAKKODY, V. (2007): Exploring relationships of shared service arrangements in local government, in: Transforming Government: People, Process and Policy, 2007, Vol. 1, No. 3, p. 271–284.

JANSSEN, M./JOHA, A./ZUURMOND, A. (2009): Simulation and animation for adopting shared services: evaluating and comparing alternative arrangements, in: Government Information Quarterly, 2009, Vol. 26, No. 1, p. 15–24.

JANSSEN, M./WAGENAAR, R. (2004): An analysis of a shared services centre in e-government, in: Proceedings of the 37th Hawaii International Conference on System Sciences, Hawaii 2004.

Kagelmann, U. (2001): Shared Services als alternative Organisationsform: Am Beispiel der Finanzfunktion im multinationalen Konzern, Deutscher Universitäts-Verlag, Wiesbaden 2001.

Kim, W. C./Mauborgne, R. (2009): How strategy shapes structure, in: Harvard Business Review, 2009, Vol. 87, No. 9, p. 72–80.

Klausen, K. K. (1997): NPM in the Nordic countries: A vitalization of or an end to the Scandinavian model?, in: Proceedings of the International Public Management Network Summer Workshop, June 25–27, Potsdam 1997.

Lacity, M. C./Fox, J. (2008): Creating global shared services: lessons from Reuters, in: MIS Quarterly Executive, 2008, Vol. 7, No. 1, p. 17–32.

McIvor, R./McCracken, M./McHugh, M. (2011): Creating outsourced shared services arrangements: lessons from the public sector, in: European Management Journal, 2011, Vol. 29, No. 6, p. 448–461.

Miskon, S./Bandara, W./Fielt, E./Gable, G. (2009): Understanding shared services: an exploration of the IS literature, in: Proceedings of the 20th Australasian Conference on Information Systems, December 2–4, Melbourne 2009.

Murray, J. G./Rentell, P. G./Geere, D. (2008): Procurement as a shared service in English local government, in: International Journal of Public Sector Management, 2008, Vol. 21, No. 5, p. 540–555.

Niehaves, B./Krause, A. (2010): Shared service strategies in local government: a multiple case study exploration, in: Transforming Government: People, Process and Policy, 2010, Vol. 4, No. 3, p. 266–279.

Sako, M. (2010): Outsourcing versus shared services, in: Communications of the ACM, 2010, Vol. 53, No. 7, p. 27.

Schulman, D. S./Harmer, M. J./Dunleavy, J. R./Lusk, J. S. (1999): Shared Services: Adding Value to the Business Units, Wiley, New York (NY) 1999.

Schulz, V./Brenner, W. (2010): Characteristics of shared service centers, in: Transforming Government: People, Process and Policy, 2010, Vol. 4, No. 3, p. 210–219.

Sedera, D./Dey, S. (2007): Everyone is Different! Exploring the Issues and Problems with ERP Enabled Shared Service Initiatives, in: Proceedings of the 13th Americas Conference on Information Systems.

Taylor, F. W. (1911): The Principles of Scientific Management, Harper & Brothers, New York (NY)/London 1911.

Tomasino, A. P. (2011): Shared service organizations in the public sector: the case of public safety networks, in: Proceedings of the 17th Americas Conference on Information Systems, August 4–7, Detroit (MI) 2011, available at: http://aisel.aisnet.org/amcis2011_submissions/125/, accessed: October 10, 2012.

Tomkinson, R. (2007): Shared Services in Local Government: Improving Service Delivery, Gower, Hampshire 2007.

Triplett, A./Scheumann, J. (2000): Managing shared services with ABM, in: Strategic Finance, 2000, Vol. 81, No. 8, p. 40–45.

TURLE, M. (2010): Shared services: an outline of key contractual issues, in: Computer Law & Security Review, 2010, Vol. 26, No. 2, p. 178–184.

ULBRICH, F. (2006): How government agencies translate the shared services idea, in: *LUNDEBERG, M./MÅRTENSSON, P./MÄHRING, M.* (eds.), IT and Business Performance, Studentlitteratur, Lund 2006, p. 113–134.

ULBRICH, F. (2008): The Adoption of IT-Enabled Management Ideas: Insights from Shared Services in Government Agencies, EFI – The Economic Research Institute, Stockholm 2008.

ULBRICH, F. (2009): Implementing centers of excellence: A case study, Proceedings of the 15th Americas Conference on Information Systems, August 6–9, San Francisco (CA) 2009, available at: http://aisel.aisnet.org/amcis2009/696, accessed: February 29, 2012.

ULBRICH, F. (2010a): Adopting shared services in a public-sector organization, in: Transforming Government: People, Process and Policy, 2010, Vol. 4, No. 3, p. 249–265.

ULBRICH, F. (2010b): Deploying centres of excellence in government agencies, in: Electronic Government: An International Journal, 2010, Vol. 7, No. 4, p. 362–379.

ULBRICH, F./BORMAN, M. (2012): A resource dependence perspective on modelling interorganisational IS collaborations, in: Proceedings of the UKAIS Conference, March 27–28, Oxford 2012.

ULRICH, D. (1995): Shared services: from vogue to value, in: Human Resource Planning, 1995, Vol. 18, No. 3, p. 12–23.

UTTERBACK, J.M./ABERNATHY, W. J. (1975): A dynamic model of process and product innovation, in: Omega, 1975, Vol. 3, No. 6, p. 639–656.

WAGENAAR, R. W. (2006): Governance of shared service centers in public administration: dilemmas and trade-offs, in: Proceedings of the 8th International Conference on Electronic Commerce, Fredericton (NB) 2006.

WANG, S./WANG, H. (2007): Shared services beyond sourcing the back offices: organizational design, in: Human Systems Management, 2007, Vol. 26, No. 4, p. 281–290.

WEGENER, A. (2007): Kommunale Dienstleistungspartnerschaften: Mit Shared Services zu einer effektiveren Verwaltung, Bertelsmann, Gütersloh 2007.

WISSKIRCHEN, F./MERTENS, H. (1999): Der Shared Service Ansatz als neue Organisationsform von Geschäftsbereichsorganisationen, in *WISSKIRCHEN, F* (ed.), Outsourcing-Projekte erfolgreich realisieren: Strategie, Konzept, Partnerwahl, Schäffer-Poeschel, Stuttgart 1999, p. 79–111.

Successful Management of Transition Projects in Finance Shared Services Organizations

STEPHAN BOOS

Siemens AG, Global Shared Services

Executive Summary

Mainly from 2010 to 2012, *Siemens* drove a comprehensive global infrastructure bundling program. As a major part of that program, more than 300 transition projects were conducted in the area of transactional accounting. Based on the practical experiences gained from this program, five major success factors could be identified:

- First of all, it is essential to have an explicit ***mandate – supported by agreed 'Guiding and Key Design Principles' and commitment from top management and the governance function*** – to run such a program.
- Secondly, a ***clearly defined service scope*** ('Activity Split' by service line) and a formal 'Deviation Request and Approval' process in order to save time and efforts is required.
- Further, ***a sufficiently staffed, well-qualified and highly motivated team,*** i.e. dedicated and experienced project managers and subject matter experts in headquarters and Shared Services Centers, is indispensable.
- Closely linked to this is ***effective management of the entire transition program and the individual projects,*** including tools helping to plan, to direct and to monitor the progress, the ramp-up of required resources and related costs as well as to support proactive risk-management.
- Finally, ***continuous and intensive communication,*** individually tailored to meet the stakeholders' needs, is a prerequisite for close and beneficial partnership, in particular with customers and the governance function.

Best practice discussions show that most of these criteria apply likewise to transition projects in the areas of Human Resources and Supply Chain Management Services.

1 Introduction

By transferring business support processes into a Shared Services Organization (SSO), various benefits can be exploited. Besides freeing up top management from tasks distracting their focus from core business, the notable advantages are improvements in the fields of the service itself: Quality, accuracy, timeliness, transparency and compliance. However, the most tangible benefit is the opportunity to achieve material short-term cost reductions. For instance, a study conducted by *KPMG* and the *University of Erlangen-Nuremberg* focusing on the top-selling German companies provides evidence for realized cost savings in the range of 5 to 35%[1]. Experiences made during the *Siemens'* 'Finance Bundling' program referred to within this article corroborate these results.

In practice, the question for any organization wishing to achieve these benefits is how to get there. How to leverage cost advantages and bundling effects from moving work to a SSO as quickly as possible ('lift and drop' phase)? And taking it further, how to generate additional value in the medium to long term by further harmonization, optimization and automation of processes ('change' phase)?

The vehicle to achieving these goals is an efficient and effective transition process, i.e. the structured transfer of transactional activities from a 'donating entity' into a SSO which can also be referred to as the 'receiving entity'.

The purpose of this article is to provide an overview of the factors of success identified by a global organization which successfully conducted more than 300 single transition projects of different size, complexity and duration in the area of accounting transactions. This practical example of a complex global program can be explored in order to identify what is key to successful transition projects based on the front-line experiences of the project team. This article is written from the perspective of the SSO focusing on project management aspects.

2 Strategic and Organizational Framework

2.1 Strategic Approach and Major Objectives on the Corporate Level

In 2008, *Siemens*[2] re-designed its global organizational structure. Business competencies were assigned to the three Sectors 'Industry', 'Energy', and 'Healthcare', with a fourth Sector 'Infrastructure & Cities' being added later. Its global set-up was transformed into a new regional cross-border structure encompassing 20 (later 14) Clusters. In this context, the central

---

1 Cf. *PAMPER/FISCHER* (2007), p. 22.

2 Founded 165 years ago and supporting its customers in more than 190 countries, *Siemens* is a diversified global player providing innovative products, technologies, solutions and comprehensive know-how in the areas of industry, energy, healthcare, and infrastructure. Key financials (FY 2011, ending Sep 30, 2011): New orders 85.6 billion Euro, sales 73.5 billion Euro, net income 6.3 billion Euro, total assets 104.2 billion Euro, 360,000 employees; cf. online: www.siemens.com (download Aug 19, 2012).

program 'Bundling Regional Infrastructure' was launched, comprising the Human Resources, Information Technology and Finance work streams, targeting the enhancement of effectiveness, efficiency, flexibility, compliance, and standardization on the one hand and the reduction of overall complexity and cost on the other[3].

The respective Finance Bundling program, the reference case for this article, focused on creating a new regional structure for financial governance and control as well as infrastructure tasks, which should also deliver transparent and sustainably optimized functional cost of finance. Further, an over-riding goal of the program was to achieve process and quality improvements and a high penetration rate for the SSO.

The Finance Bundling program was declared as mandatory for the Sectors and Clusters, i.e. it was launched by a decision on board level and was driven by the *Siemens* CFO, Corporate Finance and the senior management team with the purpose of achieving challenging business targets on a Cluster level applying certain centrally given principles, definitions and instructions. The 'Activity Split' – describing and governing on a detailed level which organizational unit is responsible for which part of the relevant accounting processes – was defined by the governance function Corporate Finance in close cooperation with Sectors, Clusters and the SSO. The Finance Bundling program comprised all relevant finance and accounting functions, i.e. governance and controlling, transactional accounting, financial services, taxes as well as supporting activities, such as communications. However, the focus of this paper will be on transactional accounting, referring to those accounting activities which are repeatable, dividable, transferable, centrally manageable, scalable and associated with manageable risks or – in other words – most ready to be transitioned into a SSO.

2.2 Boundaries and Challenges for the Shared Services Organization

Within *Siemens*, Global Shared Services (GSS) was founded in 2006 based on preceding local initiatives. GSS is run as a separate organizational unit, leveraging its global footprint to render mainly transactional services to the operational and central units within the company. That means GSS acts as a captive service provider and is an integral part of the *Siemens* group as one of the global cross-Sector services. GSS' stated mission is that the services are provided in a professional, customer-oriented, quality-focused, transparent and cost-competitive manner. Within the *Siemens* group, the legal entities have to conclude worldwide harmonized Service Level Agreements (SLAs). A 'Cost Plus' charging model applies to handle transfer pricing. By bundling transactional activities and making them 'core' to the SSO, synergies and economies of scale can be exploited for the entire group. GSS is divided into three main Business Lines: Accounting & Finance Services (AFS), Supply Chain Management Services (SCMS), and Human Resources Services (HRS), which are each responsible for articulating their own business strategy, service scope definition and product lifecycle management. The second organizational dimension reflects the regions focusing on customer relationship management and comprising Europe, the Middle East and Africa (EMEA), Asia/Australia, and the Americas. The third dimension is GSS Global Operations which manages the five 'Delivery Centers' (Czech Republic, Portugal, India, China, Latin America) and

---

3 Cf. SIEMENS CORPORATE FINANCE (2011), p. 7.

has the mission of providing and optimizing overall Center infrastructure. Global Operations is comparable to a global supply chain management organization in operational business. The smaller so-called 'Delivery Units' (UK, Singapore, US) represent a kind of 'bridgehead' or front office and customer interface role offering 'local products'. In addition to that, the Delivery Center in Germany has specific tasks supporting the central units of the corporate headquarters. The overall organization has historically grown from individual regional initiatives to a global set-up with its headquarters in Germany, due to the proximity to governance and main operational customers.

The biggest challenges of the Finance Bundling program from the perspective of the SSO include:

- The ***quick set-up of an effective global program management*** steering more than 300 single transition projects and adhering to a demanding schedule of two years,
- the ***fast ramp-up***[4]***, on-boarding, and training of highly motivated Center teams*** endowed with adequate accounting knowledge and language skills; for instance, with regard to the Shared Services Center in Czech Republic this meant ramping up an additional workforce of approximately 50% compared to the existing AFS team in the Center, which involved adding 16 new languages and more than 50 new entities/customers,
- the ***adherence to the given budget constraints*** while ***avoiding any negative impact on daily operations*** as well maintaining customer satisfaction at the required level, particularly for the crucial closing and reporting processes of the company.

3 Management of Transition Projects

3.1 Fundamentals

The Project Management Institute (PMI) defines a ***'project'*** as "a temporary endeavor to create a unique product, service, or result"[5] and ***project management*** as the "application of knowledge, skills, tools, and techniques to project activities to meet the project requirements"[6]. Project management represents the use and integration of certain ***process***es which can be grouped into the ***phases*** "initiating, planning, executing, monitoring and controlling, and closing"[7]. According to the PMI, managing a project encompasses the identification of requirements, the addressing of stakeholder needs, concerns and expectations as well as the "balancing of competing ***project constraints***"[8]: Scope, quality, schedule, resources, budget, and risk. When considering more than one project within the given scope, in project man-

4 'Ramp-up' includes the hiring of new employees, but also the re-assignment of personnel of the existing organization.

5 *PMI PMBOK* (2008), p. 5.

6 *PMI PMBOK* (2008), p. 6.

7 *PMI PMBOK* (2008), p. 6 and p. 43.

8 *PMI PMBOK* (2008), p. 6.

agement literature the term ‘***program***’ is used and interpreted “as a group of related projects managed in a coordinated way”[9] to exploit synergies and obtain control.

For the purpose of this article, ***management of transition projects*** shall be defined as a systematic process of planning, implementing, monitoring and controlling the transfer of certain activities measured as workload of full-time equivalents (FTE) from one organizational or legal unit (‘donating entity’ or ‘customer’) to another (‘receiving entity’ or ‘SSO’) in order to achieve given targets leveraging supporting methodologies and tools.

Usually, such ***activities*** are transactional in nature, which means they are repeatable, transferable, and therefore scalable work packages commonly to be found in the areas of accounting and finance (focus of this article), procurement services, or HR services. However, by reaching a higher level of maturity the SSO may go beyond the purely transitional realm and may also begin to offer specific ‘value-add services’.

Specific ***program and project targets*** are regularly related to scope (e.g. number of entities), quality (e.g. avoidance of booking errors during stabilization phase and later operations), customer satisfaction (e.g. reaching defined levels of customer and user satisfaction indices), time (e.g. 3 to 6 months including stabilization phase until sign-off of a transition), human resources (number of project/transition managers, number team leads and team members in the Center to be ramped-up), procurement (e.g. sourcing of temporary resources or Information Technology [IT] services), costs/results (e.g. project costs in terms of own man days, travel expenses, consulting and IT cost; savings gained by the transfer), risks (e.g. avoidance of delays, bottle neck situations, legal and/or tax issues), and communications (e.g. regular reporting to identified stakeholders). Program management has the challenge of meeting these multiple and wide-reaching targets while also proactively handling the corresponding management areas by applying supportive methodologies and tools.

Throughout this article, the following ***dimensions related to the management of transition projects*** will be illustrated:

- The ***institutional or organizational dimension*** of the program/project management and the human resources required;
- the ***process dimension*** comprising the phases planning, implementation, monitoring and controlling;
- the ***dimension of management areas*** to be considered and handled, i.e. overall program/project integration, scope, quality, customer satisfaction, time, resources, procurement, costs/results, legal and taxes, communications, and risks;[10]

9 *PMI PMBOK* (2008), p. 9.

10 The approach is derived from the so-called “Knowledge Areas” in the *PMI PMBOK* (2008), p. 43; however, the aspects of ‘customer satisfaction’ and ‘legal and taxes’ were added and mutual dependencies as well as the selected sequence may be subject to further discussion.

➢ the ***dimension of supporting methodologies and tools***, e.g using a 'degree of implementation' (DI) approach and milestone logic to be able to track the progress as well as recommended IT applications/databases which help to handle and monitor a larger number of transition projects in terms of schedule, milestone progress, FTE ramp-up, and budget.

3.2 Organization

The term 'organization' is here meant to be the ***structural set-up of the transition program*** and the single projects from the SSO's point of view, i.e. in case of the referenced, more comprehensive Finance Bundling program it is limited to the transactional part only. Processes are outlined separately.

The *Siemens* approach was to set up a "***projectized organization***"[11], headed by a centralized transition program management being responsible for the worldwide project coordination and the direct steering of the European transition projects. 'Projectized' means that the program was broken down into Cluster projects and managed this way. The central program director was supported by a Program Management Office (PMO) assisting him in his controlling and reporting functions. The PMO was also providing the necessary 'infrastructure' to the project managers, being most of their time on site at the customers' premises. This infrastructure includes – besides a document management system and a database – the preparation and making available of project policies, procedures, guidelines in close alignment with governance and customers, presentations, schedules, checklists for the process analyses, budget spreadsheets and savings calculations, status reports and corresponding charts, lessons learned, sign-off and other templates, as well as travel management support. During the peak time, the central program management team consisted of one project director, three (junior) project managers/controllers and one team assistant.

On a Cluster project level, one senior project manager from SSO HQ coordinated the activities supported by one to three (junior) project managers. Generally, the responsibilities were assigned by country or by division/business unit, whenever synergies could be exploited due to the similarity of processes and vertically integrated IT systems. The collaboration interfaces with the Centers are described in the two Case Studies which are included as a part of this article.

The desired skill-set for a project manager working within such a global transition program includes ***experiences and competencies*** in the following areas: Program/project management in international teams, accounting and finance, Shared Services, commercial business processes and Enterprise Resource Planning (ERP) systems, company/group specific structures and processes, and language skills.

A well-considered combination of the strengths and functional know-how of certain team members, e.g. project managers and subject matter experts (e.g. closing or IT experts), can help to further optimize collaboration and transition results.

---

[11] Cf. *PMI PMBOK* (2008), p. 31.

3.3 Process

As outlined above, the PMI distinguishes between so-called project management "Process Groups" comprising the five phases "initiating, planning, executing, monitoring and controlling, closing"[12]. However, following a pragmatic simplified approach, the main program and project processes can be condensed to three phases or steps: ***Planning, implementation, and monitoring/controlling.***

This process model should not be considered as a stringent sequence of phases, rather as a closed loop or cybernetic model. Respective process steps can be applied on a program or on a project level.

On the program level, the planning phase focuses on defining the program targets, prerequisites and boundaries (e.g. mandate, key design and guiding principles, split of activities). The program organization and team, the corresponding service delivery footprint including Center responsibilities, as well as scope and roadmaps (e.g. for Clusters or business divisions) are agreed, baseline data is gathered and 'Impact Estimations' or business cases are elaborated. The implementation usually starts with one or two pilots to prove the concept. Subsequent to the pilots, the execution of the single projects, normally on an entity level, follows. Overall monitoring and controlling of the program ensures target oriented implementation and the possibility to mitigate risks early, especially delays or insufficient performance.

On the single project level – in general – the same phases apply. In the planning phase, the entity-related project organization and the team executing the transition are defined. In addition, analyses with regard to IT landscape, headcount, volume, processes and gaps compared to 'usual Center processes' are conducted. Further, recruitment, training, and work shadowing is scheduled. Implementation starts with the actual recruitment, the on-boarding and training, the work shadowing, the takeover of tasks and finally the stabilization activities. Close monitoring and controlling is required to safeguard a successful execution of individual projects.

3.4 Management Areas

The most important ***areas of transition management*** are ***scope, service quality, customer satisfaction, time, resources, procurement, costs and payback, legal and taxes, risks, communications and change management***, as well as – last but not least – overall ***integration and coordination***.

Overarching ***program integration and coordination*** refers to how to plan, start, direct, monitor and control the program in order to keep it on track and to meet the desired targets, specifically in the case of a high number of individual projects to be successfully implemented.

---

12 *PMI PMBOK* (2008), p. 6 and p. 43.

The necessary precursor to the integration and coordination efforts is the Program Charter[13] comprising mainly the strategic targets set by senior management, a mandate including roles and responsibilities, the scope description, the rough timeline with the major milestones, the 'Guiding and Key Design Principles', the 'Activity Split', and the 'Impact Estimation' per region/Cluster. Since the Finance Bundling program was launched by the *Siemens* CFO and the senior management team, the framework was defined by the governance function.

A program integration and coordination function is also needed at the level of the SSO, in order to provide guidance to the project managers and Centers. On this level, the relevant management tasks include the creation of:

- A uniform 'Transition Guide' (including routines, checklists, documentation templates),
- harmonized reporting standards on project progress, ramp-up of Center human resources and costs,
- detailed project plans, including team staffing and schedules,
- a risk management process, and
- operational indicators for process quality and Center performance.

Based on this framework and applying methods as well as IT tools, the central program manager supported by a PMO has to direct the program implementation, to monitor and control the work and progress and to manage necessary changes, for example bottleneck situations, IT interferences, unforeseen acquisitions or carve-outs, and process deficiencies.

With respect to comprehensive transition programs, the ***scope definition*** implies decision making on targeted region(s), business division(s)/unit(s) and single "donating entities".

On a project level, the service lines to be bundled into the SSO need to be selected, e.g. accounts payable, closing and reporting.

One step deeper on an activity level, a split of responsibilities and 'to dos' is required. For instance, with regard to the accounts receivable process this could include the sub-steps 'master data processing', 'imaging and archiving', 'assure tax requirements', 'review customer credit rating', and so on.

As the Shared Services Center will provide services involving cross-border transactions between separate legal entities a formal contract in the form of a 'Service Level Agreement' (SLA), including a scope description, is necessary in order to meet legal and tax requirements. More information on this area will be addressed in a later section of this article.

With respect to transition programs and projects in the accounting and finance area, maintaining ***quality*** has the utmost priority. Major quality attributes include the ***stability of underlying processes*** and the ***reliability of financial reporting***. In order to demonstrate clear achievement of this goal, the quality of processes and Center performance needs to be translated into

13 Cf. „Project Charter", in: *PMI PMBOK* (2008), p. 73 et seqq.

transparent and relevant 'Key Performance Indicators' (KPI), which are easily and consistently collected on a regular basis. They also need to be meaningful to both customer and SSO management alike.

Gathering respective data prior and after the transitions, i.e. comparing actual data to the baseline, when the process was still under the control of the 'donating entity', facilitates an unemotional, but productive discussion between customer and SSO on weaknesses and improvement measures. The same applies for the time after stabilization, when KPIs can be utilized for the purpose of permanent monitoring and continuous process and performance improvement. A pre-requisite is a well-balanced KPI set encompassing not only output, but also input indicators.

In the finance and accounting area, such KPIs reflect all major accounting processes. Most of the commonly used KPIs are performance related, e.g. 'posted vendor invoices per FTE', 'accounts payable backlog' or 'unallocated versus incoming payments' on the output side or 'vendor invoices without purchase order' or 'number of clarification requests concerning intercompany clearing' on the input side. Quality KPIs in a stricter sense could refer, for example, to 're-opens of closing system caused by SSO' or 'audit findings/deficiencies reported'[14].

From a practical point of view, a streamlined number of relevant KPIs, which can be automatically retrieved, is more useful than a very comprehensive set which is no longer operable. The practicality and cost of data gathering as well as its interpretation needs to be weighed against the resulting benefits when defining the set of KPIs. Summary and visualization in the form of a 'Quality Cockpit' or 'Dashboard' fosters acceptance, understanding, and regular use.

In addition to performance quality, another important area to be managed is ***customer and user satisfaction***, because the apparently 'objective' results shown by quality metrics can deviate from the perception of customers (decision maker level) and/or users (operations level). Thus, it is recommendable to establish an opinion survey to frequently gather feedback from customers and users related to daily Center operations, which might be negatively influenced during and after a comprehensive transition program. In this way, it is possible to identify trends and to initiate counter-measures at an early stage. Focusing on the performance of the project management teams, customer surveys also help to improve processes as well as communication and interaction with the customer. Characteristics of the SSO which can be evaluated with the use of surveys may include perceived competence, commitment, integration skills, understanding of needs, availability/accessibility, reliability, timeliness of announcements, project results, adherence to timeline, meeting of expectations, and flexibility of the project manager and his team[15]. Respective results can be visualized, for instance, with the use of a spider or a trend diagram. This management area is closely linked to that of communications.

---

14 Such KPIs related to performance and service result can be differentiated from those referring to quality perceived on customer side, like customer and user satisfaction, which is therefore outlined separately.

15 SIEMENS GLOBAL SHARED SERVICES (2012a), p. 8.

In practice, ***time*** is often seen as the most relevant parameter to be managed. The time taken to deliver project goals has a direct effect on the overall resource consumption and cost as well as on how soon the benefits of the project are felt by the business.

Time schedules on a program, regional (Cluster), business division or single entity level, as well as bar graphs, arrow and network diagrams, simplify – by visualization – target setting and planning, support the tracking of the actual progress and provide the basis for regular status reporting in a way which can be easily understood. Thus, risks of delay become obvious and necessary preventive or corrective measures or changes to the projects can be decided upon and arranged for at an early stage.

A degree of implementation and milestone logic helps to break timelines down into concrete due dates or intervals. One example is introduced below in more detail comprising the major phases of a transition project, namely 'kick-off', 'process analyses', 'recruitment and training', 'work shadowing', and 'stabilization'.

Applying this logic in the area of accounting, experiences show that on-site process analyses take about one to two weeks, recruitment, on-boarding and training take about one to three months depending on the qualification and skill-set required, and work shadowing itself lasts about one to two weeks. With regard to the latter, one session at the customer's site and one at the SSO's Center site is recommended, and it should ideally cover one or two monthly closings or at least one quarterly closing process depending on complexity. The final stabilization phase usually takes from one month to one quarter, again contingent upon the level of difficulty.

The prioritization or sequence of the single projects can be determined by using decision-making criteria such as 'projects with highest savings first', 'projects with identical or similar processes and ERP systems first', 'projects/services with low complexity first', in order to optimize the economic impact of transitions and to leverage synergies.

Referring to the derived timeframes, ***human resources management*** is the next area of interest to be addressed.

The first target of resource management is to have the right number of people with the right skill-set at the right time in the right place to handle the transitions projects and the entire program.

The same applies for the people at the 'receiving entity', i.e. the Center side, who take over the tasks. The precondition for that is the development of a location and service model prior to the start of implementation, which reflects the intended front and back office structures, mostly based on a given global Center footprint. Such a location and service model may, for instance, mean that Canada is served from a front office in the US, leveraging a back office in India for Master Data Management and Accounts Payable, or that the Scandinavian countries are served from a Center in Czech Republic.

After these central decisions have been made, the quantitative and qualitative demand for services offered by the SSO can be determined per region (Cluster) or business division. This calculation begins with rather generic assumptions which can later be updated with more detailed and accurate on-site headcount analyses. In practice, the transition potential is often overestimated at an early stage (e.g. due to a rapid 'first shot' or motivated by political target setting) which is subsequently 'talked down' to the minimum by the 'donating entity'. The reasons for this can be, for example, that the donating entity wants to minimize the FTE stipulation in the SLA. However, based on the agreed 'demand' for services, the 'supply' on the Center side is determined referring to the discussed location and service model and is then translated into a concrete ramp-up plan. For example, during the *Siemens* bundling program, GSS Center Czech Republic had to recruit a certain number of FTE to handle the demand from Cluster NWE in Scandinavia, including all the details regarding accounting knowledge per service line, requested language skills, IT know how and the like.

It is strongly recommended to track the ramp-up progress closely as part of the monthly reporting as this is one of the major risks to success. Practice has shown that a planned and properly managed temporary overstaffing (e.g. in the range of 10 – 15%) helps to compensate for start-up issues, productivity gaps and early attrition. Focusing here on the SSO, resource planning on the governance and 'donating entity' side shall not be analyzed in detail in this article.

Procurement activities refer to the sourcing of temporary staff, IT/ERP expertise, or the engagement of external consulting companies. Certain steps of processes ('sub-processes'), such as scanning, can be outsourced to specialized service providers. Further, other multinational companies use a hybrid approach to optimize their own service model and to balance volume peaks. However, regarding 'make or buy' decisions in this area, not only economic arguments are to be considered, but also quality, transparency, compliance, and protection of sensitive business data.

When it comes to the ***financial impact*** of transition projects, different benefits are pursued. The first tend to be those resulting from labor arbitrage, bundling, and fixed cost degression effects. Following the 'lift, drop, change' approach, the impacts that follow later include productivity gains as a result of harmonization, further optimization, standardization, and automation of the underlying processes.

Such benefits should be captured in 'Impact Estimations' or business cases prior to launching the projects. In order to gather meaningful and relevant results at the time when the actual impact and the achievements can be calculated (notably if those are the basis for incentive payments) a thorough and well-considered base-lining activity is a necessary prerequisite. However, in real life the unambiguous measurement of the achievements is hampered by various influences, e.g. changes in scope (carve-outs, acquisitions), processes, ERP systems, the extent of automation, business volume, the workforce itself, salaries/wages structure and amounts, and in adjustments actually done on the 'donating entity' side. The most reliable results can be achieved in the labor arbitrage area by comparing costs per FTE prior to and after the transition. But even in this case, the question is, how specifically and in what level of detail was the baseline calculated? The measurement of the bundling effect is further complicated if the FTE base-lining is 'fuzzy' and if the positive effect is temporarily reduced due to overstaffing at the time of start-up or due to required specific language skills. Fixed cost degression can reasonably only be quantified on (aggregated) cost center level and later passed on to customers via lower FTE rates or transactional prices. In addition to these benefits, 'quick wins' (e.g. replacing a manual process by a workflow or the introduction of a scanning solution to ensure 'Shared Services readiness') have a positive additional impact, which is difficult to quantify. The 'change phase' and the economic impact of process improvements and automation shall not be dealt with in this article.

Summarizing the experiences outlined above, a diligent base-lining effort is recommended, in order to define and communicate beforehand which and how savings shall be measured and reported (e.g. in a central productivity tool). Further, it is suggested to balance the efforts for determining the savings against their significance and validity, and also to consider non-financial objectives, such as transparency and compliance. With regard to the efforts related to the measurement itself, business cases on an aggregated level help to convince the stakeholders and speed-up the entire program.

The flip side of the aforementioned opportunities and benefits offered by transition projects are the associated ***risks*** which need to be made transparent, openly reported and discussed, and mitigated by preventive or corrective measures, whenever possible.

Beside tax risks, which are discussed below, the most relevant risks in this context are: Delays, the overstretching of the existing organization, increasing backlogs, material working errors and systemic process weaknesses. In addition, quality issues caused by insufficient performance of the project/Center team or by a lack of support on the customer side can result in deficiencies in the handover of processes and data. The outcome of such shortcomings may be, for instance, material booking errors and misleading financial reporting, double payments, deterioration of the relationships with suppliers in case of late payments or with customers caused by faulty dunning.

For these reasons, strict monitoring of the transition projects is required. Relevant measures could include keeping the control environment stable and efficient, establishing quality management measures, tracking SSO Center performance using relevant statistics and indicators, as well as making trainings and best/good practice sharing sessions mandatory.

A temporary overstaffing as well as an open, self-critical learning organizational culture is essential to reduce deficiencies, and to ensure quick and decisive action when risks materialize.

Even in a captive Shared Services environment, it is very important to analyze and observe potential ***legal and/or tax restrictions*** prior to starting transitions. Such restrictions may, for example, involve a general ban on near- and off-shoring activities, data protection regulations, strict local documentation and archiving requirements, or a certain quota of native workers to be considered in administrative processes.

If there is a 'go' to continue, a Service Level Agreement (SLA), – a contractual framework governing scope of services, performance indicators, compensation principles (e.g. Cost Plus Method, FTE based charging vs. transactional prices, and true-up logic, if applicable), invoicing and payment as well as cooperation and service management rules – ensures the necessary clarity between the parties involved and delivers the proper and sound documentation for tax purposes. Tax authorities assess intercompany transactions and corresponding transfer prices in the same way as for independent 'third' parties 'dealing at arm's length'[16], which is why a clear and unambiguous SLA is required. Next to the Comparable Uncontrolled Price and the Resale Price Minus Method, the most common pricing methodology in the Shared Service industry is the Cost Plus Method[17]. Cost Plus means that the fully loaded costs by the internal service provider are to be increased by an appropriate mark-up being comparable to that which is used on the external market.

It is highly recommended to agree upon group-wide applicable standards regarding SLA and transfer price documentation – ideally supported by common IT tools (e.g. a database solution with suitable approval workflows) – to minimize tax risks, but also practically to avoid unproductive internal discussions on the actual wording of the service contracts. As a rule, only specific local laws should be accepted as tolerable deviations from the standard.

Professional ***communications and change management*** is another important management area of transition projects. Sometimes considered as a negligible 'soft factor' only, target-oriented and frequent communications is key to success, in particular, bearing in mind that transition or transfer is always linked to 'giving away' certain tasks, responsibilities and resources. Thus, the underlying emotional attitude is rather critical, reluctant and defensive. Therefore, stakeholder analyses and individually tailored communications are crucial to manage their expectations and to meet their requirements. Early, true and honest communications helps to gain the necessary confidence and support from the stakeholders.

Different ways of communication should be considered including face-to-face meetings, phone calls, e-conferencing, e-mailing, web sites, as well as 'traditional' hardcopy documents and binders[18]. Content-wise, announcements to stakeholders, project reports, informational and explanatory presentations, minutes, good/best practice sharing, feedback and lessons learned documentation are part of the communications portfolio[19].

3.5 Supporting Methodologies and Tools

Of the various supporting methodologies that can be found in project management literature[20] and practice, the ***'degree of implementation'*** (DI) approach shall be discussed here. Specifically, the "Transition Guide"[21], which was developed for the planning, implementation, monitoring and controlling of transition projects, will be explained.

16 Cf. *OECD* (2010), p. 5.

17 Cf. *OECD* (2010), p. 21 and 29 et seqq.

18 Cf. *PMI PMBOK* (2009), p. 244 et seqq.

19 Cf. *PMI PMBOK* (2009), p. 260 et seqq.

20 Cf. e.g. the *PMI PMBOK* (2008).

21 Cf. *SIEMENS GLOBAL SHARED SERVICES* (2010).

The DI method provides a scale, e.g. from DI1 to DI5, for the successful execution and completion of major project steps or even on a milestone or sub-step level. In this way, it is possible to plan and track the progress of single projects or – in the aggregated view – of the entire program.

In the aforementioned Transition Guide such DIs are more specifically defined by the events 'project started', 'process analyses done', 'staff recruitment (and training) done', 'work-shadowing done', 'stabilization phase completed'. The more detailed milestones on the level below are shown in figure 1. By permanent tracking, visualization and communication of DIs, significant issues, particularly delays, attract the necessary awareness within the project team and on the stakeholder side. The need for mitigation measures becomes obvious. Further, ideally the same DI logic method can be referred to while determining whether or not planned savings have materialized. It is only at the completion of the stabilization phase, when parallel-staffing ends, that savings are realized.

A program comprising of a high number of single transition projects should not be underestimated with regard to overall coordination efforts. Even ignoring the additional complexity of each individual project, such a program is to be considered as 'mass business' calling for the application of supportive IT tools.

In the case of the Finance Bundling program, the SSO defined the requirements and features for such an ***IT tool*** called '***Transition Coordination Kit***'[22], as follows:

- Database with a user-friendly interface offering the possibility to download data into spreadsheets for further analyses,
- administration of reference and master data per entity (in scope and addressable in the 'internal market'),
- time, resource and ramp-up cost planning per entity, Center and Cluster,
- tracking of milestones, FTE ramp-up and corresponding costs,
- determination of the internal market penetration, and
- management reporting as well as documentation.

Based on these requirements, the relevant entry masks, features and reports can be derived, realized and applied on a monthly basis to administrate, track and steer the program.

For *Siemens* GSS purposes, reports that turned out to be helpful and were continuously used on a monthly basis, were:

- A visualized overall Program Status Report (e.g. using a waterfall diagram),
- Cluster Transition Status Report (comprising function, region/area, lead, traffic light, progress entity transfer, milestones achieved, next steps with due dates, required decisions, critical issues and risks), and
- Ramp-up Status Report per Center.

---

22 Cf. *SIEMENS GLOBAL SHARED SERVICES* (2011), p. 114 et seqq.

DI1	DI2	DI3	DI4	DI5
On-site kick-off held	**Process analyses done**	**Staff recruitment done**	**Work-shadowing done**	**Stabilization phase completed**
'When the key team members are nominated and the initial kick-off for the entity is held'	'When all relevant as-is analyses (base linings) are performed and project plan is finalized'	'When the SSO Center staff is recruited and transition readiness for the entity is reached'	'When the donating entity is ready to transfer tasks to receiving SSO units'	'When the donating entity transferred all agreed tasks to receiving SSO units'
Milestones: ➢ SSO transition manager(s) for the entity is/are nominated ➢ On-site kick-off held ➢ Required contractual framework agreed and signed (e.g. Consulting/Project Management Contract, Service Level Agreement; minimum Letter of Intent)	Milestones: ➢ IT analysis conducted ➢ Headcount analysis completed ➢ Process analysis performed ➢ Volume analysis performed ➢ Control requirements (RIC, SOA) analyzed ➢ Gap analysis done and process adjustments defined ➢ Work shadowing plan defined and aligned with customer	Milestones: ➢ SSO Center staff assigned, recruitment done and new employees on board ➢ Transition readiness achieved	Milestones: ➢ Brief work shadowing kick-off held ➢ IT infrastructure access established and tested ➢ Fallback scenario incl. process documentation defined ➢ Work shadowing done, "go-live"	Milestones: ➢ End of stabilization phase reached ➢ SLA finally fixed (e.g. attachments on headcount or volume/price per transaction) ➢ Sign-off of transition project

Figure 1: Transition Guide on Entity/Single Project Level[23]

[23] Cf. *Siemens Global Shared Services* (2010). Model generalized and adjusted accordingly. With regard to abbreviations used, refer to the respective section at the end of this article.

The *Finance Bundling Case Studies* shown in figure 2 and 3 provide further practical insights from project managers, who successfully executed numerous accounting related transition projects in the Clusters CEE and NWE.

Case Study 'Finance Bundling in Cluster CEE': Challenges and Success Factors

As part of *Siemens' **Finance Bundling program in Cluster CEE*** (Central and Eastern Europe), the transactional accounting activities of 33 entities – all of different size and complexity – were transferred and bundled into the GSS Shared Services Center in the Czech Republic, which operates from two locations (Prague and Ostrava). The transitions were done between 2010 and 2012 and focused on *Siemens* entities in 11 countries with different languages, businesses, processes and ERP systems as well as distinct legal regulations (the target group included EU and non-EU countries, some with MTO requirements). Accounting processes in scope were accounts payable, accounts receivable, inter-company and intra-company business, master data management, cash and bank, fixed assets, general ledger, and closing and reporting. During peak times, 3 project managers/consultants from HQ and 10 Center transition managers were involved. Approximately 170 employees were 'ramped-up' into the growing GSS organization, trained for 2–3 months and integrated into one of 12 new operational teams which were established to provide the appropriate services.

Major challenges faced during the project were in meeting the specific language requirements (e.g. Hebrew, Turkish or Hungarian) of customers of this Cluster, as well as the heterogeneous process and IT landscape. An additional complexity came from the multiple ERP system or release changes that had to be accommodated.

Key factors of success included the program management, i.e. the strict adherence to the overall project plan. Deep dives into the specific processes and IT systems of the donating entities to fully understand the end-to-end process and how best to design the Activity Split enabled optimal work-shadowing and takeover. On the receiving GSS side, professional and therefore effective recruiting processes were essential; in particular, in those cases where specific language and accounting skills were urgently required. Last but not least, overall close collaboration and permanent communication amongst all parties involved, i.e. customer, governance, Shared Services Center and central program management team, based on clearly defined roles and responsibilities proved to be indispensable for the successful execution of such a complex program.

Figure 2: Case Study 'Finance Bundling in Cluster CEE'[24]

[24] BRUCH/SCHMIDT (2012).

Case Study 'Finance Bundling in Cluster NWE': Challenges and Success Factors

Cluster NWE (North West Europe) covers the countries from Ireland and Great Britain in the West to Poland and the Baltic states in the East, encompassing in total 11 countries with 10 different languages.

Being part of the Finance Bundling (FB) program from 2009 to 2012, Cluster NWE was one of the two pilot Clusters used to prove and to align the overall approach of the intended project blueprint and cornerstones. 62 separate business entities with more than 30 different ERP systems and processes were in scope and were considered as ***major challenges***.

In order to exploit specific synergies, e.g. with already existing service structures, it was agreed to render transactional accounting services out of several Centers; entities in the UK and Ireland were bundled into the GSS Center in India for cost and language reasons, and all other entities with a few exceptions were bundled into the GSS Center in the Czech Republic, being the largest service provider for Cluster NWE.

Due to this location strategy, more intensive coordination as well as clear project structures with defined roles and responsibilities were required. In addition to the project teams in each GSS Center, which were responsible – amongst others – for the recruiting and training of the future service staff, a so-called Transition Project Team (TPT) for Cluster NWE was established in the GSS Headquarter to secure the overall coordination and adherence to the FB project blueprint and time schedule. All deviations and escalation issues and the communication to key players of Cluster NWE (e.g. Cluster CFO and Head of Accounting) and to the central FB program management team were managed by the TPT. This was done in order to ensure one consistent approach and course of action. Trustful relationships and open communication ensured that all parties pulled together and could quickly break down barriers. Daily meetings during the training phase on a service staff level, weekly review meetings on an entity level and monthly status meetings on the Cluster level provided the opportunity to discuss and settle issues quickly. During the peak transition time more than 10 transition projects on an entity level were running concurrently.

One other key factor for success was the uniform project flow as defined by the 'Transition Guide' and its requirements referring to the project plan, responsibilities, quality gates, forms and mandatory documents. This guideline was applied to each single transition project and was one of the cornerstones of the overall project's success.

Summarizing the above points, the ***key factors to success*** were the structured and uniform execution as well as the effective cooperation and communication between all parties involved.

Figure 3: Case Study 'Finance Bundling in Cluster NWE[25]

[25] DÖRING/GUSTAFSSON-KLEIN (2012).

4 Key Success Factors

Based on numerous Lessons Learned workshops held with the many affected parties of the *Siemens* Finance Bundling program, ***five key success factors*** of a global transition initiative could be identified. These workshops were held at the entity, country and Cluster/business unit levels, and involved informal discussions and structured interviews with project managers, Center heads, subject matter experts, customers and representatives of the governance function as well as customer surveys.

4.1 Clear Mandate and Agreed Guiding Principles

In general, the roll-out of Shared Services in a multinational enterprise could follow an individual 'sales approach', in which the SSO negotiates on an individual basis with each single entity or organizational/reporting unit. The alternative is a 'mandatory approach' on an aggregated regional Cluster or global level. This mandate should be communicated from the outset as non-negotiable by top management, and should be clear about the need and rationale behind the establishment of a SSO. This article, which presents the example of a multinational enterprise undergoing more than 300 single transitions into a SSO, confirms the critical importance of a clear mandate and the development of board endorsed guiding principles to set overarching goals for the entire program.

The *Siemens* Finance Bundling ***'Guiding and Key Design Principles'*** provided an unambiguous vision and comprised the following decisions:[26]

- All transactional (accounting) activities shall be transferred to the SSO.
- The SSO as the service provider shall decide on outsourcing and location options.
- Global process ownership shall be with the SSO for (sub)processes assigned to the SSO (in line with central governance framework).
- The SSO shall perform the service scope and achieve full service quality within an agreed timeframe.
- Transition and ongoing service delivery shall be monitored by applying agreed Key Performance Indicators (KPIs) to measure quality, reliability, and cost.

Having a clearly communicated mandate alleviated the need to hold separate time-consuming discussions on hundreds of individual entities. Long-lasting debates would have prevented the entire organization from making a bold move towards savings resulting from significant scalable volume and bundling effects.

---

26 Cf. *SIEMENS GLOBAL SHARED SERVICES* (2011), p. 41.

As a consequence, the recommendation is to clearly communicate the mandate, the guiding principles, targets and overall program scope and apply the given rules consequently. Exceptions should only be granted for legal, governance and/or regulatory reasons[27] and should be approved by a defined body, e.g. a steering committee with high-level representatives. Continuous commitment and support by top management and the governance function helps to keep the momentum of the kick-off phase.

4.2 Defined Service Scope

In the case of the Finance Bundling program in the planning and preparation phase, the relevant ***'Activity Split'*** was developed, dividing and assigning the responsibilities for sub-processes to the parties involved, i.e. the SSO, the country, the Cluster (region) and Sector (business).

Taking the Accounts Payable service line as an example, the sub-processes (on level one) were clearly mapped and assigned, as follows:[28]

Master data processing (accounting view)	– SSO
Imaging and archiving	– SSO
Verification and posting of invoices	– SSO
Reconciliation (vendor and General Ledger)	– SSO
Payment release / payment run	– SSO
Assure sales tax requirements	– SSO
Local regulations in addition to central group guidelines	– Country
Control process clarifications (incl. governance)	– Cluster

The aforementioned formal ***'Deviation Request and Approval Process'*** is – even on the process level – helpful to foster the further harmonization of the accounting processes on a global level and to facilitate later process optimization and automation.

4.3 Qualified and Committed Team

To be able to handle a program with a high number of single transitions, a sufficient number of qualified and motivated employees is required. This statement is as equally relevant to the central program management and the transition managers from HQ and the Delivery Centers as it is to the newly hired and trained operational teams in the Centers. A combination of dedicated, internationally experienced and team-minded project managers and subject matter experts (e.g. closing experts) in HQ and Centers is required. They should cover – as a team – broad and deep accounting knowledge as well as company specific business, process, and IT know-how. Further, a proficiency in required project management methods and tools is crucial, not to mention the need to have the relevant languages covered.

---

27 Cf. *Siemens Corporate Finance* (2011), p. 13.

28 Cf. *Siemens Global Shared Services* (2011), p. 44.

With regards to the operational, customer-facing staff a systematic, fast, but professional recruiting and training process is needed to get the right people on board. As a general rule, it is recommended to pursue a policy of deliberate and controlled overstaffing which is reduced after successful stabilization of the operations. Generally speaking, a temporary overstaffing in the first months helps to compensate for productivity gaps, required additional trainings as well as for attrition.

Further, in order to foster and speed-up newcomers' progress along the learning curve, the application of a "nucleus concept" is recommended in the Centers, i.e. one or two experienced team leads start with a number of newcomers and move to the next transition project after successful stabilization.

Projects in a difficult and complex environment are always accompanied by conflicts, disappointments and times of frustration. Proactive change management, intensive communication, team building measures, open exchange of knowledge and experiences among the team members, mutual support and target oriented incentives mitigate such hurdles and setbacks.

4.4 Effective Transition Management

In the case of a global transition program, the complexity and barriers to success should not be underestimated. Only with a target-oriented and systematic management approach – on the program and single transition project level – a successful realization will be feasible.

Firstly, an effective and streamlined program organization staffed with qualified and committed people as described above is needed, including a program management office which provides guidance and support and ensures overall integration and coordination.

Secondly, the overall program requires a diligent and thorough planning, a consistent and time-focused roll-out plan which leverages the experiences gained during the pilots, and resolute monitoring and controlling of the progress and the implementation quality.

Thirdly, the competing program/project constraints of scope, quality, time, resources, costs/payback, and risks are to be managed bearing in mind the leading strategy of the company as well as the concrete program targets.

Finally, professional methods and tools should be utilized, notably helping to track the transition progress, the ramp-up of required resources and associated costs.

4.5 Continuous Communication

Systematic communications is of utmost relevance for the project success. Identified stakeholders need to be frequently addressed in an individually tailored way in order to manage their expectations and meet their requirements focusing on the SSO's ability to execute the transitions appropriately, to ramp-up people in time and with the right skills, to ensure the quality in later operations, and to finally meet the savings targets.

Accordingly, aspects to be communicated to this audience could include – amongst others – a program mission, targets, guiding principles, schedules, regular reporting on overall status, transition progress, ramp-up, costs, quality in operations, current issues and risks, supporting communication packages, project hand books, operating instructions and the like.

The main target of the aforementioned measures is to win the confidence and support of the various affected stakeholders via the provision of true and honest communications. Ultimately, the success of communications and expectations management has a large bearing on the overall success of global transition projects.

5 Outlook

Bundling during the 'lift and drop' phase is just the first step on the journey towards a stable, reliable, competitive and accepted SSO. After having leveraged cost competitive Center locations and the first bundling effects, the important next step – as part of the 'change' phase – is to systematically analyze, benchmark, harmonize, further optimize and automate the underlying processes. This needs to be done – in close cooperation with the customer and the governance function – by moving from a sub-process view to an end-to-end perspective utilizing state-of-the art enabling technologies.

Abbreviations and Selected Terms

AFS	Accounting & Finance Services
CEE	'Cluster' Central Eastern Europe, encompassing Austria with regional HQ functions and 18 other countries, thereof 11 included in the GSS scope
Center	Short for 'Shared Services Center' or 'Delivery Center' (*Siemens* term)
Cluster	Regional organization within *Siemens* group comprising a certain number of countries set up to optimize infrastructure functions and business support, e.g. CEE or NWE
Cost Plus Method	Transfer pricing approach commonly used in Shared Services business meaning that fully loaded costs at the internal service provider are charged by adding an appropriate mark-up
DI	Degree of Implementation

Donating entity	Legal entity or organizational/accounting unit handing over certain administrative tasks to a Shared Services Organization (or to a Cluster or country organization)
ERP	Enterprise Resource Planning
Finance Bundling	Comprehensive program in the areas of accounting, controlling, taxes and financial services to re-shape, harmonize and optimize the worldwide finance functions within *Siemens* group; focus in this article is the transfer of transactional accounting tasks to the in-house Shared Services Organization
FTE	Full-time Equivalent, measuring unit for the workforce of one employee
FY	Fiscal or Financial Year
GSS	Global Shared Services, the internal shared services provider for *Siemens* group, rendering a standardized global catalogue of services covering mainly the areas of Accounting and Finance, Human Resources, and Supply Chain Management
HQ	Headquarters
HRS	Human Resources Services
IT	Information Technology
KPI(s)	Key Performance Indicator(s)
MTO	Money Transfer Obligations
NWE	'Cluster' North-West Europe, comprising the United Kingdom – fulfilling regional HQ functions – as well as 10 further countries
OECD	Organization for Economic Co-operation and Development
PM	Project Management (or Program Management comprising a larger number of single projects)
PMBOK	Project Management Body of Knowledge
PMI	Project Management Institute
PMO	Project Management Office, i.e. centralized organizational unit providing project management support functions

Ramp-up	Describes the development phase and corresponding activities of a Shared Services Organization when work is being transferred from one or more donating entities, requiring a corresponding increase of the service provider's internal resources in order to handle the additional volume
Receiving entity	Legal entity or organizational/accounting unit, regularly a Shared Services Organization (or a Cluster or country organization), receiving certain administrative tasks from the donating entity
RIC	Risk and Internal Controls
SCMS	Supply Chain Management Services
Sector	Organizational structure within *Siemens* group being globally responsible for a defined business scope; divisions and business units represent organizational subunits of a Sector
SG&A	Selling, General and Administrative Expenses
SLA	Service Level Agreement, tax-relevant contract between the Shared Services Organization's legal entity and the legal entity of the customer ordering respective services
SOA	Sarbanes-Oxley-Act, officially titled the Public Company Accounting Reform and Investor Protection Act of 2002
SSO	Shared Services Organization(s)
Work shadowing	Systematic process of transferring knowledge from the 'donating entity' to the 'receiving entity'

References

BRUCH, C./SCHMIDT, R. (2012): Lessons Learned From the Transition Projects in Cluster CEE, in: *SIEMENS GLOBAL SHARED SERVICES* (Ed.), Internal Paper, Munich 2012.

DÖRING, M./GUSTAFSSON-KLEIN, J.-C. (2012): Lessons Learned From the Transition Projects in Cluster NWE, in: *SIEMENS GLOBAL SHARED SERVICES* (Ed.), Internal Paper, Munich 2012.

OECD (2010): Review of Comparability and of Profit Methods: Revision of Chapters I-III of the Transfer Pricing Guidelines, Paris 2010.

PAMPER, R./FISCHER, T. M. (2007): Shared Service Center Controlling, in: *KPMG* (Ed.), Ergebnisse einer empirischen Untersuchung [Results of an Empirical Study], Hamburg/ Nuremberg 2007.

PROJECT MANAGEMENT INSTITUTE (2008): Project Management Body of Knowledge (PMBOK Guide), 4th Ed., Atlanta (GA) 2008.

SIEMENS GLOBAL SHARED SERVICES (2010) (Ed.), Transition Guide, Internal Work Instruction, 3rd Ed., Munich 2010.

SIEMENS CORPORATE FINANCE (2011) (Ed.): Cluster Finance Bundling Project Book, Internal Paper, Munich 2011.

SIEMENS GLOBAL SHARED SERVICES (2011) (Ed.): Finance Bundling @ GSS Project Handbook, Internal Work Instruction, 5th Ed., Munich 2011.

Managing the Growth from a Shared Services Center Perspective

Interview with *DAN NOVAK*

Siemens, s.r.o., Global Shared Services

This interview is conducted with Dan Novak who is heading the Accounting & Finance Services Center in the Czech Republic and is also responsible for the business administration tasks of the two locations in Prague and Ostrava. Before he joined the Siemens Shared Services organization, he was working as CFO for a large Gas Turbine company within the Sector Energy. Thus, he also knows the business from the angle of those to whom the Siemens Shared Services organization provides the services.

At the point of writing, Dan Novak's daily business is primarily related to professionally manage the last miles of the worldwide bundling project "Finance Bundling" and is responsible for the service delivery to the customers from mainly North West Europe and also Central Eastern Europe. The focus of this interview will be the development phase of "lift-drop" and thus the realization of project Finance Bundling hereby especially taking the Center-perspective into consideration and the systematic management of the growth resulting from the bundling initiative.

By way of introduction, can you provide some main facts on the Siemens Shared Services Center (SSC) in Czech Republic and the role within the entire Siemens Shared Services Organization (SSO)?

The *Siemens* SSC is represented in the Czech Republic with two locations in Prague and Ostrava. With more than 1,000 Shared Services employees, this Center is one of the main Shared Services locations worldwide. The Center offers a broad range of services and covers all Business Lines of the *Siemens* SSO: "Accounting & Finance Services", "Human Resources" and "Supply Chain Management". More than 20 languages are actively used in daily business and amongst these e.g. Hebrew, Bosnian, Russian and Finnish. This broad range of languages demonstrates the customer orientation of this center serving more than 100 internal customers worldwide.

The role of specifically the financial Shared Services Center in the Czech Republic is to successfully manage the worldwide bundling project, ensure the hiring of additional resources and a smooth service delivery. The SSC in Prague is considered as one of the key players within the bundling project due to the fact that accounting tasks primarily from the Clusters in North West Europe and Central Eastern Europe are transferred to the SSC in Prague. The overall goal from a SSC's perspective is, that at the end, the customer will not realize a difference since a proper process is in place. Within the internal service business, a positive sign for high customer satisfaction is usually, if there is no noise at all.

In which way was the Siemens Shared Services Center in Czech Republic, specifically the Business Line "Accounting & Finance Services" affected by considerable growth?

As indicated before, the SSC in the Czech Republic, took over a main role in the biggest financial project *Siemens* has ever experienced. The *Siemens* SSO, specifically the business line Accounting & Finance Services (AFS) received the mandate by the *Siemens* Board to take over transactional accounting processes that were previously handled locally by the local entities. The transactional accounting activities were all related to the areas of Accounts Payables, Accounts Receivables or Closing and Reporting. These processes were bundled in the SSCs and the Centers had to recruit professionals offering the necessary language and accounting skills to take over the work. Hence, the SSC in the Czech Republic has grown to a great extent.

The goals of project Finance Bundling are to build a lean and flexible administration function, to provide faster, more efficient, less complex and highly transparent processes and to improve the overall cost position of the *Siemens* financial organization.

Finance Bundling started in 2010 and will be finalized by the end of FY 2012, having currently transferred accounting processes of more than 300 *Siemens* accounting units/entities. More than 200 employees had to be recruited for accounting tasks in the SSC in Prague and Ostrava and more than 50 new customers had to be served. Further, the language scope had to be expanded by additional 16 languages and at the same time a smooth delivery of all running services had to be ensured.

Which challenges had to be addressed when managing the growth?

The major challenges that had to be managed by the SSC in the Czech Republic were to professionally handle the transitions and at the same time guarantee a timely, transparent and high-quality delivery of services that have been recently transferred into the Shared Services environment or that were already previously handled by the SSC.

Operative challenges were in the first place the high number of accounting employees that had to be recruited, professionally on-boarded and trained. The recruiting was absolutely key to the overall success of the project, since the challenge was to find new Shared Services employees offering appropriate accounting knowledge and at the same time speaking a specific language needed in the Center.

The people aspect was definitely most challenging, since especially in the area of processes with a direct interaction to the customer, communication and language skills as well as a detailed understanding of the customers' business and environment are indispensable for a smooth transition and handling of the processes. Since the Shared Services business is driven mainly by people it is elementary to put a special focus on this area when managing the growth.

Due to project Finance Bundling it was now up to the Shared Services employees in the centers to handle the tasks that have been previously executed by the business units. Most of these new employees are young people, graduated from university, speaking multiple languages and taking this opportunity as a potential first step of their career. Especially those employees with customer contact need to have certain skills to successfully interact with the customers. Not to forget, that it is the same customer who only recently had to hand over a certain part of work to the SSC and is now a critical partner towards the service execution in the Shared Services environment. Some of the characteristics a Shared Services employee should offer are interaction skills, empathy, reliability, sensibility and of course a business-specific know-how. Closely linked to the people aspect is the motivation, since it is of utmost importance to keep the new Shared Services employees committed and engaged in what they are doing. This is definitely only possible with the help of respective human resource initiatives, such as training, promotions, job rotations to e.g. other SSCs etc.

When growing to such a great extent in only a limited period of time it is entail to put a special focus on the people side of the business to make sure the main success factor in the Shared Services business is professionally been taken care of.

How were these challenges managed in the Center - from a people and process perspective?

To guarantee a professional transition of specific accounting services from the donating entity to the SSC in Prague, a transition project team of experienced project managers and subject matter experts of the Center and also from headquarters was established. The members of this team had the common goal to analyze customers' processes, learn and document them and then transfer them into the SSC environment. When it comes to essential skills for this job, all members of the team agreed that without a high degree of communication skills as well as psychological sensitivity, the transition projects could not have been successfully realized. Unquestionably, taking over work from colleagues in the donating units and moving it to the own Shared Services base is definitely not an easy task and requires a specific intuition, since collaboration with the donating entity is elementary to gain an understanding of the current processes, their specifics and "own" way of handling.

Referring to the recruiting challenge it was highly important to use the company-internal Human Resources department and also the temporary support by a local recruiting agency helping to find the right people. One of the success factors of the recruiting was to hire young university graduates and give them the opportunity to learn the key ac-counting processes in corresponding trainings. With the help of the recruiting agencies, those people were identified, that already bring with them specific language skills. Obviously, it was then crucial to have a clearly structured and well-organized training concept in place. Actually the SSC in the Czech Republic developed an integrated training methodology that every new employee had to successfully go through to build up the necessary knowledge about Siemens in general, the SSO itself, the distinct customer they would work for and of course the precise accounting process such as Accounts Payable, Accounts Receivable or Closing and Reporting.

Not to forget, the existing service delivery had to be ensured at the same time. This means, key players had to be on both sides – supporting the take-over of new services and also ensuring a smooth service delivery of existing business. More precisely, people with a true commitment, high motivation and process expertise are needed on both sides to meet these challenges. This implies a professional people management there-by knowing exactly which skills are most reasonably placed in a specific process. Therefore, small teams with managers close to the employees had to be established strongly collaborating with each other to efficiently place resources were needed.

If you knew then what you know now, can you give one piece of advice to someone embarking on a similar journey?

From a management perspective, an important advice is to ensure a transparent and precise role description and corresponding allocation of tasks. Since a healthy balance of process know-how and accounting expertise in the operative business and also in the transition projects needs to be guaranteed in order to on-board the various new employees.

Collaboration and communication can be considered as the key to such a big project radically transforming the *Siemens* finance organization. Open discussions with the donating entity, the Cluster involved and also the colleagues on the Shared Services side are another advice for all colleagues on a similar journey.

Further, before realizing project Finance Bundling a Cluster pilot project was executed. It was an elementary step that the AFS process experts learned from these pilots before actually dealing with more than 300 transitions of project Finance Bundling in total. Cluster North West Europe was chosen as a pilot and first positive experiences were made with the transition of accounting processes of the regional company Sweden. Definitely, the key learnings were to act in a highly customer-focused and communicative way and show competency in understanding not only the business but also the "people side" of it.

After having successfully handled the growth phase, what is next for GSS AFS in Czech Republic?

Following the strategy of "lift-drop", then "change" and then "enhance and innovate", the next step after having lifted work from the *Siemens* entities and dropped it into the Shared Services environment, is to initiate the "change". For the SSC in the Czech Republic this means to strongly focus on the optimization of the accounting processes.

The main levers for this "change" are harmonization, standardization, and – where possible – automation. All this will be realized with the help of efficient best practice sharing. During project Finance Bundling the AFS employees were able to gain detailed process experience and now it is time to use this experience and start optimizing existing procedures. With the help of the process communities, experts of a special accounting area are virtually grouped together and exchanging ideas of how to make the SSO's processes more efficient, faster and transparent to ultimately realize cost savings.

This "change" phase is driven by the PIA-program which stands for Process Improvements for Accounting. The program comprises 8 projects in the areas of Accounts Payable, Accounts Receivable and Closing & Reporting set up to optimize specific accounting processes, such as the reduction of urgent payments or the harmonization of bank statements.

For the *Siemens* SSC in the Czech Republic PIA offers the opportunity to prove to be more than a transactional service provider, since detailed process knowledge and consulting on how to optimize existing processes is crucial for this phase. For all employees in the SSC PIA is a challenging and interesting next step to show their commitment and motivation to execute PIA in the same professional manner as done for project Finance Bundling. After having stabilized the processes transferred into Shared Services environment and having efficiently optimized these processes the third phase "enhance and innovate" will be initiated step by step and in close alignment with all relevant stakeholders, in particular governance and customers.

The third phase provides new challenging opportunities to all Shared Services employees to deal with new services, e.g. data consolidation and reporting as a preparation task before handing it back to the customer who will then execute the actual controlling.

To conclude, a SSC especially the one in the Czech Republic is constantly undergoing some kind of change along every relevant development phases from "lift-drop", to "change" and after that "enhance and innovate". It is essential to keep in mind, that this business is mainly people driven and that is exactly where the key focus should lie to make the changes happen.

Mr. Novak, thanks for this interview.

Part 2:

"Change" – Get to the Next Level of Shared Services Maturity and Productivity

Process Improvements for Accounting – A Systematic Approach

OTTO WENDLAND

Siemens AG, Global Shared Services

Executive Summary

Taking over transactional accounting activities from more than 300 legal entities worldwide and their subsequent bundling in the captive Service Centers was just the first step of the *Siemens*' Shared Services Organization on its evolutionary journey. The following 3-step strategy was consequently adopted:

- **'Lift and drop'** transactional tasks 'as they are' in order to leverage a cost-competitive global footprint, bundling effects and economies of scale;
- '**Change**' activities, which are now centralized in order to standardize and start automating the underlying processes to further improve quality and productivity;
- **'Enhance and innovate'** the processes, reach an even higher degree in automation and identify new 'products' and business opportunities.

Due to the fact that highly diversified multinational companies exhibit huge varieties in business processes, as reflected in multiple IT systems, the harmonization and optimization of the associated accounting processes is a real challenge but also a great opportunity to exploit further savings. A systematic approach for the launching of a Process Improvement Program like **PIA – Process Improvements for Accounting** is therefore required to overcome technical and psychological challenges.

This article briefly describes this approach, including recommendations on supporting guiding principles, the program set-up with its roles and responsibilities, practical hints for the identification and selection of potential improvement projects as well as a 'short list' of specific initiatives in the accounting environment promising a sustainable short-term impact on quality and savings.

1 Driving Change in a Shared Services Organization

Changes can happen either in reaction of an event or can be a pro-active step. In the business environment when changes are happening constantly, one of the goals could be to increase quality and reduce costs and/or make an organization leaner and less complex. Multinational companies have the advantage to generate sufficient capital and resources to have the ability to invest in greater changes affecting the whole organization. Smaller companies, on the contrary, might have some restrictions with that regard but are usually more flexible and less complex when it comes to the implementation of change.

In the following, the implementation of a change program in the Shared Services environment will be described, referring to *Siemens*[1] Shared Services Organization (SSO) and its process improvement initiatives in the area of accounting.

A Shared Services Organization is a (internal) service provider of support in the field of transactional processes. Through a transfer of these activities to a SSO, the customer or also called the 'donating entity' can benefit from cost savings through labor arbitrage, economies of scale and scope, an increase of quality and transparency over time and – last but not least – from strongly focusing on its core business without being distracted by managing administrative support processes on top of daily business.

Siemens' captive Shared Services Organization is divided into three main Business Lines: Accounting & Finance Services (AFS), Supply Chain Management Services (SCMS), and Human Resources Services (HRS), whereas the following article will focus on the first one, AFS. This Business Line made a huge step forward during the years 2010 - 2012 in terms of growth and customer acceptance.

1.1 Organizational Framework

With hundreds of legal entities and locations in more than 190 countries, *Siemens* is represented all over the world and the organization is a conglomerate of many individual structures

Siemens is, however, not only multifaceted in its organizational structure but also because of its portfolio – from Drive Technologies to Fossil Power Generation, and from Diagnostics to Smart Grid and Building Technologies in order to name only 5 of its 19 Divisions. *Siemens* grew enormously since its establishment 165 years ago. Specifically in the last decades, *Siemens* extended its business in various areas around the world by organic growth and also through mergers and acquisitions.

The consequences out of this plurality are heterogeneous processes and IT landscapes. Considering the different business areas and functions of the legal entities, this may definitely be expected when it comes to production processes and supporting IT systems. However, these differences are equally notable in administrative activities, such as procurement or accounting and finance mirroring the variety of underlying business processes.

In 2008, *Siemens* re-shaped its global structure, assigning the business competencies to the Sectors - Energy, Healthcare, Industry, and – later – Infrastructure & Cities and bundled its regional sales organization and infrastructure cross-country in 'Clusters'. In the course of this re-organization, the company-wide project 'Finance Bundling' was started aiming on the one hand to harmonize and strengthen regional governance and controlling, on the other hand to transfer defined transactional accounting tasks from the local entities to the internal Shared Services Organization and bundle them in its cost-competitive locations.

---

1 Founded 165 years ago and supporting its customers in more than 190 countries, *Siemens* is a diversified global player providing innovative products, technologies, solutions and comprehensive know-how in the areas of industry, energy, healthcare, and infrastructure.

Finance Bundling is part of a medium-term plan of AFS to make the Accounting & Finance environment within *Siemens* leaner and subsequently to harmonize, standardize, improve and automate processes. The strategic roadmap of this project as well as the major targets of each phase along the roadmap will be briefly described in the following section.

1.2 Strategic Roadmap and Major Objectives

The strategic roadmap for *Siemens*' captive Shared Services Organization was agreed with the *Siemens* Executive Board comprising the following three phases over a period of 5-years: During the first phase, the "**lift-drop**" **phase** processes were transferred as-is from the donating entity to the receiving entity[2]. As-is means the *Siemens* Shared Services Center (SSC) took over the processes as they had been processed by the donating entity until transition. Having the complexity of the overall *Siemens* structure in mind, for the SSO this implied a take-over of various procedures managed with the help of different IT tools. The main objective of this phase of the roadmap was to transfer the activities which were in scope and to guarantee service continuity by stabilizing the processes on the SSO side. Processes in scope were Accounts Receivables (AR), Accounts Payable (AP), Master Data Management (MD), Intercompany Clearing (ICC), Cash and Bank (C&B), General Ledger (GL) as well as Closing and Reporting (C&R). In some local entities with still substantial manual processes certain solutions or workflows had to be implemented upfront because otherwise the concept of transferring activities to a SSC outside the country would not have been feasible, e.g. the processing of invoices requiring either the original document or a scan[3].

After a successful transfer of the transactional tasks of the accounting processes the second phase, the **"change" phase** is initiated. As stated above, processes are usually very heterogeneous at the moment of transition. Therefore in order to achieve – besides previous labor arbitrage and economies of scale - further quality benchmarks with additional cost reductions, process improvements, standardization and automation have to be initiated. Moreover, the near- and off-shore set-up will be reviewed and where applicable additional back-office structures may be set up to achieve further labor arbitrage and economy of scale. This requires, however, a high degree of process harmonization.

The third phase, the **"enhance and innovate" phase**, will be a continuation of the previous phase, in terms of further enhancing and automating processes. Besides, this phase of the roadmap will also consider the extension of the current portfolio offered by the *Siemens* SSO. This might comprise an extension towards more expertise and specialized processes.

In the following pages, the focus will be on the "change" phase.

---

2 The donating entity in this case refers to a *Siemens* legal entity transferring transactional services to a Delivery Center, i.e. the receiving entity, which is also part of a *Siemens* legal entity.

3 In many countries the original invoices have to remain in the country. A sending of the originals by mail to the SSC for entering it into the system and then sending it back for archiving would have been either not possible due to legal regulations or too expensive and too time-consuming. With the implementation of a scanning solution, original invoices can be scanned in the country of origin, without the need to leave the country, and then sent in an electronic format to the SSC which can then process the invoice without delay. Consequently, processes were not, yet, harmonized but had to be shaped in a way to make them transferrable outside the country without complicating the performance.

1.3 Barriers and Challenges

The "change" phase brings along certain barriers and challenges. One major challenge lies in the organization itself. As described above, *Siemens* is a very complex and diversified organization and the processes and IT landscape are highly heterogeneous. Even if it is the same IT system, the releases can be different as well. Due to the fact that processes are often bound to the underlying IT system, processes can be highly different and harmonization thus becomes a challenge.

The differences arising from the business environment are also reflected in the stakeholders' opinions on certain change initiatives. A conflict may arise, when an entity runs a very specifically customized IT-system, which does not fit to others. Changes in processes and IT systems as well as organizational adjustments are therefore not always welcome, specifically when it comes to solutions which offer to standardize and harmonize existing structures and cannot reflect the individual needs and requirements of every stakeholder. Therefore to push a program with wide-reaching impact through a complex multinational organization, can be very difficult and time consuming.

Another aspect of change is the large workload which comes with such an initiative. Speaking of a company-wide initiative which is being launched centrally but with local impact, workload arising from the implementation does also affect the local entities. However, while on the central level specific project teams are usually being set up and dedicated to this project, this form of additional support is not always given at a local level. Usually local entities have to conduct projects with the available resources. Therefore, any change or project means additional work on top to the normal daily business. This bears the risk and challenge that the on-time support cannot always be guaranteed and the realization of the entire initiative might be delayed.

Moreover, the fact has to be considered that in the strategic roadmap the preceding "lift-drop" phase was already characterized by change, even though rather on the organizational than on the process level. The flexibility and openness towards additional change among the affected parties might therefore be rather low.

2 Launching a Process Improvement Program

Considering all the factual and emotional barriers and challenges in total, when launching a change initiative, a comprehensive and thorough preparation and planning, as well as professional implementation methodology is absolutely crucial for success.

The preparation of the "change" phase started already during the Finance Bundling Project and the "lift-drop" phase[4] already provided indications on the diversity of processes in place and the potential for process improvements. *Siemens* however made the decision to finish the "lift-drop" phase first before starting with improvement initiatives. This was due to the fact that it is easier to change processes once they are transitioned to Shared Service Centers,

[4] Finance Bundling was the company-wide project, mandated by the *Siemens* Management Board. The other two phases of the SSO roadmap "Change" and "Enhance and Innovate" do not have a mandate.

having dedicated management with the right skill set and experience to undergo transformation activities.

The creation of the following four "Process Communities": [5]

- Accounts Payables,
- Accounts Receivables,
- General Ledger, Asset Accounting and Closing & Reporting
- Tax & Others,

brought forward an organized best practice sharing, where potential improvement initiatives were discussed and evaluated. Internal analysis and proposals were created to achieve a common understanding of the goal. As a next step, a more detailed analysis with Sectors and Clusters was initiated.

2.1 Program Set-up

The result of the discussions within the Process Communities and with major stakeholders can be regarded as the initiation of "Process Improvements for Accounting", the PIA program. The PIA program comprises a worldwide set-up to optimize accounting processes with the help of best practice sharing to standardize, harmonize and automate accounting processes. It is not explicitly mandated by the governance function. However, the program could be considered as the natural next step for the organization to prove that the Shared Services provider can actually be the driver of change to bring about the improvements in processes as originally indicated in the Finance Bundling project.

As outlined above, change always requires the involvement of the main stakeholders in order to be successful. Therefore, the organization chart for the PIA program was set up in a way to involve all affected parties. The organizational set up of the program comprises the following roles:

- **Program Coach(es)**

  The Program Coaches or Sponsors give strategic guidance on the program. It is recommended to have at least one, but preferably two Program Coaches or sponsors. The plurality of interest in a complex company is huge; therefore it is important that the Coaches act in the interest of the whole company. They are also members of the Steering Committee and are meant to be promoters towards a successful implementation of the initiatives.

[5] The Process Communities are aimed to connect people with peers and their outputs include leading practices, guidelines, knowledge pools, technical problem- and solution discussions, working papers and strategies. Each Delivery Center assigns one or two experts per Community. Each Process Community is coordinated by fully dedicated "Product Managers" of the central Portfolio Management & Processes Team.

- **Steering Committee**

  The Steering Committee has the overall strategic decision-making power, reviews the project status and is to be informed about escalations, issues and risks. Meetings are scheduled on a quarterly basis or on special requests.

- **Advisory Board**

  Members of the Advisory Board are highly qualified experts from the Accounting & Finance organization of the Sectors and Corporate Finance as well as from Corporate Compliance. Main responsibilities of the Advisory Board are to consult PIA Program Management regarding Accounting specifics, facilitate project roll-out world wide, advise for potential Steering Committee decisions and be a sparring partner for specific PIA projects, if required.

- **Program Management**

  The Program Management's main task is the monitoring of the project progress. It acts as the operational decision–maker for the whole program and enforces the guiding principles (see below). Further, the Program Management acts as the single point of contact towards customer side and also internally.

- **Project Leads**

  For every initiative within an Improvement Program a global Project Lead needs to be nominated. He or she is fully responsible for the coordination and the success of the specific initiative.

- **Coordinators of Process Communities**

  The Coordinators of the Process Communities (e.g. AP, AR, C&R) are the main drivers for best practice sharing and process optimization. They are also responsible for the Service Life Cycle Management. Each Process Community has one Coordinator who is an expert in his or her area and advises the Project Leads. He or she aligns the projects or initiatives in the Centers, following overall process guidelines to avoid isolated applications and solutions and promotes new initiatives.

- **Sector & Cluster Representatives**

  For certain projects, specific knowledge from the customer-side, i.e. the Sectors or Clusters is helpful e.g. to solve issues in Cash Allocation, Intercompany Clearing, etc. Therefore representatives might be delegated to the program for specific tasks.

- **Center Contact & Initiative Responsible per Center**

  Each Project Lead has a counterpart on the local/regional level to drive and coordinate the rollout of an initiative within a Center. He or she has to align with the respective Project Lead regarding the status for reporting and escalation of required decisions, critical issues and risks.

In the first step, "**Guiding Principles**" were defined to create a common understanding and agreement of the goals and objectives:

- The SSO as the service provider decides on outsourcing and location options.
- The SSO has the global ownership for processes within its scope (in line with central governance framework, changes in alignment with affected Sectors and Clusters).
- Business cases for each PIA Project were to be calculated on world-wide level (a positive impact on Cluster level to be achieved, not necessarily for every company).
- Decisions of the PIA Steering Committee are binding also with regards to exceptions.

After being internally aligned, a more detailed analysis was initiated with Sectors and Clusters. Based on this, the next step of selecting the first initiatives for the program was initiated.

2.2 Identification and Selection of Improvement Initiatives

The identification of suitable initiatives for the PIA Program initially started with brainstorming within the Process Communities in cooperation with the Centers, supported by a benchmarking exercise, to also consider external practices. The objective was to prioritize the improvement initiatives that offer a faster way to improve the overall quality and standardize or automate process flows. Some initiatives were already in the pipeline but needed a clearer focus or were waiting for an official framework as the Process Improvement Program.

The initial brainstorming identified thirteen initiatives. To mention some examples: AP e-invoicing, AP and AR clarification process, automated 3-way match, AR cash allocation, GL e-voucher, GL provision tool, C&R event driven closing workflow, payment automation, workflow for small companies, etc. The analysis had shown that the opportunities are huge. The danger, however, is of getting lost with a "big approach" and therefore concentration on a few selected initiatives is recommended. Focusing is key. Therefore, the Program Management decided to assign the initiatives to at least two waves depending on the priority.

The following evaluation criteria had been defined for the selection of initiatives for wave I:

- Ease of implementation,
- Direct impact on quality,
- Yearly cost savings,
- Low complexity.

First of all, it is important to identify quick wins or "low hanging fruits" which do not require long implementation periods. If such an initiative at the same time brings notable benefits in terms of quality improvements and yearly cost savings and is not too complex in terms of implementation, the stakeholders are easily convinced of the positive aspects and benefits and would be supportive of future initiatives.

On the basis of these evaluation criteria from the original thirteen initiatives eight were assigned to wave I. The initiatives and reasons for selection are the following:

- **AP Scanning, e-Invoicing, Self-Billing:** are to be considered as a prerequisite for further improvements in subsequent processes;
- **AP Reduction of Payment Proposal Verification:** avoids double work due to a change of process sequence and improves overall quality;
- **AP Urgent Payment Reduction:** is a quick win with the implementation of payment policies and fostering discipline in process adherence;
- **AR Bank Statements:** is meant to ensure the provision of important information which is often lost in the payment chain of banks;
- **AR Remittance Advices**: is a way to increase available information for cash allocation;
- **GL Event Driven Closing Workflow**: a quality approach to streamline and automate complex closing steps.

The content of these initiatives will be described in more detail in the subsequent sections.

2.3 From Planning to Implementation and Control

For the PIA program, the same systematic project management approach was applied which was in use to successfully realize the Finance Bundling Project. To ensure relevant stakeholders are consequently involved into the program, the following 4-step-approach was developed:

- **Initial Top-Down Impact Estimation**

  A first top-down impact estimation (risk analysis, investment, quality impact, savings, etc.) has to be performed taking into consideration that all initiatives can be rolled in all Clusters/Delivery Centers.

- **Detailed Assessment/Global Business Case via Pilot Project**

  A pilot for each initiative is set up. Every SSC should only have one or two pilots in order to avoid bottlenecks, because during this phase additional resources might not be available. Based on the experience with the pilot, a detailed bottom-up assessment with global or Cluster impact estimation is performed. Cost, timeline, resources and prerequisites have to be evaluated. Each business case is expected to have a positive impact.

- **Detailed Planning for Project Initiative Rollout**

  A detailed plan including prioritized rollout is presented for approval by the PIA Steering Committee. The scope of entities has to be defined according to the operational needs of each entity.

- **Business Case Achievement Tracking**

  The implementation has to be followed up and tracked constantly. In the implementation review, business cases and achievement have to be verified and presented.

Along the four steps mentioned above, continuous reporting is essential and in the case of PIA, comprises the following: a regular update of the implementation schedule, a monthly status report including explanations for potential delays, risks and mitigation actions, a quarterly validation of quality achievements and cost reductions.

3 Implementing Selected Process Improvement Initiatives

3.1 Scanning, E-Invoicing and Self-Billing

In the course of implementing the global Finance Activity Split[6] as part of the Finance Bundling project, the Shared Services Organization took over responsibility for the majority of the AP processes, including sub-process steps imaging & archiving, verification and posting as well as reconciliation and clarification. Thus, a standard but flexible solution for receiving and processing AP paper documents was developed. Flexibility was the key to account for a diverse process baseline as well as a multitude of vertically integrated workflow and IT system landscapes with entity-level custom solutions, deviating local regulatory and business requirements.

The cornerstones of the **AP Scanning** solutions are:

- Outsourcing of scanning and OCR (Optical Character Recognition)[7] processing to external providers offering country-level "local" scanning and efficient data capture and verification services.
- Implementation of a standard corporate EDI (Electronic Data Interchange)[8] data format and interface linking providers to business-owned workflow and IT systems.
- Flexibility towards integration of electronic formats (e.g. Email PDF[9]) and more complex document types (e.g. freight invoices).
- Process harmonization and increased transparency in terms of performance benchmarking and best practice identification allowing for continuous process improvement.

By developing a standard EDI format for invoices as well as other AP documents and providing a standard interface to corporate EDI services, the service provider is able to choose external scanning and OCR service suppliers according to regional and local business requirements. Regional contracting ensures cost efficiency, comparability of service levels, the availability of fall-back supplier and thus independency.

6 The 'Activity Split' – describing and governing on a detailed level which organizational unit is responsible for which part of the relevant accounting processes – was defined by the governance function Corporate Finance in close cooperation with Sectors, Clusters and the Shared Services Organization

7 OCR enables the conversion of scanned images in handwritten or typewritten format into machine-encoded format.

8 EDI is a mean to transmit between internal systems business data and documents in electronic format.

9 PDF which is the short form for Portable Document Format is a file format which is application software independent and was developed by *Adobe Systems*.

The SSO's customers benefit from full flexibility of running costs and enhanced AP services provided on existing workflow and IT-solutions. Compliance controls improved as EDI enables electronic document archiving and retrieval within existing IT solutions. Furthermore, the implementation of the AP Scanning solution is a first step towards e-Invoicing as it provides one single data stream for the handling of paper and PDF invoices.

The pilot implementation of the Scanning solution started during the "lift-drop" phase to enable a transfer of AP activities to the Center locations. At first three European pilots were selected to establish a top-down business case and to assess the investments requirements for solution development. The assessment of solution development costs could be performed centrally due to a corporate EDI standard that defines export/import interfaces and standard message formats (e.g. INVOIC) to be exchanged between the more than 200 corporate IT-systems. Baseline data could be derived from process analysis templates of the precedent Finance Bundling project. The main challenge consisted in assessing the variety of processes and workflow solutions to be supported by the Scanning solution.

After analyzing and signing-off the business cases, the solution development started. Main changes comprised EDI interface enhancements, UNICODE[10] development for non-Latin character support and definition of workflow tool interfaces.

Roll-out planning had to account for several issues: Firstly, the implementation of the Scanning solution required setting up one external scan site per country. Thus, country-pilot companies generally were those with the highest paper volumes. After successfully stabilizing the new process at the country-pilots, remaining country entities were on-boarded. Secondly, vertically integrated IT systems and workflow solutions provided the opportunity to leverage system-based lessons learned. Country-pilots were clustered into implementation waves prioritizing high volume workflow/IT combinations. This way standard solution packages for high volume combinations were defined and refined first ensuring critical document volume levels in each country in scope. Remaining systems were approached at last when country-setup was already productive and processes of on-boarded companies stable.

To ensure continuous improvement of solution design and roll-out methodology a post implementation review was performed after implementation had been stabilized. The review covered process effectiveness, quality and efficiency targets and was performed on the basis of on-site spot-checks, interviews and documentation review. It was essential to prove business case target achievement and mitigate post-implementation service quality risks.

The **AP e-Invoicing** initiative is the second pillar of AP process optimization. Whilst AP scanning focuses on handling the paper challenge and providing a harmonized inbound process for AP documents, e-Invoicing aims at increasing the use of electronic data formats. According to *Siemens* definition, electronic invoicing comprises all areas of electronic data exchange within AP independently of the format (e.g. Email PDF, direct business-to-business EDI, web EDI).

[10] The Unicode Standard is a character coding system designed to support the worldwide interchange, processing, and display of the written texts of the diverse languages and technical disciplines of the modern world.

Key goals of the initiative are:

- Increased automation: no-touch invoice receiving, verification, booking and archiving to increase efficiency and speed whilst reducing resource requirements and cost.
- Increased transparency: process automation to provide visibility and technical prerequisites to optimize cash management.
- Increased compliance: electronic processing to foster adherence to legal, contractual accounting and quality standards.

In contrast to AP scanning, where a flexible standard solution covers all business requirements, it is not possible to tackle the e-Invoicing challenge with a "one size fits it all" approach. First of all, EDI benefits are not distributed equally across the Purchase-to-Pay (P2P) process. The Accounting & Finance stake in total process baseline cost per transaction is relatively small compared to logistics / supply chain process cost. Additionally, logistics is able to obtain additional EDI benefits via the use of "value added" features like vendor managed inventory and delivery scheduling. Thus, close reconciliation between global supply chain management and Accounting & Finance is required to ensure end-to-end perspective and prevent "silo" solutions. Secondly, not all supplier relations are equal. Global top-tier suppliers require different solutions than e.g. local low-volume indirect material suppliers.

Thus e-Invoicing efforts follow a 3 step approach:

- Centralize AP scanning solution: establish a compliant, standardized process for paper invoices providing the technical basis for Email PDF ("unstructured" electronic messages) to streamline processes and remove historic burdens. This reduces complexity, provides visibility and enables direct shift to electronic formats as cost per unit are fully flexible and do not depend on volumes.
- Replace paper and unstructured electronic formats by structured EDI: in parallel to AP scanning, a "low hanging fruit" approach for EDI integration via (a) Business-to-Business (B2B) and (b) external platform approach is followed. Preferred suppliers participate in establishing corporate standards and providing use cases for the definition of global *Siemens* standards for different supplier enablement options (e.g. B2B direct EDI, use of EDI platform, printer driver for small suppliers).
- Integrate different solutions into one corporate standard: after standards for different solutions and enablement options are defined, lessons learned and experience gathered have to be bundled into one corporate standard defining enablement options per supplier category. Additionally, clear targets have to be set in order to achieve cross-functional commitment and quick implementation.

Current scope of the second step comprises initiatives for B2B EDI and external platform solutions that will result in a test case for proof of concept, deliver business case assumptions and lessons learned. After those initiatives have been completed, an overall plan and business case for on-boarding of remaining supplier will be developed.

Self-Billing has its roots in the Automotive Industry with high inventory turns and just-in-time source models. Based on a managed inventory and delivery scheduling the supplier sends his material to the factory, where it remains on the patio. Once officially received, i.e. good receipt in the IT- system, an automated credit note is issued to the supplier (instead of a conventional supplier tax invoice) and waits for the next payment according to the due date.

The realization of Self-Billing underlies, however, several requirements:

- A high volume of invoices, a frame agreement with clear and up-dated purchase orders.
- Without respective discipline of all involved parties the whole process does not lead to the desired success. The clarification and corrections of errors would become more complex and thus more expensive.
- Statutory regulations must be taken into account. Currently, the model can only be applied in Europe, North America and Australia / New Zealand. Whereas few emerging economies have partially made provisions in their laws to enable this type of process, the BRIC-countries[11] do not permit self-billing at all.
- The initiative is only suitable for domestic supplies of production material, not for services due to goods receipt process issues.
- It is not suitable for variable prices unless there is an automatic update of purchase conditions, e.g. copper surcharges based on spot rates.

Generally, the customer and supplier must consent to operate in form of Self-Billing. Once agreed, the supplier cannot send invoices anymore. The agreement outlines the frequency of settlement and which commodities are covered. The link between supplier receivable and self-billing invoice is the delivery note, i.e. the delivery note number must be entered during goods received process in order to be printed on the self-billing invoice.

Within the PIA program the pilot Self-Billing was only implemented for direct materials. Roll-out related to indirect material is planned for catalog materials (e.g. stationary) and fixed price services (e.g. rental) with periodic invoice plans. The pilot showed that there are issues in data quality such as price lists are not up-to-date, goods receipt are being booked after invoice receipt etc. Significant effort goes into selection of suppliers, preparing agreements, communicating and following up with suppliers, i.e. evaluation of central team in discussion with Procurement.

Presently Self-Billing showed good results with high volumes in a highly disciplined environment, but there are legal restrictions in a number of countries.

[11] The BRIC-countries comprise the emerging countries Brazil, Russia, India and China.

3.2 Reduction of Payment Proposal Verification

A lot of time and effort is spent on checking, clearing of debit open items and approval of payment proposal before the payment run is being processed. In addition to that compliance controls, so-called "High Risk Payments" and random checks are to be performed.

The concept is that activities such as clearing, quality and compliance checks can be done directly after invoice posting. Transactions not approved for payment should be marked with a payment block. Thus, the payment proposal should only select open items "due" and "approved for payment", omitting the necessity of additional checks and approvals before the payment run. Only the exception list needs to be reviewed and corrected. In the ideal scenario the payment run is simply a scheduled job that automatically triggers the transfer of the payment file to the bank system and prompts the bank signatory to authorize the payment batch. Considering that corresponding cash is available, further checks can be abolished.

Due to the anticipated controls, i.e. before the payment proposal, this initiative is to change the sequence of the process and might require some adjustment in the IT-system.

Automatic payment processing (job scheduling) will be set up with automatic controls which:

- Exclude invoices with debit open items or AR-AP netting instruction from automatic payment run by blocking the open items.
- Automatic check report for duplicate invoices based on payment proposal is performed between payment proposal and payment run where duplicates are blocked automatically for payment.
- Automatic payment run is restricted to real invoices, i. e. no down payment requests, no donations etc.
- All special cases, i.e. debit open items exist on the supplier account, AR/AP-netting instruction exists, suspected duplicates, other items appearing in the exception log are reviewed on the next day and cleared manually or by a subsequent payment run that is started online by an AP-agent.

3.3 Urgent Payment Reduction

In some entities a large number of **Urgent Payments** (payments on demand) is necessary to attend to the requirements of Sectors and Clusters. Within *Siemens* the number of Urgent Payments is estimated to be about 100,000 per year worldwide, but concentrated in some regions. The reason for such a high number lies in weak process discipline prior to the payment proposal and the scheduling of normal payments. Some entities just pay once a month. The effort for such a process generally exceeds the normal payment patterns because of the missing routine and extra steps. Above all, it is unplanned and disrupts operations. The delivery centers have to maintain some spare capacity to be able to cope with "emergency" payments.

A pilot was chosen as a best practice initiative where the ratio of urgent against normal payments was the key criteria while choosing the pilot. An analysis to find the reasons followed. Major issues are of organizational or commercial nature, e.g. payment terms like cash on delivery or a too low frequency of regular payment runs.

Urgent Payment Reduction follows a three step approach:

- Spreading of more discipline and scheduling of e.g. weekly payments to reduce the number of extraordinary payments in peak times.
- Standardization and extension of payment terms in form of generally applicable policies.
- Definition of exceptions for "emergency" payments.

At a corporate level the variety of payment terms were standardized and reduced to a minimum. The deviation process was intentionally impeded by demanding the signature of the entity's Chief Financial Officer (CFO) or the Head of Accounting of the company. This measure turned out to be very efficient, because most of the exceptions were avoided. On the local level, the payment schedules were adjusted to enable timely payment. Specific rules were defined for payments, e.g. regarding tax, court orders and significant cash discounts.

This initiative does not require any financial investment but it is all about consequent adherence to defined procedures. Therefore this initiative is a quick win, but needs permanent follow-up.

3.4 Bank Statements

The matching of open items of receivables with the incoming payment is still largely manual. IT-systems offer this function, but for substantial improvement high efforts to customize are necessary over a longer period of time. *Siemens* internally implemented a system some years ago for the legal entity *Siemens* AG and its various internal entities. But the rollout outside Germany was not really successful.

The achievable automation ratio is mainly driven via the input delivered by the customer as well as the flexibility of used cash allocation software in order to interpret available information. The relevant information which invoices to be cleared with a certain payment can be received in two different ways: as "note to payee" in the bank statement position of the payment or as a remittance advice. Which way to prefer is driven by various factors as for example capabilities of the bank clearing system (number of characters) and business type (number of invoices paid by the customer). The preferable solution should always be the bank statement as it requires no additional logistical effort.

Due to a limited capacity of characters in some of the worldwide bank clearing systems, remittance advices will be the solution of choice in many countries. In this case it is important to receive the payment advice timely in an acceptable level of quality. Challenges are text recognition for paper and images as well as handling of different electronic formats. The customers pass valuable information about their payments to bank, e.g. the invoice numbers. But in the case of several invoices being paid often some of the invoice numbers are lost during bank clearing, some in the banks, some in the clearing systems and others even within *Siemens*. The first analysis showed a quick win.

This initiative was, however, not as easy to implement due to several reasons:

- Loss of information; in some cases this information is only available in the case the customer uses a more expensive cash transfer. Anyway it is hardly possible to change a bank clearing system of a country or a bank group.
- The variety of regulations in each country and the diversity around the globe requires a more detailed and time consuming analysis, i.e. practically in all countries the companies and banks have to be contacted before a final conclusion for further rollouts.
- Possible bottlenecks in the banks like the cut-off of information provided by the customer as well as the use of new bank services (e.g. virtual accounts) have to be evaluated.
- On top on this, 2014 the Single European Payments Area (SEPA) will be introduced, which brings the still available free characters to 140, which is good for some countries with 28 today, but bad for those, who have hundreds of characters available. In Austria just as an example the allocation rate, which improved substantially during the last years due to intensive maintenance of the IT-systems, will drop because of missing data.

3.5 Remittance Advices

The sooner the payment advices are available the earlier cash allocation can be conducted. So the goal has to be to improve the process of payment advices. Currently, some IT-systems allow sending out of emails once the payment run is performed. This is an automated service. The information exists in the customer's IT-system and is being transferred automatically to the supplier's IT-system. The prerequisite is the implementation and maintenance of a corresponding data base for this mailing exercise, i.e. a customer's investment to ease mainly the supplier's job in the accounting area.

In one company in Germany more than 50 % of the payments were covered by remittance advices, yet the automatic cash allocation from one customer to another showed inexplicable variations. The average was around 42 % of all open receivables, but some had very low allocation rates, others very high. The key for improvement was again an individual analysis of the top hundred customers. It was found that some sent faxes, which were not recognized by the OCR software. Others had hundreds of invoices, which were not recognized in the normal process due to "time out". So the maintenance, and this is valid for all OCR software solutions, was intensified together with the sales departments and the customers. As a consequence, the allocation rate could be brought up to an average of 66 % in the selected population. Actually some individual rates improved from 3 % to 98 %.

It is obviously not possible to achieve a 100 % allocation rate and the benchmark for each country is still unclear. However the initial results are satisfactory and promising for the rollout. This project requires detailed analysis and consequently a clear scope definition of the countries with potential to adopt this initiative.

3.6 Event Driven Closing Workflow

The Event Driven Closing Workflow is an electronic workflow to secure, monitor and control simultaneous financial closings. At month end, the Accounting & Finance community suffers, because of some last minute issues, sometimes because of an omission somewhere within the company. To control the closing steps, some checks are available in the ERP systems, but most of the companies use Excel and sometimes boards to monitor the status.

With Finance Bundling, a smooth financial closing initially became a challenge because the process is dependent on precise information and communication and is even more complicated at a country or a cluster level. Now separating tasks according to the Finance Activity Split and bundling most of them in one of the SSC worldwide, specific attention needs to be put on the following fields:

- **Communication** requirements increase with the concentration of activities from company to country level and even more at a cluster level.
- **Process conformity** necessities increase with higher number of companies in the financial closing period.
- **Quality** of financial closings needs to remain consistent even with increasing demands, a challenge particularly for smaller entities.
- **Standardization** is a must to improve productivity and to guarantee high quality.

Today the closing calendar is already very tight and does not offer substantial opportunities to save time, i.e. only small time savings might be realized. Looking at the two main solutions offered on the market, the implementation costs are very high and cost savings of only around 10 % can be achieved. Other initiatives contribute generally much more to savings, whereas time reduction is not tremendous. The main driver to continue with the Event Driven Closing Workflow is to improve and guarantee the desired quality in a complex environment. Furthermore, the more IT-systems are unified in the company, less is the implementation effort.

The Event Driven Closing Workflow is, however, the most controversial initiative. It is not easy to convince all involved parties and to align the existing closing process to one "corporate workflow". It is not only about implementing the software and adapting it to the company's workflow but this involves automation of multiple steps. Furthermore, communication workflows are to be defined and customized according to the requirements, i.e. alerts in case of necessary planned decisions or in the case of errors detected by plausibility checks in the system.

3.7 Additional Future Initiatives

In the following some examples will be given which were also results of the initial brainstorming but have been assigned to wave II of the PIA project due to reasons, such as scope, dependency and complexity.

- **Initiative: AP Clarification Process**

  As Accounts Payable is at the end of the P2P (purchase-to-pay) process chain any errors and omissions in the preceding process steps have to be clarified and corrected in order to ensure that only justified liabilities are recorded and paid to suppliers. Obtaining the requisite information to complete an AP-transaction can be truly challenging.

  The objective of this initiative is therefore to analyze root causes of inefficiencies and delays, to address insufficient data quality and lack of process discipline at the source, and to work with all stakeholders to install a lean and prompt clarification process.

  Different workflows are still in operation due to the high variety of IT systems in place. The investigation and evaluation would require substantial man power to investigate. Despite the high productivity potential this initiative was therefore postponed to wave II.

- **Initiative: AR Clarification Process**

  Similar to the AP process, a harmonized and streamlined clarification workflow between customer and the SSO is to be introduced for Accounts Receivable to reduce clarification effort in the cash allocation process. This should lead to better control and follow-up of communication. At the moment there is no such workflow in place.

  In order to reduce the amount and duration of unallocated receivables, it is essential to provide the agent with an easy to use tool to send queries to either the end customer (payee) or to the right contact in the own organization.

  In order to start with this initiative, first the initiative for cash allocation has to be solved. Thus, this initiative was shifted to wave II.

- **Initiative: AP Automated 3-Way Match**

  The best invoice is a matching invoice, i.e. matching in all aspects is based on the purchase order, the evaluated good receipt and the electronic invoice (scanned, PDF, EDI, WEB platform, etc.). So it can be recorded and paid without additional approval steps.

  Though the automated 3-way match is a standard functionality in ERP systems, in reality only a few companies are ready to accept this concept. The main barrier lies in trusting the accuracy of source data, e.g. price lists or purchase orders being up-to-date in the IT-system. A robust control framework of source data is required in order to place reliance on automatic invoicing and payment processes.

  The prerequisite for this initiative is a high quality and electronic information in processes prior to the 3-way match. First initiatives to solve these issues have higher priority. They require high discipline from all participants. This initiative with very high productivity potential was postponed to wave II.

➢ **Initiative: AP/AR Master Data Management**

Master Data Management requires very high quality assurance as it is the basis for smooth processes in AP and AR. Therefore the content has to be maintained and revised regularly in order to avoid any risk due to incorrect master data. A special focus is on eventual compliance risks. Two internal tools are currently under evaluation. An external "cloud system" was also analyzed. However, protection of sensitive data has to be adequately considered in this context.

The standardization of master data is under discussion in various parts of the company. In a consequence, this initiative with productivity potential was moved to wave II.

➢ **Initiative: GL e-Voucher**

The automation of GL postings with the help of a uniform and standardized template and approval workflow is not so easy because of the high variety of booking issues.

A GL e-Voucher tool is expected to bring the following benefits that are not always in place with the existing solution: user-friendliness, low maintenance effort, available plausibility checks, usage of reference documents, workflow that manages approvals and escalation process and approvals from mobile devices.

The discussions on the activity split in some issues are still under discussion with Sectors, Clusters and Corporate Finance.

4 Conclusion and Outlook

The "lift-drop" phase (Finance Bundling) as a precedent step of the "change" phase (Process Improvement for Accounting) proved to be the right way for paving the way for process improvement initiatives – not the other way round or both phases in parallel. A bundling of processes in one location facilitates the implementation of process improvement initiatives enormously.

Nevertheless, a change program requires a professional preparation, planning, prioritization of initiatives as well as a formal scope. The efforts of each initiative have to be well evaluated against their benefits as changes are not always welcome by every stakeholder and the enforcement without substantial paybacks is not an option from an economic point of view.

The PIA program had been started with eight initiatives, which were selected due to their ease of implementation, their direct impact on quality, cost savings and lower complexity. On the basis of these initiatives a second wave will be started after the first wave has been implemented.

As soon as a certain degree of process harmonization and automation has been achieved and the processes are stable, the next step of the strategic roadmap, the "enhance and innovate" phase can start. With this step of the evolutionary journey, the *Siemens* Shared Services Organization wants to achieve a level of service maturity in order to be seen as trusted partner within the Accounting & Finance community.

Abbreviations and Terms

AFS	Accounting and Financial Services
AP	Accounts Payable
AR	Accounts Receivables
B2B	Business-to-Business
BRIC	Brazil, Russia, India and China
C&B	Cash & Bank
C&R	Closing & Reporting
Donating entity	Legal entity or organizational/accounting unit handing over certain administrative tasks to a Shared Services Organization (or to a Cluster or country organization)
EDI	Electronic Data Interchange
Finance Bundling	Comprehensive program in the areas of accounting, controlling, taxes and financial services to re-shape, harmonize and optimize the worldwide finance functions within *Siemens* group; focus in this article is the transfer of transactional accounting tasks to the in-house Shared Services Organization
GL	General Ledger
ICC	Intercompany Clearing
IT	Information Technology
MD	Master Data
OCR	Optical Character Recognition
P2P	Purchase-to-Pay
PIA	"Process Improvement for Accounting" program within *Siemens*
PDF	Portable Document Format by Adobe Systems
Ramp Up	Describes the phase of a shared services provider's development in which work is being transferred consistently from multiple donating entities to the receiving entity/entities, requiring a corresponding increase of the service provider's internal resources in order to handle volume.

Receiving entity	Legal entity or organizational/accounting unit, regularly a Shared Services Organization (or a Cluster or country organization), receiving certain administrative tasks from the donating entity
SEPA	Single European Payments Area
SSC	*Siemens* Shared Services Center(s)
SSO	*Siemens* Shared Services Organization(s)

Leverage Finance Shared Services (FSS) to Optimize Overall Corporate Performance

ANNETTE HÄUSSER

HeidelbergCement AG

Executive Summary

In order to compete in today's global and rapidly changing environment, organizational set-ups and processes are continuously under close scrutiny. Over the past two decades Shared Services have become established globally as an organizational model for the delivery of administrative support processes. While the initial focus was on finance processes, companies started applying the model also to IT, HR, procurement, and real estate; just to mention some. Shared Services are considered as vehicle to streamline support functions while maximizing the benefits of both centralization and decentralization and minimizing their respective drawbacks at the same time.[1] As such, Shared Services can improve the overall competitive position and a corporation's success respectively.

This article addresses the contribution of Finance Shared Services to the overall performance of corporations. This includes a study that explores how and in which areas Finance Shared Services can be leveraged to optimize overall corporate performance. The study uses an in-depth survey approach. Through a combination of literature review and in-depth interviews with Shared Services Center managers of 22 multinational corporations the article reveals numerous areas in which Finance Shared Services can positively influence corporate performance. On the one hand, a direct influence to profit and loss can be derived. On the other hand, the findings suggest there are also areas with an indirect value to profit and loss. Arguments have been made that for value creation certain prerequisites have to be fulfilled. Also evidence was being found that there are limitations in today's setups which hinder Shared Services from being fully realized. It seems, even experienced companies have not overcome all challenges adherent to Shared Services.

The structure of the article is as follows: starting with an overview about the emergence of Shared Services and their relevance in today's organizations[2], it continues by highlighting theoretical considerations on the constructs of performance. Herewith, the lacking common understanding of performance and issues adherent to measuring are highlighted. Subsequently, the author elaborates on preconditions for value creation with Shared Services. The paper then sets out to explore the multifarious realms for value contribution revealed from the interview information. As there is existing evidence that the benefits of Shared Services have not fully realized the article also addresses current limitations of Shared Services implementations, which prevent further value creation; and finally where the interviewees see further potential for value creation with Shared Services. This section exceeds the scope of Finance.

1 Cf. *KEUPER/OECKING* (2006), p. 478.

2 The relevance of Shared Services depends on a number of company characteristics. *VON GLAHN* (2007), p. 7 et. seq., provides an overview of impacting factors which highlight that especially multinationals are in scope which include but are not limited to turnover, existence of multiple allied companies, company size, and the extent of specialization.

1 Relevance of Shared Service Centers in Today's Organizations

For a vast majority of multinational corporations global competitiveness is key to survival. In seeking ways to increase their profits, organizations today have continuous discussions about capabilities, which ensure the organizations remain competitive and efficient. Actual topics are downsizing, outsourcing, right shoring and redesigning how an organization operates to get the most out of economies of scale and scope. Although the nature and impact of current industry dynamics vary by markets, margin pressure and therefore cost pressure is omnipresent.

While focus was put on primary processes, support processes have long been neglected in this discussion. Nevertheless, there is huge potential that can be leveraged by eliminating inefficiencies in supporting business functions. This is now widely accepted and the Shared Services model is considered as one opportunity to improve efficiency and effectiveness of support processes by applying market mechanisms within the company.[3]

Shared Services implies managing back office functions as a business. As such, the back office functions have to be treated as a portfolio of activities and capabilities. Moreover, service receiving organizational units should not just be regarded as customers but transformed into educated customers which consume resources with thought to cost, exactly knowing which costs incurs related to a specific service.[4]

Considering the broad proliferation of Shared Services in today's multinational corporations one can state that Shared Services are more than a trend.[5] With regards to the number of Shared Service Center implementations *BANGEMANN* revealed a number of 4.000 Shared Service Centers worldwide of which around 120 are operated in Germany, 1.200 in Western Europe and 500 in Eastern Europe.[6] More than 75 % of the Fortune 500 companies report running one or more Shared Service Centers.[7] For the German DAX this is also around 75 %.[8] The wide spread adoption of this organizational setup can be regarded as evidence for its importance.

A short look back to the triggers and how the whole Shared Services development started: At the end of the 1970s, starting 1980s American organizations began centralizing supporting functions to reduce and control costs. As the markets became more dynamic throughout the '80s, companies put higher focus on customer needs and market proximity. In order to respond to these developments also internal support functions were again shifted back into the decentralized organizations looking for higher flexibility. As a consequence, divergence of internal support processes throughout the corporation entailed higher total costs for the service delivery. It didn't take long for market dynamics to create pressure on the cost structure of the companies.

---

3 Cf. *REISS* (2007), p. 147.

4 Cf. *LACITY* et al. (2008), p. 15.

5 Compare citation translated from German: „FSSC is not a trend but an established organizational form within corporations"; *ERNST&YOUNG* (2008), p. 6.

6 Cf. *BANGEMANN* (2011).

7 Cf. *ACCENTURE* (2010), p. 3.

8 Cf. *OSHRI* (2012).

Although there is no common agreement on the origin of Shared Services, its first appearance within US companies was applied to the finance function.[9]

Ford can be considered as the pioneer regarding the development of Shared Services. In 1981, the corporation established a Shared Service Center for Finance and Accounting. This is the first case of a company taking the decision, after having set up divisions before, to get back to a central model which differs from regular centralized organizational units.[10] The centralized unit was established as service function with defined service offerings and a related pricing.

Following the successful concept, an increasing number of organizations started the implementation of Shared Services in the 1980s and especially the 1990s. Until the mid-1990s, Shared Services were predominantly a US based phenomenon. Only then did European companies slowly start implementing the concept as well. The late adoption by European companies was driven by the more complex environment these companies operated in, e.g. different cultures, different languages, multiple currencies, and a variety of governmental laws and regulations.[11]

Several developments have facilitated the adoption of Shared Services, particularly within European companies:

- Developments in Information Technology

  The proliferation and commoditization of internet technologies as well as the advances in telecommunications have facilitated the interconnectedness of decentralized organizational units enabling the site independent delivery of administrative business processes. Such technologies are forming the backbone of today's IT infrastructure. *JOACHIM*[12] even states that the numerous Shared Service Centers can be seen as a result of the technology available today.

  The availability of Personal Computers was certainly one first step towards improvements in business processes. Progress in the development of transistors and faster as well as cheaper microprocessors paved the way for Personal computers; the first ready assembled one being placed on the market in 1977.[13] The early '80s can be regarded as kind of establishment phase while the final breakthrough for the business community only took place some years later in the late '80s.

  The emergence of Enterprise Resource Planning (ERP) Systems enabled the planning of the entire finance and inventory management along the whole value chain. Supporting the integration of all parts of the value chain using web based ERP applications, it can be stated that ERP software has played an important role in modeling today's SSC organizations.[14]

---

9 C.f. *QUINN* et al. (2000), *ULBRICH* (2003), and *DAVIS* (2005).

10 Cf. *DRESSLER* (2007), p. 37.

11 Cf. *DRESSLER* (2007)., p. 37 et seq.

12 Cf. *JOACHIM* (2001).

13 Cf. *LAUBE* (2008).

14 Cf. *JOACHIM* (2001), p. 35.

- Globalization

  The past two decades have significantly changed the relationships between nations and individuals. Markets and businesses all over the world face increasing connectivity and interdependence, which has been dramatically sped up by the advances in telecommunication, transportation, infrastructure and the rise of the internet. The elimination of barriers by standardizing international economic laws and policies reduces transactions cost and therefore stimulates international businesses. The added complexity by doing business internationally has to be addressed and Shared Services are considered as one way doing that.

- Development of a common corporate language/language skills

  English developed as European lingua franca.[15] It has become the language of Economics and Science. As companies operate in an international environment they have to adopt a common language for internal communication.

  Many of today's adults didn't study English during their school career. The new interest in English can clearly be seen in the globalization and the related required language skills. Today, 90 % of all European pupils study English during their compulsory school career.[16] The EF English Proficiency Index Report states that within Europe English language skills are remarkably good. This can be seen as one facilitating factor for companies operating in an international environment.

- European Union and the Euro

  The European Union is the largest international single market in the world. Corporations of member countries benefit from increasing profitability as transaction costs for buying and selling foreign currencies are eliminated for businesses between member countries.[17] Due to the gained price transparency from having a single currency there is greater competition in goods and services. When it comes to investments in other countries the uncertainty caused by exchange rate fluctuations is eliminated.[18]

  With the harmonization of standards, a reduction in paper work and the allowance for member state citizens to move freely between other countries trade barriers have been removed. The EU has also introduced measures to harmonize company law across Europe. As a result, companies benefit from easier access to funding, a clearer and more effective legislation, the protection of shareholders, creditors and employees as well as a reduction on the administrative burden of businesses.

---

15 Cf. *NICKERSON* (2000), p. 1.

16 Cf. *N. N.* (2008).

17 Cf. *EUROPEANUNION* (2012)

18 Cf. *CENUSE/DRIGA* (2010), p. 63.

While the above described developments facilitated international trade, the closer interconnectedness has also added complexity. For backoffice functions Shared Services is an approach to address this complexity.

2 Corporate Performance

Corporate performance is a widely discussed topic in economic research. Numerous authors investigate how to best measure performance and what to leverage in order to improve performance.[19]

A closer examination of how Shared Services can boost the company's performance requires a deeper understanding of the performance construct.

2.1 Performance Definition

A review of relevant literature reveals that there is no common understanding of what the term performance is actually referred to. Despite its frequency of use authors lack providing an explicit definition of its precise meaning. The following statement by Meyer and Gupta is an apt quotation summarizing the research status: "There is a massive disagreement as to what performance is and that the proliferation of performance measures has led to the paradox of performance, i.e. that organizational control is maintained by not knowing exactly what performance is."[20]

Apparently, definitions differ amongst different fields in different contexts.[21] In physics performance is defined as the amount of work performed during a period of time $P = \Delta W/\Delta t$. In informatics performance refers to a data processing system's ability to execute tasks. Even staying within the business context, we face different subject matters.

While in production management the activity is emphasized, organization theory concentrates on fast and cost effective processes. In economics performance is referred to as productivity. Business administration often equates performance with monetary value. For management accounting performance is the companies output in monetary terms.

From the variety of definitions the author has picked the following two as they can well be applied in the Shared Services context offering two different perspectives on performance. According to the business dictionary performance is defined as: "The accomplishment of a given task measured against preset known standards of accuracy, completeness, cost, and speed."[22]

---

19 Cf. *Neely* et al. (2000), p. 1120 et seq, *Melnyk* et al. (2004), p. 209 et seq, and *Bititci* et al. (2005), p. 3.

20 Cf. *Meyer/Gupta* (1994), p. 309.

21 Cf. *Samsonowa* (2012), p. 23.

22 *Dictionary* (2012).

LEBAS/EUSKE come to the following conclusion: "We take the position that performance is the sum of all processes that will lead managers to taking appropriate actions in the present that will create a performing organization in the future (i.e., one that is effective and efficient). In other words we define performance as doing today what will lead to measured value outcome in the future."[23]

Both definitions aim on the one hand for the capability of producing a desired result, achieving an objective or solving a targeted problem which basically equates to effectiveness (doing the right things) and on the other hand to the effort to produce a specific outcome, meaning efficiency (doing the things right).

It is important to understand that performance is a relative concept, requiring judgment and interpretation. It needs a set of parameters or indicators that describe the process through which the various types of outcome and results are achieved.[24] Therefore, adequate measures need to be identified, described and specified.

The following section addresses the measurement topic and highlights the specifics that have to be taken into account for performance measurement in the Shared Services context versus measuring in other organizational contexts.

2.2 Performance Measurement

Performance measures are considered as essential to effective management processes as they convey information about activities within an organization.[25] Recent research has revealed a positive effect of Performance Measurement and Management Systems on various areas such as human resource management, organizational competences, organizational behaviours, or operational effectiveness as well as reputation and customer satisfaction.[26] Performance measures can be expressed in both financial and non-financial terms.

For many decades, traditional accounting measures were financially oriented. In the 1980s critics started getting louder as authors blamed the measures for being internally focused and backward looking as well as focused on inputs rather than outputs. In addition they were responsible for encouraging short-term decision making and dysfunctional behaviour. Popular financial performance measures are Sales figures, Return on Sales (ROS), Return on assets (ROA), Profits (Profitability), ROI as well as the Market Share.

The shortcomings of financial measures led to the identification and expansion of measurements considered to be critical for success in competitive environments. This is the quality aspect of products and processes, the skill set and motivation of the workforce, reliable and streamlined processes as well as high customer satisfaction and customer loyalty and the company image. These measures are often classified as non-financial performance measures.

23 *LEBAS/EUSKE* (2007), p. 127.

24 Cf. *LEBAS/EUSKE*, p. 130.

25 Cf. *SIMONS* (2000), p. 3 et seqq.

26 Cf. *DYDUCH* (2008), p. 26.

Frameworks have been designed which support a more balanced performance measuring. The probably most popular one is the Balanced Scorecard developed by *KAPLAN/NORTON*.[27] Widely known are as well the supportive performance measures matrix by *KEEGAN* et al.[28], the SMART pyramid[29], the Results/Determinants Matrix[30] or the Performance Prism developed by *Andersen Consulting* in cooperation with the Center of Business Performance of the Cranfield School of Management.[31]

While these frameworks allow for categorization and communication of corporate performance and try to enforce a balanced measurement of both financial and non-financial aspects they do not explicitly describe what exactly should be measured.

When it comes to measuring in a service context, studies have revealed the significant challenge that is inherent to measuring in service operations.[32] This is mainly because input – output relations are not as clear as for goods production. As there is a large diversity of services with own characteristics, lessons learned from available case studies are difficult to transfer. Unfortunately, cross-case analysis is missing which would allow judging if context relevant findings are generalizable.[33] Therefore, there exists no general model for measuring in service contexts which could be applied to Finance Shared Services.

Based on literature review *JÄÄSKELÄINEN* et al. list a number of generic contingency factors affecting performance measurement. Such factors are seen in organizational size and structure, the industry sector, external factors like the political environment or industry competitiveness, strategy, purposes and needs for measurement, resources available for development, social practices and organizational culture and existing measurement and information systems.[34] The authors state that these contingency factors are as well applicable to service operations.

In addition they present service specific contingency factors. Customer's involvement in service provision, the role of intangible inputs and varying level of demand are considered as factors dedicated to choosing what to measure. As designing measures output complexity, focus on impacts and repetitiveness of service processes are mentioned.[35]

27 Cf. *KAPLAN/NORTON* (1992).

28 Cf. *KEEGAN* et al. (1989).

29 Cf. *CROSS/LYNCH* (1988/89), and *DIXON* et al. (1990).

30 Cf. *FITZGERALD* et al. (1991), and *FITZGERALD/MOON* (1996).

31 Cf. *NEELY* et al. (2001).

32 Cf. *GRÖNROOS/OJASALO* (2004), and *BERRY/BENDAPUDI* (2007).

33 Cf. *JÄÄSKELÄINEN* et al. (2012), p. 44.

34 Cf. *JÄÄSKELÄINEN* et al., p. 45.

35 Cf. *JÄÄSKELÄINEN* et al., p. 46.

The paper will later apply these specifics for measuring performance of services to Finance Shared Services once the areas for value contribution have been specified.

3 Preconditions for Shared Service Center's Value Contribution

Due to the fact that expectations of SSCs are often high for many corporations it is difficult to realize set objectives. Many executives even fail in achieving the promised results.[36] This is especially true as a large number of stakeholders are involved, requiring a series of complex, interrelated objectives.[37]

Therefore, given the apparent contradiction between the promise of shared services and some of the reported negative experiences, it becomes visible that in order to make optimal use of an organization's Shared Service Center a number of influencing factors have to be analysed and reacted to.

Some authors[38] talk about "critical success factors" that apply to the majority of organizations. Success factors can be distinguished into ones that refer to setting up a Shared Service Center (conceptual factors) and ones that are important for running a Shared Service Center and developing it overtime (operation oriented factors).

3.1 Conceptual Factors

- Strategy

  According to *JOHNSON/SCHOLES*, strategy can be understood as "the direction and scope of an organization over the long term, which achieves advantage in a changing environment through its configuration of resources and competences with the aim of fulfilling stakeholder expectations."[39] Moving towards Shared Services implies a fundamental change with regards to the set-up and configuration of administrative support functions as well as a pervasive transformation of roles and responsibilities. The implementation of Shared Services has long-term implications for a great part of the organization and therefore cannot be rolled back easily. Hence, the decision of whether and how to implement Shared Services can be considered as strategic in nature.[40] Scholars hold the opinion that the move towards Shared Services should be aligned with the overall corporate strategy.[41] While primary strategic objectives can be seen in cost leadership, quality improvements and concentration on core competencies the strategy how to pursue the service transfor-

36 Cf. *LACITY/FOX* (2008), p. 17.

37 Cf. *JANSSEN* et al. (2009), p. 16.

38 Cf. *BADER* (2008), *MULANI* (2009), p. 26, and *WENDEROTH* (2011), p. 21.

39 Cf. *JOHNSON* et al. (2008), p. 3.

40 Cf. *SU* et al. (2009), p. 383.

41 Cf. *SCHULMAN* et al. (1999)

mation alternatives in order to make business more efficient and effective needs to be thoroughly assessed and decided on. One related decision is around the topic whether or not to implement the obligation to contract.

- Organization

  The introduction of new resources, roles and processes in the course of a Shared Service implementation necessitates a new governance structure.[42] Depending on the size and scope of the shared service unit the structure varies.[43] Among other decisions this can imply a separate legal entity, which usually signifies a new start and facilitates the move towards a customer oriented service culture. Neglecting the vital necessity for a new governance structure may provoke inefficacy.

- Processes

  Another important aspect to acknowledge is the selection of applicable processes. While at the beginning usually transactional processes are in scope the spectrum gets amplified over time. One of the key considerations with regards to processes in the context of setting up a Shared Service Center is whether processes should be standardized and harmonized before or after the move into the Shared Service organization. While the consolidation of existing processes in a centralized environment reduces the efforts for planning and designing prior to implementation this takes the risk of multiple inefficient processes in the central location. Whereas the final decision is highly dependent on the starting situation as well as the strategy and set objectives consultants tend to recommend the development of certain standards prior to bundling.[44]

- Location selection

  In literature and practice three different location alternatives are discussed. Choosing a location in the same country as the retained organization(s) we talk about "onshoring". A location in a different country but the same continent would be classified as "nearshoring". Moving the SSC organization to a different continent would be referred to as "offshoring". The key challenge with regards to the sourcing decision inheres in the very careful consideration of both hard and soft facts of each location. In addition, the sourcing strategy needs to be supported by the company's culture.

3.2 Operation-oriented Factors

- Change Management

  In principal, people prefer staying with what they are accustomed to.[45] Change is often even negatively conceived. As the implementation of Shared Services requires major changes with regards to people's values, their beliefs and attitudes, their roles and responsibilities a comprehensive strategy that enables a business transformation on this scale is needed. People fear the loss of their job, loss of control or are just afraid of the

---

42 Cf. *JANSSEN/JOHA* (2008), p. 46.

43 Cf. *WENDEROTH* (2011), p. 22.

44 Cf. *PURTELL* (2005), p. 4.

45 Cf. *SCHNEIDER* (2010), p. 5.

unknown.[46] Crucial to success is a proper understanding of who the stakeholder groups are and what their expectations look like in order to identify barriers of change. In this course an in-depth cultural assessment should be conducted as well. The definition of the change management strategy along with a detailed transition planning including the allocation of dedicated resources and people as well as the definition of performance targets should take place in the conceptualization phase. During the implementation main target is the reduction of anxiety and resistance of change. This should be facilitated by a clear communication strategy creating a dialogue with the employees. A critical factor throughout the different change management phases is the strong and continuous executive support and sponsorship.[47]

- Service level agreements

  In the Shared Services context Service Level Agreements (SLAs) are used to describe and define the relationship between the service provider (Shared Service Center) and the client (retained organization). Key reason is the attempt to implement a marketplace environment.[48] This service contract records a common understanding of the service scope, operation principles, availability, target performance, responsibilities including customer duties as well as the pricing and billing mechanism. Metrics have to be defined and regularly measured in order to check whether the parties comply with the agreement. Strong service levels are recognized as one success factor provided that they are kept simple and do not lead to a bureaucratic infrastructure.

- Organizational culture

  Another important topic influencing the result can be seen in the organizational culture: Does it support the model or are there at least good ideas how to change the corporate culture and does the organization have the right people that can promote the change?

  Extremely positive effects can be derived from a culture of accountability.[49] Encouraging employees to participate in decisions about processes and routines will comfort them in taking over responsibility and ownership.[50]

It has to be emphasized that the configuration of each success factor can take shape in different forms. As organizations differ in numerous aspects one from another there is no one fits all strategy or implementation plan. The various factors have to be tailored to the respective organizations characteristics.

---

46 Cf. *PURTELL* (2005), p. 5.

47 Cf. *JANSSEN/JOHA* (2008), p. 47.

48 Cf. *WENDEROTH* (2011), p. 23.

49 Cf. *DERVEN* (2011), p. 60.

50 Cf. *CHAN* et al. (2004), p. 20.

4 Finance Shared Service Center's Value Contribution

The following section highlights the main areas for value contribution derived from the interview information.

The selection of companies interviewed for the study was mainly based on the fact that the companies have extant experience with the Shared Services model having at least one Shared Service Center established and being present in Shared Services networks which are focussing on the exchange of best practices and knowledge sharing with regards to the further development of the corporations' Shared Services organizations. The majority of companies interviewed are listed on the German DAX or on the Fortune 500 list.

The main benefits expected from a Shared Service implementation in Finance are seen in cost reductions, quality improvements and better compliance. Measures and their related effects can either have a direct impact on profit and loss (P&L) or affect it indirectly.

4.1 Direct Value to P&L

4.1.1 Bundling Effects

The first cost effect comes from bundling activities in one or a significantly reduced number of locations compared to the setup before. Just bundling usually allows the reduction of personnel as it permits a better usage of the available capacity. Also absence management requires in total less personnel. Another effect can be obtained from a reduction of overhead as larger groups allow for a higher span of control.

Bundling is directly related to the sourcing strategy and location decision. An onshore approach can have a positive cost effect by negotiating a different tariff for the newly created organization. Near shoring and offshoring usually mean the decision for a low cost location. This results in considerable labour arbitrage.

4.1.2 Harmonization and Standardization Effects

As a consequence of decentralized environments, processes have evolved differently; usually smaller groups were involved delivering these processes.

If a higher number of people are involved in a process,the process is subjected to higher level of scrutiny and as a consequence, a higher attention to improvement.And, if the same process is executed in a different way in the same location, it is most likely that management will look for best practices and unify processes. Hence, harmonization of processes can be seen as a direct consequence of bundling. The harmonization of diverse processes facilitates their standardization. This convergence then drives economies of scale. Ideally the standardization takes place down to the lowest level of the process hierarchy, which can be split into the following five levels:

- Level 1: Business Process Area, e.g. Finance
- Level 2: Process Group, e.g. Accounts Payable
- Level 3: Business Process, e.g. Invoice Verification
- Level 4: Business Process Step, e.g. Match Purchase Order
- Level 5: Business Process Activity, e.g. Reconcile Quantity

Only then is a consistent process execution possible according to an underlying common documentation. Highly standardized processes in turn are a prerequisite for an economically reasonable use of technology. In return, in order to push standardization of processes down to the lowest level common IT infrastructure and business applications are a prerequisite. Accordingly, standardization of processes needs to accompany the standardization of business applications.

4.1.3 Effects from Leveraging Technology

Providing a reasonable degree of standardization from business processes IT tools can be real cost killer. Eliminating human effort can result in huge cost avoidance, given the transactional volumes justify the investment. As shared services bundle activities and therefore handle increased volumes it can be regarded as door opener for the use of leading-edge technology. Such applications can speed up the flow of information between corporate divisions, subsidiaries and external partners, allowing companies to respond quickly and monitor activities with greater efficiency.[51]

- Scanning and OCR

  In Accounts Payable for instance, instead of manually keying invoice information into the ERP system and then filing the paper document a scanning software could capture the paper document which would then be processed by an optical character recognition (OCR) program. A successful OCR would read all relevant invoice details and save the data to the ERP tables.

- E-invoicing

  Receiving electronic invoices in a structured format provides the advantage that it obviates the need for both scanning hard- and software and OCR technology. The structured information can just be uploaded into the ERP system and the further processes from there. With regards to providing electronic invoices to own customers costs can be saved for printing, putting invoices in an envelope and mailing.

- AP workflow/Invoice verification

  Instead of sending a paper invoice to a respective approver a workflow with the applicable invoice attached could electronically be routed to the approving person. Once approved, the invoice can automatically be posted and the payment be released.

---

[51] Cf. *SUNGARD/AVANTGARD* (2010), p. 5.

In case a purchase order (PO) is available and the goods receipt note (GRN) is posted the workflow can automatically match the invoice against PO and GRN details and in case of consistence post the invoice and release the payment.

Both scenarios significantly speed up the process and reduce cycle times. The benefits of such a shortened cycle time can be the realization of cash discounts. In addition, timely payments can be ensured which prevents supplier dunning and reduces corresponding efforts.

- Self-billing/Evaluated receipt settlement

  Instead of receiving an invoice from the supplier the purchaser produces an automated payment to the supplier on delivery of purchased goods. Once the delivery is confirmed in the system the ERS produces the invoice based on the product/price information of the contract. This procedure reduces the amount of invoices to be processed in the Accounts Payable department. Potential invoice variances get prevented and reconciliation tasks eliminated.

- Intercompany processing

  If goods or services are sold between two companies (different company codes) belonging to the same organization it is referred to as intercompany transactions. Instead of manually triggering sales orders, processing deliveries and running the corresponding billing this can be set up as automated process.

  Having a proper intercompany process in place eliminates unwanted journals and adjustments, manual entries and reconciliations and speeds up the close process.

- Dynamic discounting

  Dynamic Discounting describes the arrangement between a purchasing organization and its supplier whereby payment for goods or services is made early in return for a reduced price or discount. The arrangement allows to accelerate payment based on a sliding discount scale whereas the earlier the payment, the greater the discount.

  As manual process, capturing changing price reductions and varying payment terms was basically impossible. Web portals facilitate the handling and providers estimate a potential saving of 0.5 % of the annual spend.[52]

- Cash allocation

  In Accounts Receivable the manual allocation of customer payments to the respective customer account and the corresponding settlement of the account can be replaced by IT support. The software would read the bank transfer details and match the payment to the customer account and automatically settle the account. In case there is a discrepancy between the invoice amount and the amount paid a workflow triggers respective steps for clarification.

---

52 Cf. *Taulia* (2012).

- Effective collections management

  In classical sales organizations exacting payments is usually perceived as necessary evil. The use of technology in this context can automatically issue dunning letters if invoices are overdue for a predefined period of time. The entire dunning process can be built in the system and automatically trigger the respective actions. It can even hand over cases where collection efforts failed to a collecting agency. On the one hand this results in less personnel requirement, on the other hand the software allows for a complete overview of outstanding receivables. In addition, there is proven successes of dunning in a timely manner, which eventuates in a shorter DSO ratio (days sales outstanding),which again positively impacts the working capital.

- Effective credit management

  System supported credit management can accelerate sales decisions and simultaneously reduce credit risk. Based on numerous facts like the customers' payment performance, amount of debt, etc. the system creates a credit rating, which again influences the amount of credit granted to new or existing customers. This can significantly reduce the risk of write-offs.

- Double payment testing

  Weak processes now and then lead to the fact that payments are effected more than once. Automated double payment testing can identify such cases and recover the payments from the supplier.

Although there are multiple areas where Shared Services have a positive influence on the cost structure, it is not only the cost aspect in which Shared Service Centers can contribute to the overall corporate performance.

4.2 Value From Quality

Disseminating and imposing successful practices helps driving process effectiveness. Incorporating such best practices with standardized processes error rates get reduced. First of all, process variants are limited so staff has clear instructions. In addition, limiting the number of options people gets specialized in the various activities. Automation by leveraging technology augments this effect as it eliminates human failure.

From standardization also consistent and comparable results can be derived which results in a higher quality of management reports which again builds a more reliable basis for decisions.

Data management, no matter if it is technical data, accounting data, chart of accounts, suppliers data, customer data or asset data, has been a neglected task in many organizations. As the accuracy of such data is precondition for unbroken processes it is highly important having standard requirements for this data and proper process that ensures their accuracy. In addition, a cleansing process and the responsibility for it is required. Organizations that incorporated the master data management in the Shared Service Center and built a corresponding framework profit from more efficient processes which such data as input factors.

Correct master data is also important to reach high automation degrees. Only if the master data is correct the process can run through without human intervention. Therefore, a prerequisite for successful tool implementations can be seen in accurate master data.

Another example: if pricing information in the system is not correct and therefore a wrong billing is issued customers tend to use this one wrong invoice as excuse also not to pay others. This again has an impact on the DSO and working capital.

To climb up the quality ladder continuous improvement is required. This is a topic, which Shared Services brought to the administrative area. While it was firmly established in the production management administrative or back office functions were not in focus.

A culture of continuous improvement helps drive both efficiency and effectiveness. Continuous process improvements allow for higher service levels over time.

This usually effects a higher customer satisfaction. Setting up continuous improvement programs which incentivize the participation of the employees to generate new ideas or share their experience in order to streamline existing processes has a positive impact on both employee satisfaction and process maturity.

Furthermore, employees are benefiting from the service and high quality culture. They become experts in high quality finance processes which can have a positive impact for their future career development.

4.3 Value From Higher Transparency

Documented process operations help to ensure that processes are executed in a consistent manner. IT tools allow that certain process steps have to be followed. They basically enforce the compliance with defined rules and regulations.

System supported access rights and permission levels help enforce the segregation of duties.

Apart from that, high transparency that allows keeping track of who did what reduces the risk of fraud. One example can be listed from travel and expense management. Systems supported the companies travel guideline can be applied to expenditures. The system checks if the rules were followed. In case someone books a business class flight even though only economy was allowed a note would directly go to the person's boss. This could be followed by disciplinary measures. Just being aware of that risk many individuals comply with given rules. In this example this would save the company ready cash.

Transparently generated figures are comprehensible and one can trust to compare apples with apples. In those times when all processes were different and calculations differed as well, ratios were not really comparable. This resulted also in high efforts for the auditors that tried to understand the figures. In a shared services environment, apart from fewer locations that have to be audited, there is less need to question the figures. All is very transparent and if controls are abided by is easily visible. Therefore, SSCs contribute to more efficient audits, which result in significant savings when it comes to the overall audit cost.

If processes are supported by a standardized IT environment on global scale a lot of information can be retrieved from the system which used to be quite some effort to gather and consolidate in the past. Here we can see efficiency gains in reporting generated from a more transparent environment.

Another example could be a supplier that needs information about the status of his invoice payment. If there is a self-service tool available providing this information, there is no effort at all for the corporation. In the opposite case the corporation needs to better staffed in the AP department to answer such questions.

In order to improve processes they have to be transparent. Only then one has the possibility to see where process inefficiencies are. Therefore, high transparency in combination with measurement can be seen as trigger for process improvements, which again lead to higher efficiency and effectiveness.

4.4 Indirect Value to P&L

4.4.1 Value From Expansion Towards More Knowledge-driven Processes

Having experienced the positive effects from Shared Services for transactional processes companies expand their value creation agenda. This involves the migration of roles to the center that people in the past would have said these should not be in a service center but proximate to the businesses.

Such value adding finance function processes can be seen in budgeting, strategic Finance planning, performance reporting and analytics, management information and controlling.[53]

The shift of activities as mentioned above helps freeing up finance people remaining onsite and giving them space to engage in business partnering as they should then be able to spend more time and resources on their core jobs.

By concentrating these activities in reduced number of locations the processes can also benefit from the professionalization in the service delivery. Higher quality in such processes leads to a better basis for decision-making.

4.4.2 Expansion of Value Beyond Shared Service Center Processes

One could wonder whether the value of shared services extends beyond the processes within the SSC. From an end-to-end business process perspective Finance Shared Service processes often form the end of the process chain. Discrepancies in earlier process steps become evident in the Center as they tend to cause issues there. For instance, a bad quality purchase order can lead to a broken invoice verification process. In the SSC an analysis can drill down from which organization units the problems are caused, even down to the responsible clerk. This information offers a valuable lever to improve the PO quality in the future. In smaller organizations such errors might not even be considered as an issue due to low processed volumes. But processing high volumes the absolute amount of non-compliant POs becomes much more evident and causes inefficiencies.

---

[53] Cf. *N. N.* (2012), p. 13.

Such inefficiencies beyond the FSS can only become evident and influenced if the Finance processes are properly integrated and streamlined.

Another example can be seen in the improvement in the way that inventory is managed. Companies face the issue that inventory is received but not recorded into the books and later sold. This leads to the necessity of big inventory adjustments. If the payment process in the FSS foresees a matching of invoice with PO and the recorded inventory (GRN) the missing GRN posting becomes evident. This way the FSS can play a big part in ensuring that this information is reported timely and accurately and that results are reliable.

4.4.3 Value From Reduced Complexity and Higher Flexibility

Delivering services from a reduced number of locations and standardizing processes at the same time goes hand in hand with a reduction of complexity. Merging legal entities also contributes to a reduced complexity.

In such an environment system implementations are simplified. Rather than going to x locations it is only a limited number of locations where hardware and software needs to be installed, people being trained and later maintenance have to be cared for. System implementations especially benefit from standardized processes, as process variants can be limited to a minimum.

Modular and service oriented architectures make it possible to integrate and disintegrate potential new business components efficiently and effectively. Modular components are either internally shared or outsourced to an external provider.[54]

Shared Services offer a CEO a base to grow. While in the past a local finance presence had to be established Shared services enable an integration of new acquisitions. This provides the flexibility to quickly add new business units and expand geographically and pursue rapid growth strategies. This is extremely helpful when companies need to respond to the marketplace.

Also the sale of entities is much easier as the impact of even partial divestments can be managed much more effectively within the Shared services structure.

Hence, by reducing complexity businesses can respond to opportunities faster. And, the more integrated an SSO is with the company's strategic goals, the more adaptable it can be in a constantly changing environment.

4.4.4 Value From the People Component

In a larger organization the possibilities to point up attractive career paths are much broader compared to a small organizational unit. For young talent, realistic and attractive career paths are a strong argument influencing their decision for which company to engage. Having a top performing finance organization in place can be an advantage in the war for talent.

---

[54] Cf. *Janssen/Joha* (2008), p. 37.

The shared services organization can also be leveraged to develop new talent and prepare them for executive positions some place in the organization.

The fact that the services delivered by the FSS are the core competence of this organizational unit and a valuable product to their customers drives higher employee job satisfaction and retention compared to delivering some administrative support and being considered as overhead.

Also, the understanding of delivering a valuable product that should be always improved wherever possible positively supports the employee's mindset of continuous improvement. Such a culture encourages innovation, which in return truly drives best practices. Empowering employees by cross-group learning and sharing of good practices produces a pool of knowledge and substantial capabilities with critical expertise.

Correctly implemented the improvement is not only looking at the finance process but the whole business process. Operating in such a way, employees transform the FFS into an engine that continuously drives changes and implements them to the corporation.

4.4.5 Value From Better Control Systems

If a company has fewer sites an increase in compliance and control and consistency on a global basis can be achieved more easily.

Shared services can effectively drive controls by designing the control framework. Also the deployment and assessment of controls can all be driven from Shared services. Usually specialist teams deliver these activities.

SARBANES-OXLEY and similar regulatory efforts have driven compliance up the corporate agenda.[55] The very changes of new legislation added new realms of complexity to the compliance framework. As operating in a central and standardized environment fosters a stronger control environment the risk of failing to comply with the *SARBANES-OXLEY* regulations is significantly reduced. Therefore, also the risk of potential sanctions is minimized. On an ongoing basis cost for compliance is much lower compared to the funding which is normally necessary in a decentralized, non-standardized environment.[56]

5 Measuring the Value Contribution in Finance Shared Services

As stated in the theoretical considerations of performance and its measurement, there are challenges adherent to measuring in the services context. This applies as well to Finance Shared Services. Nevertheless, stakeholders need to understand the value that derives from Finance Shared services and therefore measurement is crucial. The importance of this be-

55 Cf. *LIDDELL* (2010), p. 4.

56 Cf. *PURTELL* (2005), p. 4.

comes obvious by the statement of one SSC manager: "If stakeholders don't understand that Shared Services is adding value the value is basically lost."

Applying the traditional financial measures used for the overall organizational performance measurement does not work for many Finance Shared Services as they are mostly set up as cost center vs. profit or investment center. Transfer prices are usually calculated based on consumption with a small mark up in order to comply with tax regulations. Neglecting this fact, the missing profit generation would create a wrong picture about the real value added in case traditional financial measures were used.

The importance of non-financial measures becomes obvious. For the definition of these measures applicable contingency factors have to be taken into consideration. The following assumptions can be derived from applying identified contingency factors to the Finance Shared Services context.

With regards to size, the Shared Services model is mostly implemented in multinational corporations, implying a certain complexity and scale. Such organizations often require more advanced measurement systems and outcomes are more difficult to analyse and interpret.

From the industry sector no real impact can be derived as finance processes can be regarded as industry independent.

The purpose and need for measurement are both internally and externally motivated. While stakeholders might have an interest in following the development over time requiring indicative measures of business performance, internal measures have more likely an operational motivation in order to control the service operation. Actual service performance metrics for managing the service operations are required in this case.

The resources available for development of performance measures impacts upon the number and granularity of metrics collected. Organizations with sufficient resources may have the tendency to over-engineer the measurement system. Practitioners advise to use only a small number of meaningful KPIs per process. Otherwise executives and staff might run the risk being more occupied with KPI report generation than dedicating their time to analysis and deriving actions for further improvement.

Finance processes today are heavily dependent on technology to gather information about process details such as error rates, cycle times or number of transactions. This simplifies measurement as information can more easily be obtained; on the other hand, executives need to mitigate the risk of building too complex measurement systems just because metrics are easily obtained.

With regards to organizational culture, for most organizations measuring the performance of administrative support functions is rather new. Dealing with measures in this context requires a change in the staff's mind-set. This needs to be fostered as part of the measurement implementation.

Customer's involvement in the service process can be considered as rather low for Finance Shared Services. This reduces the complexity in measuring the outcomes and simplifies taking adequate measures in order to adjust the performance level.

Output complexity in Finance Shared Services depends on the finance service as such. While for transactional areas like accounts payable or accounts receivable the output is quite clear budgeting and forecasting activities are rather complex. Identifying adequate measures is therefore the more difficult the higher the output complexity.

With regards to the focus on impacts it has to be clear what exactly has to be achieved with the measure and carefully evaluated to avoid that dysfunctional effects are triggered with the measure.
For the Finance Shared Services context we can assume a high repetitiveness of the processes which allows for comparison over time (base lining) as well as external benchmarking.

In order to capture the entire contribution of Finance Shared Services to the overall corporate performance it is suggested to apply the findings from the contingency factors to a comprehensive measurement framework considering non-financial performance measures. The can be distinguished into:

- Effectiveness measures: capturing the quality aspect, e.g. error free processes
- Efficiency measures: capturing reliable and streamlined processes, e.g. Invoice paid per FTE
- Compliance measures: capturing adherence to regulations, e.g. no. of violations
- Strategy measures: capturing adherence to defined strategy, e.g. level of customer satisfaction

For all types of measures benchmarking is crucial. This becomes particularly important for KPIs since they are only indicative of associated performance.[57]

Further development of the SSC organization towards higher value creation has to be a hybrid of maintaining absolute consistency and continuous improvement and innovation.

The inherent dichotomy in that mixture can be solved by closely measuring all steps in innovation and change.[58] KPIs enable such measurement.

To make the contribution visible, Shared Services executive are encouraged to communicate this value contribution to the overall corporate performance.

57 Cf. *LIVIU* et al. (2008), p. 193.
58 Cf. *WHITWORTH* (2010), p. 5.

6 Current Limitations for Further Value Creation

The majority of organizations are working within a heterogeneous IT landscape resulting both from decentralized management and acquisitions. This heterogeneity impedes full standardization as at least on activity level processes differ. SSC staff needs to be able to handle multiple systems and process variants. With regards to efficiency this can be seen as one obstacle.
With regards to the harmonization of the IT landscape or the implementation of additional process facilitating applications an additional limiting factor are IT resources. Interviewees state a constant shortage of IT resources. As system support is a huge driver for efficiency but also quality and transparency the shortage of dedicated resources supporting requested system implementations impedes further value add.

Furthermore, poor master data quality is identified as problematic area. It leads to broken processes which increase operational costs for detecting and correcting errors. As a consequence, the potential of automation cannot fully be explored.

Organizational interfaces are often a drawback when it comes to end to end business process optimization efforts affecting different functions across the value chain. This seems to be symptomatic for many organizations. One interviewee stated: "The less you own a process the less value you can bring". Thus, a direct mandate from senior management with regards to the ownership of a process is required to effectively trigger improvements and ensure overall alignment. The lack of such a mandate makes SSC organizations struggling with end-to-end process optimizations. As a consequence, end-to-end process optimization needs to go hand in hand with organizational restructuring.

Another obstacle to progress indwells in corporate culture. The willingness to organize more processes and functions in a shared services model is not present in a number of organizations. There is still mental reservation against the model.

7 Future Potential

Shared services have to be understood as a journey whose capabilities for value creation depend on the maturity of the company. This can be examined from different perspectives.

Staying with existing processes interviewees state that future potential can be derived from higher standardization and consequent higher automation.

As companies come to higher maturity levels we likely will see a broadening range of back office functions being organized in a shared services model. Future potential can especially be seen in streamlining the processes of IT, HR, purchasing, controlling, and logistics.

There is also evidence that Shared services will develop more into the business partnering role away from pure transactional processing. The recipe that contributes to significantly better financial performance and business resiliency can be seen in the combination of operational excellence and business insight.

Another lever can be seen in the higher concentration of back office activities on regional and global basis. Apart from higher potential for economies of scale and scope, better possibilities for compliance enforcement are a trigger.

Today, most shared service organizations are captive centers. This is mainly due to historical reasons. Starting the Shared Services model the process and IT landscape is usually very heterogeneous resulting in high complexity. Most organizations decided for addressing this complexity first themselves. Outsourcing in such a state was apprehended with quality issues and even higher costs. Having reached a certain level of maturity, we can now observe that companies start the shift towards a hybrid model of captive and business process outsourcing (BPO). The hybrid promises the acceleration for taking the existing model to the next level of performance. Organizations can benefit from the providers' expanding global footprint, enhanced analytics capabilities, established operational excellence as well as their significant and ongoing investment in tools, technology but also process and industry expertise.

8 Conclusions

The findings of the study suggest that there is a broad spectrum of leverages for Finance Shared Services corporate performance can benefit from. Factors like bundling, the harmonization and standardization of processes or the usage of technology in order to automate processes have a direct impact on profit and loss by reducing operating costs.

In addition, a number of areas were identified which indirectly influence profit and loss. By reducing complexity and creating higher flexibility the Finance Shared Services supports the company in rapidly responding to changing business environments. Examples have shown that Finance Shared Services can even create value beyond finance processes. Also, the Shared Services model cannot only be applied to transactional processes but as well to more knowledge driven ones. These can benefit from higher professionalization and create value from that. Furthermore, evidence was found, that people capabilities can better be leveraged with the Shared Services model. Better control systems enforce compliance with company laws and regulations and can support the alignment with the overall corporate strategy.

Overall, the various initiatives result in higher quality and transparency which can have both direct and indirect impacts on the cost position.

In order to realize these benefits a carefully executed strategy, the redesign and reorganization of roles and responsibilities, standardization of both processes and IT applications as well as proper change management can be seen as critical management issues. With regards to measuring the benefits, especially non-financial measures are capable of capturing the value. Defining the measurements, a number of contingency factors have to be taken into consideration.

To fully leverage the Shared Services model identified limitations have to be overcome. Also, stated further potential can only be leveraged once challenges are addressed and a certain maturity is reached.

In the future, strategic reasons will become the main factor for the higher penetration of shared services within leading edge companies. These reasons are economically, technically, politically, strategically and organizationally motivated. Having key functions concentrated in centrals units, the formulation of effective strategies and their consistent deployment across the organization is much easier. As such, the adoption of Shared Services by an organization can be seen as an attempt to restructure the organization as a whole towards greater effectiveness.

Abbreviations and Terms

AP	Accounts Payable
CEO	Chief Executive Officer
DSO	Days Sales Outstanding
ERP	Enterprise Resource Planning
ERS	Evaluated Receipt Settlement
EU	European Union
FSS	Finance Shared Services
FTE	Full-time Equivalent, measuring unit for the workforce of one employee
GRN	Goods Receipt Note
HR	Human Resources
IT	Information Technology
KPI(s)	Key Performance Indicator(s)
OCR	Optical Character Recognition
P	Power
P&L	Profit and Loss
PO	Purchase Order

ROA	Return on Assets
ROI	Return on Investment
ROS	Return on Sales
SLA	Service Level Agreement
SSC	Shared Service Center
SSO	Shared Services Organization(s)
T	Time
W	Work

References

ACCENTURE (2010): Driving High Performance through Shared Services, online: http://www.accenture.com/SiteCollection_Documents/PDF/Accenture_Driving_High_Performance_through_Shared_Services_Accenture_Capabilities_Qualifications.pdf, download: 6-22-2012.

BADER, R. (2008): Erfolgsfaktoren von Shared Services: Strategische und Operative Aspekte im Visier des Managements, Saarbrücken 2008.

BANGEMANN, T. (2011): Ungenutztes Potenzial in Shared Services, online: http://www.personaler-online.de/typo3/nc/personalthemen/suche-in_artikeln/detailansicht/artikel/ungenutztes-potenzial-in-shared-services.html, date: 09-13-2011, download: 07-25-2012.

BERRY, L. L./BENDAPUDI, N. (2007): Health Care: A Fertile Field for Service Research, in: Journal of Service Research, 2007, p. 111–122.

BITITCI, U. S. et al. (2005): Measuring and Managing Performance in Collaborative Enterprises, in: International Journal of Operations and Production Management, 2005, p. 333–353.

CENUSE, M./DRIGA, I. (2010): Advantages and Disadvantages of the Euro, in: Annals of the University of Petrosani Economics, 2010, p. 61–68.

CHAN, L. L. M. et al. (2004): In Search of Sustained Competitive Advantage: The Impact of Organizational Culture, Competitive Strategy and Human Resource Management Practices on Firm Performance, in: International Journal of Human Resource Management, 2004, p. 17–35.

CROSS, K. F./LYNCH, R. L. (1988/89): The SMART Way to Sustain and Define Success, in: National Productivity Review, 1988/89, p. 23–33.

DAVIS, T. R. V. (2005): Integrating Shared Services With the Strategy and Operations of MNEs, in: Journal of General Management, 2005, p. 1–17.

DERVEN, M. (2011): Advancing the Shared Services Journey through Training, in: T+D, 2011, p. 58–63.

DICTIONARY, BUSINESS (2012): Performance, online: http://www.businessdictionary.com/ definition/performance.html, download: 08-09-2012.

DIXON, J. R. et al. (1990): The New Performance Challenge: Measuring Operations for World-Class Competition, Homewood 1990.

DRESSLER, S. (2007): Shared Services – Historie und aktuelle Relevanz, in: is report, 2007, p. 36–40.

DYDUCH, W. (2008): Corporate Entrepreneurship Measurement for Improving Organizational Performance, in: Journal of Economics & Management, 2008, p. 15–40.

ERNST&YOUNG (2008): Financial Shared Service Center – Wertbeitrag oder Strohfeuer?, 2008.

EUROPEAN UNION (2012): Economic and Monetary Affairs: Stability and growth, online: http://europa.eu/pol/emu/index_en.htm, download: 08-07-2012.

FITZGERALD, L./MOON, P. (1996): Performance Measurement in Service Industries – Making it Work, London 1996.

FITZGERALD, L. et al. (1991): Performance Measurement in Service Businesses, London, 1991.

VON GLAHN, C. (2007): Shared Services: Gestaltungskonzepte zur Bereitstellung von IT-Leistungen in multinationalen Konzernen, Berlin 2007.

GRÖNROOS, C./OJASALO, K. (2004): Service Productivity: Towards a Conceptualization of the Transformation of Inputs into Economic Results in Services, in: Journal of Business Research, 2004, p. 414–423.

JÄÄSKELÄINEN, A. et al. (2012): A Contingency Approach to Performance Measurement in Service Operations, in: Measuring Business Excellence, 2012, p. 43–52.

JANSSEN, M./JOHA, A. (2008): Emerging Shared Service Organizations and the Service-oriented Enterprise: Critical Management Issues, in: Strategic Outsourcing: An International Journal, 2008, p. 35–49.

JANSSEN, M. et al. (2009): Simulation and Animation for Adopting Shared Services: Evaluating and Comparing Alternative Arrangements, in: Government Information Quarterly, 2009, p. 15–24.

JOACHIM, A. (2001): Central Office, in: Financial Management (14719185), 2001, p. 34.

JOHNSON, G. et al. (2008): Exploring Corporate Strategy: Text and Cases, 8, 2008.

KAPLAN, R. S./NORTON, D. P. (1992): The Balanced Scorecard. Measures That Drive Performance, in: Harvard Business Review, 1992, p. 71–79.

KEEGAN, D. P. et al. (1989): Are Your Performance Measures Obsolete?, in: Management Accounting, 1989, p. 45–50.

KEUPER, F./OECKING, C. (2006): Shared-Service-Center – The First and the Next Generation, in: *KEUPER, F./OECKING, C.* (Eds.), Corporate Shared Services: Bereitstellung von Dienstleistungen im Konzern, Wiesbaden, 2006, p. 476–502.

LACITY, M. C./FOX, J. (2008): Creating Global Shared Services – Lessons from Reuters in: MIS Quarterly Executive, 2008, p. 17–32.

LACITY, M. C. et al. (2008): Global Outsourcing of Back Office Services: Lessons, Trends, and Enduring Challenges, in: Strategic Outsourcing: An International Journal, 2008, p. 13–34.

LAUBE, H. (2008): Wie der Computer zu Hause einzog, online: http://www.ftd.de/it-medien/it-telekommunikation/:ftd-serie-die-geschichte-der-it-revolution-wie-der-computer-zu-hause-einzog/334916.html, download: 7-26-2012.

LEBAS, M./EUSKE, K. (2007): A Conceptual and Operational Delineation of Performance, in: *NEELY, A.* (Ed.), Business Performance Measurement: Theory and Practice, Cambridge, 2007, p. 125–139.

LIDDELL, J. (2010): Top 10 Developments that Changed Shared Services, CSC News, 2010, 10-13-2010.

LIVIU, C. et al. (2008): Strategic Control and the Performance Measurement Systems in: Annals of the University of Oradea, Economic Science Series, 2008, p. 189–194.

MELNYK, S. A. et al. (2004): Metrics and Performance Measurement in Operations Management: Dealing with the Metrics Maze, in: Journal of Operations Management, 2004, p. 209–217.

MEYER, M. W./GUPTA, V. (1994): The Performance Paradox, in: Research in Organizational Behaviour, 1994, p. 309–369.

MULANI, N. (2009): Maximizing Worldwide Effectiveness with a Centrally Led Operation, in: LOGISTICS MANAGEMENT, 2009, p. 25–26.

N. N. (2008): Schüler in der EU lernen Fremdsprachen nun früher, online: http://europa.eu/rapid/pressReleasesAction.do?reference=IP/08/1754&format=HTML&aged=0&language=DE&guiLanguage=en, download: 08-06-2012.

N. N. (2012): 5 Steps to Successfully Launch a F&A Shared Services Center, in: The Controller's report, 2012, p. 13–14.

NEELY, A. et al. (2001): The Performance Prism in Practice, in: Measuring Business Excellence, 2001, p. 6–13.

NEELY, A. et al. (2000): Performance Measurement System Design: Developing and Testing a Process-based Approach, in: International Journal of Operations & Production Management, 2000, p. 1119–1145.

NICKERSON, C. (2000): Playing the Corporate Language Game: An Investigation of the Genres and Discourse Strategies in English used by Dutch Writers Working in Multinational Corporations, Amsterdam (NL) 2000.

OSHRI, I. (2012): The German Economy is Leveraging Shared Services, online: http://www.ssonetwork.com/sourcing-models-strategy/articles/the-german-economy-is-leveraging-shared-services/, download: 08.29.2012.

PURTELL, K. (2005): Shared Service: A Benchmark Study, 2005.

QUINN, B. et al. (2000): Shared Services: Mining for Corporate Gold, London (UK) 2000.

Reiss, M. (2007): Marktwirtschaft im Unternehmen – Vom „Mythos Markt" zum Modell der Hybridkoordination, in: Zeitschrift für Management, 2007, p. 146–166.

Samsonowa, T. (2012): Industrial Research Performance Management: Key Performance Indicators in the ICT Industry, Berlin/Heidelberg, 2012.

Schneider, F. (2010): Saving Money at Kingfisher: The Less Obvious Way, CSC News, 2010, 10-13-2010, p. 5–6.

Schulman, D. S. et al. (1999): Shared Services – Adding Value to the Business Units, New York (NY) 1999.

Simons, R. (2000): Performance Measurement and Control Systems for Implementing Strategy, Upper Saddle River (NJ) 2000.

Su, N. et al. (2009): Shared Services Transformation: Conceptualization and Valuation from the Perspective of Real Options, in: Decision Sciences, 2009, p. 381–402.

SunGard/AvantGard (2010): The Next Generation Shared Service Center – What Have We Learned?, online: www.sungard.com/avantgard, download: 08-16-2012.

Taulia (2012): Dynamic Discounting: New Possibilities for AP, online: http://www.taulia.com/platform/dynamic-discount-optimizer.html, download: 08-12-2012.

Ulbrich, F. (2003): Introducing a Research Project on Shared Services in Governmental Agencies, Reykjavik (Iceland) 2003.

Wenderoth, M. (2011): Critical Success Factors of Shared Service Projects – Results of an Empirical Study, in: Advances In Management, 2011, p. 21–26.

Whitworth, J. (2010): Key Performance Indicators as a Tool to Add Value, CSC News, 2010, 10-13-2010, p. 4–5.

Visualize and Monitor Shared Services Quality by a Corporate Dashboard

Interview with *Oliver Wolf*

Siemens, s.r.o, Global Shared Services

One of the most difficult tasks shared services managers face is measuring and demonstrating value returned to their stakeholders. How can the value of Shared Services be measured, specifically in terms that are quantifiable and meaningful to customers and senior management? How can it also, at the same time, be guaranteed that this analytical measurement is actually useful as performance and analytical tools by the shared services leadership team?

In this interview, Oliver Wolf shares some of the hints, best practices and pitfalls he has learned while developing a Quality Dashboard tracking the performance of Shared Services Centers with the help of analytical metrics.

What is the idea behind the Quality Dashboard and why was the implementation a necessary step for the Siemens Shared Services Organization (SSO), specifically for the Business Line Accounting & Finance Services (AFS)?

The implementation of a Quality Dashboard was an important step for the *Siemens* Shared Services Organization (SSO), and was closely linked to the strategic development phase of "lift-drop". In this phase, the *Siemens* SSO focused on the systematic transition management of specific accounting tasks that were previously handled independently in the *Siemens* Clusters or Sectors, i.e. in the regions and in business units. The overarching project overseeing these transitions was called Finance Bundling and can be considered as one of the most important projects ever to face *Siemens* Financial Community and to change it in a fundamental way. One of the key prerequisites to realize a project of this size is the solid mandate by the managing board.

Even though the mandate committed the regions and businesses to support the bundling of transactional tasks in the Shared Services Organization, the Centers nevertheless have had to establish an integrated quality concept to prove that the level of service quality can actually be maintained or ideally improved. The Quality Dashboard was established within the financial SSO to measure quality before and after the transitions for the key services taken over from the business units. In doing so, a fact-based discussion with internal customers about service quality can be ensured. Due to the fact that within *Siemens* various Enterprise-Resource-Planning- (ERP)-systems are in use, the need for a KPI reporting based on centrally available data is very important. One solution for this problem was provided by the usage of centrally available compliance data regarding the Purchase-to-Pay Process, which is retrieved by the respective ERP systems.

How were the Key Performance Indicators (KPIs) selected?

When setting up the Quality Dashboard for the *Siemens* SSO, the first step is to find a common understanding of how Shared Services metrics should actually be defined. The following four ideas are used as a basis for the development of the Quality Dashboard in the area of Accounting & Finance Services.

The metrics should be...

- ...based upon consistent, measurable data
- ...expressed in an unambiguous way and defined in an objective, reproducible way
- ...suitable for the structured monthly reporting within the SSO and to its customers
- ...simple to collect (in terms of effort, process, time and cost)
- ...easy to understand and to present
- ...actionable and not simply 'nice to have' general information.

Another basic premise for the set-up of the Quality Dashboard is to deliver actionable information rather than just data. So the intention is to actually create metrics that analyze the data available within the necessary context in order to provide a solid decision-making basis for customers and internal management.

After having aligned the basic assumptions for the specific metrics in the Quality Dashboard, the next step is to define the recipients of the reporting and to understand their individual interest in the Dashboard. Examples of questions used to systematically analyze the interests of the relevant stakeholders include:

- Who is interested in the metrics?
- What do they want to know?
- How can they be visually attracted?
- How often do they need to know?
- Why do they want to know it?
- What will they do with this information?
- What do we expect as a result?

With the help of the basic assumptions and a systematic analysis of the target group of the Dashboard, the next step is to create the actual Key Performance Indicators (KPIs). Especially in the Accounting & Finance area, a variety of KPIs are in use and the approach is to first of all select those KPIs that would truly matter for the defined target group. Furthermore, it was decided to measure KPIs prior to the transition to the SSO (on the customer side) and after the transition (on the SSO side). The KPIs are developed for the variety of core services offered by the *Siemens* Shared Services Organization – for example, in the area of accounts payable, KPIs include the average number of posted 3rd party documents per Full-time Equivalent (FTE) and per month. It is of high importance to isolate the relevant processes and then select the right level of analysis for the key performance indicators. The metric should not be too detailed, but should rather reflect a solid basis that management can easily understand without being involved in the details of accounting. Additionally, all KPIs should have clearly defined inputs, outputs and impacts. Specifically referring to the impacts, the visualization with the help of traffic lights, harvey balls etc. should not be underestimated. It is essential to make sure the rating criteria are applied uniformly on a global level and differences are measured based upon the same criteria.

One of the key success factors when developing the KPIs is the continuous alignment with the major stakeholders and the design of appropriate feedback loops. From the beginning, the focus lies on involving the customers, the governance and the shared services management in the development process to increase the acceptance of the KPIs in the Quality Dashboard.

What does the Quality Dashboard look like today?

The Quality Dashboard includes 12 KPIs in the areas of accounts payable, accounts receivable and closing and reporting. The reporting and the development of the KPIs is published on a monthly basis and two main purposes can be identified: firstly, the establishment of a discussion basis enabling a fact-based discussion with customers and secondly, the internal monitoring of the individual Center performance.

The KPIs are calculated in a uniform way, using consistent data formats and formulas guaranteed with the help of centrally available data sources or new extractor programs. Moreover, the Quality Dashboard includes input (customer responsibility) as well as output (SSO responsibility) related KPIs in order to create a complete end-to-end picture. The Dashboard can be accessed via the company's intranet and offers filter possibilities so that each individual recipient can nominate and define areas of interest, such as region, Shared Services Center and reporting period.

The first high-level view a visitor sees is the pie-chart for every KPI and the corresponding color-code according to the actual performance. If the visitor is now interested in learning more about a specific KPI, a single mouse-click guides him into the level below where a trend analysis on the upcoming months may also be accessed.

Which sources provide input for the monthly KPI reporting? How is continuous objectivity of the figures achieved?

Depending on the respective services in the area of Accounting & Finance such as accounts payable, accounts receivable and closing and reporting, the underlying databases actually differ from each other. But for all databases, the principle of being governed and hosted from a central *Siemens* perspective applies. This enables a fact based discussion as the relevant data is extracted from centrally accepted databases and compiled using uniform formulas.

A continuous objectivity is also achieved by opening the Quality Dashboard to dedicated key customers. By giving access rights to defined key customers, the *Siemens* Shared Services Organization demonstrates its commitment to transparency and customer orientation.

What would be your recommendation for other companies wanting to introduce quality reporting in a Shared Services environment?

Primarily, the collaboration and stringent communication with key stakeholders is one of the prerequisites when developing a Quality Dashboard. If you start involving customers, governance or other groups of interest right from the beginning, chances are high that they will accept the final set-up of the Dashboard more easily since they actively participated in the development phase.

Further, another piece of advice is to avoid using only history to set the standard for future performance. History is not the only reliable baseline for future performance measurement since new requirements and impacts need to be constantly taken into consideration. Look for objective impacts in order to determine how "red" or "green" statuses should be defined.

When it comes to the actual visualization and the variety of options you have, e.g. dashboards, scorecards or reports, the principle of how to attract the audience in the most efficient way should be applied. Dashboards provide indicators, estimates and summarizing charts to help senior managers make strategic decisions. The design principle of dashboards is to keep them simple and emphasize critical information in the most prominent way. Another advantage of dashboards, and also one of the main reasons why the visualization via dashboard is chosen for GSS, is that often dashboards can be automated and generated automatically from existing databases. In fact, more than 80 % of the KPIs of the Shared Services quality dashboard in the Accounting & Finance area are generated automatically, meaning that manual effort is kept to a minimum.

Nevertheless, scorecards offer a management system with integrated measurement and reports helping to present details on a deeper level. Finally, it is up to the key stakeholders to express their wishes and thoughts on the actual visualization of the metrics. One of the major findings for the *Siemens* SSO is that the higher one climbs in the hierarchy, the simpler and faster the key messages should be conveyed. By introducing the Shared Services Quality Dashboard the systematic measurement of the SSO's performance has improved to a great extent, however, necessary enhancements such as fully automatic data retrieval still need to be realized.

Taking the challenges into consideration, the objectivity and the consistency of the databases are definitely the most important factors to focus on when implementing a Quality Dashboard. Last but not least, it is of utmost importance to closely align with all relevant stakeholders at every development step to make sure they fully support the use of the Dashboard.

How would you define the future development stages of a Quality Dashboard?

'You cannot manage what you do not measure' is an old management saying that is still accurate today. Unless something is systematically measured and reported, management attention cannot be directed to whether specific processes are improving or deteriorating over time or to which parts of the process needs immediate attention. Looking at the strategic development phases of the *Siemens* SSO, the Quality Dashboard was introduced in the "lift-drop" phase where specific accounting processes were bundled into the Shared Services Centers. Moving to the next phase - the "change" phase - improvement and optimization of the processes managed by the SSO is expected by internal management and the customer base. Of course, continuous tracking and analysis during this "change" phase can be used to identify and publicize whether expected improvement eventuates, making a Quality Dashboard indispensable to all concerned.

Taking the next step forwards, the third development phase of the SSO is referred to as "enhance and innovate" by GSS. In this phase, the focus is on creating new portfolio elements and the introduction of automation wherever possible. Again, the continuous measurement of quality metrics provides a transparent tool that can be used to guide the realization of this strategic step.

Looking at the actual set-up of the Quality Dashboard and the selection of KPIs, the goal is to entirely automate the KPI retrieval in order to keep the manual effort involved to an absolute minimum. This means that the desired next development stage of the Quality Dashboard is the total automation of the Dashboard where only minor plausibility checks need to be executed.

Mr. Wolf, thanks for this interview.

Process Quality and Performance in a Shared Services Environment

MATTHIAS LOHRMANN and *ALEXANDER RIEDEL*

KPMG AG Wirtschaftsprüfungsgesellschaft

Executive Summary

Shared Services Organizations work closely with their clients to design, implement and enact service processes. This shared responsibility poses particular governance challenges that cannot be fully addressed through conventional service level management or end-to-end performance indicators such as cycle times.

Rather, effective managerial analysis and control of processes in a Shared Services environment requires appropriate concepts to comprehensively assess process quality in the sense of design and implementation, and process performance in the sense of execution. To ensure effective control, the underlying concepts of process quality and performance should enable to delineate the responsibilities of Shared Services Organizations and clients, and reflect the overall targets of the organization to ensure effective control.

This chapter develops a corresponding approach by analyzing the impact of Shared Services processes on organizational targets, deriving concise dimensions of process quality and process performance in a Shared Services environment. On that basis, it provides frameworks to support process quality and process performance assessment which can be refined to a concrete application scenario.

1 Motivation

Shared Services Organizations (SSOs) are mostly focused on executing standardized activities within business processes[1] based on formal interaction with service clients (SCs). In this context, the concept of *Business Process Management* (BPM) has achieved wide acceptance since the early 1990s.[2]

Typical BPM lifecycle models for SSOs range from process design and implementation over process enactment to process performance measurement, services charging, and process control. In this context, organizational responsibilities for process design and implementation on the one hand, and process enactment on the other hand alternate between SSOs and SCs. This characteristic poses particular *governance challenges* which apply to the entire BPM lifecycle, as summarized in figure 1.

---

1 Cf. *Workflow Management Coalition* (1999), p. 10 et seq.

2 Cf. *van der Aalst/ter Hofstede/Weske* (2003).

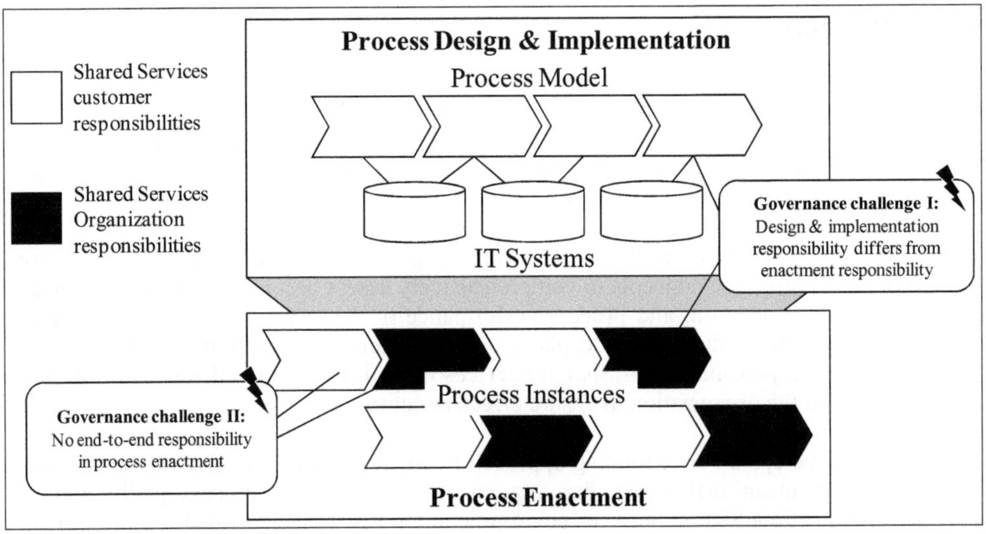

Figure 1: Governance challenges in a Shared Services environment

Governance challenge I pertains to the SSO's bearing responsibility to enact activities within process without being responsible for process design and implementation, which is typically governed by SCs. This may lead to issues with regard to the optimization of process design and implementation, services charging, and the execution of process control.

Governance challenge II pertains to the lack of end-to-end process responsibility. SSOs generally rely on process input provided by their SCs. End-to-end optimization will require driving each activity in an end-to-end process towards overall optimization. This is difficult without an overarching governance role. Moreover, proper process performance measurement, services charging and process control may be impeded.

Note that, in principle, both governance challenges exist in conventional organizational structures as well. In this case, however, it is often possible to manage emerging governance issues by referring to common leadership. For instance, an accounting department within a business unit (BU) might refer to BU management to resolve issues with the BU procurement department. Shared Services, however, aggravates the issues at hand because it deliberately creates a "market" situation resembling dealings between independent parties – it is in the best interest of each party to "sub-optimize" within its own domain. The provision of appropriate master data by a Shared Services customer is a good example in this regard.

To address the governance challenges described, Shared Services Organizations mostly rely on *Service Level Agreements (SLAs)*. SLAs constitute formalized agreements between or within organizations to govern mutual obligations regarding the provision of services. They have been pioneered in the field of information management and comprise issues such as quality of services (QoS) or collaboration duties on the customer side.[3] SLAs, however, are aimed at backwards-oriented control with regard to minimum requirements for both parties. They are thus limited in their ability to drive future-oriented continuous optimization of busi-

3 Cf. TRIENEKENS et al. (2005).

ness processes as required in today's competitive environment. Moreover, SLAs typically include end-to-end performance indicators which are, for instance, derived from common external benchmarking metrics.[4] However, these indicators fail to delineate the impact of SSO and SC responsibilities (cf. Example 1). They are thus not apt to effectively control future behavior of involved parties.

Example 1: Performance Indicators in SLAs. Cycle times are a typical example of performance indicators included in SLAs. Since they are defined in an end-to-end manner without considering lead times in differing parties' contributions to individual tasks, they are, however not suitable for to control individual behavior. For a typical example of a corresponding conflict case, consider increased cycle times caused by the SSO waiting for master data entry by the SC. In this case, the SSO may fail to fulfill its SLA without bearing responsibility for the underlying defect.

Beyond service level management, this chapter therefore looks into techniques to address process governance challenges which are of particular relevance to SSOs. We stipulate that the governance challenges lined out can be alleviated by implementing effective assessment methods for *process quality* as a result of process design and implementation, and *process performance* as a result of process enactment.

By creating appropriate transparency on existing issues and optimization potentials, these concepts could be used to counterbalance the governance constraints between SSOs and SCs. Accordingly, the contribution of this chapter can be summarized as follows:

- *Defining dimensions of process quality and process performance* which are effective to address governance challenges in Shared Services environments.
- Designing a framework for the *assessment of process quality.*
- Categorizing indicators and evaluating available options for *the assessment of process performance.*

The remainder of this chapter is structured as follows: Section 2 discusses relevant BPM lifecycle stages to illustrate the typical split of responsibilities between SSO and SC. Section 3 develops criteria for effective process quality and performance assessment, and deducts definitions for both terms. Sections 4 and 5, respectively, look into process quality and process performance assessment in more detail, including related work on both concepts. Section 6 concludes the chapter with a discussion of results and an outlook on future developments.

---

4 Cf. CAMP (1989).

2 Business Process Management Lifecycle Stages for Shared Services Organizations

Lifecycle models have proven as a valuable tool to categorize BPM activities.[5] Accordingly, figure 2 summarizes lifecycle stages of particular relevance to Shared Services Organizations.

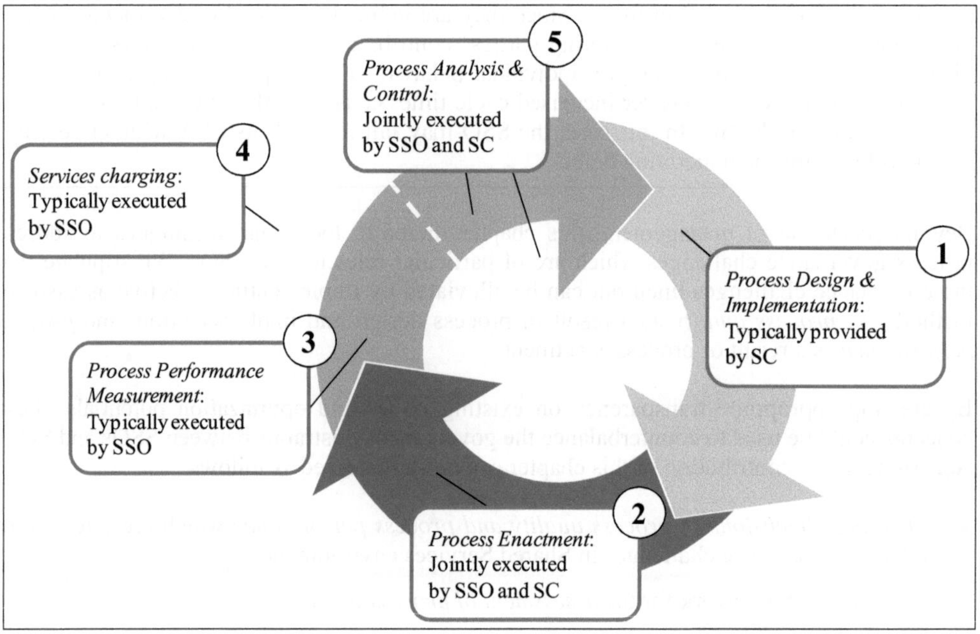

Figure 2: BPM lifecycle model for Shared Services Organizations

As described in figure 1, SSOs assume joint responsibility for the BPM lifecycle together with their customers. Along the BPM lifecycle stages, these can be described as follows:

- Information systems or other assets reflecting a formal or informal underlying process model are typically provided by clients.[6] Accordingly, responsibility[7] for *process design & implementation* lies with the SC.
- *Process enactment* is generally executed jointly by the SSO and its SCs in the sense of an end-to-end process. Typically, the SSO relies on its SCs regarding required process input such as making data available, taking decisions or approving results.

---

5 Cf. *WESKE* (2007), p. 11 et seqq.

6 Information systems apt to incorporate formal process models are designated as *process-aware information systems* (PAISs), cf. *REICHERT/WEBER* (2012). Formal process models can, for instance, be defined in the Business Process Model and Notation (BPMN) language; cf. *THE OBJECT MANAGEMENT GROUP* (2011).

7 Note that *responsibility* for design and implementation of information systems generally lies with the IT function, while *accountability* in terms of requirements definition, testing and final approval lies with technical functions (e.g., human resources management). For reasons of simplicity, we will refer only to the term *responsibility* in the context of this chapter.

- *Process performance measurement* is mostly executed by the SSO by assessing performance indicators such as cycle times. Results are, however, provided to SCs as well, for instance, in a so-called *dashboard* tool.
- *Service charging* is typically executed by the SSO in reconciliation with SCs. Charging may be based on budgetary indicators (e.g., cost plus 6%, allocated by revenue) or transactional volumes. In many cases, budgets or volume prices are renegotiated on a yearly basis.
- *Process analysis & control* is executed jointly by the SSO and its SCs, generally on the basis of process performance measurement results: As described above, feedback into process design and implementation is to be executed by SCs since they govern, for instance, the respective IT systems. Feedback into process enactment must be executed by both parties for the respective work share. Note that constructs to measure *process quality and performance* constitute tools to be applied in this lifecycle stage.

Example 2 illustrates SSO and SC work shares for a sample process.

Example 2: BPM Lifecycle. Consider the management of incoming invoices. Scanning invoices, matching against purchase orders and goods receipts, obtaining invoice approvals and managing escalation in case of differences constitute typical tasks for Shared Services.

Regarding *process design & implementation*, the execution of the related activities relies on the business process design implemented in SCs' logistics and accounting systems. Applying a Shared Service Centers' own workflow system[1] is still an exception in this standard situation. *Process enactment* is executed jointly: the SSO relies on procurement and materials management data provided by its customers, who are also responsible to approve invoices if required. Accordingly, *performance measurement* results, e.g., the number of invoices managed in comparison to personnel resources available, will reflect the performance of *both* parties involved. Obtaining SSO performance measures not biased by client performance is particularly difficult

On that basis, it is difficult to consider, for instance, the proper availability of supplier master data for payment terms in *service charging*, although this will be a major determinant of effort incurred. Likewise, the Shared Services options to execute *process analysis & control* to foster improvement of master data availability are limited.

Table 1 matches SSO process governance challenges[8] against relevant BPM lifecycle stages to further illustrate the issues at hand.

BPM Lifecycle Stages	**Governance Challenge I: Differing design & implementation vs. enactment responsibilities**	**Governance Challenge II: No end-to-end responsibility in process enactment**
Process design & implementation	SSO requirements may not be captured, leading to underperforming process implementations.	n/a
Process enactment	SSO activities are not optimally supported by process design and implementation.	Activities are not required to provide optimum results for subsequent steps if these are executed by a different party.
Process performance measurement	Data access to information systems operated by the client may be limited.	SSO/SC performance is difficult to delineate since only end-to-end performance can be measured in many cases.
Service charging	Impact of differing process design and implementations on SSO enactment effort difficult to delineate, may lead to costs-by-cause principle violations.[9]	Impact of client activities on SSO enactment effort difficult to delineate, may lead to costs-by-cause principle violations.
Process analysis & control	SSO's feedback into design & implementation impeded by differing organizational responsibilities.	No end-to-end process control due to differing organizational responsibilities, may lead to ongoing "sub-optimization" on the activity level instead of overall optimization on the process level.

Table 1: Governance challenges in the BPM lifecycle for Shared Services Organizations

8 Cf. section 1.

9 To obtain a "true and fair view"; cf. INTERNATIONAL ACCOUNTING STANDARDS BOARD (1989).

3 Understanding Process Quality and Process Performance

This section derives definitions for process quality and process performance. Both constitute "goal-bound artificial constructs" in the sense of the design science paradigm[10], and their effectiveness should be evaluated along "criteria of value or utility".[11] Therefore, this section sets out by defining appropriate effectiveness criteria for both constructs. We then discuss organizational targets in relation to processes in a Shared Services environment. On that basis, we define both process quality and process performance.

3.1 Effectiveness Criteria for Process Quality and Performance Constructs

To obtain appropriate effectiveness criteria for process quality and performance constructs, we re-consider the resolution of governance challenges in Shared Services scenarios as our relevant use case.[12] Assessment methods for process quality and performance are to be applied in the *process analysis & control* lifecycle stage. Accordingly, our effectiveness criteria are derived from criteria for *managerial analysis and control.*[13]

- *Congruence to organizational targets:* If process quality and performance assessment constructs are to be used to analyze and control process design & implementation and process enactment, respectively, measures must reflect desired actions.[14] For application in the area of BPM, two aspects are of particular relevance:
  - *Comprehensive coverage:* Process quality and performance assessment must reflect the full scope of organizational targets associated with the process.
  - *Exclusive coverage:* Process quality and performance assessment may not be biased by including aspects that are of no relevance regarding organizational targets.
- *Reflection of responsibilities scope:* Effective quality and control measures must reflect the scope of responsibilities of actors involved. In other words, end-to-end measurement might indicate present issues, but will not point out whom to approach for corrective action. Measures thus need to be *delineated* accordingly.
- *Transparency and retraceability:* Organizational acceptance is a major prerequisite to convert analysis results into effective control measures. The most common impediment in this respect is the conviction of stakeholders that measurement and analysis results fail to properly reflect actual performance. Accordingly, an appropriate, i.e. transparent and retraceable, *standard* has to be applied to performance and quality assessment.[15] Note

---

10 Cf. SIMON (1996).

11 Cf. MARCH/SMITH (1995).

12 Cf. section 1.

13 Cf. EPSTEIN/HENDERSON (1989).

14 Cf. KENNERLEY/NEELY (2002).

15 Cf. EISENHARDT (1985).

that technical "jargons" encountered in many organizations and professions can also be considered as a means of managerial control in this regard.[16]

- *Cost of computation*: This aspect as a criterion to appraise organizational control methods has been developed with the concept of bounded rationality.17 The criterion reflects efficiency considerations generally valid for analysis and control in an economic context: cost and effort incurred may not exceed benefits gained. As sub-aspects, consider the requirement to properly formalize measures to enable automated measurement, and a good integration with the existing landscape of tools and systems, e.g. for workflow management.

Note that the first and second effectiveness criteria, *congruence to organizational targets* and *reflection of responsibilites scope*, refer to the actual semantic content of assessment constructs, while the third and fourth criteria, *transparency and retraceability* and *cost of computation*, relate to practical applicability and usability. Accordingly, *congruence to organizational targets* and *reflection of responsibilities scope* are of special relevance as our *primary effectiveness criteria.*

In the following, we will use the effectiveness criteria lined out to appraise both related work and our results. In the sense of a design principle, the primary effectiveness criterion also serves as a starting point for the design of our proposals.

3.2 Processes and Organizational Targets

To align further progress with our primary effectiveness criterion, *congruence to organizational targets*, this section discusses organizational targets related to process design & implementation and enactment in the context of SSOs. A sound understanding of relevant organizational targets and the respective interrelations is a key prerequisite to develop an effective notion of process quality and performance.

According to common definitions[18], business processes are designed, implemented and enacted to achieve a business objective, to fulfill a policy goal, to satisfy a customer demand etc. In the following we, refer to this notion as to the *results specification* of a process. In this respect, it is important to understand that business objectives cannot simply be expressed by a set of tasks to be executed by a process. Rather, results specifications can be defined by relating desired resulting states to appropriate criteria, as illustrated by Example 2.[19] Note that this also includes required compliance criteria.

---

16 Cf. *OUCHI* (1979).

17 Cf. *SIMON* (1978) and *MARCH* (1978).

18 Cf., for instance, *DAVENPORT/SHORT* (1990), *HAMMER* (1990) and *WESKE* (2007).

19 For a formal definition of business objectives; cf. *LOHRMANN/REICHERT* (2012a).

> *Example 2: Business Objectives.* In the management of incoming invoices, the results specification of the invoice approval process cannot be expressed as "invoice approved". Rather, the relevant approval criteria, such as "purchase order available", "goods receipt available", "management approval available" etc. must be considered as well.
>
> Accordingly, the results specification would have to be defined by relating the desired states of "invoice approved" and "invoice declined" to the respective criteria. For "invoice declined", this might also include "escalation procedure triggered" as an additional requirement.
>
> A business process addressing this results specification would check the relevant criteria to determine the concrete desired state for each invoice, and act accordingly. With respect to fulfilling the results specification, it would not matter if this was done manually or, for instance, with the support of a workflow system.

Moreover, each process requires the availability of *resources* to be implemented and enacted. The economic context of *business* processes demands that resources are consumed sparingly. This corresponds to the more general notion of economic efficiency.[20] Figure 3 provides an overview on the resulting organizational target dimensions and their interdependencies:

- Regarding *results specifications*, we can distinguish two dimensions of organizational targets:
  - *Goal Effectiveness* refers to the contribution of the results specification set to overall organizational targets. This is a characteristic of the results specification instead of the process. In other words, a results specification can be considered as effective if its contents are of value to the organization in relation to the resources to be consumed to fulfill the results specification. In the context of Shared Services, goal effectiveness generally falls into the responsibility of SCs.[21]
  - *Process Effectiveness* refers to a process's achieving its results specification. Since SCs and SSOs share the responsibility for *process design & implementation* and *process enactment*, the responsibility for process effectiveness is also shared between SCs and SSOs. Each process requires the availability of resources to be enacted. Accordingly, we can discern between *formal effectiveness* in the sense of the process enabling to achieve its results specification in principle, and *full effectiveness* in the sense of limiting resources required to be available to achieve a results specification to a reasonable degree.
- *Efficiency* refers to the consumption of resources in relation to the results specification fulfilled. During *process design & implementation*, resources are consumed by, for instance, the implementation of workflow management systems.[22] During *process enactment*, resources are mainly consumed by using personnel. Similar to efficacy, this organ-

20 Cf. *THE ECONOMIST* (2012).

21 Moreover, the degree of complexity associated with effectiveness assessment considering the integration of processes into the overall value chain of the organization must be considered as prohibitive for formalized assessment (cf. the *transparency and retraceability* and *cost of computation* criteria).

22 For reasons of simplicity, we do not discern capital expenditures from operational expenditures here.

izational target lies in the shared responsibility of SCs and SSOs. A process is efficient if it reasonably limits its consumption of resources.

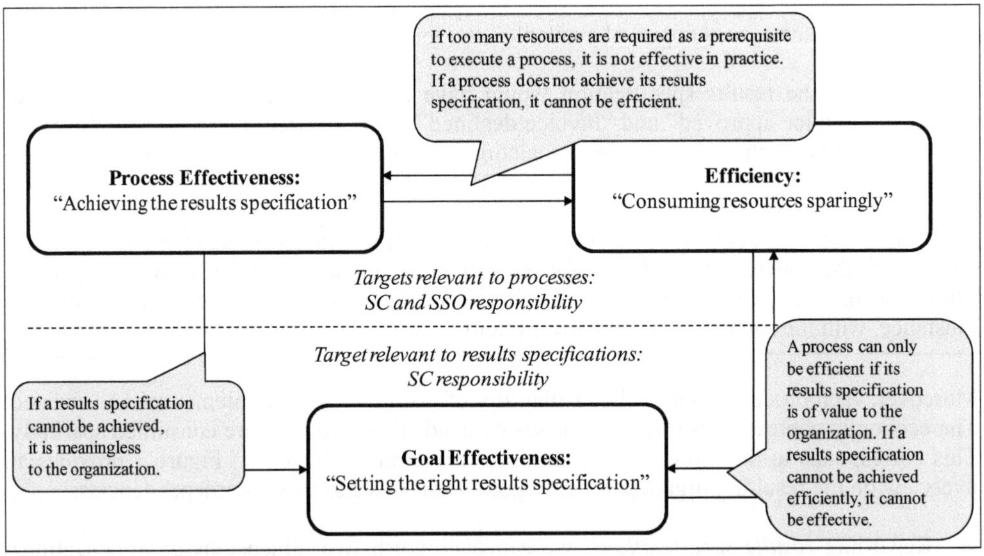

Figure 3: Organizational targets for business objectives and processes in a Shared Services context

As described above, *goal effectiveness* is a characteristic of the business objective associated with a process, and lies solely in the responsibility of SCs. Thus, only *process effectiveness* and *efficiency* constitute organizational target dimensions suitable for the assessment of process quality and performance. In the following, we therefore consider *process effectiveness* only, and refer to *effectiveness* in short.

By demanding a reasonable limitation to resources required to be available or consumed, full effectiveness and efficiency both require subject matter expert judgment. Example 3 illustrates *goal effectiveness*, *process effectiveness* and *efficiency* as organizational target dimensions.

Example 3: Organizational Target Dimensions. Again, consider the management of incoming invoices executed by a SSO together with its SC.

If the process could be eliminated by, e.g., switching to a credit note procedure (i.e., the supplier would check payment advices instead of the customer checking invoices), the results specification of having invoices managed would not be *goal-effective.*[23] This is, however, not an issue that can be addressed by means of BPM.

In terms of process effectiveness, if the process failed to acquire appropriate management approval for high-value invoices, it could not be considered as *formally effective.* If the process failed to timely address invoices that require manual approval, e.g., because of the underlying workflow lacking an escalation procedure, the process would not be *fully effective.* In this case, the process would unduly assume the availability of responsible managers.

If the process would involve undue amounts of manual effort, e.g. because it would require invoice data to be entered manually into the data base instead of automated scanning, the process would not be *efficient.*

Accordingly, relating availability and consumption of resources, respectively, to the achievement of a results specification lies at the core of assessing effectiveness and efficiency of processes. This view is summarized in figure 4.

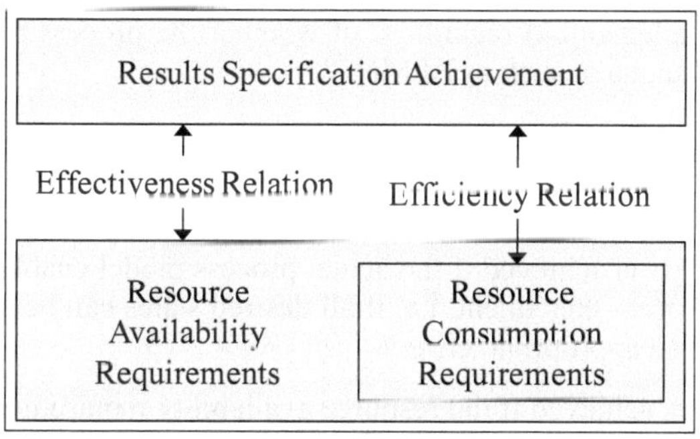

Figure 4: Business objectives vs. resources: effectiveness and efficiency relations

Note that this section's discussion of organizational targets with regard to processes in Shared Services Organizations is based on comparatively abstract targets which should be valid for organizations in a generic way. Instead, it would also be possible to seek a more direct relation to the vision and strategy of an organization if such are available. Consider, for instance, a competitive strategy based on speed to market or customer satisfaction. These topics might be directly incorporated into organizational targets applied to business processes, which would, in turn, impact our discussions in the following sections. However, the decisive factor in this context is the top-down, derivative approach of deducting an understanding of process quality and performance from organizational targets, and to further refine this understanding with appropriate indicators, reflecting the primary effectiveness criterion from section 3.1.

23 This example was cited by *DAVENPORT/SHORT* as well as *HAMMER* as the initial proponents of business process reengineering; cf. *DAVENPORT/SHORT* (1990) and *HAMMER* (1990).

3.3 Dimensions of Process Quality and Process Performance

In the sense of the design science paradigm, concise definitions for process quality and process performance serve as "constructs" to facilitate effective discussion of the underlying notions.[24] In comparison to fully-fledged sets of quality or performance indicators, they are not apt to be employed directly for quality or performance assessment, but allow deriving more detailed methods on the basis of a sound common understanding. The main advantage of this derivative "top-down" approach is that it provides a measure of control over the completeness of quality and performance measures. This aspect constitutes a challenging issue for the common approach of determining relevant indicators "bottom-up": in that case, it is not possible to ensure that all relevant dimensions of quality or performance are covered.

In the following, we apply the organizational targets of *effectiveness* (as stated above, we consider only *process effectiveness* here) and *efficiency* to the relevant BPM lifecycle stages, thus defining the dimensions of *process quality* and *process performance.*

In process design & implementation, it is possible to formalize a process model which is then implemented through a workflow system, a process-aware information system etc. Likewise, a process model may exist only implicitly in the form of policies or guidelines, as organizational knowledge[25] or as customizing of an ERP system. Process quality assessment is obviously easier if a formal process model is available. Considering the actual situation in organizations, this may, however, not constitute a strict requirement. In the following, we therefore refer to an *actual process* model as to the result of process design & implementation (e.g., an information system implemented) regardless of whether the process model has been formalized with a modeling language such as BPMN.[26]

During process design & implementation, the relevant organizational target dimensions are impacted as follows:

- *Formal effectiveness* is achieved if the actual process model enables to achieve its results specification in process enactment, i.e. if all desired states can be achieved under consideration of the related appropriate criteria.
- *Full effectiveness* is achieved if the resource availability requirements posed by the actual process model towards results specification achievement in process enactment are judged as reasonable by subject matter experts.
- *Efficiency* is achieved if the resource consumption requirements posed by the actual process model towards results specification achievement in process enactment are judged as reasonable by subject matter experts.[27]

---

24 Cf. *MARCH/SMITH* (1995).

25 Cf. *LEHNER* (2000).

26 Cf. *THE OBJECT MANAGEMENT GROUP* (2011).

27 In this context, resources consumed during process design & implementation (mostly capital expenditures, e.g., information system implementation cost) are not considered. These must be addressed in the course of business case assessment for the respective investment project. We assume this view because "sunk cost" should not impact actual quality assessment of processes.

Accordingly, these aspects constitute the dimensions of *process quality*.

Process enactment builds on process design & implementation – its impact on organizational targets is delimited by the actual process model. To present a "true and fair view" in the sense of *reflection of responsibilities scope*, effective process performance assessment therefore delineates process performance from process quality. This means that process performance needs to be defined more narrowly in comparison to process quality. Moreover, instead of the "model level" of process quality, process performance is assessed on the level of process instances in the sense of individual cases handled.[28]

Accordingly, during process enactment, the relevant organizational target dimensions are impacted as follows:

- From *formal effectiveness* to *compliance:* If a process instance adheres to its process model, we may assume that its results specification is achieved for the purposes of performance assessment.[29] The challenge of formal effectiveness in process enactment thus corresponds to compliance to internal and external regulations. Accordingly, *compliance* replaces the more general *formal effectiveness* as a process performance dimension.
- From *full effectiveness* to *model completion* and *timeliness:* If a process instance requires the availability of resources that are neither given by the process model nor consumed (cf. *efficiency*), this is only relevant if it leads to the instance terminating although it should be completed as per the model. Accordingly, *model completion* replaces the more general full effectiveness. In this context, cycle times can also be considered as an availability issue: *timely* availability of process results impacts organizational targets if subsequent processes need to be kept available while waiting for the instance to complete. Since process models typically do not address cycle times, and practical experience suggests that process models generally *can* be enacted on time, this is an issue of process performance.[30]
- *Efficiency*: In a Shared Services environment, resource consumption during process enactment typically pertains to human effort.31 This can be considered from two perspectives: labor capacity in an SSO, and processing effort incurred on the SC side. This distinction reflects the fact that SSO resources are usually committed to the process, which does not pertain to SC resources. Accordingly, efficiency in process enactment needs to consider labor capacity required and utilized in an SSO, and additional processing effort incurred in an SC.

---

28 Cf. *Workflow Management Coalition* (1999).

29 If the process model does not address the business objective, this is an issue of process quality, but not of process performance.

30 Note that in typical transactional shared services processes, cycle times result from the process instances' idle periods between processing steps. Typical process modeling languages provide message event and timer constructs to model this issue; cf. *The Object Management Group* 2011. However, these mechanisms are not commonly used.

31 In this respect, "tangible" direct material typically does not occur. However, human effort needs to consider not only direct labor cost, but also overhead such as the cost of office space.

The aspects described constitute the dimensions of *process performance.*

The dimensions of process quality and performance described can now be used to derive more detailed quality and performance indicators. The underlying structure reflecting organizational targets ensures that all relevant dimensions are addressed appropriately – if assessable quality or performance indicators cannot be found, we still may achieve transparency on the gaps of the quality and performance assessment system.

4 Assessing Process Quality

Since available approaches on business process quality are not specifically aimed at Shared Services environments, this section discusses existing work in general before we describe our solution towards process quality for SSOs and SCs.

4.1 Available Results on Business Process Quality

Approaches relevant to business process quality can be broadly divided into three groups: General management concepts applicable to business process quality, BPM concepts focusing on quality-related individual aspects of business processes, and more comprehensive frameworks for business process quality.

General management concepts applicable to business process quality are well exemplified by qualitative and quantitative benchmarking and the balanced scorecard.[32] They provide us with useful clues for our work process quality like, for instance, the balanced scorecard concept of mutually orthogonal "scorecard dimensions". Nevertheless, as they are not based on a BPM paradigm, they cannot fully cover our field without further efforts at detailing and adaptation.

On the other hand, BPM concepts focused on particular related aspects, such as the workability of a process model, are based on a BPM paradigm, but are not aimed at providing a comprehensive grasp of process quality as demanded by our primary effectiveness criteria.[33] Like general management concepts, they are thus apt to provide relevant insights, but not a comprehensive solution to the issue at hand.

More to our point, there are attempts at developing integrated business process quality frameworks.[34] These are generally based on systematizing quality attributes derived from related work, e.g. from software engineering. While this methodology duly ensures that available results are properly considered, it cannot ascertain *congruence to organizational targets*, our first effectiveness criterion, since completeness and exclusivity of quality characteristics cannot be ensured.

---

32 Cf. *CAMP* (1989) and *KAPLAN/NORTON* (1992).

33 Cf. *VAN DER AALST* (1998), *BECKER/ROSEMANN/VON UTHMANN* (2000) and *MENDLING* et al. (2006).

34 Cf. *HERAVIZADEH/MENDLING/ROSEMANN* (2009) and *HEINRICH/PAECH* (2010),.

To provide a relevant contribution beyond available frameworks, we thus approach process quality from a different perspective. By employing a deductive design approach, we aim at providing a clear link between organizational targets and quality measures, and at ensuring that all organizational targets are reflected. This also pertains to addressing the scopes of responsibility of SSOs and SCs as a characteristic of particular relevance in a Shared Services context.

4.2 Process Quality in Shared Services Environments

Based on the dimensions of process quality discussed in Section 3.3, we can now derive appropriate quality indicators. Quality indicators are assessed by inspecting the actual process model. If no formal process model is available, process mining techniques may be employed to obtain process models from ERP or other information systems log data.[35] Due to the typical IT infrastructure in a Shared Services environment, this is a viable solution in many cases.

To assess process quality, we need to consider the effectiveness and efficiency relations resulting from the model (cf. figure 1). To determine the effectiveness and efficiency relations, we traverse the process model in order to determine viable "traces", i.e. the existing alternatives how the model may be enacted.[36] Each trace is amended with information on resource availability and resource consumption requirements. Example 3 demonstrates the approach.

Example 4: Effectiveness and Efficiency Relations Determined by Traces. Reconsider the invoice checking process we already used in previous examples. In terms of traces, the process can be executed as follows (note that resources to be *consumed* must always be *available* as well):

Traces: Activities	**Resources to be Available**	**Resources to be Consumed**	**Results**
Scan invoice Match purchase order Match goods receipt Post invoice	Scanning system (SSO) PO system (SC) MM system (SC) FI system (SC)	Clerk time, 5 min (SSO) n/a n/a n/a	Invoice accepted
Scan invoice Match purchase order Identify invoice owner Create purchase order ...	See above	Clerk time, 5 min (SSO) n/a Clerk time, 5 min (SSO) Clerk time, 15 min (SC) ...	Invoice accepted, purchase order created
...	...	...	...

The first trace corresponds to the expected case: all data required are available, so the invoice can be matched and posted automatically. In the second case, the purchase order is missing. Thus, the invoice owner needs to be identified, and a purchase order needs to be created before the "standard case" can resume.

35 Cf. *van der Aalst/Weijters* (2004).

36 Cf. *Rozinat/van der Aalst* (2006).

For complex processes, it makes sense to conduct trace analysis on the basis of sub-processes that occur for multiple traces. Analysis results can thus be re-used.[37] With the progress of process mining tools, we expect automated support to be widely available soon for process model analysis on the basis of traces.[38] This will simplify quality assessment.

The assessment of *formal effectiveness* is then conducted as follows: all desired resulting states as given by the results specification must be covered through appropriate traces. In this respect, it is important that each trace properly considers the conditions that may be bound to desired resulting states, e.g. when the process requires taking decisions.[39]

Full effectiveness as well as *efficiency* can then be assessed by matching desired resulting states and resource availability or consumption requirements, respectively, as given by the possible traces. Unlike *formal effectiveness*, this step requires the knowledge of subject matter experts, since it must be judged whether resource requirements posed by the process model to individual desired resulting states can be considered as reasonable. To further facilitate expert judgment, however, it is possible to provide a criteria catalogue structuring assessment, in particular by addressing particular "reasons of poor quality".[40] The contents of the criteria catalogue can be considered as *quality indicators*. Note that, depending on the concrete application scenarios, an individual quality indicator may pertain to both *full effectiveness* and *efficiency*. This is because, ultimately, quality indicators are aimed at identifying resource waste in process models, regardless of whether resources are required to be available or actually consumed. To additionally support developing a comprehensive set of quality indicators, we distinguish between quality indicators addressing individual tasks *(task level)*, the sequence of tasks (*control flow level*)

The following tables summarize relevant quality indicators for process models. We used relevant process design best practices from literature as a starting point.[41] Based on our experience from corresponding client projects, we adapted, excluded and amended content as required with regard to the effectiveness and efficiency relation (literature-based indicators marked with "*"). Note that quality indicators are to be used to identify "reasons of poor quality" as described above, and that not every "best practice" makes sense in every situation.

---

37 An approach towards this issue, i.e. the consolidation of dependencies in goal and process models, can be found in *LOHRMANN/REICHERT* (2012a).

38 Cf. *VAN DONGEN* et al. (2005).

39 A fully formalized description of the procedure, including its integration with BPMN, is available in *LOHRMANN/REICHERT* (2012b).

40 Cf. *DALE* (2007).

41 Cf. *REIJERS/LIMAN MANSAR* (2005). Empirical validation can be found in *LIMAM MANSAR/REIJERS* (2005).

Quality indicators	Description	Impact on full effectiveness/efficiency
Task level		
*Task elimination**	Each task in a process should clearly contribute to a desired process result, input required to realize the result, or taking required decisions. Otherwise, the task should be removed.	Resources associated with the task are required no more.
Elimination of resource waste in tasks	Each task should be scrutinized regarding its effectiveness and efficiency relations on task levels: it should be assessed whether resource availability / consumption requirements are appropriate considering task output.	Reduced resource requirements.
*Triage**	Tasks can be divided into more specialized tasks to make use of specialized resources, or to reduce the workload of highly qualified resources. In particular, this pertains to the handling of exceptions.	Economies of scale/ specialization effects, reduced factor cost when replacing highly qualified resources.
*Task composition/ decomposition**	The split of process activities into individual tasks mainly follows the change of tools and roles to be employed. Composition/decomposition thus can be used to control when process participants and tools should change. Today's concept of employee "empowerment" can be fostered by composing tasks to larger entities.	Reduced resource requirements from specialization effects (see *Triage*) or reduced interfacing and setup efforts.
*Interface standardization**	Frameworks like EDI or allow to use standardized interfaces which can be supported by readily available tools. The same considerations apply to the underlying comprehensive data base of ERP systems.	Reduced resource requirements during design & implementation.
*Task automation**	Tasks can be partially or fully automated by using IT systems instead of manual effort (e.g., scanning of invoices). Note that task automation might also require re-arranging control flow	Lower effectiveness (tool must be available), higher efficiency.

Table 2: Quality indicators

Quality indicators	**Description**	**Impact on full effectiveness/efficiency**
Control flow level		
Process mapping	In principle, the overall value chain of an organization can be divided into processes and sub-processes in an arbitrary manner. To reduce resource requirements, however, processes should be mapped into an overall process landscape to represent end-to-end management of business transactions, thus counterbalancing the prevalent functional organization. Division into sub-processes should then follow changes in granularity of process output to reduce model complexity (for example, managing invoices vs. managing payment runs as part of the purchase-to-pay process).	Reduced resource requirements for coordination and interfacing efforts.
Fail-first strategy (also known as resequencing* or knock-out)	Early check of available resources enables to abort process instances that cannot be completed, eliminating further resource requirements for the instance.	Reduced resource requirements.
Task re-arrangement: Sequentialization	Parallel tasks can be sequentialized to enlarge the scope for the fail-first strategy.	Reduced resource requirements, but may impact timeliness in process performance (see below).
*Task re-arrangement: Parallelization**	Sequential tasks can be executed in parallel unless they require each other's output as input. This impedes the fail-first strategy, but may foster timeliness in process performance (see below).	Higher resource requirements in case of intermittent instance abortions, but may foster timeliness in process performance (see below).
Task re-arrangement: Branching	Tasks can be eliminated (cf. *Task elimination*) from process *instances* selectively by splitting the process model into branches that are only executed if appropriate conditions are fulfilled.	Reduced resource requirements.
Buffering	Buffering tasks to enable their processing as a "batch" may reduce setup times if setup is more specific to the task than to the instance.	Reduced resource requirements per instance.

Table 3: Quality indicators (continued)

Quality indicators	Description	Impact on full effectiveness/efficiency
Control flow level		
Interface bundling	Tasks can be re-arranged in a way to minimize organizational or technical interfaces. As this may contradict the fail-first strategy, it is relevant when interface efforts exceed expected fail-first gains.	Reduced resource requirements to manage and setup interfaces.
Workflow tools	Workflow tools can automate the routing of control flow in a process, thus reducing manual communication effort	Requires availability of workflow tools, reduces manual processing effort.
Governance level		
Qualification of human resources	Human resources should be well-qualified to the tasks assigned. Over-qualification, on the other hand, will cause increased costs. While *Triage* addresses the process being designed accordingly, the appropriate mechanisms of resource assignment per instance must also be in place.	Reduced resource requirements through lower "human" factor costs.
Customer responsibility (similar: *Split responsibilities**)	Each process interface across organizational boundaries (e.g., between SSO and SC) leads to governance effort to ensure the quality of upstream output / downstream input. This may be reduced by bundling responsibilities to avoid interfaces (e.g., accounting being responsible to enter payment terms).	Reduced resource requirements in subsequent task.
End to end consolidation (economies of scope) (similar: Order assignment*)	In the sense of case management, the number of staff involved when handling an individual instance can be minimized. This saves effort when instance-specific setup effort (e.g., to get familiar with the case) exceeds task-specific setup effort. In this case, the number of individually modeled tasks *can* be reduced for lower model complexity.	Reduced resource requirements for instance-specific setup, but higher resource requirements for task-specific setup.
Functional consolidation (economies of scale)	If task-specific setup effort exceeds instance-specific setup effort, the number of (specialized) tasks processed by an individual staff member can be maximized.	Reduced resource requirements for task-specific setup, but higher resource requirements for instance-specific setup.

Table 4: Quality indicators (continued)

5 Measuring Process Performance

This section discusses general characteristics for effective process performance measurement in terms of content and procedure. Relevant literature beyond the more general approaches discussed in Section 4.1 with regard to process quality mostly addresses tools and technology-focused methods. Thus, we present an overview of performance measurement tools as means to support practical applicability.

5.1 Characteristics of Effective Process Performance Measurement

Operational process performance is to be measured in terms of compliance, model completion, timeliness, and efficiency (cf. Section 3.1). In this regard, two major challenges are to be considered. Both pertain to properly *delineating* process performance from influencing factors that exceed the scope of control of SSO and SC actors while enacting a process. This corresponds to the *reflection of governance scope* effectiveness criterion.

- Process performance is to be delineated from process quality. I.e., process performance assessment must not be impacted by the quality of the underlying actual process model.
- Process performance of subsequent actors is to be delineated from process performance of preceding actors. I.e., process performance assessment must not be impacted by the performance delivered by other parties.

These challenges illustrate that traditional end-to-end performance indicators, such as the volume of documents processed per capacity, are not sufficient. While they may serve as an indicator of existing issues when compared to quantitative benchmarks, they do not suffice to appropriately identify "weak spots" to enable actual control.

Actually required performance indicators must generally be derived from dimensions of process performance (cf. section 3.3) *and* the concrete process in question. Nevertheless, it is possible to generally match types of performance indicators against performance dimensions. The completeness of a set of indicators can thus be ascertained, and remaining gaps become apparent (cf. *congruence to organizational targets*). By applying corresponding design principles, the delineation challenges can be considered at the same time. Note that process performance is measured by considering individual process instances and can be consolidated by analyzing mean or median values as well as measures of variance. Tables 5 and 6 present an overview on resulting performance indicator types.

Performance dimensions	Performance indicator types	Design principles
Compliance	Process pattern-based compliance analysis: occurrence of process instances not matching the process model.	Deviations are caused if a task is enacted although it is not foreseen in the process model for the respective current state of the process instance. In that case, the corresponding actor has triggered a compliance deviation. By assigning deviations to actors, it is possible to delineate between SSO and SC responsibilities. It is possible that the SC requests the enactment of deviating tasks from the SSO, for instance to handle exceptional cases. These events need to be noted accordingly to maintain delineation between SSO and SC performance. If this occurs frequently, it may be necessary to adapt the process model. The concept of process schema evolution has been developed to address this topic for operational business processes.[42]
Model completion	End point analysis: occurrence of process instances not terminating with final tasks/ events as defined by the process model.	In case of deviations, the actual terminating event is to be recorded. It is important to note that premature termination may be caused by the respective tasks actor or by missing preconditions caused by defective preceding tasks or processes, e.g. in case of missing master data. The analysis depends on a defined maximum cycle time since tools cannot determine whether an instance has actually terminated or is just "sitting idle". As an alternative, special tasks to record can be introduced at defined points in the model. This is effective if experience suggests standard reasons of premature termination because of defect preceding tasks or processes.
Timeliness	Cycle times analysis: cycle times on task/activity level, calculated on the basis of start/end events.	Cycle times are to be recorded by task. Based on task-actor assignment, it is thus possible to aggregate cycle times per instance for actors, the SSO, or SCs. Cycle times of individual tasks correspond to the time lag between the task being enabled and the task being completed.

Table 5: Performance indicator types

42 Cf. REICHERT/WEBER (2012).

Performance dimensions	Performance indicator types	Design principles
Efficiency	Process pattern-based efficiency analysis: occurrence of efficient vs. inefficient traces.	To prepare for efficiency assessment, process traces as enabled by the process model are to be amended with resource consumption information (e.g., on the task level) and/or classified as "efficient" or "inefficient". For "inefficient" traces, analysis is required regarding responsibility for the underlying defect (e.g., missing data). Efficiency-related defects can thus be delineated between SSO and SC. The more detailed resource consumption per trace has been analyzed, the more detailed efficiency assessment is facilitated. Resource consumption information per trace can also be aggregated for actual trace volumes. The results can be compared to labor capacity at the SSO to determine how effective SSO resources are managed. Note that this analysis does not make sense on the SC side since SC labor resources are typically not dedicated to Shared Services processes.

Table 6: Performance indicator types (continued)

Note that process performance assessment can be supported by appropriate tools as presented in the following section. This allows largely automating the procedures involved, up to visualizing results for presentation to senior management.

5.2 Performance Measurement Tools

Today's IT environments allow supporting process performance measurement in various ways. This section shortly summarizes available options including application examples.

As a prerequisite for most performance indicator types, it is necessary to track process enactment on a case-by-case basis by logging appropriate events, e.g. the completion of tasks. This can be achieved by using *workflow management systems (WfMS)* which generally provide logging and analysis facilities.[43] Note that comparable facilities are also provided by *enterprise resource management (ERP) packages* and *middleware tools.*[44] In certain cases, ERP packages provide the additional advantage of directly linking into resource requirements, e.g. through activity-based costing modules. Note that the provision of a tracking facility is one of the major reasons to implement a WfMS or an ERP system, since this capability can also help to address legal compliance issues.

---

43 Cf., for instance, *WORKFLOW MANAGEMENT COALITION* (1999).

44 Middleware tools are used to integrate diverse application landscapes by providing standard interfaces to other software packages in the sense of a data broker. Cf. *Interface standardization* in table 2.

Dedicated *tools for process performance* management are increasingly offered by vendors.[45] While they may follow a template approach to facilitate the definition of performance indicators for certain application areas, they still require data extraction, staging and integration methods. This is not the case when using "native" WfMS or ERP systems. Note that similar techniques have been developed under the notion of "process intelligence".[46]

Process mining tools do not only enable to deduct process models from enactment logs, but typically enrich extracted process models with additional information like, for instance, cycle times, actors or the relative prevalence of patterns.[47] Thus, process mining tools may allow to implement process performance indicators with the additional advantage of directly matching indicators against actual process models.

Business intelligence (BI) tools are aimed at managing and presenting information extracted from transactional systems such as ERP systems. The techniques employed range from data extraction and cleansing to analysis and visualization tools and are well-suited to be used in a process performance measurement context. As opposed to dedicated process performance management tools, BI tools do not provide pre-defined content in terms of indicators etc. However, this disadvantage may be more than compensated by advanced data management and visualization facilities, which constitute major challenges in typical process performance management projects, and possibly the fact that BI tools are already in use in many organizations.

6 Conclusion

In this chapter, we lined out the requirement of assessing process quality and performance as part of the BPM lifecycle between SSOs and SCs. We discussed effectiveness criteria to guide the evaluation of respective solutions, looked into the impact of processes on organizational targets, and deducted generic dimensions of process quality and process performance on that basis. We described a framework to assess process quality as well as generic types of indicators for assessing process performance, which can be supported by appropriate tools.

In summary, we revisit the cornerstones which are particularly relevant for effective process quality and performance assessment as a means of managerial analysis and control. We described these cornerstones in the form of the effectiveness criteria discussed in Section 3.1:

- With regard to *congruence to organizational targets*, we deducted our results from an analysis of the impact of Shared Services processes on organizational targets. A structure of quality and performance dimensions reflecting organizational targets helps to ensure a comprehensive, but exclusive set of measures.

45 Cf., for instance, SOFTWARE AG (2012).

46 Cf, for instance, CASATI et al. (2002).

47 Cf. VAN DER AALST/WEIJTERS (2004).

- To be fully effective as a means to exercise control, quality and performance measures must reflect organizational responsibilities – in an ideal case, responsibility for measure results lies with an individual actor or team. *Reflection of responsibilities* scope was addressed by delineating process performance from process quality, and by providing design principles supporting the delineation of SSO and SC process performance.
- *Retraceability and transparency* must be ensured in the adaptation of process quality and performance assessment to a particular application scope. However, a clear link between organizational targets and quality as well as performance measures supports this requirement.
- *Cost of computation*, finally, can be addressed by appropriately automating procedures through the use of corresponding IT tools – in particular, process mining applications to obtain actual process models for quality analysis, and, besides process mining, ERP, WfMS, and BI to facilitate process performance assessment.

Future research will further refine process quality and performance measures with regard to particular fields of application, such as accounting, HR or IT services. Moreover, additional work is required to fully utilize available IT tools for automated process quality and performance assessment. By significantly reducing the effort involved with assessing an individual process, this will be crucial to further integrate effective process quality and performance concepts into business process and Shared Services management.

References

BECKER, J./ROSEMANN, M./UTHMANN, C. VON (2000): Guidelines of Business Process Modeling, in: *VAN DER AALST, W./DESEL, J./OBERWEIS, A.* (eds.), Business Process Management: Models, Techniques, and Empirical Studies, Berlin/Heidelberg 2000, pp. 241–262.

CAMP, R. C. (1989): Benchmarking: the Search for Industry Best Practices that Lead to Superior Performance, London 1989.

CASATI, F./DAYAL, U./SAYAL, M./SHAN, M. (2002): Business Process Intelligence, online: http://www.hpl.hp.com/techreports/2002/HPL-2002-119.pdf?jumpid=reg_R1002_USEN, date visited: 8/05/2010.

DALE, B. G. (2007): The Received Wisdom on TQM, in: *DALE, B. G./VAN DER WIELE, T./VAN IWAARDEN, J.* (eds.), Managing Quality, 5th edition, Hoboken 2007, pp. 58–73.

DAVENPORT, T. J./SHORT, J. E. (1990): The New Industrial Engineering: Information Technology and Business Process Redesign, in: Sloan Management Review, 1990, No. 4, pp. 11–27.

EISENHARDT, K. M. (1985): Control: Organizational and Economic Approaches, in: Management Science, Vol. 31 (1985), No. 2, pp. 134–149.

EPSTEIN, M. K./HENDERSON, J. C. (1989): Data Envelopment Analysis for Managerial Control and Diagnosis, in: Decision Sciences, Vol. 20 (1989), No. 1, pp. 90–119.

HAMMER, M. (1990): Reengineering Work: Don't Automate, Obliterate, in: Harvard Business Review, Vol. 68 (1990), No. 4, pp. 104–112.

HEINRICH, R./ PAECH, B. (2010): Defining the Quality of Business Processes, in: *ENGELS, G./ KARAGIANNIS, D./MAYR, H. C.* (eds.), Modellierung 2010, Bonn 2010, pp. 133–48.

HERAVIZADEH, M./MENDLING, J./ROSEMANN, M. (2009): Dimensions of Business Processes Quality (QoBP), in: *ARDAGNA, D./MECELLA, M./YANG, J.* (eds.), Business Process Management Workshops 2008, Berlin/Heidelberg 2009, pp. 80–91.

INTERNATIONAL ACCOUNTING STANDARDS BOARD (1989): Framework for the Preparation and Presentation of Financial Statements, online: http://eifrs.iasb.org/eifrs/bnstandards/en/framework.pdf, date visited: 13/04/2010.

KAPLAN, R. S./NORTON, D. P. (1992): The Balanced Scorecard: Measures that Drive Performance, in: Harvard Business Review, Vol. 70 (1992), No. 1, pp. 71–79.

KENNERLEY, M./NEELY, A. (2002): Performance Measurement Frameworks: A Review, in: *NEELY, A. D.* (eds.), Business performance measurement: theory and practice, Cambridge (MA) 2002, pp. 145–155.

LEHNER, F. (2000): Organisational Memory, München 2000.

LIMAM MANSAR, S./REIJERS, H. (2005): Best Practices in Business Process Redesign: Validation of a Redesign Framework, in: Computers in Industry, Vol. 56 (2005), No. 5, pp. 457–471.

LOHRMANN, M./REICHERT, M. (2012a): Efficacy-aware Business Process Modeling, in: *RINDERLE-MA, S./DADAM, P./ZHOU, X.* (eds.), 20th Int'l Conf. on Cooperative Information Systems, Berlin/Heidelberg 2012, accepted for publication.

LOHRMANN, M./REICHERT, M. (2012b): Modeling Business Objectives for Business Process Management, in: *STARY, C.* (ed.), Proceedings of the 4th International Conference on S-BPM ONE – Scientific Research, Berlin/Heidelberg 2012, pp. 106–126.

MARCH, J. G. (1978): Bounded Rationality, Ambiguity, and the Engineering of Choice, in: Bell Journal of Economics, Vol. 9 (1978), No. 2, pp. 587–608.

MARCH, S. T./SMITH, G. F. (1995): Design and Natural Science Research on Information Technology, in: Decision Support Systems, Vol. 15 (1995), No. 4, pp. 251–266.

MENDLING, J./MOSER, M./NEUMANN, G./VERBEEK, H.M.W/VAN DONGEN, B.F./VAN DER AALST, W.M.P. (2006): Faulty EPCs in the SAP Reference Model, in: *DUSTDAR, S./FIADEIRO, J. L./SHETH, A.* (eds.), International Conference on Business Process Management 2006, Berlin/Heidelberg 2006, pp. 451–457.

OUCHI, W. G. (1979): A Conceptual Framework for the Design of Organizational Control Mechanisms, in: Management Science, Vol. 25 (1979), No. 9, pp. 833–848.

REICHERT, M./WEBER, B. (2012): Enabling Flexibility in Process-aware Information Systems: Challenges, Methods, Technologies, Berlin/Heidelberg 2012.

REIJERS, H. A./LIMAN MANSAR, S. (2005): Best Practices in Business Process Redesign: An Overview and Qualitative Evaluation of Successful Redesign Heuristics, in: Omega, Vol. 33 (2005), No. 4, pp. 283–306.

ROZINAT, A./VAN DER AALST, W. M. P. (2006): Conformance Testing: Measuring the Fit and Appropriateness of Event Logs and Process Models, in: Business Process Management 2005 Workshops, Berlin/Heidelberg 2006, pp. 163–176.

SIMON, H. A. (1978): On How to Decide What to Do, in: Bell Journal of Economics, Vol. 9 (1978), No. 2, pp. 494–507.

SIMON, H. A. (1996): The Sciences of the Artificial, Cambridge (MA) 1996.

SOFTWARE AG (2012): ARIS Process Performance Manager, online: http://www.softwareag.com/corporate/products/aris_platform/aris_controlling/aris_process_performance/overview/default.asp, date visited: 25/06/2012.

THE ECONOMIST (2012): Economics A-Z, Keyword: Efficiency, online: http://www.economist.com/economics-a-to-z/e#node-21529488, date visited: 25/06/2012.

THE OBJECT MANAGEMENT GROUP (2011): Business Process Model and Notation: Version 2.0, online: http://www.omg.org/spec/BPMN/2.0, date visited: 10/12/2011.

TRIENEKENS, J. J./KUSTERS, R. J./RENDERING, B./STOKLA, K. (2005): Business Objectives as Drivers for Process Improvement: Practices and Experiences at Thales Naval The Netherlands (TNNL), in: Information and Software Technology, Vol. 47 (2005), No. 2, pp. 67–79.

VAN DER AALST, W. M. P. (1998): The Application of Petri Nets to Workflow Management, in: The Journal of Circuits, Systems and Computers, Vol. 8 (1998), No. 1, pp. 21–26.

VAN DER AALST, W. M. P./WEIJTERS, A. J. M. M. (2004): Process Mining: a Research Agenda, in: Computers in Industry, Vol. 53 (2004), No. 3, pp. 231–244.

VAN DER AALST, W. M. P./TER HOFSTEDE, A. H. M./WESKE, M. (2003): Business Process Management: A Survey, in: *VAN DER AALST, W. M. P./TER HOFSTEDE, A. H. M./WESKE, M.* (eds.), International Conference on Business Process Management 2003, Berlin/Heidelberg 2003, pp. 1–12.

VAN DONGEN, B. F./MEDEIROS, A. K. A./VERBEEK, H. M. W./WEIJTERS, A. J. M. M./VAN DER AALST, W. M. P. (2005): The ProM Framework: A New Era in Process Mining Tool Support, in: *CIARDO, G./DARONDEAU, P.* (eds.), Applications and Theory of Petri Nets, Berlin/Heidelberg 2005, pp. 444–454.

WESKE, M. (2007): Business Process Management, Berlin/Heidelberg 2007.

WORKFLOW MANAGEMENT COALITION (1999): Workflow Management Coalition Terminology & Glossary 3.0, online: http://www.wfmc.org, date visited: 11/03/2009.

A Conceptual Model for Measuring the Service Quality of Shared Services Organizations

STEFAN RÖDER and *FRANK KEUPER*

Steinbeis University Berlin

Executive Summary

Current measures of internal service quality (SQ) do not adequately capture internal customers' perceptions of SQ provided by human resource (HR) Shared Services Organizations (HRSSOs). In order to gain a better understanding of the construct and its ability to predict important internal service outcomes, namely customer value (CV), satisfaction (SAT) and behavioral intentions (BI), this paper outlines a conceptual model of internal customer perceptions of SQ provided by HRSSOs. The model is based on a wide body of marketing and IS literature as well as qualitative pre-studies. Thus, a multidimensional, hierarchical scale for measuring HRSSO service quality is proposed. The scale is embedded in a structural model for the internal HRSSO context and simultaneously considers the relevant relationships between the aforementioned key constructs. Furthermore, the development process of the survey instrument and a proposal for a validation procedure are proposed.

1 Introduction

Next generation HRSSOs are expected to deliver a better quality of service at lower costs, meaning HR departments are having to spend more time on transformational activities.[1] The introduction of web-based and employee interaction technologies have enabled HRSSOs to expand the range of services they provide, and at the same time has dramatically changed the way employees handle their HR-related issues.[2]

An in-depth literature review reveals that there is still no generally accepted terminology for the Shared Services concept.[3] Based on an analysis of 17 academic explanations[4] and additional expert interviews, the HR Shared Services concept can be defined as a HR service delivery option positioned between HR centralization and HR outsourcing on the HR service delivery continuum.[5] Meanwhile, the intention of companies implementing the HR Shared Services concept by establishing a specialized (internal) independent organizational unit (HRSSO) is twofold: first generation HRSSOs primarily aimed to realize economies of scale and economies of scope through the bundling, harmonization, standardization and IT-enabled automation of previously decentralized and heterogeneously executed HR-related support activities. In addition to this, next generation HRSSOs additionally focus on providing a higher level of service, enabling their internal – and if applicable external – customers to concentrate on their core competencies.[6] *RÖDER/KEUPER*[7] offer insight into the wide range of potential description criteria for HRSSO arrangements.

---

1 Cf. *FARNDALE/PAAUWE/HOEKSMA* (2009).

2 Cf. *VOLLMER/FISCHER/ROEDER* (2008).

3 Cf. *VON GLAHN* (2007), and *ULBRICH* (2008).

4 Cf. *ROEDER/KEUPER* (2009), p. 206 et seq.

5 Cf. *VON GLAHN* (2007).

6 Cf. *KEUPER/OECKING* (2008).

7 Cf. *ROEDER/KEUPER* (2009).

There has only been limited academic research – not to mention the lack empirical evidence – on the extent to which the ex-ante promised benefits have been realized[8], or on how to successfully implement and operate an HRSSO. The lack of face-to-face contact, employee representation, clarity regarding process ownership as well as IT issues have been identified as the main problems related to HRSSOs from the employees' perspective. Line managers have reported an increased workload rather than time savings, preventing them from concentrating on their primary role and strategic issues and wasting resources. Consequently, [..] these problems "have reduced the quantity and quality of services for both employees and line managers, and [..] have led to rising levels of dissatisfaction."[9]

FARNDALE/PAAUWE/HOEKSMA[10] found the greatest challenge to be a lack of performance data: "The companies surveyed stated the main problem as not having performance data on how well the [HRSSO] is operating, despite the original aims of wanting to cut costs and improve service quality."[11]

So far there has been a lack of empirical research into the linkages between internal service encounter constructs, eg. SAT, CV and BI. Further research is needed into the context-specific dimensions, items and scales of SQ as well as the relationships to the aforementioned constructs. In our literature review we were only able to identify one study, conducted by *WESCHKE*[12], where SQ expectations were both integrated into independent and dependent variables implying higher correlations.[13] *WESCHKE* herself underlines the fact that structure equation modelling should have been conducted to explore the construct relationships instead of a regression analysis.[14] Moreover, the application of SERVQUAL is still the subject of controversial academic debate regarding its theoretical and methodological foundation.[15]

Consequently, there is a need for a more holistic, theoretically as well as empirically well-founded and practice-oriented measurement model.[16] Given these requirements, the Internal Service Barometer concept developed by *BRUHN*[17] is considered to be particularly appropriate in the HR Shared Services Context. Hence, this paper describes the conceptualization of a specific model for measuring SQ and the detection of relevant linkages. As the research is still in progress, only qualitative (empirical) concepts are presented. The paper's contribution towards future research is discussed in the final section.

---

8 Cf. *KAGELMANN* (2001), and *VON GLAHN* (2007).

9 *COOKE* (2006), p. 221.

10 Cf. *FARNDALE/PAAUWE/HOEKSMA* (2009).

11 *FARNDALE/PAAUWE/HOEKSMA* (2009), p. 556.

12 Cf. *WESCHKE* (2008).

13 Cf. *WESCHKE* (2008), p. 110.

14 Cf. *WESCHKE* (2008), p. 110.

15 Cf. *BUTTLE* (1996), *LEE/KETTINGER* (1996), and *GOUNARIS* (2005).

16 For such a measurment model cf. *RÖDER* (2012).

17 Cf. *BRUHN* (2003).

2 Conceptual Model

2.1 Research Framework

To assess internal SQ, *BRUHN*[18] refers to the framework of national customer indices (e.g. the European Performance Satisfaction Index).[19] He conceptualizes the Internal Service Barometer "as a regularly determined general measure of customer satisfaction with internal services and their drivers and impacts within a company."[20] This measure is based on a structural model which takes internal SQ as a latent endogenous variable that directly determines two exogenous non-observable variables: comprehensive internal customer satisfaction and internal customer retention. Moreover, *BRUHN* hypothesizes that internal customer satisfaction is directly linked to internal customer retention.[21] A questionnaire was compiled and pre-tested to evaluate the causal model. It included multi-item scales that were derived from academic literature or were purpose-made for each of the model's constructs. Using empirical data obtained from a quantitative study conducted in cooperation with a pharmaceutical company further scale validation steps were undertaken and the hypothesized relationships were subsequently tested using a partial least squares regression.[22]

BRUHN/GEORGI[23] suggest the application of the Internal Service Barometer concept with the addition of a modified service profit chain for Corporate Shared Services Centers. They describe the development and empirical testing of an internal service barometer for a banking group's Shared IT Service Center. It is assumed that "workplace IT" and "system IT" are subdimensions of the key construct "service offering" and that the customer orientation construct positively influences the level of value perceived by the customer, leading to a higher level of customer satisfaction. It is assumed that satisfied customers who perceive receiving a high level of value from their IT department are more loyal, e.g. they have less interest in third party providers' offerings, whereas dissatisfied customers who perceive a low level of value are less loyal, e.g. the word-of-mouth communication regarding the IT department is negative.[24]

Considering these findings from previous research and results from interviews with HR Shared Service Center customers, we propose a context-specific internal service profit chain as our research framework, considering SQ an endogenous latent variable and CV, SAT and BI as exogenous constructs.

18 Cf. *BRUHN* (2003).
19 Cf. *BRUHN* (2003), p. 1192.
20 *BRUHN* (2003), p. 1192.
21 Cf. *BRUHN* (2003), p. 1192.
22 Cf. *BRUHN* (2003).
23 Cf. *BRUHN/GEORGI* (2008).
24 Cf. *BRUHN/GEORGI* (2008), p. 180 f.

2.2 Definition and Measurement of the Model Constructs

2.2.1 Internal Service Quality

SQ is often conceptualized in academic literature as a HRSSO customer's attitude resulting from an individual transaction-specific performance perception and can be described as a multidimensional, higher-order construct.[25]

The three primary dimensions - structure quality, process quality and output quality – are adapted from *DONABEDIAN*[26] because of their applicability in various service contexts, their empirical foundation[27] and their compatibility with the three-phase service encounter model developed by *HILKE*[28]. The concept of "structure quality" deals with the setting in which the HR Shared Service occurs and includes e.g. the accessibility of well-educated customer contact staff via various communication channels as well as convenient operating hours. "Process quality" focuses on what happens during the service encounter, whereas "outcome quality" reflects the result of the service encounter. All three dimensions are interlinked, meaning that a good structure quality positively influences process quality, which in turn facilitates a positive service encounter outcome.[29]

We undertook an extensive literature review not only of texts based on the HR Shared Service delivery model, but also of studies on measuring (internal) service quality in various (internal) service settings and studies on evaluating electronic service quality due, in particular, to the growing importance of electronic service delivery channels.[30] Studies[31] assessing the success of technology-based self-service products as well as employee portals were also reviewed. Furthermore, qualitative data were obtained from semi-structured interviews (pre-study 1) with a total of 33 researchers, practitioners and consultants as well as internal HRSSO customers within a software company and a telecommunication company both headquartered in Germany. As a result, we propose the following dimensionality:

- Structure quality (STR)
  - *Access*, which encapsulates measures that evaluate the reachability of the HRSSO. Aspects, such as convenient business hours and the availability of various communication channels are considered.
  - *Expertise*, which especially focuses on the professional competence of the HRSSO´s customer contact employees (1st level support) and specialists (2nd or 3rd level support).
  - *Data*, which covers the relevance, correctness, completeness etc. of facts and figures (e.g. master data or customer contact history) aggregated by the HRSSO to provide valuable information.

---

25 Cf. *LAPIERRE* (1996), *DABHOLKAR/SHEPHERD/THORPE* (2000), *BRADY/CRONIN* (2001), *DAGGER/SWEENEY/JOHNSON* (2007), *DABHOLKAR/THORPE/RENTZ* (1996), *FALK* (2007), *FASSNACHT/KOESE* (2006), and *LIU* (2005).

26 Cf. *DONABEDIAN* (1980), p. 80.

27 Cf. for example *FALK* (2007).

28 Cf. *HILKE* (1989).

29 Cf. *HOECK/KEUPER* (2001).

30 Cf. *KEUPER/ROEDER* (2009).

31 Cf. *SUGIANTO/TOJIB* (2006), *HO/KO* (2008), *TOJIB/SUGIANTO/SENDJAYA* (2008), and *URBACH/SMOLNIK/RIEMPP* (2009).

- Process quality (PROC)
  - *Interaction*, which consists of measures that focus on the quality of the service encounter itself including personal interaction (i.e. friendliness and helpfulness of the customer contact employee) as well as technological aspects (e.g. ease of use).
  - *Control*, which comprises measures regarding the customer´s perception of the traceability of the service delivery (e.g. receiving a status notification).
- Output quality (OUT)
  - *Fulfillment*, which includes indicators of the service delivery output (e.g. accuracy, punctuality or adherence to prior agreements).
  - *Security and privacy*, which consists of measures that focus on the protection of personal data and confidentiality.
  - *Follow-up-care*, which covers measures of relevant post-delivery service (e.g. complaint handling).

In order to verify the construct dimensionality we created an initial item pool based on the literature review and participant feedback obtained from pre-study 1. The feedback from the study was used to check the relevance of theoretically-derived items and to extend the initial item pool. Items were added, found to be completely irrelevant or were modified to suit the HRSSO context. The resulting item pool consisted of 140 potential construct-related indicators.

As suggested by *UHRICH*[32], we conducted a delphi survey (pre-study 2) to reduce the number of items. 40 internal customers from the HRSSO of a telecommunication company headquartered in Germany took part in the first round. They were asked to evaluate the relevance of every item on a 3-point scale (1 = item is relevant; 2 = item could be relevant; 3 = item is completely irrelevant).[33] The average score given to each item was subsequently calculated. In line with the delphi method, the panel participants (N = 31) were surveyed for a second time after the first round's results had been reported. The participants were thus led to compare their previous ratings with those of the other panel members. Finally, several item reduction algorithms were carried out on the delphi survey results and in accordance with *FALK*[34], items were deleted from the pool if less than 60 % of the respondents had rated them with a "1". As a result, 60 items were excluded along with six further items that were dropped following participant feedback citing a lack of clarity.

Following this, we used an item-ranking approach[35] (pre-study 3). To implement this we developed an on-line questionnaire and a pool of HRSSO internal customers (N = 86) was asked to select the top 20 most relevant indicators. A total of 64 questionnaires were completed with 39 surveys (group 1: 21; group 2: 18) considered appropriate for further analysis. As a result, 26 items were identified as representing various facets of the construct from the customer perspective.

---

32 Cf. *UHRICH* (2008).

33 Cf. *BEARDEN/NETEMEYER/TEEL* (1989).

34 Cf. *FALK* (2007).

35 Cf. *UHRICH* (2008).

To ensure the content validity the results of all three pre-studies were discussed intensively with a group of six researchers and practitioners who had participated in the first pre-study, aiming, in particular, to refine the item wording. We subsequently reduced the basis for further validation steps from 140 items to 44.

In line with *MELDAU*[36] we argue that single service quality attributes influence the overall service quality, but that customers are unable to differentiate between the indicators during the perception process. In pre-study 1 the majority of respondents could not name context-specific service attributes without the support of the interviewer. Furthermore, *MELDAU* points out that the halo effect, which implies that the customer´s evaluation of single service quality aspects is dependent on the overall judgment of service quality, exceeds the formative influence of single service attributes in the corresponding service quality evaluation.[37]

In order to verify the influence of structure quality, process quality and output quality on the overall internal service quality perceived by the HRSSO customer, overall internal service quality is modeled as an independent construct measured by two items.[38]

2.2.2 Internal Customer Satisfaction

In line with marketing literature[39] SAT is specified as reflective and conceptualized as a (positive) emotional state of a HRSSO customer resulting from an individual comparison of the HR Shared Service expected and received taking into account all relevant aspects of the customer-HRSSO-relationship so far. In our study, SAT is measured with three items including overall customer satisfaction[40], the extent to which prior expectations are met[41] and the comparison to an ideal.[42]

2.2.3 Internal Customer Net Value

We conceptualize the CV construct as the HRSSO customers' perceived trade-off between what the customer receives and what the customer gives up.[43] This results in a high-order formative construct with two components: convenience benefits and perceived sacrifice.

In line with *FORNELL*[44], who states that a latent variable may be associated with both formative and reflective measures, CV is to be evaluated in our model by using a combination of reflective and formative indicators. Hence, the convenience benefit component is measured with three reflective measures including time saving, time- and location-independence.[45] The sacrifice component is measured according to two formative indicators adapted from *SWEENEY/*

---

36 Cf. *MELDAU* (2007), p. 118.

37 Cf. *MELDAU* (2007), p. 119.

38 Cf. *BABAKUS/BOLLER* (1992), *CRONIN/TAYLOR* (1992), *FALK* (2007), and *OLIVER* (2009).

39 Cf. e.g. *BHARADWAJ/MATSUNO* (2006).

40 Cf. *WESCHKE* (2008)

41 Cf. *BRUHN/GEORGI* (2008).

42 Cf. *BRUHN* (2003), and *BRUHN/GEORGI* (2008).

43 Cf. *ZEITHAML* (1988).

44 Cf. *FORNELL* (1982).

45 Cf. *HEINONEN* (2004).

SOUTAR[46] which evaluate the amount of time and effort internal customers have to invest to receive services from the HRSSO.

In addition to the recommendations made by *MACKENZIE/PODSAKOFF/JARVIS*[47] concerning the development and assessment of formative measures, three additional reflective items have been adapted from prior research[48], namely the customers' perception that the benefits received exceed the sacrifices, the customers' belief that they are receiving good value for the effort invested and the customer's perception of the extent to which the HRSSO meets minimum requirements.

2.2.4 Internal Customer Behavioral Intentions

As researchers have found BI to be a good predictor of actual customer behavior[49]. we focus solely on BI.[50]

To meet the specific requirements of this study, e.g. effective service level agreements foreclosing the internal customers' freedom to change the service provider[51], we use five carefully refined indicators from academic literature to measure BI as a reflective exogenous latent variable: the customer's 1) willingness to say positive things about the HRSSO to others (eg. supervisors, colleagues etc.); 2) cooperation intentions; 3) probability of reusing the HRSSO when give a free choice, 4) probability of continuing to recommend the HRSSO and/or 5) to continue using the HRSSO when the customer is consulted on the matter.[52]

2.3 Linkages of the Model Constructs and Hypotheses

In the relevant literature, support can be found for service quality being an antecedent of consumer satisfaction.[53] The positive linkage between SQ, SAT and BI has also been discussed intensively in marketing literature.[54] Furthermore, support from empirical studies can be found regarding the positive relationship between SQ and CV[55], SQ, CV and SAT[56] or CV, SAT and BI[57]. Moreover, it is argued by several researchers that customer perceived value is a stable construct for predicting customer behavior.[58] For self-service encounters *SHAMDASANI* et al.[59] found SQ, CV and SAT to be "critical antecedents" to BI. Additionally, *CRONIN* et

46 Cf. *SWEENEY/SOUTAR* (2001).
47 Cf. *MACKENZIE/PODSAKOFF/JARVIS* (2005).
48 Cf. e.g. *CRONIN/BRADY/HULT* (2000).
49 Cf. *FISHBEIN/AJZEN* (1975).
50 Cf. *BRUHN/GEORGI* (2008).
51 Cf. *DAVIS* (1993), p. 303.
52 Cf. *BRUHN/GEORGI* (2008).
53 Cf. e.g. *SHAMDASANI/MUKHERJEE/MALHOTRA* (2008).
54 Cf. *ZEITHAML/BERRY/PARASURAMAN* (1996), and *DAGGER/SWEENEY/JOHNSON* (2007).
55 Cf. *SNOJ/KORDA/MUMEL* (2004).
56 Cf. *HU/KANDAMPULLY/JUWAHEER* (2009).
57 Cf. *MCDOUGALL/LEVESQUE* (2000).
58 Cf. *CRONIN/BRADY/HULT* (2000), and *HU/KANDAMPULLY/JUWAHEER* (2009).
59 Cf. *SHAMDASANI/MUKHERJEE/MALHOTRA* (2008), p. 132.

al.[60] revealed both the indirect effect of SQ and CV on BI and the indirect effect of CV and SQ on BI. A direct positive linkage between SQ and BI has been reported in numerous studies.[61] With reference to several researchers[62] we propose overall SQ to be a true mediator of the relationship between SQ dimensions and BI.

Numerous authors question the linearity of cause-and-effect-chains as depicted in figure 1. The asymmetry between SQ and SAT is discussed by *FALK/HAMMERSCHMIDT/SCHEPERS*[63], whereas the non-linearity between SAT and BI is explored by *ANDERSON/MITTAL*[64] among others. We also adopt these positions for the internal service context. Furthermore we also explore the asymmetry of the SQ-CV-, the SQ-BI- and the CV-BI linkage.

Consistent with the aforementioned findings from previous research in the external context, figure 1 shows (as arrows) the hypothesized positive, direct and indirect relationships to be tested.

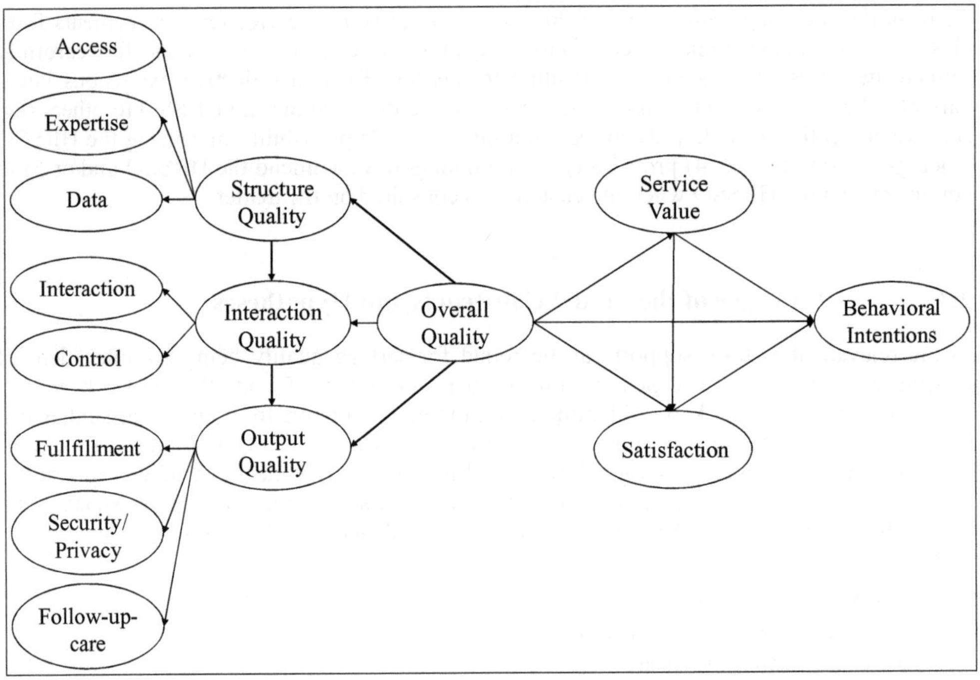

Figure 1: Conceptual model

---

60 Cf. *CRONIN/BRADY/HULT* (2000).

61 Cf. for example *BOULDING* et al. (1993), and *CRONIN/BRADY/HULT* (2000).

62 Cf. *WOODSIDE/FREY/DALY* (1989), *DABHOLKAR/SHEPHERD/THORPE* (2000), and *DAGGER/SWEENEY/JOHNSON* (2007).

63 Cf. *FALK/HAMMERSCHMIDT/SCHEPERS* (2009).

64 Cf. *ANDERSON/MITTAL* (2000).

3 Proposal for a Practice-oriented Research Design

3.1 Instrument Construction

To provide the most suitable procedure to assess the conceptualized structural model, we drafted an online questionnaire that included the four key construct variables. The test items will be evaluated by internal HRSSO customers using a five-point rating scale (1 = strongly agree, 5 = strongly disagree) enabling powerful statistical test procedures. A "no answer" option will provide less biased data.

Having intensively discussed draft wording-, design- and technical-related issues within our research team, we sent our questionnaire by e-mail for pre-testing to selected marketing researchers and HRSSO customers who had participated in pre-studies 1–3 (N = 14). The questionnaire was revised based on the pre-testers' feedback and comments on the clarity of instructions and item wording. The following tables contain the final item pool.[65]

ID	Item
STR1	*The HRSSO* is easy to contact.
STR2	... service hours meet my needs.
STR3	... offers numerous communication channels.
STR4	The communication channels are easily available when I need them.
STR5	… are easy to use.
STR6	… perform well.
STR7	Information provided by *the HRSSO* is up-to-date.
STR8	… understandable.
STR9	… correct.
STR10	*The HRSSO* provides all the information necessary regarding my inquiries and requests.
STR11	Overall, I would say *the HRSSO* complies with all necessary requirements to provide excellent services.

Table 1: Items for measuring the structure quality of a HRSSO

Item No.	Statement
PROC1	The *HRSSO's* personnel understand my specific needs.
PROC2	… listen to me carefully.
PROC3	… have a professional manner (contact via phone/[e-]mail etc.).
PROC4	… give me individual attention.
PROC5	… deal with me in a caring manner.
PROC6	… explain things in a way I can understand.
PROC7	… are polite.
PROC8	… instill confidence.
PROC9	… understand that I rely on their knowledge to solve my inquiries and my requests.
PROC10	… are willing to help me.

Table 2: Items for measuring the process quality of a HRSSO

65 Cf. RÖDER (2012).

Item No.	Statement
PROC11	… carry out their tasks competently.
PROC12	… are well informed.
PROC13	If necessary the HRSSO informs me regularly about the status of my inquiry or my request.
PROC14	… sends a confirmation once my request has been carried out.
PROC15	Overall, I would say the **process quality** provided by the HRSSO is excellent.

Table 3: Items for measuring the process quality of a HRSSO (continued)

Item No.	Statement
OUT1	I am convinced that *the HRSSO* uses my personal data accurately.
OUT2	… treats my inquiries and my requests with discretion.
OUT3	… ensures the confidentiality of my personal data.
OUT4	*The HRSSO* is reliable.
OUT5	… is effective.
OUT6	... handles my requests promptly.
OUT7	… answers my inquiries respectively handles my requests almost error-free.
OUT8	… keeps waiting time to a minimum.
OUT9	… aims at answering my inquiries respectively handling my requests directly.
OUT10	… frequently conducts surveys to check the service quality provided.
OUT11	… reminds me of necessary steps to make sure that my request is handled successfully.
OUT12	When a problem occurs, *the HRSSO* shows a sincere interest in solving it.
OUT13	*The HRSSO* handles complaints immediately.
OUT14	Overall, I would say that the output quality of *the HRSSO* is excellent.

Table 4: Items for measuring the output quality of a HRSSO

The following tables show items derived from literature[66] to measure the constructs within the effect chain.

ID	Item
SV1	*The HRSSO* provides me the service I request.
SV2	Advice given by *the HRSSO* is helpful.
SV3	I quickly receive the information I need.
SV4	I benefit from *the HRSSO* to be a point of contact for HR-related inquiries and requests fast and easy to access.
SV5	The benefit I receive from *the HRSSO* exceeds my expenditure of time.
SV6	*The HRSSO* meets my minimum service requirements.
SV7	Collaborating with *the HRSSO* is convenient.
SV8	The communication channels offer time flexibility to me.
SV9	Overall, I value *the HRSSO* greatly.

Table 5: Items for measuring the service value provided by a HRSSO

---

66 Cf. RÖDER (2012).

ID	Item
SAT1	Overall, I am satisfied with the service I received from *the HRSSO*.
SAT2	Overall, the service of *the HRSSO* meets my expectations.
SAT3	Compared to an ideal HR service provider *the HRSSO* performs well.

Table 6: Items for measuring the internal customer satisfaction[67]

ID	Item
BI1	If I am asked I would say positive things about *the HRSSO* to my superior or other professional colleagues.
BI2	I recommend my superior to keep on doing business with *the HRSSO* if she/he seeks my advice.
BI3	I encourage my superior to utilize services from *the HRSSO* more often if she/he seeks my advice.
BI4	I consider *the HRSSO* as my primary service provider for HR inquiries and support.
BI5	In future, I remain willing to work together with the HRSSO constructively.

Table 7: Items for measuring the internal customer behavioral intentions[68]

In order to measure the overall service quality as perceived by internal HRSSO the following item might be used: "Overall, I would say the service quality of *the HRSSO* is excellent."[69]

3.2 Proposal for a Data Validation and Analysis Procedure

To validate our conceptual model, the final questionnaire will be used as a data collection instrument at multinational companies running a HRSSO. Participating companies benefit from a holistic 360° identification of relevant factors influencing customer perceived SQ in the HRSSO context, which can be utilized as the basis for future investment decisions. The companies also gain important management insights into 1) the optimization of structures and processes, 2) the transferability of best practices into other Shared Services units and 3) the relevant aspects of hiring and educating customer contact employees of the HRSSO as well as second or third level support employees.

In line with recommendations made in relevant literature[70], the reliability and validity of the measurement models will be ensured by adopting a multi-step approach that uses an appropriate structure equation modeling method to test our hypotheses including first and second generation test criteria.

Based upon reliable and valid measurement models, both the directions of the relationships and the linearity between the model constructs as hypothesized in our conceptual model will be tested through estimating a linear, a quadratic and a cubic function for each linkage followed by a fit analysis comparing the linear model with the non-linear model with the highest

67 Cf. *BRUHN* (2003), p. 1195.

68 Cf. *BRUHN* (2003), p. 1195, and *RÖDER* (2012).

69 Cf. *RÖDER* (2012).

70 Cf. *CHURCHILL* (1979), and *PING* (2004).

explanation power. Due to the exploratory nature of our research we will additionally employ Neural Structural Relationships (NEUSREL) – a state-of-the art causal path modeling and exploring technique developed by *BUCKLER*[71] to uncover (a priori unknown) nonlinearities.[72]

4 Conclusion

So far in theory and in practice there is a lack of a theoretically well-founded, multidimensional model to measure internal service quality in the HRSSO context and its linkages to relevant service outcomes. Moreover, during our literature review we found no problem adequate measures for CV and BI. Hence, this long-term research project makes various contributions:

- We conceptualize a multidimensional high-order measure for SQ as well as a context-specific CV- and a BI-construct.
- Our conceptualization procedure as described above can be applied to other internal service contexts.
- Context relevant linkages as well as the linearity assumption between SQ, CV, SAT and BI will be uncovered.

Data will be collected from a multinational company running an HRSSO to empirically validate our conceptual model. The analysis and interpretation of these data is the foundation for refining our model and optimizing it for practical application leading to better management decisions regarding staff and IT among others.

However, the conceptual model focuses solely on HRSSO and the internal customers′ point of view. Further research should also consider the HRSSO management perspective as well as the integration of results gained from the model′s application into a holistic controlling tool.

71 Cf. *BUCKLER* (2001), and online http://www.neusrel.com.

72 For such an analysis procedure cf. *RÖDER* (2012).

Abbreviations

BI	Internal Customer Behavioral Intentions
CV	Customer Value
HRSSO	Human Resources Shared Services Organization
ID	Identification (Number)
NEUSREL	Neural Structural Relationships
OUT	Output Quality
PROC	Process Quality
SAT	Internal Customer Satisfaction
STR	Structure Quality
SQ	Internal Service Quality

References

ANDERSON, E. W./MITTAL, V. (2000): Strengthening the Satisfaction-Profit-Chain, in: Journal of Service Research, Vol. 3 (2000), No. 2, p. 107–120.

BABAKUS, E./BOLLER, G. W. (1992): An Empirical Assessment of the SERVQUAL Scale, in: Journal of Business Research, Vol. 24 (1992), No. 3, p.253–268.

BEARDEN, W. O./NETEMEYER, R. G./TEEL, J. E. (1989): Measurement of Consumer Susceptibility to Interpersonal Influence, in: Journal of Consumer Research, Vol. 9, March, p. 183–194.

BHARADWAJ, N./MATSUNO, K. (2006): Investigating the Antecedents and Outcomes of Customer Firm Transaction Cost Savings in a Supply Chain Relationship, in: Journal of Business Research, Vol. 59 (2006), No. 1, p. 62–72.

BOULDING, W./KARLA, A./STAELIN, R./ZEITHAML, V. (1993): A Dynamic Process Model of Service Quality: From Expectations to Behavioral Intentions, in: Journal of Marketing Research, Vol. 30 (1993), February, p. 7–27.

BRADY, M. K./CRONIN, J. J. (2001): Some New Thoughts on Conceptualizing Perceived Service Quality: A Hierarchical Approach, in: Journal of Marketing, Vol. 65 (2001), No. 3, p. 34–49.

BRADY, M. K./CRONIN, J. J./HULT, G. T. M. (2000): Assessing the Effects of Quality, Value, and Customer Satisfaction on Consumer Behavioral Intentions in Service Environments, in: Journal of Retailing, Vol. 76 (2000), No. 2, p. 193–218.

BRUHN, M. (2003) Internal Service Barometers: Conceptualization and Empirical Results of a Pilot Study in Switzerland, in: European Journal of Marketing, Vol. 37 (2003), No. 9, p. 1187–1204.

BRUHN, M./GEORGI, D. (2008): Kundenorientiertes Controlling von Corporate Shared-Services durch Interne Kundenbarometer, in: *KEUPER, F./OECKING, C.* (Eds.), Corporate Shared Services: Bereitstellung von Dienstleistungen im Konzern, 2nd edition, Wiesbaden 2008, p. 71–190.

BUCKLER, F. (2001): NEUSREL: Neuer Kausalanalyseansatz auf Basis neuronaler Netze als Instrument der Marketingforschung, Göttingen 2001.

BUTTLE, F. (1996): SERVQUAL: Review, Critique, Research Agenda, in: European Journal of Marketing, Vol. 30 (1996), No. 1, p. 8–32.

CHANG, H.-H./WANG, Q.-H./YANG, W.-Y. (2009): The Impact of E-Service Quality, Customer Satisfaction and Loyalty on E-Marketing. Moderating Effect of Perceived Value, in: Total Quality Management, Vol. 20 (2009), No. 4, p. 423–443.

CHURCHILL, G. A. (1979): A Paradigm for Developing Better Measures of Marketing Constructs, in: Journal of Marketing Research, Vol. 16 (1979), No. 2, p. 64–73.

COOKE, F. L. (2006): Modeling an HR Shared Services Center: Experience of an MNC in the United Kingdom, in: Human Resource Management, Vol. 45 (2006), No. 2, p.211–227.

CRONIN, J. J./TAYLOR, S. A. (1992): Measuring Service Quality: A Reexamination and Extension, in: Journal of Marketing, Vol. 56 (1992), No. 3, p. 55–68.

CRONIN, J. J./BRADY, M. K./HULT, G. T. (2000): Assessing the Effects of Quality, Value, and Customer Satisfaction on Consumer Behavioral Intentions in Service Environments, in: Journal of Retailing, Vol. 76. (2000), No. 2, p. 193–218.

DABHOLKAR, P. A./THORPE, D. I./RENTZ, J. O. (1996): A Measure of Service Quality for Retail Stores: Scale Development and Validation, in: Journal of the Academy of Marketing Science, Vol. 24 (1996), No. 1, p. 3–16.

DABHOLKAR, P. A./SHEPHERD, C. D./THORPE, D. I. (2000): A Comprehensive Framework for Service Quality: An Investigation of Critical Conceptual and Measurement Issues Through a Longitudinal Study, in: Journal of Retailing, Vol. 76 (2000), No. 2, p. 139–173.

DAGGER, T. S./SWEENEY, J. C./JOHNSON, L. W. (2007): A Hierarchical Model of Health Service Quality: Scale Development and Investigation of an Integrated Model, in: Journal of Service Research, Vol. 10 (2007), No. 2, p. 123–142.

DONABEDIAN, A. (1980): Explorations in Quality Assessment and Monitoring: The Definition of Quality and Approaches to its Assessment, Ann Arbor (Mich.) 1980.

FALK, T. (2007): Elektronische Dienstleistungsqualität: Konzeption, Messung und Identifikation asymmetrischer Effekte auf die Kundenzufriedenheit, Wiesbaden 2007.

FALK, T./HAMMERSCHMIDT, M./SCHEPERS, J. J. L. (2009): The Service Quality-Satisfaction Link Revisited: Exploring Asymmetries and Dynamics, in: Journal of the Academy of Marketing Science, Vol. 38 (2009), No. 3, p. 288–302.

FARNDALE, E./PAAUWE, J./HOEKSMA, L. (2009): In-Sourcing HR: Shared Service Centres in the Netherlands, in: The International Journal of Human Resource Management, Vol. 20 (2009), No. 3, p. 544–561.

FASSNACHT, M./KOESE, I. (2006): Quality of Electronic Services: Conceptualizing and Testing a Hierarchical Model, in: Journal of Service Research, Vol. 9, No. 1, p. 19–37.

FISHBEIN, M./AJZEN, I. (1975): Belief, Attitude, Intention and Behavior: An Introduction to Theory and Research, Reading.

FORNELL, C. (1982): A Second Generation of Multivariate Analysis, New York 1982.

VON GLAHN, C. (2007): Shared Services: Gestaltungskonzepte zur Bereitstellung von IT-Leistungen in multinationalen Konzernen, Berlin 2007.

GOUNARIS, S. (2005): Measuring Service Quality in B2B Services: An Evaluation of the SERVQUAL Scale Vis-à-Vis, in: Journal of Services Marketing, Vol. 19 (2005), No. 6, p. 421–435.

GREMLER, D. D./BITNER, M. J./EVANS, K. R. (1994): The Internal Service Encounter, in: International Journal of Service Industry Management, Vol. 5 (1994), No. 2, p. 34–56.

HEINONEN, K. (2004): Reconceptualizing Customer Perceived Value: The Value of Time and Place, in: Managing Service Quality, Vol. 14, No. 2/3, p. 205–215.

HILKE, W. (1989): Dienstleistungs-Marketing, Wiesbaden 1989.

HO, S.-H./KO, Y.-Y. (2008): Effects of Self-Service Technology on Customer Value and Customer Readiness: The Case of Internet Banking, in: Internet Research, Vol. 18, No. 4, p. 427–446.

HOECK, M./KEUPER, F. (2001): Empirische Untersuchung zur Auswahl und Kompetenz von Beratungsgesellschaften, in: Die Betriebswirtschaft, Vol. 61 (2001), No. 4, p. 427–443.

HU, H.-H./KANDAMPULLY/JUWAHEER, T. D. (2009): Relationships and Impacts of Service Quality, Perceived Value, Customer Satisfaction, and Image: An Empirical Study, in: The Service Industry Journal, Vol. 29 (2009), No. 2, p. 111–125.

KAGELMANN, U. (2001): Shared Services als alternative Organisationsform. Am Beispiel der Finanzfunktion im multinationalen Konzern, Wiesbaden 2001.

KANG, J./JAMES, J./ALEXANDRIS, K. (2002): Measurement of Internal Service Quality. Application of the SERVQUAL Battery to Internal Service Quality, in: Managing Service Quality, Vol. 12 (2002), No. 5, p. 278–291.

KETTINGER, W. J./LEE, C. C. (2007): Perceived Service Quality and User Satisfaction with the Information Services Function, in: Decision Sciences, Vol. 25 (2007), No. 5/6, p. 737–766.

KEUPER, F. (2001): Strategisches Management, Munich 2001.

KEUPER, F./OECKING, C. (2008): Shared-Service-Center – The First and the Next Generation, in: *KEUPER, F./OECKING, C.* (Eds.), Corporate Shared Services: Bereitstellung von Dienstleistungen im Konzern, 2nd edition, Wiesbaden, p. 475–502.

KEUPER, F./ROEDER, S. (2009): Shared Services Automation: Results of An Empirical Survey, Hamburg 2009.

LAPIERRE, J. (1996): Service Quality – The Construct, its Dimensionality and its Measurement, in: *SWARTZ, T./BROWN, S. W./BOWEN, D. E.* (Eds.), Advances in Services Marketing and Management – Research and Practice, Greenwich (CT), p. 45–70.

LIU, C.-M. (2005): The Multidimensional and Hierarchical Structure of Perceived Quality and Customer Satisfaction, in: International Journal of Management, Vol. 22 (2005), No. 3, p. 426–435.

MACKENZIE, S. B./PODSAKOFF, P. M./JARVIS, C. B. (2005): The Problem of Measurement Model Misspecification in Behavioral and Organizational Research and Some Recommended Solutions, in: Journal of Applied Psychology, Vol. 90 (2005), No. 4, p. 710–730.

MCDOUGALL, G. H. G./LEVESQUE, T. (2000): Customer Satisfaction with Services: Putting Perceived Value into the Equation, in: Journal of Services Marketing, Vol. 14 (2000), No. 5, p. 392–410.

MELDAU, S. (2007): Qualitätsmessung in Dienstleistungscentern, Wiesbaden 2007.

OLIVER, R. L. (2009): Satisfaction. A Behavioral Perspective on the Consumer, 2nd edition, New York 2009.

PARASURAMAN, A./ZEITHAML, V. A./BERRY, L. L. (1994): Reassessment of Expectations as a Comparison in Measuring Service Quality: Implications for Further Research, in: Journal of Marketing, Vol. 58 (1994), No. 1, p. 111–124.

PING, R. A. (2004): On Assuring Valid Measures for Theoretical Models Using Survey Data, in: Journal of Business Research, Vol. 57 (2004), No. 2, p. 125–141.

RÖDER, S. (2012): Dienstleistungsqualität von Personal-Shared-Service-Organisationen aus Kundensicht, Berlin 2012.

RÖDER, S./KEUPER, F. (2009) Qualitätsorientierte Steuerung von Shared-IT-Service-Organisationen, in: *KEUPER, F./WAGNER, B./WYSUWA, H.-D.* (Eds.), Managed Services: IT-Sourcing der nächsten Generation, Wiesbaden 2009, p. 203–236.

RUIZ, D. M./GREMLER, D. D./WASHBURN, J. H./CARRIÓN, G. C. (2008): Service Value Revisited: Specifying a Higher-order, Formative Measure, in: Journal of Business Research, Vol. 61 (2008), No. 12, p. 1278–1297.

SHAMDASANI, P./MUKHERJEE, A./MALHOTRA, N. (2008): Antecedents and Consequences of Service Quality in Consumer Evaluation of Self-Service Internet Technologies, in: The Service Industries Journal, Vol. 28 (2008), No. 1, p. 117–138.

SNOJ, B./KORDA, A. P./MUMEL, D. (2004): The Relationships Among Perceived Quality, Perceived Risk and Perceived Product Value, in: Journal of Product and Brand Management, Vol. 13 (2004), No. 3, p. 156–167.

SUGIANTO, L.-F./TOJIB, D. R. (1996): Modeling User Satisfaction with an Employee Portal, in: International Journal of Business and Information, Vol. 1 (1996), No. 2, p. 239–255.

SWEENEY, J. C./SOUTAR, G. N. (2001): Consumer Perceived Value: The Development of a Multiple Item Scale, in: Journal of Retailing, Vol. 77 (2001), Summer, p. 203–220.

TOJIB, D. R./SUGIANTO, L.-F./SENDJAYA, S. (2006): A Conceptual Model for B2E Portal User Satisfaction, in: Proceedings of the International Conference on Business and Information, Singapore 2006.

UHRICH, S. (2008): Stadionatmosphäre als verhaltenswissenschaftliches Konstrukt im Sportmarketing: Entwicklung und Validierung eines Messmodells, Wiesbaden 2008.

ULBRICH, F. (2008): The Adoption of IT-enabled Management Ideas. Insights from Shared Services in Government Agencies, Economic Research Institute, Stockholm School of Economics (EFI), Stockholm 2008.

URBACH, N./SMOLNIK, S./RIEMPP, G. (2009): Measuring the Effectiveness of Employee Portals, in: Proceedings of the 15th Americas Conference on Information Systems, August 6th–9th, San Francisco (CA) 2009.

VOLLMER, M./FISCHER, B./ROEDER, S. (2008): Next Generation Shared Services – Automatisierung als Trend, in: *KEUPER, F./SCHOMANN, M./GRIMM, R.* (Eds.), Strategisches IT-Management, Wiesbaden, p. 279–316.

WESCHKE, K. (2008): Kulturelle Passung als Erfolgsfaktor bei HR Shared Services: Eine empirische Studie im internationalen Servicekontext, Saarbrücken 2008.

WOODSIDE, A. G/FREY, L. L./DALY, R. T. (1989): Linking Service Quality, Customer Satisfaction, and Behavioral Intentions, in: Journal of Healthcare Marketing, Vol. 9 (1989), No. 4, p. 5–17.

ZEITHAML, V. (1988): Consumer Perceptions of Price, Quality, and Value: A Means-end Model and Synthesis of Evidence, in: Journal of Marketing, Vol. 52 (1988), July, p. 2–22.

ZEITHAML, V./BERRY, L. L./PARASURAMAN, A. (1996): The Behavioral Consequences of Service Quality, in: Journal of Marketing, Vol. 60 (1996), No. 2, p. 31–46.

Part 3:

“Enhance and Innovate” –
From a Service Provider to a Strategic Partner

Shared Services for Smaller Entities

KAI ZABEL

Heraeus Holding

Executive Summary

Shared Services is an organizational concept well introduced for years. Over the last years the scope of services provided and organized in Shared Services was continuously extended. The main directions of scope extension run along the following lines[1]:

- Geographical extension,
- Functional extension (Finance, HR, Procurement, etc.),
- Extension along the process chains,
- From purely transactional to value adding tasks.

This article discusses approaches to extend services in a different and often neglected direction, the extension to smaller entities.

Integrating smaller entities into a Shared Service program provides in particular benefits in the area of process stabilization, quality and improved compliance. Relative to the size of the smaller entities efficiency and cost reductions can be reached as well.

Beside potential business case issues the size of the remaining organization is one of the key issues when dealing with Shared Services for smaller entities. In order to overcome this issue two approaches exist: On the one hand a very comprehensive scope of services can be applied in order to make the Finance department in the smaller entity redundant. On the other hand the remaining Finance activities can be bundled and integrated into a larger department or a newly founded General & Administration department.

The integration of Services for smaller entities in a Shared Service Center requires additional organizational considerations. Integrating services for smaller entities into an existing Shared Service organization requires a solution for the additional services taken over and the customer relationship management. Separating the services for a smaller entity into a specialist group might lead to disadvantages regarding process efficiency but provides benefits regarding service quality. Hybrid approaches come with additional requirements regarding center internal communication.

Extending Shared Services to smaller entities is possible, offers benefits and shows the strength of the Shared Service idea. Dealing with smaller entities requires rather customized concepts to than dealing with larger entities. This is in particular true for the remaining organization in the smaller entity as well as the center internal organization. The extension to smaller entities should be motivated primarily by a wish for more stabilization of processing in smaller entities, the quality and an improved compliance rather than purely from cost savings.

[1] Cf. *Bangemann* (2005), p. 227 et seqq.

1 Introduction

Two generic types of Shared Service programs can be differentiated: Firstly there are those companies imitating top-down the ramp-up and roll-out of Shared Services with a pre-defined and mandated scope of services and entities to be included in the program. The design of the Shared Service program follows in general the normal principles of economic behavior: Balance implementation effort and effect. This general approach normally leads to a definition of a minimum size of an entity to stop at or certain countries to be excluded.

Secondly, approaches exist were each and every Shared Service migration project is obliged to demonstrate economic benefits. Again this design leads to a situation leaving smaller entities most likely out of scope as project efforts in most cases exceed the monetary benefits.

When dealing with Shared Service concepts for smaller entities another issue becomes obvious: The size of the remaining organization. In case process splits are applied in the same way as for larger entities very often the remaining organization gets below a critical size required in order to secure performance of the de-central activities throughout a year.

If all these approaches lead to a situation not to include smaller entities why than thinking about smaller entities in the context of a Shared Service project?
In order to find an answer to this question this article is divided into following parts:

1. Definition of terms used throughout the article;
2. Benefits gained from an integration of smaller entities;
3. Generic approaches on how to deal with smaller entities;
4. How to organize Shared Services for smaller entities;
5. Conclusions

2 Definitions

When talking about Shared Services in this article the key focus is on Finance Shared Services. Some of the considerations can be transferred to other functions like Human Resources or Procurement as well but do not necessarily fit in all cases. Following this limitation an entity is considered to be a legal entity which normally is the relevant unit for a Shared Service Center for Finance as nearly all transactions come back to a legal entity especially in those processes closely linked to Accounting.

The term "smaller entity" is a context sensitive term depending on the overall size and set-up of a company. To get closer to a usable definition for this article the differentiation between technical entities and stand-alone entities will be introduced in following table (see table 1).

Criteria	Technical entity	Stand-alone entity
Reason for running entity	➢ Legal ➢ Tax ➢ Customs ➢ Accounting reasons ➢ Other non-business related reasons	➢ Business reasons ➢ Sales ➢ Service ➢ Trading ➢ Production ➢ etc.
Staffing	➢ No dedicated finance staff	➢ Dedicated finance staff
Business Process Sourcing	➢ Finance services performed by finance staff of other entity ➢ Outsourced services	➢ Dedicated finance staff of the entity

Table 1: Differentiation between technical entities and stand-alone entities

When talking about smaller entities in the context of Shared Services technical entities are not taken into consideration. Normally services for technical entities are provided by the Finance staff of one of the stand-alone entities of the company. These technical entities are normally migrated to Shared Services together with the stand-alone entity providing the service.

The differentiation between "smaller" entities and medium or large entities can be supported by some relevant decision criteria which are basically oriented on the "normal" approach to design a Shared Service program, the expected economic benefits and the stability of the remaining organization. To provide some orientation the following table provides concrete numbers. However, the classification of an entity to one of the classes depends on the individual case.

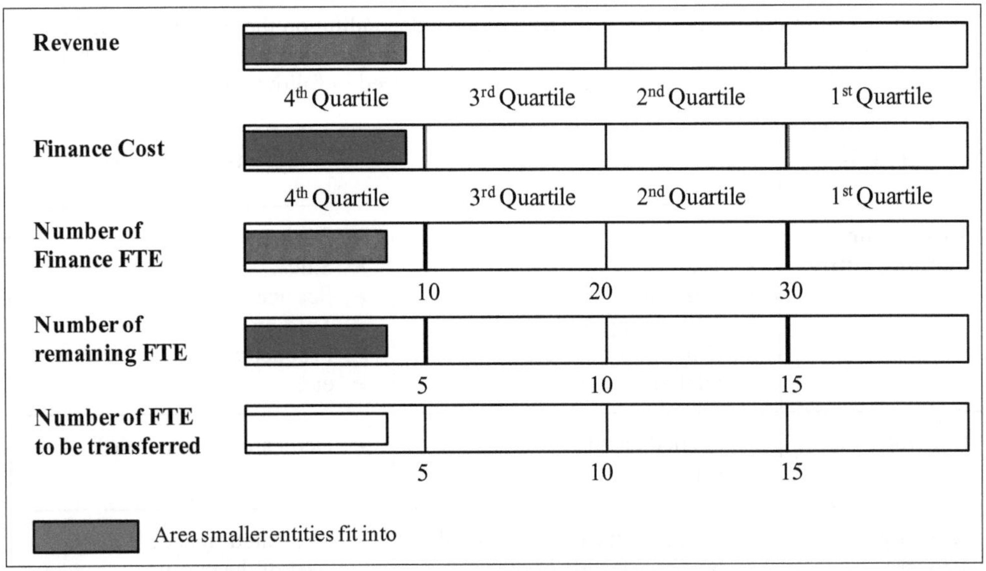

Figure 1: Decision criteria to identify „smaller" entities

Revenue and Finance Cost are very often used in order to design the Shared Service Program in the first spot. Very often a clear top down definition is chosen saying that those entities should be taken into account which count for approx. 80 % of total revenue or respectively approx. 80 % of total Finance staff. The 4th quartile companies are then very often not even analysed.

Taking the staffing situation as a criteria is rather focusing on the question if a) a positive business case can be expected or b) if the remaining organization is big enough to secure stable operations of the remaining tasks. Even in a situation where Shared Services is a mature business process sourcing model for a company it becomes difficult to show monetary benefits if the number of transferred Full-time Equivalents (FTE) is smaller than 4 FTE.

As a rule of thumb we assume that Shared Service programs resulting in a Shared Service Center with more than 40 FTE are likely to provide a positive business case. Programs resulting in a Shared Service organization with more than 300 FTE will provide in 100 % of all case a positive result. However these numbers are not really helpful for our topic as they

- Do not provide an indication for an individual migration project,
- Provide an accumulated number for larger and smaller entities,
- Accept that some of the in scope entities will not contribute positively to the business case.

Stability of a remaining organization depends on the risk not to be able to perform the assigned activities and tasks in particular in case of unexpected leave of personnel, holidays or illness.

3 Benefits From Integrating Smaller Entities Into Shared Services

Integrating smaller entities to the Shared Service concept comes with several benefits:

- Stabilization of processing,
- Quality improvements due to further specialization,
- Improved process compliance,
- Improved scalability,
- Very often cost reduction.

Smaller entities depend much more on the individuals working in the Finance department than larger entities. Very often they have a very broad knowledge of all types of accounting processes and transactions. The negative impact of having concentrated this broad knowledge into a relatively small number of people is obvious. In case of holidays, illness or key persons are leaving the company the risk of not being able to continue processing or erroneous processing increases disproportionally in comparison to larger entities. In particular for consolidated entities this risk is not only a risk for the individual entity but for the whole group. Taking a strategy of risk mitigation in this point must be an important agenda item for the key decision taker in an organization as the materialized risks related to this point could easily become enormous.

Some processes or activities appear in smaller companies very seldom. Smaller entities face difficulties in handling in particular these special or rarely appearing cases. To make sure that an appropriate level of knowledge in those cases, is available is relatively expensive for a smaller entity. But improving the processing quality in general means securing the adequate processing of rarely appearing cases in particular. Executing finance processes in a Shared Service environment is coming with the clear benefit of operating Finance on a higher level of knowledge and experience.

Similar to the processing quality is the process compliance. In order to safeguard or ensure a high level of process compliance a system of process controls needs to be implemented. Controls in general limit process efficiency as they cause extra effort besides the pure processing. In order to balance the effort for process controls and the requirements of process efficiency two things are necessary:

- Standardized processing and a
- High level of automatic or system integrated controls

Both, standardized processing and control automation are easier to handle and to implement in a scenario where processing is centralized.

One of the principles while talking about compliance is the so called 4-eyes principle. This principle foresees to split activities to several people to ensure that one person performs an activity while a second person – performing one of the following process steps – cross-checks the result of the activity before. For example the capturing of a purchase order should be separated from performing the invoice verification. The invoice posting again should be split from executing the payments. Implementing an activity split in a smaller entity securing the 4-eyes principle is much more difficult – if possible at all – than in larger units.

When dealing with smaller entities in the context of a Shared Service project you hear often the argument that you cannot cut out 0.x of a person. This argument highlights clearly one of the issues: Regardless the number of transactions smaller entities must keep capacities for processing on board. A flexible adaptation to a changing number of transactions is much more limited in smaller entities than in larger units like a Shared Service Center. The following figure tries to illustrate the differences regarding scalability of smaller entities and larger units. Very often volumes of smaller entities can be integrated to larger units without the need to increase the capacities as the impact is too small to have an effect.

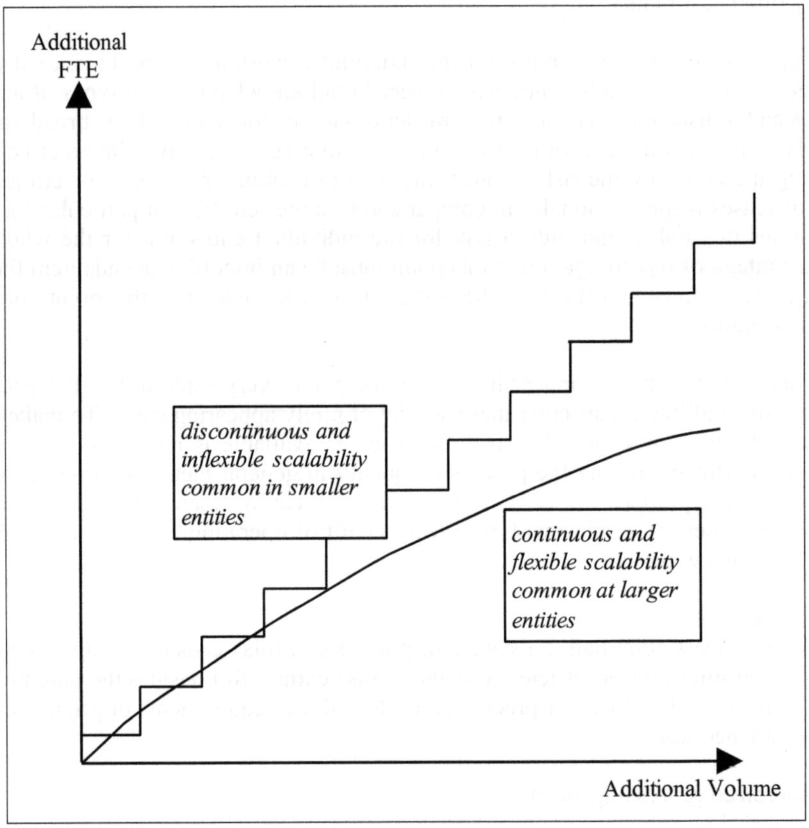

Figure 2: Scalability in smaller and larger entities

Especially due to the effect described above the relative cost savings for smaller entities are often significantly higher than for larger entities. Sources for the relatively high cost savings are

- Efficiency gains due to economies of scale bigger than in larger entities due to
  - Limited scalability in smaller units;
  - Limited specialization effects;
  - Small transaction volumes do often not lead to additional capacity requirements.
- Salary arbitrages
  - Depending on country of smaller entity and Shared Service Center;
  - Generalist in smaller entity with relatively high salary vs. specialist with payments adapted to tasks.

However, as mentioned in the very beginning, the absolute savings do often lead to a negative decision on migration projects for smaller entities. Having listed the benefits of a potential integration of smaller entities to a Shared Service program shows clearly that good reasons exist to take smaller entities into account. However dealing with smaller entities in Shared Services is linked to some key requirements and approaches different to those for medium or larger entities.

4 Generic Approaches on how to Deal With Smaller Entities

Taking the above mentioned following key findings can be summarized:

- Shared Service projects with stand-alone business cases will often lead to unsatisfactory business case results for smaller entities.
- The affected smaller entities will face issues with the remaining organization. The size of the remaining organization is likely to fall below a critical size.
- Benefits from integrating smaller entities to a Shared Service scenario exist in particular from a quality, risk and compliance point of view.

The integration of smaller entities to a Shared Service scenario requires the fulfilment of key pre-requisites which need to be fulfilled:

- Integrating smaller entities to Shared Service is in line with the organizational strategy of the respective company.
- The smaller entity is using the same ERP system as other entities served from the respective Shared Service Center
- Take over all Finance activities

- Contact partner for Finance matters will still be available in the smaller entity

In all Shared Service projects a key success factor is the fit with the overall company strategy and the top management support. Dealing with smaller entities this topic becomes much more important due to the fact that no major savings can be expected and costs are related to a Shared Service project.

The following list shows the main reasons for Shared Services[2]

- Lower costs,
- Higher quality,
- Lower risk,
- Standardized processes,
- Leverage technology,
- Encourage a 'one company' mindset,
- Increased productivity,
- Economies of scale,
- Improved controls,
- More timely and accurate information.

Main strategic driver for a Shared Service project that includes or targets smaller entities must be the non-monetary benefits and here in particular the quality, risk and compliance topic. If this is the case investments or reduced savings can be well accepted.

In situations where companies are re-organizing and trying to find new solutions in particular for smaller entities Shared Services can become a vehicle to drive and support the targeted change. If the Shared Service projects is primarily a cost saving project smaller entities will most likely fall out of scope for the above mentioned reasons.

> *"An integrated ERP is still the major enabler and ERP in general is viewed as the most useful IT solution (68 %) to support the SSO approach"*[3]

This in particular is the case for smaller entities. All the benefits listed above will disappear if the respective smaller entity is not conducting the relevant activities on an integrated ERP system. There is no necessity that the smaller entity is using the same ERP system as larger ones, but benefits will only appear if either other larger companies served by the Shared Service center are using the same ERP system or if all smaller entities to be served from a Shared Service center are using the same platform. The fact that the ERP system must support a decentral processing does not need to be mentioned separately.

---

2 Cf. BANGEMANN (2005), p. 7.

3 BANGEMANN (2005), p. 65.

In case a smaller entity is using a stand-alone system and is supposed to use this system in future as well the additional complexity added to the Shared Service center is out of balance with the benefits mentioned before.

Shared Service scenarios for Finance very often focus on the Accounting processes in particular Accounts Payables, Travel & Entertainment, Accounts Receivables, Fixed Assets, General Ledger and Period End Closing and in less cases Cost Accounting and Standard Management Reporting. In particular Controlling activities, Tax and Treasury activities are left out. In smaller entities in particular the Accounting processes take the majority of time. Controlling is somehow completing the tasks. Tax and Treasury topics are frequently handled by the Finance Management of the smaller entities.

Commonly the smaller entities are Sales & Service units of a company. Due to this fact in particular the Accounts Receivable activities are taking a larger portion of the effort and here in particular the collection activities.

Taking an average Finance department of a smaller entity with a total capacity of 8 FTE, we will find a split prior to Shared Services similar to the example in figure 3

Process	Local	SSC
Accounts Payables, Travel & Expenses	1,8 FTE	
Accounts Receivables	2,5 FTE	
Fixed Assets	0,1 FTE	
General Accounting	1,6 FTE	
Controlling	1 FTE	
Tax & Treasury	0,5 FTE	
Finance Management	0,5 FTE	

Figure 3: Local Activity Split prior to Shared Service in a small entity

Applying now an average Shared Service split to this example, we would come to an activity split according to figure 4. The remaining organization now is sized 4 FTE. Of course a remaining Finance organization with 4 FTE could keep the lights on. However, cost savings cannot be expected in such a scenario.

Process	Local	SSC
Accounts Payables, Travel & Expenses	0,2 FTE	1,6 FTE
Accounts Receivables	1 FTE	1,5 FTE
Fixed Assets		0,1 FTE
General Accounting	0,8 FTE	0,8 FTE
Controlling	1 FTE	
Tax & Treasury	0,5 FTE	
Finance Management	0,5 FTE	

Figure 4: Standard Shared Service activity split applied for a smaller entity

An alternative approach now could be to eliminate the Finance department completely. In such a scenario the following actions need to be taken (per process):

- Accounts Payables
  - Incoming invoices to be forwarded (paper or preferably as scanned documents) to Shared Services by the remaining local administration (non-Finance).
  - Direct contact of Shared Services to supplier and local ordering units.
  - Travel requests either entered to a system by the traveler or forwarded (mail or scanned document) to Shared Services.
- Accounts Receivables
  - Physical collection (if in place) to be performed by the sales department or a larger sister company operating in the same country/region.
  - Direct contact of Shared Services to customer on Finance matters
- General Ledger
  - Take over all General Ledger activities to Shared Services including local GAAP and tax accounting;
  - Period End Closing activities completely steered by the Shared Services Center;

- Controlling
  - Either transfer Controlling activities to a higher level in the company organization or
  - Keep Controlling function as the Finance representative in the smaller entity
- Tax & Treasury
  - Transfer activities either to a larger company in the organization or to a center of expertise
  - Tax activities can also be outsourced to a local service provider

In an organization shrinking as described above no real need for a dedicated Finance Management exists. However, a Finance counterpart or representative is required. This could be in the one scenario a person dealing primarily with the remaining Controlling parts. Alternatively a manager General & Administration can be established taking over beside other[4] also the Finance Management activities.

Taking this approach the remaining finance organization can consist of 1 to 2 FTE focusing primarily on Controlling and remaining local Finance activities.

According to my experience this is the essential point when dealing with Shared Services for smaller entities: Either take it completely including all Finance processes respectively activities or leave it out of scope. The scope for a Shared Service driven re-organization of a smaller entity should take the most aggressive approach possible to overcome the issues and difficulties mentioned above and to transform the Finance department from the current situation to a meaningful and stable new organization including Shared Services. This does not necessarily mean that all processes have to move to Shared Services (however, this could well be the case). As mentioned above the Finance Management will become part of these transformation considerations as well.

All the statements made so far relate to a scenario where purely the Finance function is in scope of a Shared Service project. During recent years the concept of Business Services – a shared service including more than one administrative function – became more and more popular. Dealing with smaller entities in the context of Business Services opens by far more options regarding split of activities, benefits to provide, monetary impact of a transformation but also regarding the restructuring of the remaining organization.

4 E.g. Human Resources, General Administration.

5 How to Organize Shared Services for Smaller Entities

When integrating smaller units into a Shared Service Center two different approaches are currently used in practice:

- Separate department dealing only with smaller and technical entities providing full scope services,
- Integrating smaller entities into the existing departments.

The first approach combines all Finance services for a smaller entity into one department with a dedicated person serving the respective entity (see Figure 5). This model makes sense if all services together count for 1 FTE or less. If this is the case an entity gets a direct and named contact to ask all questions and handling all operative issues appearing. On the other hand it is beneficial to keep the things together as the entities are too small to provide benefits from a split service with multiple interfaces.

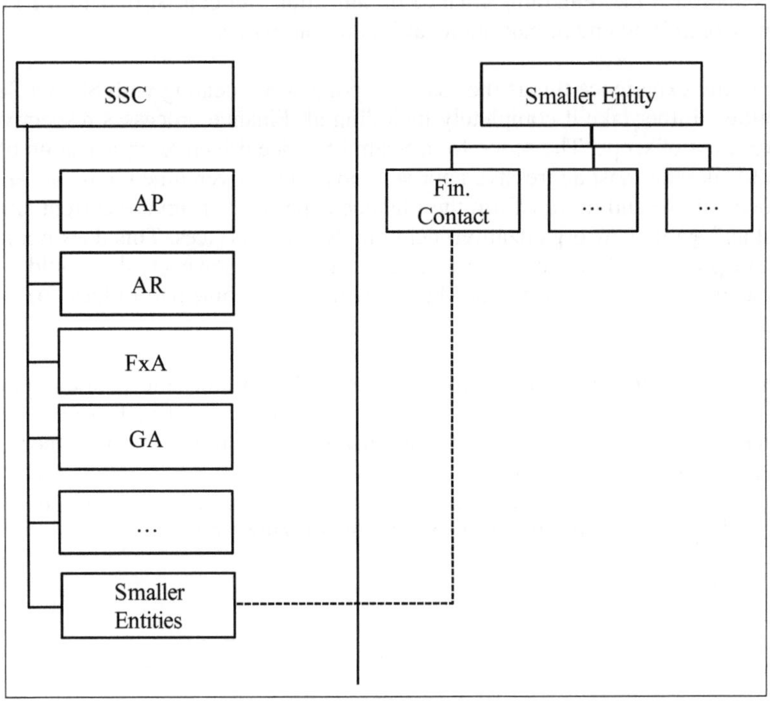

Figure 5: Dedicated department serving smaller entities

For entities with capacities required above 1 FTE it makes sense to arrange services along the standard way of the internal organization of the Shared Service Center (see figure 6).

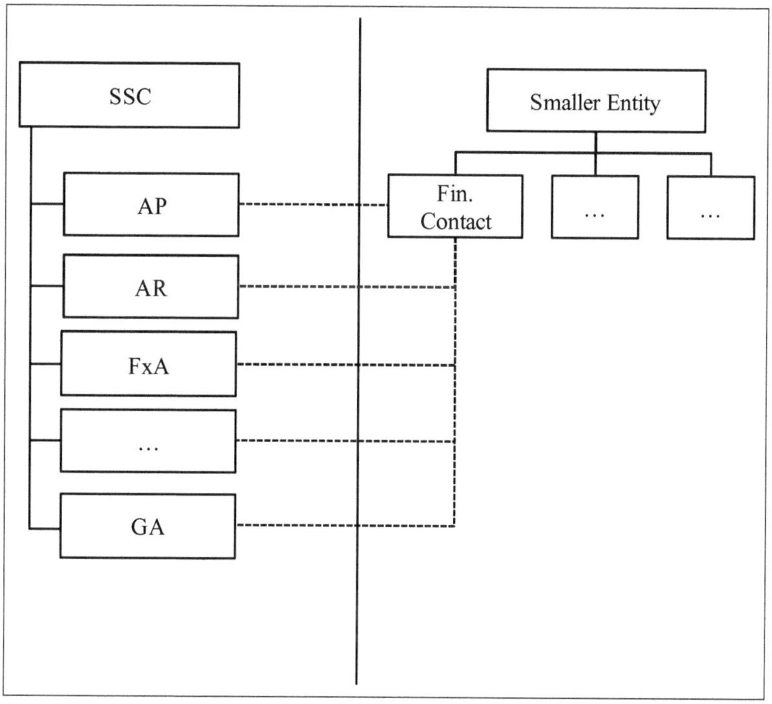

Figure 6: Service for smaller entities fully integrated in SSC structure

Most centers organize their services in two dimensions, a more activity or process oriented view and a geographical, business or system view. For Finance for example the activity or process view would split by Accounts Payables, Travel & Expenses, Accounts Receivables, Fixed Assets and General Accounting. Following this approach the services for smaller entities would be split accordingly. The second type of differentiation could be by country (geographical view). An organization designed along the different ERP systems used would help to avoid hands-off in daily work and support the specialization regarding systems used. Differentiating between the types of business would help to specialize along business and types of transactions. Here a split could, for instance differentiate between production entities and sales and service entities.

Beside these general ways of organizing Shared Service Centers you find very often a "key contact" concept, were individuals are named as primary contact for entities in case of issues, concerns, escalation needs or the need to discuss options or process improvements.

As mentioned in the chapter above it is recommended to take as much services on board as possible in order to overcome issues related to the smaller entities. This as a consequence leads to a broader non-standard service scope for the Shared Service Center. When considering the option 2 to integrate services for smaller entities to the existing departments the question *"What do we do with the remaining service scope?"* is still open.

In these cases it could make sense to take a hybrid approach, splitting the standard services to the existing departments and combining the additional services to a separate group with dedicated people performing the non-standard tasks and securing the client contact regarding all types of services (see figure 7).

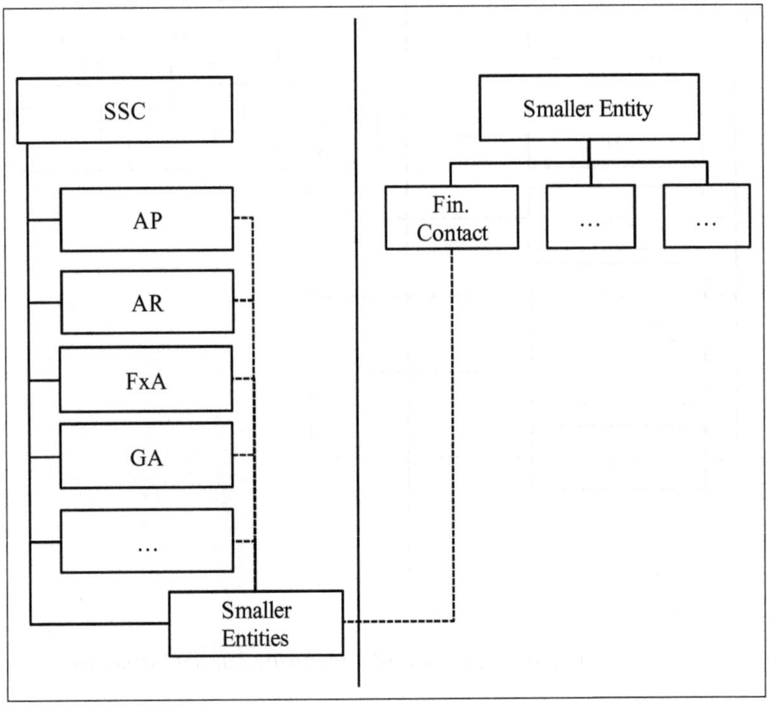

Figure 7: Hybrid organization of services for smaller entities

6 Conclusions

Summarizing the above, following conclusions can be drawn.

- An extension of Shared Services to smaller entities can be reasonable focusing on quality, compliance, standardization and risk reduction rather than short term cost savings.
- Integration of smaller entities make most sense at a point of time when Shared Services are mature.
- In order to avoid instability in the remaining organization it is recommended to take all activities into consideration for Shared Services or alternative sourcing models (e.g. business process outsourcing).
- Most likely a non-standardized service scope extending the standard service scope will be the result.

- The reorganization of the remaining organization is much more relevant when dealing with smaller entities.
- Serving smaller entities in a Shared Service Center will most likely lead to special solutions for the internal organization with a team focusing on serving smaller entities.
- The integration of smaller entities will provide benefits in particular regarding scalability, quality, risk mitigation and compliance. Cost benefits are likely to appear but will most likely not balance with the cost related to the project.

Abbreviations and Selected Terms

AP	Accounts Payable
AR	Accounts Receivable
ERP	Enterprise Resource Planning
FTE	Full-time Equivalent, measuring unit for the workforce of one employee
FxA	Fixed Asset Accounting
GA	General Accounting
Ramp-up	Describes the development phase and corresponding activities of a Shared Services Organization when work is being transferred from one or more donating entities, requiring a corresponding increase of the ser vice provider's internal resources in order to handle the additional volume
SLA	Service Level Agreement, tax-relevant contract between the Shared Services Organization's legal entity and the legal entity of the customer ordering respective services
SSC	Shared Service Center
SSO	Shared Services Organization(s)

References

BANGEMANN, *T.* (2005): Shared Service in Finance and Accounting, Aldershot/Burlington 2005.

Shared Services as Integrated Business Partners Manage End-to-End Processes

JOACHIM JÄCKLE and *SEBASTIAN WOLF*

Henkel AG & Co. KGaA

Executive Summary

Shared Services in today's business environment are mostly implemented for rather transactional activities. An enlarged scope of activities can be a starting point to follow an End-to-End process management. End-to-End means that processes are optimized from the real start to the end of the comprehensive processes. Key challenges organizations have to cope with in this context are the number of process variants, interfaces between process steps and organizational units, adequate service levels, and a possible scope enlargement from transactional toward mid-office activities. To fully leverage the benefits of Shared Services, appropriate organizational structures and governance mechanisms are needed. An integrated Shared Service Organization includes both a service delivery unit on the one hand and a process owner unit on the other hand. With this approach, Shared Service Organizations can act as a real business partner and can offer a platform and enabler for an End-to-End process optimization. Finally, to reach the status of an integrated business partner, organizations need to undergo a transformation which has to be in line with the overall corporate strategy. It is required that the strategy is also cascaded and reflected from a process, system, performance measurement, and people/talent perspective.

1 Introduction

Shared Services and Shared Service Centers in today's business environment are an important lever to increase effectiveness and efficiency of processes and to reach organizational change. The typical focus of Shared Services are transactional and repetitive processes especially of overhead functions like finance, purchasing, or IT. Although first potentials are nowadays frequently leveraged, running Shared Services offer much more potential than expected when optimizing processes from an End-to-End perspective. End-to-End optimization requires a change of mindset in companies since the process organization needs to exist and to act on par with its internal counter parts, i.e. it should behave like a business partner.

In our paper, we elaborate the changes within Shared Services when they transform to an integrated business partner who is managing End-to-End processes. Our argumentation and the remainder of the paper is structured as follows. We describe the underlying fundamentals in the next section and describe common assumptions which can be typically found in organizations in the context of shard services today. We especially address the context of Shared Services, key objectives and the activities which are in scope of Shared Services. The main section afterwards focuses on our understanding how a Shared Service Organization, acting as business partner, can manage End-to-End processes. First, we define End-to-End processes, second, we describe the key elements of an End-to-End process management, and third, we describe the organizational set up of integrated Shared Services organizations. Before summarizing and concluding our paper, we address the path of organizational transformation from transactional Shared Services to integrated business services. We discuss the way how to steer and implement the change processes, we analyze the possible impact on roles within organizations, and finally we reflect key success factors of the transformation.

2 Fundamentals of Shared Services

2.1 Overview: Outsourcing, Shared Services and Shared Service Center

In academic literature as well as in business practice, there is no common understanding and general definition of Shared Services and Shared Service Centers. Basically, Shared Services describe – from a managerial perspective – the provision of services by an organizational unit for more than one receiving organizational units within a larger organization or a group. Typically, the services were previously processed in all or at least in most of the involved receiving organizational units. By using Shared Services, the receiving organizational units share the resources of the service provider which is typically called a 'Shared Service Center' (see figure 1).

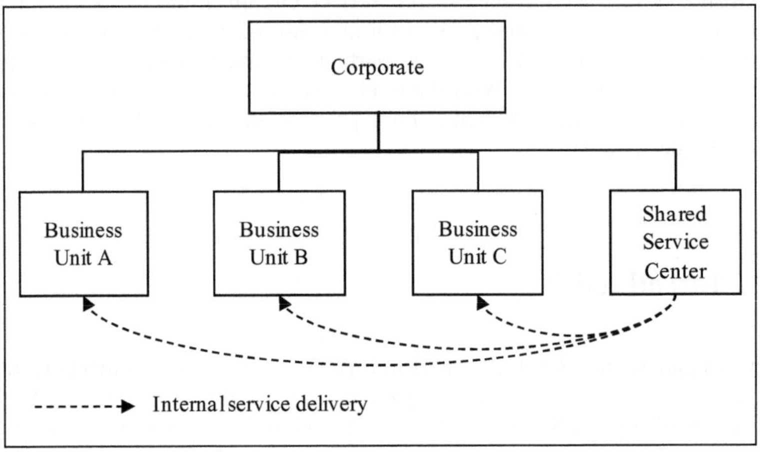

Figure 1: Basic organizational set with Shared Service Center[1]

In scope of Shared Services and Shared Service Centers are processes and activities which are not assessed as a core business process to reach the respective organizational strategies.[2] In most of nowadays cases, this applies especially for activities of support functions like finance, human resource management, purchasing, or IT.[3] Within those functions, especially the transactional activities are in focus of Shared Services. In an ideal situation, those activities can be easily separated from other activities, are processed with a high frequency, and are – in the best case – already standardized within the organization.

Shared Services and Shared Service Centers are often mixed up with outsourcing of processes. There are specific characteristics of both concepts, but the distinction is – especially in business reality – not always 100 % clear. Both have in common that from the viewpoint of a decentral organizational unit, e.g. a business unit, a service is transferred to another organizational unit. One difference between both concepts is linked to the possibility to influence the service delivery of the organization. In an organizational setting using a so-called captive Shared Service Center, the service provider still belongs to the group, thus, the corporate orga-

1 Cf. *KAGELMANN* (2001), p. 50.

2 Cf. *SCHULMAN* et al. (1999), p. 2.

3 Cf. *BANGEMANN* (2005), p. 15.

nizational unit can strongly influence the service delivery. In contrast, the outsourcing provider is owned by a separate organization and the level of influence by the receiving entity is rather limited. Whereas knowledge is retained within the organization by using an internal Shared Service Center, outsourcing to a third party provider might increase the dependency toward the service provider.

2.2 Objectives and Attributes of Shared Services

Key objective of Shared Services is a higher value creation for organizations driven by an increase of efficiency and effectiveness. Efficiency, on the one hand, by pooling resources, leveraging technology investments, and generating economies of scale typically in a low-cost location. Effectiveness, on the other hand, by harmonizing and standardizing processes as well as identifying and implementing best practices resulting in enhanced service levels.[4]

Shared Services typically comprise non-core business processes to reach corporate or business unit strategies. For a Shared Service Center, these processes are core activities.[5] Key attributes of a Shared Service Center are the focus on the delivery of activities and services within pre-defined standard processes. The Shared Service Organization delivers those processes for their internal business partners and strives for continuous improvement at competitive cost levels. To achieve this, those units leverage technology investments, standardization and harmonization.

Besides the key objectives mentioned above, companies setting up or running Shared Services can gain from further tangible and intangible benefits:[6]

- Tangible benefits which are often linked with leveraged technologies can be found for example in the areas of working capital management and purchasing. With the standardization of processes linked to accounts payables, accounts receivables and inventories, net working capital and related cost can be reduced. From a purchasing perspective, standardized processes and databases enable the consolidation of the supplier base supporting negotiations for better price, service, and payment conditions.
- Intangible benefits can exemplarily be found in an increase of agility in organizational transformations or in a changed mindset of the workforce. Using the knowledge and the learning from running standardized processes at a Shared Service Center makes the deployment of best practices or a scope increase of processes easier and faster. Especially the adoption of best practices and a continuous scope increase of Shared Services support an increase of process and result accuracy as well as consistency of information. Furthermore, Shared Services can have positive effects on employee satisfaction and mindset. Whereas personnel of support functions in a Non-Shared Service Organization might feel that their job is a non-core or "not really required" activity, employees in Shared Service Organizations are engaged in delivering core processes for these organizations. Thus, running Shared Services promotes "one company-thinking" and should positively influence employee satisfaction and motivation as well as team orientation.

---

4 Cf. *SCHULMAN* et al. (1999), p. 10.

5 Cf. *SCHULMAN* et al. (1999), p. 7.

6 Cf. *SCHULMAN* et al. (1999), p. 13 et seq.

2.3 Activities in Scope of Shared Services

Activities offered by Shared Service Centers have, on the one hand, certain commonalities and, on the other hand, can be clustered in transactional and expertise-based services.[7] Nevertheless, transactional activities are today still the main area of Shared Services organizations.

Activities operated as a shared service in a Shared Service Center have commonly a rather generic nature, i.e. they are not linked to a specific business unit or tied to a certain location. Inherently, they are typically requested in the same or at least in a very similar way by various or all business units within the group. The business units are the internal customer and normally the only receiver of Shared Services. Furthermore, Shared Services can be characterized by a certain volume of service requests and a clear potential for standardization.

Although typically transactional services are in focus of Shared Services and Shared Service Centers, activities further up of the value chain can also come into the scope of a Shared Service Organization. Against this background, Shared Services and Shared Service Centers can be clustered into transactional and expertise-based services, respectively centers of transaction and centers of expertise.

Transactional services are especially administrative, process-oriented activities with a high frequency of repetitions and high transaction volumes. The content of the services and their set up is quite homogenous, i.e. processes with a high homogeneity. Furthermore, room or need for individual behavior as well as economical risk of the activities is rather limited. Since they typically need rather larger levels of resources and offer opportunities for standardization, economies of scale can be realized and, thus, cost reduced. By leveraging potentials of running transactional services in centers of transaction or centers of scale, services can be delivered faster, at a lower cost, and with higher service levels.[8]

Expertise-based services have typically rather lower transaction volumes and are less standardized. Those services are of higher strategic importance and they are critical to reach organizational objectives. Due to the fact that activities are rather specific and knowledge-intensive, expertise-based services are typically bundled in centers of expertise or in corporate centers. Those organizational units bundle expert knowledge and offer consulting service within an organization. Thus, whereas the scope of transactional services and centers of transaction is rather on standard activities, expertise-based Shared Services focus on steering the organization toward its corporate goals.[9]

Figure 2 summarizes the reflection of possible processes in Shared Service Centers along two dimensions: on the one hand 'process homogeneity', and on the other hand 'strategic importance'. As described above, expertise-based services provided by centers of expertise are strategically important but are typically not very homogenous. Transactional services which are in scope of centers of scale are – in contrast to expertise-based services – characterized with high homogeneity and rather low strategic importance. Following the common understanding in academia and business practice, centers of scale are referred to as Shared Service Center. We will basically also follow this conception, however, the previous argumentation

---

7 Cf. *BECKER/KUNZ/MAYER* (2009), p. 23 et seq.

8 Cf. *ULRICH* (1995), p. 16.

9 Cf. *ULRICH* (1995), p. 16.

shows that the scope of Shared Service Organizations may be much wider than pure on transactional services.

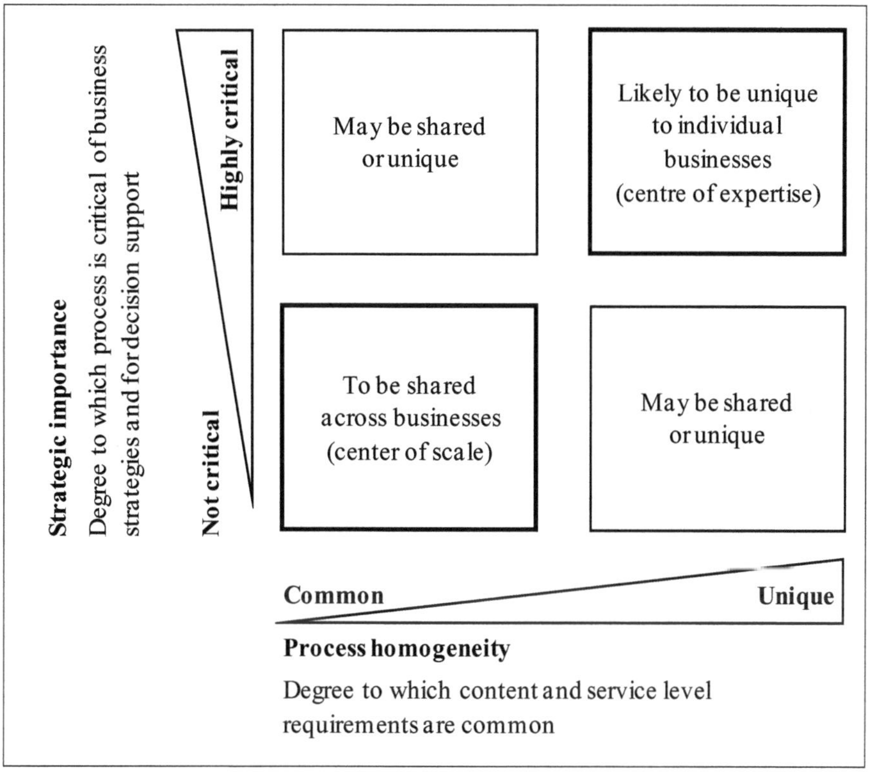

Figure 2: *Process inclusion matrix*[10]

In terms of size and organizational characteristics, the implementation of Shared Services and the set up of Shared Services centers are especially relevant for rather larger and complex multinational organizations.[11] The underlying rationale can be described according to following key drivers:[12]

- Multinational organizations have in most cases multiple local entities which have on a stand alone basis not a sufficient size to set up individual service functions.
- Transaction volumes are rather higher in larger organizations and certain minimum volumes are required that the benefits out of the single transactions overcompensate the cost of setting up the Shared Service Organization.
- Larger organizations are typically more specialized and higher degrees of specialization help to generate economies of scale.

10 Cf. *BANGEMANN* (2005), p. 26.

11 Cf. *SCHULMAN* et al. (1999), p. 4 et seq.

12 Cf. *KEUPER/OECKING* (2008), p. 477 et seq.

- Within large decentralized organizations, business units are able to focus on their key strategic activities of their operations by using adequately performed Shared Services for non-core activities.[13]

2.4 Summary of Fundamentals of Shared Services

The fundamentals of Shared Services, which can be assumed as a common understanding in business practice and which will be the underlying basis for the following elaboration of the next levels of Shared Services, can be summarized as follows: Shared Services are selected internal services which are delivered by one (or a limited number of) organizational unit(s) and utilized by other (receiving) organizational units within a group. The activities are characterized by a high degree of homogeneity and a rather limited strategic importance, i.e. typically transactional services based on pre-defined and harmonized standard processes within support functions of organizations. Key objectives are gains in efficiency, e.g. cost reductions by leveraging technology investments and generating economies of scale, and effectiveness, e.g., enhanced service levels and quality by realizing best practices through process standardization and harmonization. All in all, companies can leverage several potentials with this approach. However, to some extent they limit themselves since Shared Services can – when they act on par with their internal customers and reflect processes from an End-to-End perspective – deliver much more benefits and can contribute stronger to reach organizational goals.

3 From Transactional Activities to End-to-End Processes and Business Partnering

3.1 End-to-End Approach

As described above, typical focus of Shared Services are rather transactional activities. To leverage full potentials of Shared Services, organizations start to strive for enlarging the scope of Shared Services. One of the key ideas in this regard is the intention to look into activities and processes from an End-to-End perspective.

End-to-End process management means to look into processes from one end to the other end. Or in other words: from the start to the end. Managers tend to define the start of a process as the entry point in their area of responsibility and the end of a process as the point of activity where a certain output leaves their area of responsibility. Such an area of responsibility, which can also be described as an organizational silo, can be for example a department or a corporate function. When those managers aim for process improvement, they often only focus on their silo and do not adequately consider process steps outside from their individual scope. Thus, it seems obvious that this approach of process improvement not reflects the spirit of a real End-to-End process management and hinders reaching comprehensive process improvements. For an End-to-End process optimization, it is a clear need to analyze, understand, document, and then improve all activities embedded in the overall process.

13 Cf. *SCHULMAN* et al. (1999), p. 10 et seq.

Based on those considerations, we therefore define an End-to-End process as a comprehensive process which starts at the beginning of a chain of activities and ends at a logical final activity of the process. For the process definition and for the analysis, a pragmatic approach should be chosen. In the beginning of an End-to-End initiative, the process might comprise only the activities of two departments. In the course of the improvement, more and more activities of various departments are included. At the end or in an extreme case, the optimization of the process starts prior to the entry point of the whole company and ends after the departure point of the whole company. That means in particular that processes cross different organizational units and departments. The crossing in some processes can go beyond the business unit and supporting functions. Thus, it is of course wise to look into processes even beyond the boundaries of a company to ensure that interfaces are also properly in shape. Especially for the last aspect, there are more and more examples in business practice. E.g., there are many initiatives to link ERP systems of suppliers and of customers with the own systems landscape in order to optimize processes even beyond the own company.

3.2 Key Elements of End-to-End Process Management

To come closer to what End-to-End process optimization really means, it seems to be appropriate to analyze evidence for not optimized processes. In general, there are four elements in the context of an End-to-End process management which should be addressed:

1. there can be too many process variants
2. there can be unclear interfaces between certain process steps
3. there can be an unjustified or unwanted level of service
4. there can be only transactional activities in scope

To improve the overall processes, it is required to deeply analyze the respective situations and strive for improvement of the situation.

3.2.1 Number of Process Variants

At the starting point of a process optimization, in many cases there are certain activities that are not harmonized or standardized. In some cases, most of the activities are harmonized, but some steps are differentiated and process variants are implemented (see figure 3). Those differences can be manifold: It is possible that there are process variants on parts of an End-to-End process or that there are complete different processes with the same objective. In business practice, the differences to be considered occur typically in various dimensions. In most cases, process variants can be detected between organizational units, e.g. strategic business units (SBUs), or between regions or countries.

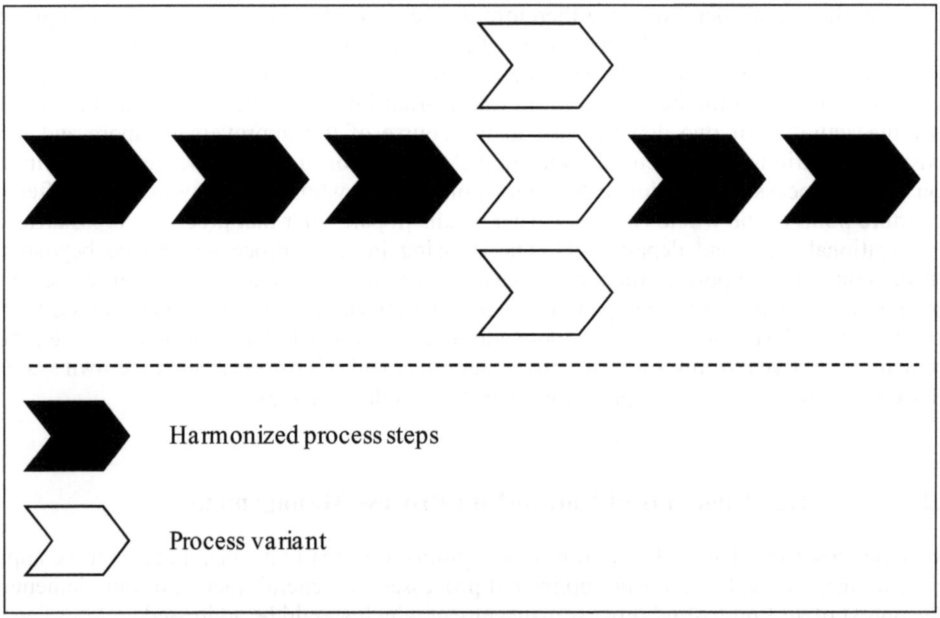

Figure 3: Process variants within harmonized process

A typical example where process variants can be detected is the order-to-cash process. Whereas most of the process activities are harmonized, it happens for example that the way how customer deductions are managed may be differently processed between SBUs. Another example is the collection process of a customer order which is managed differently across different SBUs.

An example for the other dimension of different process activities is the existence of process variants between regions or countries. It is not uncommon that subsidiaries in different countries argue that local legal requirements are the reason for exceptions from a standard process. This can be a reality despite of operating one basically harmonized ERP system. Working on one technical platform helps as an enabler to run harmonized processes, however, it does not necessarily mean that processes or activities are standardized. It can be that tables and configurations are differently implemented or used across different entities. For sure, sometimes differences are really required. But, in most of the cases in business reality we see more exceptions implemented than exceptions required.

Another case to be mentioned is the situation that a portion or even most of the activities of an End-to-End process are harmonized, but which has many different interfaces to partnering units. This is the typical case for an order-to-cash process of a diversified company with more than one SBU and a centralized finance function. The centralized finance function has a harmonized process, but this harmonized process needs to be linked to different activities within the different SBUs. Although those heterogeneous activities may probably have the same objective and are quite similar, already small differences of the interfaces may increase the complexity and reduce the overall efficiency of the operations. – This aspect is also closely linked with the broader aspect on unclear interfaces between process steps which will be discussed in the next section 3.2.2 “Unclear Interfaces”.

Besides the order-to-cash process, master data is also a topic which is in business practice frequently confronted with a high number of process variants. Different conventions across regions or countries, changes of the underlying standard settings in basic processes, mergers and acquisitions, or overly individualized payment terms on the supply and on the customer side lead to a variety of terms and congested master data. As a result, complexity increases and effectiveness in the processes is reduced. Additional resources are often required when multiple or at least not harmonized payment terms are in place. E.g. when additional payment runs are required or also when master data needs to be maintained. Payment term harmonization is also critical from a net working capital management perspective. For example, if a company negotiates on a global level payment terms with its suppliers and those payment terms are not always implemented in the local systems, a negative financial impact is frequently the case.

Process variants are in any case of off-shoring or the case of a migration of processes to Shared Service Centers a key topic. Typically, companies are confronted with situations of having too many process variants which lead to inefficient process management. Possible synergies in terms of common management of one process cannot be realized and cause extra cost until the process steps are further standardized. Besides cost and efficiency benefits, process harmonization and standardization also leads to other synergies and risk reductions, e.g. in regards to work organization. For example, it makes it easier to manage fluctuation, maternity leaves, or simply vacation of the employees.

3.2.2 Unclear Interfaces

For most processes, several organizational units or departments are involved. This involvement leads to a certain complexity and unclear interfaces between the different departments and another key element of missing End-to-End optimization.

A typical reason for those inefficiencies may be the lack of assignment of clear roles and responsibilities between sending and receiving unit. Each department receives input information for certain activities, works on a certain result as an output and delivers it to the receiving department. However, the output of an organizational unit does not always fit the requirements of the receiving unit. The content may be wrong or only understandable on the sending side. It may be the case that the receiver of the information is not the one who really needs the information, e.g. he only needs some information and only transfers other information to the next receiving entities. The typical origins of problems linked with interfaces are wrongly de-fined roles and responsibilities between business partners. There is the need that sender and receiver of information are well defined and aligned. Also it must be clear which information in which layout and structure has to be delivered by a sender. This is only possible by looking into the process from an End-to-End perspective. Only then employees in the process are able to have a big picture view. An optimization only between two business partners is in most of the cases not enough. For example, in the purchase-to-pay process supplier information are entered into the systems as one of the first steps. Although not obvious, some supplier information might be required only at the very end of the process. As a result, the information might not be added to the system in the first steps, but since required at the end of the process, it is added later with much higher efforts.

Unclear responsibilities are also frequently a problem with regard to process interfaces in not well designed processes. In such unclear cases, the situation may occur that problems are on the table but do not find a clear owner. In consequence, the interfaces between certain departmental units are not in order and not well managed. The order-to-cash process offers again one typical example: when customers make deductions from the invoiced prices the reasons can be manifold. It can for example be that (a) the quality of the delivered products was wrong, (b) that the assigned invoiced price does not match with the contract, or (c) the normal deduction for a discount. Different organizations have to deal with the different root causes. In addition, the incentive scheme of the different departments normally differs as well. As a result, the deductions process is inefficient and the company looses money.

A focal prerequisite to manage processes and especially interfaces, are clear process descriptions on high as well as on detailed level. Whereas at a high level of abstraction all processes look aligned and clear, the situation on a detailed level is often different. Thus, high level descriptions are not enough to secure clear interfaces and smoothly running processes. It is necessary that processes are described and documented on a very high level of detail. However, the pure documentation is also not sufficient alone. It is necessary that people are trained on the basis of the documentation.

Interface optimization initiatives addressing activities of different organizational units, unclear responsibilities, or system landscapes are a key challenge within organizations. However, the full End-to-End approach should also consider interfaces with external partners like suppliers or customers to leverage all process improvement potentials as well as to design optimal processes.

3.2.3 Service Level

Analyzing End-to-End processes, it is often the case that the service levels of the different process steps and activities vary and are not homogenous or that service levels are unjustified offered. Origin of this situation is in most of the cases that many activities in a company have been developed over time and now exist in their way because at one point in time there was a need for them. The question whether a process is needed or not is not repeated very often. Also it is clear that the process design is not always challenged and it is difficult to reduce a level of quality when every receiver of a service is happy with the quality of a service. Nevertheless, there can be hidden uncompetitive cost structures in areas where the company does not necessarily compete. The art is to organize processes in the supporting functions in a way that the service level does meet the necessary level of quality.

One example for this thought can be found within the context of Human Resources (HR): In the past, in many companies the HR organization had teams physically around their internal counterparts and customers. A major portion of HR work, however, was more administrative in nature than business partnering. Bundling those administrative services can help to improve the quality of the services and reduce the cost at the same time. As a key tool, many processes have been changed by introducing so called self services. Enabled by IT systems, HR self services give employees and their managers the possibility to get relevant information from a system or to enter certain master data like private postal addresses, etc. directly into a system. Whereas in the past, this type of work was physically done by HR employees after receiving the information, e.g. per telephone call or email, from the employee, the employees now frequently do these themselves. As a first perception, service levels are reduced, however, objectively this is not true in most of the cases.

Homogeneity of service levels can also be improved in the course of the transition of activities to Shared Service Organizations. When several activities of a process are performed by various organizational units, it happens quite often that the service levels differ. They might differ between the activities of the process or – when the same activities are performed by various preparers – between the preparers. In consequence, the users or receivers of the services might complain or would always approach the preparer with the higher – but perhaps not required – service level. Or, assuming a situation where an activity with a high service level follows an activity with a lower service level: in such a case it is probable that much more efforts are required for the second activity than it would be required if also the first activity has a high service level.

As a conclusion, transferring activities to a Shared Service Organization helps smoothing the service levels. It might be also required to reduce service levels by eliminating activities. This all means change for an organization; however, initiatives in this context help to optimize processes from an End-to-End perspective.

3.2.4 Limitation of Transactional Scope

Shared Service Organizations run – as mentioned before and common sense in business practice – in most of the cases transactional activities. Analyzing process chains or processes from an End-to-End perspective, it gets often obvious that not all activities within the process have a pure transactional repetitive character. Such tasks, which have less routine work character, can be better described as mid-office activities and are so far often not processed by the Shared Service Organization. In consequence, it happens quite often that the process flows are interrupted, interfaces need to be managed, and the overall End-to-End process is not running smoothly.

With an increasing maturity of Shared Service Organizations, Shared Service Centers and their staff can more and more cope with increasing demand in terms of quality and quantity. With this development, also mid office tasks will come more in the focus of Shared Services (see figure 4). The clear benefit of such scope increases is that processes can be improved from a real End-to-End perspective. In such a situation, the receiving organizational units clearly specify their demands and the Shared Service Organization acts as a business partner and delivers an optimal End-to-End process.

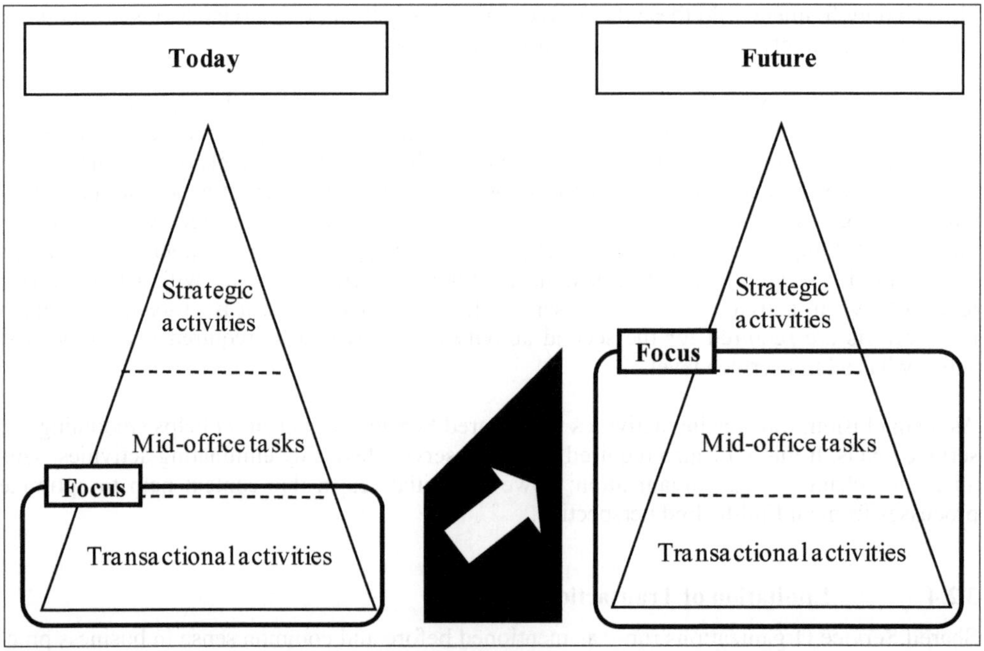

Figure 4: Scope increase of Shared Services

The scope increase from transactional activities to mid-office tasks is not limited to the 'typical' processes for Shared Service Center. With this development, processes beyond typical functional areas get into the focus of Shared Services. In a mid term perspective, more and more business processes, e.g. customer services, will also be in the scope of Shared Service Organizations.

The challenge of a possible limitation due to the focus on transactional activities differs between the processes. For example, the activities of the purchase-to-pay process have mainly a transactional character and the few mid-office activities can be easier integrated in the course of an End-to-End optimization. But, there are also other examples: shifting reporting activities to a Shared Service Organization requires a more complex transformation (see also section 4 "Transformation From Transactional Shared Services to Business Partnering"). Much more activities have mid-office character and the role descriptions of employees need to be adjusted in the shared service and in the retained organization since a major portion of their working scope is affected.

Organizations which limit their shared service scope to transactional activities are confronted with other risks. I.e. if a process is fragmented including activities with a transactional and with a non-transactional character, the number of interface increases. As a result, processes are more complex and an End-to-End optimization is getting more difficult.

In consequence, the prevailing view in business practice that only transactional activities are in scope of Shared Services is not enough. It is rather the case that companies with this understanding limit themselves and miss opportunities with Shared Services. A mindset change is required; however, in most of the cases, this is worth it and the kind of activity should not be a limitation.

3.3 Shared Services as Integrated Business Partners

After having implemented Shared Service Centers and after having off-shored activities, the question is what can be a logical next step of organizational development in the context of Shared Services. In many cases, the next level is an integrated Shared Services organization. Sometimes this organization is called integrated business services (IBS) or global business solutions (GBS). This next level can only be reached when a wide range of things come together.

It starts with the fact that such a change must be wanted. The starting characteristic of an IBS or GBS organization is the mindset to move not only transactional activities to Shared Services but – as described above – also mid-office or even front office activities. With this approach, complete processes can be part of the new organization. One clear advantage of such a way forward is the opportunity to win synergies from End-to-End process optimization. It is clear, however, that each move into this direction requires a large commitment from all parties involved. This is not always given from the beginning of the initiative. As a consequence, Shared Services are not only a transaction center anymore where easy tasks are dumped. In the contrary, the concept only works if the Shared Service Organization is seen as a valued business partner and process competence center. At this stage of typical discussions, two questions are frequently raised: First, can Shared Services improve End-to-End processes? And second, would a process optimization also be possible without running Shared Services? Answering the first question is typically rather easy. When properly set up, shared service can enable End-to-End process improvements. To realize this, all activities – transactional and mid-office tasks – of the End-to-End process needs to be considered and optimized. The answer regarding the second question is not that easy. For sure, process optimization initiatives would also be somehow possible without running a Shared Service Center. Nevertheless, since standardization and harmonization are in most of the cases key objectives of process optimization initiatives, a shared service approach with its inherent benefits does support a process optimization in most of the cases.

One major stumbling block is the organizational differentiation between a service delivery unit on the one hand and a guideline responsible unit on the other hand. If End-to-End process optimization is really a target, it is necessary – alone worth it for acceptance reasons – that the process owner organization must be part of the Shared Service Organization as well. But to be clear, the process owner organization does not have the role of service delivery but has the role of designing processes and support the implementation of process changes with expertise and project management. Other elements of a process organization are a global and regional footprint. In addition, on a local level key users and process experts are necessary. These roles for certain processes can also be found in Shared Service Centers. To manage a global process, certain exchanges of information are necessary and decision making bodies for changes in processes have to be established. All in all, it is noticeable that an IBS/GBS only will be successfully working on processes when such expertise is part of the organization.

With this development, an IBS/GBS has left the focus on service delivery and transactional tasks only. Furthermore, running Shared Services does not mean that all activities of an End-to-End process need to be performed in a Shared Service Center location-wise. Especially due to the fact that mid-office tasks are also in scope of the process, it can be that the activities of the overall process are processed in both a Shared Service Center and in the retained organization. Thus, with the described developments, Shared Service Organizations can be organized virtually as well.

When setting up an IBS/GBS organization, the governance of the system is critical. What happens is that retained organizations hand over tasks and responsibilities to the Shared Service Organization where the process management is bundled as well. With this the degree of central influence on a process is increased. The governance model has to ensure that the retained organizations are still involved in the right way of steering the processes because in many cases the changes of processes will also influence the retained organization. To find the right balance in this sensitive topic, the company culture has to be taken into account.

For example, for most processes, more departments are involved. When looking at the source-to-pay process, this is typically finance, purchasing, and to some extent also the supply chain organization. Whereas this process at a first glance looks rather simple, it is actually very complex with an enormous amount of single activities. Along with the first shared service initiatives, especially modular activities along process steps are moved to the Shared Service Organization. To further enhance its shared service, organizations strive towards setting up End-to-End processes. With the End-to-End process optimization and the possible shift to an IBS/GBS, all activities of the process are centralized in one Shared Service Organization. Whereas in the past, separate teams of purchasing and finance processed the tasks, one team is now taking care of the process. Bringing all involved parties organizationally together, the objective to reach a comprehensive process steering covering all relevant process steps from sourcing to payment activities can be reached. This adjustment of the governance and the team structure helps to increase speed, reduce complexity, and improve service levels.

To conclude, integrated Shared Services organizations can serve as process platform and enabler for End-to-End process optimization. And, they are the logical next step for Shared Services acting as valued business partners of their internal customers.

4 Transformation From Transactional Shared Services to Business Partnering

4.1 How to Steer and Implement Change?

An increase of the scope of Shared Services, a reengineering of a process, or a change of the service delivery mode always has an impact on the organization and leads to a certain transformation of the organization and requires adequate change management procedures. To ensure that objectives are reached, a comprehensive steering and change management approach needs to be implemented. Such an approach comprises underlying strategies, processses, systems as well as performance measurement.

Starting point of the transformation process is a clear strategy definition. What are the overall purposes and the directions of the – eventually changed – shared service initiative? Whatsoever is changed in the scope of the Shared Services, precise definitions are of utmost importance and a key success factor to reach organizational objectives. Based on the strategies, individual objectives can be cascaded and elusive activities should be avoided. For the assessment if objectives are reached, specific key performance indicators need to be implemented to track progress of the change and the effectiveness of the measures. Clear responsibilities are at this stage also important to guarantee accountability of the responsible managers. However, any constitutional activities at this stage should not only focus on single processes of a Shared Service Organization or the whole organization, scope needs to cover all End-to-End activities. Thus, the starting point of all strategy definitions and cascading activities needs to be the overall group strategy. Shared Services can be an important lever to reach corporate strategies, but full potentials can only be leveraged if the shared service strategy embracing activities from End-to-End is embedded in the corporate strategy as well as in the strategies of other corporate functions and business units.

As soon as constitutional elements like strategies, objectives, performance measures, and responsibilities are defined, organizational changes need to be implemented on operational level. Activities can be clustered into three steps enabling change.[14]

First, organizational structures need to be implemented or adjusted. At this stage organizational structure comprises also relevant processes and IT systems. This means that planning, forecasting and reporting contents and processes need to be set up, aligned – content wise with strategies and process wise with involved parties – and finally implemented. Planning and forecasting are very important for Shared Services to steer for example resource availability and, reflecting the objectives on effectiveness, utilization levels. Especially utilization levels need to be forecasted seriously to be well prepared to smooth peak and low times. In this phase, typically service level agreements needs to be set up between the Shared Service Organization and the receiving organizational units. Before contracting the agreements, a clear alignment – and commitment – is required, what and how the services are delivered. Focal questions are what are the variants in the processes and what service levels are expected. Is it already satisfactory to provide a service "just good enough" or on "world-class" level? Those are typical questions, which, first, need to be in line with the overall strategies and, second, need to be agreed between the involved parties. For all involved parties it must be transparent that those decisions are in most of the cases also the key drivers to reach respective objectives. A higher number of process variants is typically more complex, requires more resources and at the end might diminish cost reduction ambitions. However, a higher number of process variants might be essentially required by a business unit to gain additional revenues which are at the end higher than the additional cost. Nevertheless, relevant factors need to be adequately tracked by key performance indicators which need to be consistently defined and implemented in the respective IT systems to ensure full transparency and allow fact-based decision making for involved parties.

Second step to enable the transformation is the selection and qualification of the team. Depending on the defined strategies and objectives, personnel on the respective levels needs to be selected, recruited, and/or qualified. At this point it is important that required profiles in Shared Service Organizations strongly differ (see also chapter 4.2 "Impact on Organizational Roles"). The requirements for positions with nearly pure transactional tasks differ from the

[14] Cf. *DAVIS/MCLAUGHLIN* (2009), p. 51 et seqq.

requirements which are needed for mid-office tasks or the requirements for positions which manage single or even End-to-End processes. In business practice, companies sometimes tend to hire personnel with profiles qualified for only transactional activities although they want to staff them on positions with more complex tasks. A rethinking is required for those cases: more complex positions require different profiles. Although salaries might be higher for those candidates, gains from higher effectiveness and efficiency as well as reduced fluctuation should over compensate higher costs. Besides aspects regarding selection and recruitment, qualification is a key challenge in any transformation process which needs to be carefully considered. In a shared service context, focus is especially on processes. How processes work, how they are linked, and foremost how processes can be improved are the focal topics which need to be addressed in the design and the set up of the qualification programs. There needs to be a balance of program standardization, to realize also efficiency gains on this point, and tailoring to the specific roles. This means that employees performing transactional activities need the understanding how the process works and what is their specific "to do" in the process chain. Other roles which steer, manage or even design End-to-End processes need to be qualified in aspects like process management, process improvement, business strategy, and – quite often insufficient reflected – how to document processes appropriately. Competencies in process documentation are not only required for documentation of single processes in a Shared Service Organization. Such knowledge and experiences are also very important and a critical success factor in the phase of analyzing the process in an operational business unit which will be transferred to a Shared Service Organization. Inadequate documentation often hinders leveraging the full potentials of shared service initiatives. To conclude and reflect this step, selection, recruitment, and qualification are very important and are also – and this aspect should not be neglected – the basis to retain resources, i.e. personnel and know-how, within the organization.

Third, to motivate people and to steer activities, adequate salary and incentive structures need to be implemented. To anchor objectives it is important to link incentives to the critical key performance indicators. Definition of those indicators should reflect the typical requirements to define such measures, e.g. they should have a clear link to the overall strategies, and ideally they should be controllable by the employee. In consequence, a careful selection of key performance indicators is required to ensure, on the one hand, a comprehensive measurement, and, on the other hand, an appropriate selection for the respective role owners.

4.2 Impact on Organizational Roles

Traditionally, Shared Services are linked to "back-office" or rather transactional activities. As described above, maturity and especially scope increases towards End-to-End process management in organizations have also major influences on the talent or role perspectives. I.e. some roles are changing, some roles can even be omitted, and foremost new roles are emerging.

Running or implementing Shared Services leads to changes of roles in organizations. Although Shared Services are in place to free up resources of employees in other organizational units[15], this does not obligatorily mean that activities do not have to be performed anymore. It's rather the case that activities are analyzed, decomposed, and – after analysis and improvement – composed again. In consequence, roles and activities related to certain roles are

15 Cf. *SCHULMAN* et al. (1999), p. 3.

changing. Whereas this procedure is nowadays nothing uncommon for transactional activities, as soon as Shared Services manage End-to-End processes, this is getting also the normal case for enhanced activities like mid-office processes or, in general, activities which are not only transactional.

In the course of process improvements, some roles in organizations using Shared Services can be even omitted. If Shared Services are in place to manage comprehensive End-to-End processes, organizations should also strive for complexity reduction. By leveraging potentials of complexity reductions, some single processes or process steps might be left out or can be consolidated with other activities. Roles for those activities can be in consequence omitted. However, although some roles might be omitted, changing roles or foremost new roles are the more relevant outcome of a case in which Shared Services act as business partner of End-to-End processes.

The increasing scope of Shared Services leads to the emergence of new roles in organizations. The role of a process owner or process manager for Shared Services becomes a permanent role. The owner of the role typically manages an End-to-End process in its full scope. Starting point for such role is the project manager who is setting up Shared Services or new processes in a Shared Service Center. With the increasing importance of Shared Services, those roles become common positions which should also be grouped under one organizational umbrella. This follows – as described above – also the increasing trend toward stand alone operations for Shared Services which are implemented in "integrated business services" organizations. The role of the process manager for a shared service encompasses all process relevant activities from analysis of existing process, over decomposition and composition of process steps, to the definition of performance indicators. One key task of the process manager is to capture and pick up the needs to the internal customers of the Shared Service Organization. Therefore, the owner of this role needs to be equipped not only with competencies of process management, he/she needs strong communication skills and also a sound business knowledge as well as business acumen. Such competencies enable the owner of the role to act on a par with its internal counterparts and to drive the necessary change within the organization. Finally, since change in most of the cases triggers some portion of resistance in an organization, the owner of the role needs the capabilities to properly cope with such situations. I.e. he/she needs persuasiveness and also a good portion of power of endurance. In consequence, it is required for the project manager of an End-to-End process that all above mentioned facets are given to fully leverage the potentials of Shared Services.

4.3 Success Factors at a Glance

Reflecting arguments, experiences, proposals, and possibilities of Shared Services acting in an End-to-End mode, the relevant success factors can be basically clustered in three groups: (1) systems, (2) governance, and (3) people. All facets of those three groups should be considered in the course of End-to-End endeavors for Shared Services and are at the end also the key drivers if potentials can be leveraged or not. Although those key aspects should cover the most relevant facets, it is obvious that they cannot include every possible point.

First, systems serve as an enabler for successful Shared Services. They become even more important when Shared Services cover full End-to-End processes. At this point, systems should be interpreted in broader sense, from basic IT infrastructures to end user application landscapes. As a successful enabler, systems need to be – assuming a global organization – globally harmonized and standardized. Whereas in business practice, questions about availability of documentations, missing links between systems, or only semiautomatic interfaces are quite often still on the agenda, there is the clear need for harmonization to reach the given objectives of value adding Shared Services. In the course of harmonization, there needs also be a balance between system complexity and comprehensiveness. As discussed above, there might also be the consequence that a shared service initiative leads to an intended reduction of service levels (e.g. due to a reduction of variants) which would also need to be reflected in the system architecture. Or, the harmonization of master data could – or rather should – be the outcome. An example for this is the reduction and harmonization of payment terms: Although not all possible options might be available afterwards and at the first glance the service level is decreasing, the possible positive result of complexity reduction – and also on net working capital if properly implemented – should compensates this. At the end, harmonized systems are – properly designed and implemented – a key success driver for Shared Services. Especially following the emerging trend toward End-to-End process coverage, harmonized systems can – if they are also designed scalable – the basis for growth.

Second, if Shared Services getting mature within an organization, e.g. by delivering End-to-End process solutions, adequate governance structures are needed. As described above, those organizational units should be independent within the group and act like in a market oriented context. It might be even the case that the Shared Services are set up in an independent legal entity. However, they should be at least under the responsibility of a senior management member. Such a stand-alone organizational setting will foster and strengthen the culture to strive for service orientation and continuous process improvement by best practice deployment. For most organizations undergoing a shared service transformation, this means a change of the organizational structures offering also the opportunity to break silos in organizations. Besides the basic organizational set ups, operational relationships between providing and receiving organizational units need also to be agreed and contracted. Service level agreements are today the typical instrument for this purpose. With those agreements, the involved parties clearly document their expectations what are the services to be delivered, what are the defined service levels, how are the service levels measured, what are the variants of the process, etc. At the same time, with those service level agreements, it is documented what is – and what is not – in the scope of the shared service. Additionally to those aspects, the timing of the transformation should also be documented. There needs to be a sound transformation plan which on the one hand reflects that change needs some time, but on the other hand sets clear ambitions and roadmaps to foster agility. This is especially of utmost importance when the shared service transformation is embedded in other organizational change programs; in such cases, the momentum of those initiatives should also be leveraged for the shared service programs.

Third, people are the last of the three key success factors. Foremost, adequate employees for the respective roles are required. As described above, besides employees performing transactional tasks, more qualified personnel is required to allow running End-to-End processes in a shared service context, i.e. personnel performing mid-office tasks and especially process managers steering the activities. Besides required personnel, mindset needs to be changed within the organizations using comprehensive shared service approaches. Only if the personnel is open for change, allows thinking out of the box, or strives for continuous improvement, the full potential of shared service can be leveraged. One important supporting factor for a mindset adoption is the full commitment and dedication of the top management, often described as the 'tone at the top'. When top management appreciates Shared Services, the organizations will be recognized as valued business partner within an organization and not only an extended workbench for other organizational units. Nevertheless, this can also only be the case if Shared Services deliver the agreed results; and this heavily depends on the structures, the governance models and foremost on the people directly or indirectly involved in the processes.

5 Summary and Conclusion

Shared Services are in today's business environment mostly implemented for rather transactional activities. But, with this approach organizations limit themselves since Shared Services can deliver stronger benefits when they follow an End-to-End approach and are properly implemented within the organization. End-to-End means that processes are not harmonized in organizational silos; moreover, activities need to be optimized from the real start to the end of the comprehensive processes.

Organizations striving for an End-to-End optimization have to cope with four elements: First, they need to limit the number of process variants. Second, they need to align interfaces between process steps efficiently; especially when activities are performed by different organizational units. Third, service levels should be on a proper level, a sufficient and adequate quality is for processes with a limited strategic relevance from cost vs. benefit perspective often appropriate. Fourth, organizations should not limit their shared service initiatives to transactional activities; End-to-End process optimization might also include rather mid-office tasks.

To fully leverage the benefits of Shared Services, an appropriate organizational structure and governance mechanisms is needed. An integrated Shared Service Organization includes both a service delivery unit on the one hand and a guideline responsible unit on the other hand. With this approach, Shared Service Organizations can act as a real business partner and can offer a platform and enabler for an End-to-End process optimization.

To reach the status of an integrated business partner, organizations need to be transformed. During this transformation, it is critical that overall strategies are the starting point and processes, systems, and performance measurement aspects are cascaded accordingly. Furthermore, the talent perspective needs to be considered appropriately since such a change has a strong impact on roles which need to be filled properly. Within the transformation, three key success factors can be identified which should be carefully considered: adequate systems, proper governance, and the right people on board.

As a final conclusion, many companies use today share service and benefit from them. However, to fully leverage potentials of Shared Services, a mindset and approach change is required. If Shared Service Organizations act as integrated business partners, an End-to-End process optimization is getting easier and companies should come closer to realize more benefits with Shared Services.

References

BANGEMANN, T. O. (2005): Shared Services in Finance and Accounting, Burlington 2005.

BECKER, W./KUNZ, C./MAYER, B. (2009): Shared Service Center. Konzeption und Implementierung in internationalen Unternehmen, Stuttgart 2009.

DAVIS, T.R. V./MCLAUGHLIN, L. P. (2009): Breaking Down Boundaries, in: Strategic Finance, Vol. 90 (2009), April, pp. 47–53.

KAGELMANN, U. (2001): Shared Services als alternative Organisationsform. Am Beispiel der Finanzfunktion im multinationalen Konzern, Wiesbaden 2001.

KEUPER, F./OECKING, C. (2008): Shared-Service-Center – The First and the Next Generation, in: *KEUPER, F./OECKING, C.* (Ed.) Corporate Shared Services. Bereitstellung von Dienstleistungen im Konzern, Wiesbaden 2008, pp. 475–505.

SCHULMAN, D. S./HARMER, M. J./DUNLEAVY, J. R./LUSK J. S. (1999): Shared Services: Adding Value to the Business Units, New York et al. 1999.

ULRICH, D. (1995): Shared Services: From Vogue to Value, in: Human Resource Planning, Vol. 18 (1995), pp. 12–23.

Developing and Selling New Portfolio Elements in a Captive Shared Services Environment

NICOLE DREHER

Siemens AG, Global Shared Services

Executive Summary

Shared Services Organizations (SSOs) are considered as powerful enablers of enterprise benefits when effectively implemented and managed. As a consequence, the implementation of SSOs is regarded as one of the "hot topics" when it comes to leveraging opportunities to cut costs and improve quality within an organization.

Introduced in the 1980s when companies were searching for a way to reduce especially administrative costs, Shared Services have evolved to a comprehensive and flexible tool for improving processes, enabling technologies, ensuring quality and reducing cost.[1] Once the Shared Services concept is implemented, the focus switches to maintaining the momentum and continuously proving the benefit delivered from a SSO. This is automatically linked to the SSO's opportunity to develop along defined phases, such as the "lift-drop" phase and thus the bundling of transactional activities, the "change" phase and with that the optimization of transferred processes, and finally the "enhance and innovate" phase referring to the preparation of selling new or additional services out of a Shared Services environment.

The focus of this article will be placed on the accounting and finance side of the Shared Services environment represented by the *Siemens* Shared Services Organization, specifically the Business Line Accounting and Finance Services. In detail, it will be dealt with the rather future-oriented third development phase ("enhance and innovate", referred to above) and thus focus on carefully enhancing the existing service portfolio following a systematic approach of selecting the right ideas for new services.

The use of a SSO is either mandated by management, or may be freely chosen by a business unit based on the SSO's ability to create a compelling value and generate real benefits. But what if it comes to marketing and selling Shared Services? A special emphasis of this article will be placed on exploring the way in which a captive SSO gets to market and sell new services.

Starting with a detailed analysis of the as-is-situation by making use of a classical SWOT analysis and *ANSOFF*'s Matrix, the next step is to outline a systematic concept of developing new ideas that can be added to the portfolio and sold within a captive environment. After having selected the new service offerings, a comprehensive approach – the "6 Shared Services Ps" – is applied to systematically develop the marketing and sales strategy of new services along the Shared Services relevant areas of product, price, place, promotion, people and perception management. The measures and initiatives derived along the "6 Shared Services Ps" give a clear hands-on guidance and a practical implementation advice on how to sell services in a highly sensitive environment – thereby taking political as well as emotional obstacles into consideration.

In a nutshell, Shared Service business is a "hot topic", but it is easy to get burned…

[1] Cf. *KULHALI* (2010, p. 2.

1 Introduction

The *Siemens* Shared Services Organization (SSO) acts as an internal, "captive" service provider and supports the business units by freeing them up to meet the challenges in their operative business. In doing so, the SSO lets them focus on their core business by taking over administrative support services centrally. The SSO portfolio consists of Accounting & Finance Services, Human Resource Services, Supply Chain Management Services and specialized regional expertise-based services. The *Siemens* Shared Services Organization ensures the delivery of services at competitive and benchmarked prices as well as service levels whilst committing to agreed performance and quality as well as cost reduction (savings) targets.

The role of the *Siemens* SSO as a zero profit organization is embedded in the vision which clearly states to focus on strengthening the *Siemens*' competitiveness by providing and continuously improving cost effective and high quality services for the worldwide business.

In the course of this article the focus will be placed on the Shared Services area "Accounting & Finance Services" employing about 2,500 employees in five main Shared Services Centers (SSCs) around the world.

During the last two years the financial Shared Services Organization of *Siemens* has grown enormously. This is mainly due to the company-wide bundling infrastructure projects, one of them the 'Finance Bundling' project. In this project the company's finance world was reshaped and the financial SSO received the mandate by the company's board to take over specific transactional accounting processes that were previously handled locally by the respective legal entities. As a consequence, the accounting processes were bundled into the regional SSCs which had to recruit professionals offering the necessary language and accounting skills to be able to seamlessly take over the work.

The overall strategy of the financial SSO describes three organizational development phases: "lift-drop", taking over the work from the "donating" local (legal) entities and dropping or bundling it into the regionally centralized SSCs; the "change" phase including the harmonization and automation of services; and the third phase "innovate & enhance" to intensify the automation of processes and enhance the service portfolio. At the time of writing, the *Siemens* SSO is finalizing the "lift-drop" phase and has initiated the "change" with the help of a program called PIA (Process Improvements for Accounting). Further, the SSO is systematically preparing for the third development phase, specifically with regard to logical enhancements of the existing service portfolio.

This article explores the process of identifying new portfolio elements in the area of financial Shared Services and elaborates a distinct marketing concept to sell new portfolio elements in a captive Shared Services environment. In chapter 2, the focus will be the analysis of the as-is-situation, while chapter 3 outlines the systematic approach of finding suitable ideas to enhance the existing portfolio. Chapter 4 presents a marketing concept of selling new Shared Services internally to the company's operational business units. Within the following, when talking about the term 'product' it is being referred to the actual services offered by a SSO.

2 Strategic Analysis of the Siemens Shared Services Environment

In this chapter the strategic analysis of the *Siemens* Shared Services environment, specifically focusing on the Accounting and Finance area, will be outlined. In doing so, the basis for the next chapters will be established. Based on that the concept of selecting new ideas for new portfolio elements as well as the marketing and sales approach for a captive SSO will be derived.

The investigation comprises a SWOT analysis realized in the *Siemens* Shared Services environment outlining the strategic focus areas for the financial SSO. In a second step, *ANSOFF*'s matrix will be applied in the *Siemens* Shared Services area to elaborate the potential ways of further growth regarding the current portfolio. To round off the picture, the current service portfolio of the SSO will be mapped on a classical product lifecycle in order to draw conclusions with regards to potential further development opportunities.

2.1 Identification of Strategic Focus Areas for a Captive SSO

The SWOT analysis is considered as a general technique that finds suitable applications across diverse management functions and activities and is commonly used as an elementary part of the development of a company's strategy. Performing a SWOT analysis comprises identifying and recording the strengths, weaknesses, opportunities and threats of a task, department or organization[2]. The analysis typically takes into account internal resources and capabilities (strengths, weaknesses) as well as external factors to the organization (opportunities, threats)[3]. The ultimate goal of the SWOT analysis is to identify focus topics, both within and outside of the organization, and embed them into the overall strategic approach[4].

To synthesize precise output messages of this tool, the SO-, ST-, WO- and WT-strategies have been derived from the ideas developed around strengths, weaknesses, opportunities and threats. The SO-strategy focuses on "using strengths to exploit external opportunities", the ST-strategy on "using strengths to deal with external threats", the WO-strategy on "exploiting opportunities and thereby overcoming weaknesses" and the WT-strategy puts emphasis on "overcoming internal weaknesses and thereby reducing threats"[5].

The SWOT-analysis, geared towards the *Siemens* financial SSO, has been developed by consolidating input from SSO managers around the world. As a first step, strengths, weaknesses, opportunities and threats were identified with the help of a classic brainstorming approach. In a second step, the focus areas were identified by formulating the ST-, SO-, WT- and WO-strategies.

---

2 Cf. *BRUHN* (2003), p. 77 et seqq.

3 Cf. *MORSE* (1998), p. 59.

4 Cf. *GRIFFIN* (2008), p. 68 et seqq.

5 *MÜLLER-STEWENS/LECHNER* (2011), p. 225 et seqq.

Looking at the internal opportunities and strengths first, management agreed that the *Siemens* financial Shared Services Organization has great and motivated staff offering a high potential with regard to its expertise in the area of accounting processes. This is supported by the fact that the SSO has a global footprint and is able to cover every time zone necessary to continuously provide global services and reach a high number of customers. Secondly, servic-es to be offered by the SSO are clearly defined through the company-wide bundling project. In this project a clear guideline about the allocation of processes (activity split) was used as a basis for the new process ownership.

	Opportunities: ➢ High customer penetration ➢ Leverage *Siemens*-wide process know-how ➢ Leverage global footprint	**Threats:** ➢ Captive service provider ➢ Changing customer business ➢ Image improves slowly
Strengths: ➢ Great people and skills pool ➢ Process expertise ➢ Presence in every time zone, global locations ➢ Pockets of best in class technology ➢ Clearly defined products	**SO-Strategy:** Use knowledge available to anticipate customer needs and grow portfolio (new products) **→ Customer/Portfolio**	**ST-Strategy:** Use process expertise to achieve industry benchmarks by managing and automating financial transactional processes **→ Process Optimization**
Weaknesses: ➢ Complex organization ➢ Lack of standardization & harmonization ➢ Cost opportunities not fully leveraged ➢ Image/attractiveness of the SSO as employer	**WO-Strategy:** Develop global 'people program' to increase attractiveness internally and also externally **→ People**	**WT-Strategy:** Drive cost optimization by benchmarking **→ Financials**

Figure 1: SWOT Analysis in the Siemens SSO Environment

Looking at internal weaknesses, the organization was rated as rather complex due to multiple organizational layers (in a matrix) and the resulting ambiguity with regards to respective responsibilities. Additionally, the potential for harmonization and standardization can be further leveraged to sell accounting services at an even lower price. A substantial problem is the image and attractiveness of the SSO as an employer within the entire company due to the fact that the value and benefit of Shared Services is not always recognized, and the perception that the SSO concentrates on mundane, highly repeatable and non-expert functions.

The image issue is also considered as a "threat" in the external view, i.e. the problem of moving from the image of being a "mandated supplier" to a "strategic partner" competently managing administrative services by bundling, standardization and automation of processes. More threats from the external side result from the fact that the SSO is captive, serving only internal customers, and further that it must be able to offer services across the diverse customer businesses and heterogeneous IT-landscape of the company's business units.

When the SSO managers were asked to think of external opportunities, they all agreed that the *Siemens* internal SSO has built great customer relationships mainly due to the bundling project. After the professional take-over of accounting processes from more than 300 operational units, the expectation is now to leverage these relationships as well as the detailed company knowledge gained through the experiences of various bundling activities.

As a next step, the strategic focus areas were derived based on the brainstormed ideas:

- **"Weaknesses-opportunities-strategy":** Develop a global 'people strategy' to increase attractiveness within the SSO and also towards customers by emphasizing global, intercultural diversity of the organization.
- **"Weaknesses-threats-strategy":** Drive cost optimization by bench-marking without compromising on quality and in doing so fulfill customer expectations on Shared Services within the company.
- **"Strengths-opportunities-strategy":** Use know-how that is already available to anticipate customer needs and grow the SSO portfolio by implementing new value-adding products.
- **"Strengths-threats-strategy":** Use process expertise to achieve industry benchmark by managing and automating financial transactional processes.

The resulting "4 Strategy Statements" serve as short- to mid-term focus areas indicating the key topics to be concentrated on by the management. Bearing in mind that these Strategy Statements need to be realized as structured initiatives, the concrete projects behind each statement in terms of corresponding milestones and responsible persons have to be defined.

Looking at each of the Strategy Statements in detail, it can be stated that the first people-related topic is already being addressed and a specific article on the people concept within the *Siemens* SSO can be accessed via the article "Personnel Management" in the section 'enablers and prerequisites' of this book. The second and third focus areas are also dealt with in the SSO and within the scope of a specific article on 'Process Improvements for Accounting' which may be accessed in the chapter "change" of this book.

This leaves the focus area three – the systematic growth of the current Shared Services portfolio – as the main topics to be elaborated in this article.

2.2 Development of Opportunities to Enhance the Shared Services Portfolio

To generate strategic options to grow the financial SSO portfolio, *ANSOFF*'s diversification matrix is applied. By considering alternative ways to grow – either by expanding existing products or by branching into entirely new areas – four product-market combinations can be applied:[6]

6 Cf. *KOTLER/BERGER/BICKHOFF* (2010), p. 35.

	Existing products	New products
Existing market	Market penetration	Product development
New market	Market development	Diversification

Figure 2: ANSOFF's *Matrix applied*[7]

Referring to the first alternative of fully leveraging market penetration, this opportunity has been almost entirely exploited for the *Siemens* financial SSO, as the worldwide bundling project involved the SSO taking over global accounting tasks for all major operational units. This applied to the existing service portfolio in the areas of accounts payable (AP), accounts receivable (AR) and closing and reporting (C&R). As a consequence and only referring to the *Siemens* financial SSO, the opportunity to leverage existing products on the existing market is very low and cannot be considered as a concrete opportunity to grow the Shared Services portfolio.

Taking new markets as an opportunity for growth is currently not an option, as the *Siemens* SSO is captive and currently not allowed to sell services to other markets outside the existing internal *Siemens* market. The strategic option of opening up to external customers may be considered as a potential future step but cannot be applied as a strategy to grow the SSO portfolio at the time of writing. The option of diversification and thus the selling of new products in a new market cannot be considered as an opportunity to grow either, since this would also require tapping into new, external markets.

Based on this analysis, the alternative offering the highest strategic fit to the current development phase of the *Siemens* financial SSO is the product development route, and thus the focus on the existing market and customer relationships to develop and sell additional service offerings.

2.3 Service Lifecycle Management for a Shared Services Portfolio

When it comes to the products, or rather services offered by the financial SSO, the current portfolio can be visualized with the help of figure 3 (below) which defines the distribution of current portfolio elements across the product life cycle. As a theoretical basis, the product life cycle differentiates between four phases: introduction (embryonic phase), growth (product takes off, attracting an early majority of buyers), maturity (buying behavior and competitor activity more predictable) and decline (or saturation phase, during which sales falls drastically).[8] Of course, the question can be raised – how can internal processes that will always be executed (e.g. booking activities) be logically allocated to a life cycle? Considering the fact that the

7 KOTLER/BERGER/BICKHOFF (2010), p. 35.

8 Cf. ADCOCK/HALBORG/ROSS (2001), p. 374.

Siemens financial SSO is in the middle of the optimization ("change") phase and manual work is – if possible – replaced by automation, the actual service execution will change to a great extent: less employees will be used for specific processes and this is automatically linked to a significant reduction in cost. Therefore, if the SSO plans to develop towards being a strategic business partner, the actual life cycle of the services needs to be taken into consideration and planned in the long run.

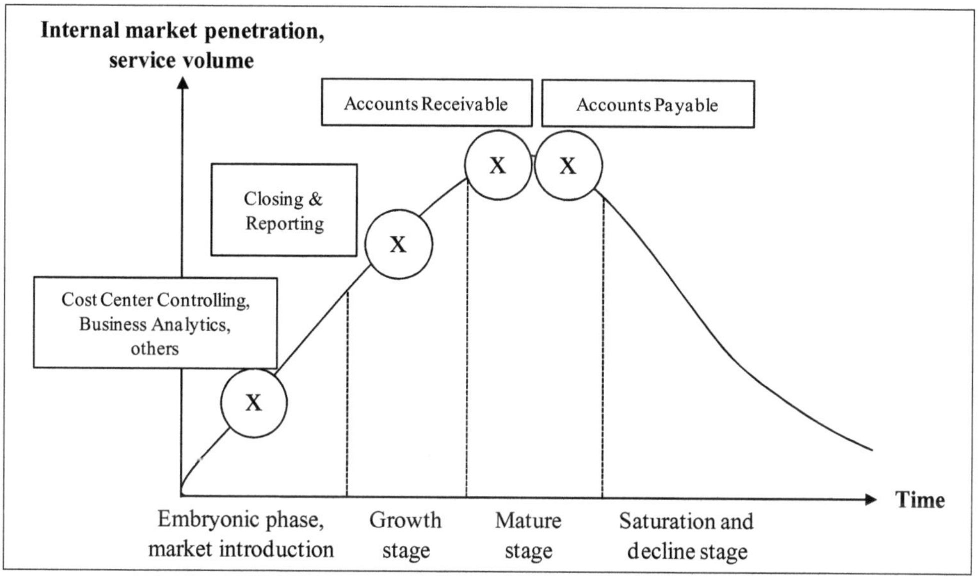

Figure 3: The Siemens Financial Shared Services Lifecycle

The two products accounts payable and accounts receivable can be allocated to the "mature stage". This is due to the worldwide bundling project and the resulting transfer of especially accounts payable and accounts receivable processes into the SSCs. For these two products, the maximum internal (accessible) market penetration has already been reached, as the SSO has taken over accounting tasks of more than 300 operational units worldwide. Looking at the mature stage that has already been reached for accounts payable and accounts receivable, it has to be taken into consideration that further (accessible) market penetration for these services is limited.

The service closing and reporting may be allocated to the growth phase of the lifecycle, since the SSO is in the middle of taking over more and more processes in this area. However, within approximately one to two years this service will move to the same stage as accounts payable and accounts receivable and the result is predictable: to gain additional volume in the light of the increasing automation and to follow the strategic direction of developing from a mandated service provider to a strategic partner for the *Siemens* operational units, the financial SSO has to develop product ideas and start launching selected services to make their way along the service life cycle.

3 Selection of New Portfolio Elements

When it comes to selecting the right ideas for new Shared Services portfolio elements it is essential to bear in mind that these ideas should be chosen on the one hand offering a relevant customer benefit and on the other hand guaranteeing a high strategic fit into the Shared Services Organization.

Within the following the systematic approach of selecting the right ideas within the *Siemens* Shared Services organization will be outlined following a three-step-approach of firstly identifying relevant selection criteria, secondly developing a scoring model and thirdly actively using a matrix as a basis for a decision making process in a Shared Services environment.

3.1 Identification of Relevant Selection Criteria

The identification of relevant selection criteria – to be used to decide if an idea is of high relevance or if it offers low potential – is executed in three main steps (see figure 4): Gathering qualitative (1) and quantitative (2) criteria and then clustering the selection criteria into groups (3).

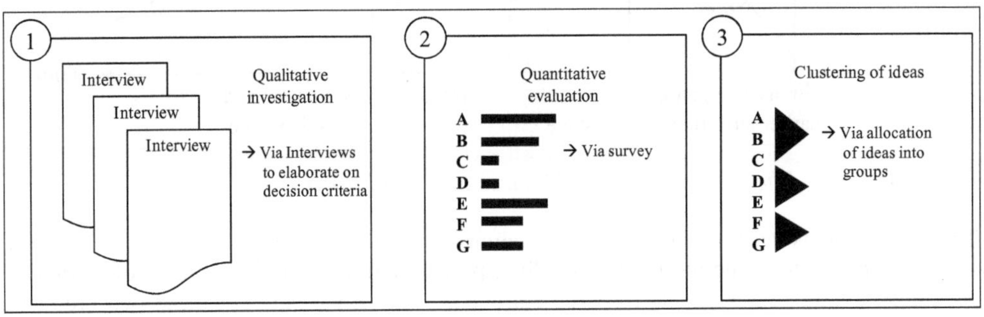

Figure 4: The identification of selection criteria for new portfolio elements

First of all (step one), qualitative interviews are carried out to elaborate the criteria of why an idea should be chosen. Referring to the *Siemens* SSO, the interviews were executed with employees of the SSO in close contact with customers i.e. those employees interacting with the customers on a regular basis and at the same time providing a deeper understanding of the service delivery within a SSO. In addition, customers may also directly be asked to state their opinion. Looking at the results collected through qualitative interviews, the following selection criteria were identified.

Focus should be on services that meet the following criteria:

- Cost reduction can be realized by bundling into Shared Services environment
- Customer must have a certain need for process

- Customer must be freed up and relieved by handing over process to SSO
- Process is not influencing customers' yearly/quarterly results in any way
- Process is not part of customers' core business
- Process offers opportunity to leverage economics of scalc
- Process is transactional and can be clearly described
- Process is rule-based and easy to repeat
- Process can be centralized and potential for global roll-out exists.

After having identified the relevant criteria listed above, a quantitative survey (step 2) is executed to choose the topics of highest importance. In this case, the quantitative investigation is executed with the help of an online questionnaire where the respondents have the opportunity to rate the listed criteria according to their individual preferences. Again, referring to the *Siemens* SSO, the respondents are employees in frontline contact with customers, who have a reasonable knowledge of the strategic set-up of the Shared Services Organization. The sample of respondents is also taken from all global locations.

Using this evaluation and technique of rating importance, the criteria are clustered into groups of related ideas (step 3). In this case, two main categories are identified: the "Customer benefit" and the "Shared Services fit".

3.2 Development of the Shared Services Scoring Model

After the selection criteria has been collected, evaluated and clustered into two main categories, the next step is to derive an efficiency analysis. This efficiency analysis, or the so-called Shared Services Scoring Model, is used to evaluate individual ideas to enhance the existing portfolio along the chosen characteristics.

As mentioned above, the Scoring Model divides the selection criteria into two groups referring to the "Customer benefit" and the "Shared Services fit". The latter comprises multiple aspects that are again grouped into the "management of services" e.g. referring to the fact that the process needs to be repeatable, implementable, able to be offered out of a regional hub etc. and the "mid-to-long-term strategic view" including for instance the potential to harmonize and automate certain parts or the overall process to be transferred.

This Scoring Model can be efficiently used to create a practical short-list from a variety of ideas for new Shared Services offerings. The *Siemens* SSO uses this Scoring Model to reduce the number of ideas to a handful of selected concrete proposals. This was decided during a management meeting when all Center Heads of the Finance SSO came together and brought with them their ideas for further services offerings. These ideas were either developed together with the customers or in some cases, a single customer has specifcally asked for a new service. During the management meeting, all ideas were evaluated with the help of the Scoring Model and the collected characteristics in order to filter the long list to approximately three ideas that the organization wants to move forward with. The evaluation per portfolio enhancement idea was handled with a simple rating from "++" to "--" (see figure 5).

GSS AFS Portfolio Enlargement Scoring Model			
Portfolio Enlargement Idea/ Decision Criteria	**Idea 1** Center:	**Idea 2** Center:	**Idea 3** Center:
Customer Benefit			
Cost effect Further increase of professionalism of services Free up customer to focus on core services			
Total			
Shared Services fit			
Management of services...			
Repeatability (economies of scale) Clear definition Implementability Centralization possible Predictability of risks			
Mid-to-long-term strategic value...			
Expected results Harmonization and standardization potential Automation potential Quality improvement to be expected Proximity to existing portfolio Potential to move from local to global Potential to enhance service with increasing value-add Employee motivation/ retention effect			
Total			

Figure 5: The Shared Services Scoring Model

3.3 Deviation of the Shared Services Matrix

After the selection criteria is identified, evaluated and grouped, the Scoring Model is developed helping the Shared Services management to evaluate the individual ideas to further enhance the Shared Services portfolio. The outputs of the Scoring Model are entered into a matrix according to the "customer benefit" – "Shared Services fit" indicators.

Each portfolio enhancement idea can now be categorized according to the score reached in the Scoring Model. After having placed all evaluations of the ideas in the matrix, the next step is to choose those ideas offering the highest "Customer benefit" while guaranteeing a high "Shared Services fit". An example is visualized in figure 6, where those ideas in the upper right quadrant would be selected as having most potential and represent the basis for the next steps of selling the chosen services within a captive environment.

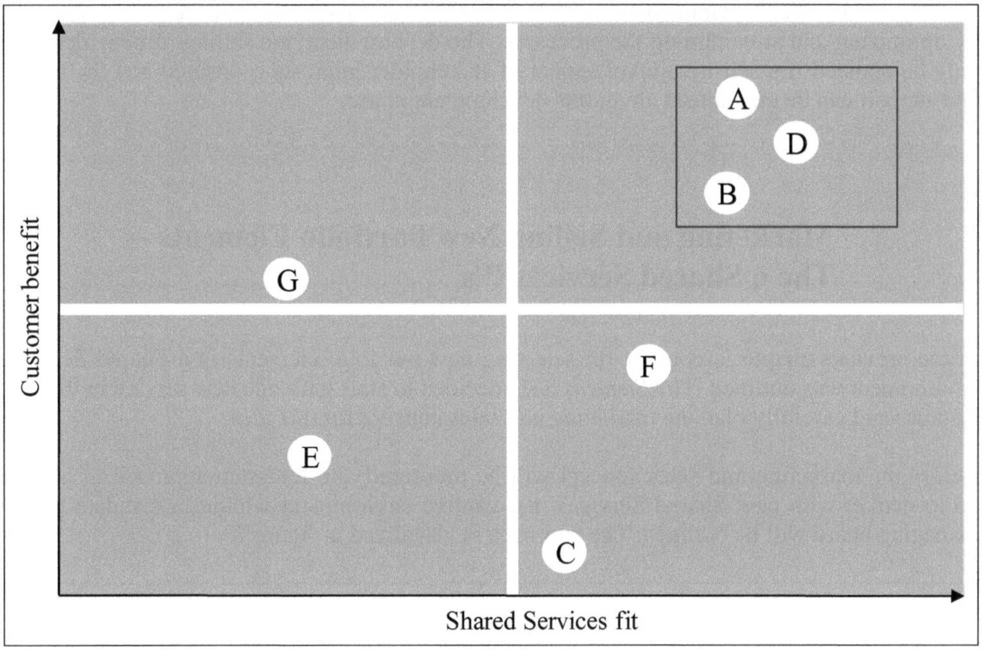

Figure 6: The Shared Services Portfolio Enhancement Matrix

3.4 Implications for Practice

It is essential to mention that this approach represents a basis for a decision making process referring to the selection of new portfolio elements in a Shared Services environment. This approach has already been successfully applied within the *Siemens* SSO and offers the flexibility to be used in other SSOs in the same way.

However, the respective environment of the SSO needs to be taken into consideration, thereby focusing on the fact that Shared Services was and still is a highly sensitive topic linked to handing over a certain degree of (man-) power to the SSO and at the same time reducing the work on the side of the donating entities. Nevertheless, as soon as the operative entities recognize the value of the internal SSO, chances are high that further processes are transferred into the SSCs.

This is closely linked to the fact that the internal SSO has to deal with different stakeholders: the governance department (Corporate Finance) and the customers represented in the case of *Siemens* by the Sectors and Clusters. If a SSO intends to develop in the direction of selling further services, it is indispensable to include these stakeholders into the planning process and continuously update them on the next steps and projects that are planned.

To conclude, one piece of advice is to focus on a limited number of high-potential enhancements at a time, rather than kicking off too many portfolio enhancement projects at once. Bearing in mind that the *Siemens* SSO is currently in the phase of stabilizing the transferred accounting activities and systematically optimizing these projects, the major expectations by the stakeholders is to guarantee a smooth service delivery and realize further cost reductions by optimizing and streamlining the processes. The development and selling of new ideas can only be realized if a sensitive involvement of stakeholder interests is ensured and the buy-in and support can be guaranteed along this development phase.

4 Marketing and Selling New Portfolio Elements – The 6 Shared Services P's

In the previous chapter a concept for selecting new portfolio elements in a Shared Services environment was outlined. The *Siemens* SSO decided to start with one new service in the first instance and carefully plan the marketing and sales concept for this idea.

Before the marketing and sales concept will be presented, the four-step-approach of how to go to market with new Shared Services in a captive environment without a mandate by the managing board will be outlined. The approach is visualized in figure 7.

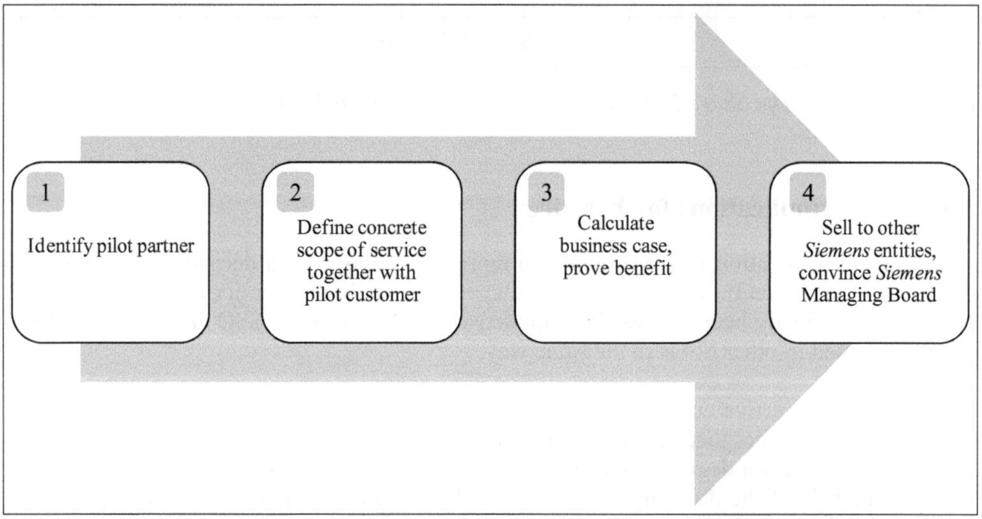

Figure 7: The four-step-approach to marketing & selling Shared Services

In the first step, the focus is to find a collaboration partner for the realization of a pilot project. Especially in this phase, existing customer relationships are taken into consideration if there is potential to sell "more" than what is already offered after the worldwide bundling project (AP, AR, C&R).

Especially for those operational units experiencing a high cost pressure, the thought of handing over work to the SSO and thereby achieving a clear cost effect is obvious. Nevertheless, potential pilot customers need to be convinced of the benefit and their chance to influence the scope of service.

As soon as the partner is identified, the next step is to shape the service offer together with the customer. It must be taken into account that not every service exists in a form that makes it suitable for transfer to a Shared Services Organization and receive immediate benefits from that. Rather, in a joint collaboration between customer and the SSO, the service "package" to be transferred to a SSC needs to be set up in a reasonable way to achieve the expected results when transferred to the SSO. Specifically, the services to be transferred need to offer the characteristics described in chapter 3 (e.g. cost effect, repeatability, customer free-up etc.).

In the third phase, after having identified a pilot customer, having realized the first transitions and stabilized the work on the SSO side, a business case on the actual financial results will be calculated. The target is to achieve labour arbitrage effects out of the transfer from a rather high-cost country e.g. Germany to locations offering higher cost effectiveness e.g. the Czech Republic. Further, a bundling effect is to be achieved, especially by leveraging employees being in charge of services within the current portfolio, that now get less and less complex due to the on-going process optimization (automation). These employees are thus 'freed-up' to take over new challenges leading to an increased motivation and loyalty within the SSO.

With the results of the business case covering the financial benefits of the transition and the lessons-learned experienced during the pilot, the selling to other operational units will become easier. Further, if the pilot customer is satisfied with the results of the SSO and is convinced of the benefit, there will likely be a recommendation to other entities to move into the same direction. Aside from this, a managing board can be convinced with the calculated business case, the results from the transition and the voice of the customer to announce a mandate e.g. for a worldwide bundling project.

When marketing products, commonly the "4 Ps" of the marketing mix[9] are applied (see figure 8). These '4 Ps' refer to the necessity of focusing on product, promotion, price, and place simultaneously in one aggregated strategy. This concept has now been mapped to a Shared Services environment and two further Ps have been added to the traditional approach to make it more applicable to the challenges of Shares Services.

The two additional perspectives are: "people" and "perception management". The selection of the two additional Ps is due to the fact that Shared Services business is all about people and further, one of the key factors on the journey to become a strategic partner is to systematically increase the positive perception by internal clients.

9 Cf. *KOTLER/ARMSTRONG* (2009), p. 17.

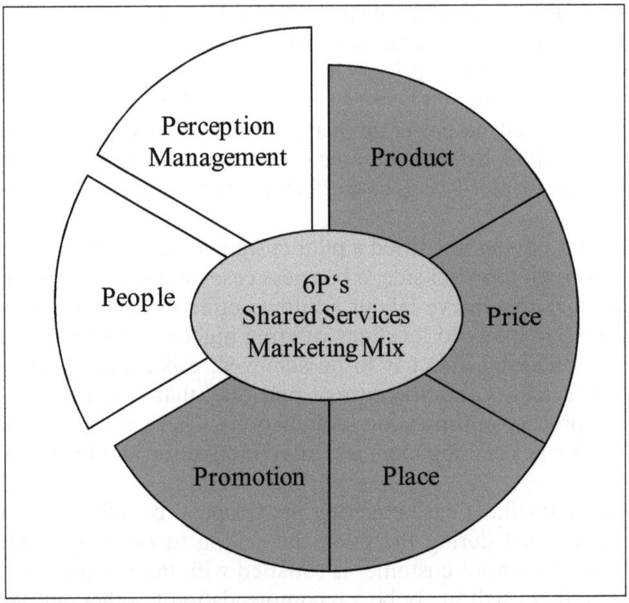

Figure 8: *The "6 Shared Services P's"*

4.1 Product/Service Management

In the Shared Services environment, the actual "product" is a service, intangible and highly subjective when being evaluated. Thus it is not easy to convince customers that a SSO may actually execute the same service in a cheaper and more effective and efficient way. Literature as well as practice cite characteristics such as quality, the underlying process or brand name as mainly influencing the product. The most relevant characteristics for a product or service come together in the Unique Selling Proposition (USP). Having a USP can be defined as saying or doing something about a product that is unlike what anyone else offers. In other words, it is unique and 'one of a kind'[10].

The USP for any new service to be offered out of the *Siemens* SSO is definitely the cost aspect achieved by labor arbitrage. To further differentiate the service, additional aspects can be added, e.g. an increase in quality and transparency due to the bundling of services; the free-up of customers who can now focus on their core tasks, since the SSO takes over the non-core and administrative side of the business; the business knowledge about the entire company and internal processes gained through the bundling project; best practices, that may be leveraged out of existing communities; systematic process standardization and automation to decrease manual effort, and last but not least the service culture the SSO has built up during the previous years serving various operational business units with a variety of different ERP-systems. Table 1 outlines the Unique Selling Proposition as well as further differentiation as-pects regarding the selling of new services out of a Shared Services environment:

10 Cf. *SCHULTZ/DOERR* (2009), p. 13.

Savings	After project Finance Bundling, the SSO can do "more" to achieve further savings for customers
Quality and Transparency	The SSO focuses on systematic quality improvement by optimizing processes step-by-step
Free up Customers	The SSO takes over non-core services and makes them core for them
Business knowledge	The SSO is an internal service provider and has great expertise in *Siemens*' processes
Best Practices	The SSO identifies and deploys best practices quickly and globally
Process Standardization	The SSO develops streamlined process standards that can be maintained and improved quickly
Service Culture	The SSO treats business units like customers and offer services they value

Table 1: Shared Services Differentiation and Unique Selling Proposition

4.2 Price Management

Transferring the topic of Price Management into the Shared Services environment, especially when it comes to selling new services, the price for the actual service delivery as well as all agreed service levels need to be documented in a Service Level Agreement (SLA). In this SLA, business units and the SSC firstly negotiate and then agree upon the specific services to be delivered, specific requirements and parameters, unit and total costs and further, how the costs will be charged and the time frame for service delivery.

The purpose of the SLA is to establish a dialogue between the client and the SSO and to identify services to be provided at the agreed level. Directions and objectives of the collaboration can be aligned and thus the SLA is considered as a basis for successful partnership. When it comes to the content of the Shared Services SLA, it does not differ from a classical SLA including services and levels, costs, expectations, performance measures and targets. The principles of an SLA are obvious: it should be simple, clear, communicated, continuously monitored and all costs should be included.

4.3 Place Management

From a Shared Services perspective, Place Management leads to the question of the location of service delivery. Looking at the pilot project for a new service, the decision will be made in a way to select a rather "mature" SSC to host the service, so that the already strong customer relationships could be easily leveraged.

Obviously, after a successful pilot in the selected SSC, other centers could start their own projects and can learn from the experiences made in the pilot. In the case of the *Siemens* SSO and similar to the worldwide bundling project the actual service delivery – after a beneficial pilot – would be executed with a focus on customer proximity.

Further, a back-office collaboration may be taken into consideration, e.g. for the highly transactional parts of the new services, but this again is only possible after having ensured the agreed level of performance in the front-office center and a structured concept outlining those service parts with relatively low customer contact (e.g. establishing a report out of an existing database). The underlying principle is to always focus on quality when selecting the right place of delivery.

4.4 Promotion Management

With regards to Promotion Management, there are two logical routes to promote the new services (see figure 9). The first option is that existing customer relationships can be utilized to actively sell more. Especially those customers who can already recognize the value of SSOs and have established a close partnership with the internal service provider can be consulted to jointly define the scope for an enhanced package of services offered out of the SSO environment.

Looking into the second opportunity, the set-up of a Shared Services "Sales Team", or "Customer Relationship Management (CRM) Group", it can be generally stated that companies that mandate the use of Shared Services do not include this function and may not see the value of marketing, selling and building relationships in their business model.

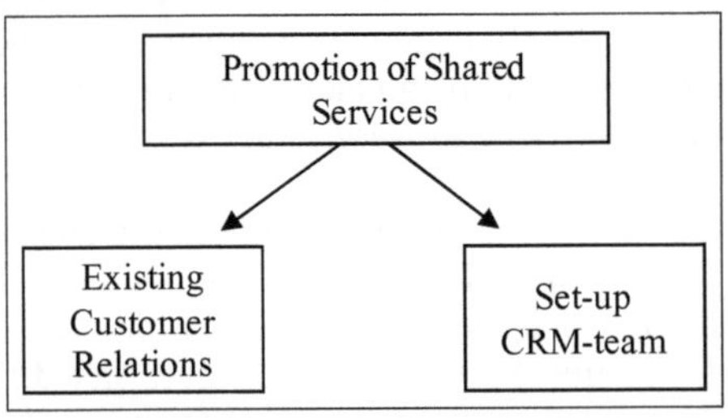

Figure 9: Two options to promote Shared Services

Based on that, what would be the responsibilities of a Shared Services "CRM-team"? They can add value by taking on the role of a moderator between customer and provider with the goal of having a mutually beneficial solution to open issues. One main responsibility is to visit, understand and communicate with the business units. Further, the team is responsible for:

- developing a plan and corresponding customer presentation that promotes the Shared Services and increases business systematically,
- identifying issues and concerns referring to the existing service delivery,
- identifying any additional opportunities to serve the business units,

- improving the relationships with the customers in an interpersonal way.

A challenge for the Shared Services CRM Team is definitely to cover the various fields of potential customer interest in such a way that trust is always built and compounded upon. Especially for the financial SSO, this would have to be reflected in a broad expertise around the existing and the potential new portfolio.

Further, an alternative to a distinct CRM Team would always be that those employees of the SSO that are already in close contact with the customers based on their role (e.g. head of the SSC) may take over the CRM-task in addition to operational tasks. In doing so, the customer is already used to the existing Shared Services contact and in the best case a relationship of trust is already established and may serve as a basis for further collaboration.

4.5 People Management

Due to the fact that the Shared Services business is driven mainly by people, it is a logical addition to the existing classical 4Ps of marketing. During the "lift-drop" phase and thus the bundling project, the SSO has built various new employees in the Centers around the world that now execute the tasks that have been previously handled independently by the business units. Most of the new employees are young people, newly graduated from university, speaking multiple languages and taking this opportunity as a potential first step of their career. In the following text, an excerpt of different characteristics (especially for those employees with customer contact) will be outlined that are of considerable importance for any new recruit to a SSC. In particular when it comes to selling new services, it is the first contact between the employee of the SSC and the customer deciding upon the definition of the future relationship.

It is commonly accepted that a Shared Services Organization's contact person – no matter at which point they get in contact with the customer – needs to have interaction skills, generally known as the ability to ask, listen, relate and care[11]. Further, customer service representatives should aim to know as much as possible about their client's business and needs. Of course, customers buy and like being consulted by people they are comfortable with, particularly if contact people can convince based on their in-depth knowledge, commitment to the company and absolute reliability. Individualized care and empathy are additional characteristics that a Shared Services employee should offer to serve internal customers in an authentic way.

Moreover, with the rather repetitive work in a SSO, e.g. posting hundreds of invoices per day, it is crucial for the SSO to provide the employees with motivating, balancing programs in order to decrease attrition.

Two such examples that have been applied to good effect at the *Siemens* SSO include specific a career development program that selects committed and motivated people from each SSC and gives them the opportunity to jointly work on a common project in the Shared Services environment and finally present the results in front of the SSO's management.

---

[11] Cf. *GOODMAN* (2000), p. 28.

The second example is the job rotation program, where the SSCs exchange key players amongst locations and in doing so give their employees the opportunity to live and work in foreign countries and come back with helpful intercultural experiences. To sum up, it is crucial to offer a variety of human resource initiatives to the employees of a SSO to ensure motivation and commitment.

4.6 Perception Management

The dimension of customer Perception Management intends to actively influence the customers' view of a company, meaning the image customers automatically have in their minds as soon as they hear the company's name. The individual perception plays a key role when selling new services, since only with a positive picture of the SSO in mind the customer is willing to hand over more tasks to a SSC. *MELEWAR/KARAOSMANOGLUPATERSON*[12] identified four elements of corporate identity management mainly influencing the customers' perception: **corporate culture**, **corporate strategy**, **corporate communication** and **corporate image**. In the following text these four areas will be considered in relation to a Shared Services environment, elaborating the possibilities to systematically improve customers' perception towards a SSO.

Corporate culture includes the organization's core values, beliefs and behavior. These internally created values influence customers through the contact by people who effectively live these internal values. This means, frustration, demotivation or fears of the employees of the SSO have a direct impact on the corporate culture and therefore need to be eliminated as far as possible with the help of corresponding human resource initiatives (see chapter 4.5).

Corporate strategy determines what the company produces, how it develops in a certain time frame, with whom it cooperates etc. This overall strategy is directly linked to the customer's view of trust and assurance. Due to the transfer of activities from operational units to the SSO, the customer's view of the overall strategy might be affected, e.g. customers might consider the decision by the *Siemens* managing board to move specific processes to the SSO as inappropriate or customers may not recognize the overall strategic fit and financial benefit that lies behind the transitions. As a result, the strategy needs to be communicated step-by-step involving all major stakeholders in the final decision making. Without their buy-in and active support, the strategy chosen by a SSO is not likely to be realized within the organization.

Corporate communication is associated with the manner of how the company communicates with its stakeholders. Here, communication plays a highly important role: the earlier affected employees on customer side are informed about the upcoming changes, of transferring certain activities to a SSC, the more efficiently firms may eliminate rumors and speculations. This implies specific information provided using personal interaction through the responsible CFO on the donating side, management representatives or letters and other informative materials.

12 Cf. *MELEWAR/KARAOSMANOGLU/PATERSON* (2005), p. 61.

Corporate image can be referred to as the "net result of the interactions of all the experiences, impressions, beliefs, feelings and knowledge that people have about a company".[13] The corporate image is therefore a highly emotional and subjective topic that can only be systematically geared towards a positive direction by proving step-by-step the benefit and the actual value-add of Shared Services. The corporate image can then be considered as the result of the mentioned initiatives in the areas of culture, strategy and communication.

4.7 Implications for Practice

All action items identified within the analysis of the "6 Shared Services Ps" to effectively market and sell new services to the internal customers need to be mapped into a so-called "Marketing & Sales Roadmap". All roadmap elements should then be linked to detailed action plans, which offer comprehensive allocations of responsibilities as well as milestones, deadlines and costs involved.

Furthermore, a systematic change management concept needs to accompany the realization of the initiatives to motivate involved employees to play an active role in the realization of this concept. In addition, a comprehensive tracking and controlling of achievements should be added to the implementation to make sure all deadlines and milestones are achieved.

5 Conclusion and Outlook

Two concepts – both with reference to the third development stage of the *Siemens* Shared Services Organization "enhance and innovate" – have been developed: the first one refers to the systematic selection of new elements to be added to the existing Shared Services portfolio and the second concept – the "6 Shared Services P's" – has been explored in its ability to facilitate the marketing and selling of the new ideas when a formal mandate does not exist.

As a baseline, a detailed analysis of the as-is-situation of the *Siemens* SSO accompanied by a SWOT analysis and Ansoff's Matrix is executed in order to spotlight the key focus areas for the internal service provider to systematically and logically grow the portfolio. From here, the selection concept for new Shared Services portfolio elements is derived including a step-by-step approach of identifying selection criteria (e.g. the cost effect), setting up the Shared Services Scoring Model and a corresponding matrix used as a basis for joint decision making within a management team.

After having chosen a new service to offer, the concept of the "6 Shared Services Ps" derived from the classical marketing mix gives clear guidance on how to efficiently succeed in selling additional services within a captive environment and without a mandate by the managing board. The "6 Shared Services Ps" comprise a comprehensive package of measures to market and sell new services along the areas of **product** (presenting the Unique Selling Proposition and the differentiation of the service), **price** (as captured in the Shared Services SLA), **place** (site selection), **promotion** (via existing customer relations or a specialized CRM-team),

[13] *BERNSTEIN* (1984), p. 125.

people (where the main focus is to motivate young professionals with the help of human resource initiatives), and **perception management** (a 4-step approach combining corporate culture, strategy, communication and image).

The two concepts were both developed for the *Siemens* Shared Services Organization but due to their flexible set-up and general validity may offer guidance for any other internal Shared Services provider.

Depending on a SSO's maturity, the marketing and selling of additional services may be considered as a valuable strategic step to expand the service portfolio and increase the support of operational business units within the company to ultimately improve the overall competitiveness. While in the first place new services are all geared towards transactional, administrative activities, to gain customers' trust and confidence, in a second step more and more services requiring a higher degree of expertise may be transferred to SSCs. As a consequence the marketing and selling of services is always a first step to initiate the new business and therefore both concepts, the selection of ideas and also the "6 Shared Services P's" are considered as indispensable factors to systematically develop and sell new portfolio elements within a Shared Services environment.

6 Abbreviations and Terms

Center	Short for "Shared Services Center" or "Delivery Center" (*Siemens* term)
Donating entity	Legal entity or organizational/accounting unit handing over certain administrative tasks to a Shared Services Organization (or to a Cluster or country organization)
Finance Bundling	Comprehensive program in the areas of accounting, controlling, taxes and financial services to re-shape, harmonize and optimize the worldwide finance functions within *Siemens* group; focus in this article is the transfer of transactional accounting tasks to the in-house Shared Services Organization
HQ	Headquarters
KPI	Key Performance Indicator
Ramp-up	Describes the development phase and corresponding activities of a Shared Services Organization when work is being transferred from one or more donating entities, requiring a corresponding increase of the service provider's internal resources in order to handle the additional volume
Receiving entity	Legal entity or organizational/accounting unit, regularly a Shared Services Organization (or a Cluster or country organization), receiving certain administrative tasks from the donating entity

SLA	Service Level Agreement, tax-relevant contract between the Shared Services Organization's legal entity and the legal entity of the customer ordering respective services
SSC	Shared Services Center(s)
SSO	Shared Services Organization(s)
USP	Unique Selling Proposition, real or perceived benefit of a good or service that differentiates it from competitors and gives its buyer a logical reason to prefer it over others.

References

ADCOCK, D./HALBORG, A./ROSS, C. (2001): Marketing Principles and Practice, Essex 2001.

BERNSTEIN, D. (1984): Company Image and Reality – A Critique of Corporate Communications, London 1984.

BRUHN, M. (2003): Relationship Marketing, Management of Customer Relationships, Essex 2003.

GOODMAN, G. S. (2000): Monitoring, Measuring and Managing Customer Satisfaction, New York (NY) 2000.

GRIFFIN, R. W. (2008): Fundamentals of Management, Mason 2008.

KOTLER, P./ARMSTRONG, G. (2009): Principles of Marketing, Essex 2009.

KOTLER, P./BERGER, R./BICKHOFF, N. (2010): The Quintessence of Strategic Management: What You Really Need to Know to Survive in Business, Berlin/Heidelberg 2010.

KULHALI, S. (2010): A Structured Approach to Establishing Shared Services, in: Infosys (Ed.), White Paper, London 2010.

MELEWAR, T. C./KARAOSMANOGLU, E./PATERSON, D. (2005): Corporate Identity: Concept, Components and Contribution, in: Journal of General Management, Vol. 31 (2005), No. 1, 2005, p. 59.

MORSE, S. (1998): Successful Product Management, London 1998.

MÜLLER-STEWENS, G./LECHNER, C. (2011): Strategisches Management. Wie strategische Initiativen zum Wandel führen, Stuttgart 2011.

SCHULTZ, M./DOERR J. (2009): Professional Services Marketing: How the Best Firms Build Premier Brands, Thriving Lead Generation Engines, and Cultures of Business Development Success, New Jersey (NJ) 2009.

Controlling Shared Services (CSS) – Managing Capabilities for the Digital Age

DOMINIC STEPHENSON, ROMAN BECKER, PATRICK LANGE, THILO RAU und *ALEXANDER RIEDEL*

KPMG AG Wirtschaftsprüfungsgesellschaft

1 Introduction and Purpose of Article

Winston Churchill may have said it best: "A pessimist sees the difficulty in every opportunity, an optimist sees the opportunity in every difficulty."

Staying competitive in globalized markets while developing business in a low growth environment presents the most formidable challenge for many executives today. Every more often, executives turn to our practice at *KPMG Advisory* for insight and direction on how to maintain a healthy balance between cost and quality. Particularly in the controlling organizations, executives are asked not only to deliver valuable business intelligence, but also to create value by structuring their teams in a cost-conscious manner. Moreover, many executives in controlling organizations are eager to attest their function's value contribution to the firm by supporting operational and financial managers with strategic business intelligence and meaningful analytical fire power. These executives seek comparative advantages from the interdependencies among processes, systems and people and hence manage their organizations increasingly according to proven business fundamentals.

In this article, *KPMG Advisory* shares insights into recent trends in organizational development for controlling, argues which service delivery model has proved to deliver the highest benefit, and suggests decisive measures to create sustainable advantages – both in terms of costs and quality. As a management consulting team, *KPMG* foresees that non-transactional operations in administrative functions – such as strategic planning or business performance management – will become increasingly subject to "industrialization" in the way transactional, highly repetitive activities have been subject to standardization, automation and centralization. Interestingly, the "industrialization" of transactional controlling activities today shows the same disruptive side effects it has had in the manufacturing revolution a century ago. Fortunately, the lessons learned in transition management back then will serve well today to prevent old mistakes from being repeated.

KPMG affirms that many manufacturing principles from the automotive industry and other industries found their way into the strategic management of today's service delivery models – examples include process optimization, specialization, and outsourcing. Controlling activities are increasingly managed strategically, thereby reaping benefits from key business management fundamentals. For example, *Ford* "industrialized" areas of accounting and financing as a countermeasure in the early 1980s to increase efficiency in administration. In the aftermath of the oil crisis, demand for American cars fell, and consumer preference shifted towards more economical cars (losing market shares to Japanese manufactures) while the overall volume in financing/leasing application rose (credit applications and risk management). Interestingly, *Ford* finds itself facing similar challenges again in the aftermath of the financial crisis of 2008.

Current discussions with *KPMG* clients confirm that many executives foresee the establishment of "controlling factories" – supporting the CFO in sustaining the overall financial viability, helping engineers/marketers develop the right products for customers and providing plant manager with critical business intelligence to optimize production processes as well as identifying comparative cost advantages. In fact, many clients consider rigorous "industrialization" a prerequisite for further advances in effective controlling. Advances that capitalize on technological innovations such as data mining and analytics are powered by modern computer systems.

We suggest that non-transactional processes – typically untouched by large Shared Services Organizations (SSOs) transformation projects – generate value by transferring them into Centers of Competence (CoCs) and by optimizing their management. Non-transactional processes are suitable for consolidation because specialists pool their knowledge and offer their skills to the company as a whole. Therefore, economies of scope and specialization effects can be realized. This insight from our clients represents a real opportunity – available to responsive and well-prepared businesses.

2 Definitions Regarding Controlling Shared Services

In this chapter, we outline the current shared services landscape and review its current developments. Following this review, we make the case for Controlling Shared Services (CSS) and introduce a framework of controlling processes and their characteristics.

2.1 Status quo of Shared Services Organizations

The development of SSOs is based on the principle of internal service performance and has its origins in the division of labor. Early steps towards a shared services center concept as we know it today were already taken during the 1920s, when *General Motors* (GM) introduced a divisional structure and consolidated various support functions for all units into one separate organizational division that was not located at the corporate headquarters. *GM* was aware of the redundant structures that went hand in hand with decentralization and emphasized the service character of that division.[1]

During the early 1980s, corporations increased customer orientation by moving closer to the clients and by establishing highly decentralized service organizations. In turn, the resulting inefficiencies soon caused Ford to centralize areas of the financial and accounting system and to introduce explicit agreements of performance and price, the so-called Service Level Agreements (SLAs). In 1984, *General Electric* (GE) consolidated several accounting processes from over 50 locations into four Shared Service Centers (SSCs). Both companies have been regarded as pioneers of the SSC concept ever since.[2]

That concept was soon adopted by many American corporations. Until the mid-1990s, application was mainly limited to Anglo-American companies and their corporate subsidiaries. It was only later that the SSC concept gained acceptance in Europe, making its way into all industries as a popular means of cutting costs and driving corporate standards. Today, most international companies have consolidated different parts of their corporate functions in SSOs in one way or another. Apart from accounting and financial processes, services relating to HR, IT, and procurement are also increasingly delivered out of SSOs. The processes in these functions are particularly suitable due to their level of standardization. Furthermore, these processes are characterized by a high proportion of routine and low decision activities.

---

1 Cf. *DRESSLER* (2007), p. 11.

2 Cf. *KAGELMANN* (2001), p. 69.

Due to its popularity, the concept of shared services evolved into many different variations. The following key factors define “shared service center” according to considerations from *DRESSLER*[3] and *MOLL*[4]:

- SSOs are legally independent responsibility units where the execution of support processes is consolidated.
- To the SSOs, those processes are core processes with the objective to increase the overall shareholder value by optimizing processes in terms of cost, quality and time.
- A market-oriented service delivery is ensured by explicit Service Level Agreements (SLA).

After three decades, SSOs have proved to be capable of realizing saving potentials of up to 40 % at best practice companies. The full saving potential is a combination of different factors. The bundling of support processes into a SSO creates economies of scale in comparison to decentralized delivery of processes, and economies of scope by a common and recurrent usage of know-how and indivisible assets. Both effects have a positive impact on costs per unit. Standardization of processes is a prerequisite for specialization, which in turn has positive effects on throughput time and quality of processes. Optimization of processes directly affects the throughput time and quality. Throughput time and quality in turn have effects on the costs of a process. Positive side effects of optimization and standardization include the reduction of overall complexity of processes and improved automation potential. Processes are partially automated and interfaces minimized. A global SSO location provides additional leverage for optimizing factor and infrastructure costs and for capturing arbitrage effects.

Initially, SSOs focused on transactional activities characterized by high volume and low qualification profiles. As SSO acceptance grew not only in terms of penetration but also in terms of scope, companies started to incorporate more sophisticated tasks. Bundling higher-skilled personnel and processes will leverage expert knowledge and service competence. This concept is known as center of competence and represents a second type of SSC besides the traditional center of scale. In Germany, we saw that many companies started centralization of higher-skilled activities for the corporate functions accounting, IT and HR, as well as procurement. However, a shift of those higher-skilled processes into a SSO and center of competence has played no major role so far. We expect high-skilled activities to be increasingly shifted into dedicated SSCs.

Why has the controlling function not yet played an important role in SSOs? Controlling, as a business service, was initially excluded from SSO considerations due to the “non-transactional” nature of the activities. This perspective changed, however, due to ever increasing cost and efficiency pressure during the recent economic and financial crisis. Today, corporations consider enlarging the scope of SSOs to include controlling processes. So-called “reporting factories” are gaining popularity, deployed for the preparation of periodical and standard reports. Those management reporting activities are indeed well suited for a transfer into an SSO. We currently conduct a comprehensive study on controlling functions in order to test *KPMG's* theoretical framework on CSS operations.

---

3 Cf. *DRESSLER* (2007).

4 Cf. *MOLL* (2012).

2.2 Framework of Controlling Processes

As the operation of the controlling function varies across companies and industries, a common framework of controlling processes is required to determine our scope.[5] We apply the *IGC*[6] controlling process model as basis for our considerations.[7] The model provides a general overview covering all relevant controlling functions for companies across all industries. Further, we categorize the controlling processes in terms of their strategic relevance because they reflect typical layers of a controlling organization (see also figure 1):

- Strategic Controlling
- Business Performance Management
- Management Accounting

Strategic controlling includes the following processes: strategic planning, risk management, and business partnering. The corporate strategy developed by the business has to be aligned and evaluated with strategic controlling in order to ensure a consistent derivation of corporate objectives, including the breaking down into organizational units and an assessment of the financial impacts on the company. Risk management has to ensure the long-term existence of the company. The continuous identification and control of factors having a positive or negative influence on the value of the company builds a crucial objective and has attracted significant attention in the course of the current financial and economic crises. Finally, strategic controlling also includes business partnering. One main objective can be summarized as interaction with the operational units by providing the knowledge and experience to translate a strategy and planned initiatives into a long-term business plan. Decision support represents an additional key objective of strategic controlling.

Business performance management focuses on short- and mid-term planning, as well as reporting and includes the following: operative planning and budgeting, functional controlling, forecasting, and management reporting. Operational planning and budgeting supports the realization of strategic objectives. Planning assumptions and top-down goals are set and individual plans and budgets are created to derive short- and medium-term objectives. Consolidation of the individual budgeting plans helps validate a company's strategic goals. Forecasting data has to be processed and expected deviations have to be analyzed to support the development of countermeasures in achieving corporate objectives. Management reporting creates and delivers decision-relevant information to top management. An effective reporting system meets legal and management requirements, provides performance transparency, and delivers data as basis for operational decision making. Functional controlling focuses on the controlling of various functions of a company, such as R&D, production, distribution, staff, or IT.

---

5 Cf. *ANTHONY* (1965), p. 28, and *WISSKIRCHEN/MERTENS* (1999), p. 91.

6 The *INTERNATIONAL GROUP OF CONTROLLING* (IGC) has the objective to establish the professional role and image of the controller and the coordination and development of a matching controlling conception.

7 Cf. *INTERNATIONAL GROUP OF CONTROLLING* (2011), p. 19 et seq.

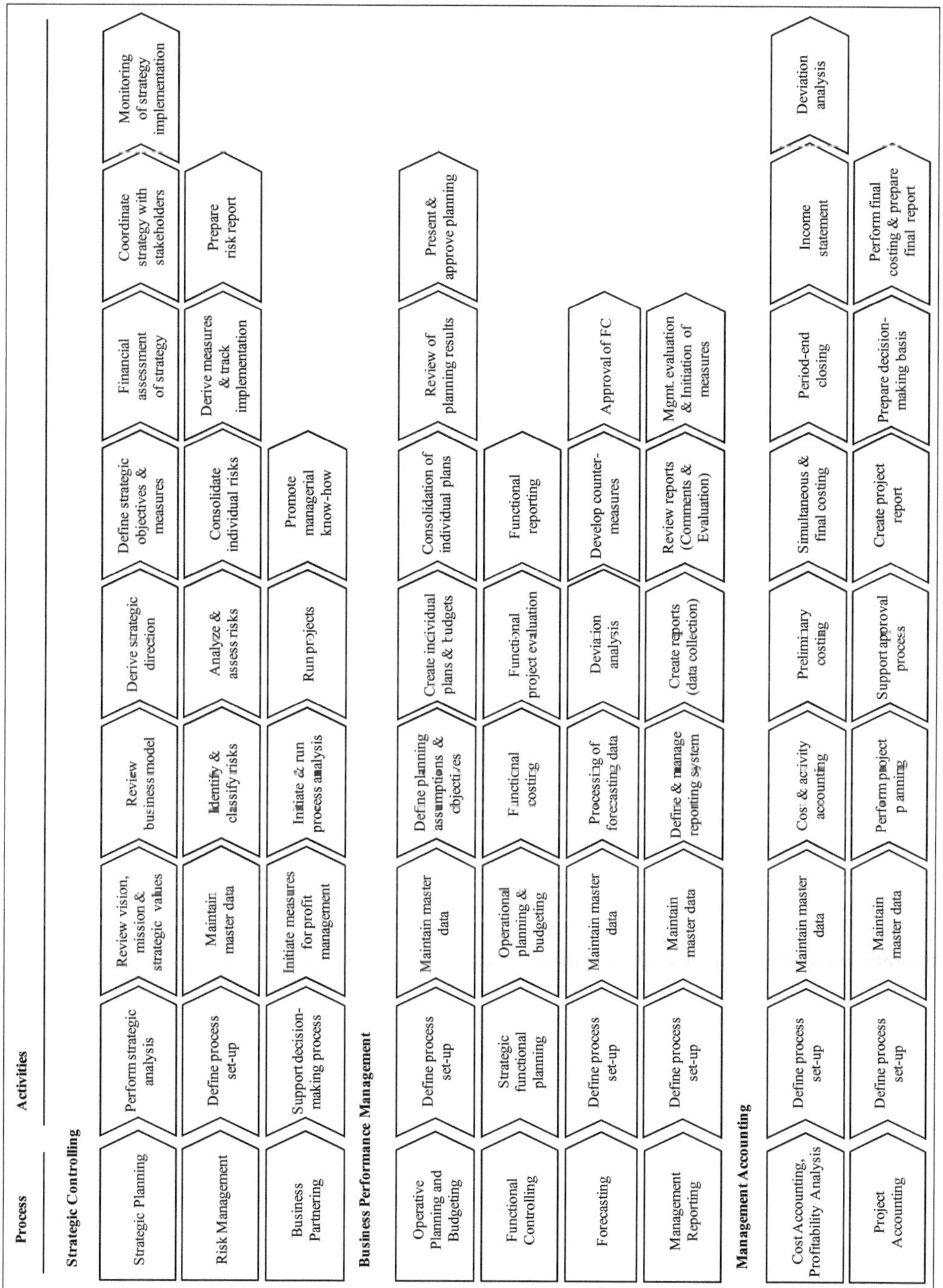

Figure 1: Controlling Process Model

Management accounting includes cost accounting, activity accounting and product costing, as well as project accounting. Cost and activity accounting creates transparency through proper allocation of costs, benefits and revenues. Preliminary costing generates a rough estimate of the expected costs, while final costing provides an accurate view on current and actual costs. Period end closing is also part of the cost accounting process. Project accounting supports the evaluation, selection and prioritization of projects in the planning execution, control as well as completion. The results of the project planning form the basis for the approval process. Management accounting is often considered the "backbone" of the operational controlling system.

2.3 Characteristics of Controlling Processes

After outlining the relevant controlling processes, we want to analyze the different skill levels required for performing the different controlling processes to derive feasible sourcing options for CSS organizations conclusively. We distinguish among high, medium, and low skill levels.

For example, high skill level tasks *("expertise-driven")* include complex analysis such as the assessment of an investment proposal. The controller challenges the business case, detects potential risks, and derives conclusions considering dependencies between the investment decision at hand and that of concurrent investment proposals. High skill level activities are typically not standardized (except formal requirements like templates, procedures, etc.) and require a thorough understanding of controlling as well as the underlying business.

Medium skill level tasks *("competence-driven")* comprise more standardized activities compared to those of expert-driven tasks. Analyzing variances in the course of a monthly reporting process is as typical as is the reconciliation with the business. To perform these kinds of activities, a fundamental knowledge of the business and controlling structure is required. Comprehensive understanding of the underlying reporting system represents an important factor. For example, the implementation of new reporting requirements is considered a medium skill level task.

Low skill level profile *("transaction-driven")* represents the third category, focusing on the highly standardized tasks. Data collection and preparation of controlling reports as well as executing standard closing procedures are considered low-skill. These kinds of activities can represent very time- and resource-consuming controlling tasks. The required expertise to collect and prepare data to perform standard closing procedures consists of basic understanding of controlling and can be learned in a short period of time. Although they are not complex, these activities are crucial as they build the basis for all advanced business analyses at Business Performance Management and Strategic Controlling.

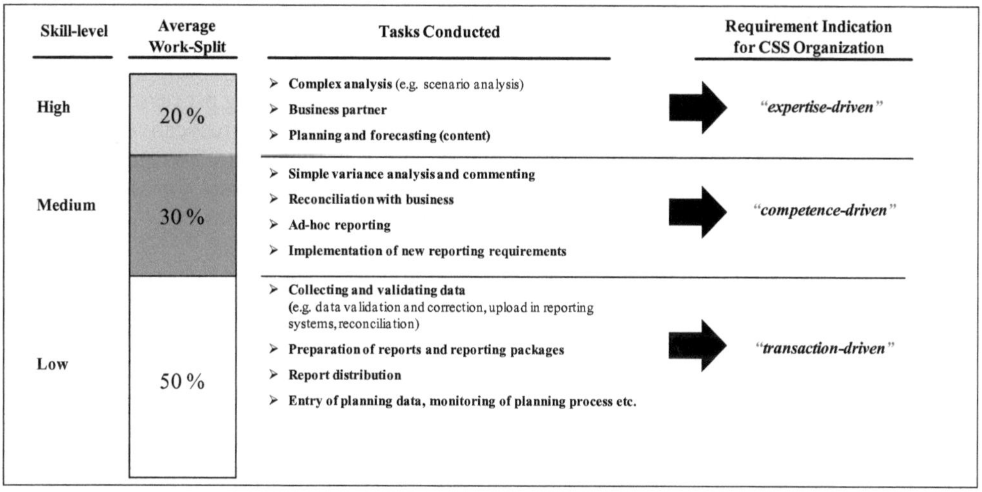

Figure 2: Average Controlling Work-Split Distribution

Based on our consulting experience and insights into several controlling functions as well as interviews with our clients, we observed the following average work-split distribution per skill level: 20 % of the overall controlling workforce of a company can be categorized as high level activities and 30 % as medium, while 50 % are low level. From an end-to-end perspective, the specific insight into controlling processes is that the majority of controlling processes require a mix of these skill levels depending on the individual process-step (activity). We illustrate this fact with the following example: Strategic planning requires a consolidated financial statement for each business segment/unit as baseline and starting point of the long-term planning. The collection of the underlying data from various reporting systems and subsequent consolidation requires only low-level data processing skills. The validation of the consolidated results requires at least medium level skills because reconciliations are performed based on business specific competences. The final validation and actual planning requires high-level skills in order to interact with the business based on profound expertise.

In order to increase the efficiency within controlling processes, a higher level of specialization of activities and processes has to be achieved. In comparison with the manufacturing industry, Controlling has to change its delivery model from individual production to mass production. Or, in other words, we need a high degree of specialization to achieve the expected cost savings. Based on our experience in various projects, this change has to be made under consideration of the skill levels described above. The developed classification is to be understood as a generic model, which has to be customized in detail according to company-specific circumstances. Nevertheless, there are no doubts that "transaction-," "competence-", and "expertise-"driven activities imply different requirements for CSS and their delivery centers.

3 Sourcing Options for CSS

So far, we have set the scope of our investigation in terms of controlling processes we consider relevant, and also discussed required skill levels in general and their respective proportions in a typical controlling organization. This chapter describes the relevant CSS center types and introduces relevant criteria for selecting appropriate controlling processes for each CSS center. Moreover, we present a feasible activity split for controlling processes.

In this context, we start with the discussion of different center types and their specific characteristics. Subsequently, we develop a systematic approach to analyze the processes in terms of suitability for CSS. Finally, we conclude the chapter by providing an overall activity split/sourcing option model for the entire controlling function.

3.1 Center Types for CSS

Based on our experience and defined skill levels in chapter 2.3, we need different center types to fulfill the requirements. The different center types and their characteristics are discussed in this chapter before we start to define the controlling processes suitable to be shifted to and conducted by SSC. Taking this into account, we distinguish between transaction-, competence-, and expert-oriented CSS center types and discuss major differences.

Type	Center of Scale	Center of Competence	Center of Excellence
Objectives	➢ Economies of scale ➢ Increasing efficiency ➢ Better scalability	➢ Bundling of competence ➢ Stronger governance by standardization ➢ Increased quality	➢ Bundling of expertise ➢ Business Partner
Process	➢ Repetitive tasks ➢ Often transactional and standardized processes ➢ Less business specific content, knowledge and systems necessary ➢ Low skill requirements	➢ Competence driven task ➢ Methods and business specific knowledge and systems necessary	➢ Expert driven tasks ➢ Strategy, business or segment specific content necessary
People	➢ Low qualification ➢ No expertise required ➢ Short training time	➢ High qualification ➢ Expertise required ➢ Long training time	➢ High qualification ➢ Highly specialized experts required ➢ Knowledge of business division ➢ Several years of experience

Figure 3: Overview CSS Center Types

Shared service centers yield economies of scale. To realize the same benefits in controlling, the switch from single to mass production has to be made, implying splitting activities into basic, medium, and high analytic categories, each being delivered by individual center types. We define three different center types (see illustration above): Center of Scale (CoS), Center of Competence (CoC), and Center of Excellence (CoE) in order to analyze the Controlling function concerning possible sourcing options. The CoS is the typical SSC type for transactional processes like accounts payable and should be selected by corporations which consider establishing an SSC. The CoC has experienced a significant growth in recent years but its potential is still to be fully utilized on a macroeconomic perspective. In accordance to the discussed skill levels required for the different controlling functions, we define a CoE as a visionary center type, assuming that there is no retained controlling organization in the business units.

Centers of scale, also known as "reporting factories," improve the efficient delivery of transactional services. By bundling activities of several business units/legal entities in one "factory," operational costs can be significantly reduced by means of economies of scale. In addition, the CoS enables corporations to drive process optimization very efficiently, as optimization initiatives can be managed centrally, which also increases the standardization level of processes. Improving scalability is also one of the objectives companies are aiming at, especially when the market is volatile. In this case, the flexibility to adapt to market changes plays an important role. CoS often focus on the reduction of cost factors which are particularly driven by labor arbitrage effects, and on real estate cost reduction if the center is located offshore.

The different types of processes that are carried out within the center are a distinguishing feature of SSCs. Typically, CoS activities have low strategic relevance and minor importance for the decision making process.[8] The activities operated in a CoS are executed in large numbers/repetitions and high volumes with transactional character.[9] The degree of standardization is high and should be maximized in order to fully lever economies of scale effects.[10] The standardization of processes leads to shorter cycle times, while experience and specialization effects contribute to the increasing of process efficiency.[11] Economies of scale are driven by improved resource utilization and higher volumes at lower unit costs.

According the skill level categorization and outlined process characteristics, the CoS requires employees with a low qualification profile and no major controlling experience. These employees can typically be trained within a short period of time to conduct the activities in the CoS.[12]

In contrast to a CoS that predominantly focuses on economies of scale, a *center of competence* (CoC) aims at specialization effects by means of activity bundling. CoCs aim at the bundling of competences, considering activities with higher complexity. By operating a central CoC unit, corporate governance regarding controlling activities is more easily ensured (e.g., reporting standards, evaluation standards, costing standards). In addition thereto, the level of standardization can be maintained more effectively compared to the decentralized execution of controlling operations. By sharing expertise across business units within the CoC, the overall quality also increases, leading to an improved decision process within corporations.[13]

Processes conducted in a CoC differ significantly from those performed in a CoS in terms of their characteristics. The main distinction lies in the know-how/expertise requirements as well as in the transactional volume. In order to conduct non-transactional processes like deviation analysis, ad-reports or budgeting support, a certain level of expertise and experience is re-

---

8 *MOLL* (2012), p. 42.

9 Cf. *BECKER/KUNZ/MEYER* (2008), p. 24.

10 For more details about Economies of Scale see also *HUNGENBERG/WULFF* (2007), p. 154 et seq.

11 Cf. *HENDERSON* (1974).

12 Cf. *KLINGEBIEL* (2005), p. 780.

13 Cf. *KAGELMANN* (2001), p. 89, and *DEIMEL* (2008), p. 197.

quired. Processes in the CoC have a far more transformational character and are executed in comparatively smaller volumes than CoS processes.[14] Due to a lower degree of automation, the processes require more independent decision making of the CoC-employee. Nevertheless, we consider all processes operated by a CoC to be a standard process to a certain extent. Processes which cannot be standardized at all are excluded in our definition of CoC. Finally, the analytical character of the processes implies a higher interaction between the CoC and the customers/business units compared to a CoS.[15]

Taking into consideration the skill levels discussed in chapter 2.3, a CoC requires highly qualified employees with sophisticated expertise in controlling and in the business itself. The period of time to onboard new employee is significantly higher compared to a CoS because the know-how/expertise level is higher.[16] Employees of a CoC should be viewed as internal experts giving advice to the business units and bringing process knowledge into the division. In this context, sharing experience plays an important role in solving problems with the business units. Furthermore, process engineering know-how is required because the CoC-employees are also responsible for the implementation of defined processes and their maintenance.

Besides the CoS and CoC discussed above, we define the *Center of Excellence* (CoE) as a visionary center type which is currently not relevant for CSS organizations but will have to be considered in the long-term in the course of the strategic development of CSS. According to our vision, there is potential for almost the entire traditional controlling organization in a CSS organization to be shifted, leaving the business units with very few controlling operations. Further investigation is necessary to finally identify potential sourcing options and implications in this respect. Nevertheless, we provide initial considerations in this direction by discussing the CoE concept as an important center type in this context.

A CoE aims at the bundling of expertise and business partnering. Cost saving is not the main driver but increases the effectiveness of the controlling function. Bundling of expertise facilitates the sharing of knowledge, leading to an increase in the overall quality. The CoE acts as a business partner for the business units in order to challenge and support the planning and strategy process by contributing top-quality experience and expertise. As several strategic controlling activities are already conducted centrally in a corporate controlling department, we conclude that these processes should be included in the CoE.

Unlike a CoC, the CoE operates processes where no standardization is possible. Activities are highly expert-driven in terms of controlling experience as well as business knowledge of the company. We assume that all controlling processes with strategic relevance are operated by a CoE. The definition of guidelines and methods is one lever in order to ensure a uniform controlling system.

To operate a CoE, highly skilled personnel is required. Business-specific know-how is relevant not only on an operational level but especially concerning strategic business development. Employees need to understand the entire business and controlling system of the company, which requires sophisticated theoretical and practical qualification.

---

14 *BECKER/KUNZ/MEYER* (2008), p. 24.

15 Cf. *ULRICH* (1995) and *MOLL* (2012), p. 42.

16 Cf. *KAGELMANN*, (2001), p. 89, *SCHEFFNER* (2008), p. 647, and *DEIMEL/ISEMANN/MÜLLER* (2006), p. 202.

The different center types are theoretical categorizations, while companies in practice often operate hybrids or combinations of these center types, performing both transactional and transformational processes.[17] Nevertheless, the distinction is relevant in order to assign the controlling activities in scope of our investigation to the different center types.

3.2 Criteria to Evaluate Sourcing Options

Since we conclude that controlling processes overall must be operated in different centers types due to the different skill levels required (high, medium, low), we need criteria reflecting this. Hence the challenge lies in the design of skill-based criteria enabling a skill-based assignment of controlling processes and activities to the appropriate operating unit.

We view a CoE as a vision, subject to further investigation. Hence we do not consider the CoE as a sourcing option in the following, but we will provide initial considerations and conclusions. To decide whether controlling activities are suitable to be operated in a CSS center (either CoS or CoC) or not, we develop a systematic approach to support this decision process. Note that the assessment of processes according to the different criteria in individual cases is not trivial, and the decision has to be made in accordance to company-specific configurations of the processes. Based on our experience and conducted projects, we conclude that decisions should be based on the following set of criteria:

- Business-specific reason for local execution
- Intensive coordination needs that would require geographic proximity to the (internal) customer/business units
- Uniqueness of a process
- Standardization potential of a process
- High processing volumes
- Short training time and little expertise/know-how
- Profound business-specific know-how required/process with high decision proportion

The first criterion for local retention of a process is a *business-specific* reason; this criterion represents an exclusion criterion for the CSS suitability. Process-specific reasons are, for example, elements of the production controlling where short response-times are required. Another example would be the production variance and error cause analysis, which often require close collaboration with the production organization.

The traditional need for close *proximity to the user of data/business units* may be an additional factor to reject establishment of a CSS center. However, this common argument is increasingly counteracted by widespread availability of high-speed data and video networks, making it easier to collaborate regardless of location. In fact, our project experience shows that consequent use of crowed-sourcing methodologies helps advancing knowledge sharing and management significantly. For example, successful analyses and meaningful data find their way into the latest reports, in turn motivating employees to contribute more in order to gain instant

[17] *FISCHER/STERZENBACH* (2006), p. 38 et seq.

recognition from a company-wide audience. The quality of cooperation among coworkers still varies significantly among companies and among business units within companies, so that personal communication or consulting service will remain important irrespective to the latest technological achievements.

The third criterion focuses on the *uniqueness* of a process. If a process and its demands are common across multiple business units, resources are bound to be bundled in CSS. Due to the demand in multiple units, economies of scale and specialization effects can be realized and thus process execution in a CSS center is potentially more efficient. If a process is unique, the question arises whether it can be standardized or not. Only those processes which cannot be standardized seem impractical for a CSS center.

The *standardization potential* of (sub-) processes is one of the most important criteria because processes which cannot be standardized at all are impractical both for use in a CoS or in a CoC. Despite the fact that a comprehensive analysis and conclusion of potential CoE-processes is not in scope of this article, we assume that several of those processes are predestined for a CoE. For example, the financial analysis of an acquisition initiative could very well be performed by a strategic controller of a CoE.

A high *process volume* indicates the potential for efficiency gains that can be realized (remember that we already discussed the criteria above, hence all the processes we consider here are not unique, meaning that they can be standardized). Any increase of the standardization level or reduction of process time bears a great potential for economies of scale. Hence these processes are suitable for a CoS. A low process volume does, however, indicate smaller economies of scale; in this case, benefits lie mainly in the realization of economies of scope. The decision whether a low volume process should be conducted by a CoS or CoC, depends on the process complexity and corresponding training time/expertise required.

The period of *time to train* the employees is an indicator in terms of complexity of a process. Long training periods indicate a fairly complex process, while short training periods suggest that little expertise is required to conduct the process. As the CoS is characterized by personnel with a low qualification profile, we conclude that processes with short training periods qualify for a CoS because only a low level of expertise is required.

Processes with a high decision proportion indicate complex decisions, typically requiring a comprehensive understanding of business know-how as well as controlling expertise. Hence, the requirement of profound *business-specific know-how* or a high *decision proportion* is an exclusion criterion for a CoC. As the required skill-level of those processes is presumably high, it can be concluded that those activities should be performed by a CoE.

Our systematic approach to derive an activity split for CSS (focusing on CoS and CoC) is summarized and illustrated by the decision tree below (see figure 4). In the following, we apply this systematic approach to the discussed controlling processes in scope, in order to develop an activity split for the entire set of controlling operations.

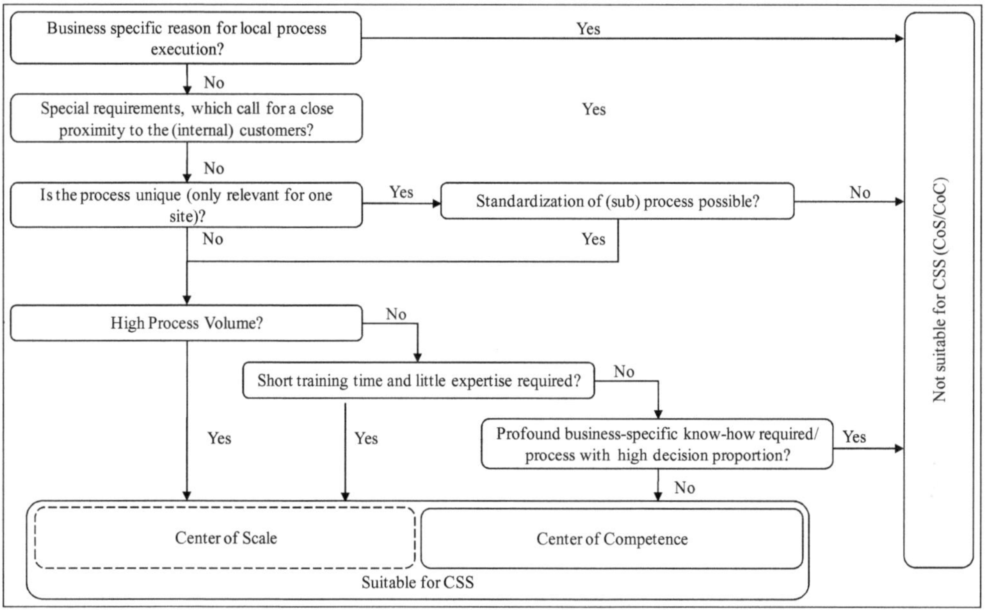

Figure 4: Approach to Derive an Activity Split for CSS

3.3 Development of an Activity Split for CSS

In the course of the implementation of a CSS center, the definition of the activity split builds one of the most important elements. In this context, companies are facing the challenge to decide on the level of detail on which processes shall be analyzed and "split" (between the different operating entities) while limiting the risk that too many interfaces between the involved parties may lead to inefficient and ineffective controlling processes. From a theoretical point of view, it may me reasonable to assign as many activities to the CSS center as possible, but if this leads to too many interfaces of a process from an end-to-end perspective, we highly recommended that several activities be aggregated to a sub-process to reduce process fragmentation and coordination complexity. This balancing requires profound experience, which is the reason why experienced consultants typically provide support to companies in this phase of a CSS project.

To develop the activity split, each sub process has to be reviewed in the context of the decision tree criteria developed in chapter 3.2. To provide an example, we discuss the activity split for the process of Management Reporting as one part of our controlling process model. The order of activities illustrated below represents the chronological order of the sub-processes/activities.

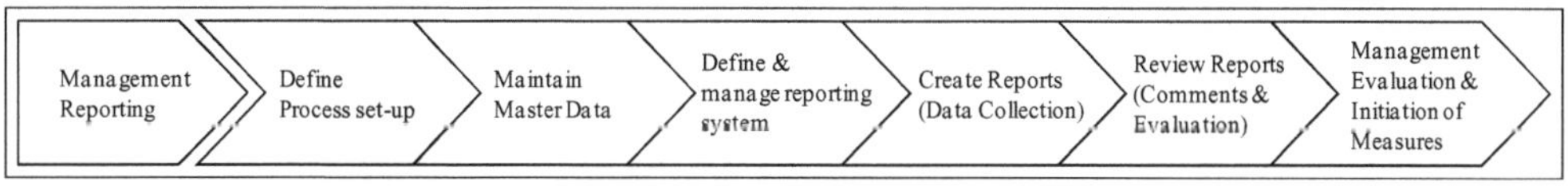

Figure 5: Management Reporting Activities

The *definition of the process setup* is typically standardized at a group-wide level, with little or no variation for the different business units. New reporting requirements based on management decisions are group-wide, resulting in the adoption of standard reports and master data requirements. A business-specific reason for local process execution of standard reports as well as a close proximity to business units can be declined, in order to ensure consistent and standardized group-wide management reporting. The definition of the reporting process setup is typically not unique and occurs infrequently (annually or quarterly). As this process requires comprehensive knowledge of the reporting system and processes but no profound business knowledge and only minor decision proportion, we conclude that these activities should be conducted by a CoC

The *maintenance of master data* should be highly standardized and performed by a central entity. Depending on the reporting level (group/business unit) BI solutions or ERP systems are the sources of management reporting. Mere technical master data maintenance is a standardized process controlled by IT-enabled access rights. The process volume might vary between high/low depending on the company, but irrespectively thereof, the know-how requirements to perform these activities are pretty low. In many cases, these kinds of activities are already centralized in practice and are definitely suitable to be operated in a CoS.

The *definition and management of the reporting system* focuses on the reporting system and underlying IT solutions. Based on the business requirements defined by the management, the controlling division has to incorporate and ensure these in the reporting system and manage necessary changes. Local execution requirements as well as close proximity can be excluded because the reporting systems are typically on a global scale. The process itself is not unique and has (depending on the company) generally a low volume because changes of reporting requirements are typically not a frequent event. The management of reporting systems is of course an ongoing activity to safeguard the entire reporting process; however, we assume a relatively low volume. The activities require know-how of the reporting system and general controlling experience to understand the requirements, but not profound business know-how. Hence we conclude that this process is suitable for a CoC. Depending on the complexity of the reporting system and/or required changes, this activity might require the involvement of highly skilled professionals not typically found in a CoC (according to our definition), but based on our experience and market insights, this effect can be neglected.

The *preparation of reports (data collection)* is a highly standardized activity without business specifics and should be performed in a similar manner across business units (if differences are significant, companies should strive for standardization anyway independent of CSS considerations). Nevertheless, differing requirements could result due to heterogeneous IT infrastructure or ERP programs. Many different interfaces and stand-alone solutions require special knowledge for data extraction, but even in these cases, a short training will likely prevent this from becoming a "show-stopper" for the migration into a CSS organization. If large corporations make constant harmonization and alignment efforts, it is safe to assume that the data collection and preparation of reports can be bundled globally for most international groups. Data collection for standard reports takes up a fair amount of time of the reporting process and has to be performed on a regularly basis. Given the short training time and the low amount of expertise required, it is predestined to be performed in a center of scale.

For the *evaluation and commenting of reports*, no business specific reason is evident to execute the process locally. Even though involved controllers often argue that the close proximity is essential to understand potential deviations, we argue that understanding of a deviation and commenting on it, respectively, are basically standard procedures. Local expertise is not essential to evaluate deviations, but it is needed to explain them. Hence, interaction between a CSS center and the local units is important. As we conclude that the general evaluation and commenting process is quite a standardized process requiring a certain level of competence regarding controlling and business, we assume that this process is suitable for a CoC.

The *management evaluation and initiation of the suggested measures* is per definition a local activity requiring business unit/site-specific expertise and knowledge. The development of measures is often driven by deviations of actual versus planned performance. Therefore, in-depth knowledge of any potential cause and countermeasure is essential. The management (depending on the magnitude of the measure, this may be at legal entity, country, region, business unit, or corporate level) is responsible for defining these measures, while the controlling department is responsible for detecting deviations and potential causes, and especially for evaluating and assessing potential options in terms of their feasibility and financial impacts.

By applying our assessment approach on all of the controlling activities defined in-scope (see chapter 2.2), we have developed the following activity split for the controlling function (see figure 6). The developed activity split provides a general overview of potential sourcing options companies have when they consider implementing a CSS organization. Due to company-specific circumstances and requirements, this split has to be adopted and also analyzed on a case-by-case basis.

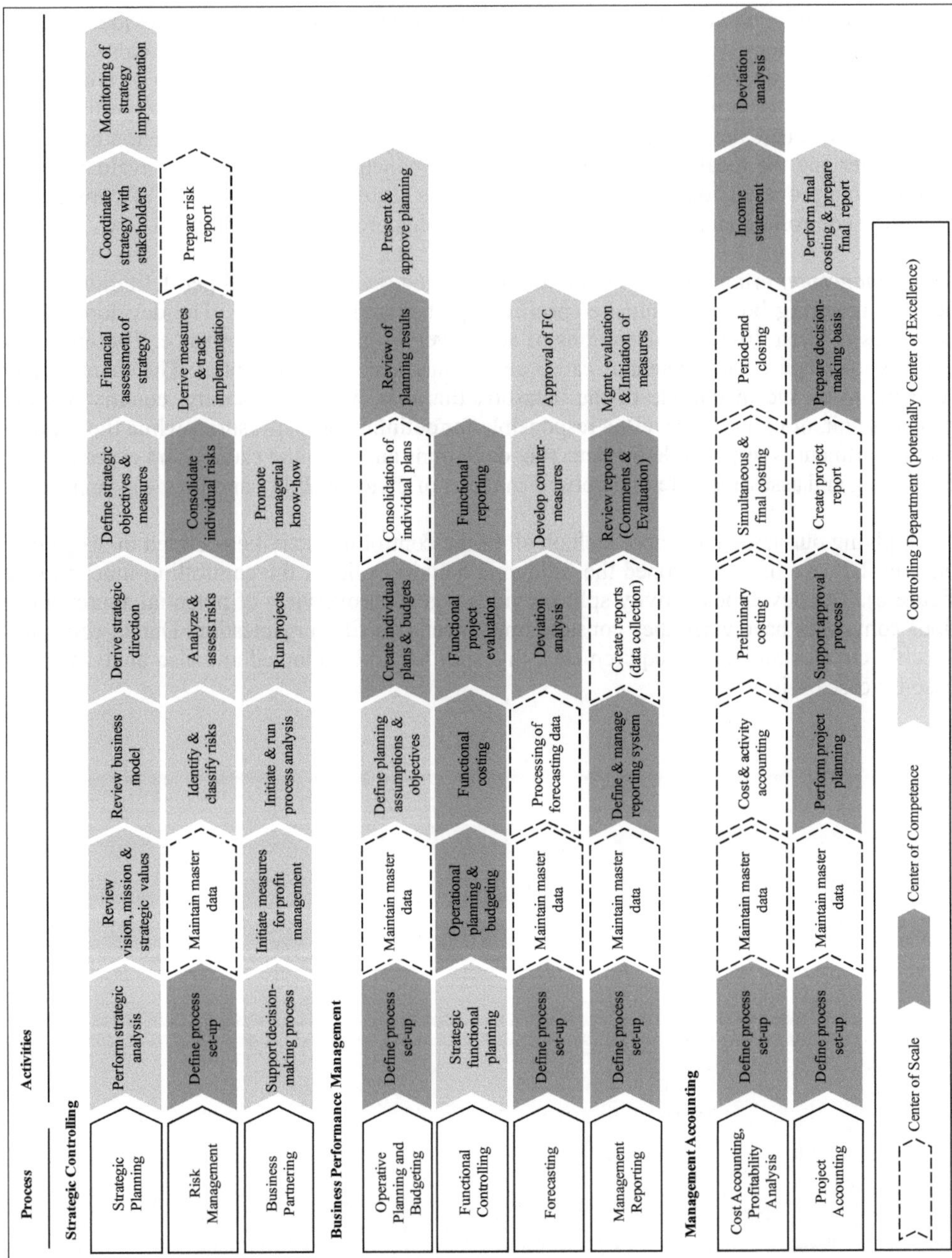

Figure 6: Activity Split for a Controlling Function

4 Crucial Elements of the Implementation of Controlling Shared Services

From our transformation experience in local as well as global projects, four elements are deemed crucial for a successful transition of controlling processes into a CSS organization. Also, in chapter 4.2, we evaluate the potential risks as well as opportunities arising during a CSS transition.

4.1 Transformation from Traditional Setup to a CSS Organization

Transforming an established controlling organization is no small endeavor. Successful implementation is – in our experience – dependent on sensible handling of the following factors:

- Decisiveness of change
- Suitability of implementation approach
- Sensibility to people and to issues involving change of management

Decisiveness of change: Implementing a CSS organization requires the full commitment of a firm's finance community, including CFO, staff council, and other accountable individuals within the donating entity, depending on the legal backdrop of the transition. Risks and rewards of the transition will need to be communicated upfront to ensure business continuity during the transition; failure to do so will spark fundamental discussions about design, purpose, or feasibility in the middle of the transition and could jeopardize the entire project. Particularly in controlling, once job descriptions are altered and entire jobs are being eliminated in the donating entity, it would be challenging to reinstate the previous situation – or at least costly. Longstanding and accomplished employees have their previously varied activities reduced to rather standard tasks, often accompanied by loss of a prestigious work title.

From past project experience, commitment to change needs to be communicated from the top of the organization down into the affected departments. A clear vision accompanied by tangible benefits to the organization at large will help argue the case for change. From the outset, top management needs to state clearly that no exceptions to common design principles will be granted unless legally necessary. Neglecting to communicate decisiveness and commitment to a vision, again, will spark a plethora of filing for exceptions, alienate top personnel and prolong the transition period unnecessarily with respective impact on financial payback.

Suitability of implementation (parallel vs. sequential): Establishment of a CSS organization differs in key aspects from a common shared service organization. As typically 50 % of the controlling activities are non-transactional and, more importantly, are performed by numerous employees "part-time" as well as dispersed over the organization, a differentiated implementation approach is deemed necessary.

The most suitable implementation approach for transaction-based processes is considered "lift drop change," e.g., for transferring repetitive, highly standardized data processing activities. Entire jobs are "lifted" out of the donating entity and migrated ("dropped") into the SSC as if the same employee would perform his task just from another location. This approach assumes that only basic knowledge of the value flow and underlying reporting systems is required and that the SSC center design is free from limitation of legacy systems, people or processes. Depending on the sophistication and urge for standardization, processes and systems will be standardized either during or after the transfer to the final organization. Hence the most common implementation approaches are: lift-drop-change or lift-change-drop, respectively. Depending on the overall transaction/data volume, sequencing a transition by easily alternating heterogeneous units, regions or business units helps building experience as well as confidence. Controlling activities are also suitable for a parallel transfer approach; for example, collection and validation of data from various sources in order to prepare and distribute standard reports for the different addressees represents a classic “lift-drop” scenario. Those controlling activities occur in the course of the monthly reporting cycles and also include standard closing procedures (e.g., technical valuation runs). They do not require sophisticated business and financial analytic expertise. Neither do they require direct and frequent communication with the business (besides minor reconciliations during the data validation processes). Given the characteristics of these exemplary activities, those processes are suitable to be delivered through a center of scale often called “reporting factory,” and typically are transferred by a “lift-change-drop” approach.

We would like to emphasize that most controlling processes are not suitable to be transferred in a sequential approach. Processes left back in the originating department as well as processes lifted into CSS will have to be redesigned from scratch.

As described above, formerly heterogeneous roles are subsumed and specialized. In analogy to the industrial revolution in the automotive industry, production is transformed from individual manufacturing to a large scale, specialized production. Also, in analogy to the global sourcing strategies of today’s automotive companies, production sites bundle different skill levels (e.g., engineering in Germany, component assembly in India realizing labor arbitrage).

Parallel implementation is essential in the transition to a CSS center because a CSS center represents a special case of shared service organization. “Change” in the local department needs to precede any transfer activity. The non-transactional nature of many controlling activities requires the separation of jobs locally before they are transferred to a dedicated CSS organization. To obtain a clear vision of the job description (separation) in its optimal end-state, early decisions on collaboration modes between departments and analytical teams as well as infrastructure (systems) should not be developed alongside the transition. Only the parallel implementation approach ensures a successful transfer and creates effective options to deal with temporarily unmotivated local staff.

A transfer of extensive knowledge from the donating entity into the receiving CSS without losses is essential because many activities performed are competence-driven and require methodological, business-specific knowledge and understanding of the value flow (including the underlying reporting systems).

Separation of activities preceding the transfer will often result in the creation of “split-heads” because local experts need to separate their competence and thus reduce their overall workload. Without clearly differentiated job descriptions, which also mirror the desired steady-state in the CSS, local controlling heads will struggle with the allocation of activities and risk not reaping the benefits of readily transferable activities. Moreover, establishing CSS structures in parallel allows testing and eventually transferring analytical responsibility swiftly.

Running structures in parallel is not only costly, but also inherently unstable. Therefore, running local and central responsibility side by side for a limited period of time will allow for proper work-shadowing, ensuring business continuity and quality assurance, but also requires decisive project management to be transferred into the desired state soon.

Sensibility to people and to issues involving change of management: Recruiting, training and retaining personnel represent capital challenges in any transition project. Particularly the proposed parallel implementation approach results in two challenges: How to transfer specialized activities from one person to another? How to motivate previous owners of analytical activities and reallocate their spare time? For example, we often advise to kill two birds with one stone: create a long-term career perspective for the transition manager and offer her the position of CSS lead. Offering the transition manager – which by definition is a temporary role only – a long-term career perspective has been key in our past transition projects. Additionally, this option is advisable because recruiting an external expert without intimate understanding of the firm's operations is risky.

4.2 Risks and Opportunities

Organizing the controlling function as shared services has several advantages; cost reduction is being the top consideration. By central service delivery, the number of employees necessary to provide the service can be reduced. Transferring to more favourable wage agreements, as well as benefiting from government incentives and tax benefits, may significantly reduce staff cost.[18]

Standardization of processes represents another common objective of establishing shared service organizations. Standardizing the number of different systems reduces the cost of system integration and maintenance. Consolidation increases the bargaining position, leading to better rates and terms. Best-practice processes can be implemented, resulting in a more efficient and effective execution of processes.

Specialization fosters transparency of processes, leading to higher process quality and flatter organizational structures. By outsourcing the support processes into shared service organizations, the business units are refocused onto their core business and productive activities. Management capacities are relieved from administrative burdens; therefore, SSOs contribute to the pursuit a firm's corporate and business strategy.[19]

With respect to employee motivation, target agreements and bonuses that are directly linked to certain key performance indicators may help to foster effective resource and talent allocation. Additionally, knowledge management is advanced due to exploiting existing knowledge through concentration into one location.[20] Employees can directly exchange and harmonize knowledge.

---

18 Cf. *SCHULMAN* et al. (1999), p. 16.

19 Cf. *SCHULMAN* et al. (1999), p. 35, *DRESSLER* (2007), p. 94, and *MOLL* (2012), p. 31.

20 Cf. *KAGELMANN* (2001), p. 77.

These benefits in particular were supported by a CFO panel in 2007.[21] 83 % of respondents pursued cost-reduction target, 75 % mentioned economies of scale, 64 % pursued improvements in process quality, 57 % needed to reduce cycle time, 56% aimed for increases in service quality, and 49 % needed to refocus on core business as a reason to establish SSCs to finance their organization. More recent studies, on the other hand, show that process standardization and compliance requirements have become equally important.

Risks particularly associated with the implementation of CSS structures include high implementation costs, as well as complex interfaces management as a result of new activity splits. New interfaces may have a negative influence on the quality of services through increased needs for coordination, and perhaps also through slower response times – at least temporarily.

If processes are not sufficiently standardized, the heterogeneity of processes is associated with higher cost of operation. Cost in adapting existing IT infrastructure and employee training are also aspects of change to be professionally managed during a transition from a traditional setup.

As indicated before, the expected long-term increase in motivation has to be weighed against the short-term risk of demotivation of employees during the implementation phases. Highly qualified staff in particular could leave the company if they are faced with a major organizational change, lower wages or a higher degree of specialization.

Some clients have moved straight from a traditional "elaborated" set-up to a highly efficient and specialized reporting factory including center of competence organization in controlling. The finance leadership of those clients recognizes the prospect of a transition project as a "golden" and highly welcomed opportunity to radically alter the company's internal admiration and perceived value contribution. Their decisive leadership and delivered results have inspired other functions to rethink their processes, people and system management – in radical ways. Therefore, some of our clients name the sheer opportunity for fundamental change as key benefit for controlling and for the company at large.

5 Conclusion

Establishment of SSCs is commonplace in organizational development today. This includes reporting factories (also known as CoS) in controlling functions that are gaining popularity among leading corporations. Empirical evidence shows that fundamental business principles of separation, standardization and specialization are also increasingly applied to non-transactional activities - for example to business performance management.

KPMG advisory affirms that many clients are contemplating establishing centers of competence for controlling activities and embrace the opportunity for change. The typical transition risks such as implementation cost, distraction from daily operations, and business continuity are outweighed by the gain in strategic knowledge. In fact, many clients perceive the estab-

21 Cf. *Horváth & Partners* (2008).

lishment of CSS in controlling as a prerequisite to capitalize on technological advances of the digital age, such as data mining and the analytical power of modern IT.

The promise of Controlling Shared Services represents a real opportunity available to responsive and well-prepared businesses – presuming their decisiveness to change, appropriate selection of implementation approach, and sensible dealing with people and change management issues.

Abbreviations and Terms

CFO	Chief Financial Officer
CoC	Center of Competence
CoE	Center of Excellence
CoS	Center of Scale
CSS	Controlling Shared Services
ERP	Enterprise Resource Planning
HR	Human Resources
IT	Information Technology
SLA	Service Level Agreement
SSC	Shared Service Center
SSO	Shared Services Organization

References

ANTHONY, R. N. (1965): Planning and Control Systems, Boston (MA) 1965.

BECKER, W./KUNZ, C./MEYER, B. (2008): Shared Service Center – Konzeption und Implementierung in internationalen Unternehmen, Stuttgart 2008.

DEIMEL, K. (2008): Möglichkeiten und Grenzen des Wertmanagements durch Shared Service Center, in: *KEUPER, F./OECKING, C.* (eds.), Corporate Shared Services, 2nd Edition, Wiesbaden 2008, pp. 191–221.

DEIMEL, K./ISEMANN, R./MÜLLER, S. (2006): Kosten- und Erlösrechnung, München 2006.

DRESSLER, S. (2007): Shared Services, Business Process Outsourcing und Offshoring, Wiesbaden 2007.

FISCHER, T./STERZENBACH, S. (2006): ZP-Stichwort: Shared Service Centers, in: Zeitschrift für Planung und Unternehmenssteuerung, No. 17, pp. 123–128.

HENDERSON, B. (1974): The Experience Curve Reviewed – How Does It Work?, Boston (MA) 1974.

HORVATH & PARTNERS (2008): CFO-Studie 2007 – Reorganisation im Finanzbereich. Stuttgart 2008.

HUNGENBERG, H./WULFF, T. (2007): Grundlagen der Unternehmensführung, Berlin 2007.

INTERNATIONAL GROUP OF CONTROLLING (2011): Controlling-Prozessmodell, Freiburg 2011.

KAGELMANN, U. (2001): Shared Services als Organisationsform – Am Beispiel der Finanzfunktion im multinationalen Konzern. Wiesbaden 2001.

KLINGEBIEL, N. (2005): Shared Service Center, in: Das Wirtschaftsstudium, Vol. 34 (2005), No. 6, pp. 777–782.

MOLL, L. (2012): Strategische Erfolgsfaktoren von Shared Services im Personalbereich, Wiesbaden 2012.

SCHEFFNER, J. (2008): Industrialisierung des Controllings, in: Der Controlling-Berater, No.5, pp. 637–657.

SCHULMAN, D./DUNLEAVY, J./HARMER, M./LUSK, J. (1999): Shared Services – Adding Value to the Business Units, New York 1999.

ULRICH, D. (1995): From Vogue to Value, in: Human Ressource Planning, Vol. 18 (1995), No.3, pp. 12–23.

WISSKIRCHEN, F./MERTENS, H. (1999): Der Shared Services Ansatz als neue Organisationsform von Geschäftsbereichsorganisationen, in: *WISSKIRCHEN, F.* (ed.), Outsourcing-Projekte erfolgreich realisieren, Stuttgart 1999, pp. 79–111.

Operational Risk Management as Shared Service Center of Excellence (CoE)

MARIJN JANSSEN, JÜRGEN H. M. VAN GRINSVEN and *ANTON JOHA*

Delft University of Technology

Executive Summary

Organizations are looking for way to mobilize their knowledge which is often distributed among the many organizational departments and business units. Centers of Excellence (CoE) are focussed on retaining, utilizing and developing knowledge, whereas Shared Services Centers (SSC) are focussed on the efficient service provisioning to many users. The basic premise of SSC is that services that are provided by one organization or department can be provided to users with relatively little effort resulting in economics of scale and scope. In contrast to many SSCs the aim of CoE is not only service provisioning, but also to foster knowledge in the area of the CoE. Both SSCs and CoE are a strategic decision having a long term impact that cannot easily be undone. As such the decision, introduction and management needs dedicated attention.

In this chapter we focus on the challenges of combing CoE and SSC into a Shared Service Center of Excellence (SSCoE). We analyze the basic concepts and identify a case study at a financial organization, in which the operational risk management (ORM) function is organized as a SSCoE. ORM is aimed at the identification and mitigation of operational risks in an organization and its surroundings. ORM is a knowledge intensive process which needs the involvement of experts. ORM can be a continuous activity that is integrated in business processes like mortgage and other financial services, but also activity for a business such as the management of risks assets. For all these activities indepth and up-to-date expertise is necessary. As such, organizations establish a SSCoE as their operational risk management (ORM) to ensure the concentrating of these expertise in a single semi-autonomous business unit, The SSCoE is part of the primary processes as it performs tasks in these processes, as well has a support function of advice on ORM and keep track of the latest requirements and developments. By being involved in the process in case be viewed as a Shared Business Process Center (SBPC), whereas the other function can be viewed as a Shared Knowledge Center (SKC). The combination of both has the advantage that all activities in one way related to ORM are concentred in a single business unit.

The findings show that the ORM SSCoE provides a focal point for knowledge development, supporting implementation and operations. Although the benefits of a CoE are often easily be determined and explained, the introduction, realization and operation of CoE might be more difficult and the actual achievement of these benefits requires the overcoming of management challenges like resistance and having clear procedures. Once a CoE is introduced management attention is needed to ensure its sustainability. In particular a challenge is to keep the focus on both efficient service provision and utilization and development of knowledge It should be ensured that the CoE operates efficient and knowledge dissemination is outreached to all organizational parts. A SSCoE needs substantial governance mechanisms to ensure its proper functioning.

1 Introduction

Shared Services have been hailed as a way to improve efficiency and services levels at the same time[1], although creating them might be more difficult.[2] The introduction of Shared Services can provide a wide diversity of advantages. In many financial institutions activities are distributed over many departments resulting in a huge fragmentation. Often departments of the financial institutions are unaware of each other activities and are not working together leading to different points of view and fragmented responsibilities. This results not only into a large duplication of activities, but also in the fragmentation of expertise and knowledge over many departments. By bundling the development, maintenance and use of services, the costs can be shared among the users, innovations out-of-reach might become feasible, and the money freed can be used to improve service levels without any of the agencies having to give up their autonomy. As such all kinds of organizations are looking for possibilities to enhance the collaboration among these departments and one way of doing this is by bundling all activities and expertise in a single semi-autonomous unit. This is often called Shared Services Center (SSC) or Shared Services Organizations (SSOs).[3]

There are many definitions of SSCs in the literature.[4] *BERGERON*[5] defines a SSC as a "a collaborative strategy in which a subset of existing business functions are concentrated into a new semi-autonomous business unit that has a management structure designed to promoted efficiency, value generation, costs savings and improved service for the internal customers of the parent corporation."[6], whereas *JANSSEN/JOHA/ZUURMOND*[7] define a service as "the concentration of dispersed service provisioning activities in a single organizational entity."[8] All these definitions of Shared Services have slightly different nuances.[9] Despite the many definitions there is consensus about the essence of Shared Service Centers. A *Shared Service Center* is an organizational arrangement in which the provision of services are consolidated within a single area of an organization. It typically replaces arrangements where there is a duplication of efforts among different business units.

Shared Services vary regarding the nature and type of services being shared as well as the extent to which they are shared among users.[10] They may range from sharing simple IT services to sharing complete business processes. Shared Services exist in different areas include payroll processing, accounts payable, call centers, IT services and so on. SSC have become a common service delivery model in many organizations. Often SSCs support different ser-

---

1 Cf. *JANSSEN/JOHA* (2006).

2 Cf. *ULBRICH* (2006).

3 Cf. *ULRICH* (1995), *BERGERON* (2003), and *ULBRICH* (2009).

4 For an overview cf. *SINGH/CRAIKE* (2008), and *SCHULZ/BRENNER* (2010).

5 Cf. *BERGERON* (2003).

6 *BERGERON* (2003), p. 3.

7 Cf. *JANSSEN/JOHA/ZUURMOND* (2009).

8 *JANSSEN/JOHA/ZUURMOND* (2009), p. 16.

9 Cf. *QUINN/COOKE/KRIS* (2000), *BERGERON* (2003), *ULBRICH* (2006), and *LONGWOOD/HARRIS* (2007).

10 Cf. *BERGERON* (2003).

vices[11], are developed having a variety of motives in mind[12] resulting in a variety of different business models.[13] Hence, SSC should not be considered as a single business model, but as a range of business models.

Centers of Excellence (CoE) represent the best practice of managing knowledge.[14] CoE are aimed at leveraging knowledge and making them available to the rest of the organization.[15] CoE are a group of people who are in a same juridical entity. They can be on a single geographical location, but might also be distributed around the globe. Sometimes people are both part of the CoE and part of another department to ensure the cross-fertilization of knowledge among the enterprise. CoE have often a clear focus on a particular area and brings in members having different backgrounds and expertise to ensure that all knowledge that might be needed is available. Although CoE can have a formal structure and clear responsibilities, it can also have an informal structure in which the people from different organizational units work together in expertise groups. As outlined by *MOORE/BIRKINSHAW* this might be risky as the daily priorities might be given all the attention at the expense of knowledge building. Often CoE are complemented with expertise from outside organizations, like consultancy and research. Especially in organizations, in which limited expertise is available, the latter might be a desired strategy.

The aim of this chapter is to investigate the role of knowledge in Shared Services Centers and to understand the implementation challenges. We do this by investigating Shared Business Process Center and Shared Knowledge Center, which combination results in a Shared Service Center of Excellence (SSCoE). Next we investigate a case study in which both service provisioning and knowledge play a crucial role. This is followed by discussing the advantages and management challenges. Finally we draw conclusions.

2 Background

2.1 Shared Services

The rationale for Shared Services originated from various developments. First, technology enables to remotely provide services. Technology trends like cloud computing and Software-as-a-Service enable innovative forms of service provisioning. Another development is the increasing globalization, in which companies are distributed over many geographical locations resulting in more decentralization. Both results in the need for new forms of services provision, whereas retaining the knowledge inhouse and improve service provisioning. Utilizing, retaining and assimilation of knowledge is especially important in knowledge-intensive industries like the financial industry. There are several characteristics that make a SSC unique.[16]

---

11 Cf. *BERGERON* (2003).

12 Cf. *JANSSEN/JOHA* (2006).

13 Cf. *JOHA/JANSSEN* (2001).

14 Cf. *MOORE/BIRKINSHAW* (1998), p. 81.

15 Cf. *MOORE/BIRKINSHAW* (1998), p. 81.

16 Cf. *BERGERON* (2003), *SINGH/CRAIKE* (2008), and *SCHULZ/BRENNER* (2010).

First, there are several users which are often different departments). Second, there are predefined agreements made concerning what the SSC should deliver against what price. Third, the SSC has a certain amount of freedom to arrange and operate its own activities within the larger organizations context.

Shared services provide a range of different elements and can be viewed as a collection of different business models. SSCs can take many forms and descriptions vary in the literature.[17] Shared services can have different configurations, that might change during the design and implementation phase and should be viewed as a range of business models. The business model (BM) relates the organizational strategy and operational processes and systems.[18] *KEEN/QURESHI*[19] view business models as an instrument for addressing how to balance value between the customers and the provider. *AL-DEBEI/AVISON*[20] developed a unified business model conceptual framework based on a literature survey. Four primary BM dimensions, including value proposition, value architecture, value network and value finance, are distinguished by these authors. These elements form an ontological structure describing a business model.

The sharing of services is not easy and can be done in various ways. Each logic used to cluster services might result in other types of SSCs.[21] The modularization of service scan be based on type of products, functionality, expertise and information systems.[22]

1. *Products*, e.g. financial and insurance products;
2. *Functionality*, e.g. collecting payment or paying claims;
3. *Expertise*, e.g. operational risk management (ORM);
4. *Information Systems*, e.g. infrastructure.

These four criteria are not mutually exclusive. For example ORM can be viewed as a product that is delivered to other organizations, it can be viewed as a functionality that can be performance, as a type of expertise that is needed within banks and insurance companies. Whereas in the past often relatively simple services were shared, nowadays complete business processes are shared among users and operated by SSC. SSCs can consists of tens, hundreds or even more people. This makes it paramount to manage not only the service provisioning, but also to manage knowledge.

In contrast to Shared Services and SSCs, CoE are not primarily focussed on service provisioning. *MOORE/BIRKINSHAW*[23] define a CoE as "*a small group of individuals recognized for their leading-edge, strategically-valuable knowledge, and mandated to leverage and/or make that knowledge available throughout the global firm*".[24] CoE are focussed on retaining and

---

17 Cf. *JANSSEN/JOHA* (2006), *BORMAN* (2010), and *NIEHAVES/KRAUSE* (2010).

18 Cf. *HEDMAN/KALLING* (2003).

19 Cf. *KEEN/QURESHI* (2006).

20 Cf. *AL-DEBEI/AVISON* (2010).

21 Cf. *JANSSEN/JOHA* (2008).

22 Cf. *JANSSEN* (2008).

23 Cf. *MOORE/BIRKINSHAW* (1998).

24 *MOORE/BIRKINSHAW* (1998). p. 81.

utilizing knowledge for the organization. In our view this does not have to consider a small group and it is not necessary to distribute knowledge throughout the whole organizations, as one reasons for a CoE can be the concentrations of this. Instead of distributing the knowledge in the firms, a CoE might be focussed on concentrating it with the SSC. CoE combined with SSC has both a focus on service provisioning and on knowledge and is called a Shared Service Center of Excellence (SSCoE). We will discuss both elements in the next subsections.

2.2 Shared Business Process Center

Business processes are sequences of tasks resulting in a notable outcome. Shared services can be used as part of business processes. Figure 1 shows that by unbundling activities from several business processes (top) and concentrating them in a Shared Business Process Center (SBPC) (bottom) these activities are performed by the SSC. Once such a center is created it can be used to provide services to other business processes. A SBPC enables the creation of flexibility for developing new business processes, as new business processes can be constructed from existing services. This is similar to the concept of Service-oriented architectures, in which new processes can be created by utilizing readable existing (technical) services. Shared Business Process (SBP) can potentially be used as a solution to overcome fragmentation of responsibilities by ensuring that all similar activities are concentrated in one accountable business unit.

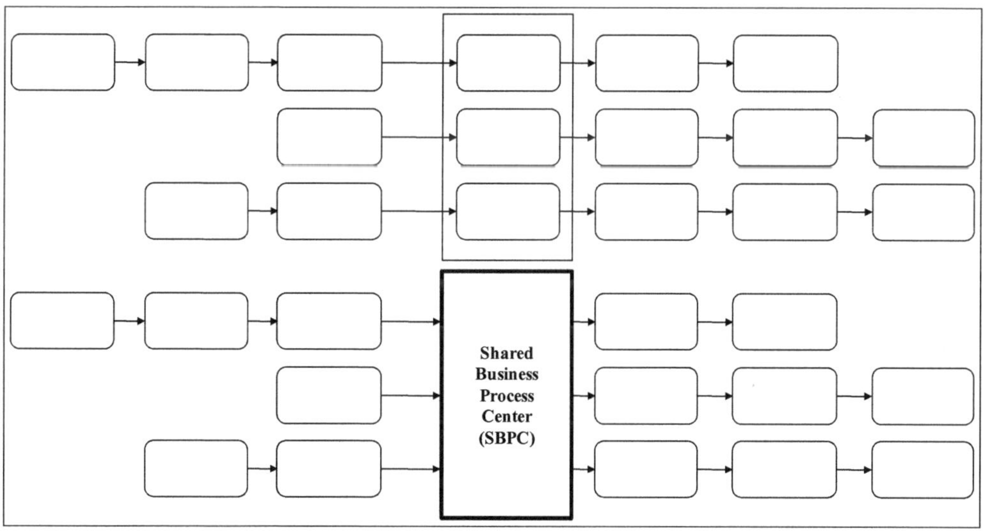

Figure 1: Shift towards Shared Business Process Center

SBPC can be viewed as management structure for better alignment of the organizational structure with the strategic objectives. In the 1960s and 1970s this resulted in more centralized organizational structures to profit from economies of scale and scope, whereas in the 1980s and 1990s more decentralized forms are explored to stay close to the customer needs. SSC can be viewed as a hybrid model between centralization and decentralization, as SSC tries to capture the advantages of both centralization and decentralization resulting in the combination of advantages.[25] The aim of a SSC is to retain close to the user and react quickly to changes, while at the same time benefiting from economies of scale and scope.

2.3 Shared Knowledge Center

In today's global economy knowledge utilizations has become more important. SKCs are aimed at concentrating and sharing knowledge. In figure 2 it is shown that the expertise is unbundled (left) from the departments and concentrated into a SKC (right). Experts that were formerly part of a line department have now become part of a SSC. The advantage is that all experts can now be found in a single organizational unit which makes it easier to assimilate knowledge and extending the current knowledge or building new knowledge.

Additionally, all experts together represent usually more and diverse expertise than a single expert has. They can share practices and knowledge easier discuss with each other. Moreover, they might utilize the same decision support systems, instead of having their own systems. Furthermore they can step in if necessary. If somebody is ill or does not have the specific expertise they can be replaced by one of the other experts. Finally, they might have more career opportunities. Within their previous departments they are often only one member of a small experts group, whereas in a CoE they are with many experts and they can be more easily promoted.

The drawback of the construction is that the expertise is detached from the line drawback. The connection with the former departments might become more loosely over time. Therefore, job rotating and having governance mechanisms contributing to the connection between the CoE and the business departments is crucial to overcome this drawback.

25 Cf. *HODGKINSON* (1996), and *JANSSEN/JOHA* (2004).

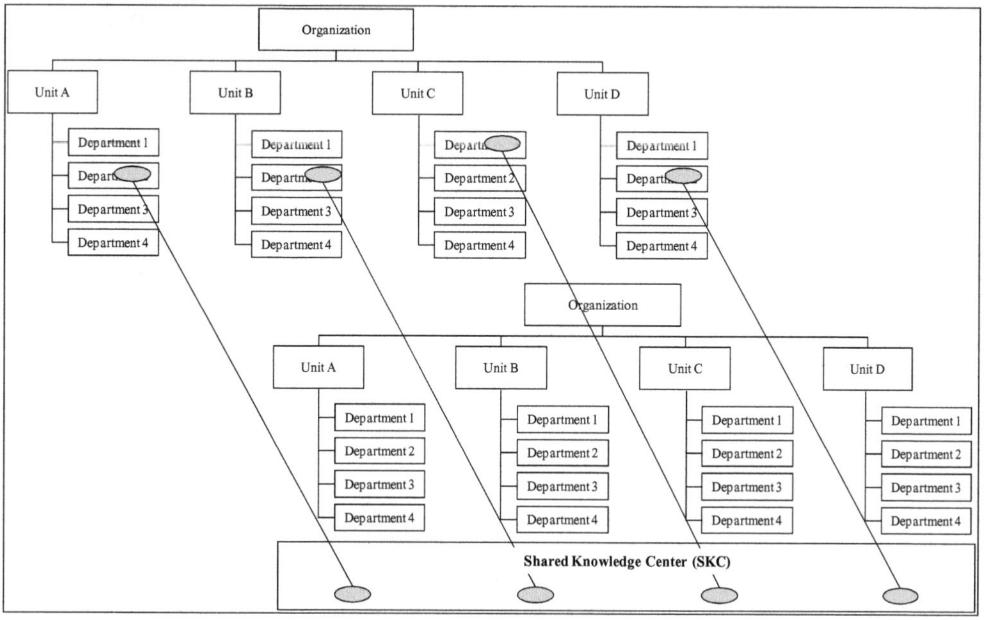

Figure 2: Shift towards Shared Knowledge Center

2.4 Shared Service Centers of Excellence

Shared Service Centers of Excellence (SSCoE) are aimed at leveraging knowledge and making it available to the rest of the organization.[26] CoE are a group of people who are in a same juridical entity. They have the freedom to organize them, and the organization has stated expectation concerning their contribution to the organization. Although they do not provide operational services to the organizations, they make their knowledge available. As such there are many similarities between SSCs and CoEs. In particular CoE can be arranged as a kind of Shared Service Centers (SSC) in which formerly fragmented expertise is bundled. Furthermore, they might also provide services.

In the next section a case study will be investigated in which SBPC and SKC are combined in a single center.

[26] Cf. *MOORE/BIRKINSHAW* (1998).

3 Case study – Operational Risk Management Center

3.1 Background

Operational Risk Management (ORM) is often viewed as a core activity of financial institutions as it influence it long term viability. Over the last decades a number of investments have been made in ORM at various levels of the organizations. Organizations are looking for solutions to improve their ORM and reducing their costs at the same time. ORM can be defined as "the identification and mitigation of operational risks in an organization and its surroundings"[27]. There is consensus about the basic elements of a definition of an operational risk, i.e. the risk of direct or indirect loss resulting from inadequate or failed internal processes, people and systems or from external events.[28]

The need for a professional ORM functions for banking and insurance companies become clear after the failures of companies like Barings and Enron. This resulted in the introduction of all kind of legislation like Basel II. Compliance to these new legislation rules required that ORM should be implemented as a separate function within organizations. In the company under study this resulted in the implementation of ORM in the various business units of the organizations. The business units took their own approach and ensured that they had the necessary expertise and procedures in place. After a while the management of the large insurance firm in the Netherlands was confronted with different and even contradicting recommendations as visualized in figure 3. Eight different departments of this financial institution approached ORM for the four primary processes (making offers, accepting, mutating and damage handling) from their own perspective.

The current situation in many financial institutions is characterized by a hierarchical structure organized around business functions, which are often geographically fragmented. The different departments act autonomous and hardly communicate with each other resulting in fragmentation of tasks and responsibilities. Moreover, due to this fragmentation it is difficult to obtain an integral view on ORM. As a result the management incidentally received eight different reports, which might include different and even opposing recommendations. All this resulted in unclear decision making processes, assignment of resources and a distrust in the recommendations given by experts. Reports from certain departments were considered to be more credible and received more attention than the reports of other departments. Furthermore, this resulted in the undesired situation that the amount of attention a department received was often important for the assignment of resources: the more attention (priority) the more resources. Hence, each department tried to get as much attention as possible, which was not based on the expertise available. In times of economic recession this was even amplified due to ever decreasing budgets.

27 *GRINSVEN* (2007).

28 Cf. *RMA* (2000).

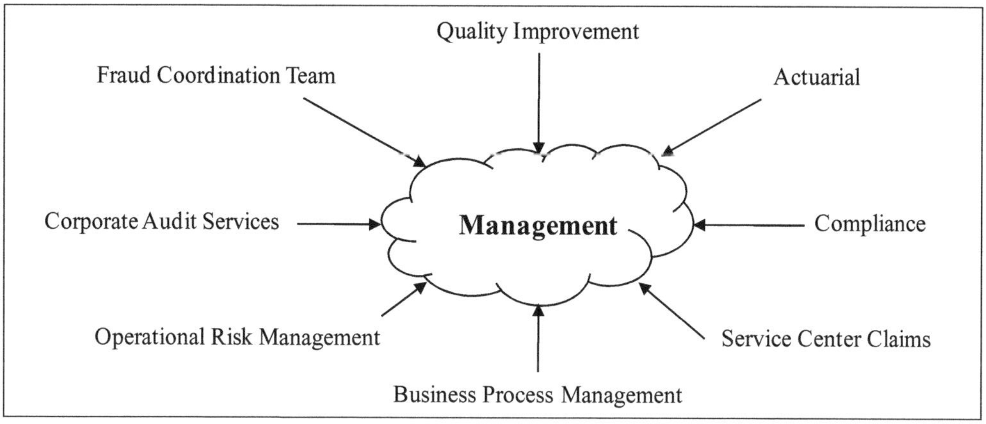

Figure 3: *Overview of reporting business function to management*[29]

3.2 Implementation

The organization undertook a major reorganization by introducing a SBP in combination with the concentrating of ORM knowledge. The goal of this reorganization was to deal with the difference in recommendation and make better use of the knowledge within the company. The approach taken was to create a Shared Service Center of Excellence by the unbundling and concentration of business processes in an autonomous business unit. In these processes confidential information concerning operational risks often plays an important role and companies want to retain this information in-house. A SSC as SBP was not only expected to deal with the fragmentation, but also to provide economies of scale while at the same time retaining experiences within the organization and ensure high levels of information security by keeping information within the SBP. The reorganization was motivated by a document explaining the current problems and benefits of the desired organizations. Based on this, the SBP for ORM was introduced at the large insurance firm. Within the ORM-SBP the knowledge was concentrated and the formerly fragmented field of responsibilities was concentrated in the SSC as schematically already depicted in figure 2. This ORM-SBP ensures that one recommendation is presented to the management and the risks are clarified and a uniform decision is made based on the integral considerations of many factors.

The introduction of the SSCoE caused a lot of resistance. Line managers felt that their control of the ORM function was threatened and the size of their departments will be reduced as persons would be transferred from their own department of the SSCoE. During the reorganization process it was initially not clear for all persons who would be transferred to the SSCoE and which would remain in the organization. This resulted in speculation about who was (not) going to move to the SSCoE. Furthermore, the reorganization was also aimed at reducing the number of employees resulting in speculations about who was going to stay and who would be fired. All this contributed to inefficiency, resistance and uncertainty by the staff.

29 GRINSVEN (2010).

After the introduction of the SSCoE it became clear that the embedding within the existing process was not well-designed. Although it was clear which business processes would be executed by the SSCoE it was at the beginning not clear when a process would be initiated. The responsibilities of the SSCoE and the inputs and outputs of the SSCoE were not clearly defined. Over time it became clear that it was not defined which knowledge was necessary.

After being in operation for a time it became clear that visibility of the SSCoE was not arranged properly. While the SSCoE is well known to the persons directly before and after the activity they performed in the business process, they were not visible or known by others within the business process and a large number of business units were ignored by them resulting in a local implementation of the ORM function. Another reason mentioned by the interviewees for the local implementation of the ORM function was that the SSCoE was considered as bureaucratic and disconnected from the local situation in which the business unites operated. They were merely interested in their own tasks without having an understanding of the end-to-end process and the customer needs. They were more and more focussed on retaining their expertise, conducting the ORM activities and ensuring compliance with tasks, instead of making business.

3.3 Challenges

The case study illustrates typically challenges when introducing a SSCoE. The SSCoE was introduced as a way of better exploiting its geographically dispersed expertise. While the advantages of the SSCoE model are clear the management challenges are significant. To accomplish the objectives it is important to define how the SSCoE should look like, how the relationship with the line departments will be maintained and a strategy to deal with resistance is necessary, as the shift in balance of power can lead to large counterforce's.

The implementation process of the SSCs can be roughly divided into three main stages, imitating, implementing and operating stages. During the (1) *initiating* stage the main decision concerning how to reallocate the human resources and systems are made. During the (2) *realization* stage the decisions that are made in the business case are realized. In the stages, *operating* stage the SSC should be functioning and supporting the day-to-day operations.

Table 1 clearly illustrates that implementation challenges can be found during the whole implementation life-cycle. During the realization there is a huge risk that the focus is on making the service provisioning work and that the knowledge part is neglected. This might easily result in persons leaving the center or even the organization. The combination of focus on operational functions and making use of knowledge has a tension. The first results often in a focus on smooth functioning, well-defined processes that are efficient, whereas the latter requires unstructured processes, freedom to develop knowledge and ultimately resulting in competitive advantage. Competitive advantage is created by better understanding the risks, the possible impact and developing new products and mechanisms to manage ORM. The combination of efficiency and competitive advantage focus might be viewed as inherently conflicting. Nevertheless the case shows that the combination is useful as the knowledge is used in the operational processes and in this way feedback is gained about the usage, which results in the development of new knowledge. Management attention should be given to overcome these challenges. A center needs substantial governance mechanisms to ensure its proper functioning.

Implementation stage	Typical challenges
1. Initiating stage	➢ No clear problem analyses and no clear understanding of the need and use of knowledge ➢ Too optimistic business case ➢ Unclear requirement ➢ No change management approaches ➢ No top-management commitment ➢ Lack of vision ➢ No sense of urgency
2. Realization stage	➢ Resistance of people ➢ Lack of commitment ➢ No clear processes and procedures ➢ Unclear division of responsibilities ➢ Lack of budget for unforeseen circumstances ➢ No communication ➢ Moving away from people ➢ Shift towards operational activities instead of retaining knowledge
3. Operating stage	➢ Retaining knowledge ➢ Connecting to the business organization ➢ Balancing operating services and assimilating and developing knowledge ➢ No communication between departments ➢ Shifting ambition which needs to reconsideration of the implemented arrangement ➢ Retaining knowledge and job rotation

Table 1: Overview of implementation challenges

The operational risk management center provides a focal point for knowledge development, supporting implementation and operations. The interaction and services exchange and sharpen the expertise through is usage. As such feedback on the outcomes and decision and ensuring a closed loop learning is essential. By bundling the experts in SSCoE there exists a wide range of opportunities that experts learn from each other. Experts combine and build on prior experience to create new techniques or ideas. In addition individual team members might lose the knowledge over time unless it is somehow institutionalized in the system. Institutionalizing is also necessary for transferring knowledge to new employees. In our case study only a few persons were updating their knowledge, whereas others were primarily providing services and utilizing the knowledge of these persons. Thus, we conclude that SSCoE might improve the focus to harness the experts' knowledge and at the same time to warrant operational efficiency in the execution of business processes.

4 Conclusions

Shared Service Centers (SSCs) are a way to provide similar services to a large number of users in this way advantaging of economies of scale and avoiding fragmentation. Centers of Excellence (CoE) are a particular type of SSC which is aimed at concentrating knowledge. Combining them results in a Shared Service Center of Excellence (SSCoE) business model. A SSCoE can solve the problem of the fragmented allocation of tasks and functions and at the same time use knowledge as a source for competitive advantage, as was done for Operational Risk Management (ORM) in our case study. A SSCoE combines a Shared Business Process Center (SBPC) and a Shared Knowledge Center (SKC).

SSCoE as a SBPC bundles and concentrates the primary business processes in an autonomous business unit, responsibilities are concentrated and the management is provided with one, uniform, recommendation concerning ORM. This resulted in substantial economies of scale and scope. In our case study the SSC has also the function as a SKC, which is able to answer questions related to ORM. A SSCoE is created by combining both the SBP and SKC model. The combination has the advantage that by sharing of services efficiency gains are achieved, whereas by sharing knowledge competitive advantage can be created. The main challenge is to develop, leverage, and disseminate knowledge among the experts which should be facilitated by an environment stimulating this.

The introduction of CoE represents a decision having a big impact and should be realized based on a reorganization process like in our case study. Challenges are found in the introduction, realization and operation phase. Thus, during the whole life cycle management attention is necessary and the type of organizational arrangement might need to be changed. Challenges might have a social, but also a more technical nature and might include resistance, sense of urgency, lack of procedures and alienation with business. Once these challenges are overcome experts' knowledge can be harnessed and operational efficiency gained.

Abbreviations

CoE	Centers of Excellence
ORM	Operational Risk Management
SBPC	Shared Business Process Center
SKC	Shared Knowledge Center
SSC	Shared Services Center
SSCoE	Shared Service Center of Excellence
SSO	Shared Services Organizations

References

Al-Debie, M. M./Avison, D. E. (2010): Developing a Unified Framework of the Business Model Concept, in: European Journal of Information Systems, Vol. 19, No. 3, pp. 359–376.

Bergeron, B. (2003): Essentials of Shared Services, Hoboken (NJ) 2003.

Borman, M. (2010): Characteristics of a Successful Shared Services Centre in the Australian Public Sector, in: Transforming Government: People, Process and Policy, Vol. 4, Nr. 3, pp. 220–231.

Grinsven, J. H. M. (2007): Improving Operational Risk Management, Doctoral Dissertation, Delft University of Technology, Delft 2007.

Hedman, J./Kalling, T. (2003): The Business Model Concept: Theoretical Underpinnings and Empirical Illustrations, in: European Journal of Information Systems, Vol. 12, No. 1, pp. 49–59.

Hodgkison, S. L. (1996): The Role of the Corporate IT Function in the Federal IT Organization, in: *Earl, M. J.* (ed.), Information Management: The organizational dimension, Oxford, pp. 247–269.

Janssen, M. (2008): Exploring the Service-oriented Enterprise: Drawing Lessons From a Case Study, Paper presented at the Hawaii International Conference on System Sciences (HICSS-41), Hawaii (US) 2008.

Janssen, M./Joha, A. (2006): Motives for Establishing Shared Service Centers in Public Administrations, in: International Journal of Information Management, Vol. 26, No. 2, pp. 102–116.

Janssen, M./Joha, A. (2008): Emerging Shared Service Organizations and the Service-oriented Enterprise: Critical Management Issues, in: Strategic Outsourcing: An International Journal, Vol. 1, No. 1, pp. 35–49.

Janssen, M./Joha, A./Zuurmond, A. (2009): Simulation and Animation for Adopting Shared Services: Evaluating and Comparing Alternative Arrangements, in: Government Information Quarterly, Vol. 26, No. 1, pp. 15–24.

Janssen, M./Joha, A. (2011): Types of Shared Services Business Models in Public Administration, 12th Annual International Conference on Digital Government Research (d.g.o 2011), Digital Government Innovation in Challenging Times, University of Maryland, College Park MD, June 12–15, pp. 26–35.

Keen, P. W. G./Qureshi, S. (2006): Organizational Transformation Through Business Models. A Framework for Business Model Design, Paper presented at the Proceedings of the 39th Hawaii International Conference on Information Systems, Hawaii (US) 2006.

Longwood, J./Harris, R. G. (2007): Leverage Business Process Outsourcing Lessons to Build a Successful Shared Business Service Organisation, Stamford 2007.

Moore, K./Birkinshaw, J. (1998): Competitiveness and Global Leadership in the 21st Century, in: The Academy of Management Executive, Vol. 12, No. 4, pp. 81–92.

Niehaves, B./Krause, A. (2010): Shared Service Strategies in Local Government – A Multiple Case Study Exploration, in: Transforming Government: People, Process and Policy, Vol. 4, No. 3, p. 266–279.

QUINN, B./COOKE, R./KRIS, A. (2000): Shared Services: Mining for Corporate Gold, Upper Saddle River (NJ) 2000.

RMA (2000): Operational Risk: The Next Frontier in: The Journal of Lending & Credit Risk Management, Vol. 82, No. 6, pp. 38–44.

SCHULZ, V./BRENNER, W. (2010): Characteristics of Shared Service Centers, in: Transforming Government: People, Process & Policy, Vol. 4, No. 3, pp. 210–219.

SINGH, P. J./CRAIKE, A. (2008): Shared Services: Towards a More Holistic Conceptual Definition, in: International Journal of Business Information Systems, Vol. 3, No. 3, pp. 217–230.

ULBRICH, F. (2006): Improving Shared Service Implementation: Adopting Lessons From the BPR Movement, in: Business Process Management Journal, Vol. 12, No. 2, pp. 191–205.

ULBRICH, F. (2009): Implementing Centers of Excellence: A Case Study. Paper presented at the AMCIS 2009 San Francisco (CA) 2009.

ULRICH, D. (1995): Shared Services: From Vogue to Value, in: Human Resource Planning, Vol. 18, No. 3, pp. 12–23.

Future Trends in Finance Shared Services Organisations

FRANK HELBING, THILO RAU and *ALEXANDER RIEDEL*

KPMG AG Wirtschaftsprüfungsgesellschaft

Executive Summary

Shared Services Organisations are viewed as an important driver to improve efficiency and achieve cost-savings for finance and accounting functions. In theory, Shared Services provide a clear set of benefits: Cost reductions, better services and increasing efficiency of resources. Today, more than 90 % of all large multinational Western companies already operate Shared Service Centres (SSCs).

In recent years, global competition has increased: Irrespectively of what markets a company dominated ten years ago, many former market leaders lost their top position against innovative companies with flexible internal structures. These flexible structures can be supported by Shared Services Organisations. Four main drivers have been discovered that shape the future of Shared Services: Globalisation & complexity, profitability despite cost pressures, demographics, and advances in information technology. First, if companies do business in more than 150 countries, then approximately 150 local accounting and tax regulations have to be met, which naturally drives complexity. Second, expenses regarding finance and accounting activities offer only a low economic benefit because a customer is not willing to pay for these services. Third, viewing the demographic side, China's and India's population and their number of college graduates will increase, while Germany's population is already decreasing and the number of graduates cannot keep pace with China. Fourth, information technology becomes more powerful, enabling Centres to process and store more data. This also leads to the application of cutting edge data analysis tools to support process analysis and optimisation efforts. Improved collaboration tools and faster networks enable SSCs to source services from the best possible location internally as well as from the cloud externally. An increase of profitability through economies of scale can be facilitated by bundling and centralising processes from many business units into one or a few big Centres, which naturally provides huge optimisation potential. Additionally, offshoring Shared Services plays an important role in achieving labour arbitrage gains, as finance and accounting related processes are labour intensive, but easily learnt and executed. However, with increasing IT capabilities, more and more process activities can be automated, which leads to a decreasing share of manual work. As a result, the overall impact of labour arbitrage effects is declining.

Shared Services will become a strategic decision for C-level executives: Keeping services in-house if a critical mass can be achieved and the process design leads to competitive advantages, or radically outsource the process to business process outsourcing (BPO) providers to achieve significant cost savings. However, BPO providers are generally seen as barriers to process innovation. Overall, the share of IT costs will switch positions with personnel costs at SSCs. During the next decades, additionally the share of skilled staff will increase, as more and more competence-based decisions, which cannot be automated, will be moved to the Centres. Attracting and managing bright people with the optimal finance and accounting skills will be the challenge for SSCs. As modularisation of processes from the cloud increase, the location of the Shared Service Centres will not be as important as it is today. The SSC can then source several services from other providers, which provides flexibility and scalability.

The evolution of Shared Services can therefore be summed up as follows: The responsibility and governance of finance processes will be fully taken away from the business units of the parent company and be transferred to the Shared Services Organisations. The parent company will only be concerned about receiving the right data with the desired quality at the right time at acceptable costs.

1 Introduction and Description of Purpose

1.1 Status quo of Shared Services Organisations

In recent years, Shared Services Organisations have been viewed as an important driver to improve efficiency and achieve cost-savings for back-office functions like finance and accounting, human resources, and procurement. *BERGERON*[1] already assigns Shared Services a strategic management function, both for the parent company and for itself:

> "Shared Services is a collaborative strategy in which a subset of existing business functions is concentrated into a new, semiautonomous business unit that has a management structure designed to promote efficiency, value generation, cost savings, and improved service for the internal customers of the parent corporation [...]."[2]

From a different perspective, Shared Services are nothing more than an internal reduction of duplication of processes and facilities as well as sharing of assets.[3]

The main task of a Shared Services Organisation is to execute a process centrally. Simply put, processes are a set of activities that are pursued to accomplish a specific objective. There are complex and cross-functional processes like the end-to-end process purchase-to-pay, which starts at issuing a request note for a certain good or for services, and finally ends at paying the vendor. This set involves several stakeholders of different organisational units, in general the business unit, such as the purchasing department and the accounts payable department. Processes can also have a narrow focus, like invoice handling, which can be a process itself, but also a sub process of the aforementioned purchase-to-pay process.

During the 1980's, manufacturing companies started building their production facilities offshore to gain labour arbitrage effects. Over the past two decades, this form of globalisation began to transform service industries as well. With increasing technological advantages and plummeting telecommunication costs, many service jobs and back-office functions and process parts have been internationalised, sending this kind of work to China, India, the Philippines, and other countries with low wages.[4]

In theory, Shared Services provide a clear set of benefits for the parent company: Cost reduction, better services, reduction of tied management capacity, and bundling activities in one profit centre by increasing efficiency and economies of scale, while also decreasing personnel requirements. The growth during the past 20 years has been extraordinary. Approximately 40 % of all S&P 500 companies ran a Finance function SSC in 1995. Nowadays, it is expected that more than 90 % of all large multinational Western companies gain advantages through Shared Service,[5] usually operating more than one centre on a global scale and spreading across continents. The main question this article provides an answer to is the following: As more than 90 % of large corporations already have Shared Services, what will be next?

---

1 Cf. *BERGERON* (2003).

2 *BERGERON* (2003), p. 3.

3 Cf. *SAKO* (2010), p. 28.

4 Cf. *FARRELL* (2004), p. 82 et seqq., and cf. *DAVENPORT* (2005), p. 100 et seq.

5 Cf. *DRESSLER* (2007), p. 19.

Looking at it from a different perspective: What has to be next for Shared Service Centres to maintain the parent company's competitiveness over the next decades? How can parent companies utilise their SSCs better to gain competitive advantages?

1.2 Scope and Purpose

Shared Services are usually linked to transactional processes, and – in general – without a visible outcome for the external customer or supplier of the company. Even though they have a major impact on service quality, these processes are generally seen as overhead cost which result in general and administrative (G&A) expenses on the income statement. In other words, it affects money that is spent on running the business rather than production, selling and marketing. Such processes are, for instance, finance processes like purchase-to-pay, human resource processes such as payroll services, or information technology-related processes such as infrastructure or application management. Typically, transactional processes consist of simple and recurring activities that can be easily learnt and executed within a short period of time.[6]

G&A costs take a significant share of a company's expenses. More importantly, this share has remained steady between approximately 6 and 7 % of the total sales revenue at German DAX companies over the past 12 years, excluding the banking and insurance sectors. At the same time, however, companies were able to reduce their cost of goods sold (COGS) by approximately 3 to 4 %, from 70 to 66 %. To explain the impact in a simplified way: If an average revenue of 40 billion EUR per year is assumed, a decrease in G&A cost of absolute 1 % equals an annual savings potential of 400 million EUR. Figure 1 shows the relative development of G&A versus COGS as of 2006.

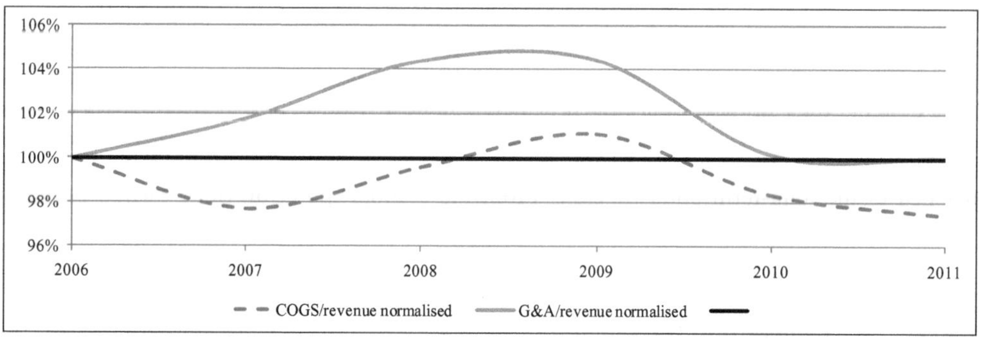

Figure 1: Development of G&A and COGS at DAX30 companies

The main scope of this article is to analyse the future of Finance Shared Services. Today, finance processes still require a lot of human interaction and effort to be executed in a timely manner and in a desired quality. During the past two decades, companies were interested in bundling activities of many business units within one or many Shared Service Centres, usually within the region of the affected business units' locations. Such finance processes are typically the accounts payable process, which processes and pays a vendor's invoice; the ac-

6 Cf. *DRESSLER* (2007), p. 23.

counts receivable process, which issues bills to customers and ensures the customer pays the invoice; and the reporting process, which aggregates the company's financial data into a consolidated financial statement. These processes are transactional by nature, and will be the main scope of this article.

Future needs for Shared Services Organisations are not solely dependent on the specifics of the company itself, such as business model, strategic direction, size and location. Furthermore, this article assumes that factors not under managerial control will shape the future more significantly than those under control. Management actions of the next decades are influenced and will be mainly driven by external factors. The authors provide a direction for Shared Services Organisations managers to proactively shape the future of the organisation. This article proposes that the future of Shared Services Organisations will strongly be influenced by three external and one internal driver, as shown in figure 2: Globalisation & complexity, demographics and advances in information technology on the external side, and the natural urge to increase profitability as an internal driver.

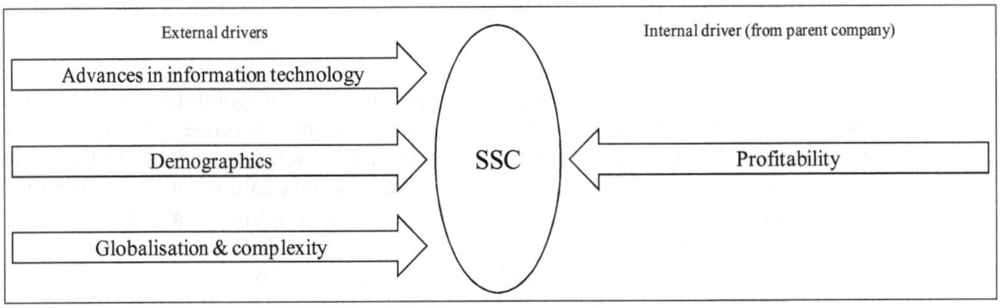

Figure 2: Drivers that shape the future of SSCs

This article is strictly to be distinguished from traditional and commonly known maturity and/or lifecycle models for Shared Services. Maturity is per *Oxford dictionary* definition a state of being fully grown or developed, which is logically followed by a decline. This article argues that Shared Service Centres have to adapt to their environment. Since environments are, have always been, and will always be volatile and changing; a mature state cannot be reached in the long-term point of view. From the authors' point of view, Shared Services Organisations will follow an evolution during the next decades, and not a lifecycle's path.

1.3 Conceptual Background

This article presents a framework for the evolution of Shared Service Centres developed from economical influences. The development of this framework evolved from research concerned with analysing both theoretical and practical influences on Shared Services. Chapter 2 provides an overview of the drivers from figure 2. The next section then outlines the implications of the drivers for future trends. The drivers have been set into a context from which the corresponding trend is then derived. Throughout that section, the implications of the several drivers affect the trend to a greater or lesser extent. The following table 1 provides a matrix that connects trends and drivers with the corresponding context of how the drivers influence the particular trend. Within each section management implications are presented at the end. The article concludes with a brief summary of the trends as well as an outlook.

Trend	Context	Globalisation and Complexity	Profitability	Demographic Developments	Advances in Information Technologies
Centralisation into Shared Services	Achieve economies of scale	✓	✓		
Offshoring and Outsourcing of Shared Services	Gain labour arbitrage		✓		✓
Shared Services Become a Strategic Decision	Maintain competitiveness	✓	✓		
Process Automation and Controlling rather than Execution	Increase automation rate		✓		✓
Shared Services as Shared Competence	Process competence topics	✓		✓	
Shared Services from the Cloud	Source from the best location			✓	✓

Table 1: Overview of trends and corresponding drivers

Therefore, the aim of this article is to develop a detailed understanding of the future challenges and naturally evolving trends that Shared Service Centre managers and C-level executives of the corresponding parent company have to consider. The drivers and trends described lead to an understanding of general challenges and potential strategies for addressing these challenges.

2 Drivers that Shape the Future of Shared Services Organisations

2.1 Globalisation and Complexity

Competition these days is not like it used to be: simple constellations such as "big corporation A versus big corporation B versus big corporation C," or "Europe versus America versus Japan". Irrespectively of what markets a company dominates today, it appears to be highly likely that it will not dominate the same market over the next ten years. Just imagine companies like Sony or Nokia that have produced world class products in certain areas and are currently facing huge economic challenges. As it appears, competition is now driven by small, innovative, and in some cases even unorthodox companies who better understand customers by looking far beyond what is possible today. Just think of companies like *Apple*, *Google*, or *HTC*, which today produce faster than ever known, matching customer requirements better than others do. Remember what these companies were doing one to two decades ago: *Apple* was close to bankruptcy, *Google* had not even been founded, and *HTC* was a white label manufacturer of cell phones for companies like *Deutsche Telekom* and *Vodafone*.

Today, customers have almost unlimited access to information on products and services worldwide through the Internet. Global connectivity of data sources has driven globalisation for the past two decades. That trend is unlikely to pause or even stop. Markets are as transparent as they have never been before. This new transparency is even more important for companies acting in mature industries, where similar products and/or services are compared on prices rather than on features. For example, more and more companies are gaining advantage because of centralised purchasing departments with huge global supplier databases. These databases contain almost daily information about products, prices, and – as best practice – a vendor rating. If screws are cheaper in Mexico than in Brazil, they'll be almost automatically bought in Mexico. Global contracts are being managed centrally, especially for goods or services that can easily be substituted.

There are generally two drivers of complexity in organisations. On one hand, there is the complexity of the organisation itself, and on the other hand, the complexity of cross-national regulations. Hence, one could argue that the complexity of the structure reflects the complexity of the environment.[7] For example, if a company manufactures just a few products and sells them to a well-specified market, the organisational structure should be quite simple. However, globalisation will force more and more organisations to cross national borders during the next decade. For example, *Siemens* is active in about 190 countries today,[8] whereas currently the *United Nations* accounts for 193 member states.[9] In other words, companies like *Siemens* have to take into account up to 190 local reporting, tax and tariff regulations. Nonetheless, there are small and medium-sized businesses which operate in probably a handful or up to 50 different countries. Undoubtedly, that global trade will develop further, and smaller firms are surely following bigger companies like *Siemens* and increase the number of countries from which they source and/or where they sell products, although unlikely at an extent like *Siemens*. By contrast, international standards like IFRS are becoming more and more accepted, thereby replacing local standards. Furthermore, transparency increases by global access to publications and sources regarding local standards. Both developments support a central management of growing organisational complexity.

Global economy is very volatile and competitive through the tight connection of many markets. A market's volatility is primarily described by fluctuations in demand and changes in customers' preferences. To remain competitive, the pace at which organisations update their processes and internal routines must be adapted to the market's volatility. For companies acting in these dynamic markets, Shared Service approaches appear very valuable to maintain competiveness and to handle complexity.[10]

2.2 Profitability

General and administrative expenses represent a large portion of a company's overall expenses. At the same time, however, these expenses offer only a low economic benefit because a customer is not willing to pay for these services. A company's goal is therefore to minimize G&A expenditures. However, these processes still require much human interaction today, and

---

7 Cf. *THOMPSON* (1967), p. 70.

8 Cf. online *SIEMENS* (2012).

9 Cf. online *UN* (2012).

10 Cf. *AKSIN* (2008), p. 243.

therefore a relatively large number of people. Especially in the context of economic downturns and increasing volatility, fixed costs are a big challenge to administrative functions because high personnel costs in good economic times remain high personnel costs in economically bad times, during which their portion of overall costs even increases. Additionally, the finance function has not changed much over the past decades. The age structure is usually quite disadvantageous for many companies: Quite a few people are working in accounting departments for more than a decade. If an average annual wage increase of just 2 % is assumed, it naturally results in 50 % higher labour costs after 20 years. However, given the complexity of the activities, highly skilled staff is required to execute many administrative tasks these days. In general, corporations need to be able to quickly adjust their administrative tasks to economic requirements. An in-house flexibility to handle volatile workloads is advantageous to corporations. However, it should be clear that in this context, flexibility obviously implies more services at less cost assuring faster response times.

2.3 Demographic Developments

Demographic change and its impacts are challenges that every company has to deal with in the upcoming decades. For instance, there is a shrinking, older population combined with an extraordinary deep impact on the available labour force in Germany. Its population reached its peak at 82.5 million people in 2003. During the last decade, this number decreased slightly by 1 % to 81.7 million people in 2010. This is just the beginning of a trend that will last for the next fifty years. According to the Federal Office of Statistics in Germany, the German population will be approximately 70 million in 2050. This is a drop of about 13 %. Because of the demographic change, the impact on the available labour force is even wider than the general impact on the population. In 2010, the German labour force was about 41.5 million people. This number will decrease by 28 % to approximately 29.5 million in 2050.[11] Taking a global look on population growth, the development in Germany is quite similar to the overall situation in Europe. Over the next 40 years, the European population will decrease by 3 % from 810 million in 2010 to 790 million people in 2050.

On the other hand, the population of the United States will increase by 30 % to 404 million. Asia expects growth rates of 25 % to 5.100 billion people during the same time period. In other words, Asia's population is expected to be 6.5 times larger than the European population by 2050, and up to 12 times larger than the population of the United States.[12] The Asian development is mainly driven by China and India. Between 2010 and 2050, China's population will increase by 6 %, from 1.338 billion to 1.417 billion. India's growth is even more impressive: Starting at 1.171 billion in 2010, India will pass China between 2020 and 2030, reaching a population of 1.614 billion people by 2050.[13]

---

11 Cf. online *Statistisches Bundesamt* (2012a).

12 Cf. online *Worldbank Research Center* (2012).

13 Cf. online *Worldbank Research Center* (2012).

2.4 Advances in Information Technologies

IT infrastructure can be seen as a basis for the establishment of Shared Services Organisations because it shapes and influences a company's processes and, more often, even requires an organisation to adjust its processes to meet the logic of the underlying IT system.[14] Hence, the development of the IT infrastructure and the performance of the networks are key indicators and will drive the idea of Shared Services. There are three main "laws" which direct the development of information technology for Shared Services Organisations.

First, according to *GERALD BUTTERS* of the *Lucent's Optical Network Group*, the amount of data coming out of an optical fibre doubles every nine months. This statement, also known as Butters' law of photonics, describes the rapid progress happening in the network industry.[15] In other words, the cost of transmitting data decreases by half every nine months. Therefore, the opportunity of shifting large amounts of data across countries and company entities is possible and will continue to increase during the years to come.

Second, based on observations of network speed and capacity, an outstanding rise can indeed be recognised. But while shifting and sending large amounts of data, one needs the ability to store them. Similarly to the item described above, there is another technology rule which is called *KRYDER*'s law. The focus of *KRYDER*'s law is development of disk drives. Since disk drives were introduced in 1956, the density of information it can record has swelled from a paltry 2,000 bits to 100 billion bits per square inch.[16] This is an increase of 50 million times, and the development is not likely to end anytime soon. Or in other words, the capacity per US dollar spent is doubling every 18 to 24 months. These days, modern technologies such as cloud storage enable companies to store almost unlimited amounts of data.

Third, there is the issue of processing power and the ability to standardise and automate processes through IT. According to *GORDON MOORE*, co-founder of *Intel*, the number of transistors on a chip roughly doubles every two years.[17] This expectation, expressed nearly 40 years ago, is well-known as "*MOORE*'s law". Over the years, a debate has been arisen as to when the time will have come for the law to fail. As of today, however, the rule is still valid, constituting a good indicator for the progress regarding the chip industry.

Figure 3 illustrates the development of the aforementioned IT capabilities. It can clearly be discovered that data transmission is the fastest developing trend. It can be concluded that information technology will be a key enabler for the Shared Services Organisations of the future. IT becomes more powerful, enabling Centres to process and store more data. At the same time, more data can be sent faster between Centres and countries than before, which will be the most important driver.

---

14 Cf. *AKSIN* (2008), p. 243.

15 Cf. *NIXON* (2009), p. 129.

16 Cf. *WALTER* (2005), p. 1.

17 Cf. *INTEL* (2005), p. 1.

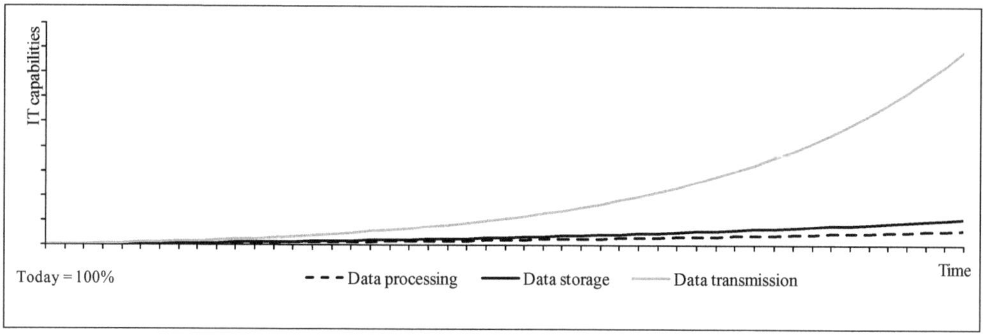

Figure 3: *Development of IT capabilities*

3 Future Trends in Finance Shared Services

3.1 Centralisation into Shared Services

Shared Services is a centralisation process by itself. The concept of the experience curve is not new. It simply describes the relation between cumulated output and its costs. Production costs usually decrease by 10 to 30 % with each of cumulative output.[18] These cost advantages can be gained if many business units have the same input, use similar facilities and systems to process the input and have an equal output of their products. These interrelationships surely exist and have to be considered.

> "Practice makes perfect. A thing can always be done better not only the second time but each succeeding time by trying. Everybody knows that. But how many people know that the pattern of improvement can be sufficiently regular to be predictable?"[19]

Without any doubts, competition has already been intensifying on a global base, and this trend will continue. In turn, companies have to search for new ways to cope with a toughening competition. However, increasing competition is not a new strategic factor to consider for companies. *PORTER*[20] released his five forces that describe the rivalry within an industry in 1979.[21] Within the past three decades, numerous competitors have emerged globally, growth in mature industries has slowed down, and many products and services lack differentiation, but more importantly, competitors are diverse in strategies, origins and culture. The main problem is that finance processes are supporting processes which fail to contribute significant, if any, value to the company and are only a driver to costs – yet it turns into a competitive advantage if these finance processes are supporting the overall business in the best possible way with the lowest possible cost: This is the challenge for Shared Services over the next decade.

---

18 Cf. *GHEMAWAT* (1985), p. 144.

19 *HIRSCHMANN* (1964), p. 125.

20 Cf. *PORTER* (1979).

21 Cf. *PORTER* (1979), p. 137 et seqq.

Therefore, further centralisation will influence the evolution of Shared Services for the upcoming decade. A continuing concentration of previously dispersed activities and corporate functions will leverage economies of scale, increasing the buying power of the purchasing function and even allowing for further specialisation, as existing resources are better utilized than they are nowadays. However, centralisation of services and functions is only possible to the extent that economies of scale can be leveraged. This means that processes have to be harmonised and standardised at a global level. However, centralisation is not to be interpreted as the one and only mass service, as transactional processes are, per definition, decision-based. Still, centralisation offers great advantages in terms of economies of scale. However, simply bundling several similar, but somehow diverse, processes in one organisational unit is not enough. For such large scale implementations, the general process itself has to be reconsidered to provide a common basis for harmonisation and standardisation.

One problem arises because many processes are dispersed across different business units and locations, mainly due to global complexity and heterogeneously grown companies. Initially, this provides a huge challenge for standardisation and redesign of processes to gain desired cost-advantages. However, under an increasing pressure to reduce cost, companies and their Shared Services will be forced to eliminate waste in their processes. Finally, companies have to be able to deliver the right product and/or service at the right time to their customers while utilising their resources at the best possible way. This requires both parties to rethink the way they interact with each other, defining input variables and desired outcome more accurately than it is done today. Especially accounting departments produce reports, sometimes even redundant, which are addressed to a small number of people. Research shows that smartly redesigning the G&A processes can account for 35 % of a company's G&A savings potential simply by eliminating process activities that do not contribute to the business.[22] In the past, analyses of transactional processes have been costly and did not fully result in the expected outcome. It was time-consuming to interview key personnel, conduct workshops, and analyse outdated process documentation. Today, cutting-edge data mining techniques can help businesses to fully analyse their transactional processes, giving insights into deficiencies and improvement potential. Processes, process steps, and activities can now be benchmarked internally as well as externally, providing management with a huge lever to increasing the overall performance, quality, and cost of transactional processes.

The automobile industry has already faced the aforementioned challenges. For about 40 years, car manufactures were not able to decipher why *Toyota's* cars were cheaper and produced faster while providing a higher quality than those manufactured elsewhere, for instance in Detroit. The underlying principles were finally discovered in the book "The machine that changed the world" by *WOMACK/JONES/ROOS*[23] which highly influenced not just automakers, but all production companies by introducing lean manufacturing principles. To be even able to decode these principles, the authors had to raise 5,000,000 USD.[24] The main question one could ask is: Why did it take 40 years to decipher them? Simple answer: *Toyota's* production principles were radically different to those accepted by automakers' senior executives, and it took four decades to change their biases. For example, *Toyota* radically reduced the amount of inventory and all safety nets by implementing the famous just-in-time system, called "kanban," which means that parts would only be produced to supply the demand of the next step.

22 Cf. *ROGERS/SAENZ* (2007), p. 30.

23 Cf. *WOMACK/JONES/ROOS* (2007).

24 Cf. *WOMACK/JONES/ROOS* (2007), p. 4 et seqq.

This system was simply designed to use containers that were sent back to the previous step if they had been used up. However, it took even *Toyota* approximately 20 years to fully implement all of the initial ideas.[25] These kind of initial ideas have still to be developed for finance-related processes. Until now, there has not been much pressure to rethink certain flows and activities, but substantial pressure will arise in this area during the next decade. Lean concepts as they are applied in almost every plant have to be applied to invoice processing, order management, and reporting activities. Pacesetters regarding radically changing processes and biases have yet to emerge - although a development towards lean processes should be evident.

Taking a look at lean management approaches, even transactional finance process activities can be split into three categories: First, activities that actively contribute value to a process, like initiating timely payment of vendors. Second, activities that do not add any value but are required with regard to regulations and other policies, for instance certain SEC requirements – and third, activities that are simply waste of resources, such as rework due to errors, loop-backs, and the like.

It can be concluded that in order to achieve economies of scale, processes from many business units will have to be bundled and centralised in one or a few big Shared Service Centres. These Shared Service Centres will then consist of executing harmonised and standardised processes. To standardise their finance processes globally, companies have to radically rethink the current process design and detect inefficiencies and harmonisation potential, just as *Toyota* did with the application of lean management principles to its famous *Toyota* Production System. Especially in environments with many transactional activities, differences between to-be and as-is process used to be difficult to detect. Today, however, modern methodology such as the process mining approach can easily discover and document harmonisation and improvement potentials of processes among many business units.

3.2 Offshoring and Outsourcing of Shared Services

Dispersed processes become centralised in one or many Centres worldwide. The more work is performed in one Centre, the more staff is required. This leads to a high labour arbitrage potential when selecting a location with low labour costs. Companies have always focused on reducing their costs of production, shortening their lead times and improving their levels of productivity. During the 1970's, manufacturing companies began hiring firms in other countries to manage less-than-essential-processes to increase their own efficiency, which is known as "outsourcing." But these savings alone turned out to be insufficient. Later, even manufacturing processes were shifted to low-wage countries in order to cut expenses. Management expert *PETER DRUCKER* said that the fastest growing industry in America during the 1990's was outsourcing.[26] Back in the 1970's, it was the textile industry that first shifted production off shore. As a result of the Multifibre Arrangement (MFA) of 1974, Western companies shifted production to less developed countries such as Bangladesh and Sri Lanka. Those countries did not have any textile industry at the time but were also part of the MFA, which allocated a certain amount of textile export to each country.[27] Besides the effects of this agreement, low wages in particular became a key driver for offshoring. Today, about 8 % of

---

[25] Cf. *WOMACK/JONES/ROOS* (2007), p. 62.

[26] Cf. *CORBETT* (2004), p. 5.

[27] Cf. *DÜRR* (2001), p. 28.

all textile import to Europe comes from Bangladesh, outperformed by China which accounts for 42 % of EU textile imports.[28] Globalisation accelerated the structural change enormously during the 1990's through decreasing transportation costs and the appearance of free-trade-agreements. Additionally, the increasing capabilities of global communication even allowed for offshoring information-driven services.

Globally competitive automotive manufacturers have also been outsourcing to countries with lower labour costs for decades now. Together with the textile industry, car manufacturers were among the first to adopt the practice offshoring. Today, India is considered a competitive player in the automotive manufacturing outsourcing industry. In fact, offshore manufacturing of car parts in low-wage countries increased from 7 % in 1995 to 28 % in 2007.[29] This increase is even higher than in the textile offshore production.

Three distinct types of benefits have since been associated with outsourcing:[30] First, achieving best practice and enhancing cost discipline and control. Second, improving service quality and being able to focus on core competencies. Third, gaining access to new technology and skills in order to enhance the development of products and services and reduce capital costs. However, firms were only able to reap these benefits because of several critical developments: First and most importantly, communication and computer technology have evolved so rapidly that outsourcing became not only possible and manageable, but very attractive. Second, the massive differences in wages, production costs and – often – tax and tariff structures between the Western world and less developed countries made offshoring a viable business model. Finally, commercial, cultural and political globalization has enabled companies to accomplish work on a global scale.

Additionally, the development of labour cost levels and the question whether labour arbitrage is possible and sustainable in the future is of interest as well. According to the *Economist Intelligence Unit*,[31] there is quite a difference concerning the wage growth amongst the important regions. As figure 4 shows, China and Brazil are the only regions with a significant increase in real wage growth.

28 Cf. online *EUROPEAN COMMISSION* (2012).

29 Cf. *IDW* (2007), p. 1.

30 Cf. *KAKABADSE/KAKABADSE* (2002). p. 189 et seqq.

31 Cf. online *EIU* (2012).

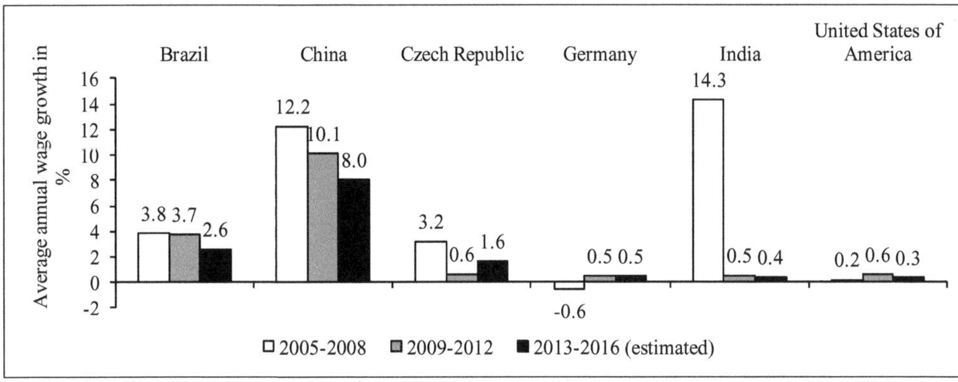

Figure 4: *Average annual wage growth from 2005 to 2016*[32]

Nevertheless, the difference between cost levels in Germany and China is obvious, as figure 5 shows. However, there are many factors you have to keep in mind. One of the most important aspects of this topic is the regional disparity within one country. If labour is shifted to China or India, the regional and local wage level gaps can be huge. Megacities like Shanghai or Beijing are much closer to a European level than rural areas in the Western parts of China. On the other hand, well-educated young people drive urbanisation and will only be available around these cities. Ultimately, there must be a trade-off between high cost savings due to labour arbitrage, and the skill level of the employed staff. In total, these are reasonable indicators that the area of gaining long-term advantages through significant labour arbitrage effects will come to an end sooner rather than later. For instance, if a skilled Chinese worker earns 50 % more than the average Chinese, applying the average growth rate between 2005 and 2016 of 10.1 %, China is likely to reach German wage levels by the early 2030s.

In general, customers have become more informed on price, reliability, and availability issues. They have greater access to alternative sources of supply and therefore demand products and services in a more customised manner at a lower price. The Internet has been providing global access to a multitude of products and services and through instant communication typical time and distance constraints are of decreasing significance.[33] However, there is currently no transparency in the market of G&A costs since most services are kept in-house and are bound to one's own SSC. How do companies know that costs are significantly lower at an equal level of service, if outsourced?

[32] Cf. online *EIU* (2012).

[33] Cf. *Piercy/Lane* (2005), p. 249 et seqq.

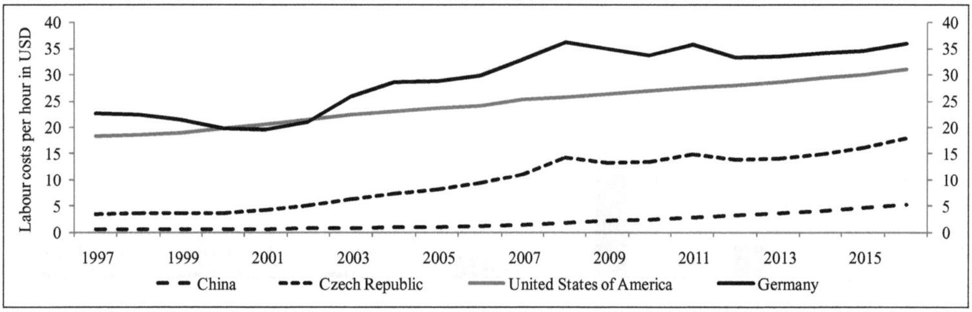

Figure 5: *Development of labour costs per hour in USD*[34]

The extent to which developments in technology, cost inequities, and globalisation continue to make outsourcing attractive will determine the future of outsourcing as a strategic operating model. It must be concluded that offshore sourcing plays an important role in achieving labour arbitrage gains in labour intensive industries, such as Shared Services with a high degree of transactional processes.

3.3 Shared Services Become a Strategic Decision

Shared Services drive profitability of the parent company. There has to be a clear business case: First, the cost advantages have to offset the initial costs of implementing Shared Services Organisations. Implementation costs can be seen as fixed and independent from the corresponding transaction volume the SSC has to handle because matters such as activity splits, location decisions, and adjustments of IT systems are independent from the planned transaction volume. Second, rationalisation gains are typically larger at multinational heterogeneous corporations which deal with more inefficiency in their internal processes than smaller companies do. In other words, the resulting costs per transaction of Shared Services can be easier offset at larger companies than at smaller ones.[35] These facts are also supported by *KPMG* research, as is shown in figure 6: The G&A costs at German DAX30 companies account for 5.0 % of total costs over the past six years, whereas MDAX, SDAX, and TecDAX companies show significantly higher shares at 5.5 %, 5.6 %, and 7.2 %, respectively.

Initially, dealing with Shared Service Centres is costly for companies. Given the fact that more than 90 % of the companies already have Shared Service Centres in place, it must be concluded that larger companies achieve higher cost savings at their G&A costs than smaller companies do. It must also be concluded that a critical mass is required to implement and maintain captive Shared Services. Companies now have to decide whether they achieve competitive advantage through cost reduction or through custom process execution. If the strategic direction is to reduce cost of the finance function and a critical mass cannot be reached, BPO may be an alternative to consider for transactional processes like accounts payable, accounts receivable, or even reporting processes.

34 Cf. online *EIU* (2012).

35 Cf. *AKSIN* (2008), p. 244, and cf. *DAVENPORT* (2005), p. 102.

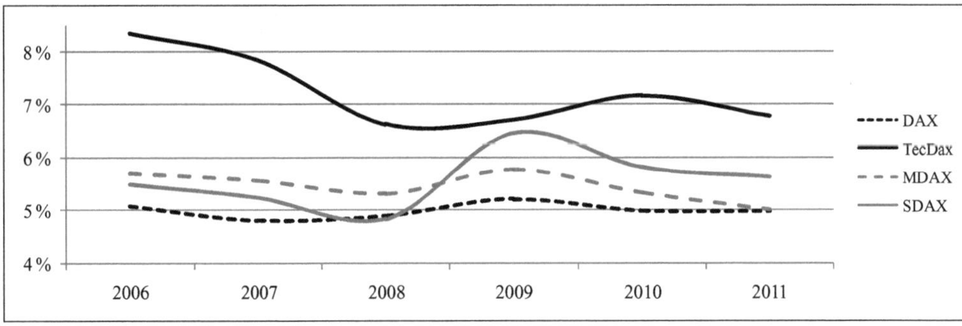

Figure 6: Leveraging economies of scale at DAX companies

However, it is expected that even though complexity is increasing during the next decades, there will be intrinsic motives within every organisation to identify homogeneous parts in their processes which will then be bundled in Shared Services to deal with. This article therefore argues that environmental complexity does not necessarily result in organizational complexity. Hence, it can be concluded that multinational corporations are running their own Shared Service Centres. In turn, it can also be said that the more complex processes become, the less improvement potential can be gained through Shared Services because processes are too diverse to be bundled and centralised. However, with increasing complexity of processes, re-engineering needs naturally arise for the harmonisation, standardisation, and finally simplification of processes which will in turn increase the importance of Shared Services Organisations. This article assumes that there are potentials to harmonise and bundle between 70 and 80 % of a company's finance processes within Shared Service.

It should not be a company's goal to benchmark a competitor's processes, but to develop one's own vision about how processes may lead to competitive advantages and about how to exploit them. The more a process facilitates competitive advantage, the more it will stay under tight parental control. The same principle applies to risks associated with the process: The higher the risks, the less likely a process will be moved to a Shared Service Centre. It can therefore be concluded that Shared Services will become a strategic decision and an opportunity to achieve competitive advantages. However, what if a company is not large enough to reach and exceed a critical mass? Then, it only has to decide between keeping processes and Shared Service captive and designing as well as executing them to gain competitive advantage or, alternatively, radically outsourcing the process to BPO providers to achieve cost efficiency.

3.4 Process Automation and Controlling rather than Execution

In their influential book "Competing for the future" *HAMEL/PRAHALAD*[36] argue that restructuring is ultimately a dead-end for companies.[37] Getting processes executed by Shared Services will not be enough to survive in tough economies. Shared Services need to radically re-engineer their processes to eliminate needless work while aiming at satisfying customers, reducing cycle

[36] Cf. *HAMEL/PRAHALAD* (1994).

[37] Cf. *HAMEL/PRAHALAD* (1994), p. 11 et seq.

times and improving quality at the same time. If needless work is eliminated and processes are standardised and executed in a stable manner, advances in technology can be exploited. However, a high rate of automation for transactional processes is ultimately paramount to a shifting of the ways in which processes are executed towards Shared Services Organisations. Best-in-class companies have a three-way match success rate of approximately 95 %, which means that 95 % of all invoices can be approved automatically. According to an internal *KPMG* benchmark database, the median of all research companies is at about 65 %. Through advances in technology, an overall automation rate of 80 % appears feasible.

At first glance, however it might seem obvious that processes performed by computers are cheaper and faster than those performed by humans. However, in many situations this is not the case today. There are still quite a few tasks at Shared Services Centres that are manually executed. How is the information on paper-based invoices transformed in bits and bytes? One could implement highly sophisticated scanning solutions with cutting-edge optical character recognition (OCR) software, which interprets 8 out of 10 invoices without any errors. It remains unknown, however, on which invoices some minor errors occur. Therefore, the risk of dealing with faulty information is quite high. For instance, it could finally result in the release of payments to the wrong bank accounts or balance sheet misstatements. That risk can be covered by manually verifying the scanning results, invoice by invoice. Today, especially in countries with low labour costs, manually typing out the information of all the invoices without any automated solution is still cheaper and, overall, results in fewer failures. However, as IT capabilities will become more advanced, powerful and accurate, it can be concluded that the cost of accurate end-to-end process automation will be lower than manually executing these processes. Finally, human interaction is only required if the process deviates from the standard implementation, that is, either for the handling of exceptional situations, or when dealing with special requirements which are not implemented and for which an implementation would be too expensive, due to its rare occurrence and/or complexity. Even if it were possible to achieve 100 % automation from an IT perspective, the cost to implement and maintain the algorithms would by far exceed the gains achieved through such automation.

However, as more and more activities will be performed by computers, manual input is only required at a minimum, and yet required to resolve issues a computer cannot handle. Ultimately, this requires the placing of specialists for information technologies and process experts within Shared Services Organisations. It will shift process know-how away from the parent organisation, having the processes managed right at Shared Services Organisations. However, this also requires governance, technology, and management responsibility and competencies located at the Shared Service Centre. Even if Shared Services are captive organisations, a certain degree of autonomy has to be provided by the parent company. As processes become more and more automated, the actual cost per transaction is likely to decrease.

The following figure 7 describes the relationship between total costs and automation rate. Costs for automation basically cover IT costs. Without any automation in place, human interaction is at a maximum. However, at 100 % automation, human interaction is still required with respect to server administration etc. Logically, the impact of pure labour costs plummets with high automation in place. The minimum of the total cost curve describes the optimum of automation, which is expected to be between 60 % and 80 %. This optimum automation rate (minimum of total costs) will increase in the future with rising staff costs and dropping automation costs.

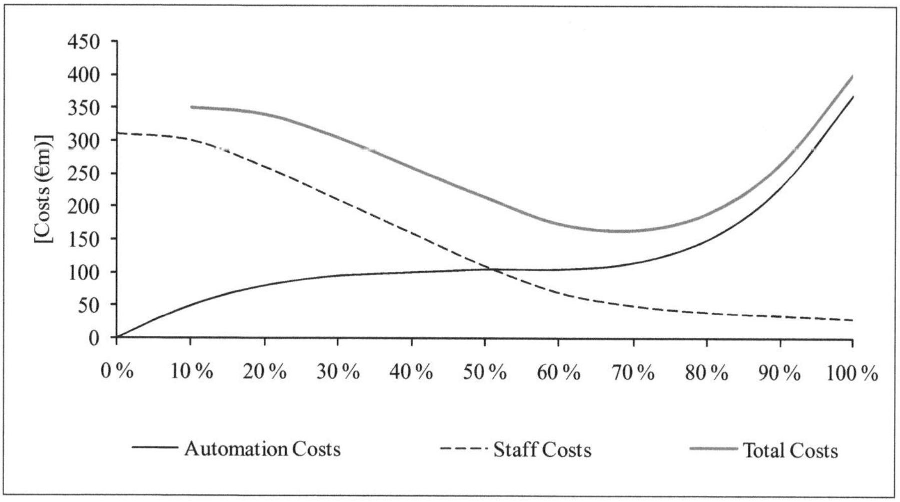

Figure 7: *Relation between IT and labour costs*

Today, the implementation of new IT systems is of minor interest for Shared Services. IT costs only cover about 10 % of a Shared Service Centre's expenses for transactional processes while personnel cost account for 80 %. The other 10 % is required overhead. However, if information technology advances and transactional processes can be standardised and automated, interactions of humans can be reduced to a minimum.

For example, the share of a company's invoice volume distribution today is as follows: Approximately one third of a company's invoices are below 1,000 EUR. In total, invoices below 10,000 EUR account for three quarters, which represents only one third of a company's purchasing volume. Typically, these invoices are the ones that require the most effort because in many cases, the creation of a purchase order was not mandatory before. If this is the case, Shared Services waste a significant amount of time and effort by identifying the correct account assignment objects, such as profit centre and the responsible department that can acknowledge the product or service received and finally approve the invoice. Without any process automation, invoices with low volume are nowadays treated the same way as invoices regarding complex large volume purchase orders. With modern technologies such as electronic invoices through EDI standards in place, invoice processing can be easily automated. Additionally, detecting main issues at invoice processing is made easier with help of modern data analysis technologies. For instance, vendors issuing low quality invoices that typically cannot be automatically matched against a purchase order can easily be discovered.

In summary, the share of IT costs will switch positions with personnel costs and account for the larger share in the future. Modern technologies and advances in technology help Shared Services Centres automate many activities which are currently still performed by humans. However, exceptions and competence-based decisions are unlikely to be automated completely, as the implementation and maintenance of the IT and algorithms exceed the benefits.

3.5 Shared Services as Shared Competence

With automation in place, staff would only intervene if IT systems issue exceptional occurrences that need to be resolved manually. This provides a huge opportunity for management to enrich the jobs of finance staff. The equation is that simple: For instance, automate the treatment of low volume invoices while shifting the freed-up work time to check, verify, and approve complex high volume invoices, and while reliably ensuring that local tax regulations are met and the service acceptance is performed accurately. While 'mainstream' processes can be automated in about 80 % of all cases, the other 20 % can therefore be regarded as exceptions to the default process. Handling those exceptions under complex and detailed accounting guidelines, local Generally Accepted Accounting Principles (GAAPs), and tax regulations is challenging. Additionally, these regulations are likely to change more often than they used to do, which requires specialists whose knowledge is up-to-date. By now, one can assume that specialists may be located at the company's business units and subsidiaries. However, the specialists would only have a third of their normal workload because the simple tasks have been eliminated from the daily task schedule. This provides the opportunity to share the special knowledge across many business units from diverse locations and to specialise even more. This would ultimately enrich the staff's jobs and move them from the parent company to the company's Shared Service Centre. That will have significant implications because Shared Service Centres then need to attract bright and well-educated personnel to be competitive and to deliver the right services to their parent. The widely-known so-called 'war for talents' will be as significant for Shared Services Organisations as it is common for certain industries such as German engineering companies today.

With high automation in place, labour arbitrage effects do not play a significant role in terms of location. The following figure 8 describes that impact. The higher the rate of automation, the brighter the required people have to be. Overall, this effect does not reduce total labour costs, but it lowers the optimum rate of automation.

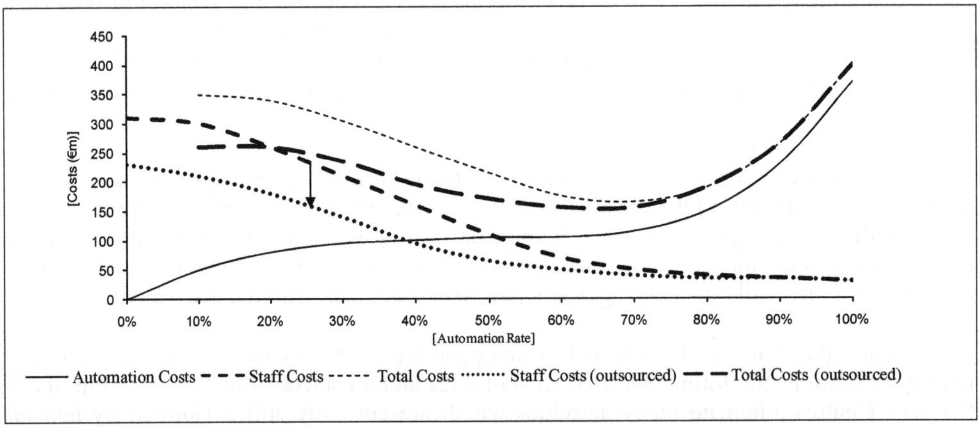

Figure 8: Impact of labour arbitrage and automation

As a result of globalisation, ever higher challenges for the accounting of organisations are arising. Often, several accounting frameworks have to be regarded simultaneously. In addition to national GAAP and national tax-law, the International Financial Reporting Standards (IFRS) are playing an ever-increasing role for multinational organisations. In particular, publicly traded companies are required to prepare their consolidated financial statements in accordance with IFRS. The *International Accounting Standards Board* (*IASB*) has set for itself the goal of publishing high quality accounting standards, thereby contributing to the global harmonisation of accounting. Such harmonisation represents the internationalisation of economic life, and at first glance, it seems to bring a number of simplifications. Global unified accounting standards generally lead to an increasing comparability of financial statements and facilitate access to international capital markets. A standardized, supra-regional application of the IFRS may also bring significant simplification for multinational groups. Ideally, the accounting of all group companies could be unified, which should result in several advantages.

In practice, however, the opposite is true. The application of IFRS is only mandatory for consolidated financial statements of publicly traded companies. With respect to the preparation of single financial statements, local GAAP is still predominating[38]. Moreover, specific national tax regulations have to be taken into account. These facts lead to increasing requirements for organisations although harmonisation of accounting should have the opposite effect. The main reason for the increasing requirements for the accounting of organisations is the application of IFRS itself. In recent years, there has been a distinct increase of the complexity of IFRS, and this momentum is unlikely to pause or stop. The currently applicable standards comprise approximately 650 pages.[39] Additionally, there are comprehensive explanations and interpretations to be regarded. As figure 9 shows, the overall extent of IFRS has more than tripled since 1995.[40] Moreover, the content of some standards is so comprehensive and complex that proper application is associated with enormous effort. Even today, many organisations are simply overwhelmed by the complexity of IFRS[41].

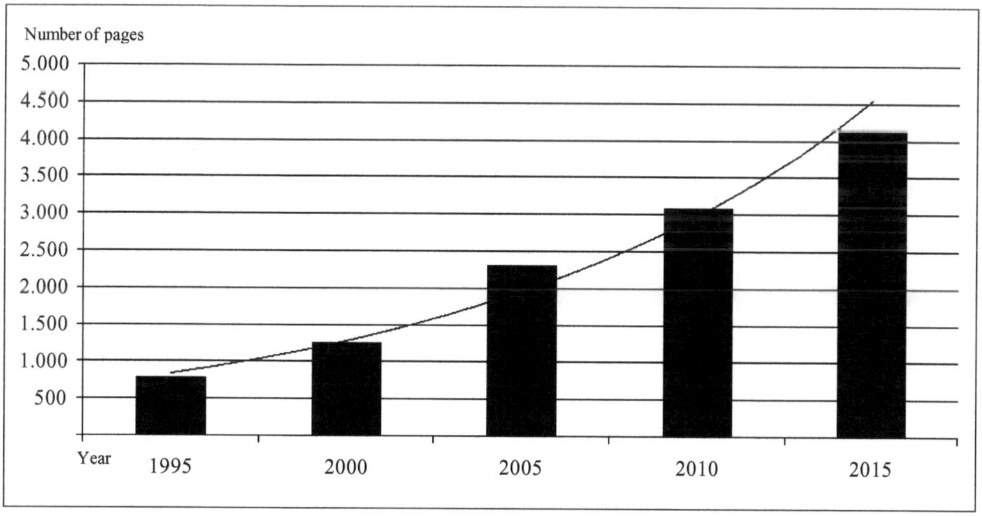

Figure 9: *Development of extent of IFRS*

---

[38] Cf. *KÜTING* (2012a), p. 1.

[39] Cf. *KÜTING* (2012b), p. 300.

[40] Cf. *FÜLBIER/KUSCHEL* (2012), p. 929 et seqq.

[41] Cf. *KÜTING* (2012b), p. 297 et seqq.

The purpose of IFRS is to provide information that is useful in making economic decisions. For example, to meet this purpose, the IASB intends a comprehensive implementation of the fair value concept.[42] Where possible, the fair value is to be determined by current prices in an active market. In most cases, however, this is not possible, thus the fair value has to be determined by the application of complex valuation models. Generally, this kind of valuation is based on subjective planning data bearing a high degree of uncertainty. This approach inevitably leads to an increasing susceptibility to error.

In Germany alone, consolidated financial statements of publicly traded companies consistently contain significant misstatements. In recent years, the auditing of such financial statements by the German Financial Reporting Enforcing Panel showed that one out of four financial statements contain significant misstatements. According to the Panel, the majority of errors are attributable to the enormous complexity of IFRS.[43] This complexity is also criticised by the auditors.[44] *KÜTING*[45] notes that the application of IFRS is associated with enormous effort, the regularity of the application can only be verified by the auditors, and that accounting has become unintelligible.[46] Meanwhile, the high complexity of IFRS is further pushed by its dynamic changes. For the future, the IASB working plan proposes numerous amendments, which are, in relation to their extent, comparable to a new introduction of IFRS.[47] These developments, for example, lead to a higher specialisation of people working within finance processes. To achieve economies of scale, there will be pressure to use this kind of highly-skilled people on a wider scale. This, in turn, will require the ignoring of country and company boundaries, leading to the implementation of shared competence centres.

As mentioned above, the German work force will decrease rapidly in the future. Nevertheless, Germany is in a leading position when it comes to the availability of education and knowledge. In 2010, a total of 2.18 million students graduated from German colleges and universities, which is a share of 2.6 % of the whole population. In total numbers, India and China outperform Germany with 14.9 million and 29.3 million graduates, respectively. However, the share of graduates on total population in India is only 1.2 %, and in China 2.1 %.[48] Nevertheless, the labour force in both countries cannot be compared to the level in Germany. In 2010, the Indian labour force of 460 million people was eleven times, and the Chinese labour force, totalling 786 million, was 19 times larger than Germany's. However, according to a research paper of *GOLDMAN SACHS*[49], the work force of India and especially China will decrease over the next 40 years. The impact in China will be much more significant than in India, because of China's ageing population caused by its one-child policy.[50]

---

42 Cf. *MEYER/BRAUN* (2012), p. 300.

43 Cf. *DPR* (2012), p. 2 et seqq.

44 Cf. *IDW* (2011), p. 3 et seqq. and *WPK* (2011), p. 3 et seqq.

45 Cf. *KÜTING* (2012b).

46 Cf. *KÜTING* (2012b), p. 304.

47 Cf. *LOITZ/GLASNER* (2011), p. 2789.

48 Cf. online *STATISTISCHES BUNDESAMT* (2012b).

49 Cf. online *GOLDMAN/SACHS* (2010).

50 Cf. online *GOLDMAN SACHS* (2010), p. 4.

Nevertheless, these countries have and will have a large number of professional and skilled people available. Also, along with growing welfare in these countries, the educational level is likely to increase further. However, this development has another side to be considered: The more people are well-educated, the higher the demand for more interesting activities in day-to-day work. Especially in strongly industrialised countries with well-educated people, simple transactional process steps like manually typing out invoice data into the system appear very unpopular. Automation will eliminate this kind of activities to a large extent and switch work from transactional to decision and knowledge-based activities. However, these kinds of activities require workers with a higher skill level. As described in figure 10, ever more knowledgeable workers are required to facilitate the Shared Service Centre of the future, while the need for workers performing simple transactional activities will decrease.

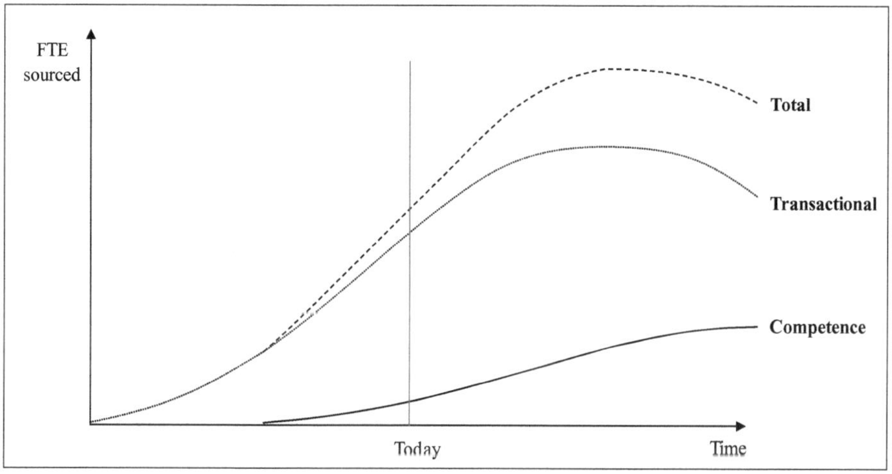

Figure 10: *Development of transactional and competence staff*

It can be concluded that on one hand, low-skilled activities will be further automated and therefore the number of people working within transactional processes will decrease. On the other hand, the required level of skills of Shared Service Centre staff working in competence-driven processes will increase in the future. Attracting bright people with the required finance and accounting skills which cover several accounting frameworks will be the challenge for Human Resources at Shared Service Centres. As a consequence, the location of the Shared Service Centre will not be as important as it is today, as the skills of staff will be more important than the achieved labour cost savings.

3.6 Shared Services from the Cloud

Today's world is more volatile and complex than it was twenty years ago. During the recent financial crisis, the Dow Jones Industrial Index (DJII) crushed down and lost about 7,000 points within just 15 months, which almost corresponds to a drop of 50 %. As a matter of fact, earlier crises did not reach such magnitude at all. First, having a look at the "Black Monday" in 1987, the DJII dropped by just 500 points, and it took about 3 years to reach the initial level. Second, during the so-called "dot-com" crisis around the year 2000, the index lost approximately 3,500 points; subsequently, it took only 30 months to reach the pre-crisis level of 11,500 points again. Finally, after *Lehman Brothers* crashed, leading to the 2007 financial crisis, the *Dow Jones* needed just 24 months to reach its old level. These numbers are a significant indicator that – given an increasing interconnection of global trade and markets - the fluctuations become even bigger at an increasing pace, which ultimately leads to future challenges companies have to deal with.[51] Given the context of increasing economic volatility, finance functions have to design flexible processes and structures because currently, high fixed costs of finance functions in good economic times remain high fixed costs of finance functions during economically bad times. To cope with volatile markets, there is the need for fixed costs to transfer to variable costs. Additionally, flexible services of the future have to account for a globally increasing complexity of accounting regulations.

Advances in technology facilitate service-oriented approaches, leading to new organisational structures within the Shared Services Organisations. Imagine modularised services, or centre of competences which are structured around traditional Shared Services Organisations with its single obligation to provide strategic direction for the modularised centre, defining interfaces between its customer and itself with its several modules. Each module can be located at the best possible location or even split across different locations, which become then virtually bundled in a single module. However, this approach requires a high degree of standardisation at the customer and well defined organisational design principles as well as interfaces between the company and the service provider. However, the management effort to coordinate the modules might increase significantly because "the different pieces must work together, and the whole must accomplish more than any subset of its parts."[52] But once designed properly, management attention can focus on integrating the single components and assisting customers in using these modules. To illustrate this idea in a simplified way, just imagine the power of smart phones today: Managing contacts and calendars, sending and receiving emails; executing applications and taking high quality photos; providing almost unlimited storage space and computing power through cloud services – an impressive complexity in features nobody could have even imagined two decades ago are now being managed by a small device and its operating system, respectively. Such new organisational structures have yet to emerge.

Additionally, if G&A processes or their sub processes become enormously standardised, they can easily be modelled within IT systems. There are possible providers who may offer these kinds of standardised process modules with the ability to, e.g., activate and respectively deactivate certain compliance control sets on the fly, if required. Possible providers may be: First, ERP software providers who already provide the extensive underlying IT systems and then offer standard interfaces to its own modules. Second, Software as a Service (SaaS) providers who already offer specialised modules for certain finance activities and then integrate additional services into its software. Third, BPO providers who already offer a full set of activities and services which can then be flexibly connected to the Shared Service Centre according to needs.

These days, cloud computing is nothing more than delivery of processing power and storage as a service. Processing power and storage can then be sourced according to a company's needs, easily increasing or decreasing storage capacity, for instance. The more automation is in place, the more tasks can therefore be delivered as a service from the cloud, as shown in figure 11. The Shared Service Centre then, in one way or another, simply rents the service

---

51 Cf. online *MARKT-DATEN* (2012).

52 Cf. *BALDWIN* (2000), p. 5 et seq.

rather than executing it in-house. With further increasing collaboration capabilities, why should the cloud be restricted to information technology only? Human services that perform competence-driven activities can also be sent to the cloud if standard communication and collaboration interfaces are in place.

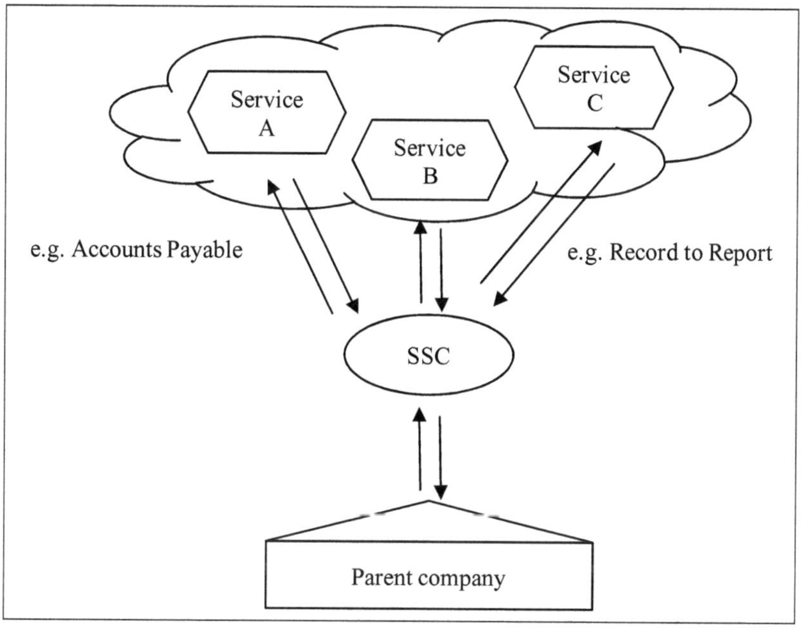

Figure 11: SSC as interface between the cloud and the parent company

In summary, modularisation and/or service from the cloud offer a couple of advantages for both sides: First, it makes increasing complexity manageable because it splits complex processes into manageable parts. Second, it enables parallel work and improvements while assuring business continuity. Third, it tolerates volatility and uncertainty. With cloud services in place, the business itself is only concerned about providing the correct input for Shared Services Organisations and receives the desired results according to a defined service level agreement. The Shared Services Organisations can then source several services from other providers. However, the end-to-end process responsibility and governance has then to be fully managed by the Shared Services Organisations.

4 Conclusion and Outlook

Today, more than 90 % of large multinational corporations already have Shared Services Organisations that bundle activities. The evolution of Shared Service Centres is mainly driven by external factors. The next evolutionary steps are increasing cost-effectiveness and leveraging advances in information technologies. Information technologies can account for up to 80 % of transactional activities that are currently performed by humans. However, this automation can theoretically be driven towards 100 %. But from a business perspective, a trade-off between services, quality of the performed services, standardisation, and costs will take place.

Supporting processes such as accounts payable and accounts receivables are generally seen as drivers for cost. However, this is likely to change soon. There is still significant potential for additional improvement and cost savings. Reduced costs will, in turn, lead to increased profits. Shared Service Centres shall therefore rather be seen as profit centres than as cost drivers.

Large multinational companies will have the opportunity to adjust their processes at their own Shared Service Centres, while smaller firms have to buy standardised services from BPO providers. This will ultimately be the only way for smaller firms to compete with larger companies, especially in traditional and mature industries. Processes may be standardised in a way that the companies completely lose influence over the process itself. It rather delivers a specified input to the Centre, while receiving a defined output from the provider. If the provider is in-house, the own "black box" can be adjusted to meet the company's requirements. If not, the company has to adjust its interfaces to connect to the standardised interfaces of BPO providers. However, BPO providers are generally not seen as a driver for innovation. And yet, innovation in finance processes is a big challenge and a requirement for companies, Shared Service Centres, and BPO providers during the next decades in order to achieve competitive advantage. If processes are outsourced, however, data protection and confidentiality still create a big obstacle to overcome. Business models and structures that account for data protection have to be developed; the issue of data protection, however, exceeds the scope of this article.

As automation will have a significant impact on designing and executing processes, human interaction will decrease during the upcoming decades. Gaining advantages from labour arbitrage will be of low importance compared to today's focus. More importantly, the location with the best educated people will have an impact on the location of the Centre. Ultimately, the Shared Service Centre will be virtualised with services sourced from the cloud. Cloud technologies and further improvements of collaboration methods will enable Shared Service Centres to have the work executed from the best possible source without caring about the location of the source.

However, fully outsourcing processes provides a significant risk for companies. For example, some activities and related documents are prohibited to physically leave the country. Certainly, if input and output can be standardised, it is easier for companies to switch between services and locations, which in turn reduces the dependency on one provider. In return, if companies are able to switch between service providers, cost transparency naturally emerges and transactional processes and services can be easily compared and sourced from the best possible provider.

Companies that will be leading their industries in the future are the companies that were the first to radically challenge the execution and design of their finance and accounting processes. It took Toyota between 20 and 40 years to implement their initial ideas of a new production system. Today, car manufactures are able to build a car with thousands of parts, whereas up to hundreds of parts are sourced from different vendors. Furthermore, carmakers are even able to tell a couple of months in advance the exact date the customer can get his car. At the same time, accounting departments are not able to process invoices with simple and very limited input variables such as price, amount, and purchase order number to get an invoice automatically matched, approved, and paid timely.

This article offered a general road map for Shared Service Centres for the next one to two decades. Described trends have been derived from main drivers and challenges that shape the future of the overall economy especially tailored to Shared Services Organisations. Companies have to take a closer look at their back-office finance functions. Future models of Shared Services appear even more valuable to companies than today, providing higher quality at lower costs. Today, SSCs are just gaining momentum at the beginning of their evolutionary path.

Abbreviations and Terms

BPO	Business Process Outsourcing
COGS	Costs of Goods Sold
DJII	Dow Jones Industrial Index
G&A	General and Administrative (expenses)
GAAP	Generally Accepted Accounting Principles
IASB	International Accounting Standards Board
IFRS	International Financial Reporting Standards
MFA	Multifibre Arrangement
OCR	Optical Character Recognition
SaaS	Software as a Service
SSC	Shared Services Centre

References

AKSIN, Z./MASINI, A. (2008): Effective Strategies for Internal Outsourcing and Offshoring of Business Services: An empirical investigation, in: Journal of Operations Management, Vol. 26 (2008), pp. 239–256.

BALDWIN, C./CLARK, K. B. (2000): Design Rules: The Power of Modularity, Cambridge (MA) 2000.

BERGERON, B. (2003): Essentials of Shared Services, Hoboken (NJ) 2003.

CORBETT, M. (2004): The Outsourcing Revolution – Why it makes sense and how to do it right. Chicago (IL) 2004.

DAVENPORT, T. (2005): The Coming Commoditization of Processes, in: Harvard Business Review, June 2005, pp. 100–108.

DPR (2012): Tätigkeitsbericht 2011, online: www.frep.info/presse/taetigkeitsberichte.php, date visited: 22/06/2012.

DRESSLER, S. (2007): Shared Services, Business Process Outsourcing und Offshoring, Wiesbaden 2007.

DÜRR, A. (2001): Soziale Verantwortlichkeit in globalen Produktionsnetzwerken: Erkenntnisse aus der Bekleidungsindustrie, Berlin 2001.

EIU (2012): The Economist Intelligence Unit: Data tool, online: http://data.eiu.com/Default.aspx, date visited: 27/06/2012.

EUROPEAN COMMISSION (2011): Textiles and Footwear, online: http://ec.europa.eu/trade/creating-opportunities/economic-sectors/industrial-goods/textiles-and-footwear/, date visited: 17/07/2012.

FARRELL, D. (2004): Beyond Offshoring: Assess Your Company's Global Potential, in: Harvard Business Review, Vol. 82 (2004), No. 12, pp. 82–90.

FÜLBIER, R./KUSCHEL, P. (2012): Komplexitätszunahme in der IFRS-Rechnungslegung? – Versuche der Systematisierung und indikatorbasierten Messung, in: Der Betrieb, No. 17 (2012), pp. 929–937.

GHEMAWAT, P. (1985): Building Strategy on the Experience Curve, in: Harvard Business Review, Vol. 63 (1985), No. 2, pp. 143–149.

GOLDMAN SACHS (2010): Die BRICS nehmen Fahrt auf, online: http://www.goldmansachs.com/gsam/docs/funds_international/brochures_and_sales_aids/fund_literature/rb_brics_de.pdf, date visited: 25/06/2012.

HAMEL, G./PRAHALAD, C. K. (1994): Competing for the Future, Boston (MA) 1994).

HIRSCHMANN, W. B. (1964): Profit from the learning curve. In: Harvard Business Review, Jan/Feb 1964, pp. 125–139.

IDW (2007): Importe – Der Konkurrenzdruck steigt. Pressemitteilung 14/2007, Köln.

IDW (2011): Presseinformation, online: www.idw.de/idw/portal/d606110, date visited: 25/06/2012.

INTEL (2005): Moore's Law, online: http://download.intel.com/museum/Moores_Law/Printed_Materials/Moores_Law_2pg.pdf, date visited: 25/06/2012.

KAKABADSE, A./KAKABADSE, N. (2002): Trends in Outsourcing – Contrasting USA and Europe, in: European Management Journal, Vol 20 (2002), No. 2, p. 189–198.

KÜTING, K. (2012a): HGB oder IFRS?, in: Der Betrieb, No. 13 (2012), p. 1.

KÜTING, K. (2012b): Zur Komplexität der Rechnungslegungssysteme nach HGB und IFRS, in: Der Betrieb, No. 6 (2012), pp. 297–304.

LOITZ, R./GLASNER, K. (2011): Embedded Accounting, in: Der Betrieb, 2011, p. 2789–2797.

MARKT-DATEN (2012): Daten Chart/Download, online: http://www.markt-daten.de/daten/2006 djia.txt, date visited: 25/06/2012.

MEYER, H./BRAUN, R. (2010): Fair Value als Treiber der Komplexität von IFRS, in: Betriebs Berater, No. 30, 2010, pp. 1779–1782.

NIXON, SD (2009): U.S. National Security in New Times, in: Frontiers of Engineering: Reports on Leading-Edge Engineering from the 2008 Symposium, 2009, National Academy of Engineering, Washington, p. 127-132.

PIERCY, N. F./LANE, N. (2005): Strategic Imperatives for Transformation in the Conventional Sales Organization, in: Journal of Change Management, Vol. 5 (2005), No. 3, p. 249–266.

PORTER, M. E. (1979): How Competitive Forces Shape Strategy, in: Harvard Business Review, March/April 1979, p. 137–145.

ROGERS, P./SAENZ, H. (2007): Make Your Back Office an Accelerator, in: Harvard Business Review, March 2007, Vol. 85 (2007), No. 3, p. 30.

SAKO, M. (2010): Outsourcing versus Shared Services, in: Communications of the ACM, Vol. 53 (2010), No. 7, p. 27–29.

SIEMENS (2012): FAQ – Siemens Global Website, online: http://www.siemens.com/about/en/index/faq.htm, date visited: 01/06/2012.

STATISTISCHES BUNDESAMT (2012a): Bevölkerungsstatistiken, online: https://www.destatis.de/DE/ZahlenFakten/GesellschaftStaat/StaatGesellschaft.html, date visited: 23/03/2012.

STATISTISCHES BUNDESAMT (2012b): Absolventenstatistik, online: https://www.destatis.de/DE/ZahlenFakten/LaenderRegionen/Internationales/Thema/Tabellen/Basistabelle_Studierende.html, date visited: 25/06/2012.

THOMPSON, J. D. (1967): Organizations in Action: Social Science Bases of Administrative Theory, New York (NY) 1967.

UN (2012): The United Nations at a Glance, online: http://www.un.org/en/aboutun/index.shtml, date visited: 01/06/2012.

WALTER, C. (2005): Kryder's Law, in: Scientific American Magazine, No. 8 (2005), pp. 32–33.

WOMACK, J. P./JONES, D. T./ROOS, D. (2007): The Machine That Changed the World, New York (NY) 2007.

WORLDBANK RESEARCH CENTER (2012): Data by indicators, online: http://data.worldbank.org/indicator, date visited: 23/03/2012.

WPK (2011): Stellungnahme zur IASB Agenda Consultation, online: http://www.wpk.de/pdf/WPK-Stellungnahme_21-11-2011.pdf.

Shared Services in 2020

KAI-EBERHARD LUEG and *FRANK KEUPER*

Siemens AG, Global Shared Services and *Steinbeis University Berlin*

Executive Summary

An in-depth literature review reveals that there is still no generally accepted terminology on the Shared Services concept.[1] Based on the analysis of 17 scientifically substantial definitions of the Shared Service concept[2] and additional expert interviews the Shared Service concept is an internal service delivery option positioned between centralization and outsourcing as the two turning points of the (internal) service delivery continuum.[3]

While first generation Shared Services Organizations (SSOs) primarily aimed to benefit from cost reductions as a result of labour arbitrage advantages, economies of scale and economies of scope gained through the bundling, harmonization, standardization and IT-enabled automation of prior decentralized and heterogeneously executed support activities, next generation SSOs are expected to deliver intelligent services at better quality and lower costs, spending more time on transformational activities.[4] The consolidation of IT infrastructures and application portfolios as well as the introduction of new web-based and customer interaction technologies have enabled SSOs to expand the range of services they provide, to increase their effectiveness and efficiency simultaneously, and at the same time have fundamentally changed the way customers handle their support-activity-related issues.[5] Hence, the number of companies establishing a SSO or transferring processes to an existing SSO as a key element of a broader transformation leading from a cost factor to a value adding business partner is growing. Meanwhile, SSOs are seen as a key enabler for business units and companies to concentrate on their core competencies.

The Shared Services journey has not finished, yet. In this article we try to think a litte bit "out of the box". After a short introduction we explore selected strategic (chapter 2), structural (chapter 3) and technological trends (chapter 4) which might influence the Shared Services journey until 2020.

1 Introduction

Though the importance of SSO as a key element of a modern internal administration and service delivery is growing, there has only been limited academic research not to mention scientifically generated empirical evidence – except from the study published by *PAMPER/ FISCHER*[6] – on the question if and to what extent the ex-ante promised benefits have become real[7] or how to implement a successfully operating SSO.[8] Moreover, *HOLLICH* et al. criticize:

---

1 Cf. e. g. *DRESSLER* (2007), *VON GLAHN* (2007), *PÉREZ* (2008), *SINGH/CRAIKE* (2008) and *BECKER/KUNZ/MAYER* 2009, p. 18.

2 Cf. *RÖDER/KEUPER* (2009), p. 206 f.

3 Cf. *VON GLAHN/KEUPER* (2008), p. 18 et seqq.

4 Cf. e.g. *FARNDALE/PAAUWE/HOEKSMA* (2009).

5 Cf. e.g. *VOLLMER/FISCHER/ROEDER* (2008).

6 Cf. *PAMPER/FISCHER* (2007).

7 Cf. *KAGELMANN* (2001), p. 49, and *DRESSLER* (2007), p. 26.

8 Cf. *COOKE* (2006), p. 212.

"Most of the research is vendor and consultant driven."[9] In most cases studies show theoretical and methodological gaps, which particularly limit their appropriateness to meet managerial challenges. The most important issue is that due to a lack of a consistent terminology it is impossible for researchers to identify the population of SSO. Hence, quantitative study findings are statistically not representative[10] and explanatory power of empirical results is limited. Consequently, results from empirical studies in the SSO context always have to be interpreted very carefully in view of their theoretical and methodological limitations. However, completely without doubt many companies have gone a step closer towards second generation SSO and will do so to an even greater extent in the future. In this regard it is of prime importance to focus on relevant trends within three interdependent action areas: strategy, structure and technology.

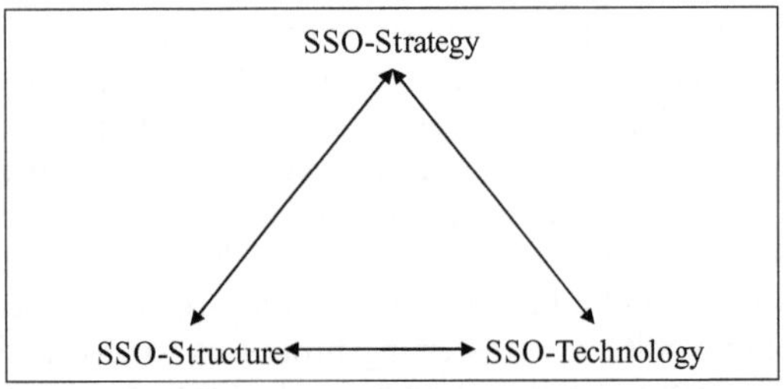

Figure 1: Interdependent SSO-related action areas

2 Strategic Trends

The intended purpose of companies implementing the Shared Service concept by establishing a specialized (internal) self-operating organizational unit[11] is twofold: While first generation SSO primarily aimed to benefit from cost reductions as a result of labour arbitrage as well as economies-of-x effects (e.g. economies of scale, of scope or of network integration) gained through the bundling, harmonization, standardization and IT-enabled automation of prior decentralized and heterogeneously executed support activities, second generation SSO additionally focus on providing higher service levels enabling their internal – and if applicable external – customers to concentrate on their core competencies.[12] Consequently, second generation SSOs simultaneously strive for a higher level of effectiveness and efficiency (see figure 1).

This finding is in line with latest research results from *The Hackett Group*[13] or *ZILLNER* et al.[14]. At the moment SSOs try to become more "service centric" paying attention to unit cost reductions while having a service value focus. A higher degree of effectiveness is expressed by service level excellence. To deliver superior results SSOs implement service management

---

9 *HOLLICH* et al. (2008), p. 29.

10 Cf. e.g. *KAGELMANN* (2001).

11 A deeper insight into the variety of potential description criteria for SSO arrangements derived from literature has been discussed in detail by *RÖDER/KEUPER* (2009).

12 Cf. *KEUPER/OECKING* (2008), p. 478.

13 Cf. *THE HACKET GROUP* (2012).

14 Cf. *ZILLNER* et al. (2012).

frameworks, establish Shared Knowledge Centers[15], and integrate multiple functions within a global business service organization.[16]

The next evolutionary stage will be "value-centric". In future SSOs will have a more sophisticated performance profile acting as a service-oriented entity, serving internal and sometimes (especially when lacking appropriate size) also external customers, delivering unit cost reductions, service value and having a farer reaching business value focus.[17] Increasing business value generated by next generation SSOs results from the ability to innovate processes and improve decision making processes. One big lever will be Big Data management. Hence, we assume next generation SSOs to become a widely accepted strategic business partner focusing both on effectiveness and efficiency improvements. Consequently, the complexity level of customer-supplier-relationships as well as of services will grow (see figure 2).

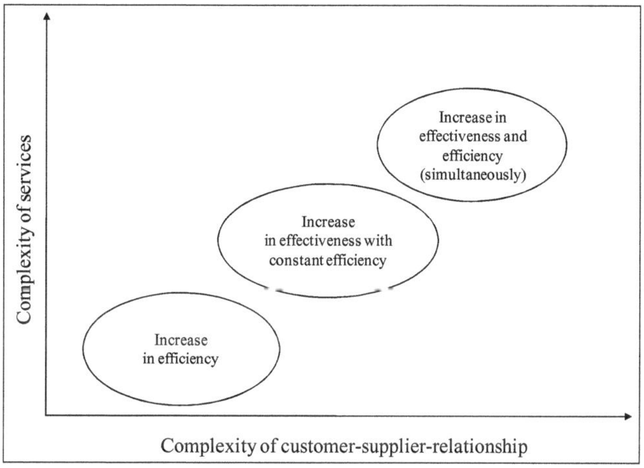

Figure 2: Changing focus of SSOs[18]

Handling these complexity dimensions also means that responsible managers will have to pay much more attention on people- and communication-related aspects during the Shared Service journey. Planning and communication as well as knowledge transfer initiatives will become as important as technology improvements or benefit tracking to foster innovation. A study conducted by *Deloitte* in 2011 supports our expectations (see figure 3).

The *Deloitte* study especially reveals that recruiting is of prime importance. Undoubtly, hiring well educated and highly motivated staff is becoming a key challenge for SSO managers – not only because of dramatic demographic changes. In addition to that systematic and sustainable talent management programs will be one of the top-priority action items on the agenda of SSOs executive agendas. Managing the Shared Services journey as depicted in figure 2 means that next generation SSOs requires both generalists and specialists, who can handle increasing complexity. Thus, there will be a job evolution within SSOs ranging from rules-ba-

15 Cf. e.g. JANSSEN/VAN GRINSVEN/JOHA (2013).

16 Cf. THE HACKET GROUP (2012).

17 Cf. THE HACKET GROUP (2012).

18 KEUPER/OECKING (2008), p. 488.

sed processing to judgment-based processing to knowledge-based processing.[19] This job evolution within a Finance-SSO (FSSO) can be characterized as described in table 1.

	Job Evolution	Know-how	Problem Solving	Accountability
Operational Maturity	Rules-based processing (traditional)	➢ Task-focus ➢ Applies relevant basic financial principles ➢ General knowledge of function	➢ Applies standard techniques to routine problems with limited variables	➢ Receives detailed instruction on work routine
	Judgement-based processing	➢ Proficient understanding of financial processes, principals, theories and concepts and organizational policies, procedures, goals, and strategies	➢ Exercises judgment within generally defined practices and procedures ➢ Selects methods and techniques for obtaining solutions	➢ Receives general instruction frequently
	Knowledge-based processing (true Shared Services)	➢ Comprehensive knowledge of financial processes, principals, theories, and concepts and organizational policies, procedures, goals and strategies	➢ Faces complex issues ➢ Drives innovation, in-depth assessments ➢ Considering many variables and potential consequences	➢ Functions independently with limited work direction

Table 1: Job Evolution in next generation SSOs[20]

[19] Cf. *CUSTIS/HILTON/SEQUEIRA* (2008), p. 21.

[20] *CUSTIS/HILTON/SEQUEIRA* (2008), p. 21.

3 Structural Trends

There are three fundamental support models for Shared Services:[21]

- *Center of Scale Services*, which "handle routine transactions by leveraging economies of scale and standardization"[22] (e.g. accounts payable or payroll)
- *Center of Expertise Services*, which handle complex non-routine activities (e.g. income tax issues)
- *Corporate Steward Services*, which handle "activities requiring high levels of expertise to corporate management" (e.g. government relations or risk management).

Aiming at a higher level of effectiveness and efficiency we expect these fundamental support models to change regarding their structural organization. Globalization and new technologies[23] enable next generation SSOs to create Shared Services Networks (SSN).[24] A recent study conducted by the *Steinbeis Center of Strategic Management*[25] in cooperation with *SAP* in 12 multinational corporations running one or more SSOs for various services revealed that there is no "standard" organizational structure. SSOs structures change dramatically. In line with other researchers and experts[26] we expect SSOs to "become a focal company within a network of service providers."[27]

At the moment lots of experts discuss about multifunctional SSOs. From our point of view it is plausible to assume that future SSOs will often be a conglomerate of various functional-oriented types of Shared Service Centers within an SSO. So, the Finance Shared Service Center (FSSC) could be organized as a "classic" Corporate Shared Service Center (CSS) due to its critical role for the whole company, while Procurement Shared Service Centers (PSSC) could be organized as cooperatively-arranged SSOs. Both the FSSC and the PSSC can be part of a global SSO. Hence, next generation SSOs can choose between different organizational structures, which in their specific case fit best in view of the highest level of effectiveness and efficiency. Cutting a long story short, next generation SSOs pay special attention to an effective and efficient network as well as cooperation management.[28]

21 Cf. *UHL/FISCHER* (2012).
22 *UHL/FISCHER* (2012), slide 8.
23 Cf. chapter 4 in this article.
24 Cf. *KEUPER/OECKING* (2008), p. 492.
25 Cf. online http://www.steinbeis-scsm.de.
26 Cf. e.g. *KEUPER/OECKING* (2008).
27 *KEUPER/OECKING* (2008), p. 494.
28 Cf. *KEUPER/OECKING* (2008), p. 495.

4 Technological Trends

During the lift and drop phase companies operating an SSO benefit from cost reductions through labour arbitrage and economies of effects (e.g. economies of scale, economies of scope and economies of time). The positive impact of IT-technology is twofold. On the one hand it reduces the cost per transaction and on the other hand it is the basis for further qualitative improvements.

According to a study conducted by *The Hackett Group* in 2010 automation is a key factor for next generation SSOs. More than 50 % of the respondents stated that automation and self services are the most influential cost reduction factors going forward. 80 % of the companies plan to invest more in automation technologies (e.g. Electronic Data Interchange [EDI]) and 91 % expect more initiatives regarding the development and operation of new automation technologies.[29] With regard to automation we especially expect higher investments in document scanning and imaging as well as workflow and data processing automation tools. These "commodity" technologies are the basis for successfully operating SSOs. But, next generation SSOs will have to go further: FSSCs for example import, process and manage large data volumes from numerous sources, but so far as a rule, they do not analyze these data to improve and accelerate decision making processes. Thus, we predict, that building and operating specialized data analyzing groups either integrated in a running SSO or established as a completely new Shared Service will grow rapidly. These derive relevant management implications from identified patterns within unstructured data. Hence, next generation SSOs will evolve from simple transaction-processing units to knowledge-intensive business units delivering visible value to their stakeholders. Automation and data analysis will provide mid- to long term the biggest improvement levers for SSOs.

Another key success factor for next generation SSOs is the effectiveness and efficiency of their knowledge management. Therefore, modern knowledge management tools have to be developed and implemented (e.g. search engines, how-to-databases or collaboration tools). Such tools are fundamental for cross-border operations management as well as innovation management. In order to handle complex customer inquiries SSO personnel need fast and simple access to up-to-date information. If a service agent has solved a non-routine problem, he/she should be able to make his solution available for other colleagues to avoid duplication of work. Moreover knowledge database tools help SSOs to save money regarding the onboarding of new staff.

With regard to innovation management knowledge management helps organizations pursue continuous process improvement — an ongoing challenge for SSOs. Knowledge management database solutions can help organizations capture, organize, track, manage, and prioritize ideas for innovation. They can be implemented so that anyone within the organization can generate and contribute ideas, which helps the company capture ideas from the employees — not just management. These applications can also give managers the tools they need to avoid losing or ignoring good ideas. Most of all, at many companies, knowledge management technologies may already be available in the organization through the IT function.[30]

---

29 Cf. *THE HACKETT GROUP* (2010).

30 *DELOITTE* (2011).

DELOITTE (2011a): Shares Services: From "If" to "How". Insights from Deloitte`s 2011 Global Shared Services Survey, 2011.

DELOITTE (2011b): Technology-enabled Shared Service Centers: The Vital Role of Strategic Planning, online: http://www.deloitte.com/assets/Dcom-UnitedStates/LocalAssets/Documents/IMOs/SharedServices/us_sdt_technologyenabledsscs_11112011.pdf, date: 2011/11/11, download: 2012/10/11.

JANSSEN, M./VAN GRINSVEN, J. H. M./JOHA A. (2013): Operational Risk Management as Shared Service Center of Excellence (CoE), in: *KEUPER, F./LUEG, K.-E.* (eds.), Finance Bundling and Finance Transformation – Shared Services Next Level, Wiesbaden 2013, pp. 365–380.

KERMANSHAHCHE, K. (2012): Shared Services and Healthcare Cloud: A Strategy for Adoption, online: http://www.intel.eu/content/dam/www/public/us/en/documents/reports/shared-services-healthcare-cloud-presentation.pdf date: 2012/18/04, download: 2012/30/11.

KEUPER, F. (2001): Strategisches Management, München/Wien 2001.

KEUPER, F. (2004): Kybernetische Simultaneitätsstrategie, Berlin 2004.

PAMPER, R./FISCHER, T. M. (2007): Shared Service Center Controlling, in: *KPMG* (ed.), Ergebnisse einer empirischen Untersuchung [Results of an Empirical Study], Hamburg/Nuremberg 2007.

PWC (2012): German Entertainment and Media Outlook 2011–2015, Frankfurt/Main 2011.

RÖDER, S./KEUPER F. (2012): Wie HR-Shared-Service-Center effektiver werden, online: http://www.steinbeis.de/publikationen/transfermagazin/transfer-032012/wie-hr-shared-service-center-effektiver-werden.html, date: 2012/11/07, download: 2012/30/11.

THE HACKETT GROUP (2010): Annual GBS Performance Study, 2010.

THE HACKETT GROUP (2012): Annual GBS Performance Study, 2012.

UHL, A./FISCHER, M. (2012): Approaching the Digital Enterprise – Shared Service Center 3.0, Presetation during the SAP Business Transformation Summit 2012, Budapest 2012.

VONGLIS, J. (2011): Vision of Shared Services: What the Future Could Look Like, online: http://www.businessofgovernment.org/blog/strategies-font-color-redcut-costsfont-and-improve-performance/vision-shared-services-what-futu, date: 2011/11/14, download: 2012/12/02.

WIKIPEDIA (2012): Holography – Overview and History, online: http://en.wikipedia.org/wiki/Hologram, date: 2012/11/14, download: 2012/12/02.

ZILLNER, M./ENDERS, W./SEITZ, S./SCHEUBLE, F. (2012): Financial Shared Service Center on the Rise toward valuable business partners – 2nd Generation FSSCs, in: *PWC* (ed.), 2012.

Part 4:

Selected Enablers and Prerequisites for a Successful Development of a Shared Services Organization

A Sustainable Approach to Transition Projects – Change Management

VANESSA EGLI

Siemens AG, Global Shared Services

Executive Summary

Over the last decade, the financial organization of *Siemens* has changed significantly. Following a classic bundling approach and in order to achieve economies of scale, *Siemens* entities all over the world started to consolidate highly repeatable, transaction-heavy accounting and finance work to an internal organization, called Global Shared Services (GSS). From these beginnings, GSS has not stopped on its path of transformation and the GSS of today barely resembles the organization of one decade ago.

The pace of change embarked upon by ramping up such Shared Service Centers is not to be underestimated. First, the Shared Services provider needs to rapidly absorb new employees with a broad range of process and language skills to suit the growing customer community. Secondly, if a 'Lift and Drop' transition methodology is being employed – whereby processes are absorbed 'as is' from the donating entity and without major incoming process standardization steps – the Shared Services provider also needs to cope with a growing process complexity while staying on top of local compliance and legal regulations. The internal pressure to take over and perform often completely new processes or process steps under time pressure – to the same quality, or better, than the donating entity performed them – can become overwhelming for teams and managers.

Added to this, the Shared Services provider, especially that which caters to a captive market, operates in an environment of acute attention from varying stakeholders and governance partners – the corporate, governance, compliance and customer communities – and the complexity of the stakeholder community will obviously increase exponentially during the transition months. Despite the constant change and growth, service and quality levels need to be maintained and improved upon in order to maintain the goodwill and support of this growing group of stakeholders. Growth at the expense of user and customer satisfaction is not an option.

The conundrum of achieving such rapid organizational change while still keeping all affected parties aligned, supportive, and 'pulling in the same direction' – and while also ensuring that the performance and motivation of internal teams does not suffer – can be achieved to a great extent with the use of good change management practices.

Change management, as a business discipline, focuses on the 'people' dimension of organizational strategy. In essence, change management takes a humanistic (rather than a process or systematic) view of organizations. The core assumption is that organizations are the sum of all of those people working for it and that sustainable strategic change can only be achieved by engaging and supporting all employees and managers in the journey of change. Further, it posits that excellence can *not* only be achieved by cutting edge technology and processes; rather, that relevant changes in the mindset, aspirations and competencies of the employees is also necessary in order to create sustainable and 'felt' organizational change that can drive an organization into new levels of performance, into new markets, and allow it to follow more challenging and rewarding business strategies.

This article explores the way in which change management has been used, and can be used, to support the successful execution of transition projects, referring to the *Siemens* Finance Bundling global project as a specific example. The focus is primarily on the changes that need to be led within the *receiving* organization – in other words, the Shared Services provider whose scope grows out the global transition.

In particular, this article explores how a global Shared Services provider can divide its internal transition into concrete phases – 'Lift and Drop', 'Change', and 'Enhance and Innovate' – and how the change management strategy can be specifically adapted per phase. These different phases of a large global transition project represent the different maturity levels of the receiving organization, implying different 'people' needs along the change journey.

It is important to note that the views and opinions provided in this article are based strongly on the experience of the project team and management within the global Shared Services provider at *Siemens* – Global Shared Service (GSS). The change management considerations and conclusions derived over the course of the project have influences – for example, the culture of *Siemens* and the global heterogeneity of the many entities with the *Siemens* finance community – which may or not apply to other multinationals pursuing a similar strategy of Shared Services.

1 Change Management at *Siemens* Global Shared Services

Siemens Global Shared Services (GSS) utilizes change management across the board and on all projects of a certain size, due to the core conviction that change management contributes to organizational success by:

- pro-actively and systematically supporting the organizational changes required to achieve corporate goals
- enabling people to understand the changes and be committed, and enabling them to build the skills needed to 'live' the required changes
- increasing the motivation of people sustainably and their active contribution towards change.

Further, through the application of change management practices, the following negative effects of large change projects may be proactively avoided. These negative effects include:

- negatively impacting employee or even customer satisfaction due to the project implementation
- productivity drops due to this dissatisfaction from employees, or as a result of employees feeling 'change fatigue'
- the business case for the project not being achieved as originally set out in the project definition, due to a lack of commitment to the changes implied in the project (active or passive 'change resistance')
- only achieving 'superficial change' as a result of the project, with target groups quickly returning to the 'way they have always done things' instead of living the new processes and/or behaviors needed to make change sustainable.

GSS has a defined change management methodology[1] integrating certain core change management interventions into the globally-used standard project management methodology, which all project managers in all locations are required to follow.

In order to leverage the people of an organization for any type of change, the following areas typically need to be addressed by a change management strategy:[2]

- the leadership of change – empowering leaders at all levels of the organization to effectively explain and promote the changes happening in the organization and why they are important
- relationships and collaboration – proactively informing and involving those stakeholders (both inside and outside of the organization) most affected by the changes in order to minimize resistance and maximize buy-in
- awareness and commitment – ensuring that core strategic goals are translated into effective messages that can be cascaded throughout the whole organization, orienting everyone towards the desired destination
- employee engagement and its effect on performance – recognizing that superior performance only comes from engaged and motivated employees
- competency development – being able to recognize which competencies are needed now and in the future to achieve organizational objectives, and having the right strategies for training and supporting employees build up the required skills.

2 Redefining the Transition Roadmap in terms of 'People'

Often it is tempting to speak of large projects in terms of the 'concrete' end result – for example, one might define how the organisation structure, processes, technological landscape, level of automation, or business model will change from time point A to time point B. Judging success or arrival at the agreed end point is relatively simple: Are the processes up and running? Is the computer system 'live'? Is the new organizational unit operational?

Judging success from a change management perspective is slightly problematic and much more subjective. For example, it is much harder to prove or to demonstrate that the culture of a group of people has become more entrepreneurial, or that a certain competency has increased for the majority of line managers within a defined time frame.

However, multiple years experience in running transition projects at GSS has certainly led to the belief that addressing the people-side of change, and not just the technological or process sides, leads to a project that is considered to have been more successful and that is better accepted both internally and by the various stakeholder and governance groups.

1 Cf. *Siemens Global Shared Services* (2011).

2 These points reflect the experience of Siemens Global Shared Services (GSS) throughout the last decade of transition, and are based in part on classic change theory such as *John P. Kotter*'s '8 Step' approach to leading change. Cf. *Kotter* (1996).

How does a change manager begin devising a strategy for a large global transition project? The important first step is to define the project goals and scope in terms of 'people' components, such as the knowledge and skills, competencies, practices, behaviours, values and attitudes that will be needed to make the project a sustainable success.

For example, the Finance Bundling project mission[3] – with specific regard to GSS Accounting and Finance Services (AFS) – was broadly defined as follows:

> *"The ultimate goal of Finance Bundling for GSS is to realize savings for our customers. GSS AFS leverages savings potential by bundling all transactional accounting activities of the Siemens entities in the corresponding GSS Delivery Center(s) and by enhancing the standardization and automation of key accounting processes [...] In addition to realizing savings for our customers, GSS AFS is committed to acting as a trusted strategic partner for our many customers by constantly seeking opportunities to improve and optimize the many processes for which we are responsible. We are dedicated to the constant pursuit of improved service quality and transparency in a spirit of entrepreneurial partnership with our customers."*

While the ultimate goal may well be the delivery of savings, the mission also makes many references to 'people' topics. Being 'committed to act as a strategic partner' implies a group behaviour that should be demonstrated by GSS managers and executives in their dealings with customers in the sectors, regions and companies. The implication is also that a higher level of skill needs to be built and supported within the organization in order to be able to identify topics and areas for improvement that have a high strategic relevance for the customer community. Displaying a 'spirit of entrepreneurial partnership' is a mindset that must be fostered by leaders and internally promoted. It is the role of change management to extract the people components of the overall mission and strategy, and think about the 'building blocks' that need to be put in place within the organization to make them a reality. Competency plans, training, communications, and leadership actions are examples of such building blocks.

It is important to recognise that GSS, for its own internal purposes as a receiving organization, has made a distinction between the phases of its strategic roadmap and refers to the following three distinct phases:

- Phase 1 – 'Lift and Drop'
- Phase 2 – 'Change'
- Phase 3 – 'Enhance and Innovate'.

The personnel and performance strategies of each phase necessarily differ, meaning that the change management strategy should be adjusted and focused to each phase at hand. The three transition phases, and the recommended change management strategy, are explored in more detail throughout the rest of this article.

---

3 Cf. *SIEMENS* (2011b).

3 'Lift and Drop' Phase – The Change Challenge of the Shared Services Provider in 'Ramp Up'

The 'Lift and Drop' phase of a transition project is in effect a 'Ramp Up' phase for the service provider, a highly dynamic phase in which work is transitioned from multiple donating entities to a receiving entity or entities. For GSS Accounting and Finance Services (AFS), this meant a three to four year effort (including planning) in which individual Siemens entities transitioned accounting and financial processes or sub-processes to GSS according to a defined activity split per process.

Obviously, the people issues at the **donating** entity are more focused on keeping stability and performance high despite the unrest that comes when parts of processes are withdrawn and teams either made smaller or redirected to new tasks. One of the core challenges for management and human resources within the local organization is in retaining the resources with the depth of skills to perform adequate knowledge transfer to the receiving entity. It is understandable that in such a transition project, the local business units may 'push-back', question the sense of the new business model, and argue against either the timing or scope of the transition. This creates an environment of political 'noise' which needs to be managed if the project is to be successful. The importance of change sponsorship in overcoming this challenge is discussed below.

From a people perspective, the challenge for the **receiving** entity is in rapidly absorbing the process, including its necessary local variants, and growing this capability in the receiving organization. The combination of process skills and required language skills to serve the growing number of customers at the desired quality presents a huge challenge to the recruiting activities of the human resources department. As each wave of transition proceeds, the receiving entity grows in complexity from both a service delivery and customer relationship management perspective. The more rapid the ramp up and the larger the waves of transitions, the harder the receiving entity has to work in order to develop the correct supporting functions and processes (for example, the Customer Relationship Management function and the corresponding roles and responsibilities).

The main change priorities for the 'Lift and Drop' phase for the receiving entity can be summarized as follows:

- having a clear mandate for change –also called having a 'Case for Change' – to overcome the resistance that may result from the donating entities (local business units)
- having effective and visible change sponsorship to help promote the overall strategy and need for change
- ensuring stakeholder alignment ('one direction') and clear relationship management responsibilities
- speed and completeness of knowledge transfer for process steps/processes being transitioned
- supportive human resources policies for rapid recruiting and on-boarding within the receiving entity

- solid competency development plans for the many new employees in a ramp up environment, with focus on both 'hard' and 'soft' skills.

Each of these change priorities is elaborated in more detail in the following sections.

3.1 Clear and Agreed Mandate for Change

A mandate for change – also called the 'Case for Change' – is a brief and compelling statement of the change expected to be achieved by the overall transition project. An effective Case for Change may be formulated by answering the following questions:

- why are we doing the project?
- if we do not do this project, what is the 'missed opportunity' to the organization?
- how will the overall organizational success be threatened if the project is not attempted or is done badly?
- what are the benefits of the project – to the organization as a whole, to the stakeholders, and to the end users or recipients of the project?

Winning support at the beginning of a transition project comes from ensuring that the case for change is globally communicated, understood and accepted. For example, in order for GSS to have been able to begin with the first Finance Bundling transitions with the cooperation of the donating entities, this mandate for change needed first to have been globally communicated and cascaded by the *Siemens* Board and Corporate Finance as the governance function.

An effective change mandate makes a strong link between the project goals and the overall strategic objectives of the organization, and is best personally delivered by a person with considerable expertise and influence within the topic area – the so-called "Change Sponsor".

3.2 Change Sponsorship

Moving to a Shared Services structure is a fundamental change for an organization, being in effect a complete shift in business model. It can cause debate and resistance as different parts of the organization question the sense of moving to a Shared Services model, the pace of transition, the scope of what is to be transitioned, and concern over ongoing quality and cost of the processes being delivered. Of course, fears and concerns around redundancies within the donating entities always accompany transition projects and need to be handled sensitively.

While discussion and debate is a natural part of change, in order for the transition to gain momentum and gain critical mass, clear direction and change sponsorship is required. The overall change sponsor is usually the overall process or topic owner and for a large global transition project would ideally be someone at board level. The change sponsor needs to be visible to the entire organization and have the influence to resolve issues and make binding decisions.

The success of any change management effort relies to a great extent on how visible and vocal the change sponsor is; how often they speak to the topic, sell the positive aspect of the changes, and how they deal authentically and honestly with resistance and skepticism. However, in a large global transition, change sponsorship needs to go further than just one person. 'Strong corporate-executive advocacy is important in the journey [...] Continuous, consistent senior leadership endorsement of the Shared Services Organization – combined with appropriate monitoring and enforcement – is a must."[4]

Of course, as the Shared Services Organization develops and matures, the strong need for top-down enforcement or mandate would ideally drop, being replaced by a growth in the internal competence of sales and key account management. This is explored more in Section 5 – 'Enhance and Innovate Phase'.

3.3 Stakeholder Management

The sheer size of the *Siemens* finance global transition project led to a complex and large group of stakeholders in the sectors and clusters who needed to be constantly informed about the transition project' goals, milestones, and progress. Although GSS was not directly accountable for stakeholder management for the Finance Bundling program (this was a Corporate Finance responsibility), it is clear that the operating environment is more favorable for the Shared Services provider when the business stakeholders have a positive perception from the outset. Any time invested in boosting stakeholder support in the early years of a transition project can avoid time spent later repairing a 'damaged brand' when those same stakeholders have become customers.

Stakeholders are a critical consideration in all change projects and initiatives because:

- they are well-placed within the organization and have influence
- they are involved in decision making and may either actively support or block decisions
- they are often very visible to other members of the local organization (line managers, team leads and end-users), who look to the stakeholder when forming their opinions about 'the sense' of particular projects or initiatives
- they possess expertise for their respective area which can be used to make the project more successful
- if resistance is faced by the project, it usually always comes from a stakeholder or small group of stakeholders who have not been adequately involved, informed, or managed, or whose contribution has not been sought.

Because a large part of change management deals with resistance and how to minimize it, Stakeholder Management is crucial for projects that span multiple regions and business areas. Creating the right communications channels to cover the required breadth and depth of the stakeholder community can be complicated, ensuring that the information is cascaded as far as it needs to go, while at the same time being targeted to the unique needs of each stakeholder group.

---

4. Cf. *DELOITTE DEVELOPMENT LLC* (2009).

One of the most effective ways to lower resistance is by fostering collaboration, for example, by inviting key stakeholders to be a part of certain project activities or to have a chance to help design end state processes. The project might also want to develop a quick means of 'taking the pulse' of the stakeholders' sentiment from time to time to confirm if it is in fact improving in aggregate. Stakeholder sentiment tends to exist in direct correlation with the strength and visibility of change sponsorship (see previous section).

In the global project Finance Bundling, a large amount of time was spent on fostering relationships with and seeking to understand the concerns of the many stakeholders of the project, especially during the planning, requirements gathering, and pilot phases of the global transition project. In retrospect, this proved to be a time consuming but ultimately important step, and a lever for project success.

3.4 Knowledge Transfer

The strategic imperative of the 'Lift and Drop' phase is to enable seamless ramp up for the service provider. From a people perspective, this means ensuring that there is a careful matching of the availability of resources handing over and also taking over certain process steps from those who currently do the work.

Indeed, the ongoing availability of process experts at the donating entity, who are required to take part in knowledge transfer activities such as work-shadowing, was identified as one of the critical risks for GSS during the transitions from customers to the Shared Services Organization. In reality, the experience from the *Siemens* Financial Community is that key experts in individual companies *did* show strong work ethics and remained in their positions to take part in the necessary knowledge transfer activities. This is attributed to the considerate, fair, and honest communication – as well as early involvement of workers councils – that was cascaded throughout the organization in partnership with local human resources professionals.

3.5 Recruitment and Competency Development

Obviously, a ramp up situation requires that the receiving entity has fast access to the right talent pools, and the 'right' talent for a Shared Services provider needs to tick multiple boxes. Process and ERP system 'know-how' is obviously required, but an equally important consideration is language skills. Depending on the global footprint of the Shared Services provider, one hub could end up needing to operate in upwards of 10 or even 20 different languages. GSS' experience during ramp up for Finance Bundling is that the ability to find the right language resources is a much greater constraint on transition plans than system or process know-how.

Example: 'People' Aspects of the ramp up of the *Siemens* Global Shared Services (GSS) Lisbon Delivery Center 2009–2012

Consider the following experience from the GSS Lisbon Delivery Center during the ramp up phase of Finance Bundling; between 2009 and 2012, the Center grew in scope from serving 6 to 72 customers from 18 different countries and speaking a total of 11 languages. The local HR department reviewed close to 2,000 candidates in order to employ the final 180 staff. 80% of this growth was actually achieved in the 12 months from April 2011 to April 2012. The effort required to attract such a high number of candidates in an already competitive employment market was immense – other global players such *Cisco*, *Microsoft*, *Fujitsu*, *Mercer*, *Apple*, *Solvay*, and *Adidas* were in competition for the same resources. In the end, recruitment activities in Lisbon alone were not enough, and targeted campaigns were launched in the 'donating' countries speaking the required languages.

The competition for resources also depended strongly on the perceived brand equity of '*Siemens*' and proves that corporate identity and perceived culture are topics that have relevance to the Shares Services provider.

Recruitment is only half of the challenge during ramp up. The GSS Lisbon Center also needed to grow an internal competency for rapid employee onboarding and training. The number of training hours delivered to all employees grew over the transition years from 5,000 hours in 2009, to 35,000 hours in 2011. The training content and methodology were revised in order to condense the learning into shorter time frames and to ensure onboarding staff were job and customer ready. At the same time, an ever-growing number of team leaders and service delivery managers needed to be trained in the necessary leadership competencies to support these new teams and ensure that service and quality targets were reached.

Training is not just a once-off and upfront concern; after the initial training provided to support new employees, progressive training modules are required to keep bringing improvements in service quality across the board.

3.6 Post 'Ramp Up' Challenges

While ramp up seems like only good news for the growing Shared Services provider, it can leave a 'hangover' for subsequent phases. The risk is that the organization grows so fast that it is no longer one unified organization acting in the same way. In other words, the risk is that it is a random collection of parts, instead of one truly unified organization. Performance across service offerings and regions may be 'patchy', which is no basis for improving measures of customer and user satisfaction and brand image across the board. This risk sets up the direction of the change priority for the Change Phase (post ramp up) – using the organizational culture to gain unity and consistency. The unique change management challenges of this phase are discussed in the next section.

4 'Change' Phase – A New Challenge for a New Phase

The 'Lift and Drop' phase is typically centrally orchestrated, due to the need to carefully time and coordinate activities between the donating and receiving entities. 'Lift and Drop' implies equal amounts of effort on both sides of the equation. However, once the receiving entity moves into the 'Change Phase', the focus becomes entirely internal. The donating entity, now called the customer, becomes concerned with the cost-quality relationship and moves into the role of a service user, receiving pre-defined information from the service provider (achievement of Key Performance Indicators agreed in Service Level Agreements (SLAs), for example). At the same time, the receiving entity, now called the service provider, which has taken on the huge amounts of processes and process variants, may turn attention inward to stabilization, optimization and productivity boosting initiatives.

Seeking opportunities for change that result in efficiencies and an improved cost position is crucial to the long term success of a Shared Services provider. In the 'Lift and Drop' phase, quick wins through labour arbitrage and the first bundling effects are possible. However, the challenge post-transition is to keep delivering year-on-year savings. This can only be achieved if, every single year, process improvements, modifications, and optimizations are made – hence the name 'Change Phase'. The changes, instead of being led centrally, could originate from any part of the service provider organization. The challenge is how to identity best practice (desirable changes) and leverage it to all service units and regions so that the savings that derive from the changes are maximized.

In this phase, robust internal and external comparisons are made in order to arrive at an optimal delivery model for the services provided to the user community and the effort is taken to make sure that the 'desired' delivery per service is replicated across the whole organization. Redundancies and duplications are driven out wherever they are discovered. Changes may also be needed in the structure of the organization, for example, new functions such as Quality Management may be needed to bring attention to topics which can be considered important strategic levers in the new phase.

It will come as no surprise, then, that an organization finding itself in this 'Change' phase will benefit from the application of change management principles. Using a strong change management methodology and training managers in its application gives those managers the skills and confidence to recognize opportunities for change and to successfully bring about sustainable change in their respective area of responsibility. Further, working to increase the general appetite for change is crucial. It cannot be assumed that all managers perceive change as positive; in fact, even the most talented and technically competent managers can be innately adverse to change. The change management effort in this phase is therefore not only about giving the organization the *skills* to change, it is also about building a *will* to change – an overall belief that the sum of changes successfully executed will open new markets and options for the overall organization.

The overall implication is that the receiving entity must take the next step along the maturity curve; instead of passively receiving processes in the form they existed at the customer site, the entire organization must be ready to recognize and propose suitable process and service delivery changes. This requires a differing skill set from managers and teams as opposed to the previous 'Lift and Drop' phase. The competencies required for success in this 'Change Phase' include, for example; quality management, process reengineering, strong Shared Services Industry knowledge, internal collaboration and knowledge sharing, the ability to consult and guide the customer as a true process expert, and the ability to drive up professionalization and productivity at all levels of the organization.

Some of the main change priorities for a Shared Services provider in a 'Change Phase' can be summarized as follows:

- driving appropriate cultural change from the top down (appropriate in the sense that the cultural elements need to match the overall organizational strategy of *where it wants to go*)
- supporting management, especially middle management, in their role as change agents for the organization
- ensuring true collaboration, both internally and externally, in the constant pursuit for worthwhile and impactful improvements
- increasing focus on retention strategies in the face of constant focus on savings and standardization efforts – keeping the right people with the process expertise and service excellence for the coming transformation phase.

Each of these change priorities is elaborated in more detail in the following sections.

4.1 Developing the Right Organizational Culture

In 2008, *Deloitte* surveyed 35 Shared Service leaders and asked them to nominate the greatest challenges to the 'advancement of global shared services'. The number one identified challenges, with 52 %, was internal culture.[5] In the previous 'Lift and Drop' section, it was noted that perceived culture of a Shared Services Organisation has a role in attracting talent during ramp up and in that respect can provide competitive advantage.

In the 'Change Phase', culture continues to provide competitive advantage, but for different reasons. The importance of culture is that it helps provide signals to the entire organization as to which behaviours are expected and rewarded. If the role of corporate strategy is to set out the roadmap towards long term growth and viability, then the role of corporate culture is to drive behaviours *en masse* – for all teams from top to bottom – in order to allow the strategy to come alive in an operational sense, and in a way that is tangible to the service user and customers.

For a Shared Service provider in the 'Change Phase', the relevant behaviors for success typically include:

- complete service orientation (customer focus)
- the ability to innovate
- the ability to collaborate
- rapid best practice sharing

5 Cf. *DELOITTE DEVELOPMENT LLC* (2009).

- ability to execute with speed
- commitment to quality
- non-silo thinking
- end-to-end process focus.

These behaviors, taken together, create an organization that is more mature than the one described in the previous section. Whereas success under 'Lift and Drop' comes from the ability *to do the work for the customer as it was done previously (by the customer)*, success in this phase comes from the ability to recognize every opportunity for process improvement and to make it happen quickly and across the entire organization.

Changing culture takes a long time, but that is no reason to ignore its role as a strategic lever. Some success factors for managing culture in the right direction include:

- having published and well communicated organization values, which are fully aligned with the desirable behaviors as listed above
- strong leadership, with global and local leaders displaying the stated desirable competencies and values, and also willing to make clear leadership actions to support desired organizational change
- global unity – while localizations in process may be required, organizational culture should be consistent at all locations
- performance reviews and policies that are consistent with the stated values.

4.2 Turning Middle Managers into Change Agents

Organizations undergoing large scale change often create a 'squeeze' on operational middle managers; on the one hand, they are encouraged 'by the top' to execute and be a role model for which ever change is seen to be most important. At the same time, they themselves do not have limitless capacity and attention to devote to the new changes and are just as prone to develop change fatigue as anyone else.

Nonetheless, managers are the logical change agents within any organization, and they are in a position to guide and motivate with their words and actions. One of their most important tasks is to translate the organizational strategy into daily operational practices that are unambiguous and understood by all teams.

In order to drive change within their own areas and help to move culture, managers need support from the respective HR unit in developing soft skills as well as hard skills. Such soft skills include the ability to manage resistance, networking and collaboration skills, communication skills, and the ability to motivate others. Managers need not only to be trained in these skills, but need to be given the chance to practice them while being given feedback on progress.

4.3 Organizational Collaboration

An organization can only change as fast as it can share knowledge and ideas across the organization. Change occurring in isolated pockets does not bring strategic advantage, and there is great scope for Shared Services Organizations to integrate activities across functions. "Mature Shared Services Organizations are taking a holistic view of the entire enterprise, improving productivity not only in a single function but breaking down silos and integrating processes across functions."[6] For example, integration between the Accounting & Finance and the Supply Chain processes in order to bring about greater accuracy and speed in procure-to-pay processes is a logical area in which benefit can be derived.

It is important to stress that collaboration is a human behavior. It is much more than simply making a knowledge sharing platform available to all employees. True collaboration stems from dialogue; being inquisitive, actively seeking information from parts of the business that are seemly non-related, and taking the time to inform others about one's own area of expertise. In this way, the topics of collaboration and behavioral (culture) change are very closely linked.

In order to maximize the added value of a Shared Services Organizations to the business users, collaboration needs to extend to the customer, for example, allowing the customer to deliver input into process optimization discussions, helping the customer perform their part of the process as well as possible, and viewing process excellence as end-to-end instead of being focused on only 'our' part of the process. Collaboration can even go one step further, for example, by collaborating with suppliers or banks for more effective master data capture and maintenance. This represents a new foundation for the relationship between the Shared Services provider and the customer as compared to the 'Lift and Drop' phase.

4.4 Employee Engagement and Retention

"Companies have found that once they establish a fully operational Shared Services Center it is difficult to keep its employees fully engaged in the face of demands for further efficiencies."[7]

The change phase is one in which there is lots of talk about driving out cost and unnecessary complexity. At the same time, it is like a 'pause' phase between 'Lift and Drop' and the phase of portfolio expansion which brings the next cycle of growth; the focus is on internal housekeeping, so to speak. Depending on how long this phase lasts for, and on how this phase is communicated internally, the risk is that the staff begin to fear that automation will reduce jobs and that opportunities for growth and development will dry up. Constant talk about process standardization and harmonization can give the impression that those who stay within the company will sink deeper and deeper into a specialized and highly technical part of a process with no scope for sideways or upwards movement.

---

6 *CECIL/WILLIAMS* (2011).

7 *KULHALLI* (2010).

It is crucial that from a communications and change management point of view, that the next expansionary phase ('Enhance and Innovate', addressed in the next section) is constantly discussed with managers and employees, regardless of when it 'officially' starts. This can help ensure that the best talent see future career path opportunities within the organization and that they are reassured that they will have a chance to build new skills in new areas of service offering.

5 'Enhance and Innovate' Phase – The Change Challenge Switches Again

The focus of the previous 'Change' phase is on process standardization and harmonization; although the phase is called the 'Change Phase', changes are only made on *existing* processes as brought over by the 'Lift and Drop' phase. 'Change' in this sense is taken to mean any change that *rationalizes* and *streamlines* the existing service portfolio and delivery. The implication is also that there is a known 'destination' of the change for the 'Change Phase' – maximum reduction of process variants within defined scope, greatest degree of automation, and the best possible performance to cost ratio.

In comparison, the degree of change in the 'Enhance and Innovate' phase is actually higher and much harder to grasp; at the outset of the phase, the service provider may not even *know* in which direction the service enhancements and innovation will logically go or how broadly, deeply or quickly they will affect the organization. The ability to identify, analyse and execute change, then, – at *all* management levels – becomes much more pronounced in this stage and a much greater criteria for future success.

During an expansion phase, Shared Service providers that provide a 'typical' service offering of Accounting and Finance, HR or IT services may chose to look into areas such as marketing, sales, research and development, and real estate. Specifically within the Accounting and Finance function, examples of services at the higher end of the expert scale may include controlling, cash collection, invoicing services, and business analytics. Generally speaking, during a service enhancement phase, the aim is to identify services with higher complexity, higher need for expert resources, and with a higher value to the end customer.

From an organizational development perspective, it is useful to summarize here the core changes that have taken place in the previous two transition phases. 'Lift and Drop' brings rapid growth in the numbers of locations, customers, internal headcount, and processes/process variants offered. In other words, the transition challenge can be summarised as how to support ambitious ramp up, while constraining cost and ensuring performance at the level that customers expect, and while also pioneering and promoting the Shared Services concept in a sometimes resistant stakeholder environment.

During the next phase, the 'Change' phase, focus shifts to how to drive the logical and impactful *internal* changes required to drive professionalization, achieve higher levels of customer satisfaction, and take action to drive down cost. In a sense, this is the phase in which the provider has the chance to deliver on the promise of the Shared Service business model; it must prove that it can identify and execute the changes needed to 'hit' the performance to cost ratio demanded by the particular market (either captive or otherwise), within the appropriate amount of time, and prove that centralized model brings clear benefits to the customers. In order to meet this challenge, changes in the IT landscape or even location strategy may be implied. New functions (for example, Customer Relationship Management) and competencies may be required to bring the requisite amount of focus on internal professionalization and on effective and supportive key account management.

The third transition phase, 'Enhance and Innovate', represents the most substantial change in the sense of venturing into the unknown. Here, the *commercial* skills of the organization come to the forefront in terms of identifying new products and services that will increase market share (without cannibalizing existing share for portfolio elements) and move the perceived image of the Shared Services provider in the desired direction. The higher the degree of 'newness' of chosen portfolio elements and decisions about the *timing* of when to introduce them, the higher the change challenge in building or attracting the required competencies. Competence must not only be built in the delivery of the new service elements, but also in the preceding analysis (identification of *which* enhancements to make) and key account support areas (*how to promote* the enhanced services to the customer).

Of course, there are also benefits to the organization of embarking on an enhancement and innovation path; it is a chance to engage the resources that may have been freed up during the rationalizing 'Change Phase' in new and more expert portfolio areas and service offerings. It also provides better career path options for employees seeking more commercial, analytical and expert roles.

Some of the main change priorities for a Shared Services provider in an 'Enhance and Innovate Phase' can be summarized as follows:

- resurgence of resistance as the Shared Services branches into new and sometimes specialist service offerings
- heightened need for overall and business-line specific leadership
- supporting the new capabilities required for this stage, for example, marketing, service life cycle management, and commercial skills
- managing the Shared Services provider brand and 'breaking from the past' in which the brand only meant repeatable, low-cost and non-expert transactional services.

Each of these change priorities is elaborated in more detail in the following sections.

5.1 Resurgence of Resistance

Stakeholder resistance is discussed in Section 3 of this article – 'Lift and Drop' Phase – and the importance of strong executive change sponsorship was emphasized. In reality, resistance to the Shared Services Organization, particularly in a captive market, is never wholly absent; it is simply a question of degree.

During 'Lift and Drop', resistance often comes from stakeholders wanting proof that the Shared Services provider is capable and delivers a real business benefit. During the 'Change' phase, resistance may be more specifically focused on cost per service or pricing methodology.

Portfolio expansion, the third phase, can bring a fresh wave of resistance. 'It is not uncommon to encounter considerable business-unit resistance when trying to expand the scope of the Shared Services Organization and add more customers.'[8] Here, it is probably not enough to rely on the top-down mandate for change, as previously discussed. It is also crucial that the Shared Services provider have its own internal competence in sales and marketing, to promote and support the growth of the products and services portfolio and to counter resistance with one-on-one fact based discussions with existing and potential customers.

In reality, it may be that *both* an internal sales competence is needed, coupled with continued support from governance. It cannot be denied that strong support 'from the top' can cut through resistance and add speed to the execution of an expansionary phase.

5.2 Heightened Need for Overall and Business-Line Specific Leadership

It has been previously mentioned that the change during this phase can be more overwhelming, simply because the end destination is less clear than for the preceding two phases. For Phase 1, 'Lift and Drop', the end state is more or less known: Transfer the maximum amount of defined processes to the central Shared Services provider from all defined donating entities. For Phase 2, 'Change', the end state is also clear: the most cost-efficient and streamlined delivery model for a set of standardized services. However, in the third phase, the end state is unknown and highly dependent on the internal skill of the Shared Services provider in executing the phase.

To avoid paralysis from ambiguity, or from 'too many options', it is important that the leadership team – both global and function-specific – is ready and able to provide a sensible framework to encourage enhancement work to start. It also needs to be done in a way that is efficient, meaning that information must be flowing optimally at the higher levels of the organization to be able to recognize and stop duplicate work and to leverage success quickly. Barriers to change (for example, open questions around *who* funds innovations or how costs of portfolio development should be covered) need to be dealt with decisively and in a timely manner by leadership. Only by being seen to be acting in the interests of bringing about successful change, will the whole organization hear the message that this new change – enhancement and innovation – is the critical priority.

---

8 Cf. *DELOITTE DEVELOPMENT LLC* (2009).

5.3 Moving into New Competency Domains

In the previous section, reference was made of some of the competencies that are required for the 'Change Phase'. In this section, the more specialised competencies required for driving enhancement and innovation are explained.

Success in this area of service enhancement requires an orchestrated approach between Portfolio Management (bringing the product/service expertise and the vision of how services can be developed over time through different stages of maturity) and Customer Relationship Management (CRM) (bringing the customer relationship expertise). One without the other is not sufficient. Portfolio management skills without customer relationship management could result in a list of services and enhancements that are not seen as a priority or as attractive by the market. Similarly, focus solely on CRM as a source of innovation ideas could result in a 'wish list' that makes little commercial sense to the Shared Services provider or involves excessive investment that cannot be recouped.

Portfolio management skills may include:

- Shared Service industry expertise
- collaboration skills (especially vis à vis the customer)
- product/service design principles
- commercial/start up skills
- consulting skills (to customer)
- IT and data analytics (to identify opportunities together with customer).

Customer relationship management skills at this stage need to have moved beyond simply having one clear contact point to the customer and needs to more proactively support the search for appropriate innovations and enhancements for specific customers or customer groups. The specific skills required may include:

- negotiation skills
- data analysis and interpretation skills
- advanced issue resolution skills
- 'need creation'/marketing
- proactive communication (not just escalation management).

Ultimately, once the Shared Services provider has an enhanced service offering, growth will only be achieved with stronger emphasis on sales and marketing. For many Shared Services providers, especially those with origins in the captive market scenario, this can be a radically new mindset and skill set to have to develop or attract. In summary, some of the most important skills that the Shared Services provider needs to develop in this regard are:

- customer retention strategies
- targeted cross-selling
- one-to-one marketing
- advanced marketing
- service lifecycle management
- deep knowledge of the customers' business drivers per functional area.

These three lists taken together represent a large need for appropriate competencies to support the prerogatives of enhancement and innovation. In order to make it possible, or at least to have a plan to move forward, tight integration is needed between change management and HR. Knowing the required competencies and skills is simply the first step. It is also helpful to be able to define the level at which the competency is required. It may be useful to define a high level competency map and to audit the organization to find out the gap between the existing skill levels and that which is ideally required. Human resources then needs to be able to define to which extent the skill set can be generated internally (within the given time) as opposed to brought in from external sources.

It must also be said that the ease in which these higher level competencies can be built, and how quickly, is a direct result of human resources strategies in the preceding two phases. The first determinant is obviously the skill level of the resources absorbed during ramp up, and to what extent 'expert' skill sets were attracted in comparison to skills that may have been more important at that time i.e. language skills. The second determinant is the success of retention strategies of the best or most expert resources during the 'Change Phase'. The length of the change phase, and the nature in which it was communicated, will have had a bearing on the degree of attrition vs. retention that will take place. This of course has an impact on the skill 'starting point' for the third phase, 'Enhance and Innovate'.

5.4 Managing the Shared Services Brand

All of the best internal enhancements and innovations achieved during this third phase mean nothing if the 'story' of the new and improved Shared Services provider is not transported in a believable and authentic way to the customers. Perceptions of an organization from the past can linger, and rarely keep exact pace with reality. The reality is that the amount of internal transformation that happens between Phase 1 and Phase 3 of transition is massive; the Shared Services provider that has been discussed in this section, 'Enhance and Innovate', bears little resemblance to the fledgling Shared Services Organization undergoing ramp up in the 'Lift and Drop' phase – although the latter is exactly what the customer may remember.

In order to help perception keep pace with reality, the Shared Services provider needs to have a strong hold on communication and to make sure that it is globally consistent in terms of key messaging so that gains in image are made across the board. Success stories and examples of service enhancements and innovations need to be constantly promoted.

However, communication is just one option, with actions much more important. In order to be truly recognized as a partner to the business, capable of suggesting and executing value-adding enhancements, the Shared Services provider needs to try to be more present wherever the customer is. An invisible, thick-walled 'back office' is hardly the image needed for ongoing and sustainable success. In this sense, the Shared Services provider should seek to be at customer events where processes, innovations and projects are discussed; should become involved on customer projects as a subject matter expert, or sit on business project steering committees; and should seek industry recognition and awards in areas in which the customer will take notice. Only by being 'seen' as an organization with the same competence and business drivers as the customer community, can the Shared Services provider gain the overall trust needed to be a true partner and a force for change within the market.

6 Conclusion

The separation of the strategic development of a Shared Services Organization into three distinct phases – and the unique 'people' challenges that need to be answered in each phase – is a structure that has worked well for *Siemens* Global Shared Services during recent years. Such a split into different phases may not be appropriate for other Shared Services Organizations, nor may other organizations choose to use the same terminology for the steps along its development path. Regardless, this article seeks to raise and discuss some of the change management considerations and approaches that may be employed as a Shared Services Organization progresses from start-up to high value-adding business partner to its customers. By keeping commitment, motivation and skills for change in focus, the Shared Services provider gains speed and precision in its strategic development, and maximizes its chances for sustainable success.

Abbreviations and Terms

AFS	Accounting and Financial Services
Donating entity	Legal entity or organizational/accounting unit handing over certain administrative tasks to a Shared Services Organization (or to a Cluster or country organization)
Finance Bundling	Comprehensive program in the areas of accounting, controlling, taxes and financial services to re-shape, harmonize and optimize the worldwide finance functions within *Siemens* group; focus in this article is the transfer of transactional accounting tasks to the in-house Shared Services Organization
GSS	Global Shared Services, the internal Shared Services provider for *Siemens* AG, providing a standardized global catalogue of services covering the Accounting and Finance, Human Resources, and Supply Chain Management areas.
Ramp Up	Describes the phase of a Shared Services provider's development in which work is being transferred consistently from multiple donating entities to the receiving entiy/entities, requiring a corresponding increase of the service provider's internal resources in order to handle volume.
Receiving entity	Legal entity or organizational/accounting unit, regularly a Shared Services Organization (or a Cluster or country organization), receiving certain administrative tasks from the donating entity

References

CECIL, B./WILLIAMS, L. (2011): Up then Out? Shared Services Strategies that Help Promote Best Practice, Bangalore (India) 2011.

DELOITTE DEVELOPMENT LLC (2009): Taking Shared Services to the Next Level – Towards a Portfolio Approach for Shared Services Optimization, 2009.

KOTTER, J. P. (1996): Leading Change, Boston (MA) 1996.

KULHALLI, S. (2010): A Structured Approach to Establishing Shared Services, Bangalore (India) 2010.

SIEMENS GLOBAL SHARED SERVICES (2011a): Change Management Guideline, published internally, Munich 2011.

SIEMENS GLOBAL SHARED SERVICES (2011b): Finance Bundling @ GSS Project Handbook (2011), Version 5.0, Munich 2011.

Service Business Is People Business – Strategic Personnel Management in a Global Shared Services Organization

SUSANNE SOMMERER

Siemens AG, Corporate Human Resources – Global Shared Services

Executive Summary

Focusing on the actual core business and transitioning of administrative non-core processes to a Shared Services Organization (SSO) has been a trend in the global business world for a couple of years now. SSO have proven to be a successful way to support the business not only in terms of cost savings through making use of cost competitive locations, but also through process optimization in general or the implementation of new enabling, productivity ensuring technologies.

But transferring business processes from the 'donating entity' to an (internal) SSO has also a major impact on a core 'production factor': the employees. In order to be able to provide the same services seamlessly to the customer in the promised quality and time, the SSO Human Resources (HR) department needs to make sure that at the right time, the right number of employees with the required business skills is available. In this quickly growing and evolving environment, the requirements can change at a high pace. This brings along many challenges, from hiring the right people and providing qualitative services on the one hand, to fostering training, development and engagement strategies on the other hand.

The Shared Services Industry (SSI) is widely perceived as an industry that does not offer many individual development options, but offers repetitive, low level and low pay jobs in an environment characterized by constant time and cost saving pressure. The creation of an attractive employer brand, or the Employee Value Proposition (EVP), goes hand in hand with the strategic approach on how the workforce will be managed in a Shared Services Organization (SSO).

In a nutshell: considering people development and engagement/retention management is crucial when defining the people strategy. Clearly committed measures ensure that all required professional competencies and skills are available in time on all employee levels and, furthermore, they foster talent and key player retention. Equally important, they help to manage the desired attrition, and to keep the unwanted, cost intense attrition as low as possible. In fact, with the appropriate people management approach, attrition can be managed towards an optimum, which in the end impacts again on the cost effectiveness of a shared services provider. How the HR organization and the responsible management of a SSO can jointly ensure a successful Personnel Management - considering all relevant external (e.g. economic, educational, social environment) and internal influencing factors (e.g. the strategic and organizational boundaries within the company) will be elaborated in this article. Hereby strategic Personnel Management will be analyzed in the light of two dimensions: the commonly known Human Resource Lifecycle and a typical strategic business roadmap of the SSO. Further, important success factors and selected 'real life' HR initiatives, applied within a SSO of a multinational company, are described.

1 Introduction

1.1 Subject

In this paper, the specifics of Strategic Personnel Management in a **Shared Services Organization (SSO)** shall be reflected upon. A SSO can be defined as an (in-house) supplier providing – dependent on its maturity level – transactional administrative and expertise to support customers thus leveraging cost advantages by labor arbitrage, economies of scale and scope as well as producing other benefits such as harmonized and improved quality standards and transparency.

Strategic Personnel Management covers the target-oriented mid- to long-term planning, implementation and controlling of human resources related measures, typically following the process from "hire to retire" of an employee. In more detail, this human resource lifecycle covers the following steps and activities:

- **Definition and planning of manpower requirements**: business based deduction of required skills, determination of the quantity of human resources needed, location and timeline (strategic workforce planning);
- **Attraction of people**: evaluation of the most successful recruiting channels to attract potential candidates;
- **Selection of candidates**: appointing candidates from the application list according to clearly defined criteria and requirements;
- **Employee on-boarding and integration**: ensure employee commitment, understanding and productivity from the very beginning through orientation and introductory workshops and business related training;
- **People development**: skill and capability enhancement through training and assignments, career development plans, succession planning etc.;
- **Employee engagement and retention management**: development and fostering of healthy employer brand and implementation of retention measures to avoid unwanted attrition;
- **Separation and termination of work relationship**: application of appropriate processes: retirement, separation by mutual consent, dismissal by employer and resignation.

When developing and elaborating the Personnel Management Strategy for a Shared Services Organization, many frame-setting dimensions[1] need to be considered by management and HR partners. The most crucial are:

[1] HR literature offers a rich spectrum on these aspects, a good encompassing graphic can be found in *EHNERT* (2009), p. 105.

- External business environment, related to economic, educational, social and demographic conditions or new service trends in the Shared Services Industry[2].
- Internal business environment, related to the given organizational structure, the HR organization as well as the overall business and SSO strategy.

This article focuses on the above mentioned influencing factors as they have the most immediate impact on the Personnel Management approach for the SSO of a multinational company.

1.2 Factors of Influence

In the course of globalization and more intensive competition on international markets, companies need to significantly reduce their costs. This is particularly valid for companies in industrialized countries which face increasing competition from emerging countries, where the overall labor cost level is usually lower. One solution is to transfer non-core processes and specifically scalable transactional tasks to SSOs, which can realize cost advantages through leveraging a global footprint, based on near- and off-shoring options.

Considering the **external factors** from a Shared Services perspective, specific attention needs to be placed on the environment, in which a SSO conducts its business. The global footprint which is key to the overall cost position represents its organizational and local set-up, in terms of Headquarters (HQ) and local Shared Services Center (SSC) locations. However, when selecting the Center location(s) – besides the labor costs – qualitative factors such as the education system, demographic structure[3], availability of potential staff with a defined set of business and language skills as well as the competition around these people at the location have to be taken into account.

On the one hand globalization and competition has a positive effect on the SSO as more and more companies are applying the concept, on the other hand due to this growth the SSO environment has become equally competitive, in particular in certain near and off-shore boom locations, e.g., in the Czech Republic, on the Iberian Peninsula or in India. This has a tremendous impact on the local labor market and SSOs see themselves constantly competing for the same people. This is a factor which can determine the overall success or failure of a SSO and therefore requires the highest attention from the HR side.

When talking about an internal, or captive, Shared Services Organization, one **internal factor** influencing the Personnel Management Strategy is definitely the overall company's organizational structure. It makes a profound difference whether a SSO has to provide services to a company which is located only in one location or whether this company is spread globally in different locations. Required language skills and time zones have to be reflected in the Shared Services Center concept. Consequently, depending on the complexity of a SSO's organizational model the coordination of global HR topics requires ongoing exchange between central

---

2 In a research report by *ACCENTURE* (2011) about a study of more than 100 shared services related individuals across 16 countries worldwide, almost half of the interviewees indicated that they expect to become a provider of new value-add services (e.g. analytics) or atypical services (e.g. legal) over the next five years

3 According to the Employer of Choice Framework developed by *Siemens* in 2012, the share of employees with the age of >= 55 ranges from 14 % in Germany to 22 % in the US. In China, 74 % of employees are 35 years and younger; in India, core region for the SSI, 69 % belong to the age group 35 or below.

and local HR as well as the respective managers of the business. While the central SSO HR department takes a more strategic role[4] on a global level, the local HR is the operational partner for the local SSC dealing more with the day-to-day tasks[5].

Besides the organizational aspect, the overall business strategy strongly influences the SSO's Personnel Management Strategy. For instance, a company's decision to expand its business, e.g. in the form of acquisitions, or to carve-out certain units or to increase or decrease the volume of Shared Services consumed, affects the SSO regarding its location concept, its size, skill-set needed and the like. Business strategies of this kind have to be reflected in the SSO's strategic roadmap. Volume, timeline, requirements as well as budget are the determining factors. This again obviously has an equally important influence and is a determining factor on the Personnel Management Strategy of the SSO HR, in terms of how many people with which education, at what time and which location need to be available.

In order to make this more concrete and tangible, the internal SSO of *Siemens*[6] will be taken as an example. The *Siemens* SSO strategic roadmap is defined according to the following three phases: (1) "lift-drop", (2) "change" and (3) "innovate and enhance". Every business phase brings along specific HR related requirements.

During the "lift-drop" phase, administrative processes (e.g. related to accounting and finance) which are in the defined scope are being transitioned 'as they are' from the donating entity to the receiving SSO and bundled in the respective Center. On the SSO side this phase is usually characterized by employee mass ramp-up, rapid competency and knowledge building in the SSC. Depending on the volume of full-time-equivalent (FTE) to be transferred, for the local HR function this means extensive advertisement and hiring activities which can keep the entire HR department busy for months. Only in some cases, recruitment from the external market can be limited, if the local HR department can access a pool of internal resources which were made available due to the automation and standardization of some processes and can therefore be deployed for new customers.

This is where we approach the next phase of the strategic business roadmap, the "change" phase. While the previous phase was characterized by the transfer of processes "as-is", this phase focuses on the professionalization of processes in terms of process standardizations, improvements and automations. This has an impact on HR related topics, as the content of jobs may change, notably in the course of ongoing automation. While jobs requiring lower knowledge and skill levels may drop away, new high level expertise functions, such as Quality Management or Process Management become apparent.

4 Due to the diversity of a global SSO regarding culture, customer requirements, locations, national regulations etc., centrally defined employee related activities should be based on organization wide agreed and implemented values

5 On the basis of centrally defined guidelines, local HR can adapt the general strategy to the local specifics and needs (e.g. in form of trainings or engagement activities).

6 Founded 165 years ago and supporting its customers in more than 190 countries, *Siemens* is a diversified global player providing innovative products, technologies, solutions and comprehensive know-how in the areas of industry, energy, healthcare, and infrastructure.

This trend can also be observed in the third phase of the strategic business roadmap of the *Siemens* SSO, the “enhance and innovate” phase. This phase builds on the previous phase by further automating existing processes, but also foresees the expansion of the portfolio to new and more knowledge based services. The development from standard to high-end or totally new products again impacts the Personnel Management Strategy in a way, that available resources have to be either trained on the new processes and/or people with new skill-sets have to be recruited in order to meet the new requirements. Furthermore, it also offers also professional and personal development options and thus a long-term perspective for the Center teams.

2 Specifics of Strategic Personnel Management in a Shared Services Organization

The internal and external influencing factors bring along some SSO specifics, which will be elaborated in more detail in the following section. In doing so, the typical Human Resource Management Process will serve as a guiding theme for the analysis.

2.1 The Strategic Human Resource Lifecycle

As described above, the Personnel Management Strategy has to follow closely the underlying business strategy and the derived demand. The main target is to meet the business requirements in terms of having available the right number of people with the requested skill-set, at the right location and on time.

2.2 Key Management Areas of the Human Resource Lifecycle

2.2.1 Definition and Planning of Manpower Requirements

The process step “Definition and Planning of Personnel Requirements” of the Human Resource Management process is specifically applicable for the “lift-drop” phase of a SSO which is still emerging or extending its service volume. In terms of business and people this phase brings along the biggest change for the affected company units. Equally for the SSO this stage of the process is of utmost importance.

Before being able to develop the Personnel Management Strategy, it first of all necessitates the identification of the required skills, capabilities and number of people in a certain location. Referring this to the location and service concept, e.g. master data management services are provided from a Center in India or closing and reporting services from a Center in CZ Republic, the number of people to be recruited for every location can be determined. Depending on the quantity[7], the global set up and the hiring timeline, the local HR departments might

[7] At peak times, the HR department might be confronted with the hiring of hundred people per month.

need to request temporary capacities from central HR colleagues or engage external companies to support the whole hiring process.

In terms of qualitative aspects, a careful definition of employee competencies – based on the actual requirements of the business – is a core prerequisite for the next planning steps. The competencies and skills have to be described by the SSC in standard job profiles, giving a clear job description as well as an indication of the expected level of practical business related experience.

During the "change" but also "enhance and innovate" phase the job requirements should be continuously reviewed and mapped with the current business demand as they can differ from the "lift-drop" phase. In comparison to this phase, job requirements in the "change" and "enhance and innovate" phases are rather determined by the need of business expertise. This may lead to additional challenges in attracting the more highly qualified candidates in a competitive labor market environment.

2.2.2 Attraction of People

The process step "Attraction of People" is a decisive factor for the final success of a hiring process. Especially, when hundreds of people need to be ramped up in a short period of time, it is important to have an effective recruitment concept in place to guarantee a constant number of candidates in the pipeline. Depending on the local labor market, the business requirements and hiring scope, various channels e.g. internal job advertisements, referral schemes, HR agencies or through co-operations with universities need to be considered accordingly and widened if necessary.

The Shared Services Industry is often confronted with a common perception that positions within a SSO are unattractive, as they are "low end and low cost" jobs, offering practically no personal development options over time. This requires upfront, long-term investments for the amelioration of the industry's image[8] and the company's brand. When considering the potential scale of a "lift-drop" phase, an effective and appealing advertisement concept is key to the success of this phase in terms of having a sufficient pool of applicants available.

One concept helping to achieve a certain job appeal for potential candidates is the Employee Value Proposition (EVP). "The EVP for an organization can be understood as a reflection of the employment experience that individuals have while being a member of that organization. It refers to the complete package of experiences and benefits employees are likely to gain in return for their contribution, effort, creativity, commitment and loyalty."[9] In a global SSO, this package can differ from country to country, as it is strongly influenced by cultural specifics and by what people consider as a real personal benefit.

Generally a strong EVP is not only important during the set-up phase, the "lift-drop" phase, but also during the "change" and "enhance and innovate" phases. As mentioned above, in the latter two phases the HR departments are often confronted with the need of attracting new employees with stronger analytical skills, expertise as well as creativity who are the target

8 Developing specified Corporate Master Studies on Service Management in cooperation with local universities or the enhancement of the local education system towards a specialization in this area are supportive approaches, for the latter cf. e.g. *SRINU/KOMRAIAH* (2008), p. 42.

9 *THOMPSEN* (2010), p. 52.

group of many other SSOs. Often the job descriptions do not differ materially from one SSO to another. A good EVP can therefore be the determining factor for a candidate to apply for a specific SSO.

One part of a good EVP is the offering of clear development perspectives to new employees within the organization. The importance and effects of development options on the overall attractiveness of an employer has to be kept in mind already at the stage of attracting potential candidates. For a smooth transition of processes the SSO requires a sufficient number of employees, who are the knowledge carriers/experts in their area of responsibility and who help to ensure the achievement of business goals. If these people cannot see any personal development opportunities they will most likely look for other employers. In particular, in a booming Shared Services market such as India, the loss of potential candidates can become a critical factor and therefore plays a crucial role in the overall Personnel Management Strategy.

2.2.3 Selection of Candidates

If the Personnel Management Strategy was successful so far, at the end of the attraction period a 'candidate long list' will be available for the "Selection of Candidates".

There are various ways to handle the candidate selection process. The most common are individual interviews in person or via phone, but there are also other forms, such as centralized assessment centers, online tests or the outsourcing of selection steps to HR agencies. Here again, the general approach does not differ tremendously from normal hiring processes in other business areas. However, what comes into play again in the environment of a SSO, is the quantity of required employees and the timeframe within which the employees should be in place.

Flexibility in the selection process is requested, as the requirements can quickly change from a quantitative perspective, in terms of number of employees to be recruited, but also from a qualitative perspective in terms of changing capability and skill requirements. During the "lift-drop" phase, the stage of a quick, mass ramp up, it is important to quickly achieve a short list of candidates exhibiting the required skills. This can be achieved through online pretests in combination with a temporary support from HR agencies in peak times. During the "change" and "enhance and innovate" phases, the hiring might be more determined by the ramp-up of employees of smaller scale, however, with more specific skills. The more knowledge-based the delivered services are, the more specialized candidates need to be hired. In this case individual interviews in person or via phone, involving team leads or service line managers to ensure that candidates dispose of the right skills, are more appropriate.

During the selection future talent development already needs to be considered. Candidates should also be chosen according their ability and willingness to develop into more complex topics, a team lead role or to aim for an international development over time. This ensures a solid talent pipeline and reduces the risks coming with unwanted attrition.

Generally it is important to understand, that candidate selection requires close cooperation between the responsible management and the HR organization. Only if both partners have a mutual understanding of business and people related requirements, will the hiring process be a success.

2.2.4 Employee On-Boarding and Integration

As soon as the candidates have been selected, another critical phase of the Human Resource Management process starts, namely the employee "On-boarding and Integration". *THOMPSEN*[10] describes the relevance of this phase very clearly: "Depending on how it is conducted, this stage of the Human Capital Cycle has the potential to do one of two things: either it sets talented people on the performance fast track or it sends them fleeing for another offer."[11]

Specifically in the Shared Services Industry, where competition for employees is very high and employees quickly leave a company for slightly better offers, the first weeks and months of an employment are decisive – in particular during the mass-ramp up period, the "lift-drop" phase but also throughout the other two business phases. Here again the intensity can change – from a more 'mass on-boarding' driven approach ensuring fast operational productivity to more stable and organized, encompassing and involving organizational identity creating programs.

"To ensure the delivery of a service […] the know-how of service employees is especially relevant in the first instance."[12] This seems to be a commonplace at first glance, but for a Shared Services Organization, this statement gains critical weight. Following *PÉREZ*' argument, the right know-how to ensure customer satisfaction consists not only of professional expertise but also of company specific knowledge, including a certain familiarity with the company culture, informal "rules of the game", people, their net-works and so on.

During the employee on-boarding and integration phase two aspects are therefore crucial: Firstly, the support of team leads, service line managers and HR during the administrative on-boarding phase, the establishment of contacts to other colleagues and management as well as the orientation within the company. Secondly, it is the preparation of new employees on the job, in form of specifically designed training and seminars. Defined on-boarding and training programs ensure that employees are set on track quickly, and that the SSO is able to roll out its service to various different customers.

At the end of the on-boarding and integration phase all employees should have a clear picture about the SSO, the relationships within the organization including customers and their business, his/her role and contribution to business success, company culture and service mindset.

2.2.5 People Development

"Employees are increasingly considering career development prospects in an organization apart from the financial aspects while making career choices."[13] This is an important thought when talking about "People Development", notably in the SSI environment.

First of all, this point relates directly to the attractiveness and EVP of a company. If a SSO is not able to provide development options, it risks loosing its key players or new candidates to competitors who seem to be more attractive in this regard. The current work place is then only seen as a suitable training step in the CV that helps to boost the personal market value

---

10 Cf. *THOMPSEN* (2010).

11 *THOMPSEN* (2010), p. 63.

12 *PÉRÉZ* (2008), p. 152; translation of German quote to English by the author

13 *PADHI/NAGESH* (2008), p. 158.

before changing to another Shared Services Organization. Secondly, a continuous development of employees, their skills and capabilities is crucial for the organization's business success, which, in the end, lies in the responsibility of its managers. As service business is people business, employee development needs to play a major part in the strategic management discussions – and needs to materialize in a way, that people can actually "feel" the development related activities and options being offered to them – rather than just being confronted with theoretical statements and concepts.

While the first aspect relates mainly to the "lift-drop" phase of the SSO's strategic business roadmap, where it is important to attract the right people through respective offers, the second aspect relates mainly to the "change" and "enhance and innovate" phases. As already described above, the factor of success for the latter phases is to either hire new employees exhibiting the required skills or to further train and develop the existing teams so that they can cope with the new requirements.

People development has many facets: knowledge related development activities, such as classroom or on the job trainings for the various job levels, but also talent programs, job rotations and succession planning. The basis is usually an annual performance review process, consisting of a clear individual target setting related to overarching business targets, target achievement review and feedback dialogue between employee and manager. Employee development is the stage in the Human Resource Management process that takes most of the time. It is a process over years and has to be constantly reviewed from three perspectives: the employee, the manager and the organizational point of view[14].

- **Employee – Driver of own Career**

  For the employee it is important to understand that he/she is responsible for his/her own career. By a realistic self-assessment of capabilities and ambitions, open discussions on career aspirations as well as the striving for new development measures, the employee can be a driver of his/her own career.

- **Manager – Partner & Decider**

  The manager can be a partner and decider in the development phase of the employee by leveraging the potential of the employee by defining demanding targets, tasks and responsibilities, by regularly conducting development dialogs as well as through the promotion of the employee for career opportunities to other areas/units.

- **Human Resources - Consultant**

  HR can take over a consulting function for parties, the employee and the manager, with the necessary expert advice regarding the elaboration of development plans, training measures, identification of job opportunities as well as the supporting HR tools and processes.

For the individual development planning it is crucial that employees and managers have a clear overview on career options and the requirements related to the respective development steps. It cannot be emphasized enough that clear individual target setting, transparent measurement criteria, frequent feedback dialogues with the manager and individual development

[14] *SIEMENS AG/CHR CU GSS* (2012.

discussions should be a natural part of a SSO's Personnel Management Strategy and Culture. Thereby, national cultural aspects[15] have, however, to be kept in mind to achieve the intended results.

2.2.6 Employee Engagement and Retention Management

Considering that the delivered service quality is strongly linked to motivation and commitment of employees as well as reliability and continuity in service delivery, "Employee Engagement and Retention Management" is a key topic in the strategic Personnel Management discussion between management and HR organization.

'High pressure – monotonous work flow – limited career options – comparably low income' are common prejudices that need to be constantly kept in mind by the management of a SSO, when evaluating attrition rates. In particular in countries with a well developed SSI, retention is a serious topic: "No matter what extent of fun is created in the work environment; youngsters fail to cope with the continuous stress. (…) Most of the youngsters face the common problems of odd shifts, long working hours, repetitive nature of work, insufficient holidays and call volume (number of calls)."[16] Figures discussed in the market, report an attrition rate in the range of 25–35 % in offshore locations such as India, caused by moves to other, better paid jobs, moves to another country, family reasons or going for higher studies.

In order to achieve service reliability and continuity beyond the sensitive starting phase "lift-drop" and the equally challenging "change" phase, effective employee engagement programs and retention measures need to be implemented to mitigate or eliminate these critical points. However, all efforts will only be successful, if they are embedded into a well-balanced catalogue of individual, team and organization related measures. As said previously, the needs and perceptions of individual employees can differ enormously. But this is just half of the success: only if this mix of measures is being constantly perceived by the employees, e.g. through realized development steps (of peers) and regular internal employee communications, will there be a significant increase in employee engagement and retention.

From a management perspective, a stable and motivated team fosters two core success factors which are relevant throughout the whole business roadmap strategy: service and process quality improvements and cost savings. High employee engagement will in general materialize in a higher service orientation and quality, which can be measured in customer satisfaction surveys. This supports the SSO to win additional customers (also for new services) over time. Cost-wise, a reduced unwanted attrition rate saves the company substantial sums that would have been spent on replacing qualified employees[17], handling business shortfalls or performance failure and mitigating an unfavorable reputation.

---

15 *BUDHWAR/BJÖRKMAN/SINGH* have observed in their study on India that "(…) in the present system there is relatively less participation of individual employees regarding their goal setting (though few companies claim they are doing it). This reflects the hierarchical nature of Indian society. Perhaps, a more participative approach could be beneficial (…)"; cf. *BUDHWAR/BJÖRKMAN/SINGH* (2009), p. 129.

16 *SRINU/KOMRAIAH* (2008), p. 37.

17 Costs for on-boarding and training of a new employee are estimated at about 30–50 % of the annual fully loaded costs in practice.

2.2.7 Separation and Termination of Work Relationship

Terminating a work relationship can be an administrative process, but this stage of the Human Resource Management process is definitely one of the most sensitive ones. The "Separation and Termination of Work Relationship" can happen because it was thoroughly planned (e.g. due to retirements, time contracts for seasonal/peak capacity demand), but also can often come as a surprise.

In the planning phase of the strategic Personnel Management, attention is being drawn on having the right people in the right place at the right time. This quantitative requirement is determined by different variables as described above, e.g. the increase or decrease of customers and business volume, the level of automation, or the increase or decrease of service portfolio elements being offered. Depending on the actual business requirements – the number of required employees can go up but also down – a termination of a work relationship can therefore be non-desired or partly desired.

The non-desired attrition is the more critical one for the HR department as it usually comes at short notice and concerns highly skilled employees. A re-staffing is often difficult, time-consuming and costly. In the event of such a case, it is important to identify the reasons behind and derive mitigating actions in order to prevent such a situation in the future. An exit interview with the concerned employee is one means to investigate and discuss the reasons for the employee's resignation. Also, it is a chance for the organization to make the employees "understand their value before they walk out of the door."[18] Based on the results from the exit interview, management and HR need to work on an action plan, if appropriate and feasible. In areas with many competing SSO this is a crucial point, as otherwise the EVP of a Shared Services Organization will quickly get damaged, and result in hiring difficulties as well as high capacity replacement costs. This, in the end, will have a negative impact on the SSO's overall productivity.

'Normal' or planned attrition (e.g. related to retirements, temporary workforce or exits in booming emerging markets) helps to adjust the Center size and the qualification mix according to actual demand in a socially responsible manner.

Summarizing the impact of the Human Resource Management process in the context of a SSO business strategy; it becomes clear that in this extremely performance and cost driven environment a high quality Personnel Management is key to success.

---

18 *THOMPSEN* (2010), p. 93

3 Selected Examples of Personnel Management Methods and Initiatives in a Shared Services Organization

"Having the right human capital in the organization [...] provides the edge that is not easily replicated by a competitor.[19]" With this statement it becomes evident, that Personnel Management is one of the management key responsibilities – and that management needs to understand this responsibility not as a "routine HR process driven by HR", but as its own core task. The HR organization is the strategic partner to develop and implement or advise on suitable tools and measures enabling management to develop their people professionally.

For the reference case of the *Siemens* SSO the following described examples of Personnel Management approaches have been successfully implemented. One major success factor was the high acceptance of the suggested approaches and an outstanding management commitment to introduce them sustainably throughout the globe.

3.1 Career @ Shared Services – A Toolbox

Considering the fact that individual development perspectives play an important role for employee retention already from the recruiting phase on, the outlining of possible career opportunities within the *Siemens* SSO proved to be very important. This is dedicated to provide (potential) employees and management with a maximum transparency on:

- the SSO career principles,
- the SSO job landscape and respective job profiles, and
- available development measures.

In addition to that, elements such as a personal career compass for employee self-assessment, a sample of development paths and testimonials or supporting material for development and staff dialogues have proven to be helpful to support managers and employees when talking about career.

The **career principles** of a SSO comprise general values and build the foundation of the development culture of a company. It is crucial to say that once agreed, career principles need to be a constant part of the strategic people discussion. Only then the principles will become a natural part of the company's DNA.

Obtaining knowledge on the personal preferences and motivation drivers should always be the first step of a personal career planning process – and a continuing process over time. Through self assessment, which can be conducted with the help of the **career compass** tools, employees can get a picture about themselves in order to make a thorough career decision.

19 PADHI/NAGESH (2008), p. 156.

A **job landscape** gives an overview of all possible job roles in the different organizational units of the SSO and points out possible vertical and horizontal developments. A job landscape differs from an organizational chart in a way that it gives a functional view instead of a person or reporting line related picture of the organization. For a global SSO it is important to ensure a worldwide alignment regarding the (generic) description of jobs and their positioning within the job landscape. This is a very time consuming effort, however, the organization, employees, management and, not to forget HR, can benefit from a joint common understanding when talking about development possibilities. Therefore, when developing a job landscape and job profiles for an organization, it is recommended to set up the project organization globally to gain a maximum of (local) management commitment and input from all involved stakeholders. Ideally the respective job profiles can be accessed through the job landscape for a comprehensive overview on content and requirements or key learning topics of the functions. Depending on local regulations a job landscape can also be broadened to job grades or payment groups. As a proof of concept, real life examples on personal career development within the SSO or across the company can be published as well. This helps the organization to increase its credibility towards the employees as they can follow up on their peers' real professional development.

When talking about the individual learning requirements, a catalogue of globally or locally available **development measures** completes the picture and provides valuable input for the development dialogue between manager and employee,. The offers should give hints on technical and personal trainings, assessments and also on job developments. Ideally, this catalogue is enriched with training material for managers on how to successfully conduct development and staff dialogues.

3.2 Fast On-boarding and Enabling of Middle Management

A *Siemens* SSC organized the introduction and integration of new employees based on a structured program worked out by local HR and the local management representatives. The program was formed of information packages, smart movies with welcoming words from the CEO/CFO, a virtual intro on the SSO and SSI in general, an introduction on the SSO's global people development framework, and some best practice sharing ideas like "Lunch with the Management" to support networking.

In another approach, independently of their future function, new employees in the *Siemens* SSC undergo an internal training program before they start the work shadowing at the donating entity's location. To provide some examples, the Accounting & Finance Services (AFS) related program consists of local module-based training concepts with the following content:

- Introduction training for new employees;
- Basic accounting training;
- Accounting & Finance Services specific trainings per job level;
- Training on the job;
- Other training modules on e.g. *SAP*, Excel, languages, compliance, Service Mindset;
- Refresher/Enhancement training.

These training modules have been harmonized globally over time. For this, a global training network with representatives from all SSC has been established under the roof of a global training initiative, headed by a team member from the AFS HQ management, who ensures continuous improvement through best practice sharing, alignment and decision making on mandatory and optional contents. At the end of every module certain quality controls are conducted in the form of tests in order to examine the individual employee's knowledge on the above mentioned topics and his/her readiness for the job.

Additionally, in order to involve the new employees as quick as possible in day-to-day business a 'buddy concept' was applied where experienced employees were asked to act as coaches and mentors for the new employees. A slightly different approach with the same result of quickly integrating new employees and fostering training on the job is the 'nucleus strategy'. In this case one team lead of an already experienced team is taken out and assigned to a new team, which consists of (mainly) new employees without any experience in the company or the specific business. This approach is notably effective in mass ramp-ups, when new employees need to quickly achieve a certain level of business know how.

Specifically in the growth phase of a SSC it is possible that the number of employees increases very quickly and it is required to put in place a middle management level, in the form of team leads. In the case of the SSO roadmap phase which has been described above, the team lead positions usually need to be filled with people from the teams itself. This can lead to the situation that employees become promoted into a team lead role at a rather early point in their career. The essential management competencies, such as entrepreneurial leadership for this defined area of responsibility, therefore need to be developed in parallel and very quickly.

Training focusing on management and leadership skills are usually part of the local standard training portfolio and local HR and the SSC management ensure that employees who are new to a leadership role receive the appropriate training in time. Nevertheless, management recommends to take action at an earlier point in time, namely when selecting employees to also consider the employee's potential to grow into a team or service line lead role. At the same time, HR would be required to proactively support the skills and capability development of new employees in a structured way from the moment of their hire by offering a tailored-to-need set of management and leadership training.

Case Study: Middle Management Academy

In order to foster the development of the middle management, a *Siemens* SSC has initiated a Middle Management Academy offering six leadership related training modules, for beginners but also for more experienced leaders.

A more business management focused program that has been centrally developed by the HQ Operational Excellence team for team leads and middle management, is the KPI-based management training program. Its major objective is to initiate the re-orientation of the SSC towards a KPI-based management and leadership style. KPI based management is a general state-of-the-art approach for managing service business on a day-to-day basis in an entrepreneurial way. With applying the KPIs, management on all levels has a system to recognize problem areas early and ensure prevention, conduct root cause analysis and define countermeasure, share best practices, ensure continuous improvement and generation of savings.

Case Study: Middle Management Academy (continued)

The chosen training approach – highly interactive discussions on case studies – supports the commitment to the new leadership method as participants have an immediate transfer of the necessary "know how and do how" which they can apply in their day-to-day tasks.

The training is framed by key note speeches by the SSC heads on "Using KPIs". These introductions have proven to be a real success factor for the training itself, but also for the acceptance of the new, KPI based management style in general. Very suitable is also the split in different target groups for the training sessions Management only, Team Leads only, Management and Team Leads jointly.In every session the specific topics and needs can be addressed. In particular, for team leads it is important to acquire the new knowledge and discuss questions independently from their line managers. Only the last training session takes place jointly and this is where managers and their team leads negotiate on how KPI problem solving, best practice sharing, target setting and continuous improvement will be managed together. An important prerequisite for this negotiation is that the respective target groups have worked out their personal perspectives on these topics during the sessions before.

The KPI training is mandatory to all team leads and managers as well as the operational excellence heads of the global SDU. The content of the training is supposed to be modified according to further organizational development.

3.3 Internal Talent Program and Short-term Rotation

Due to its requirements, the majority of SSI's employees belong to the generation born between 1977 and 2000. According to a synthesis of many studies[20], this generation the so-called "Gen(eration) Y" can be characterized by the following selected, job related aspects:

- Own career must have a meaning;
- If promise not kept, fast disengagement;
- Life long learning is seen as normal;
- Communication takes place in social networks;
- Working with other bright and creative people is aspired;
- Security in terms of income and personal flexibility is wanted.

This generation will one day take over the workforce lead in the economy. Some people of the "older" part of this generation already hold leading positions or are on the verge of doing so. University is not sufficient to prepare them for management or leadership roles. For them and also the younger colleagues it is therefore important to be prepared in an optimal way. To meet their expectations, needs and desires an international talent program is a suitable approach.

20 *SIEMENS* (2010b).

Case Study: New Horizons – Talent Program

➢ **Program goals**

Experience cooperation in an international network with colleagues from other Business Lines, Centers and locations, learning from others, exposure to top management

➢ **Organizational responsibility for program**

Central HR and project sponsor from SSO HQ Business Line. The latter ensures management commitment, which will be expanded through the entire organization by revolving business line sponsorship. HR and sponsor elaborate program frame and meeting agendas, organize trainings and other required logistics. Participants organize themselves as a group by nominating a group coordinator.

➢ **Target group and selection of candidates**

15 acknowledged local talents from all SSC's, who are in the company for at least two years, early in their career, maximum early team lead experience, not yet a member of other central talent programs and not yet assigned to tasks with high management attention, short term 'ready to develop date' for next development step; candidates to be proposed by management and local HR through a clear process (during annual performance review phase), pre-selection by central SSO HR and program sponsor, final release by top management.

➢ **Program structure**

➢ One year of ongoing cooperation in five small teams on specifically defined projects, that have an actual benefit for the SSO overall; project management responsibility lies within project teams, project coaches from HQ act as door openers, sparring partners and consultants;

➢ In total three on-site weeks at the SSO HQ, with SSO business related workshops and presentations, management chats, project management work, presentation and personal skills trainings, project team work sessions;

➢ Together with project coaches, status presentation to SSO top management and related feedback discussions;

➢ In total three virtual intermediate sessions with presentations on work status (between the on-site sessions);

➢ Final results presentation to the global SSO management team in the course of a global conference.

➢ **Communication**

Program articles on each session are published in the SSO newsletter. In addition, an intranet page with all encompassing information on the program, the projects and the participants is set up. Senior Management takes ownership of this program and communicates its success to their leaders in the SSO board.

The talent program is well acknowledged by participants and top management. It has become a topic in the day-to-day communication between employees and managers, as it is seen as a privilege to be a member of this talent program. As a succession of the program, an alumni network is recommended to ensure that the grown talent networks continue to exist. With having demonstrated their capabilities and skills on a global platform, it will become easier for those involved to gain support for their individual development.

Case Study: International Short-term Job Rotation

Another approach that has been tested is the short term job rotation for employees between more established and just recently ramped-up AFS delivery teams. The intended goal was to share operational knowledge and to set up a culture of AFS internal consulting. Critical success factors for such a program are:

- Sound preparation of candidates for the assignment already in the home unit (e.g. train the trainer and/or communication and intercultural training, preparation of catalogue of local best practice examples, preparation of learning requirements);
- Assignment of a clear set of tasks that have to be accomplished during the rotation period (e.g. collection of new best practices, identification of improvement areas and solutions for saving measures,…);
- Immediate integration of employees in local improvement projects after their return from the assignment abroad to ensure practical transfer of learning;
- Integration of the job rotation program in an ongoing global rotation framework to foster a climate of constant learning and improvement.

SSO always have to face the conflict of employee engagement and -development, both being topics which need to be invested in, and the fact, that as a cost center, the organization is not supposed to spend 'the customer's money' on too many and too expensive people related measures. Considering the fact that a number of employees in the SSI come from "Gen Y and see constant learning as a natural part of their working life, an appropriate local and global budget for the implementation of the HR strategy should be ensured.

As mentioned earlier, it is important to support employee related measures with suitable communication (e.g. via internet homepage, news letters, announcements at 'town hall meetings' and 'chats with the management') to make employees aware of the efforts, a company is taking for the benefits of its staff. Nevertheless, the participants are the most important promoters: If they feel the program makes a difference and supports them in their development, that it is worth walking the extra mile by taking over an extra work load in addition to the daily job, they will talk about it to their peers and make it attractive to new candidates. Only if this happens the company has managed to establish a valuable and sustainable development module.

3.4 Engagement Surveys

As already briefly addressed above, Employee Engagement is a key success factor for employee and customer satisfaction. Moreover, it contributes to a company's competitiveness in many ways. Accordingly, it is important for a SSO to develop an individual and appropriate approach for a global Employee Engagement Management, which equally gives room for local and culture specific solutions.

The key aspects that have to be observed when talking about Employee Engagement are the employee's rational understanding and support of the strategic goals and values; an employee's emotional attachment to the company and the motivation and opportunity to "walk the extra mile" to contribute to the organization's success.

In order to be able to measure the employee's degree of engagement, in many companies employee surveys are conducted. In a SSO the participation rate and results are tracked as Key Performance Indicators (KPI) and are used in the global individual target setting for managers. Thus, responsibility for motivating employees to participate in the survey, and thus giving their feedback on how they feel about their job with the company, has been allocated to the SSO's management level. This approach also ensures management support for a sustainable development and implementation of suitable local measures. However, as an organization with a global footprint, a Shared Services Organization can benefit a lot from ongoing best practice and idea sharing around engagement measures.

Case Study: Global Engagement Survey

Employee Engagement is key for employee satisfaction, customer satisfaction and the competitive edge of a company. The survey makes it easy for everybody in the company to express how they act and what they think and feel about a range of topics such as management culture, internal cooperation and working relationships. It provides feedback from all *Siemens* employees as a basis for our organization's further development and it plays a key role in sustaining success as a company

The *Siemens* Global Engagement Survey is conducted annually and provides a basis for rethinking the current Personnel Management Strategy. For that reason a Global Survey Expert Network has been set up in the SSO, consisting of representatives from all organizational units around the globe and is coordinated by an HR business partner from central Shared Services HR. The members of the network are appointed by executive management and are the partners for defining, developing and implementing local measures, based on the survey results. The network meets virtually on a monthly basis. All representatives introduce and discuss their local engagement activities and the achieved degree of implementation. With this approach, the SSO can benchmark in the hosting company in terms of topic awareness amongst employees and participation rate.

The fields of activity that are in the focus to increase employee engagement and retention encompass amongst others: salary and bonus topics, a reward and recognition system (monetary and non-monetary), learning and career initiatives (e.g. Career @ Shared Services), management training, social engagement, special office facilities (e.g. gym, canteen, improvement of transportation), or extended communication activities such as employee newsletters and town hall meetings. These examples offer only a small insight in the list of activities. Depending on the cultural background of the employees and the location of the SSC individual elements get different weight, but contribute in their overall variety to a continuous global increase of employee satisfaction.

3.5 Motivation and Retention Measure "Gamification"

A new approach which evolved on the market and has already become a part of the *Siemens*' motivation and retention measures is "Gamification". It is a concept applying game design thinking to non-game applications and should provide a moment of excitement to the teams through competition inducing elements. Thereby business related forms of competition are set up between teams, where for example the team in the Accounting & Finance business with the least errors in the posting of vendor invoices gains an award. "Gamification has been called one of the most important trends in technology by several industry experts. Gamification can potentially be applied to any industry and almost anything to create fun and engaging experiences, converting users into players."[21] This kind of measure is, for instance, very successful in India, of course depending on the given local culture and demographic structure.

Case Study: Motivation and Retention Initiative "Gamification" in SSC India

The *Siemens* Shared Services Center in India has launched the 'India Grand Prix Season', a 'Formula 1' game amongst employees to increase productivity and customer satisfaction. 19 groups of 20–30 members have been created and all employees within GSS India are participating in this game. The goal of each team is to earn points for speed or gasoline in order to make the own team race car faster than others. Every team has to prepare and earn points for 10 race days spread throughout the month.

Each team member can earn points for the team's race car by exceeding goals that were set for daily performance or by extraordinary laud by the customers or by submitting improvement suggestions through '3i[22] scheme'. At the same time – if there is a decrease in quality or any escalation - the race car is slowed down due to a 'pit stop' the car has to go through. The members of a team are working closely together and are extremely enthusiastic about finding their own best strategy to win. Furthermore, the teams have created their own logos and team equipment to demonstrate their unity.

The results after the first days of the game being 'live' are amazing: Employees are very eager to win the competition and the team spirit is great. And above all, the quality and productivity has been increased during a very critical time of quarterly closing and we see a boom in 3i suggestions.

---

21 COLLINS (2012).

22 The *Siemens* internal 3i Program encourages employees to constantly initiate and implement improvements in the company on their own initiative. Suggestions relating to occupational health and safety and to environmental protection within the company are particularly important.

3.6 Succession Planning

Succession planning helps to identify and develop internal employees with leadership potential and thereby ensures a company's solid pool of people who can take over leading roles either immediately or in the course of a defined timeframe. A SSO should reflect its succession planning for management functions according to the actual knowledge and experience related requirements of a position, but also according to the business roadmap and its required management capabilities [23].

If a person has been identified as a potential candidate for a future management position, she/he will be subject to a structured succession planning. In so-called succession planning sessions, which mostly take place in the course of the performance reviews, the individual candidates are being discussed under performance and potential perspective. If a candidate turns out to be a potential immediate successor, the challenge for the organization is to maintain motivation and engagement of the candidate to avoid her/him leaving the company, in case an immediate succession cannot be realized. Other people related methods, from the field of employee engagement and retention management, have to be applied then by the responsible manager. If a candidate is seen as an ideal candidate within a clear period of time, learning requirements, either technical, intercultural or personality related, can be defined and linked to concrete development measures.

The overall crucial point is to establish dynamic succession planning which enables real individual development towards the intended functions rather than just implementing an administrative Personnel Management process. A good approach to make succession planning more development oriented for a SSO was to link the success story of realized development measures to the official succession planning presentation, which is held by the SSO management to its managing board annually.

4 Conclusion

Service business is people business. This simple statement is the point at which strategic Personnel Management for a SSO achieves a different dimension and perspective compared to Personnel Management of any other business type. Besides the fact that the success of a SSO is strongly related to the knowledge and capabilities of its employees, also their engagement and motivation plays a vital role, as both will be perceived by the customer through many channels. The SSO-required personal and professional skills are being determined by the maturity level of the existing service portfolio – and the future product development. *EHNERT* observes in her study on sustainable human resource management, that "One of the main problems in making an investment into the future workforce is that many companies report today, that they are underlying continuous change and restructuring processes (…). Under these conditions it is nearly impossible to predict which skills, competencies, and qualifications are needed in the future."[24] This may be true for a number of other businesses, but the SSI can actually profit from this development. By constantly following up on the business

23 For examples of typical service developer competences that can be relevant cf. *KEITH* (2010), p. 156 et seq.

24 *EHNERT* (2009), p. 118.

development and challenges of their customers, managers of a SSO can be ahead of time in their strategic business development, service portfolio and organizational design planning[25]. Accordingly, the HR strategy of a SSO needs to be developed further focused on the future, driving topics like e.g. organizational design and leadership models (empowered organization), or sourcing strategies (internal-external, local-global, technology enabled).

For the HR departments the specific employee related requirements bear a number of challenges, when developing a sustainable Personnel Management Strategy: "Considering the fact, that sustainability [...] is linked almost exclusively to micro level issues such as occupational health and safety, work-life balance, or diversity, and social responsibility"[26], the HR organization as a key partner for overall SSO success needs to constantly seek the exchange with management and evaluate its strategy around topics such as position evaluation, maintenance of engagement and motivation, practical career support, management of attrition towards an optimum, or how budget related development restrictions in terms of global job rotations and future oriented training programs can be handled. It is important to consider that also key players and more senior staff – both essential for the stability of teams – should strongly benefit from people related initiatives. If this leadership and development culture has reached a level of stability and continuity, the organization has accomplished the most challenging part in terms of its staff. New management trends like Gamification can then be a fun creating 'add-on' for the employees, but sight on the true human resource related challenges for management and HR, namely the perception of the SSI and the characteristics of its jobs as such, will not be lost.

In fact, this is only half of the success story. Of course, also HR organizations are required to build up and constantly further develop their capabilities. Besides the classical HR knowledge areas and activities, change management, stakeholder communication, organizational and HR strategy development are core capabilities to support the business. Also, the HR partners need to develop a solid understanding of the SSO's business development. This requires a close exchange between management and HR. So, if management and HR succeed in establishing a cooperation and culture of trust, openness, innovation and appreciation throughout all business phases, a SSO is on the right way to achieve its roadmap targets with the full support of its employees: being a trusted business partner.

---

25 Cf. also *Justice* (2012).

26 *Ehnert* (2009), p. 112.

Abbreviations and Selected Terms

Donating entity	Legal entity or organizational/accounting unit handing over certain administrative tasks to a Shared Services Organization (or to a Cluster or country organization)
Finance Bundling	Comprehensive program in the areas of accounting, controlling, taxes and financial services to re-shape, harmonize and optimize the worldwide finance functions within *Siemens* group; focus in this article is the transfer of transactional accounting tasks to the in-house Shared Services Organization
FTE	Full-time Equivalent, measuring unit for the workforce of one employee
HQ	Headquarters
KPI	Key Performance Indicator
Ramp-up	Describes the development phase and corresponding activities of a Shared Services Organization when work is being transferred from one or more donating entities, requiring a corresponding increase of the service provider's internal resources in order to handle the additional volume
Receiving entity	Legal entity or organizational/accounting unit, regularly a Shared Services Organization (or a Cluster or country organization), receiving certain administrative tasks from the donating entity
SSC	Shared Services Center(s)
SLA	Service Level Agreement, tax-relevant contract between the Shared Services Organization's legal entity and the legal entity of the customer ordering respective services
SSO	Shared Services Organization(s)
Work-shadowing	Discuss, understand and apply the processes of the "donating entity" and transfer the knowledge to the "receiving entity"

References

ACCENTURE (2011): Trends in Shared Services – Unlocking the full potential, online: http://www.accenture.com/us-en/Pages/insight-trends-shared-services-unlocking-full-potential.aspx, download: 20.07.2012.

AUER, CH./SIEBERT, M. (2012): Einer für alle, in: *Siemens* World, 2012, No. 5, p. 2.

BHATNAGAR, J. (2009): Talent Management Strategies in India, in: *BUDHWAR, P. S./BHATNAGAR, J.* (Eds.), The Changing Face of People Management in India, New York 2009, pp. 180–199.

BUDHWAR, P./BJÖRKMAN, I./SINGH, V. (2009): Emerging HRM Systems of Foreign Firms Operating in India, in: *BUDHWAR, P. S./BHATNAGAR, J.* (Eds.), The Changing Face of People Management in India, New York (NY) 2009, pp. 115–136.

COLLINS, A. (2012): How Gamification in Purchase to Pay is Having an Impact on Employee Engagement, online: http://www.sharedserviceslink.com/file/95065/how-gamification-in-purchase-to-pay-is-having-an-impact-on-employee-engagement.html, download: 16.08.2012.

EHNERT, I. (2009): Sustainable Human Resource Management. A Conceptual and Exploratory Analysis from a Paradox Perspective, Heidelberg 2009.

HAHN, D./TAYLOR, T. (Eds.) (2006): Strategische Unternehmensplanung – Strategische Unternehmensführung, Berlin/Heidelberg/New York 2006.

HANNA, N. K. (2010): Enabling Enterprise Transformation. Business and Grassroots Innovation for the Knowledge Economy, New York 2010.

JUSTICE, C. (2012): The Death of Outsourcing, KPMG International Shared Services and Outsourcing Advisory, online: http://www.kpmginstitutes.com/shared-services-outsourcing-institute/insights/2012/pdf/death-of-outsourcing.pdf, download: 16.08.2012.

KALTENBACHER, S. (2011): Integration bei Mergers & Acquisitions, München/Mering 2011.

KEITH, H. (2010): Empirische Untersuchungen zum Kompetenzprofil des Dienstleistungsentwicklers unter Berücksichtigung der systematischen Entwicklung von unternehmensnahen Dienstleistungen, Aachen 2010.

MORGAN S. J. (2008): HR management and Employee Engagement, in: *TAPLIN, R.* (Ed.), Outsourcing and Human Resource Management – An International Survey, New York 2008, pp. 26–56.

PADHI, S. K./NAGESH, T. R. (2008): Career Development and Succession Planning, in: *SITA, V.* (Ed.), Human Resources Management in India. Issues and Initiatives, New Delhi 2008, pp. 155–166.

PÉREZ, N. M. (2008): Service Center Organization. Neue Formen der Steuerung von internen Dienstleistungen unter besonderer Berücksichtigung von Shared Services, Wiesbaden 2008.

SIEMENS AG (2010a): Finance Bundling Transition Guide, Munich 2010.

SIEMENS AG (2010b): Internal Paper on Career Topics, Munich 2010.

SIEMENS AG/CHR CU GSS (2012): Internal Paper on Career@GSS, Munich 2010.

SRINU, CH./KOMRAIAH, P. (2008): HR Issues and Challenges – A study of Indian BPO industry, in: *SITA, V.* (Ed.), Human Resources Management in India. Issues and Initiatives, New Delhi 2008, pp. 35–43.

STROHMEIER, S. (1995): Die Integration von Unternehmens- und Personalplanung, Wiesbaden 1995.

THOMPSEN, J. A. (2010): Achieving a Triple Win. Human Capital Management of the Employee Lifecycle, New York 2010.

WUCKNITZ, U./HEYSE, V. (2008): Retention Management. Schlüsselkräfte entwickeln und binden, Münster 2008.

Transfer Pricing Requirements Concerning Shared Services

ARWED CRÜGER and *ANDREAS RIEDL*

WTS Steuerberatungsgesellschaft mbH

Executive Summary

Intra-group services are getting more and more important as companies are getting more and more international. Following that, tax authorities are eager to audit these intercompany transactions which can lead to double taxation and fines if the regulations concerning intra-group services are not followed thoroughly.

The transfer pricing requirements concerning intra-group services will be explained in the following. The different types of intra-group services and their specific characteristics will be regarded. It is important to note that the recipient of the service has to have a benefit from the service so that the service can be remunerated within the group. In this context there will be a special focus on shareholder services, implicit support and synergies.

Based on that, the common transfer pricing methods regarding intra-group services, the comparable uncontrolled price method, and the cost plus method will be explained. Regarding the cost plus method, the different steps of determining the intercompany price – the cost base, allocation keys, and the mark up – will be examined. Subsequently the concept of cost pools will be discussed in relation to intra-group services.

In the last chapter information concerning contracts and documentation requirements for intercompany transactions will be presented.

1 Introduction

From a business standpoint, regulatory systems concerning intra-group services are often underestimated, since the result for the group as a whole is the same regardless which company within the group pays for the services. However the fiscal administrations of the different countries focus on the amount of tax paid within the country. Therefore many countries around the world implemented regulatory systems concerning intra-group services. In addition to that intra-group services are getting more and more attention from tax auditors. A survey states that the tax authorities are increasing their transfer pricing resources and preparing for more transfer pricing penalties and disputes. Countries that are not having repositories of natural assets are focusing on service transactions and intangibles. According to the study more than 75 % of the responding authorities confirmed to focus on service transactions[1].

The regulatory systems of most countries are mostly based on the "OECD Transfer Pricing Guidelines for Multinational Enterprises and Tax Administrations". In the following the transfer pricing requirements concerning shared services will be explained. First we will lay down the different types and specific characteristics of intra-group services. Within this part we will also explain some anomalies of shareholder services, implicit support and synergies. In the second part we will focus on the transfer pricing methods that are used commonly regarding shared services and give some hints for the daily practice. After that we will

[1] Cf. *ERNST & YOUNG* (2009), p.6 et seq.

demonstrate the concept of cost pooling. At last we inform about contracts and documentation requirements in regard to shared services.

2 Types and Specific Characteristics of Intra-Group Services

In the beginning we want to take a look at the different sorts of services that can be observed between related parties. The EU Joint Transfer Pricing Forum (EU JTPF) has issued "Guidelines on low value adding intra-group services". In Annex I of these EU JTPF guidelines there is a list of intra-group services which are commonly provided between related parties. This list is grouped into the following main categories:[2]

- Information technology services
- Human resource services
- Marketing services
- Legal services
- Accounting and administration services
- Technical services
- Quality control services
- Other services

There are plenty of types of intra-group services. The OECD Guidelines list different examples for intra-group services for illustrative purposes. These examples include debt-factoring activities, where a multinational enterprise decides to centralize these activities to e.g. minimize administrative burdens or limit currency and debt risks.[3] According to the OECD shared services may also be involved regarding contract manufacturing. The producer may get extensive instruction and could bear low risks. In such cases the production company would be performing a service and should be remunerated accordingly.[4] Contract research is another example for an intra-group service according to the OECD Guidelines. In practice the research companies will often not bear financial risks as they will be reimbursed whether the research was successful or not. Furthermore the intangible property is mostly owned by the principal company.[5] The last example of the OECD Guidelines is also linked to immaterial property as it is the administration of licenses. The OECD observed that the control of licenses might be handled by a group service center in practice.[6]

---

2 Cf. *EU JTPF* (2010), Annex I.

3 Cf. *OECD* (2010), Chapter VII C 7.39.

4 Cf. *OECD* (2010), Chapter VII C 7.40.

5 Cf. *OECD* (2010), Chapter VII C 7.41.

6 Cf. *OECD* (2010), Chapter VII C 7.42.

A special category of services are the so called on call services. In connection with on call services there are often discussions regarding standby charges to ensure the availability of a service[7]. Standby charges for certain services can also be observed between independent parties and therefore they can also be charged between group companies. Of course independent enterprises would not pay a standby charge if the advantage of having services on call was negligible. The extent to which the services have been used over a period of several years should also be taken into account according to the OECD when it comes to determine if a standby fee is adequate.[8]

As between third parties, related parties have to pay each other for services they have received from each other. The remuneration for the services has to be determined considering the arm's length principle meaning related parties should pay a price for the received services a third party would pay, too. We will focus on how to determine a price at arm's length later on.

The arm's length principle also implies that the rendered service provides economic or commercial value for the recipient. Otherwise, a third party would not have paid for the service. The EU JTPF states that it is key that the service provides economic or commercial value.[9] There will also be services rendered between related parties for which a payment is not always adequate. Two of these special groups of services will be analyzed in detail within the next two paragraphs

2.1 Shareholder Services

Companies may receive an intra-group service even though they do not need it. As independent enterprises they would not be willing to pay for these services. One group of such services is known as shareholder services as it would be services that a group member (usually the parent company or a regional holding company) performs solely because of its ownership interest in one or more other group members, i.e. in its capacity as shareholder.[10] In the case of such stewardship services a charge for the services will not be accepted by most fiscal authorities. The costs for these services have to be borne by the shareholders themselves.

In its annex II the EU JTPF guidelines include a non exhaustive list of services that the EU JTPF reviewed and recognised as services that are regularly classified as shareholder costs. This classification will always depend on the specific facts and circumstances and therefore a case by case analysis should be performed. Nevertheless the following costs have to be regularly classified as shareholder costs according to the EU JTPF:[11]

---

7 Cf. *Stuffer/Reichl* (2010), p.686.
8 Cf. *OECD* (2010), Chapter VII B.1 7.16.
9 Cf. *EU JTPF* (2010), Chapter 7.1 26.
10 Cf. *OECD* (2010), Chapter VII B.1 7.9.
11 Cf. *EU JTPF* (2010), Chapter 7.4 41 and Annex II.

- Costs of activities relating to the juridical structure of the parent company itself such as:
  - Costs for the issuing of shares of the parent company
  - Cost of the board of directors of the parent company that is associated with the statutory duties of a director as a member of the board of directors.
  - Costs for the compliance of the parent with the tax law (tax returns, bookkeeping, etc.)
- Costs relating to reporting requirements of the parent company including the consolidation of reports:
  - Costs for the financial reports of the parent
  - Costs for the consolidated financial statements of the group
  - Costs for the application and compliance with cross-border tax consolidation
  - Costs for the audit of the parent
- Costs of raising funds for the acquisition of the parent company's participations
- Costs of managerial and control (monitoring) activities related to the management and protection of the investments in participations unless an independent party would have been willing to buy for or to perform for itself
  - Costs of the parent company's audit of the accounts of the subsidiary if it is carried out exclusively in the interest of the parent
  - Costs for the drafting and auditing of the financial statements of the subsidiary in accordance with the accounting principles of the States of the parent (e.g. US GAAP)
  - Costs of information technology connected to managerial and control (monitoring) activities as described above
  - Cost for the general review of the affiliates' performance if not connected to the provisions of consulting services to the subsidiaries
- Costs to reorganize the group, to acquire new members, or to terminate a division
- Costs for initial listing on a stock exchange of the parent and costs for the activities related to stock market listing of the parent, in the years after the initial listing (e.g. preparation of documents required by the stock market supervisory body).
- Investor relations' costs of the parent company as costs for press conferences and other communications with shareholders of the parent company, financial analysts, funds and other stakeholders of the parent company
- Study and implementation of the capitalization structure of the subsidiaries
- Costs for the increase of the share capital of the subsidiary

Of course there are services that are on the one hand shareholder services but on the other hand provide an additional benefit for the group company. In that case the costs for the services have to be split in an adequate manner. Regarding the remuneration the question arises if only one company or the whole group has benefitted. Furthermore the attribution of the costs has to take into account the type of industry, the type of company and the service provided so that there will be an individual allocation key for each service. A case by case approach results as the only viable way.[12]

2.2 Implicit Support and Synergies

Another anomaly that does not occur between independent companies is the so called implicit support that exists through an international group for each of the group companies. This support may induce implications on financial transactions as a group company may receive loans from third parties with better conditions then the company would receive independently. In these cases subsidiaries receive a benefit from being part of a group.

The implicit support as described above is not a typical shareholder service as each of the group companies receives a benefit from it. But even as the group companies receive a benefit the implicit support will not be regarded as an intra-group service that has to be remunerated. As described within the OECD Guidelines a group company should not be considered to receive an intra-group service when it obtains incidental benefits attributable solely to its being a part of a larger concern, and not to any specific activity being performed.[13] If a group company would issue a guarantee to another group company and the better loan conditions would be a result of this guarantee the guarantee would be like an intra-group "service" the recipient would have to pay for. As stated within the OECD guidelines it is key to distinguish between passive association and active promotion and judge each case according to its own facts and circumstances.

In that context the OECD is also addressing group synergies within its latest discussion draft on the revision of the special considerations for intangibles in chapter 6 of the OECD Transfer Pricing Guidelines and related provisions dated June 6th, 2012. Within the draft the OECD states that those synergies can take many different forms and may have an effect on the determination of the arm's length conditions of controlled transactions. They should be addressed as comparability factors.[14] It has to be seen which conclusions the OECD will draw in the final version of the revision.

12 Cf. *EU JTPF* (2010), Chapter 7.4. 44–46.

13 Cf. *OECD* (2010), Chapter 7 B.1 7.13.

14 Cf. *OECD* (2012), Chapter A.4. (vi).

3 Transfer Pricing Methods

Within the following paragraphs we want to give some details on two transfer pricing methods that are often used to remunerate intra-group services.

3.1 Comparable Uncontrolled Price Method (CUP)

In general this method compares the price paid for intra-group services to the price charged for services rendered in a comparable uncontrolled transaction under comparable circumstances ("market prices"). Differences between the two prices suggest that the conditions of the commercial and financial relations of the associated companies are not arm's length, and that the price in the uncontrolled transaction may need to be substituted for the price in the controlled transaction.[15]

According to the OECD guidelines an uncontrolled transaction is comparable to a controlled intra-group transaction (i.e. it is a comparable uncontrolled transaction) for purposes of the CUP method if one of two conditions is met:[16]

- None of the differences (if any) between the transactions being compared or between the enterprises undertaking those transactions could materially affect the price in the open market
- Reasonably accurate adjustments can be made to eliminate the material effects of such differences.

Where it is possible to locate comparable uncontrolled transactions, the CUP method is the most direct and reliable way to apply the arm's length principle. Nevertheless it can be hard to find an uncontrolled transaction that is comparable to the own intra-group service. In many cases there are major differences observable so that the CUP method cannot be used. In other cases there are differences that are minor but could also influence the price for the transaction. In these cases adjustments to the price have to be made. Concerning the adjustments it is important that the adjustments are made reasonably accurate to achieve comparability as the extents of such adjustments affect the reliability of the comparability analysis.

3.2 Cost Plus Method (CPM)

The cost plus method is based on the costs of the service providing company. The costs get transferred from the service provider to the purchaser. On top of these costs a mark up is added so that the service provider receives an appropriate profit in light of the functions and risks performed and the market conditions. The result of the costs and the added mark up can be regarded as the arm's length price for the service. The OECD states that this method is probably most useful where the controlled transaction is the provision of services.[17]

---

15 Cf. *OECD* (2010), Chapter II B.1 2.13.

16 Cf. *OECD* (2010), Chapter II B.1 2.14.

17 Cf. *OECD* (2010), Chapter II D.1 2.39.

The costs that will be charged to the purchaser of the service normally include direct as well as indirect costs. Below we will describe more details on how to determine a direct cost base, allocate the indirect costs of the service and establish a mark up.

3.2.1 Cost Basc

The OECD Guidelines state that it is particularly important to take into account differences in the level and types of expenses. It is necessary to differentiate between operating expenses and non-operating expenses including financing expenditures.[18] To maintain comparability over time accounting consistency is very important.

The cost base of a certain service includes the direct costs of that certain service plus the indirect costs of that service and an adequate portion of the overhead costs of the company as a whole. The direct costs are normally easy to read off the books. It is the indirect costs and the overhead costs of the business that are harder to determine. These costs can be calculated by using different allocation keys.

3.2.2 Allocation Key

Regarding the cost plus method it is critical to allocate further indirect and overhead costs. Different allocation keys can be used for different sorts of costs. In all cases the allocation key must lead to a result that is consistent with what comparable independent enterprises would have been prepared to accept.[19] The application of a self evident allocation key for a single service provision should not present major problems, e.g. payroll service allocated by headcount according to the EU JTPF.[20] Furthermore the EU JTPF states that the provision of more than one service under a single contract may require the deployment of several different allocation keys.[21] The application keys that were agreed on have to be regularly reviewed and consistently applied.

According to the EU JTPF the following allocation keys are in common usage:[22]

- IT: number of PCs
- Business management software (e.g. SAP): number of licences
- Human Resources: headcount
- Health and safety: headcount
- Management development: headcount
- Tax, Accounting, etc: turnover or size of balance sheet
- Marketing services: turnover
- Vehicle fleet management: number of cars

18 Cf. *OECD* (2010), Chapter II D.1 2.45.
19 Cf. *OECD* (2010), Chapter VII 7.2.4.
20 Cf. *EU JTPF* (2010), Chapter 7.5 48.
21 Cf. *EU JTPF* (2010), Chapter 7.5 49.
22 Cf. *EU JTPF* (2010), Chapter 7.5 52.

3.2.3 Mark Up

The mark up can also be deduced from comparable uncontrolled transactions. According to the OECD the cost plus mark up of the service provider for the intra-group service can ideally be established by reference to the cost plus mark up that the service provider earns in comparable uncontrolled transactions ("internal comparable"). In addition, the cost plus mark up that would have been earned in comparable transactions by an independent enterprise can be used ("external comparable").[23]

If there are little differences between the transaction underlying the comparable mark up and the service transaction an adjustment to the mark-up has to be determined. The mark up generally has to take into account the functions and risks that were performed by the service provider. In general the following rule of thumb applies: The higher the value that was added by the service provider the higher the mark up.

There are a lot of low value adding intra-group services and therefore the EU JTPF specified the determination of the mark up for these services. These services will typically only attract a modest mark up and establishing an appropriate cost base is relatively more important. The experience of the EU JTPF shows that this modest mark up typically falls within a range of 3–10 %, often around 5 %.[24]

For high value adding services it would be more appropriate to perform an in-depth analysis of the five comparability factors, including a functional analysis, as a preparation for a benchmark study. Through a benchmark study comparable mark up rates of uncontrolled enterprises can be determined. Within the range of comparable mark up rates a mark up for the service under review has to be determined based on the above mentioned analysis. The benchmarking study includes a quantitative and qualitative screening of the potential comparables.

4 Cost Pool

Besides using a classical transfer pricing method for the remuneration of intra-group services there exists also the possibility of a cost pool. A cost pool will be generated through contracts between group companies in which they agree to share the costs and risks of developing, producing or obtaining assets, services, or rights, and to determine the nature and extent of the interests of each participant in those assets, services, or rights. These contracts are called cost contribution agreements. According to the OECD each participant's proportionate share of the overall contributions to the arrangement will be consistent with the participant's proportionate share of the overall expected benefits to be received under the arrangement in a cost pool.[25] The participants of the cost pool are entitled to exploit their interests separately as effective owners. Very common are cost contribution agreements concerning joint development of intangible property.

23 Cf. *OECD* (2010), Chapter II D.1 2.40.

24 Cf. *EU JTPF* (2010), Chapter 7.7.2 61.–63.

25 Cf. *OECD* (2010), Chapter 8 B.1 8.3.

Each participant is expecting a benefit from taking part in a cost pool. A problem in relation to cost pools is to estimate the benefit relating from the cost pool. For some activities e.g. research and development the outcome of the development is highly uncertain. Furthermore it is hard to determine in certain cases if the benefit will be short or long term. The expectation of a benefit does not include a guarantee for success. Research and development activities could fail to produce valuable results. If the activity would fail over a longer period of time the participants of the cost pool should think about terminating the activity and with it the cost pool agreement.

Contributions to the cost pool by the participants have to get remunerated. In most cases the participants' costs for the contribution to the pool get reimbursed. In practice it is very important that all appropriate costs are within the pool and inappropriate costs (e.g. shareholder costs) are excluded. In a next step the costs will be split up according to the arm's length principle between the participants of the cost pool. For this matter an allocation key similar to those used in 3.2.2 can be used where it seems adequate.

Within a tax audit the following information could be requested by an auditor for the review of the cost pool according to the EU JTPF:[26]

- The company/group audit standard that is applied to the pool e.g. materiality limits; standard of proof.
- An explanation of the cost accounting method used in attributing direct and indirect costs to the pool. A description of how costs are dealt with will be needed where multi service provision centres exist.
- The basis on which costs identified as shareholder costs were specifically excluded from the pool. It may be that a separate analysis of these costs will be submitted for the sake of completeness.
- A description and analysis of the cost pool headings (e.g. IT, accounting, HR).
- The origin of any mark up applied and identification of costs allocated without mark up.
- A description and analysis of costs allocated. Detail here will particularly be in point where worldwide service costs are attributed to individual associates.
- A reconciliation of total pool costs to total allocated costs to guarantee that costs allocated are not greater than total costs.

Tax auditors are reviewing cost pool concepts more critical than regular intra-group services as they see a higher potential for a shift of profits to countries with a lower tax burden within these concepts.[27] Therefore the importance of intercompany contracts and documentation is even higher for this sort of transactions.

---

26 Cf. *EU JTPF* (2010), Chapter 7 7.2 36.

27 Cf. *KUCKHOFF/SCHREIBER* (2000), p. 346.

5 Contracts and Documentation

It is highly recommended for all intra-group services to gather information and relevant documents so that adequate transfer prices can be proven within a tax audit. In most countries there are existing documentation requirements. If a documentation report cannot be provided within a certain timeframe payments for the delay can be opposed by tax authorities in some countries. Another reason for providing a transfer price documentation lies in the shift of the burden of proof. In most countries the tax authorities bear the burden of proof after receiving a valid transfer pricing documentation report. As documentation requirements vary in each country it is necessary to assess the requirements in every country involved regarding the own transfer pricing system.

According to the EU JTPF a documentation pack considering intra-group services could contain the following parts:[28]

- A narrative
- Written agreements
- Justification of OECD methodology applied
- Verification of arm's length price applied
- Invoicing system and invoices

In practice intra-group services will be performed without written agreements quite regularly. From a documentation point of view this can lead to problems as it will be harder to prove that the transfer prices were adequate. Furthermore a third party would always require a contract and correct invoicing. According to the EU JTPF the absence of written documentation should not be the deciding factor in rejecting service provision or benefit but rather should be an element in any overall fact pattern on which a decision is based within a tax audit.[29] Nevertheless a written documentation makes it a lot easier to prove the correct application of the arm’s length principle and therefore prevent penalties.

---

28 Cf. *EU JTPF* (2010), Chapter 8 70.

29 Cf. *EU JTPF* (2010), Chapter 8 68.

References

OECD (2010): OECD Transfer Pricing Guidelines for Multinational Enterprises and Tax Administrations, Paris 2010.

OECD (2012): Discussion Draft – Revision of the Special Considerations for Intangibles in Chapter VI of the OECD Transfer Pricing Guidelines and related provisions, Paris 2012.

ERNST & YOUNG (2009): 2009 Global transfer pricing survey, n. n. 2009.

EU JOINT TRANSFER PRICING FORUM (2010): JTPF Report: Guidelines on Low Value Adding Intra-Group Services, Brussels 2010.

KUCKHOFF, H./SCHREIBER, R. (2000): Die neuen Verwaltungsgrundsätze zu den Umlageverträgen (Teil I), in: IStR, 2000, p. 346–351.

STUFFER, W./REICHL, A. (2010): Verrechnung konzerninterner Dienstleistungen über die Grenze – Aktuelle Entwicklungen im EU-Verrechnungspreisforum, in: IStR, 2010, p. 685.

Transfer Pricing Aspects of Cross-Border Service Provisions

STEFAN STEIN, WINFRIED RUH, MARCUS SELG, MARTIN TROST and *ALEXANDER RIEDEL*

Ulm University, Institute of Accounting and Auditing,
Graf Kanitz Steuerberatungsgesellschaft mbH,
MT Audit GmbH Wirtschaftsprüfungsgesellschaft
and *KPMG AG Wirtschaftsprüfungsgesellschaft*

1 Introduction

"Business goes global – taxes stay local." This statement conveniently describes the inherent conflict between the economic globalization and the national focus of taxation. Global presence and diversification constitute a prerequisite for multinational enterprises (MNEs) to ensure competitiveness in the present and in future. As a consequence, cross-border transactions between group members and permanent establishments have significantly gained in relevance. International taxation is based on a separate entity approach. Therefore, each individual entity of a MNE is subject to taxation on the related income.[1]

Since no harmonization of national income tax systems has been implemented yet, both MNEs and tax administrations are faced with complex taxation issues and the corresponding problem of double taxation. On the other hand, MNEs can take full advantage of the differrence in tax levels by the allocation of profits to low tax jurisdictions. Especially in the context of business restructurings, i.e., the cross-border redeployment of (business) functions in Germany, significant profit potentials can be reallocated within MNEs. Concerning the corporate alliance, the commercial and financial relations within the MNEs are not affected by external market forces. Therefore, the conditions – in particular the agreed prices – imposed between associated enterprises (related parties) may differ from those which independent enterprises would have agreed upon (paid) under otherwise comparable circumstances. In order to apply the separate entity approach to intra-group transactions and to ensure that each jurisdiction involved in the controlled transaction is allocated a reasonable portion of the profits, the involved enterprises have to be taxed in their transactions on an arm`s length basis.[2]

The ascertainment of an arm's length price relies on a functional analysis. In a functional analysis, the functions performed by associated enterprises in a controlled transaction and by independent enterprises in comparable uncontrolled transactions – taking into account assets used and risks assumed are identified, and the economically significant activities and responsibilities undertaken are compared.[3] Considering the results of the functional analysis, the profits of a transaction are divided between the associated enterprises taking into account that functions performed, assets used, and risks assumed correlate with a higher share in profits. Further, functional analysis is the basis for the determination of an appropriate transfer pricing method.

If the conditions contradict the arm's length principle, the host countries are authorized to adjust the agreed conditions in order to secure an appropriate tax base.[4] In reference to cross-border reallocation of business activities, the Foreign Transactions Tax Act (Außensteuergesetz) contains specific regulations on applying the arm`s length principle. It states that the value of a transfer package as a whole must correspond with the expected profit potential attributable to the transferred function.[5] The general valuation of a transfer package as a whole is deemed to be dispensable under the three escape clauses pursuant to § 1 (3) sent. 10

1 Cf. *OECD* (2010b), Preface, (5).

2 Cf. *OECD* (2010b), Preface, (5), and § 1 (1) sent. 1 of the Foreign Transaction Tax Act.

3 Cf. *Federal Ministry of Finance* (1983), p. 218, sect. 2.1.3, and *OECD* (2010b), sect. 1.42.

4 Cf. Art. 9 (1) of the *OECD* Model Tax Convention.

5 See Chapter 4.

of the Foreign Transactions Tax Act, which enable the taxpayer to rely on single arm`s length prices for the transferred assets.

2 Theoretical Perspectives on Cross-Border Tax Planning

Generally, the primary objective of an enterprise is to maximize profits. In achieving this objective, the decision-makers often have to choose between different alternatives available to the enterprise at the time of decision. To prevent companies from alternatives leading to suboptimal results, any issue on which a decision is required has to be resolved in a structured and methodical way.[6] Since the effect of a decision not only depends on the choice of an alternative but also on extraneous and partly risky factors, the interdependencies between the alternatives and the status quo have to be quantified. Based on these results, the alternatives of maximizing the expected utility in reference to the objectives and the status quo have to be selected.[7]

Due to cognitive limitations, a multitude of alternatives cause the decision-making process to become very difficult to handle. Therefore, sub-objectives should be defined, facilitating a decomposition of any complex issue into smaller fractions. As taxation affects the maximization of profits in a negative way, the effects of taxation have to be taken into account in managerial decisions.[8] A reduction of corporate taxation to MNEs for a defined period as well as a reduction of corporate taxation as a result of business restructuring is a sub-objective (minor objective) of the enterprises primary objectives.[9]

Many ways may lead to a reduction of corporate taxation, but the reallocation of functions and activities within MNEs towards low tax jurisdictions has the greatest impact on the average group tax burden.[10] Based on the deferral principle, the MNEs may take full advantage of the difference between tax levels and tax bases. To avoid an extensive reallocation of profits abroad, almost every tax jurisdiction has established an extensive transfer pricing regime including special exit taxation rules. Cross-border tax planning has to account for all positive and negative tax-influencing factors in connection with alternatives open to the company at the time of decision. Focusing on the sub-objective of reducing corporate taxation, the alternative of the lowest capitalized tax burden has to be chosen since the expected utility for the MNEs will be maximized. In this context it is important to note that the sub-objective reducing corporate taxation might be at odds with other objectives and should therefore be considered in the context of the target system.

6 Cf. *KLEIN/SCHOLL* (2004), p. 1 et seq.

7 Cf. *LAUX* et al. (2012), p. 53 et seqq.

8 Cf. *WAGNER* (1984), p. 202, and *JACOBS* et al. (2011), p. 911.

9 Cf. *JACOBS* et al. (2011), p. 916.

10 Cf. *HERZIG* (2003), p. 87 et seqq., and *JACOBS* et al. (2011), p. 914.

3 German Transfer Pricing Principles

For purposes of taxation, the analysis of business relationships between associated enterprises depends on the behavior of the enterprises having acted in the manner of parties unrelated to each other. Therefore, § 1 (1) sent. 1 of the Foreign Transactions Tax Act stipulates that transactions within MNEs have to be assessed by following the arm`s length principle. According to § 1 (2) of the Foreign Transactions Tax Act, a transaction between related parties is generally assumed if a party holds a direct or indirect ownership interest of one fourth or more (a "substantial" ownership interest) in the taxpayer or is able to exert direct or indirect control over the taxpayer, or conversely, the taxpayer holds a substantial ownership interest in the party in question or is able to exert direct or indirect control over this party. The distinction of arm`s length prices relies on different arm`s length concepts depending on the availability and quality of third-party comparable data and information. Regarding the applicable arm`s length concept, different transfer pricing methods according to the information and data available could apply. The functional analysis described below constitutes the basis of both methods, of the choice of the arm`s length concept, and of the adequate transfer pricing method.

3.1 Functional Analysis

The purpose of a functional analysis is the collection and evaluation of information and data needed to analyze controlled transactions. It is the primary objective of a functional analysis to indicate the allocation of principal business functions among independent legal entities of MNEs and to compare the economically significant activities and responsibilities as well as the valuable (intangible) assets used and the risks[11] assumed by the parties to a transaction.[12] Since the income allocation correlates positively with the functions exercised, functional analysis is of great importance for the choice of an applicable arm`s length concept as well as for the identification of the most suitable transfer pricing method.[13]

In the first step of a functional analysis, all transactions among associated enterprises which are sufficiently material to necessitate any analysis have to be identified. Concurrently, all transactions with third parties as well as transaction between third parties, comparable to the transaction under review, should be identified. In a second step, the suitable arm`s length concept and the most appropriate transfer pricing method have to be chosen.[14] The selection depends on the availability and quality of comparable information and data needed for the application of each method. If the functions undertaken by any third party enterprise in a comparable transaction differ materially from the functions undertaken by the enterprise under review, appropriate adjustments have to be made. Adjustments are only worthwhile for material differences of economically significance in functions exercised with regard to the transaction under review. If significant differences exist in the functions exercised and the risks assumed and no appropriate adjustment could be made, the controlled and the uncontrolled transactions are not comparable. According to the outcomes of functional analysis, the

---

11 Examples for risks assumed by an associated enterprise are market, investment or financial risks.

12 Cf. *Federal Ministry of Finance* (1983), p. 218, sect. 2.1.3, and *Federal Ministry of Finance* (2005), p. 570, sect. 3.4.11.4, and *OECD* (2010b), sect. 1.42.

13 Cf. *OECD* (2010b), item 1.42 and 1.45.

14 See Chapter 3.2 and 3.3.

German tax administration distinguishes between three different types of enterprises:[15] strategic leaders, enterprises with routine functions, and enterprises that perform more than routine functions without being a strategic leader.[16] The business classification has to be made on a case-by-case basis. A strategic leader is defined as an enterprise controlling the intangible assets necessary to carry out business activities in any particular way, performing the economically significant functions, and bearing the material risks. Due to the material functions undertaken and the material risks assumed, a bulk of the income of any MNEs is allocated to the strategic leader. Whether the results reported by the strategic leader are consistent with the arm´s length principle is generally impossible to determine by using comparable arm´s length data for want of comparable enterprises; instead, its profits are a residual amount.[17] By contrast, an enterprise only performing routine functions[18], utilizing minimal business assets, and bearing only minor risks, incurs no losses in the normal course of events, but rather tends to realize small but relatively stable profits (e.g. contract manufacturers, low risk distributors).[19] If an enterprise with routine functions is under review, the taxpayer should generally apply the cost-plus method for the determination of its arm`s length prices.[20]

3.2 Arm's Length Concepts

Depending on the availability and quality of information and data of comparable market transactions, § 1 (3) of the Foreign Transactions Tax Act stipulates an application hierarchy of the three possible arm`s length concepts: fully reliable arm`s length comparison, limited reliable arm`s length comparison, and hypothetical arm`s length comparison.

3.2.1 Fully Reliable Arm's Length Comparison

According to § 1 (3) sent. 1 of the Foreign Transactions Tax Act, a fully reliable arm's length price exists whenever third-party data is completely comparable, assuming terms and conditions of controlled and uncontrolled transactions are identical or any existing differences have no material impact on pricing.[21] In this case, all transfer pricing methods accepted by the German Federal Ministry of Finance are suitable; nevertheless, a preference for the application of traditional transaction methods[22] is stipulated.[23] Since transfer pricing is not an exact science, the ascertainment of a single correct transfer price is not always possible.[24] The correct transfer price may have to be evaluated within a range of fully reliable arm`s length prices

---

15 Since enterprises that perform more than routine functions without being a strategic leader are of minor relevance for the choice of the transfer pricing method, this type of enterprise will not be considered further.

16 Cf. *FEDERAL MINISTRY OF FINANCE* (2005), p. 570, sect. 3.4.10.2 and 3.4.10.3.

17 Cf. *FEDERAL MINISTRY OF FINANCE* (2005), p. 570, sect. 3.4.10.2 b).

18 E.g., intra-group services which could have been readily obtained on the open market from third party providers, simple distribution functions.

19 Cf. *FEDERAL MINISTRY OF FINANCE* (2005), p. 570, sect. 3.4.10.2 a).

20 Cf. *FEDERAL MINISTRY OF FINANCE* (1983), p. 218, sect. 2.1.3.

21 Cf. *FEDERAL MINISTRY OF FINANCE* (2005), p. 570, sect. 3.4.12.7 a).

22 See Chapter 3.3 for a definition of the traditional transaction methods.

23 By contrast, the OECD Transfer Pricing Guidelines stipulate the application of the best method rule. The best method is defined as the transfer pricing method that, under the facts and circumstances, provides the most reliable measure of an arm's length result.

24 Cf. *OECD* (2010b), item 4.8.

meeting the arm`s length principle. Hence, the taxpayer might choose a price at the bottom end of the range being most advantageous to him.[25] Assuming that the agreed transfer price does not fall within the range, tax authorities might adjust the transfer price to median of the identified arm`s length prices.[26]

3.2.2 Limited Reliable Arm's Length Comparison

Limitations in availability of completely comparable third-party data are often acknowledged. Under the assumption that only limited comparability exists, the relevant factors of third-party data considerably influencing the transfer price have to be adjusted to evaluate arm`s length prices of limited reliability. A definition specifying exactly when arm's length prices are of limited reliability is not offered in the Foreign Transactions Tax Act. Therefore, it turns out to be particularly challenging for taxpayers as well as for the tax administration to assess the degree of comparability of data and information on a case-by-case base depending on the functions undertaken and the risks assumed.[27] In contrast to the determination of fully reliable arm`s length prices, the most suitable means may be applied. The traditional transfer pricing methods as well as the transactional profit methods[28] have proved to be appropriate. Since the reliability of these arm`s length prices is lower, statistical tools (e.g. the interquartile range) or control accounts should be applied as instruments to narrow the range.[29] The tax authorities might be inclined to adjust the transfer price to the median of the narrowed range if the selected transfer price is outside the narrowed range.[30]

3.2.3 Hypothetical Arm's Length Comparison

If neither completely nor partly comparable data exists due to the heterogeneity of transaction terms and conditions, a hypothetical arm`s length price has to be determined referring to § 1 (3) sent. 5 of the Foreign Transactions Tax Act. According to the hypothetical arm`s length concept, the taxpayer must simulate a price negotiation process on the basis of a prudent and diligent business manager pursuant to § 1 (1) sent. 2 of the Foreign Transactions Tax Act. By reference to the methods of classical price theory, a negotiation range has to be established in a first step defined by the marginal price of a hypothetical seller (minimum price) and the marginal price of a hypothetical buyer (maximum price).[31] The marginal prices must – from the perspective of the enterprises involved – be commensurate with the profits anticipated at the time of the transfer, with the anticipation being based either on the exercise of the transferred function or on the exploitation of the transferred intangible asset(s) (profit potentials).[32] By reference to the profit potentials, the marginal prices and therefore the transfer price will strongly be influenced by the subjective profit expectations of the respective transaction par-

---

25 Cf. *Baumhoff* et al. (2007), p. 1463.

26 Cf. § 1 (3) sent. 4 of the Foreign Transaction Tax Act.

27 Cf. *Federal Ministery of Finance* (2005), p. 570, sect. 3.4.12.7 c).

28 See Chapter 3.3.4 and 3.3.5 for a definition of the transactional profit methods.

29 Cf. *Federal Ministery of Finance* (2005), p. 570, sect. 3.4.12.5 c) and d); this concept coincides with the *OECD* Transfer Pricing Guidelines; cf. *OECD* (2010b), sect. 3.57. Affirmative *Förster* (2011), p. 22; critical *Baumhoff* et al. (2007), p. 1463.

30 Cf. § 1 (3) sent. 4 of the Foreign Transaction Tax Act.

31 In Chapter 4.2 the calculation of the marginal prices is described for a cross-border transfer of business functions in detail.

32 Cf. § 3 (1) of the Transfer of Function Regulations.

ties.[33] After determining the negotiation range, § 1 (3) sent. 7 of the Foreign Transactions Tax Act provides that the value within the negotiation range which has the highest probability based on the bargaining power of the transaction parties should be assumed to be arm's length. Otherwise, if a value of highest probability cannot be proved, the mean value of the area of negotiation represents the arm's length price for the transaction under review.

The following figure illustrates the application hierarchy of the three different arm`s length concepts in Germany:

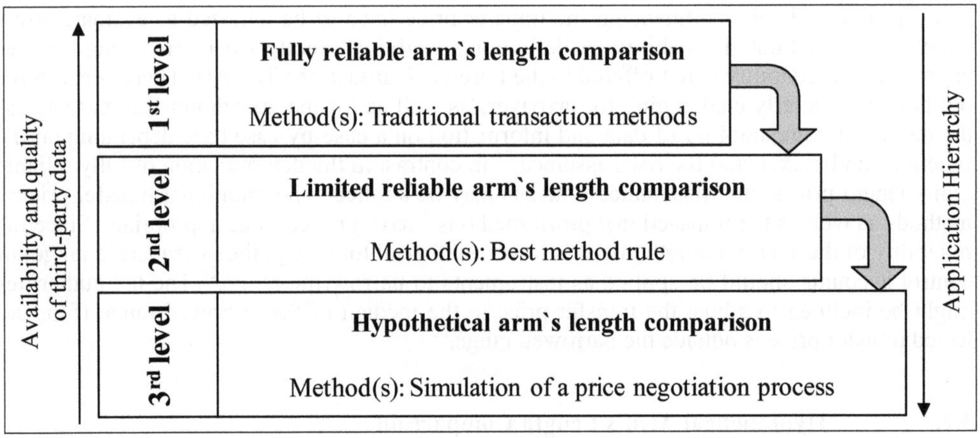

Figure 1: Hierarchy of Transfer Pricing Methods

3.3 Transfer Pricing Methods

For tax purposes, the allocation of income among associated enterprises of MNEs has to be compliant with the arm's length principle. The taxpayer must provide evidence of reasonable efforts to justify the appropriateness of transfer prices agreed upon in a controlled transaction. Therefore, he is held responsible for employing a suitable transfer pricing method.[34] In this regard, a fundamental distinction has to be made between the traditional transfer pricing methods (comparable uncontrolled price (CUP) method, resale price method, and cost plus method) and the transactional profit methods (transactional net margin method (TNMM) and (residual) profit-split method). In the view of the German tax administration, the comparable profit method does not yield results consistent with the arm`s length principle and for that reason is not accepted in Germany.[35] While the traditional transfer pricing methods rely on observable prices or gross margins in comparable market transactions for the determination of an arm's length price, the transactional profit methods break out the (expected) profits from a specific transaction of the comparable companies. Thus, traditional transaction methods are assumed to be the most direct instrument to establish whether the conditions made or imposed between associated enterprises in their commercial and financial relations are at arm`s length.[36]

33 Cf. *OESTREICHER/HUNDESHAGEN* (2009), p. 146.

34 Cf. § 2 (2) of the Profit Allocation Documentation Regulations.

35 Cf. *FEDERAL MINISTRY OF FINANCE* (2005), p. 570, sect. 4.10.3 d), and *OECD* (2010b), item 2.56.

36 Cf. *FEDERAL MINISTRY OF FINANCE* (2005), p. 570, sect. 3.4.10.3 b) and c), and *OECD* (2010b), item 2.3.

Focus shall be on the transfer pricing method most likely reflecting compliance with arm's length prices in the perspective of a prudent and diligent business manager.[37]

The selection of a transfer pricing method aims at finding the most appropriate method for the particular situation.[38] Since the selection might have a significant impact on income allocation, the implementation should be carried out with care. For this purpose, the particular strengths and weaknesses of any suitable transfer pricing method should be taken into consideration during the selection process. As mentioned above, the appropriateness of a transfer pricing method with regard to the nature of the controlled transaction under review is determined in particular on the basis of a functional analysis.

3.3.1 Comparable Uncontrolled Price Method (CUP Method)

The CUP method derives the arm's length prices directly from observable price agreements incomparative uncontrolled transactions and therefore has emerged as superior to all other transfer pricing methods.[39] The direct reference to market prices requires a full comparison of the price-determining key factors between the controlled and the uncontrolled transaction. As long as differences between price-determining factors exist, they must be eliminated by appropriate adjustments. The price agreements among related parties are compared with the prices agreed in the open market for comparable transactions between unrelated parties. This may be accomplished by an internal or an external price comparison.[40]

In the case of an internal price comparison, the transfer price of a controlled transaction is compared with prices existing in the open market which the taxpayer or an associated enterprise has agreed to with unrelated parties. By contrast, the external price comparison matches the transfer price of a controlled transaction with open market prices based upon organized exchanges, customary prices in an industry sector, or transactions between third parties unrelated to each other and unrelated to the taxpayer. Due to the generally limited degree of comparability of terms and conditions in an external price comparison, the arm's length prices should preferably be determined on basis of an internal price comparison. The compliance with the requirements for an internal price comparison corresponds in theory to the most exact and the most appropriate method for determining arm's length prices.[41] However, even minor deviations in terms and conditions of the transactions cause significant price differences, which will reduce the reliability of the ascertained arm's length prices. Due to the sensitivity of variations, the application of the CUP method has proved to be problematic in many cases, due to the fact that transactions within MNEs often contain products or services not traded in a similar way in the open market.[42]

---

37 Cf. *FEDERAL MINISTRY OF FINANCE* (1983), p. 218, sect. 2.4.1.

38 Cf. *OECD* (2010b), item 2.2.

39 Cf. *OECD* (2010b), item 2.13 et seq.

40 Cf. *FEDERAL MINISTRY OF FINANCE* (1983), p. 218, sect. 2.2.2, and *OECD* (2010b), item 3.24.

41 Cf. *BAUMHOFF* (2012), item 357, and *OECD* (2010b), item. 2.14.

42 Cf. *BAUMHOFF* (2012), item 412.

3.3.2 Resale Price Method

The resale price method is suitable if an enterprise purchases goods from or provides services to an associated enterprise and the goods or services are resold to a third party afterwards. In contrast to the CUP method, the resale price method is based on a single-sided retrograde calculation. The starting point of the resale price method is the market price of the resold goods purchased by a third party. The arm's length price is calculated backwards by subtracting an appropriate gross margin of the reseller – according to functions undertaken and risks assumed – from the uncontrolled resale price.[43] The gross margin provides coverage for the expenses incurred plus an appropriate compensation for the functions exercised and risks assumed by the reseller.

When the resale price method is applied, an arm's length price for a controlled transaction may just indirectly be derived from market prices by subtracting an arms' length gross margin from the resale price for the goods sold or services provided. Similar to the CUP method, the gross margin of a controlled transaction could be compared either by reference to gross margins on goods sold or services rendered by the reseller in comparable uncontrolled transactions (internal gross margin comparison), or by reference to gross margins of an independent reseller in comparable uncontrolled transactions (external gross margin comparison).[44] An uncontrolled transaction is assumed to be comparable if none of the deviations in terms and conditions between the controlled and uncontrolled transaction materially affect the gross margin, or if material effects are eliminated by adequate adjustments. Under conditions of the resale price method, the gross margin represents compensation for functions performed, rather than for products sold. Therefore, the functions are the strongest price-determining factor, and deviations in the functions undertaken are assumed to have a significant impact on pricing. By contrast, fewer adjustments are needed to account for product differences, as product differences have a minor impact on profit margins compared to prices.[45]

3.3.3 Cost Plus Method

The third traditional transfer pricing method constitutes the cost plus method, which provides for a progressive calculation of the arm's length price on the basis of supplier`s costs incurred in connection with the transaction under review. For the determination of decisive costs, calculation methods should be considered which usually serve the seller as basis in uncontrolled transactions. Assuming that no comparable supplies or services are provided to third parties, business management principles shall be used for the determination of the decisive costs.[46] In a second step, a profit mark-up customary in the appropriate business or industry sector has to be added to the costs.[47] Profit mark-ups ensure that an appropriate profit margin is granted to the supplier considering the market conditions and the functions exercised. Thus, the arm's length price for the controlled transaction under review compounds the incurred costs plus an adequate profit margin.[48]

43 Cf. *FEDERAL MINISTRY OF FINANCE* (1983), p. 218, sect. 2.2.3.

44 Cf. *BAUMHOFF* (2012), item 422.

45 Cf. *OECD* (2010b), item 2.2.1 et seqq.

46 Cf. *FEDERAL MINISTRY OF FINANCE* (1983), p. 218, sect. 2.2.4.

47 Cf. *FEDERAL MINISTRY OF FINANCE* (1983), p. 218, sect. 2.2.4.

48 Cf. *OECD* (2010b), item 2.3.9 et seqq.

The profit margin of the supplier in a controlled transaction should primarily be derived from corresponding profit margins which the supplier under review or an associated enterprise would be willing to charge for similar third party transactions (internal comparison). If an internal comparison is not possible, the profit margin may also be derived from surcharges of third party sellers in comparable uncontrolled transactions or from surcharges in line with the industry standard (external comparison). An uncontrolled transaction is deemed to be comparable if none of the differences between the transactions being compared or between the enterprises undertaking those transactions affect the profit margin considerably, or if the effects of such differences can be eliminated by reasonably accurate adjustments. In cases where semi-finished goods are sold between associated enterprises, the cost plus method is superior whenever these enterprises have concluded joint facility agreements, the supplier carries out only routine functions, or if the controlled transaction comprises the provision of services.[49]

3.3.4 Transactional Net Margin Method (TNMM)

The calculation of an arm's length price under the transactional net margin method, which provides one of the two transactional profit methods, is based on net margins which independent enterprises would be able to realize in uncontrolled transactions. The net margin will be derived from the net profit relative to an adequate reference basis (e.g. costs, sales, assets).[50] Similar to the cost plus method and the resale price method, an adequate net margin should primarily be established by reference to the net margins the enterprise under review realizes in comparable uncontrolled transactions (internal comparison). Net margins realized by independent enterprises in uncontrolled transactions (external comparison) may furthermore serve as a guideline. The TNMM differs from the cost plus method and the sale price method with regard to the margins applied. Whereas the standard transaction methods use gross margins, the TNMM is based on net margins considering not only the productions costs but also all other costs incurred within the production process. However, the TNMM has proved to be superior whenever the standard transaction methods cannot be applied due to a total lack or insufficiency of comparable arm's length data.[51]

3.3.5 Transactional Profit Split Method

The transactional profit split method, representing the second transactional profit method, is typically applied in the case of highly integrated operations when each party exercises more than routine functions and owns significant (intangible) assets. It seeks to eliminate the effect on profits of special conditions imposed by a controlled transaction while determining the division of profits which independent enterprises would expect to realize from engaging in a comparable transaction. This method refers to the combined profit to be split for the associated enterprises from a controlled transaction and divides this profit among the associated enterprises on an adequate basis. Therefore, the combined profits to be split should be identified and determined in a first step. Subsequently, the combined profits are to be allocated among the associated enterprises based on the relative value of the enterprise's contribution depending on the functions undertaken, the risks assumed, and the (intangible) assets applied by each party of the transaction, anticipated and reflected in an agreement made at arm's length.[52]

49 Cf. *OECD* (2010b), item 2.3.9 et seqq.

50 Cf. *OECD* (2010b), item 2.58.

51 Cf. *Federal Ministry of Finance* (2005), p. 570, sect. 3.4.10.3 b).

52 Cf. *OECD* (2010b), item 2.108.

Where external data (e.g. profit split percentages among independent enterprises performing comparable functions) are available, they can be used to assess whether the profit division between the associated enterprises is at arm's length. The arm's length profit split criteria must be documented. One weakness of the transactional profit split method is the difficulty of associated enterprises or tax administrations to get access to information of foreign affiliates.[53]

3.4 Adjustment of Income

MNEs are free in their decisions to organize their business operations and can act in their own best commercial and economic interests (managerial authority). The tax administrations do not have the right to dictate MNEs the design of their business structure and the allocation of their business operations.[54] Thus, the analysis of business relationships and the allocation of income for tax purposes shall generally be based on each specific transaction with the associated enterprise. The actual facts and circumstances are determinative in accordance with their economic substance.[55]

Consistent with the international guidelines, transactions between associated enterprises are taxed on an arm's length basis. In applying the arm's length principle, the tax administrations are authorized to adjust the prices charged on controlled transactions if the terms and conditions are not in line with those which unrelated enterprises would have agreed upon under comparable circumstances. However, transfer price adjustments by the tax administration are not contradictory to the managerial authority.

Within the German Tax Law, three legal provisions exist for income adjustments:

- Constructive dividends (§ 8 (3) sent. 2 of the Corporate Income Tax Law)
- Constructive contributions (§ 8 (3) sent. 3 of the Corporate Income Tax Law)
- Adjustment of income (§ 1 of the Foreign Transactions Tax Act).

According to § 8 (3) sent. 2 of the Corporate Income Tax Law, **constructive dividends** may not reduce the income of a corporation. A constructive dividend represents a decrease in corporate property or a prevented increase in corporate property induced by the shareholder relationship. It has an impact on the difference in value referred to § 4 (1) sent. 1 of the Income Tax Law and is not based on a profit distribution resolution adopted in accordance with the provisions of the corporate law.[56] Inducement by the shareholder relationship is present where a prudent and diligent business manager would not have accepted the decrease or prevented increase in corporate property when dealing with a third party under otherwise comparable circumstances.

The following figure illustrates the cases in which a constructive dividend could occur.

53 Cf. *OECD* (2010b), item 2.114.

54 Cf. *OECD* (2010b), item 9.163.

55 Cf. *FEDERAL MINISTRY OF FINANCE* (1983), p. 218, sect. 2.1.2.

56 Cf. § 8 (3) of the Corporate Income Tax Law, and R 36 (1) sent. 1 et seq. Corporate Income Tax Guidelines.

Constructive dividends cause			
a decrease in corporate poroperty due to		a prevented increase in corporate property due to	
a decrease in book value of an asset	an increase in book value of a liability	a prevented increase in book value of an asset	a prevented decrease in book value of a liabaility

Figure 2: Prerequisites for constructive dividends[57]

If an agreement between the corporation and its shareholder contradicts the arm's length principle and leads to a constructive dividend, an off the tax balance sheet income adjustment must be carried out when determining taxable income. Constructive dividends are generally valued at their fair market value, which might differ in some cases from the arm's length prices determined under § 1 (3) of the Foreign Transactions Tax Act.

Constructive contributions are not permitted to raise the income of the recipient corporate entity according to § 8 (3) sent. 3 of the Corporate Income Tax Law. A constructive contribution occurs where a shareholder is induced by the shareholder relationship to confer a contributable pecuniary benefit on the corporate entity outside the corporate law framework for contributions.[58] Causation by the shareholder relationship exists only where a non-shareholder acting with the care of a prudent and diligent business manager would not have conferred the pecuniary benefit to the company. This is generally to be determined by arm's length comparison.[59] In contrast to constructive dividends, only a pecuniary benefit that can be reflected on the corporate`s balance sheet can be subject of a constructive contribution. This implicates that surrenders of use cannot constitute a constructive contribution because the benefit of use cannot be reflected on the balance sheet. Non-contributable benefits of surrenders of use include, for example, services performed wholly or partially without consideration or interest benefits resulting from interest-free or low-interest loans granted by a shareholder.[60] The following figure illustrates the cases in which a constructive contribution could occur.

Constructive contributions cause			
an asset to be capitalized	an increase of book value of an asset	a liability to be eliminated	a decline of book value of a liability

Figure 3: Prerequisites for constructive contributions

A transaction is induced by the shareholder relationship and is therefore not in line with the arm's length principle if a prudent and diligent business manager would not have granted the pecuniary benefit when dealing with a third party under otherwise comparable circumstances. Constructive contributions are generally valued at their going concern value[61], in some cases being subject to deviation from the arm's length prices determined under § 1 (3) of the Foreign Transactions Tax Act.

---

57 Cf. *LANG* (2012), § 8 Corporate Income Tax Law, item 65.

58 Cf. *FEDERAL TAX COURT* (1974), p. 123, *FEDERAL TAX COURT* (1983), p. 744, *FEDERAL TAX COURT* (1984), p. 227, *FEDERAL TAX COURT* (1992), p. 333, and R 40 (1) of the Corporate Income Tax Guidelines.

59 Cf. *FEDERAL TAX COURT* (1970), p. 442, *FEDERAL TAX COURT* (1974), p. 123, *FEDERAL TAX COURT* (1992), p. 333, and R 40 (3) of the Corporate Income Tax Guidelines.

60 Cf. *FEDERAL TAX COURT* (1987), p. 348, and *FEDERAL TAX COURT* (1989), p. 633.

61 Cf. § 8 (1) of the Corporate Income Tax Law in conjunction with § 6 (1) no. 5 of the Income Tax Law.

§ 1 of the Foreign Transactions Tax Act regulates the income allocation between internationally associated enterprises with cross-border business relationships based on the law of obligations. The purpose of this provision is to protect German tax revenues against erosions caused by inadequate transfer prices.[62] In contrast to constructive dividends and constructive contributions proved to be applicable to both domestic and cross-border transactions among associated enterprises, § 1 of the Foreign Transactions Tax Act focuses on cross-border transactions only. If the terms and conditions in a cross-border business relationship among two enterprises of the same MNE are not at arm's length, the tax administration is authorized to adjust the prices charged in a controlled transaction.[63] Arm's length prices represent the decisive valuation standard under §1 of the Foreign Transactions Tax Act for inadequate transfer prices agreed in a controlled transaction. An adjustment of income under §1 of the Foreign Transactions Tax Act is permitted under all circumstances of income reduction induced by the shareholder relationship and therefore does not suspend surrenders of use of its scope of application. Whereas the legal prerequisites of constructive dividends and constructive contributions are mutually exclusive, the scope of § 1 of the Foreign Transactions Tax Act and constructive dividends as well as the scope of § 1 of the Foreign Transactions Tax Act and constructive contributions partly interfere with each other. To resolve any potential conflict, § 1 (1) sent. 3 of the Foreign Transactions Tax Act stipulates a priority for constructive dividends and constructive contributions. Only if the application of an arm's length price according to § 1 (1) sent. 1 of the Foreign Transactions Tax Act results in an adjustment more extensive than those of the other provisions, the more extensive adjustment shall be implemented in addition to the legal consequences of the other provisions. Therefore, the legal consequences of § 1 of the Foreign Transactions Tax Act shall be treated as subordinate to those of constructive dividends and constructive contributions.

4 Reallocation of Business Activities

Reallocation of business activities is a game played by multinational corporations under supervision of the tax authorities. Proponents argue that reallocating of business activities is an important tool in a global market environment to develop market volume abroad. In many cases, the main focus simply lies in cutting costs. Small and midsize companies normally don´t take part in this game. Their business model is subject to lifelong taxation on any asset they purchase or develop, with no chance of relief or at least reducing their tax rate. However, reallocations of business activities have gained a bad reputation, as it is widely classified as a tool for aggressive tax planning, sharing this fate with excessive interest payments and "transfer pricing management."[64]

---

62 Cf. *KRAFT* (2009), § 1 of the Foreign Transaction Tax Act, item 10.

63 Cf. § 1 (1) sent. 1 of the Foreign Transaction Tax Act.

64 Cf. *KESSLER/EICKE* (2007), p. 53.

4.1 What is a Business Function?

A business function in the context of § 1 (3) sent. 9 of the Foreign Transaction Tax Act represents business activities consisting of an aggregation of operational tasks of the same kind performed by certain units or departments of an enterprise. In addition, it is an organic part of an enterprise, but not necessary constitutes a branch of activity for tax purposes.[65] A mandatory condition for the existence of a function is to carry out the same kind of operational activities, whereas, by contrast, a bundling of different tasks cannot grant the status of a function.[66] Based on these criteria, by judging the similarity of operational tasks, no concise regulation exists. Referring to the statements in the Transfer of Function Regulations, a business activity has to be distinguishable as "activity-based and object-oriented" activity.[67] In context with an activity-and object-based assignment of a business, the risk of atomization of the term function is threatening[68] because the minimum level of operational tasks to be summarized for the emergence of a function is not clearly defined.[69] To avoid an excessive application of § 1 (3) sent. 9 of the Foreign Transactions Tax Act, the application of the term "function" according to § 1 (1) sent. 2 of the Transfer of Function Regulations must be limited. Accordingly, there has to be a certain level of aggregation of similar operational activities to qualify a function as an organic part of an enterprise. The allocation of income and expenses to individual functions may be carried out, for example, on the basis of cost-earnings accounting.[70]

Examples for business functions include business activities related to management, research and development, production, distribution, transport, or marketing. Except as otherwise provided, a transfer of function within the meaning of § 1 (3) sent. 9 of the Foreign Transactions Tax Act occurs where an enterprise (transferring enterprise) conveys assets and other benefits to a different, associated enterprise (receiving enterprise) in combination with the associated opportunities and risks (transfer package[71]), or provides these for use[72] by the receiving enterprise enabling the receiving enterprise to exercise a function previously exercised by the transferring enterprise. A transfer of function may also be carried out for a limited period of time. Transactions realized within five fiscal years shall be combined to form a single transfer of function as an economic matter.[73] No transfer of function occurs where no restriction exists concerning the exercise of the function by the enterprise during the five years following the commencement of the function by the associated enterprise (duplication of function). In case any kind of a restriction occurs within the stated period, the entire transaction constitutes a single transfer of function as of the time when the restriction was arising, unless the taxpayer

---

65 Cf. § 1 (1) of the Transfer of Function Regulations.

66 Cf. *WOLTER/PITZAL* (2008), p. 797.

67 Cf. *BORSTELL/SCHÄPERCLAUS* (2008), p. 282, *BRÜNINGHAUS/BODENMÜLLER* (2009), p. 1286, *LOOKS/FREUDENBERG* (2009), p. 2515, *BORSTELL* (2010), p. 1013, and *FEDERAL MINISTRY OF FINANCE* (2010), p. 774, item 16.

68 Cf. *BORSTELL/SCHÄPERCLAUS* (2008), p. 276, *WOLTER/PITZAL* (2008), p. 796, *KAHLE* (2009), p. 558, and *BLUMERS* (2010), p. 20.

69 Cf. *BORSTELL/SCHÄPERCLAUS* (2008), p. 277.

70 Cf. *FEDERAL MINISTRY OF FINANCE* (2010), p. 774, item 166. Other view *BRÜNINGHAUS/BODENMÜLLER* (2009), p. 1286.

71 Cf. § 1 (3) of the Transfer of Function Regulations.

72 This leads to an advantage of liquidity for the transferring enterprise due to a postponed taxation of hidden assets.

73 Cf. § 1 (2) of the Transfer of Function Regulations.

makes a credible showing that this restriction has no direct economic relationship to the duplication of function.[74]

A transfer of function likewise does not occur as a result of services rendered, unless these transactions are part of a transfer of function. This applies analogously to personnel being seconded within MNE`s without any function being transferred (e.g. expatriates).[75] A business function under the perspective of amended opportunities and risks has to be regarded as a transfer package. Such transfer packages consist of a function and the opportunities and risks associated with the function as well as the assets and benefits the transferring enterprise conveys to the receiving enterprise, accompanied by the function and the services rendered in this connection.[76]

4.2 Valuation of the Transfer Package

When a function is reallocated in combination with important (intangible) assets and other benefits, risks and opportunities abroad, the legislature argues that the summation of "the prices of every individual transferred assets as part of a function is not reflecting the value of the function as a whole on a regular basis."[77] To ensure a broad taxation of values created in Germany within the meaning of a cross-border transfer of functions according to § 1 (3) sent. 9 of the Foreign Transactions Tax Act, the shifted values have to be combined and transferred in the aggregate. Taking into account all related values, the cross-border reallocation of business activities are measured quantitatively, without individual identification and valuation. Some special clauses are contained within § 1 (3) sent. 10 of the Foreign Transactions Tax Act which allow the taxpayer to avoid the valuation of the function as an aggregate (see Chapter 4.3.).[78]

4.2.1 The Approach

Whenever a function contains significant intangible assets or benefits, the German government suspects that the aggregate value of the function as a whole would be higher than the cumulative sum of the individual prices of the included items.[79] According to § 1 (3) sent. 9 of the Foreign Transactions Tax Act, the transferred items should be included in a transfer package and the package should be valued as a whole.[80] So every item of the function reallocation is considered, and it is not necessary to value every single item. Whenever a lack of fungibility and the uniqueness of the functions make it impossible to identify a limited comparable arm´s length price, the arm`s length price will usually be determined on the basis of the hypothetical arm's length comparison. Where the value of a function attributable to the transferring enterprise is determinable as an aggregate in a situation addressed by § 2 (1) sent. 2 of the Transfer of Function Regulations, this value must, in accordance with the arm's length

74 Cf. § 1 (6) of the Transfer of Function Regulations.

75 Cf. § 1 (7) of the Transfer of Function Regulations.

76 Cf. § 1 (3) of the Transfer of Function Regulations.

77 *FEDERAL GOVERNMENT* (2007), p. 86.

78 Cf. § 3 (1) of the Transfer of Function Regulations.

79 Cf. *FEDERAL GOVERNMENT* (2007), p. 86.

80 Cf. § 1 (3) sent. 9 of the Foreign Transaction Tax Act.

principle as provided in § 1 (1) sent. 1 of the Foreign Transactions Tax Act and from the perspective of the enterprise involved, be commensurate with the profits anticipated at the time of the transfer of the exercise of the function and must be allocable to that function (profit potentials).[81] The respective profit potentials shall be determined under due regard to all circumstances of the individual case on the basis of a functional analysis before and after the cross-border service provisions, considering the courses of action available and taking account of locational advantages, or disadvantages, and synergy effects. The documents that formed the basis for the enterprises decision to carry out a cross-border service provision are the starting point for the calculations. The reckoning of the respective profit potentials and the range of negotiation[82] shall be based on the after-tax profit expectations of the participating enterprise resulting by the standard defined according to § 1 (1) sent. 2 of the Foreign Transactions Tax Act, on appropriate capitalization rates[83], and on a capitalization period[84] determined in accordance with the circumstances of the function exercised.[85]

The range of negotiation is a scope of agreed prices bordered by the respective assumed prices of the shifting corporations. The minimum price in the range of negotiation according to § 1 (3) sent. 6 of the Foreign Transactions Tax Act should be equal to the compensation for the loss or reduction of the profit potential, plus the amount arising for any costs of closing.[86] The profit potential for the receiving enterprise arising from the transferred function provides as a rule the upper limit of the range of negotiation.[87] These border prices determine the range of negotiation within which prudent and diligent managers should act. Whenever a fixed price cannot be determined, the law provides that the middle of the border prices should be selected as a price for reference.[88] The marginal price, in accordance with the arm's length principle, should be within the range of negotiation and furthermore be the price independent parties most likely would accept under comparable conditions.[89] The respective marginal prices determining the range of negotiation reflect the extent of the potential profits negotiated by prudent and diligent managers of both business parties, and it is assumed that their individual bargaining power will determine which price within that range should be considered arm's length. By determining the bargaining power, the legal and economic conditions of the business parties should be taken into consideration (e.g. market position or financial conditions). The advantages and disadvantages of shareholder relationship must be disregarded. Depending on the available information, the determination of potential profits may be based on either the direct or the indirect method.[90] To determine the potential profits under the direct method, a direct allocation of revenues and expenses to the reallocated business activities has to be made by conducting only one transfer package evaluation for each business party. Under the indirect method, the value of the function-related profit potential for the entire enterprise before and after the function reallocation, respectively, has to be compared. To determine the marginal prices under the indirect method, four business valuations are needed, resulting in a

81 Cf. § 3 (1) of the Transfer of Function Regulations.

82 Cf. § 7 of the Transfer of Function Regulations.

83 Cf. § 5 of the Transfer of Function Regulations.

84 Cf. § 6 of the Transfer of Function Regulations.

85 Cf. § 3 (2) of the Transfer of Function Regulations.

86 Cf. § 7 (1) sent. 1 of the Transfer of Function Regulations.

87 Cf. § 7 (4) sent. 1 of the Transfer of Function Regulations.

88 Cf. § 1 (3) sent. 7 of the Foreign Transaction Tax Act.

89 Cf. § 1 (3) sent. 7 of the Foreign Transaction Tax Act.

90 Cf. *Federal Ministry of Finance* (2010), p. 774, item 31 et seq.

considerable investigative effort. The direct method is preferable since the evaluation effort is significantly lower.[91]

The inclusion of foreign location advantages and synergies for the determination of marginal prices and the legal arrangement relating to the selection of a price within the range of negotiation according to § 1 (3) sent. 7 of the Foreign Transactions Tax Act may have the effect that 50 percent of the foreign-realized synergies and locational advantages are being taxed in Germany. This leads to a substantial risk of double taxation, since foreign tax authorities often refuse to recognize a transfer price which causes a significant shift of taxation substrate to Germany.[92]

4.2.2 After Tax Profits

The net profits after taxes serve as a starting point for the determination of the profit potential, which a prudent and conscientious manager would deem to have a value.[93] These profits should be determined under assistance of the functional analysis and in-house calculations.[94] The term "profit" is defined as the balance of income and expenses of a period. The profits contain periodic earnings and do not take into account the liquidity effects due to non-cash expenses and income. The net profits according to § 1 (4) the Transfer of Function Regulations are determined by the expected annual results of a function adjusted by non-cash earnings.[95] In this context, the net profits include no periodization and are in accordance with the cash-flows while exercising the function. The application of cash-flows to determine the profit potential is consistent with the arm's length principle since the net present value method is usually based on cash-flows and not on profits.[96]

While determining the function-related cash-flows, synergies and locational advantages and disadvantages have to be considered under the aspect that independent parties would also consider these factors favorable while determining their marginal rates.[97] Synergies represent financial advantages or disadvantages caused by the interaction of at least two functions (e.g. cost reduction by economies of scale in procurement or higher machine utilization) and furthermore affected by a change in the financial surpluses against an isolated view of the transaction object.[98] Synergies have to be taken into consideration for the determination of the profit potentials, irrespectively of whether they already exist when a business activity is being reallocated, or whether they arise for the first time caused by a cross-border service provision.[99] Locational advantages and disadvantages consisting of specific regional circumstances (e.g. labor and material cost differences, quality of available labor and infrastructure, tax rate differences or tax subsidies) must be distinguished from the synergies and shall be used independently from other business functions.[100]

91 Cf. *OESTREICHER/HUNDESHAGEN* (2009), p. 151.

92 Cf. *HEY* (2007), p. 1308, *FROTSCHER* (2008), p. 53, and *HAAS* (2008), p. 523.

93 Cf. § 1 (4) of the Transfer of Function Regulations, and *FEDERAL MINISTRY OF FINANCE* (2010), p. 774, item 31.

94 Cf. § 1 (3) sent. 6 of the Foreign Transaction Tax Act.

95 Cf. *FEDERAL MINISTRY OF FINANCE* (2010), p. 774, item 31, and *FISCHER/FREUDENBERG* (2012), p. 169 et seqq.

96 Cf. *BAUMHOFF* et al. (2008), p. 1949.

97 Cf. *FISCHER/FREUDENBERG* (2012), p. 169.

98 Cf. IDW S 1, item 33.

99 Cf. IDW S 1, item 50.

100 Cf. *FEDERAL MINISTRY OF FINANCE* (2010), p. 774, item 93. Affirmative *SCHILLING* (2011), p. 1536.

4.2.3 Discount Period

With respect to the potential profits, the period for the expected economic utilization of a function has to be determined. The capitalization period reflects the duration of the expected economic utilization of a function. Based on economic conditions within the meaning of § 6 of the Transfer of Function Regulations, a capitalization period of unlimited duration is assumed.[101] A capitalization period of unlimited duration shall be applied whenever no credible showing of reasons for a finite capitalization period is made on the basis of circumstances of the exercise of the function and such reasons are not otherwise apparent.[102] Furthermore, the focus on a capitalization period of unlimited duration is important for legally-based appraisals in view of the legislature. The general foundation of a capitalization period of unlimited duration may lead to reduced legal stability if, in contrast, foreign tax administrations regard a capitalization period of limited duration as arm´s length.[103]

A capitalization period of limited duration may serve as a reference for the determination of profit potentials as long as the taxpayer is able to prove the existence of a capitalization period of limited duration under reliable conditions.[104] Examples of a basis for identifying a capitalization period of limited duration may include the time span of a license or patent, or a function reallocation of limited time within the meaning of § 1 (2) sent. 2 of the Transfer of Function Regulations.[105] The identified time span of a capitalization period of limited duration should basically be equal to the corresponding product life cycle. Typically, most of the involved goods, services and provisions are not worthless at the time when a capitalization period of limited duration ends. For the identified goods and other provisions at the ending point of a function reallocation, an adequate value has to be determined. In order to determine the fair value of the earning potential of the discounted cash-flows, the identified value of the goods and provisions has to be added after taxation as a terminal value.[106]

4.2.4 Discount Rate

After the determination of a discount period, the calculation of the underlying capitalization rate provides another important component. The determination of the capitalization rate, appropriate in a given case, shall take account of the tax burden and be based on the interest rate for a risk-free investment. The term “comparable risk-free investment” is determined by the time span within which the transferred function is likely to be exercised.[107] For investors, risks are far more important than the chances resulting from an investment. Therefore, investors expect an adequate reward for their risks. In order to adequately reflect the uncertainty in forecasting future cash-flows, a risk premium shall be added to the interest rate for a risk-free investment.[108] The dimension of the uncertainty will accordingly be determined by the positive and negative discrepancy of the expected cash-flows. In a nutshell, the discount rate reflects the time value of money through a risk-free interest rate, and investors claim an addi-

---

[101] Cf. § 6 of the Transfer of Function Regulations.

[102] Cf. § 6 of the Transfer of Function Regulations.

[103] Cf. *KROPPEN/ROEDER* (2012), item 156.1.

[104] Cf. § 6 of the Transfer of Function Regulations, and *FEDERAL MINISTRY OF FINANCE* (2010), p. 774, item 40.

[105] Cf. *FEDERAL MINISTRY OF FINANCE* (2010), p. 774, item 109 et seq.

[106] Cf. *IDW S* 1, item 87.

[107] Cf. § 5 of the Transfer of Function Regulations.

[108] Cf. *FEDERAL MINISTRY OF FINANCE* (2010), p. 774, item 106.

tional risk premium because of the assumed risk that the expected cash-flows might not materialize as forecasted.

4.2.5 Further Determinants of Transfer Package Pricing

In connection with the reallocation of a business activity, the transferring enterprise will be faced with closure costs such as costs for vacancy or scrap disposal.[109] The present value of the expected cash-flows out of the function at the transferring enterprise has to be increased by any closing costs in the event they are not included in the cash-flows unless no connection exists between the reallocation of the business activity and the costs for closure.[110] In situations of cross-border function reallocation within the transfer of assets, when the marginal price of a transfer package exceeds the cumulative book value of the single components of the transfer package, the hidden assets have to be exposed and taxed. The taxation of the profit reduces the real cash-flows of the cross-border service provision. In view of the tax authority, prudent and diligent managers of the transferring enterprises would have to consider the tax charge while establishing the marginal price in fact. For that reason, the marginal price of the transferring enterprise has to be raised by the transfer tax (Exit Tax Factor).[111]

Enterprises not affiliated in MNE's and unbound in their business activities will only agree to enter into businesses if they expect a benefit. Whenever several business alternatives are available, enterprises would select the alternative with the greatest benefit for them. In accordance to § 7 (1) sent. 2 and (4) sent. 2 of the Transfer of Function Regulations, such alternatives are to be considered when determining the marginal prices, provided these alternatives are actually available. Without challenging the actual business relationships, the arm's length nature of the respective marginal prices for the shifted transfer package on the basis of opportunity cost calculations has to be established. Furthermore, advantageous alternatives may strengthen the negotiating position of the parties to transactions, thereby affecting the price agreement.[112] There is no need to state all possible alternatives and their implications on the price determination of the shifted transfer package. In the opinion of the tax authorities, it may be sufficient to consider advantageous alternatives in the context of the hypothetical arm's length price.

In the following, a basic problem within the scope of cross-border service provisions shall be discussed by reference to an example: Alpha GmbH, based in Munich, Germany, is a manufacturer of car panes and in addition fixes rock chips by using its own patented sealing procedure. Both related enterprises and unrelated third parties can make use of Alpha's repair services. The expansive Alpha GmbH wants to centralize its services in the region of Eastern Europe at Warsaw, Poland, and therefore wants to transfer its service function "repair of car panes Eastern Europe" to its newly-established subsidiary in Poland, Beta Sp. Z. o. o. This service function is assumed not to constitute a branch of activity for tax purposes. In combination with the function, the patent "sealing procedure" and the special expertise of the service employees, who are regarded as essential relating to the function according to § 1 (5) Transfer of Function Regulations, are going to be transferred, whereas tangible assets will not be transferred.

---

109 Cf. *FREUDENBERG/PETERS* (2008), p. 1425.

110 Cf. *BRÜNINGHAUS/BODENMÜLLER* (2009), p. 1288.

111 Cf. *FEDERAL MINISTRY OF FINANCE* (2010), p. 774, item 118. Affirmative *SCHILLING* (2011), p. 1539, other opinion *GREINERT/REICHEL* (2011), p. 1184 et seqq., and *FISCHER/FREUDENBERG* (2012), p. 169 et seq.

112 Cf. *FEDERAL TAX COURT* (2004), p. 181, item 16.

The enterprise's intangible assets are not financially ascertained at the internal level, due to the prohibition on the capitalization of self-created intangible assets in accordance with § 5 (2) of the German Income Tax Act.

All chances and risks of the exercise of the service function are transferred to Beta Sp. Z. o. o; none of them are kept in Germany. With respect to the exercise of the service function, Alpha GmbH expects annual net profits of 100 K€ over an expected capitalization period of 5 years. Due to low labor costs, the Polish subsidiary expects an annual net profit before taxes of 120 K€. In Germany, the corporate tax rate is 30 percent, whereas the Polish corporate tax rate is 19 percent. The depreciation period of the acquired intangible assets amounts to five years. For both enterprises, a quasi-risk-less interest rate of 2 percent und an adequate risk premium of 7 percent has to be assessed. Absent determinability of the most probable arm´s length price, the median price of the settlement area according to § 1 (3) sent. 7 half sent. 2 of the Foreign Transactions Tax Act has to be identified as arm's length price. The prerequisites for application of the escape clauses (see discussion in Chapter 4.3 below) are deemed to be unfulfilled.

Years		**1**	**2**	**3**	**4**	**5**
Pre-Tax Net Profit		100	100	100	100	100
Taxes		30	30	30	30	30
Profit after Taxes		70	70	70	70	70
Capitalization Factor		0.9174	0.8417	0.7722	0.7084	0.6499
Net Present Value		64	59	54	50	45
Marginal Price Step 1	272					

Table 1: *Marginal Price of the Transferring Enterprise*

The marginal price (first step) has to be increased by the exit tax. The marginal price (first step) multiplied by the Exit Tax Factor equals to:

$$\text{Exit Tax Factor} = \frac{1}{1 - \text{Corporate Tax Rate}} = 1.4286$$

The marginal price (second step) amounts to **389 K€** (272 K€ x 1.4286) and determines the lower limit of the range of negotiation.

Years		1	2	3	4	5
Pre-Tax Net Profit		120	120	120	120	120
Taxes		22.8	22.8	22.8	22.8	22.8
Profit after Taxes		97.2	97.2	97.2	97.2	97.2
Capitalization Factor		0.9174	0.8417	0.7722	0.7084	0.6499
Net Present Value		89	82	75	69	63
Marginal Price Step 1	378					

Table 2: Marginal Price of the Receiving Enterprise

The purchase price of the transfer package will be amortized in Poland over five years. Due to depreciation-related tax benefits, the marginal price (first step) of the receiving enterprise has to be increased by the Tax Amortization Benefit Factor (TAB Factor).

Years		1	2	3	4	5
Depreciation Ratio		20 %	20 %	20 %	20 %	20 %
Capitalization Factor		0.9174	0.8417	0.7722	0.7084	0.6499
Net Present Values of Depreciation Ratio		0.1835	0.1683	0.1544	0.1417	0.1300
Corporate Tax		19 %	19 %	19 %	19 %	19 %
Tax Savings due to Depreciation Expense		0.0349	0.0320	0.0293	0.0269	0.0247
Total Tax Savings	0.1478					

Table 3: Total Tax Savings

The marginal price (second step) of the receiving enterprise has to be increased by the TAB Factor, determined as follows:

$$\text{TAB Factor} = \frac{1}{1 - \text{Total Tax Savings}} = 1.1734$$

The marginal price (second step) amounts to **444 K€** (378 (marginal price first step) x 1.1734) and therefore determines the upper limit of the settlement area. The arm's length settlement price resulting from the median price of the range of negotiation (lower limit 389 K€ vs. upper limit 444 K€) equals to 416 K€.

The following diagram illustrates the determination of the settlement price:

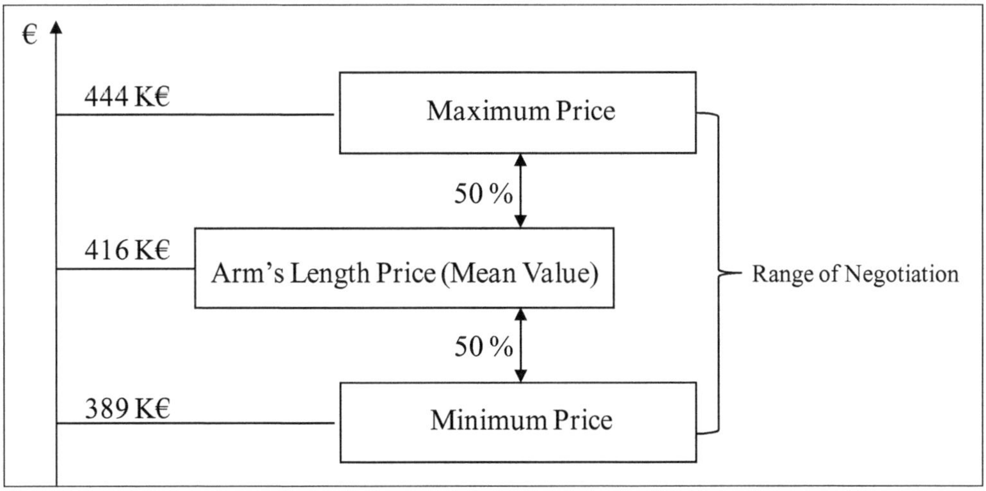

Figure 4: Determination of the hypothetical arm's length value

4.3 Escape Clauses

Generally, the transferred function should be valued as an aggregate because the value of the entire package often exceeds the cumulative prices of the single assets.[113] The evaluation of the transfer package as a whole may be waived if the conditions of one of the three escape clauses of § 1 (3) sent. 10 of the Foreign Transactions Tax Act are met.[114] If one of these three escape clauses is applicable, the assessment of the transfer package may be made on the basis of the individual prices of the single assets. In these exceptional cases, it is possible to evaluate the price by using the arm's length principle if comparative data for the components of the transfer package is available. If in fact neither restricted nor unrestricted comparable data is available, the valuation of the transfer package has to be performed using a hypothetical arm's length price.[115] The three alternatives according to § 1 (3) sent. 10 of the Foreign Transactions Tax Act are explained in the following.

The **first alternative** provides allowance for determination of individual transfer pricing if the taxpayer is able to demonstrate that no material intangible assets and benefits were subject to the cross-border reallocation of business activities. "Material" in the definition according to § 1 (5) of the Transfer of Function Regulations means that such intangible assets or benefits are necessary for the reallocation of a function and their arm's length price amounts to more than 25 % of the sum of the individual prices of all assets and benefits in the transfer package.[116]

---

113 Cf. *Federal Government* (2007), p. 86.

114 Cf. § 1 (3) sent. 10 of the Foreign Transaction Tax Act.

115 Cf. *Freudenberg/Ludwig* (2010), p. 1270.

116 Cf. § 1 (5) of the Transfer of Function Regulations.

The absence of significant assets at a cross-border service provision remains to be shown. However, this first alternative is only rarely of practical relevance.[117]

In the **second alternative**, the taxpayer has the obligation to confirm that the sum of the single transfer prices corresponds to the transfer package as a whole. § 2 (3) sent. 2 of the Transfer of Function Regulations requires that taxpayers disclose and justify the difference between the sum of single transfer prices and the value of the entire transfer package.[118] In addition, the sum of the individual transfer prices must be within the range of negotiation. The second alternative requires considerable efforts. Therefore, it is imperative to determine the value of the transfer package and furthermore the value of the individual transfer prices.[119]

The **third alternative** under § 1 (3) sent. 10 of the Foreign Transactions Tax Act was created by the EU Transposition Act of 2010. It provides that the taxpayer has to make a credible showing that at least one material intangible asset is part of the function reallocation. The term "at least" is providing the possibility that more than one intangible asset may be subject of the cross-border reallocation of business activities. Furthermore, the application of the provision requires a precise description of the material intangible asset. The valuation for all components of the transfer package – including assets as well as benefits[120] – may be based on individual transfer prices.[121]

4.4 Price Adjustment Clause

While the amount of a transfer price has to be determined at the time of the reallocation of business activities, the actual development of benefits and profit potentials after the shifting depends on future events. Such future events cannot be foreseen with certainty in advance; in fact, forecasts may prove completely wrong in retrospect. As a consequence, a discrepancy between expected and actual earnings of a function is to be expected.[122] To avoid possible negative effects, the legislator transfers the principle of the retroactive price adjustment clause on the hypothetical arm's length comparison. According to § 1 (3) sent. 11 and 12 of the Foreign Transactions Tax Act, the taxpayer is prompted to include a price adjustment clause in the contract governing the cross-border reallocation of business activities. If not such adjustment clause is included, the government is entitled to make a subsequent upward price adjustment if the actual profit performance within ten years substantially differs from the performance that was anticipated when the transfer price was determined.[123]

According to § 1 (3) sent. 11 of the Foreign Transactions Tax Act, the legislature presumes in a refutable way that at the time of the transaction, uncertainties relating on price agreements existed and that third parties would have to make an appropriate adjustment clause if significant intangible assets and benefits are part of the function reallocation. In the absence of an individually negotiated price adjustment clause, the law provides that within a time span of

[117] Cf. *GREINERT* (2007), p. 569.

[118] See also *FEDERAL MINISTRY OF FINANCE* (2010), p. 774, item 72 et seq.

[119] Cf. *FEDERAL GOVERNMENT* (2007), p. 86.

[120] Cf. *FEDERAL MINISTRY OF FINANCE* (2010), p. 774, item 29.

[121] Cf. *FEDERAL MINISTRY OF FINANCE* (2010), p. 774, item 76.

[122] Cf. *THIER* (2011), p. 2013.

[123] Cf. § 1 (3) sent. 11 and 12 of the Foreign Transaction Tax Act.

ten years, a one-time upward adjustment may be performed. This arrangement should encourage the taxpayer to make his own adjustment clauses, which allow both for upward or downward adjustments.[124] If either the taxpayer is able to prove that no uncertainties existed at the time of transfer, or independent third parties would not have included a price adjustment clause, then the statutory adjustment clause will not apply. Otherwise, the taxpayer may disburden himself from the application of the statutory adjustment clause by agreeing to an individual adjustment clause with the transaction party. The individual adjustment clause must be in line with the arm's length principle because otherwise, it fails to be recognized properly by the tax authorities, and the legal subsidiary adjustment clause will therefore be applied. According to § 9 of the Transfer of Function Regulations, a taxpayer adjustment clause that precludes any post-transactional adjustments is also assumed if, with respect to material intangible assets and benefits, licensing terms are agreed to by which the royalties payable depend upon the licensee's turnover or profits.

The application of price adjustment clauses in cases of uncertain profit expectations is rather uncommon in practice. Only in exceptional cases, ex post price adjustment clauses are included, but typically, such clauses cover no more than 3 years.[125]

4.5 Transfer Pricing Aspects Related to Shared Service Centers

Service provision consists of a series of activities that bring about benefits. From a transfer pricing perspective, a service provider is an entity providing services to other entities. Many MNEs have centralized services in order to support the manufacturing and/or distribution function ("shared service centers").[126]

In contrast to outsourcing, where an external service provider renders the service, the shared service involves internal outsourcing while recognizing the arm's length principle. An important interrelationship exists between the compensation of the reallocation of the business activity and the arm's length reward for performing the transferred business activity after reallocation. The compensation for the services rendered depends on the functions performed, the assets used, and the risks accepted by the shared service center. Provided that comparable prices for the performed function or service exist, the CUP-Method shall be preferred. In the absence of comparable prices, the cost-plus method should generally be applied.[127] Since the performed services are generally not resold, the resale price method has to be ruled out.

Internal outsourcing of service functions to a shared service center is deemed to be a transfer of business functions under German tax law.[128] Basically, cross-border transfers of business functions are taxed on a transfer price for the transfer package as a whole corresponding to § 1 (1) sent. 9 of the Foreign Transactions Tax Act if none of the escape clauses stated in § 1 (1) sent. 10 of the Foreign Transactions Tax Act apply. Therefore, the relevance of the escape clauses – especially the first escape clause – must be examined in conjunction with the reallocation of shared services. § 1 (1) sent. 10 alternative 1 of the Foreign Transactions Tax Act

124 Cf. *FEDERAL GOVERNMENT* (2007), p. 87.

125 Cf. *SCHOLZ* (2007), p. 524.

126 Cf. *BAKKER* (2009), p. 32.

127 Cf. *FEDERAL MINISTRY OF FINANCE* (1983), p. 218, sect. 3.2.3.2.

128 Cf. *FEDERAL MINISTRY OF FINANCE* (2010), p. 774, item 70.

provides that the determination of transfer prices for all relevant individual assets and services shall be accepted, provided that the taxpayer makes a credible showing that material intangible assets and benefits were neither transferred with the transfer package nor made available for use. Transferring of intercompany service functions to a shared service center is often a matter of transfer of auxiliary functions, generally not accompanied by a transfer of material intangible assets and benefits, therefore qualifying for a valuation of transfer prices on a single asset basis.[129]

Without any detailed proof, the assumption has to be made that no material intangibles assets and advantages are transferred if the following preconditions are fulfilled:

1. The receiving enterprise exercises the transferred function only with respect to the transferring enterprise and
2. the remuneration to be charged for the exercise of the function and the provision of the corresponding service is determined using the cost-plus method.[130]

Otherwise, the taxpayer must make a credible showing that no material intangible assets and benefits are being transferred. The aforementioned regulation provides for a rebuttable assumption that the compensation for the transfer of service functions must be charged in accordance with § 1 (1) sent. 9 of the Foreign Transactions Tax Act if

1. the shared service center (function receiving enterprise) independently provides the services in whole or in part to other enterprises and
2. prices (e.g. computed under the CUP-Method) are higher than the compensation payable under the cost-plus method.[131]

Insofar, a transfer of material intangible assets and benefits in conjunction with the service function is deemed to take place, and the value of the transfer package is determinable as a whole because a profit potential is being transferred abroad. Since the spreading of risks and intangible assets for transactions of the related parties is relevant for the compensation of post-restructuring services and the transfer pricing method used, as well as for the compensation for the restructuring itself, decision-makers should be aware of possible implications on taxation in conjunction with shared service constructions.

129 Cf. BORSTELL/WEHNERT (2011), item 1007.

130 Cf. § 2 (2) sent. 1 of the Transfer of Function Regulations.

131 Cf. § 2 (2) sent. 2 of the Transfer of Function Regulations.

5 Transfer Pricing Documentation

5.1 Documentation

5.1.1 Basic Documentation Requirements

The taxpayer is required to document the nature and content of its business relationships with related parties within the meaning of § 1 (2) of the Foreign Transactions Tax Act.[132] The documentation to be prepared under § 90 (3) of the General Tax Code must clearly indicate the factual situation the taxpayer is facing and furthermore to what extent the taxpayer has based these business relationships on terms, including prices, showing compliance with the principle of arm´s length principle.[133] The information to be applied shall include without limitation data of comparable transactions between unrelated third parties and of comparable transactions entered into by the taxpayer or its related parties with unrelated third parties, such as prices and business terms. The documentation must be prepared based on internal data and data on sales permitting the plausibility check of the transfer prices.[134]

5.1.2 Nature, Content, and Scope of the Documentation

The nature, content, and scope of the required documentation depend on the circumstances of each individual situation and in particular on the transfer pricing method applied by the taxpayer.[135] The documentation shall be prepared in written or electronic form to enable an outside expert to determine within an appropriate time frame the conditions of business transactions between the taxpayer and related parties and if and to what extent the arm´s length principle was observed.[136] The taxpayer bears the risks resulting from non-compliance, including the risk of being exposed to penalties.[137] Taxpayers should be aware of the need for diligent documentation and preserving of evidence, due to the imminent risk of being subject to internal audits every 5 years.

5.1.3 Transfer Pricing Analysis

The Transfer pricing analysis consists of the description of the transfer method applied, the justification of the suitability of the method applied, documents showing the calculations involved in applying the chosen transfer pricing method, and furthermore the presentation of prices or financial data of uncontrolled enterprises relied on for purposes of comparison and documentation of any adjustment calculations made.[138]

---

132 Cf. § 1 (3) sent. 1 of the Tax Procedure Act.

133 Cf. § 1 (1) sent. 1 of the Profit Allocation Documentation Regulations.

134 Cf. § 1 (2) of the Profit Allocation Documentation Regulations.

135 Cf. § 2 (2) of the Profit Allocation Documentation Regulations.

136 Cf. § 2 (1) of the Profit Allocation Documentation Regulations.

137 Cf. *EU-Commission* (2004), p. 33, item 150.

138 Cf. § 4 no. 4 of the Profit Allocation Documentation Regulations.

5.1.4 Contemporaneous Preparation of Documentation of Extraordinary Transactions

Extraordinary transactions include the conclusion or amendment of long-term contracts which have a significant impact on the amount of the income of the taxpayer derives from his business relationships.[139] Documentation of extraordinary transactions within the meaning of § 90 (3) sent. 3 of the General Tax Code must be prepared within six months of the close of the fiscal year in which the business transaction occurred.[140] Transactions to be regarded as exceptional in this context are in particular transfers of assets in the course of restructuring, and the sale of valuable intangible assets.[141] As a rule, the tax authorities shall only require the preparation of documentation for purposes of a tax field audit. Documentation has to be prepared within 60 days of the respective request, unless it relates to extraordinary transactions, in which case the deadline is 30 days.[142]

5.2 Double Taxation and the Mutual Agreement Procedure (MAP)

5.2.1 Factors for Double Taxation

A standard regulation for the taxation systems of individual countries with respect to income tax law exists neither worldwide nor across Europe. In cross-border business relationships, the tax legislation of at least two different countries has to be taken into consideration. As a consequence, one and the same content may be subject to totally different treatment under the tax legislation of different countries, which may lead to double taxation, or in rare cases, to non-taxation. As indicated in Chapter 4.2 in connection with functional reallocations due to the accounting of benefits abroad, there is a substantial risk of double taxation if the arm's length prices identified and adjusted in accordance to German principles fail to be accepted by the other country. In that case, taxation on profits in Germany is carried out without consideration of corresponding costs, leading to economic double taxation of profits.

5.2.2 Corresponding Downward Adjustments

To eliminate the problem of double taxation especially in transfer prices cases, tax administrations may consider requests for corresponding adjustments according to Article 9 (2) of the OECD Model Tax Convention. A corresponding adjustment can mitigate or eliminate double taxation in cases where one tax administration increases a company´s taxable profit as a result of applying the arm's length principle to transactions involving an associated enterprise in a second tax jurisdiction, leading to downward adjustment to the tax liability of the associated enterprise by the tax administration of the second jurisdiction. The allocation of profits between the two jurisdictions is consistent with the primary adjustment, and no double taxation occurs.[143] Based on practical experience, there is no obligation for a corresponding downward adjustment. Furthermore within the German tax regime in the context of double tax conventions, corresponding downward adjustment are rarely applied.

---

139 Cf. § 3 (2) of the Profit Allocation Documentation Regulation.

140 Cf. § 3 (1) of the Profit Allocation Documentation Regulation.

141 Cf. *EU-COMMISSION* (2004), p. 33, item 151.

142 Cf. § 146 (2a) sent. 6 to 9 of the General Procedure Code.

143 Cf. *OECD* (2010b), item 4.32.

5.2.3 Failure of Mutual Agreement

Under the assumption that an agreement among the tax administrations of different states due to divergent opinions about the arm's length nature of a settlement price is not immediately possible, international mutual agreement and arbitration procedures have to be initiated. These provide intergovernmental proceedings for the consistent application of tax treaties or application of the Convention on the Elimination of Double Taxation in connection with the adjustment on profits of associated enterprises.[144]

5.2.4 Commencement of the Mutual Agreement Procedure

Mutual agreement clauses in tax treaties generally provide for an agreement procedure on request by a taxpayer whenever measures taken by one or both treaty countries result in taxation not in accordance with the provisions of the tax treaty.[145] Where a person or a company conclude that the actions of one or both of the contracting states result for them in taxation not in accordance with the provisions of the *OECD* Model Tax Convention,[146] they may, irrespective of the remedies provided by the domestic law of those states, present their case to the competent authority of the contracting state, they are resident.[147] Only the competent authorities of the treaty countries are party to the mutual agreement procedure. The treaty beneficiary is required to contribute to the proceedings by explaining its situation and by identifying and if necessary producing its documentary evidence. Only restricted commitment of the beneficiary within the mutual agreement procedure is regulated by law.[148]

In general, the case must be presented within three years from the first notification of the action resulting in taxation not in accordance with the provisions of the Convention. Within the general adaptable time span of three years starting from the existing of the double tax convention, the commencement of a mutual agreement procedure has to be undertaken. [149]A petition for commencement of a mutual agreement procedure is admissible only if it alleges that taxation in contravention of the treaty has occurred or is impending. To the extent the tax measure has the potential to result in double taxation, the petition shall be based only on the measure to avoid double taxation.[150] Most of the German double tax conventions are based on the *OECD* Model Tax Convention. The execution of the mutual agreement convention, calls for repealing of the binding effect of § 175a of the German Tax Act.[151] To avoid double taxation, the competent authority shall endeavor, if the objection appears to be justified,[152] to find a solution to resolve any difficulties[153] by communicating directly for the purpose of reaching

[144] Cf. *Federal Ministry of Finance* (2006), p. 461, sect. 1.1.1.

[145] Cf. *Federal Ministry of Finance* (2006), p. 461, sect. 1.2.1.

[146] Some double tax conventions are in part based on the UN Model Tax Convention, as is, for example, the case with the portion of the convention between German and India governing withholding taxation.

[147] Cf. Art. 25 (1) of the *OECD* Model Tax Convention.

[148] Cf. *Federal Ministry of Finance* (2006), p. 461, sect. 3.3.

[149] Cf. Art. 25 (1) of the *OECD* Model Tax Convention.

[150] Cf. *Federal Ministry of Finance* (2006), p. 461, sect. 2.3.1. To expedite the proceedings, detailed information about the essential contents of the petition are found in sec. 2.2.3 of the *Federal Ministry of Finance* (2006), p. 461.

[151] Cf. *Federal Ministry of Finance* (2006), p. 461, sect. 4.1.

[152] Cf. Art. 25 (2) of the *OECD* Model Tax Convention.

[153] Cf. Art. 25 (3) of the *OECD* Model Tax Convention.

a mutual agreement.[154] According to Art. 25 (2) of the *OECD* Model Tax Convention, a mutual agreement procedure, is available for issues concerning the allocation of profits between associated enterprises and permanent establishments, among others. If the mutual agreement procedure turns out to be unsuccessful, an arbitration procedure ensues automatically as long as it is provided by double tax conventions.[155]

5.2.5 Commencement of Arbitration Convention

When a person or a company have presented their case to the competent authority of the contracting state on the basis of actions of one or both of the contracting states resulting in taxation not in accordance with the provisions of the ***OECD* Model Tax Convention** and the competent authorities are unable to reach an agreement to resolve that case within two years from the presentation of the case, any unresolved issues arising from the case shall be submitted to arbitration if the taxpayer so requests. The competent authorities of the contracting states shall settle the mode of application of this paragraph.[156] The filing of an arbitration committee is done by independent experts (mostly judges) not bound by the interests of the tax administration.[157] The costs of an arbitration convention occurring with tax administrations are covered by themselves. The taxpayer himself may be faced with enormous costs by tax advisory.

The provisions of the **EU Arbitration Convention** provide an alternative to the *OECD* Arbitration Convention and are applicable to petitions for commencement of a mutual agreement procedure according to Art. 25 (1) of the *OECD* Model Tax Convention.[158] If a tax authority intends to adjust the profits of an enterprise in accordance to Art. 4 of the EU Arbitration Convention, the involved enterprise has to be informed of the intended action in due time to provide the opportunity to notify the affected associated enterprises in the other contracting states. Additionally, these enterprises abroad shall be enabled to discuss the matter with their tax authorities in order to obtain a correlative adjustment.[159] Under an intentional set-off, it is only permissible to set off advantageous and disadvantageous transactions of a taxpayer with a related party if unrelated parties would have arranged a set-off of this nature in their transactions with each other.[160] The number of arbitration conventions is increasing significantly due to the insufficient personnel base of the German tax administration. On the other hand, an arbitration convention leads to the elimination of double taxation.

5.2.6 Advance Pricing Agreements

As a digression Advance Pricing Agreements (APAs) shall be discussed provided that the competent authorities accept the procedure. Transfer prices may be established based on rules of APAs among tax administrations and the taxpayer, for certain business, over an extended period of time and based on definite admittance by the tax administration. Advantages to list

---

[154] Cf. Art. 25 (4) of the *OECD* Model Tax Convention.

[155] Cf. *FEDERAL MINISTRY OF FINANCE* (2006), p. 461, sect. 1.2.2. Some of the German double tax conventions, e.g., with India, China or Russia, do not provide the opportunity of an arbitration procedure.

[156] Cf. Art. 25 (5) of the *OECD* Model Tax Convention.

[157] Cf. *FEDERAL MINISTRY OF FINANCE* (2006), p. 461, sect. 13.1.1.

[158] Cf. *FEDERAL MINISTRY OF FINANCE* (2006), p. 461, sect. 10.

[159] Cf. *EWG* (1990), sect. 2, art. 4.

[160] Cf. *FEDERAL MINISTRY OF FINANCE* (1983), p. 218, sect. 2.3.1.

may be safety oriented tax expenses for cross-border transactions, avoidance of disputes with tax administrations about the appropriateness of transfer prices, and the elimination of risk of double taxation. Disadvantages are found in time- and money consuming procedures, submitting of internal data to tax administrations and the abundance of agreements caused by amended legislation or change in conditions with the taxpayer.

6 Conclusion

The guidelines for business restructurings were set up to enhance legal certainty and to prevent erosion of the tax base. Emphasis of the guidelines is on taxation of functions as an aggregate.[161] While implementing cross-border service provisions abroad, a set of rules establishes an order of preference of methods to assess the price for a transferred function. Generally, comparable arm’s length prices for functions are impossible to determine. Therefore, the valuation for the transferred function usually shall be based on a hypothetical arm's length comparison, taking into account the expected profit potential. In the context of the German tax regime, the foreign earning potentials lead to a significant risk of economic double taxation if the foreign tax authorities decline to accept the arm's length prices established by the German principles. This risk is further increased by the fact that the German provisions do not exactly match the *OECD*-Guidelines in conjunction with taxation of cross-border business restructurings.[162] Any cross border service provision – especially outside of the EU – must be planned carefully. In a nutshell, MNEs are faced with the risk of being taxed twice. Reallocation business functions out of Germany might become a costly adventure.[163]

A function under § 1 (3) sent. 9 of the Foreign Transactions Tax Act has to be defined as a business activity consisting of an aggregation of operational tasks of the same kind performed by certain units of an enterprise. Hence, cross-border reallocations of service functions (e.g. outsourcing of service functions to shared service centers) comply with the prerequisites of § 1 (3) sent. 9 of the Foreign Transactions Tax Act. As a consequence, the displaced functions generally have to be valued as an aggregate. Since generally no profit potentials are displaced in conjunction with an outsourced service function, the first alternative of the escape clauses codified in § 1 (3) sent. 10 of the Foreign Transactions Tax Act apply, and the transferred (intangible) assets should be valued at their individual arm’s length prices. According to § 2 (2) sent. 1 of the Transfer of Function Regulations, the transfer package shall, without need for further proof, be assumed not to include material intangible assets and benefits if the receiving enterprise exercises the displaced function solely with respect to the transferring enterprise and the consideration payable in return for exercising this function is properly determinable under the cost plus method. If the receiving enterprise exercises the displaced function in whole or in part to other enterprises at prices are higher than the compensation payable under the cost plus method, a transfer of material intangible assets and benefits (e.g. know-how) in conjunction with the function is presumed. In a nutshell, the outsourcing of service functions to shared service centers might qualify for the application of § 1 (3) sent. 9 of the Foreign Transactions Tax Act in specific situations and, as a consequence, the price for the transfer

161 Cf. KESSLER/EICKE (2007), p. 56.

162 Cf. *OECD* (2010b), item 9.1 et seqq.

163 Cf. KESSLER/EICKE (2007), p. 56.

package has to be determined as a whole. Against this background, any cross-border reallocation of service function to a shared service center should be planned carefully from a taxation point of view.

The following illustration summarizes the relevant scenarios and its legal consequences in conjunction with cross-border service provisions:

	The receiving enterprise exercises the displaced service function			
	solely with respect to the transferring enterprise		**in whole or in part to other enterprises**	
	transfer of profit potentials	**no transfer of profit potentials**	**transfer of profit potentials**	**no transfer of profit potentials**
Cost Plus Method		**single arm's length prices**	package pricing as a whole	**single arm's length prices**
Other transfer pricing methods	package pricing as a whole	**single arm's length prices**	package pricing as a whole	**single arm's length prices**

Figure 5: *Scenarios of legal consequences in conjunction with the cross-border reallocation of service functions*

Based on our own long standing experiences made in practice of auditing work and corporate advisory activities, we suggest that transfer prices represent an important issue for tax audits.[164] MNEs increasingly are coming into the focus of auditors on the topic of allocating charges incorrectly or not at all between entities or enterprises within their corporate structure. This applies especially to MNEs allocating charges only to their German entities. Furthermore, the documentation and valuation of cross-border reallocations of business activities will be of great importance to future tax audits. In summary, a reliable partnership between tax advisor and taxpayer will turn out to be helpful for improving corporate processes and reducing the risks of subsequent taxation as a result of tax auditing.

[164] Cf. *SCHOPPE/VOLTMER-DARMANYAN* (2012), p.1253 et seqq.

Abbreviations and Terms

APA	Advance Pricing Agreement
CPM	Cost Plus Method
CUP	Comparable Uncontrolled Price Method
MAP	Mutual Agreement Procedure
MNE	Multinational Enterprise
OECD	Organization for Economic Co-operation and Development
TAB	Tax Amortization Benefit Factor
TNMM	Transactional Net Margin Method

References

BAKKER, A. (2009): Transfer Pricing and Business Restructurings: Streamlining All the Way, Amsterdam 2009.

BAUMHOFF, H. (2012): § 1 AStG Berichtigung von Einkünften – Einzelerläuterungen zu § 1 Abs. 1 AStG, in: *WASSERMEYER, F./BAUMHOFF, H./SCHÖNFELD, J.* (eds.), *FLICK/WASSERMEYER/BAUMHOFF*, Außensteuerrecht Kommentar, Loose Leaf Edition, Cologne 2012.

BAUMHOFF, H./DITZ, X./GREINERT, M. (2007): Auswirkungen des Unternehmenssteuerreformgesetzes 2008 auf die Ermittlung internationaler Verrechnungspreise, in: Deutsches Steuerrecht, 2007, p. 1461–1467.

BAUMHOFF, H./DITZ, X./GREINERT, M. (2008): Die Besteuerung von Funktionsverlagerungen nach der Funktionsverlagerungsverordnung vom 12.8.2008, in: Deutsches Steuerrecht, 2008, p. 1945–1952.

BLUMERS, W. (2010): Funktionsverlagerung und ihre Grenzen, in: Deutsches Steuerrecht, 2010, p. 17–21.

BORSTELL, T. (2010): Die verunglückte Funktionsverdoppelung, in: *KESSLER, W./FÖRSTER, G./WATRIN, C.* (eds), Unternehmensbesteuerung: Festschrift für Norbert Herzig zum 65 Geburtstag, Munich 2010, p. 1001–1021.

BORSTELL, T./SCHÄPERCLAUS, J. (2008): Was ist eigentlich eine Funktion?, in: Internationales Steuerrecht, 2008, p. 275–283.

BORSTELL, T./WEHNERT, O. (2011): Kapitel Q: Funktions- und Geschäftsverlagerung, in: *VÖGELE, A./BORSTELL, T./ENGLER, G.* (eds.), Verrechnungspreise, 3rd Edition, Munich 2011, p. 1607–1835.

BRÜNINGHAUS, D./BODENMÜLLER, R. (2009): Tatbestandsvoraussetzungen der Funktionsverlagerung, in: Deutsches Steuerrecht, 2009, p. 1285–1290.

EU-COMMISSION (2004): EU joint Transfer Pricing Forum – Draft – Revised Secretariat Discussion Paper on Documentation Requirements, European Commission, Brussels 2004.

EWG (1990): Übereinkommen über die Beseitigung der Doppelbesteuerung im Falle von Gewinnberichtigungen zwischen verbundenen Unternehmen (90/436/EWG), 23. Juli 1990, in: BGBl. II 1993, p. 1314.

FEDERAL TAX COURT (1970): I R 24/67 of 1970/02/19, in: BStBl. II 1970, p. 442.

FEDERAL TAX COURT (1974): I R 168/72 of 1974/08/14, in: BStBl. II 1975, p. 123.

FEDERAL TAX COURT (1983): I R 182/78 of 1983/03/09, in: BStBl. II 1983, p. 744.

FEDERAL TAX COURT (1984): I R 50/80 of 1984/11/13, in: BStBl. II 1985, p. 227.

FEDERAL TAX COURT (1987): GrS 2/86 of 1987/10/26, in: BStBl. II 1988, p. 348.

FEDERAL TAX COURT (1989): I R 8/85 of 1989/03/14, in: BStBl. II 1989, p. 633.

FEDERAL TAX COURT (1992): VIII R 24/90 of 1992/07/07, in: BStBl. II 1993, p. 333.

FEDERAL TAX COURT (2004): I R 87/02 of 2004/01/28, in: BFHE 205, p. 181.

FEDERAL GOVERNMENT (2007): Entwurf eines Unternehmenssteuerreformgesetzes 2008 v. 27.03.2007, in: Printed Matter of the German Bundestag 16/4841.

FEDERAL GOVERNMENT (2009): Law Regarding the Taxation of Transactions Involving Foreign Jurisdictions (Foreign Transactions Tax Act – Außensteuergesetz) of 8th of September 1972, in: BGBl. I, p. 1713, last amended by the Act of 8th of December 2010, in: BGBl. I, p. 1768.

FEDERAL GOVERNMENT (2011a): Corporate Income Tax Law (KStG) in the Version of the announcement of 15. October 2002, in: BGBl. I, p. 444, last amended by the Act of 7th of December 2011, in: BGBl. I, p. 2592.

FEDERAL GOVERNMENT (2011b): Income Tax Law (Einkommensteuergesetz) in the Version of the announcement of 8th of October 2009, in: BGBl. I, p. 3366; I 2009, p. 179, last amended by the Act of 20th of December 2011, in: BGBl. I, p. 2854.

FEDERAL MINISTRY OF FINANCE (1983): Principles for the Examination of Income Allocation Among Internationally Associated Enterprises (Transfer Pricing Regulations), of 23rd of February 1983, IV C 5 – S-1341 – 4/83, in: BStBl. I, p. 218 amended by Federal Ministry of Finance guidance of 30th of December 1999, in: BStBl. I 1999, p. 1122.

FEDERAL MINISTRY OF FINANCE (2004): Corporate Income Tax Guidelines (Körperschaftsteuergesetz) of 13th of December 2004, in: BStBl. I 2004, Special Issue 2, p. 2.

FEDERAL MINISTRY OF FINANCE (2005): Principles for the Examination of Income Allocation between Related Parties with Cross-Border Business Relationships as regards Duties of Investigation and Cooperation, Adjustments, Mutual Agreement Procedure, and EU Arbitration Procedures (Transfer Pricing Documentation & Procedural Regulations) of 12th of April 2005, IV B 4 – S-1341– 1/05, BStBl. I 2005, p. 570.

FEDERAL. MINISTRY OF FINANCE (2006): Bulletin on International Mutual Agreement and Arbitration Procedures with Respect to Taxes on Income and Capital, of 13th of July 2006, IV B 6 – S 1300 – 340/06, in: BStBl, I 2006, p. 461.

FEDERAL. MINISTRY OF FINANCE (2007): Regulation as to the Nature, Content, and Scope of Documentation under § 90 (3) of the Tax Procedure Law (Profit Allocation Documentation Regulation – Gewinnabgrenzungsaufzeichnungsverordnung, of 13th of November 2003, in: BGBl. I, p. 2296, last amended by the Act of 14th of August 2007, in: BGBl. I, p. 1912.

FEDERAL MINISTRY OF FINANCE (2008): Regulation on the Application of the Arm's Length Principle under § 1 (1) of the Foreign Transactions Tax Act in Instances of Cross-Border Transfers of Function (Transfer of Function Regulation – Funktionsverlagerungsverordnung) of 12th of August 2008, in: BGBl. I, p. 1680.

FEDERAL MINISTRY OF FINANCE (2010): General Administration Rule for Auditing the Accrual of Income between Related Parties in Cases of Cross-border Transfers of Business Functions of 13th of October 2010, IV B 5 – S 1341/08/10003, in: BStBl. I 2010, p. 774.

FISCHER, W. W./FREUDENBERG, M. (2012): Berücksichtigung von Besteuerungseffekten bei der Verrechnungspreisermittlung im Rahmen von Funktionsverlagerungen, in: Internationales Steuerrecht, 2012, p. 168–173.

FREUDENBERG, M./LUDWIG, C. (2010): Chancen für Gestaltungen aufgrund der geänderten Vorschriften zur Funktionsverlagerung, in: Betriebs Berater, 2010, p. 1268–1271.

FREUDENBERG, M./PETERS, H. M. (2008): Steuerliche Allokation von Restrukturierungsaufwendungen im Kontext von Funktionsverlagerungen, in: Betriebs-Berater, 2008, p. 1424–1430.

FÖRSTER, H. (2011): Die allgemeinen Verrechnungspreisgrundsätze des § 1 Abs. 3 AStG – Vergleich mit den aktualisierten Verrechnungspreisrichtlinien der OECD, in: Internationales Steuerrecht, 2011, p. 20–26.

FROTSCHER, G. (2008): Grundfragen der Funktionsverlagerung, in: Finanz-Rundschau, 2008, p. 49–57.

GREINERT, M. (2007): Verrechnungspreise und Funktionsverlagerungen, in: *SCHAUMBURG, H./ RÖDDER, T.* (eds.), Unternehmenssteuerreform 2008 – Gesetze, Materialien, Erläuterungen, Munich 2007, p. 541–582.

GREINERT, M./REICHEL, A. (2011): Einfluss von Besteuerungseffekten auf die Verrechnungspreisermittlung bei Funktionsverlagerungen, in: Der Betrieb, 2011, p. 118–1187.

HAAS, W. (2008): Funktionsverlagerungen nach dem Erlass der Funktionsverlagerungsverordnung, in: Die Unternehmensbesteuerung, 2008, p. 517–524.

HEY, J. (2007): Verletzung fundamentaler Besteuerungsprinzipien durch die Gegenfinanzierungsmaßnahmen des Unternehmensteuerreformgesetzes 2008, in: Betriebs-Berater, 2007, p. 1303–1309.

HERZIG, N. (2003): Gestaltung der Konzernsteuerquote – eine neue Herausforderung für die Steuerberatung?, in: Die Wirtschaftsprüfung, 2003, Special Edition, p. S80–S92.

IDW S1 (2008): IDW Standard: Principles for the Performance of Business Valuations, Düsseldorf 2008.

JACOBS, O.H./ENDRES, D./SPENGEL, C. (eds.) (2011): Internationale Unternehmensbesteuerung – Deutsche Investitionen im Ausland; Ausländische Investitionen im Inland, 7th edition, Munich 2011.

KAHLE, H. (2009): Ertragsteuerliche Abgrenzung der Funktionsverlagerung, in: Steuern und Bilanzen, 2009, p. 557–564.

KESSLER, W./EICKE, R. (2007): Out of Germany: The New Function Shifting Regime, in: Tax Notes International, 2007, p. 53–56.

KLEIN, R./SCHOLL, A. (2004): Planung und Entscheidung: Konzepte, Modelle und Methoden einer modernen betriebswirtschaftlichen Entscheidungsanalyse, Munich 2004.

KRAFT, G. (2009): § 1 AStG: Berichtigung von Einkünften, in: *KRAFT, G.* (ed.), Außensteuergesetz – Kommentar, Munich 2009.

KROPPEN, H.-K./ROEDER, A. (2012): Funktionsverlagerungsverordnung (FVerlV), in: *KROPPEN, H.-K.* (ed.), Handbuch Internationale Verrechnungspreise, Loose Leaf Edition, Cologne 2012.

LANG, F. (2012): § 8 Abs. 2 KStG, Teil C: Die Grundregeln der verdeckten Gewinnausschüttung, in: *DÖTSCH, E./JOST, W. F./PUNG, A./WITT, G.* (eds.), Die Körperschaftsteuer – Kommentar zum Körperschaftsteuergesetz, Umwandlungssteuergesetz und zu den einkommensteuerrechtlichen Vorschriften der Anteilseignerbesteuerung, Loose Leaf Edition, Stuttgart 2012.

LAUX, H./GILLENKIRCH, R. M./SCHENK-MATHES, H. Y. (2012): Entscheidungstheorie, 8th Edition, Berlin/Heidelberg 2012.

LENZ, M. (2010): Deutsches Außensteuerrecht, German International Taxation, Statutes and Materials, Munich 2010.

LOOKS, C./FREUDENBERG, M. (2009): Zukünftige Konfliktfelder zwischen Finanzverwaltung und Steuerpflichtigen als Ergebnis des Entwurfs der Verwaltungsgrundsätze-Funktionsverlagerung, in: Betriebs-Berater, 2009, p. 2514–2519.

OECD (2010a): Model Tax Convention on Income and on Capital: Condensed Version, adopted by the OECD Council on 22nd of July 2010, Paris 2010.

OECD (2010b): Transfer Pricing Guidelines for Multinational Enterprises and Tax Administrations, adopted by the OECD Council on 22nd of July 2010, Paris 2010.

OESTREICHER, A./HUNDESHAGEN, C. (2009): Weder Wirtschaftsgut noch Unternehmen – die Bewertung von Transferpaketen anlässlich der grenzüberschreitenden Verlagerung von Unternehmensfunktionen, in: Internationales Steuerrecht, 2009, p. 145–151.

SCHILLING, D. (2011): Bewertung von Transferpaketen – Ausgewählte Bewertungsfragen unter besonderer Berücksichtigung des BMF-Schreibens vom 13.10.2010, in: Der Betrieb, 2011, p. 1533–1539.

SCHOLZ, C. M. (2007): Die Fremdüblichkeit einer Preisanpassungsklausel nach dem Entwurf zu § 1 Abs. 3 AStG, in: Internationales Steuerrecht, 2007, p. 521–525.

SCHOPPE, C./VOLTMER-DARMANYAN, L. (2012): Konzerndienstleistungsverträge in der (steuerlichen) Praxis, in: Betriebs-Berater, 2012, p. 1251–1258.

THIER, C. (2011): Die Preisanpassungsklausel bei grenzüberschreitenden Funktionsverlagerungen im Konzern, in: Betriebs-Berater, 2011, p. 2013–2019.

WAGNER, F. W. (1984): Grundfragen und Entwicklungstendenzen der betriebswirtschaftlichen Steuerplanung, in: Betriebswirtschaftliche Forschung und Praxis, 1984, p. 201–222.

WOLTER, H./PITZAL, C. (2008): Der Begriff der „Funktion" in den neuen Regelungen zur Funktionsverlagerung in § 1 Absatz 3 AStG, in: Internationales Steuerrecht, 2008, p. 793–800.

List of Authors

Becker, Roman: Roman Becker is a senior consultant at KPMG AG Wirtschaftsprüfungsgesellschaft's consulting practice. For the past four years, he has been working as an advisor in the field of shared services, finance function optimization, IT-enabled process optimization. Industry knowledge encompasses the pharmaceuticals, private-equity, and telecommunications sector. Roman Becker holds a Diploma in Business and Engineering from Darmstadt University.

Boos, Stephan: Dipl.-Kfm., Head of Customer Projects and Commercial Head of GSS Business Line Accounting & Finance Services, Commercial Head of Business Line Supply Chain Management Services at Siemens AG, Munich/Germany, studied Business Administration at the Justus-Liebig-University in Giessen. During his professional life, Stephan has predominantly held roles in or closely related to international project management, ranging from the commercial management of refurbishment projects in nuclear power plants and decommissioning of nuclear facilities, accounting for power plant projects, management of audit and compliance projects, management of a productivity program and a start-up project in the wind power industry, to the lead of a comprehensive finance bundling program in a Shared Services Organization.

Crüger, Arwed: Dr. rer. pol., Dipl.-Vw.; since 2008 partner and leader of the transfer pricing group of WTS Steuerberatungsgesellschaft mbH, is one of the "World´s Leading Transfer Pricing Advisers" according to the recent Legal Media Group Guide and possesses longtime experience in consulting multinational enterprises in all aspects of transfer pricing.1999–2008 senior manager for a BIG4 company in the area of transfer pricing. Doctorate at the University of Halle-Wittenberg, studies at the University of Frankfurt/Main as well as at the University Hagen. Field of work and research: market analysis, design of transfer pricing systems, transfer pricing documentation, brand evaluation, ratings, mergers & acquisitions, analysis of interest and license rates, post merger integration, value chain analysis, business valuations based on the valuation standard IDW S1, valuation of immaterial property based on the valuation standard IDW S5.

Dengler, Sigrid: Since 1987, Sigrid Dengler has assumed a wide variety of roles within the global Siemens finance organization ranging from senior positions in accounting and financial reporting to the management of large-scale projects. From 2005 to 2008, she headed the financial reporting as well as the Siemens Shared Services Organization for China. From 2009 to 2011 she ran the group-wide program 'Cluster Finance Bundling' to develop and implement a new operating model for Siemens's global finance organization covering its accounting, controlling, financing and taxes functions. Since late 2011 she heads the global corporate shareholder controlling function of Siemens.

Dreher, Nicole: Nicole Dreher is a Strategy & Communication Manager for Siemens Global Shared Services, in the area of Accounting & Finance Services at Siemens AG, Munich/Germany. She holds a Diploma Degree in Business Administration and started her career within Siemens in the area of project management dealing with carve-outs. She then started to work for Global Shared Services where she took up her studies in parallel to her job at the Steinbeis University in Berlin where she is currently working on her Master in Business Administration focusing on the topic of developing and selling new services in a Shared Services environment.

EGLI, VANESSA: Vanessa Egli is a Change Management specialist with broad international experience. She has spent multiple years consulting clients in Australia, London, Switzerland and Germany on topics such as employee engagement and readiness for change, stakeholder management, and communications strategy. She holds a Bachelor of Commerce from the University of New South Wales, Australia, and the Change Management Qualification from the Australian Graduate School of Management. Devising change management strategies around large-scale IT and organization restructure programs is her specialty, and she is also a keen advocate of topics such as Diversity, Ethical Management, and Corporate Social Responsibility.

GRINSVEN, JÜRGEN H. M. VAN: Dr. Jürgen van Grinsven M.Sc. is director of Van Grinsven consultancy and expert in the field of operational risk management. He has worked for several large financial institutions. Jürgen van Grinsven holds a PhD in Systems Engineering from Delft University of Technology. His research was about 'improving operational risk management'.

HÄUSSER, ANNETTE: Dipl. Kffr.; works as Global Shared Service Center Coordinator in the Group Shared Service Center (GSSC) at the headquarters of HeidelbergCement. After her studies in Business Administration focusing on Finance and Controlling, Industrial Science and International Management, at the Friedrich Alexander University of Erlangen-Nuremberg and the Universidad de Extremadura in Badajoz (Spain), she started her career at HeidelbergCement in 2007 as trainee. As an IT business analyst within Global IT she managed several IT implementation projects before she joined the GSSC. The GSSC is responsible for the overall Finance Shared Services strategy. It supports the local Shared Service Centers in their further development by facilitating tool roll-outs, or organizing the exchange of best practices. In her role, Annette is responsible for the Shared Service Centers of Eastern Europe, North America and Africa. In addition to her role at HeidelbergCement, Annette works on her doctoral thesis about value creation with Shared Services. This is in cooperation with the School of International Business and Entrepreneurship – a Steinbeis-Transfer-Institute of the Steinbeis University Berlin.

HELBING, FRANK: Frank Helbing is a senior consultant at KPMG AG Wirtschaftsprüfungsgesellschaft's consulting practice. For the past three years, he has been working as an advisor in the field of shared services, finance function optimization, and process intelligence. Industry knowledge encompasses the diversified industrials, pharmaceuticals, and telecommunications sector. Frank Helbing holds a Diploma in Business and Engineering from Leipzig University.

JÄCKLE, JOACHIM: Dr. rer. pol., Dipl. Volkswirt; Corporate Senior Vice President Financial Operations at Henkel AG & Co. KGaA, Düsseldorf. Dr. Joachim Jäckle is responsible for the finance organization of Henkel Group in all regions/subsidiaries worldwide. In addition he leads the Shared Services program for Henkel Group. This role includes the responsibility for the captive Shared Service Centers in Manila and Bratislava where mainly finance processes are off-shored. Joachim joined Henkel 1991. Since then he held different positions in finance. Among others he was group treasurer and regional CFO for the Asia Pacific region.

JANSSEN, MARIJN: Prof. Dr. Marijn Janssen holds the chair in ICT & Governance and is director of the interdisciplinary Systems Engineering, Policy Analyses and Management (SEPAM) Master and Compliance program of the Technology, Policy and Management Faculty of Delft University of Technology (www.tbm.tudelft.nl/marijnj). His research interests are in the field of ICT and governance in particular e-government, compliance, orchestration, (Shared) Services, intermediaries, open data and infrastructures for coordinating public-private service networks. He serves on several editorial boards, is associate editor of Government Information Quarterly and the International Journal of E-Government Research and is involved in the organization of a number of conferences, including IFIP EGOV. He published over 240 refereed publications.

JOHA, ANTON: Anton Joha M.Sc. is a consultant at Equa Terra in the Netherlands and an affiliate of Delft University of Technology. His projects are mainly in the field of outsourcing and Shared Service Centers. Anton Joha holds a M.Sc. in Systems Engineering, Policy Analyses and Management from Delft University of Technology. He is involved in research about Shared Services and published many papers in this field.

KEUPER, FRANK: Prof. Dr. rer. pol. habil. Frank Keuper is director of the Steinbeis Center of Strategic Management – a Steinbeis-Transfer-Institute of the Steinbeis University Berlin (www.steinbeis-scsm.de), owner of professorship in Business Economics, in particular Convergence Management and Strategic Management at the Steinbeis University Berlin, editor and executive director of the business management trade journal Business + Innovation – Steinbeis Executive Magazin (www.businessundinnovation.de), director of the Competence Center for Strategic Management and Strategic Controlling, visiting professor at the University Tai'an (China), various lectureships at European universities, associated partner at inRESTRUCT – a member of the iKnowledge Group, and between 10/2002–08/2004 guest professor at the Johannes Gutenberg University Mainz. Doctorate and postdoctoral lecture qualification at the University of Hamburg, as well as studies at the Münster School of Business and Economics. Field of work and research: investment and financing theory, planning and decision theory, production, cost management, strategic management, convergence management, cybernetics, system theory, corporate planning and management, sales & service management.

LANGE, PATRICK: Patrick Lange is a senior manager at KPMG AG Wirtschaftsprüfungsgesellschaft's consulting practice. For the past 12 years, he has been working as an advisor in the field of shared services, post merger integration, and corporate restructuring. Industry knowledge encompasses the automotive, energy, healthcare, and aviation sector. Patrick Lange holds a MBA in finance from Chicago University and a Bachelor from New York University.

LOHRMANN, MATTHIAS: Matthias Lohrmann is a senior manager at KPMG AG Wirtschaftsprüfungsgesellschaft's consulting practice. For the past ten years, he has been working as an advisor to clients from the automotive, engineering, aerospace, and other industries. His areas of expertise include process management and optimization, the design and implementation of advanced operating models, and organizational consulting in finance and accounting and other G&A functions. Matthias Lohrmann holds a Diploma in Business and Computer Science from Regensburg University.

LUEG, KAI-EBERHARD: Kai-Eberhard Lueg holds a double role as Head of Siemens AG's Global Shared Accounting and Finance Services, and as CFO of the Siemens Global Shared Services organization. Prior to this engagement, he drove the entrepreneurial evolution of the Siemens Wind Power business unit from a startup organization to 6,000 employees in a multi-billion-euro business. His resume spans various senior management positions in both operations and business administration in an international environment, including, for example, the development of risk management systems at Corporate Audit and supporting the foundation of initial Shared Services structures at Corporate Finance.

NOVAK, DAN: Dan Novak, MSc., is Head of Siemens Global Shared Services Accounting & Finance Center in Czech Republic, studied Business Administration at Linköping University, Sweden and at Universität Hamburg, Germany. During his professional life Dan has held Chief Financial Officer positions in France, United Kingdom and Czech Republic. Working for ABB, Alstom and Siemens he has mainly specialized in international project business within the Energy sector and has also participated in a number of Mergers & Acquisition projects around the world. In recent years he has been responsible for expanding Siemens' Shared Services business in Czech Republic.

RASPER, PETER: Peter Rasper is Executive Vice President Global Finance Infrastructure and COO F&A at SAP. He is responsible for global Finance Shared Services Centers, Global Procurement, Global Facility Management, Contract Licensing and for all processes related to Finance & Administration worldwide. From 1995 to 2001 Peter held various positions within SAP such as Vice President of Finance and a member of the management team of SAP Markets with responsibility for both the EMEA subsidiary and controller for the Americas region in Corporate Controlling. Prior to joining SAP, he held various positions within the analytical division of HP (today known as Agilent). Peter holds a Diploma in Industrial Engineering from the University of Karlsruhe.

RAU, THILO: Thilo Rau is a partner at KPMG AG Wirtschaftsprüfungsgesellschaft responsible for KPMG's shared services and finance transformation practice. For the past 15 years he has led consulting projects ranging from finance and sourcing strategy, finance transformation, finance IT strategy, process optimization, shared services design and implementation. His clients include global groups in the engineering, automotive, chems and pharms, utility, and telecommunication industries. Thilo Rau holds a Diploma in Business and Engineering from Karlsruhe University. He is certified as a Wirtschaftsprüfer, Steuerberater and CPA.

RIEDEL, ALEXANDER: Dr. Alexander Riedel is a partner at KPMG AG Wirtschaftsprüfungsgesellschaft responsible for KPMG's shared services and target operating model practice. For the past 18 years, he has led consulting projects ranging from process optimization in finance to GAAP conversion, ERP systems implementation, cost optimization and organizational restructuring for back-office functions. His clients include global groups in the engineering, automotive, chems and pharms, utility, and aerospace industries. Alexander Riedel holds a Diploma in Business and Engineering from Siegen University, and a doctorate in business administration from Ulm University. He is certified as a German chartered accountant and tax advisor.

RIEDL, ANDREAS: Dipl.-Vw. Andreas Riedl is a consultant for WTS Steuerberatungsgesellschaft mbH since 2009 and member of the transfer pricing service line of WTS. Studies at the University of Augsburg. Field of work and research: market analysis, design of transfer pricing systems, transfer pricing documentation, brand evaluation, ratings, analysis of interest and license rates, business valuations based on the valuation standard IDW S1, valuation of immaterial property based on the valuation standard IDW S5.

RÖDER, STEFAN: Dr. Stefan Röder is director of the Competence Center for Corporate Planning, which is part of the Steinbeis Center of Strategic Management – a Steinbeis-Transfer-Institute of the Steinbeis University Berlin (www.steinbeis-scsm.de). His research activities concentrate on the development of business models and financial planning systems for small and medium sized enterprises, particularly in the energy sector. Furthermore Stefan is co-editor of Business and Innovation – Steinbeis Executive Magazin (www.businessundinnovation.de).

RUH, WINFRIED: Winfried Ruh is Chief Executive Officer of Graf Kanitz Steuerberatungsgesellschaft mbH and qualified bank clerk. Tax expert for third countries, especially India, China, Switzerland and France. Field of work and research: international tax law, tax planning, company tax, and general business management. Author of various publications on international tax law and cooperation partner of the Chamber of Industry and Commerce Südlicher Oberrhein as referee. Lectureship at the University of Calw (SRH), member of the expert committee "International Tax Law" at the Chamber of Tax Consultants in Südbaden. Winfried Ruh holds the title Dipl.-Betriebsw. (FH) from Offenburg University of Applied Sciences, major: controlling and taxation.

SCHMITZ, JOCHEN: Dr. Jochen Schmitz is Corporate Vice President & Controller of Siemens AG, Munich/Germany, since 2011. He studied Business Administration and Economics at the University of Augsburg and holds also a Ph.D. in the same field. During his time with Siemens he held for the first eight years various positions with increasing responsibility in Corporate Finance until he moved to the Healthcare Sector as Head of Performance Controlling. In Healthcare he was promoted CFO of the Healthcare Business Unit Molecular Imaging in Hoffman Estates, IL. After this he took helm as the CFO of the Healthcare Division Diagnostics in Tarrytown, NY and finalized his time at Siemens Healthcare by being the CFO of the Healthcare Division Imaging & Therapy Systems, Erlangen, Germany.

SELG, MARCUS: Marcus Selg is Senior manager consulting and qualified bank clerk; academic title Dipl.-Oec. from the University of Hohenheim, major: credit services and marketing. Long-term experience in financial analysis and investments. Field of work and research: transfer pricing and function shifting, strategy and restructuring consulting, and international IT compliance consulting and auditing.

SOMMERER, SUSANNE: Dipl-Geogr. Susanne Sommerer is HR Business Partner for GSS AFS, studied Economic Geography, Ethnology and Urban Planning at Ludwig Maximilian University in Munich. Susanne has held various positions during her career in environmental planning and corporate real estate, before she decided to move into HR management in 2004. Focus topics of her work are the specification and implementation of the GSS HR Strategy with focus on strategic employee development, specifically for finance related functions, international talent programs and HR communications.

STEGEMANN, KLAUS P.: Klaus P. Stegemann started with Siemens in 1973 in Berlin. Since then he held several senior finance management positions in Germany and in the US working in operational as well as central functions including being a partner within the Siemens Management Consulting Group. He currently serves as Chief Financial Officer for the Americas residing in New York.

STEIN, STEFAN: Dipl.-Betriebsw., Ph.D. student and research assistant at the Institute of Accounting and Auditing at University of Ulm. Field of work and research: commercial accounting, national and international corporate tax law; tax planning and structuring; transfer pricing.

STEPHENSON, DOMINIC: Dominic Stephenson is a senior manager at KPMG AG Wirtschaftsprüfungsgesellschaft's consulting practice. For the past eight years, he has been working as an advisor in the field of shared services, finance function optimization, IT-enabled process optimization, process intelligence, cost management, corporate planning and management. Industry knowledge encompasses the automotive, diversified industrials, pharmaceuticals, private-equity, and telecommunications sector. Dominic Stephenson holds a Diploma in Business and Engineering from Darmstadt University.

THOMAS, RALF P.: Dr. Ralf P. Thomas studied economics and business administration at the University of Erlangen-Nuremberg after completing his apprenticeship as industrial commercial and graduated with a Diploma in Business Administration. He further achieved a PhD in Corporate Taxation. Since 2008 Dr. Thomas has been CFO of the Siemens Industry Sector. Prior to that, he held various different positions within the Siemens financial community, e.g. Head of Accounting and Treasury at Siemens Ltd. in South Africa, performance controller of Siemens Medical, and after that, CFO of the business unit Angiography, Fluoroscopic and Radiographic Systems at Siemens Medical Solutions. He also headed Corporate Finance Accounting, Controlling, Reporting and Taxes of Siemens AG, assuming responsibility for Siemens' worldwide financial statements. Dr. Thomas joined the Institute of Internal Auditors in Germany as a member of the Supervisory Board and is a member of the Administrative Board of the Accounting Standards Committee of Germany where he has been elected as its Chairman. In addition, Dr. Thomas has a lectureship at the Friedrich-Alexander University Erlangen Nuremberg.

TROST, MARTIN: Martin Trost is a Certified international tax advisor and Wirtschaftsprüfer (CPA); first academic title Dipl. Betriebsw. (BA) from the University of Cooperative Education at Stuttgart, major: banking; second academic title Dipl. Math.-Oec. from the University of Ulm, major: financial mathematics. Authorized officer and senior manager with KPMG Germany, auditor, tax accountant for German and international tax law with an approval of the US PCAOB, leading an own chancery. Field of work and research: international tax advising ,international transfer pricing, IFRS/US-GAAP, compliance audit (ISAE 3402/SSAE 16), corporate finance, and mergers & acquisitions.

Ulbrich, Frank: PhD, MSc is Senior Lecturer in Information Management and PhD Program Leader at Northumbria University's Newcastle Business School, UK; Affiliated Researcher at the Stockholm School of Economics, Sweden; and Visiting Research at Carleton University's Sprott School of Business, Canada. His research concentrates on the development, strategic management, and use of information and communication technologies in the context of organizational design, managerial intent, and the impact on people. His award-winning research has appeared in scholarly journals and peer-reviewed conference proceedings. Dr. Ulbrich is member of the Editorial Advisory/ Review Boards of: Electronic Markets, Strategic Outsourcing: An International Journal, and International Journal of Sociotechnology and Knowledge Development.

Vollmer, Marcell: Marcell Vollmer holds a PhD in Politics as well as a degree in Business Administration; Senior Vice President and Chief Procurement Officer at SAP. In his role as CPO within the Global Procurement Organization at SAP he has introduced and rolled-out the shared services concept for procurement globally. Since he has joined SAP Mr. Vollmer was driving global strategic programs for SAP with a strong focus on Shared Services, Post-Merger-Integration and Performance Improvement Programs. Before joining SAP, he worked for DHL Express as a manager of several integration projects in Finance, Controlling and HR. In addition to that, he has worked as a management consultant and project lead.

Weber, Tobias: Tobias Weber is a project manager at GSS AFS Strategy & Business Development. Before joining Siemens in June 2012, he worked four years for KPMG Management Consulting in the areas of finance transformation & organizational consulting, shared services and process optimization, G&A cost optimization and IT post merger integration. He holds a Master of Arts in Finance & Accounting from Frankfurt Goethe University.

Wendland, Otto: Otto Wendland is Head of Business Line Accounting & Finance Services – Portfolio Management and Processes of Global Shared Services at Siemens AG, Munich/Germany, studied Business Administration at the University of Siegen with focus on Marketing (Dipl. Kaufmann [FH]), Logistics and International Commerce. In a career with Siemens spanning more than 30 years, he has performed – amongst others – the functions of Cluster Chief Financial Officer, several times Head of Accounting & Finance and Leader of projects for Logistics and for Shared Services of Accounting & Finance. He further led the regional introduction of a new accounting concept and US GAAP/IFRS. He has spent most of his career outside Germany in Brazil, Mexico, South Africa, Thailand, France and Western & Central Africa. One of his main goals has always been to empower people to achieve high quality via a permanent simplification and optimization of processes.

Wolf, Oliver: Oliver Wolf is Head of Service Delivery Management GSS AFS CZ and Head of GSS AFS Service Management & Business Excellence CZ. He studied Business Administration at Johann Wolfgang Goethe University in Frankfurt. During his professional life, Oliver has held various positions within Siemens Corporate Finance including Siemens US-GAAP listing preparation for the NYSE, central closing activities and audit. In addition, he has held various positions within Global Shared Services such as Senior Project Manager for cross-national transition projects and Quality Manager for GSS AFS.

WOLF, SEBASTIAN: Dr. rer. pol. Sebastian Wolf is Manager Group Financial Controlling at Henkel AG & Co. KGaA, Düsseldorf. Current responsibilities: financial business partner of Henkel's purchasing organization. Prior joining Henkel: management consultant with CTcon GmbH. International project experience in the fields of post merger finance integration, shared service organizations, and management reporting. Doctorate at the University of Gießen as well as studies at the University of Gießen and University of Karlstad. Field of work and research: management control systems, incentive compensation, changing roles of controllers, and finance transformation.

ZABEL, KAI: Dipl.-Wi.-Ing. Kai Zabel is currently project manager Shared Services Accounting for the Heraeus Holding GmbH. Beside the management of Shared Service Migration projects he coordinates and develops Governance and Compliance concept supporting the Shard Services concepts of the Heraeus Group. Prior to his current engagement he worked in a similar responsibility for Heidelberger Druckmaschinen AG. Kai Zabel started his professional career in 1997 at Arthur Andersen Managementberatung, Frankfurt followed by engagements at Deloitte Consulting and The Hackett Group. Since 1998 he deals with Shared Service projects in Finance for larger and mid-sized companies headquartered in Europe. Kai Zabel studied Business Engineering at the University of Karlsruhe with a specialization in Computer Science and Operations Research.

MIX
Papier aus verantwortungsvollen Quellen
Paper from responsible sources
FSC® C105338

If you have any concerns about our products,
you can contact us on
ProductSafety@springernature.com

In case Publisher is established outside the EU,
the EU authorized representative is:
Springer Nature Customer Service Center GmbH
Europaplatz 3, 69115 Heidelberg, Germany

Printed by Libri Plureos GmbH
in Hamburg, Germany